Walter Wanger
Hollywood Independent

COMMERCE AND MASS CULTURE SERIES
Edited by Justin Wyatt

Walter Wanger Hollywood Independent

Matthew Bernstein

Foreword by Robert Wise

Commerce and Mass Culture Series
University of Minnesota Press
Minneapolis   London

MINNESOTA

"Fritz Lang, Incorporated" was originally published by the University of Texas Press in *Velvet Light Trap* 22 (1986): 33–52. "Hollywood's Arty Cinema" was originally published by The Johns Hopkins University Press in *Wide Angle* 10, no. 1 (January 1988). "Hollywood Martyrdoms: *Joan of Arc* and Independent Production in the Late 1940s" was originally published in *Current Research in Film* (1988): 89–113; reprinted with permission from Ablex Publishing Corporation. "Institutions and Individuals: 'Riot in Cell Block 11'" was originally published by the University of Texas Press in *Velvet Light Trap* 28 (fall 1991): 3–31. "Hollywood's Semi-Independent Production" was originally published by the University of Texas Press in *Cinema Journal* 32, no. 3 (May 1993): 41–55.

First published in hardcover by the University of California Press, 1994

First University of Minnesota Press edition, 2000

Published by the University of Minnesota Press
111 Third Avenue South, Suite 290
Minneapolis, MN 55401-2520
http://www.upress.umn.edu

Library of Congress Cataloging-in-Publication Data

Bernstein, Matthew.
    Walter Wanger, Hollywood independent / Matthew Bernstein ; foreword by Robert Wise. — 1st University of Minnesota ed.
        p.   cm. — (Commerce and mass culture series)
    Originally published: Berkeley : University of California Press, 1994. With new foreword.
    Includes bibliographical references and index.
    ISBN 0-8166-3548-X (alk. paper)
    1. Wanger, Walter, 1894–1968.   2. Motion picture producers and directors — United States — Biography. I. Title. II. Series.
    PN1998.3.W345 B47   2000
    791.43'0232'092 — dc21
    [B]   99-088848

Printed in the United States of America on acid-free paper

The University of Minnesota is an equal-opportunity educator and employer.

11 10 09 08 07 06 05 04 03 02 01 00   10 9 8 7 6 5 4 3 2 1

For Natalie

I know that in an accidental sort of way, struggling through the unreal part of life, I haven't always been able to live up to my ideal. But in my own real world, I have never done anything wrong, never denied my faith, never been untrue to myself. I've been threatened and blackmailed and insulted and starved. But I've played the game. I've fought the good fight. And now it's all over, there's an indescribable peace. I believe in Michael Angelo, Velasquez and Rembrandt; in the might of design, the mystery of color, the redemption of all things by Beauty everlasting, and the message of Art that has made these hands blessed. Amen.
—Louis Dubedat, *The Doctor's Dilemma*
by George Bernard Shaw

A producer comes on the set and says, "I don't like the shoes."
—Mike Nichols, quoted by
John Gregory Dunne

Contents

Foreword

Robert Wise

Like any director working in Hollywood in the 1950s, I knew of Walter Wanger's many pictures and his extensive film career. But I had never met him before he contacted me in the fall of 1957 regarding my directing a film about Barbara Graham, the first woman executed in California several years earlier. This real life story was finally released as *I Want to Live!*

We met for lunch at the Brown Derby in Beverly Hills, then a favorite restaurant and hangout for many film people. In contrast to some film producers I had worked with, Walter was soft-spoken, quite articulate, and very much a gentleman. Although he had been out of university for many years, he still retained the style and manner of the educated Easterner.

But that style and manner did not cover his passion for the Barbara Graham story. Walter believed Barbara was innocent, and he had had some rough times with the press a few years before, so he was personally sensitive to the shoddy treatment that Barbara had received from the news media. During lunch he spoke at great length and with great anger about what Barbara had gone through during her trial, how unfair it was, and how she had been almost prejudged by the press and TV people. Later, as Nelson Gidding and I worked on the script, Walter was always determined that Barbara's shabby treatment be thoroughly dramatized.

At that luncheon Walter gave me a short, three-page synopsis of the story. Even in those bare bones, I found the story horrifying and fascinating. "People like a horror story," I told him. "This is a real life horror story if I ever saw one. Let's go." He had another great asset for the project and that was a commitment from Susan Hayward to star as Barbara Graham. In those days, and it is still true today, it was most unusual to get a major star of Susan's standing to commit to a picture without at least a completed, first draft screenplay. But Walter had it, and knowing that Susan would star definitely influenced my decision to direct the film.

Enthusiastic as he was about the material, Walter was deliberately hands-off during the actual production. This allowed me and my staff to go about the business of putting the script onto film. Of course, Walter always viewed the dailies and always gave his reaction and opinions, but he was not on the set regularly during shooting. From a director's standpoint, this is an ideal type of producer, one who lets you make the film without interference, but who gives you great support. Walter gave us the fullest support all the way through the production.

In fact, I would say Walter's greatest strengths as a producer were in finding excellent story material, carefully assembling the group that would make the film, and marketing and selling the pictures when they were finally completed. He was tireless in this last area because he always said, "It's not enough to make a good picture. You have to sell it as well, you have to get the audience into the theaters."

Throughout his career, Walter made many good pictures and several great ones. In looking over his filmography, one comes to appreciate the great range of subject matter that his films have encompassed: westerns, romantic melodramas, musicals, screwball comedies, costume films, and of course social problem films such as *I Want to Live!* Yet one also becomes aware that in many of Walter's films, there is a keen interest in social concerns, of people and how they deal with the problems they face in the world around them.

The reader will discover this in Professor Bernstein's book. It is wonderfully comprehensive in its scope and a thoroughly researched account of Walter Wanger's career. It conveys clearly his personality, the way he worked, and what he accomplished in Hollywood. *Walter Wanger, Hollywood Independent* is an excellent addition to the list of biographies about Hollywood producers who contributed so many fine pictures to our silver screen, but whose careers have been forgotten with the passage of time.

Preface

I first heard of Walter Wanger more than ten years ago while working as a research assistant to Donald Spoto on his massive biography of Alfred Hitchcock, *The Dark Side of Genius.* Spoto asked me to dig up some information about Wanger and the making of *Foreign Correspondent.* At that time, one lengthy and informative interview in Bernard Rosenberg and Harry Silverstein's *The Real Tinsel* and a few pages in Tino Balio's *United Artists: The Company Built by the Stars* composed the bibliography of writings on Wanger. But virtually every star biography and Hollywood history mentioned him repeatedly.

The more I learned about the contours of Wanger's career, the more intrigued I became. It was full of contradictions.

Wanger produced several provocative message movies and aesthetically accomplished works, from *Gabriel Over the White House* to John Ford's *Stagecoach.* His most interesting films reinforced his authority as one of Hollywood's foresighted leaders during the late 1930s and early 1940s. An unrepentant idealist and a charismatic speaker, Wanger rose to the height of his prestige when topical movies about politics were rare and articulate, college-educated producers were unheard of. Leading the Academy of Motion Picture Arts and Sciences during World War II, publishing innumerable articles, and making a barrage of speeches, Wanger always stressed Hollywood's potential to keep the American citizenry informed and to influence the world. His career was virtually a one-man campaign to have Hollywood taken seriously by cultural critics. He became a national celebrity.

Yet the overwhelming bulk of Wanger's sixty-five films was not the outstanding titles he is best remembered for, but movies devoid of social significance, plausibility, or aesthetic accomplishment, as less charitable critics were quick to note. *The New Republic*'s Otis Ferguson, for example, in 1939 accused him of "turning an A.B. degree [from Dartmouth College] into the biggest shell game even this industry has seen." Journalist Ezra Goodman wrote of Wanger's propensity to "talk about the brave new world of cinema while turning out celluloid old hat." The same dichotomies informed the box office performance of Wanger's output. A number of Wanger films made respectable profits, but many more failed to earn back their costs, and two, *Joan of Arc* (1948) and *The Reckless Moment* (1949), forced him into near bankruptcy.

I became convinced that Wanger's career was one of Hollywood's great and—except for his notorious crime of passion in 1951—untold stories. The present volume is thus intended as a resurrection of a forgotten career and an extraordinary personality. But it is also a close examination of the work of the Hollywood producer—who Thomas Schatz recently described in *The Genius of the System* as "the most misunderstood and undervalued figure in American film history."

Through the late 1970s, the prevalent view of the producer—typically promulgated by victimized writers and directors and inspired by the malapropisms of Samuel Goldwyn, the tyrannic vulgarity of Harry Cohn, and the sentimentality of Louis B. Mayer—was that the producer was an uncultured philistine. Ben Hecht once compared two Coney Island pinhead clowns, Bippo and Zippo, to production executives: "Their heads used to jiggle and they drooled a bit, but they seemed to Charlie (MacArthur) and me very much like authentic producers."

There were exceptions, of course, such as Hecht's friend David O. Selznick, Irving Thalberg at MGM, and Darryl F. Zanuck at Warner Bros. and Twentieth Century–Fox. These men were comparable to auteurs and could contribute some measure of their vision and style into their films by scripting, reshooting, and editing the work of others. This, and the excellence of many of their films, is the main reason why multiple volumes have been written about them.

Wanger was neither an auteur nor a philistine, and his significance rests, in part, on the fact that he does not fit into these categories. In fact, Wanger's methods of work render him a more typical and, perhaps, a more revealing example of how the movie producer functioned in Hollywood's classical era than Selznick and his colleagues.

Until recently, film historians lacked an appropriate vocabulary for describing the Hollywood producer's work. (Even observers and workers in contemporary Hollywood struggle with defining it.) But Balio and Douglas Gomery's analysis of the studios' corporate conduct and Janet Staiger's analysis of Hollywood's mode of production have tempered the romantic, individualistic premises of auteurism with the institutional framework of business practices. Wanger's job, and that of any producer, is best described as managerial. For each of his films, Wanger supervised the writing of shootable scripts and selected the talents and technicians to realize them: he conceived, chose, combined, and negotiated business cycles, production ideas, narratives, cultural meanings, and aesthetic traditions. These functions were offered to Wanger through Hollywood's division of labor within its mode of production. Such constraints and opportunities of working as a producer in the Hollywood studio system were some of the primary factors that influenced Wanger's achievements in Hollywood.

Equally crucial to the shape of Wanger's career was what I have termed "semi-independent production," another phenomenon that I closely examine in this book. After toiling in anonymity at the major studios for several years, Wanger went into business for himself to secure a share in his films' profits and to gain the opportunity to choose the subjects of his films. But, as was the case with Samuel Goldwyn or Selznick or other independents, Wanger's efforts were compromised for a variety of reasons.

Staiger has specified many of them. The so-called independent producers frequently used the same sources of financing—banks, financial institutions, service organizations such as laboratories—as the majors, and they had to meet comparable loan criteria (proof of their films' profit potential) to get funds for their films. They rented or purchased the same technologies that the majors used in order to maintain industry standards of quality. They took for granted and employed the same detailed division of labor that the studios evolved among departments and technicians, and they often copied any number of the studios' production management systems. And as Schatz stresses, the most successful and visible independents often used major studio facilities and borrowed their talents (stars, writers, directors, art directors), and they needed the vertically integrated companies' first-run theaters to earn the largest possible grosses on their films.

Wanger's semi-independent ventures confirm Staiger and Schatz's explanations of how and why such companies functioned in Hollywood, while providing a specific illustration of how they played out in one producer's career. But Wanger's career also confounds the conventional wisdom that defines "independent production" in terms of a producer's lack of corporate ties to a major studio. In fact, the conduct of the Wanger companies shows in new ways how the fact of corporate independence provided a producer with little freedom from major studio influence.

The classical Hollywood producer, then, was a manager of cultural trends in a highly stratified industry where corporate "independence" could hold constraints of its own. Given this framework, I realized that an account of Wanger's career would be woefully inadequate if it only recounted his personal idiosyncrasies and the making of his best films. In fact, I give Wanger's domestic life (apart from his work) comparatively little attention, in part because I am more concerned to show through my discussion of his career how semi-independent producers worked in Hollywood.

All Hollywood producers, studio-employed or independent, faced the same kinds of obstacles in Hollywood that Wanger did. What made Wanger distinctive was his individual responses to them, and these were the product of his personality and inspired by many of the social and cultural currents, specifically Progressivism and the New Stagecraft in the theater, that flourished during the first two decades of this century. An examination of these contexts clarifies the sources Wanger drew upon and his significance in Hollywood's history. It also helps to explain why Wanger never successfully resolved the central contradictions of his career—the coexistence of social relevance and irrelevance, of box office success and failure, the similarities between his "independently" produced films and those of the studios, and lastly, the disjuncture between his theories and his practice; such paradoxes were embedded in both the fabric of American culture and in the workings of Hollywood's classical era.

Chief among Wanger's strategies for success in Hollywood was his self-promotion—yet another area where his personality came into play. A forceful and energetic man, Wanger promoted himself as a celebrity, and his public persona, though rooted in his personality, was as much a production as any of his films. In his publicity, Wanger sold himself as the maverick who could not stand studio rules, the man who had to make films his own way. Publicizing himself became one tool with which Wanger could address the disparity between his idealistic intentions and the often disappointing results of his films, shape the reception of his films, and balance his sense of individuality and his need to belong.

Fundamentally, Wanger was at once a self-righteous rebel and a satisfied member of the industry against which he ostensibly railed. In an industry that thrived on the tension between standardization and differentiation in its films and its talents, this tension could be productive: in Wanger's case, it resulted in a handful of the finest films ever produced in Hollywood. But Wanger often paid a high price for it. As screenwriter Robert Soderberg once put it, "He had courage without being a courageous man—that's the toughest approach."

With Wanger as my focus, then, I have sought to weave together a chronology of economic, institutional, and aesthetic trends in American commercial movie production from the twenties through the sixties. I spend a good deal of time outlining the terms of Wanger's contracts and the production methods at the studios where he worked. These details I gleaned from studio archives and Wanger's papers. I corroborated and supplemented archival materials and Wanger's accounts of various disputes with trade press reports, particularly from *Variety*, of the business health and social status of the film industry at given periods. Although *Variety* was often inaccurate and hysterical in its reporting, I have found its bias in favor of the dominant producers in Hollywood helpful in documenting their perceptions of the market. Indeed, I hope my presentation of Wanger's historical context will prove useful in future studies of Hollywood and other individuals who worked there. At the very least, I intend this history to enrich the reader's viewings of Wanger's best available films (the Filmography indicates which titles are available on videotape).

The study of this contradictory man is not without conceptual paradoxes of its own. To examine a distinctive figure in Hollywood history and yet assert that he is worthy of study for his typicality may seem inconsistent. Insofar as Wanger encourages us to reevaluate our conceptions of the producer's function and the independent producer's place in Hollywood's oligopolistic studio system, he raises some of the most pressing questions that can be posed of Hollywood's history and the significance of its achievements.

In 1928, Broadway critic and Algonquin Table wit Alexander Woollcott recounted in the *New York Morning World* several humorous anecdotes about Wanger for the benefit of "that harried and inevitable historian," Wanger's biographer. On the centennial of Wanger's birth, I want to thank Woollcott and the many other people and institutions who assisted me more recently on this project.

Various grants supported this work. A University of Wisconsin Graduate Student Travel Fellowship funded an early visit to Los Angeles archives in 1985. A generous Fellowship for College Teachers and Independent Scholars from the National Endowment of the Humanities supported my research and writing on Wanger's early life and Hollywood career during 1989. A grant from the University Research Committee of Emory University financed my research for the final chapters of this book in the summer of 1990; another in the fall of 1993 provided the illustrations. The Ball Foundation funded a research trip to the Lily Library at Indiana University, and an Emory University Summer Faculty Development Award supported my revisions in the summer of 1992.

Many archivists provided considerable assistance when I visited their libraries: Sam Gill at the Margaret Herrick Library at the Academy of Motion Picture Arts and Sciences; the late John Hall at the former RKO archive; W. H. Crain, Prentiss Moore and Mary Mallory of the David O. Selznick Collection at the Theatre Arts Library at the University of Texas in Austin; tireless Ned Comstock at Doheny Library of the University of Southern California; Rebecca Cape and Heather Munro at the Lily Library at Indiana University; Maryann Chach in the Shubert Archive in Manhattan; Philip Cronenwett at Dartmouth College Library's Special Collections; Ed Duesterhoert in the microfilm reading room at the Memorial Library of the University of Wisconsin in Madison; Terry Geesken at the Museum of Modern Art; and most of all, Harry Miller and his courteous staff at the State Historical Society of Wisconsin in Madison. I am especially grateful to Menzi Behrnd-Klodt, Ann Bloczynski, and Joan Gilbertson who cataloged the Wanger Collection in 1983. Film archivist Maxine Fleckner-Ducey of the Wisconsin Center for Film and Theater Research facilitated my work in numerous ways.

Other archivists saved me considerable time and expense: Adelaide Elm of the Arizona Historical Society, the special collections staff at the University of Chicago Library (for the Charles Merriam papers) and at the University of Oregon Library (the Richard Collins Collection), Sheila Ryan of the Morris Library at Southern Illinois University (the John Howard Lawson papers), and Carolyn Rowlinson of the University of Stirling Library (the John Grierson Archive).

Many other film archivists and collectors provided the opportunity to screen rare Wanger films: Charles Hopkins, Jef Stier, Rene Schillachi, and Eleanor Tanin at the UCLA Film Archives in Los Angeles; Charles Silver at the Museum of Modern Art; and Emily Sieger at the Library of Congress. Finally, I am grateful to the extraordinarily generous William K. Everson, who allowed me to screen ten obscure Wanger titles from his personal collection.

I am also thankful to the many individuals who knew or worked with Wanger and were kind enough to talk or correspond with me, including the late Charles Bennett, the late Joan Bennett, Leonardo Bercovici, Edward L. Bernays, True Boardman, Peter Bogdanovich, Richard Collins, the late Robert Cummings, Rosemary Dexter, Alexander Golitzen, Jane Greer, Ted Haworth, Mrs. Leonora Hornblow, Arthur Krim, Robert Lantz, Edward Lasker, Arthur Lubin, Don Mankiewicz, the late Joseph L. Mankiewicz, the late Samuel Marx, the late Joel McCrea, Roddy McDowall, Aileen Mehle, Walter Mirisch, Maurice Rapf, Gottfried Reinhardt, Leo Rosten, Silvia Richards, the late Irene Mayer Selznick, Sylvia Sidney, the late Don Siegel, Robert Soderberg, Henry Spitz, Sonya Timmons, Etta Wanger, Don Weis, Burke Wilkinson, Dana Wynter, and Phillip Yordan.

I must say a special thank-you as well to Wanger's stepdaughters Diana Anderson and Melinda Markey Bena, and to his daughters Stephanie Guest and Shelley Wanger. Diana generously and fondly recounted growing up around Wanger and shared some of his personal correspondence with me. Stephanie and Shelley have spoken with me many times at length about their parents, and Shelley has helped me contact her father's former associates. Never once has she or Stephanie sought to impose their conception of their father on me. Both have been a patient and constant source of encouragement.

Many film scholars have offered guidance and support. Donald Spoto first pointed out to me Wanger's obscurity and was wonderfully generous in sponsoring several research trips and opening many doors; I will always be indebted for his friendship and encouragement. Similarly, John Belton insisted on the interest of Wanger's career at an early stage of my graduate career, enabled me to screen several films, and brought his keen intellect and editorial skills to bear on my first writings on the subject.

Tino Balio facilitated this project in many ways. As former head of the Wisconsin Center for Film and Theater Research, Tino secured the Wanger papers and ordered them cataloged. Years later, he persuaded me to renew my research on Wanger as a dissertation topic and served as an enthusiastic adviser. Alongside Tino, David Bordwell and Vance Kepley of the Film Studies program at the University of Wisconsin in Madison provided superb models of scholarship and pedagogy for a young film historian. I am equally grateful for their advice, encouragement, and friendship.

Other friends and film scholars have helped me with research and feedback. Professor Nancy Peterson dug up reports of Wanger in *The Dartmouth*. Jeffrey P. Kurz made several crucial contacts for me in Los Angeles which eased the course of my research. I received invaluable legal advice from the late Keenan Peck. Lutz Bacher unstintingly shared addresses, interviews, and his expert perspectives on Max Ophuls's work with Wanger. Kevin Brownlow sent me a transcript of his interview with Wanger in the 1960s. Richard Maltby sent me informative items from the Motion Picture Producers and Distributors Association and the Father Lord Papers. Patrick McGilligan graciously shared his address book of Hollywood veterans and his research on Fritz Lang. David Thomson offered the benefit of his perceptive insights into Selznick's personality and performance as a producer. Dana Polan and Thomas Schatz each in his own way gave me much appreciated, unsolicited encouragement for my work. Dana also served as a reader of my manuscript; he along with Robert Sklar and Michael Rogin made many helpful suggestions.

For other favors, I am grateful to Shaun Abshere, Joe Beck, the late Professor Marc Belth, Ms. Helen Bernstein, Alice and Robert Bond, Carolyn Brooks, Professor Donald Crafton, Jack Daniels (who let me see Stella Wanger's theater scrapbook), Dan Ford, Bill Ficks, Keith Gardner, Jeanne Hall, Denise Hartsough, Michael Patrick Hearn, John Hokkanen, Margaret Hokkanen, Professor Barry Karl, Richard Koszarski, Gavin Lambert, Al La Valley, Robert Lazzaro, Ann Louise Lipman, Amit Malhotra, Professor Russell Merritt, Larry Nardine, Tif Payne, James D. Peterson, Paul Seale, Daniel Mayer Selznick, Greg Solman, John Springer, Kristin Thompson, Henry B. Troutman, Peter Viertel, Armond White, Professor Tony Williams, and Brian Winston. Emory University Theater scholars Alice Benston and James W. Flannery read my chapters on Wanger's theatrical career and made helpful suggestions for improving them.

Film scholars Kevin Hagopian and Richard Neupert each read the first third of the manuscript with their characteristically demanding intelligence. David Pratt closely read the first completed draft of the manuscript and offered precise, compelling criticisms of my arguments and interpretations and gave me sage advice at numerous points in the writing of this book. Alan D. Williams provided expert editorial suggestions.

I am also grateful for the patience and guidance of my editors at the University of California Press. Ernest Callenbach welcomed a book on Wanger with enthusiasm, in spite of the fact that Wanger tried to sue *Film Quarterly* only months after Callenbach took it over. Ed Dimendberg inherited this project and, with Michelle Nordon, firmly shepherded it through the publication process. Diane Mark-Walker copyedited the manuscript exhaustively and improved it immeasurably.

The Film Studies Program at Emory University has been a genial, high-spirited place to teach and to complete this work. I have enjoyed discussing *Joan of Arc* with Robin Blaetz, and I have benefited from many animated and illuminating conversations with Gaylyn Studlar about Hollywood's orientalism in the teens and twenties. David Cook took time from a busy schedule to read over the manuscript and offered wise counsel and encouragement on innumerable matters.

In diverse ways, my family has offered constant help as I researched this project. Like all of my siblings, Donna Bernstein conveyed to me the pleasures of pursuing knowledge as well as the fun of going to the movies. Jay and Jill Bernstein also offered me their hospitality in Manhattan. In Los Angeles, Linda and Tony Rubin housed me for several months of research and made my trips there a sheer joy. Gene and Pam Bernstein first introduced me to the pleasures of an academic life and generously encouraged my own pursuits. In this, they emulated my parents. From my earliest years, Elayne Bernstein and Harold Bernstein fostered my interest in the arts and encouraged me to embrace learning in too many ways to enumerate. They have supported my work with affectionate interest for which I remain deeply grateful.

Finally and most profoundly, I thank Natalie Bernstein for her considerable patience and her endless enthusiasm. She has endured months of solitude and hours of indifferent movies for the sake of this project. She has typed, proofread, and otherwise enhanced my work in manifold ways over the years. Without her wise counsel and constant collaboration, this book would be much less interesting and humane. She and our exuberant sons Justin and Adam have made it all truly worthwhile.

Part One

Personal History

1

The Gentleman from the West (1894–1911)

Walter F. Wanger cut a distinctive figure in Hollywood. His colleagues spoke of his stylish Savile Row suits and his infinite charm. Jesse Lasky, Jr., who in the 1920s was at the Astoria, New York, studios where Wanger worked, described him as a "continental, worldly sophisticate": "I can still see them in my mind—Walter Wanger, Joe Kennedy, wearing spats, carrying walking sticks, pearl gray gloves in their hands, derbies, striped trousers, you know. They dressed like diplomats." "He had the air of a fellow about to be sent to the Court of St. James," confirmed Leonardo Bercovici, who authored the script of Wanger's *The Lost Moment*. Dana Wynter, star of *Invasion of the Body Snatchers*, recounts that Wanger was "such a civilized man, softly spoken, highly educated and very well tailored. His manners were Eastern-seaboard impeccable. He was a lovely, special man." This image of Wanger reappears in countless Hollywood histories and biographies.

Other talents who worked closely with Wanger were skeptical. "There were two Walter Wangers," a major studio executive remarked. "I once came into his office where he was reading *Foreign Affairs*. But I could see that under the cover was an open copy of a true detective magazine." Sara Haardt, a fledgling screenwriter in the 1920s, found him "no different from any other executive in the movie industry. His highbrow complex is a little more pronounced, he has definite social ambitions and a flair for Christian women not too unsightly."

In fact, Wanger was all of these things. He was bright, well-bred, dashing, optimistic, and self-assured. But he had his vulgar, rakish side and was also self-conscious enough to know that taste and intellect were precious commodities in a parvenu industry. The role of Hollywood gentleman came easily

3

to Wanger, but it remained for him precisely a role, one that carried pressures of its own. Wanger's childhood in an upper middle-class, well-connected, and assimilated German-Jewish milieu nurtured these contradictions in his personality.

In 1870, Wanger's father, the fifteen-year-old Sigmund Feuchtwanger, emigrated to the United States, one of an estimated two hundred thousand German Jews who arrived between 1840 and 1880. He came from Bavaria, where Jewish Germans faced the threat of government and aristocracy-sponsored reprisals after the failed 1848 revolutions. Along with thousands of German immigrants, he joined the gold miners on the West Coast.

Like Lévi Strauss—the frustrated mine owner who secured a market for denim jeans among miners—Feuchtwanger was a determined salesman. With his hair brushed straight back, his piercing eyes and sharp look suggested enormous self-confidence. Restless and energetic, he spent nearly twenty years selling and transporting jeans and finer clothes between California and Oregon. As gold fever subsided, Feuchtwanger settled in San Francisco, then a bustling port city of nearly three hundred thousand which had a Jewish population of more than sixteen thousand. He joined a prosperous clothes-making business, Neustadter Bros., which made terry cloth items, denim jeans, "boss of the road" overalls, and "standard" shirts, the ready-made garments whose manufacture was made possible by recent advances in mechanical cloth cutting.

His association with Neustadter Bros. was only half of Feuchtwanger's good fortune, for in 1890 he married their son-in-law's sister, Stella Stettheimer. Stella, born in 1869, was sixteen years younger than Feuchtwanger and a first-generation German American from Rochester, New York. Stella and her four younger siblings lived briefly in California before their father abandoned them and reportedly lit out for Australia. More than Feuchtwanger, who Wanger recalled was fond of reading Shakespeare, the Stettheimer family had an exceptionally strong interest in culture and learning.

Late in life, Wanger described the "traveling salon" of intellectuals and artists created by Stella's three younger sisters—Carrie, Ettie, and Florine—during their frequent visits to Europe. In the teens and twenties the salon was a fixed if informal institution at their apartment at the Alwyn Court on West 58th Street in New York, where they hosted—in a very proprietary manner—intimate gatherings for the likes of composer Virgil Thomson, dancer Adolph Bohm, photographer Alfred Stieglitz, painter Georgia O'Keeffe, and painter Marcel Duchamp (who gave them French lessons). Moving in such circles, the Stettheimer sisters were familiar with the avant-garde movements of the day, such as the shocking 1913 Armory Show that introduced Postimpressionist art in America, and they kept their sister and her family well apprised of the latest developments.

They were an accomplished trio in their own right, as well. Carrie Stett-heimer, who functioned as the housekeeper, made elaborate dollhouses, which are on permanent display at the Museum of the City of New York. Ettie Stettheimer was a novelist published by her friend Alfred Knopf (under the pseudonym Henri Waste), and her Ph.D. in philosophy (with a disserta-tion on William James) was a rare achievement among women in the late nineteenth century. Florine Stettheimer painted diverse landscapes and scenes from her personal life in a naive style with bright pastel colors and willowy forms. Although Florine was fearful of public exhibition in her lifetime, sev-eral of her works are held by museums as prestigious as the Whitney and the Museum of Modern Art, and she received some public acclaim for her cello-phane cyclorama set designs for the 1934 Gertrude Stein–Virgil Thomson opera, *Four Saints in Three Acts,* directed by John Houseman. Together, the Stettheimer aunts demonstrated to the Feuchtwanger children the joys of art connoisseurship and creativity.

Like her sisters, Stella Stettheimer had big cheeks, heavy eyebrows, and large eyes, but she did not share their rebellious spirit, their distrust of marriage, nor their creative ambitions. When the Stettheimers returned to Germany with their mother in the late 1880s, Stella chose to rejoin her younger brother Walter, who had married into the Neustadter family, for whom he worked in San Francisco. There she met and married his coworker, Feuchtwanger.

Walter Wanger, born on July 14, 1894, was the third of four children. Beatrice, Wanger's older sister, was the most forcefully influenced by the Stettheimer aunts, whom she accompanied on several trips across Europe. In 1932, she was named Officier D'Academie by the French government for her years of teaching modern dance in Paris under the name of "Nadja"; she died in 1944. Herbert, the next eldest, died at the age of nineteen from blood poi-soning while attending Cornell University. Younger than Walter was Henry, who attended Yale and eventually enjoyed a successful career in Wall Street finance at the firm of Loeb, Rhoades. Of his siblings, Walter felt the closest to this "kid brother." He threw big parties for Henry when he visited Holly-wood. Henry loaned him sizable amounts of money when his finances were tied up in film production in the late 1940s.

Wanger was never one to look back. It was not that he felt he had ignoble origins to hide. When his daughters asked about his childhood, he typi-cally dismissed it as uninteresting. Photos show him dressed according to fashion of the times in feminine clothes with long red curls: "When I was a little girl," he used to say. But on the one occasion that Wanger recalled his childhood publicly, he spoke of his home as providing "an atmosphere of human understanding." His parents preserved innumerable European social proprieties:

I remember my father and mother, on Sunday in their Sunday best . . . my father with a high silk hat. They would visit their friends and, if they were out, they would drop cards. The following Sunday they would remain home and courtesies would be returned. This was a polite society.

The Feuchtwanger family was a formal but close-knit household, and Walter enjoyed the attentions of his doting mother and of a nurse who spoiled him and coaxed him in German. All "conspired to give me a belief in life, beauty, and faith and protection and plenty."

Such optimism derived as well from the social advantages that the German-Jewish Feuchtwangers enjoyed and which were completely alien to such later Eastern European immigrants as Hollywood pioneers Adolph Zukor, Louis B. Mayer, Carl Laemmle, and William Fox. The Feuchtwangers' insistence on continental gentility provided a bulwark against social prejudice from below or above their upper middle-class station in San Francisco. The city proved tolerant, electing its first Jewish mayor in 1894, and the Feuchtwangers were not ostracized for either their origins or their religion; only the ponderous name "Feuchtwanger" signaled their immigrant status. Stella, who had never been able to pronounce it comfortably, in 1908 spent two hundred dollars to officially shorten the family name to Wanger (which was henceforth pronounced to rhyme with "ranger"). Walter took F. as his middle initial to memorialize the original patronym.

Although he contributed to Jewish causes in later years and rescued many of his parents' relatives from the Nazis during the late thirties and early forties, Wanger grew up a completely assimilated Jew. Stage producer Jed Harris, a friend of Wanger's in the 1920s, found him "almost proud of his ignorance of Jewish history and Jewish life in general." (Harris also claimed that, at his mother's insistence, Wanger was not circumcised at birth.) In his later years, he attended the Episcopal church with Joan Bennett. His daughters first learned of their father's Jewish background outside their home.

If the Feuchtwangers neglected their ethnic heritage, they embraced the arts and primarily the theater, which became a personal obsession in Wanger's childhood. From the early 1800s, theater and light opera were well-established institutions in San Francisco and boasted several actor-playwright-managers such as the celebrated David Belasco, who worked at the New Theater in the 1870s. San Francisco houses had featured the likes of Lola Montez, Oscar Wilde, Edwin Booth, and Sarah Bernhardt, as well as James O'Neill's portrayal of Christ in Belasco's controversial production of *The Passion* in 1879. During Wanger's early years, the reorganization of the business by the notorious Theatrical Syndicate ensured that a stream of prominent performers traveled to San Francisco theaters in their triumphant New York vehicles.

One of Wanger's clearest memories was of flipping through his mother's scrapbook of playbills and newspaper clippings from the opera and theater, where he admired the photographs of numerous fully costumed stage stars, such as Henry Miller and Maxine Elliott, and of celebrated productions such as *Quo Vadis* and Belasco's famed *The Heart of Maryland.* The playbills and scrapbooks focused young Wanger's attention on the visual elements of stage production, and he was an appreciative spectator by the time his parents took him to see Bernhardt play in *L'Aiglon,* a performance that he mentioned decades later as one of the greatest he had ever seen.

Wanger's early interest was enhanced by the family's frequent trips to Europe, taken to ease Sigmund's weak heart condition. Whether their itinerary took them to Berlin, Paris, or Rome, Wanger, like his sister Beatrice, developed a fascination with the excitement and richness of the world of the arts. Outside of the theater, he was also entranced by the parades of German military. His older daughter Stephanie Guest recalls that Wanger "would go on endlessly about when he was a little boy and his family went to Germany and he'd see all these troops. He adored the uniforms and the pageantry." Such adoration remained with him all of his life. When Cardinal Spellman died in the 1960s, Wanger could not tear himself away from the television coverage of his funeral. "Those Catholics really know how to put on a show!" he told Stephanie. As Joseph Mankiewicz put it, "Walter liked flashy trappings, an attraction that extended from the shiny, feathered helmets of Mussolini's running 'Bersaglieri' to the bouncing, shiny plumes of a Ziegfeld chorus line." Such visions only fed Wanger's connoisseurship of production design which he applied to his stage plays and films.

But Wanger's idyllic childhood was shattered in 1905 when Sigmund Feuchtwanger died of a heart attack at age fifty. Stella regretfully left her brother Walter and moved to Europe, where like her mother and her sisters she could live in greater comfort at less expense than she could in San Francisco. Though Hollywood lore had it that Wanger's parents were fabulously rich, the Wangers in fact had an annual dividend income of about $13,000 (roughly $130,000 in today's dollars). The family passed two years in Switzerland, where the children acquired a speaking knowledge of German and French. Walter attended an elementary school (the Selig Institute) near a chocolate factory in Vevey, Switzerland, where Charlie Chaplin later retired, a sojourn that confirmed Walter's affinity for Europe.

Raised in an atmosphere of gentility, up until 1905 Wanger remained free of the kind of personal hardship that had driven pioneers of the American film industry to American shores to build up a business empire. As a publicity profile in the 1930s put it, he "could never qualify in a rags-to-riches Odyssey of a film producer." Unlike an Adolph Zukor, Wanger had no need to achieve great social acceptance and power; he was born into it. Unlike a second-generation producer such as David O. Selznick, Wanger had no personal vendetta against the industry for destroying his father. Until the age of eleven, his life was secure and he could indulge in a sense of complacency about the world.

But his father's death modified all this. In many ways, it was liberating: Stella Wanger couldn't closely monitor four children, and young Walter had a great deal of time to pursue his interests without interference, a condition that strengthened his sense of independence. Feuchtwanger's death and the family's travels also must have heightened Wanger's restlessness. To writer Leo Rosten, who became friends with Wanger in the early 1940s, this was a key personality trait:

> He was a very nervous fellow. He wouldn't talk about a book he was reading without mentioning two or three other books. His conversation always darted about. This was his personality structure—it wasn't all of one piece. There wasn't any one consistent self. . . . What the core personality was, I don't know. Was it uncertainty, insecurity, anxiety? People like that seem to be trying to find themselves. He was unfocused.

Such nervous energy was also the key to Wanger's prolific career.

Wanger smoothed over his uncertainties about himself with enormous personal charm. His insecurities gave Wanger insight into how well people responded to encouragement. He had a knack for making people feel important, for giving them a sense of their unlimited possibilities. "I've never seen anybody who could have people so entranced, so quickly," his daughter Stephanie later recalled; "He was just charming." "He was someone to conjure with," says society columnist Aileen "Suzy" Mehle. "He was a magnificent friend, and when he was in love with me during the 1960s, he focused completely on me, on my career and what he thought I was capable of."

In 1907, the Wangers returned to America to be closer to the Stettheimer family. While Stella established residence in Manhattan, brother Herbert enrolled at Cornell University, and Walter attended the nearby Cascadilla Preparatory School for Boys. There he studied his father's beloved Shakespeare, as well as Chaucer, French, German, composition, and elementary math. He joined the ski club and was coxswain for the rowing team. For the rest of his life, however, with the exception of his brief career as a polo player in the thirties, Wanger was disinterested in athletics.

Staying at Delta Sigma Phi, where his brother Herbert was a member (and loaned family funds to help finance the construction of a new fraternity house), Wanger flourished. His energy, infectious sense of humor, and optimism won him many friends among the older boys. It was there that he met the future publicist Edward L. Bernays. To Bernays, Wanger at the age of fourteen was already the suave and elegant figure who would later be celebrated: "He was an outgoing, warm, personable, charming and humane young man. He was the gentleman from the west."

In New York, mother Stella renewed contact with her wealthy relatives and contacts among the German-Jewish banking families such as the Guggenheims, the Kahns, and the Warburgs (some of whom later invested in Wanger's theatrical and film ventures). But Stella's closest association was with her maternal aunt Adelaide, who had married banker Henry Seligman. The Wangers became frequent guests at the lavish Seligman home on East 56th Street and their beachside estate at Elberon, New Jersey. The Seligmans confirmed for Wanger the values and proprieties of European culture which had informed his family's existence in San Francisco, but they did so on a scale that rendered the Feuchtwangers' home quaint and crude.

"Coming from San Francisco," Wanger later recounted, "I was overwhelmed by the luxury of the Seligman homes," which included an elevator in their Manhattan house and the gold embossed buttons on the livery of their "retinue." In his view, the Seligmans wonderfully balanced their daily routines between their heritage and their present circumstances: "Although devoted to the United States and all its traditions, the luxury one encountered was European." They had imported candies, tailor-made clothing ordered from Paris shops (while Wanger was "a mere Brooks Brothers job"), and superb food. They entertained European royalty ("the new citizens of the United States offering hospitality to those who never offered it to them"), actors, journalists, and other prominent figures.

The luxuries extended to highbrow culture, which the Seligmans patronized with enthusiasm. They "had subscription seats for the opera, Philharmonic and Carnegie Hall, and eventually a box at the Metropolitan, which was considered some punkins." They also enjoyed subscriptions to "all the magazines," and they possessed "every new novel of the day." Stella encouraged Wanger to spend time with his cousin Walter, who later became a prominent banker. Wanger described him as "my beau ideal" and "always considered by my family the young man with whom I should associate when invited."

Endorsed by his mother, the Seligmans' affluence, taste, and conduct became a compelling example for Wanger. They inspired Wanger's voracious reading habit. To screenwriter Maurice Rapf, this was part of his facade. "Wanger faked his intellectualism. He would constantly refer to his reading of important books when he may only have read no more than a chapter and a review." But Rosten found it genuine. "He would read seven or eight books at a time and he would shove them at you—'Have you read this?'" Leonora Hornblow, a frequent guest in Wanger's home in the 1940s, recalled how before dinner, "one had drinks in this library. Well, many homes in Hollywood had libraries. You could call them that, but it was a hoot. But there were real books and copies of *Foreign Affairs* in *this* library and I was enormously impressed." Mankiewicz agreed:

> Walter was, one might say, too well read. He devoured, almost compulsively, any and all available newspaper and magazine accounts of political, social, and literary events throughout the literate world. He didn't just subscribe to the papers and buy the books—he *read* them. He'd always carry with him the current *Times Literary Supplement* or *The Manchester Guardian;* they served almost as identity cards for Walter. I could never figure out where or with whom he might discuss their content.

Wanger also nurtured a love of reading in his daughters and stepdaughters. When Stephanie was just eighteen months old, Wanger read to her for a half-hour before going off to work.

The Seligmans also served as a model for Wanger's personal sense of style. "He liked the best of things and he appreciated luxury," his daughter Shelley recalls. "He always dressed in the most elegant way. He made sure he had a white handkerchief in his jacket pocket and a white or red carnation or a cornflower in his lapel." Mankiewicz speculated that "all the young sons of the New York Jewish banking families must have grown up as they imagined the young lords, the young offspring of nobility grew up. They all had to have a dashing car, a haberdasher, they all had to take up racquets, or so I've been told. And I think Walter was a spin off."

Indeed, Wanger approached the New York families as an outsider, and from his description of the awe in which he held the Seligmans' wealth, there is the implication of discomfort. The Seligmans' affluence must have been intimidating as well as seductive, particularly since Stella held his cousin up for praise and expected Wanger to go into the banking business, where he was sure to prosper. "That's what my family wanted me to do," Wanger later told his daughters. Though brother Henry took it up, "I couldn't do it. It was too boring."

Instead, Wanger in subsequent years defied the Seligmans and their milieu by his decision to work in the theater and the movies. The Kahns, Warburgs, and Seligmans might socialize with performers and invest in the odd show, but they never ventured into entertainment careers. As Mankiewicz put it,

> Oddly enough, Walter Wanger does not represent a Hollywood figure. He represents a Schiff, or a Warburg, or a Frankfurter. But he did not go into stocks, did not go into bonds, real estate or oil. He wandered across a boundary and found himself in a neighborhood that he didn't recognize, but it was a hustling neighborhood, where they were selling the faces of life.

Walter was a hustler himself, determined to prove his own worth to a social circle that denigrated his chosen profession. This decision particularly outraged the Stettheimer aunts, who stopped speaking to Wanger after 1919 when he married dancer Justine Johnston and entered the film industry the following year.

Walter's rebellion extended further into the "faces of life" that he chose to mount, particularly as an independent producer. In *52nd Street* (1937), he took revenge on the Stettheimer sisters with the caricature of snobbish aunts who disown their stage producer nephew. More significantly, his friendship with Walter Seligman ended when Seligman "had the misfortune to view a film I made [*The President Vanishes*, 1934] that he considered was anti-big-business and socialistic." Seligman considered correctly: Wanger's cousin could hardly misinterpret the sentiment of the film's second scene, in which a banker conspires with a judge, a munitions manufacturer, an oil tycoon, and a press magnate to drag America into a European war.

If the milieu of the Seligmans caused Wanger any unease, it also gave him the contact with a social elite on the East Coast and in Europe which reinforced a thoroughgoing faith in his own opinions and projects. By the time he entered Dartmouth College in 1911, Wanger was, in one campus historian's words, "completely unabashed in the presence of famous personalities."

That ability sustained him in future years. For example, when a French diplomat protested that *Algiers* (1938) would hurt tourism in that country, Wanger replied:

> The majority of Americans do not know where Algiers is and this picture will be of the greatest value in publicizing the name and the locale. I am sure those who see it will want to go to Algiers and look for the counterparts of Hedy La Marr [sic] and Charles Boyer.

But Wanger was hardly content to defend himself. "I should receive the highest consideration from the French government for effecting the most constructive and popular propaganda in their behalf." And after viewing *Algiers*, the French consul enthusiastically agreed. Similarly, knowing well the value of association with celebrities and statesmen, Wanger constantly petitioned them to support his projects. In 1948 he wrote George Marshall that *Joan of Arc* was a "spiritual outrider for the Marshall Plan." Even at the low-budget studio Monogram, he asked Edward R. Murrow and Winston Churchill to endorse his films.

Hence, Walter Wanger grew up extremely well connected in financial and cultural circles, which extended from the Seligmans to the likes of the de Rothschilds of Europe, American political counselor George Beer, and Wanger's Stettheimer cousin who married Julius Ochs Adler, for several decades the general manager and vice-president of the *New York Times*. And Wanger clothed himself with the manners, charm, and poise that he studied as a fringe member of a social elite. But at the same time he felt the need not only to seek a career as an impresario but to do so in the manner of a social crusader and to try to confer a moral legitimacy on his work in the "decadent" entertainment industries. Significantly, the most passionate phrase he could summon up for one of his movies, such as *Joan of Arc* or *I Want to Live!*, was that it was "more than a motion picture." He never completely left behind the high-art biases of his aunts and the social conservatism of the New York bankers, and he continued to address the affluent and the intelligentsia in his public statements about the movies. Himself a sometime elitist, Wanger sought not to "elevate" the movies to the level of more traditional arts but to make cultural custodians appreciate the elevating "potential" in a popular mass medium.

This was the psychological basis for what many colleagues and observers perceived as Wanger's insincere posing throughout his career. Walter F. Wanger was a go-between. Although financially comfortable and socially assimilated, he retained the sense of being an interloper among both social royalty and the movie pioneers. As he rebelled against the upper-class establishment, Wanger simultaneously aspired to be accepted by it; as he outclassed his Hollywood colleagues, he tried to fit in with them.

2

The Boy Manager (1911–1914)

Throughout his life, Wanger was a devoted alumnus of Dartmouth College. In the mid-1930s, he created the Irving G. Thalberg script library and started a course in screenwriting. He served as president of the college's Alumni Association in the 1940s. Publicity profiles made his attendance there well known.

What is less well known was that Wanger never completed his degree. He was "separated" from Dartmouth for academic delinquency in early 1915 before he could graduate. Wanger's first sustained act of youthful rebellion was to ignore completely his coursework and the warnings of the college to pursue his own interests in the drama club, where he uncovered a distinctive approach to theatrical production which involved a tireless pursuit of novelty and marketing it to the faculty.

From the very beginning, Wanger refused to buckle down to the discipline of an ordinary student. As a result he was "admonished" by the college before the December break of his freshman year. The following February, he was separated. An assistant dean explained to Stella Wanger that, even though her son was "a young man of rather unusual ability and promise" and that there "has been no dissatisfaction whatever" with his conduct, Walter had "failed nine semester hours in his work" in math, biology, and even German.

Fortunately for Wanger, a remedy to the embarrassment of dismissal came in the form of another trip with his mother to Europe. During the spring and summer of 1912, between visits with his family in Euis, Wiesbaden, and Marienbad, Wanger attended lectures on English and German literature and the history of nineteenth-century art at the University of Heidelberg. His sponsor there was Victor Eckert, a drama professor and theater critic, who at summer's end wrote Dartmouth officials that Wanger had "helped" him "with his diligence and interest in every field." Wanger was readmitted on probation the following fall.

Eckert did more than help Wanger recover his place at Dartmouth. He inspired the young theater lover to explore a broad range of contemporary European playwriting and stagecraft techniques, from Stanley Houghton's Repertory Theater in Manchester to Max Reinhardt's productions in Berlin. And in Paris there was Serge Diaghilev's revolutionary Ballets Russes with Leon Bakst's sets and Vaslav Nijinsky's daring choreography for *Afternoon of a Faun*. The overwhelmed audiences included the Stettheimer sisters, who compelled the Wangers to attend a performance.

The knowledge Wanger brought back with him to Dartmouth became the essence of his success on campus, for it encompassed a range of playwrights and production methods that were barely familiar even to the most knowledgeable American theatergoers. George Bernard Shaw, Henrik Ibsen, Maurice Maeterlinck, and August Strindberg by 1911 were well-established names in America. But Wanger also knew the work of less prominent authors such as Houghton and the American Witter Bynner and had become familiar with the innovative New Stagecraft, which he deployed strategically in his first experience as a stage impresario.

The key principle guiding the new stagecraft was aesthetic unity, achieved not through the spectacular realism of Belasco or Henry Irving, but rather through highly formalized, symbolic design in which all the theatrical elements inflected a single idea. Such an aesthetic, derived in part from Richard Wagner's *Gesamtkunstwerk,* contrasted sharply with the conventional stagecraft of the era. Instead of blocking strategies centered on a charismatic leading performer, the New Stagecraft director orchestrated all the components of the settings and character movements into a compelling whole. Instead of creating set designs with an often distracting profusion of scenic detail, innovative practices espoused an aesthetic of minimal detail and evocative design derived from the theories of the English ex-actor and set designer (and the lover of dancer Isadora Duncan), Edward Gordon Craig.

In publications such as *The Art of the Theater* (1905) and in exhibitions of his design sketches, Craig argued for the use of abstract sets, for the severely controlled manipulation of lighting for expressive effects, and for an emphasis on rhythm and movement as the central force of dramatic production. His designs for the Moscow Art Theater's 1912 production of *Hamlet* signaled changes of scene only with shifting lighting schemes and gold and cream-colored screens. Seeking to free the theater from the "tyranny" of the written word, Craig declared that the actor could emote without dialogue, and that bodily movement was a superior vehicle for conveying thought and emotion.

Although anticommercial in their aesthetic, Craig's views were internationally endorsed and implemented. He disdained the majority of appropriations of his work, commenting in 1916, as one journalist put it, that "975 out of 1000 of his disciples seem to have been blind to the ideas he has been driving at." By late summer 1912, Wanger had seen Craig's ideas modified for narrative purposes by Reinhardt, George Fuchs, and other European directors. Harley Granville Barker's *The Winter's Tale* at London's Savoy Theater featured sets that suggested palace interiors through bare white walls, pillars, and gold curtains rather than extravagant detail.

But even more impressive to Wanger was the way in which Craig's predilection for "evocation rather than literal representation" became a guiding principle in the work of scenic designer Bakst and choreographer Michel Fokine, both of whom worked for Diaghilev's Ballets Russes. Fokine choreographed dances that minimized the hierarchy of conventional ballet between principals and the corps de ballet. His work with Bakst confirmed, as had the performances of Duncan, that the ballet was better suited than the theater to the evocative symbolism that Craig sought. Craig was personally offended by Bakst's jarring and luxurious color juxtapositions in his set designs, yet Bakst sought, like Craig, to "overwhelm" and "inoculate" the audience with emotion.

The most popular instance of the collaboration among Fokine, Bakst, and Nijinsky was *Scheherazade,* which tells the story of a Shah who finds his wives in an orgy with his slaves and kills all of them. The action of the dance, a representation of unbridled sexuality and violence in a paean to the irrational, shocked Parisian audiences in 1912. But Bakst's color combinations of dark green hues (for the harem curtains, throne, and various covers) and a dark blue light streaming in through the windows was entrancing. Beyond stage design, Bakst's set and costume designs had a strong and immediate effect on European interior decoration, clothing, and jewelry design.

Bakst also provided a model for Wanger's production ideas at Dartmouth and in Hollywood, not least because of the way they awed the affluent elites of Paris and London. "I am very fussy about clothes and sets," he wrote a British production manager in 1949. "That is why my pictures look a little different from some other people's pictures." In 1939, he told a reporter that the Ballets Russes and Duncan's dancing were "the greatest influence on drama, direction, lighting, costume designing and interior decoration in the past fifty years." In the 1940s, he inaugurated the *Arabian Nights* cycle of films that became a regular feature of the major Hollywood studios' low-budget output. Half a century later, discussing the impetus for *Cleopatra,* Wanger recalled how he had met Bakst and Nijinsky while a college student and how impressed he was with the Ballets Russes, with *Scheherazade* and with "all their oriental influences. I always tried to project some of that into my productions whenever I could."

Wanger was also deeply impressed by the austere Abbey Theater productions that toured North America in 1912 and introduced transatlantic audiences to the ideas of Craig. Wanger saw the troupe's productions of Lady Gregory's *Workhouse Ward* and *The Rising of the Moon* in New York in December, an experience that galvanized Wanger into his active playwriting and production at Dartmouth.

Wanger's visit to his mother in Manhattan had followed a fairly dull fall semester. He had dutifully completed his coursework, worked at the *Jack o'Lantern* humor publication, and was appointed assistant manager of the Dramatic Club, which was relatively inactive. Like most colleges at the time, Dartmouth had no theater department and college theatricals held second-class status behind athletics and fraternities. Although some New York plays toured New Hampshire, the Dramatic Club typically put on classic works (such as Oliver Goldsmith's *She Stoops to Conquer,* performed in Wanger's first year), and revues, comic operettas, and amateurish burlesques. In the fall of 1912, when the Winter Carnival was instituted (the event that Wanger in 1938 disastrously hired F. Scott Fitzgerald to dramatize), Dartmouth was not the place to try out Craig—or at least, not yet.

Wanger later claimed that his inept efforts at performing heroic or villainous roles led to his work in theater management. Jack Warren, a fellow student, later recalled that he

> was not an actor or a singer or a dancer and he would have probably dropped dead from fright if he had to appear on a platform before an audience. . . . He was a hustler, stage hand, and water boy. But he could afford to wait.

He didn't have to wait long. In early December 1912, Dartmouth announced the gift of $105,000 from Wallace F. Robinson, a financier and head of American Shoe Machinery Company, to build Robinson Hall, a student center including a small auditorium on the second floor. Excitedly, Wanger injected himself into the planning of the hall, persuading Robinson to incorporate the latest stage technology into the three-hundred-seat theater.

That same month, Wanger saw Lady Gregory's one-act play *The Rising of the Moon* (later adapted to film by John Ford). Aside from its nationalist theme, pitting an Irish revolutionary against an arresting police officer, what excited Wanger was the play's use of Craig's simplified stage decor for naturalistic drama. Narrowly aimed spotlights replaced general illumination of a set consisting of a single, overturned barrel with a poster advertising the wounded man. As one critic described it:

> In *The Rising of the Moon,* the footlights are suppressed and the stage is lighted only by two streams of apparent moonlight which come to a focus at a large barrel in the centre, on which the two most important actors seat themselves,—

while the wharf and the water in the background are merely imagined in a darkness that is inscrutable and alluringly mysterious.

Wanger realized that it was feasible, for reasons of economy as well as dramatic impact, to stage the play at Dartmouth. At the beginning of the 1913 spring term, Wanger convinced the junior prom committee to secure the performance rights.

At the same time, Wanger coauthored and staged *The Test,* a ten-minute play for the Dramatic Club's vaudeville sketch-writing contest in February 1913. His stage directions read: "Absolute dark stage except for a lighted candle on a rough table. Army cot against back wall in corner. Wireless outfit on table. Two soap-boxes and a chair are lying about." The stark contrast of light and evocative darkness directly echoed the two streams of moonlight that poured over the set of *The Rising of the Moon.* Craig had arrived in Hanover.

For *The Test,* Wanger and his cowriter were also borrowing the thesis-play aspect of Lady Gregory's work. Just as *The Rising of the Moon* evoked Irish nationalism, *The Test* demonstrated the inherent superiority of Dartmouth over certain other Ivy League colleges. On stage, a trio of undergraduates each portrayed an alumnus of Yale, Harvard, and Dartmouth, now officers in the American army serving abroad during a future war. The three, seated around a table, are cut off from their comrades. As the play begins, the men await the radio transmission of a decoding key to translate an enemy message. They are grim and tense; an enemy soldier with a machine gun waits for any one of them to step outside.

While the other Ivy Leaguers boastfully discuss the benefits they gained from attending their colleges, the Dartmouth man wistfully alludes to Dartmouth Night—a recently introduced welcoming evening for freshmen, full of speeches about the college's long and illustrious history. When the battery on the soldiers' wireless radio gives out, one of them must venture into the dangerous darkness to retrieve a fresh pack. It is the quiet, self-confident Dartmouth man who makes the essential sacrifice with a smile. The play reaches a rousing climax as he stumbles back into the cabin fatally wounded and dies under the illusion that he is attending a Dartmouth Night.

This crowd-pleaser won the Dramatic Club's "vaudeville sketch" contest and won Wanger the position of assistant manager of the Dramatic Club. Thus honored, he staged a decisively successful "vaudeville" program for the junior prom in May, consisting of a blackface performance, a violin solo, a dramatic rendering of Jack London's *To Kill a Man,* and a performance of *The Rising of the Moon,* complete with balcony-mounted lighting rigs. A noisy crowd of students abruptly rose and left as the Irish play got underway. Yet the remaining audience watched attentively—and with complete surprise—as the Dartmouth Dramatic Club realized its most technically polished and convincingly acted drama in campus memory. Though their attention was exhausted by the lengthy afternoon performance and the stuffy heat that suffused the hall, they applauded the actors enthusiastically.

Two days later, the campus newspaper carried a review by an English professor who noted that "each item of the bill . . . was given in performance a smoothness and finish that we have been educated not to expect in college productions." Those prom participants who had rudely left the performance received a thorough scolding in *The Dartmouth;* their casual attitude, reflecting the campus's general view of theatrical activities, was completely inappropriate to the new ambitions of the Dramatic Club. Meanwhile, one Professor Licklider voiced his hope that the reception of these plays "will open the eyes of the College to the brilliant possibilities of the new Robinson Hall."

That summer, a Dartmouth summer administrator appointed Wanger manager of the club's activities. But Stella Wanger expected Walter to come to Europe (and to attend a birthday party for his grandmother in Munich). Wanger's sponsor wrote Stella that Walter "has been taking hold of his work and his avocation with a vigor which promises much for his future accomplishments," and that his summer position would be "the greatest aid towards realizing his worthy ambition."

Wanger himself wrote Stella a personal plea, which indicates his clear understanding of the politics of his situation: "I have been elected business manager of the Dramatic Club which means that I will probably have the management of the new theater here when completed." But even more striking is Wanger's equation of his theater work with his search for self-esteem:

> Firstly, it is rather an honor for me as I am rather young to say the least and secondly it gives me a chance to do something and show that perhaps I am worth something anyhow—besides it will be a great satisfaction and will give me a feeling of independence if I can hold down the job and it is really a job which may lead to bigger things. . . . If I come to Europe this summer I will as usual waste most of my time and will not be adding an awful lot to my actual career—while if I stay here you can see I will accomplish something really worthwhile. . . . I feel I ought to grab this opportunity to show you as well as myself that I have serious ambitions.

More than earning an audience's approval or an administrator's endorsement, Wanger's work affirmed his identity as an imaginative and responsible impresario.

From that summer on, Wanger—with the help of some talented actors and of the generous budget allocations of the college—transformed Dartmouth's Dramatic Club from a campus afterthought to a polished harbinger of the latest theatrical trends and a worthy competitor to George Baker's famous playwriting workshops at Harvard University. The twelve-hundred-seat theater in Webster Hall was consistently packed with faculty, students, and townspeople. From all accounts, Wanger was responsible for all the major decisions regarding the program: he found the plays, negotiated for performance rights, commissioned set designs and costumes, and sometimes directed the actors.

Fresh, current drama was the guiding principle of the two seasons he managed there, and Wanger's preferences encompassed new production techniques as well as new plays. The enthusiastic Professor Licklider informed readers of *The Dartmouth* that *The Rising of the Moon* used a setting "inspired by Gordon Craig's new idea of color simplicity, an idea that began in Russia and is rapidly revolutionizing the scenic effect of the modern stage." The article's condescending tone and misleading genealogy suggests Wanger was his source. An article on Wanger's presentation of Maeterlinck's *The Intruder* informed its readers that its designer, Livingston Platt, "is to America what Gordon Craig is to England and Rinehart [*sic*] is to Germany." The Ballets Russes were another inspiration. Director Diaghilev, whom Wanger finally met in England in 1914, employed a diversity of choreographers and composers in a policy that lacked a commitment "to any particular style or movement other than a genuine interest in and appreciation for whatever was new and original." More specifically, for the musical *Ta! Ta! Tango* set in Persia, Wanger commissioned a design for gold-stenciled curtains and gold-laced ambassador uniforms from Lucille Duff Gordon's Paris studio. All this, *The Dartmouth* noted, "added to the ensemble of Oriental richness" in the manner of Bakst's work and resulted in "the most pretentious and magnificent production yet attempted" at Dartmouth.

Wanger might have chosen to apply these production methods to the classics—Aeschylus, Shakespeare, Molière—but he favored the newest works. Announcing auditions for a new season, Wanger told *The Dartmouth*, "Nothing too new or too elaborate will be refused a trial." At the end of the spring 1914 term, *The Dartmouth* reported that Wanger "is now abroad gaining new ideas from the theaters of Paris, Germany, and England, from which places he will return next fall to direct next year's dramatic season in Hanover." A 1914 press release published in the *Literary Digest* noted, "It is not Mr. Wanger's idea to present Greek tragedies and ancient comedies. He says it is his ambition to present up-to-date plays, or rather, to present plays a little bit ahead of the day." Using one-acts, Wanger planned for diversity while partaking of fresh dramatic trends.

Wanger also brought a new degree of professionalism to the tired mainstay of campus theatricals, the revue. His interest in impressing his audience, regardless of a work's cultural pedigree, encouraged him to sponsor original works such as *On to Princeton* in October 1913. *Ta! Ta! Tango*, with Bakst-inspired designs, was an original Ziegfeld Follies–style revue, which incorporated a pantomime ("The Garden of Punchanello") and a tango tournament during the second act. In the fall of 1914, Wanger staged the "flawless" self-reflexive production "But Is It Art?" described as a "mixture of violent contrasts, snappy songs, dainty songs, brilliant dances and local humor" which included an impersonation of Wanger himself. The highlight of the show was a "living cinema" parody of nickelodeon-style programs, complete with advertisement slides and out-of-tune sing-alongs.

The crowning achievement in Wanger's attempts to make Dartmouth drama equal to, or better than, the professional theater came in January 1914. Wanger obtained from Broadway impresario William Harris the rights to *The Misleading Lady,* a "theatrical crazy quilt" comedy in which an amateur actress, on a bet with a theatrical producer, attempts to obtain a coveted role by persuading its author that she loves him (Paramount Pictures later produced it in 1932 with Claudette Colbert). The Dartmouth production was performed concurrently with the play's Broadway run starring Laurette Taylor, and Wanger used Dramatic Club funds to commission sets from professional designers in Boston and costumes from Parisian clothing designers such as Callot Soeurs and Paul Poiret (the latter being one of the key innovators of orientalist fashion during the teens). Wanger arranged this coup by appealing to author Charles Goddard, a Dartmouth alumnus, and by inviting his coauthor Paul Dickey to give an opening night speech. Dickey was so impressed that he had the players perform two matinees at Manhattan's Fulton Theater (a privilege that previously had been extended only to the Yale Dramatic Association when it produced Ibsen's *The Pretenders*). These were attended by critics, producers, and play stars Billie Burke and Taylor. Taylor reviewed it favorably for the *New York Herald;* the paper's regular critic reported that the Dartmouth cast performed "as if they had done it all their lives." The Gaumont Film company shot footage of the cast.

The professionalism of the Dartmouth Theater informed not only the standards of the productions, but the operating routines of the club. Beginning in the fall of 1913, Wanger insisted against the advice of students and the administration that the drama group should stage productions during football season. He boldly scheduled the year's first production for the evening of a game against Williams College. He instituted the policy of refusing to seat late audience members during performances. For tryout sessions, he replaced classic monologues with new plays, and he took over the blocking, rehearsal, and direction of the plays from professional directors, whom the college previously had hired. Financed by the college, Wanger was able to spend money freely: he created a set design department, he produced new shows virtually every month, and he gave the club a more imposing title—the Dartmouth Dramatic Association.

Surveying Wanger's management of the club in early 1914, poet and playwright Bynner told the *New York World,* "The faculty of Dartmouth stand for all this with an equanimity that is certainly a testimonial to the boy manager's genius." The Dartmouth officials accepted his transformation of the club, and his inevitable neglect of his coursework, because his knowledge of contemporary European theater was so clearly innovative and instructive. Indeed, a review of November 1913's *The New Sin* and *Workhouse Ward* noted that the audience was packed with more faculty than students. Their reviews clearly demonstrate that the faculty was overwhelmed by Wanger's shows. One professor in October 1913 praised Wanger's "rare ability and untiring energy. To him, more than to any one person, is due the credit for what seems to be generally acknowledged a complete success." Another wrote that "the nature of [Wanger's work] is warranty against over-praise."

For two years, Dartmouth's administration overlooked his awkward academic derelictions and class scores averaging in the low seventies because of such accolades. With the endorsement of the Dartmouth faculty, which also was learning from his experiments, Wanger was able to "sell" the club activities as a form of extramural education. *The Dartmouth* expressed the hope that "the College will welcome whatever the Dramatic club has to offer it, not only for its mere diversion, but for its upbuilding in the intellectual life." Wanger told the paper that in Europe

the drama is looked upon as part of a young man's education—a necessity if you will—and all boys see the classics and respect the men actively engaged in the work. . . . America is rich in men of aesthetic taste without the practical side, or on the other hand in men of practical turn of mind without the aesthetic touch. Dartmouth will attempt to educate men who will combine both of these essentials.

He spoke from personal ideals, but also with an awareness that his academic standing depended upon it.

Ironically, Wanger barely enjoyed the privilege of staging plays in the new Robinson Hall. For its opening in November 1914, Wanger chose a Dartmouth student's original one-act, consisting of open graves and dead voices in conversation, and a three-act play by Dobbs Milton called *The Burden of Life*. His plans for an elaborate Christmas pageant complete with dwarfs were cut short when the college administration announced his "ineligibility" to continue at Dartmouth. The Christmas show was canceled so that Wanger could satisfy the school's requirements. But Wanger found his old habits hard to shake; in February 1915, he concluded his college career.

By then, it seemed as though Dartmouth needed Wanger more than Wanger needed the college. In an editorial entitled "The Dramatic Crisis," *The Dartmouth* eulogized his career:

Thus far the rise of Dartmouth in the theater world has been exclusively a remarkable triumph for Walter F. Wanger, much as he has disclaimed the fact. But the active test of his triumph will be its permanence. Only if the dramatics of the College can stand on their own legs has the apparent success been anything more than a flash in the pan.

Twenty years later, in June 1934, the Dartmouth Board of Trustees voted to grant Wanger an honorary degree, a decision made on the basis of his work on stage and in Hollywood. It henceforth became a prominent feature in his publicity.

At Dartmouth, Wanger made crucial contacts upon which he built his later career. He developed a confidence in his own discriminating taste and in his unerring sense of audience appeal. He discovered that he could meet the relentless demand for innovative presentations by keeping current with the latest experimental techniques.

An incident that occurred nearly three decades later illustrates how consistently Wanger invoked innovation as the guiding principle of all his undertakings. Upon the release of his 1939 comedy *Eternally Yours,* Wanger received a complaint from a leader of a magicians association that the film had exposed the workings of too many magic tricks. Wanger replied, in his executive assistant's words, that since the tricks exposed were explained in a thirty-five-cent magic book he had bought at a magic store, Wanger "had the right to expose them in his production [and] if these effects were in current use by magicians throughout the world that it was about time that they discard them and invent new ones to take the place of the ones exposed."

Finally, Wanger developed at Dartmouth a knack for publicity and marketing. Specifically, he wedded Progressive Era idealism and intellectual pursuits with practical commercialism to appeal to diverse audiences. And in doing so, the "boy manager" also realized that he was "worth something" after all.

3

Finding a Niche
(1915–1919)

When he left Dartmouth in 1915, Wanger was determined to become a professional theater manager. But for all of his expertise in production values and promotion, the one element lacking at Dartmouth had been a sense of risk. All of his activities were financed by the college, and his audience, in isolated Hanover, was virtually captive. Now he faced the challenge of selling tickets to the general public. Wanger's fledgling career in New York barely began, however, before it was interrupted by the advent of the Great War, an event that gave him his first and decisive contact with film production.

When Wanger came to New York in early 1915, the American legitimate stage was in the grip of a passionate argument about the proper nature and function of the theater. This debate forced Wanger to confront and define his own views about whether, and how, the theater should mediate between popular appeal and elevating subject matter. While in New York, Wanger rarely produced shows that balanced these alternatives. Since the experience was not entirely successful, it ultimately inspired Wanger to specify his own goals in the entertainment field: to elevate popular taste, but also to persuade cultural snobs to accept the level of popular taste that prevailed.

The theater argument focused on the theater monopolies that dominated the business versus the "Little Theater" movement. Since 1896, the Theatrical Syndicate—consisting of Charles Frohman, Marc Klaw, A. L. Erlanger, and Alf Hayman—had accumulated fifty houses around the country with controlling interests in five hundred more. With the formation of theater circuits, they had centralized play production in New York and controlled the booking of touring groups nationwide; in fact the Syndicate sent out the shows the Feuchtwangers enjoyed in San Francisco.

Within a decade of this theater trust's formation, Jake, Lee, and Sam Shubert, former Syndicate clients, challenged it by establishing their own booking offices and by buying and constructing new theaters in New York and around the country. They attracted such disaffected performers as Bernhardt, Minnie Maddern Fiske, and Eddie Foy by promoting an "open door" booking policy to all performers. By 1909, the Shuberts were battling the Syndicate to dominate show business.

One consequence of this rivalry was the "commercialization" of the theater, a situation that Syndicate leaders and the Shuberts defended unashamedly. Klaw, for example, argued that "the theatre is not primarily an educator of the public" but simply a form of entertainment. He and his colleagues favored musical comedies and revues that copied Ziegfeld's Follies, and the plays they promoted clearly lacked the intellectual purpose and dramatic power of the Little Theater productions. Critics bemoaned the Syndicate's exclusive preference for entertaining plays that made money in New York and on tour.

By contrast, since 1909, the Little Theater movement, inspired to a great extent by continental experiments such as Andre Antoine's Theatre Libre, typically included small, often nonprofessional, art-oriented houses whose seasons were financed through subscription rather than through ticket sales. Most prominently, Harvard graduate Winthrop Ames had launched his intimate Little Theatre on 42nd Street in 1909. Celebrated for serving tea in the lobby during matinees and coffee in the evenings, Ames's theater, where Reinhardt's *Sumurun* had its American premiere, was the model for Wanger's Robinson Hall (and at least one Dartmouth show served coffee at intermission).

Whether amateur or professional, the Little Theaters presented esoteric or modest works—frequently of European origin, such as Maeterlinck's chamber dramas, Ibsen's social criticism, Shaw's thesis plays, and some of the new plays Wanger mounted at Dartmouth—which their managers deemed to advance the art of the theater. Since the diverse playwriting movements in Europe also drew upon Craig's aesthetics in production, the New Stagecraft placed Wanger squarely within the "elevated" Little Theater movement. In fact, Wanger had couched his Dartmouth rhetoric of "elevation" and "education" in terms of the larger controversies burning in New York.

The rise of the Little Theater movement facilitated an explosion of high-art stage trends that remained unsurpassed until the 1960s. In many respects, the argument with the commercial interests was an assertion of nineteenth-century aesthetic values—be they Émile Zola and Antoine's naturalism or Wagner's symbolic renderings of mythical archetypes—against the vulgar commercialism of the new monopolies. It was also a vehement expression of larger cultural struggles taking place in America during the early twentieth century. The same impulse that inspired new, more exclusive audiences for symphonic concerts, museums, and productions of Shakespeare also informed the reaction against the Syndicate and Shubert's degrading commercialization. This sentiment came primarily from upper-class elites, whether American Anglo-Saxons or European emigré patrons such as the Seligmans. Both segments recognized the encroaching power of the growing urban masses, and they responded in part by enhancing the aura of the high arts. But, as Progressive-minded civic leaders and professionals argued, aesthetic events could be offered to the unwashed thousands to "elevate" them, providing moral instruction as well as exposure to the highest standards of art. In contemporary debate, the word "uplift" became a noun, with a logic that endorsed the Little Theater movement to its devotees.

By 1916 more than fifty little theaters were operating in the United States, and several books were published to champion the phenomenon. *Theatre Arts* began publication that year, devoted to "the creation of a new theater in America, a theater in which art and not business will be the first consideration." Arthur Hornblow, editor of *Theatre Magazine* (and father of the highly esteemed film producer, Arthur Hornblow, Jr.), in 1919 concluded his two-volume history of American theater by describing the current period as "grossly commercial and conscienceless, with not an idea above piling up the dollars":

> The average American theatrical producer, primarily a man of affairs, has had neither the time nor the education to enable him to cultivate the drama as an art. . . . The American theatre awaits a modern Moses to lead the way out of captivity.

If any director resembled Hornblow's Messiah in 1915, it was the thirty-seven-year-old actor-playwright-director Barker, then in New York to mount a repertory season of new and classical plays. And it was while working as a twenty-five-dollar-a-week "nothing sort of apprentice" to Barker, alongside stage manager Claude Rains, that Wanger entered the professional theater and claimed his place in the highbrow-lowbrow debate.

Wanger had first met Barker the preceding summer in England. Like Reinhardt, Barker, whom Sir John Gielguld called "the greatest man in the theater I ever met," specialized in synthesizing diverse trends in European stage production from the turn of the century, and his own works (such as the fantasy *Prunella*) enjoyed remarkable success. While working in London from 1904 to 1912, he mounted the plays of contemporary authors such as Arthur Schnitzler, Ibsen, Gerhart Hauptmann, Maeterlinck, premiered many of his friend Shaw's works, and was best known for his distinctive stagings of Shakespeare.

The Shakespeare plays were the kind of classics Wanger had studiously avoided at Dartmouth, and yet Barker had made Shakespeare exciting again. His reverence for the texts and his emphasis on ensemble acting led to a more abstract rather than realistic approach to scene design which focused the audience's attention on the actors and, through the actors, on the dialogue. Barker thereby used Craig's production design principles for a purpose Craig abhorred. The 1911 *A Midsummer Night's Dream* at the Savoy was a milestone in British staging technique, evoking the magical forests with simple hanging sheets of paper rather than with detailed backdrop paintings. These designs, as well as an exhibit of the New Stagecraft, were put on display in New York in January 1915 when Barker arrived.

In short, Barker was the most exciting and innovative new presence in the New York theater. For the first time, Wanger could see close up a professional producer at work, and there was much to admire. "My work is fascinating and I am most enthusiastic," Wanger wrote an acquaintance in early 1915. "Barker is a marvel." Barker's own working regimen made Wanger's prolific Dartmouth seasons look laconic. His round boyish face belied his intense drive; he was a charming but "quite literally indefatigable" taskmaster. But what Wanger found most appealing about Barker, beyond his drive and perfectionism, was the director-producer's knack for inspiring coworkers with an idealistic sense of mission.

Although Barker privately recognized that the New York public was "most alarmingly fickle," he spoke to his associates and backers of uplifting the public with productions of old classics and new thought-provoking dramas. Much as Wanger had framed the purpose of his work to *The Dartmouth,* Barker spoke of using the theater purposefully and constructively for the "education" of its audience's "imaginative faculty." Unlike Wanger's productions, however, Barker's repertory project—the presentation of different plays on alternating nights during the week—was incompatible with the commercial stage. When the Great War postponed his plans in London, Barker accepted an offer from the New Theater Millionaires (such as Otto Kahn and F. G. Bourne), who raised a mere $65,000 for Barker's season. "If he demonstrates a theatre conducted on artistic principles can be made self-supporting," *The Theatre* noted, "he is to have all the backing he wants for a permanent institution."

Hence Barker's presence in New York brought to a head the argument between the commercial interests and the devotees of the drama. When local theater managers (including Syndicate leaders Klaw, Erlanger, and Hayman) gave Barker dinner shortly after his season began, one of them derided repertory by asserting that "the money that came in through the box office window would do more to uplift the stage than all the money that could be carried in through the back door in the form of subsidies."

Unfortunately, the response to Barker's New York program proved the manager's point. Barker restaged his London production of *A Midsummer Night's Dream,* and he premiered Shaw's *Androcles and the Lion* and *The*

Doctor's Dilemma at Wallack's Theatre (where Wanger had seen the Abbey Players perform in 1912). He also mounted a production of Anatole France's *The Man Who Married a Dumb Wife,* whose sets by Robert Edmund Jones, who had previously worked with Reinhardt, represented "the first important native expression of the 'new stagecraft.'" Extending the forestage area and shifting the lighting banks to the balcony, Barker and Jones gave the New York critics plenty to debate. By April, however, he had exhausted his budget and his associates. His summer tour of Greek tragedies in Ivy League stadiums proved equally disappointing.

Barker's box office failure was not due to extravagance. In fact, theater critic and wit Alexander Woollcott once quipped that when Barker showed his staff's measly payroll to Kahn, Kahn pointed to the figures opposite each name and asked, "What are these figures? Their ages?" But efficiency couldn't overcome lack of audience interest. The Barker venture folded in the summer of 1915. Exhausted and feeling guilty about abandoning Europe during the war, Barker went to France to write a book about the Red Cross. The Little Theater movement sustained the Provincetown Players, the Washington Square Players, and the Theater Guild later in the teens. In fact, the Little Cinemas of the 1920s and the art houses of the post–World War II era modeled themselves on the little theaters. But repertory on such a grand scale was not attempted again in the United States for another decade.

The demise of Barker's venture was for Wanger a harsh introduction to the commercial realities of the theater. But Barker, in Wanger's eyes, had made an avoidable, crucial mistake: he had refused to take general public taste into account. Thirty years later, Wanger declared that the experience "taught me a real lesson about communications. I learned very quickly, in a few months to be exact, that if nobody comes to see your elevating play, nobody gets elevated. . . . No producer ever succeeded with an attitude that 'the public be damned.'"

While Wanger shared Barker's belief that theatrical events could have a salutary effect on an audience, the financial basis of production clearly necessitated popular appeal. And as his productions of *Ta! Ta! Tango* and *The Misleading Lady* at Dartmouth demonstrated, Wanger had no personal objections to commercialism as long as the work was novel. That college officials perceived Wanger as a champion of high art was a mere coincidence due to the fact that the European stagecraft that animated the Little Theater was simply the latest innovation Wanger discerned.

Unlike Barker, Wanger felt no dissatisfaction with the intellectual substance or the organizational system of the commercial theater. For him, innovation in the theater, and later in the movies, depended on astute choices of material. The challenge was to provoke an audience within a familiar and comfortable framework. His logic was not just to uplift the general audience, but in effect to persuade an elite to go slumming. This was a central paradox of his career in theater and films—his desire to earn approval from cultural arbiters of taste without championing the high art that they admired.

Interestingly, the Barker experience by itself did not persuade Wanger that art theater was incompatible with grand entertainment. Until 1920, Wanger's professional producing efforts vacillated between light entertainment and more serious work. For instance, in the fall of 1915, he briefly worked in a small-scale Follies company, about the furthest he could travel from Barker's example. He joined Elizabeth Marbury, a sixty-year-old agent whom P. G. Wodehouse and Guy Boulton described as "dear, kindly, voluminous," and whose clients included the illustrious Jacques Feydau, Georges Bataille, James M. Barrie, Arthur Wing Pinero, and W. Somerset Maugham.

Marbury's American Play Company on West 42nd Street specialized in what Wodehouse and Boulton described as "musical comedy on a miniature scale—musical comedy [typically composed by Jerome Kern] with not more than two sets, eight to twelve girls and an orchestra of eleven." Marbury asked Wanger to manage *See America First,* the first professional work of former Harvard law student Cole Porter. After several out-of-town tryouts, this parody of patriotic musicals—featuring dancer Clifton Webb and heiress Ann Morgan—ran for just fifteen performances in March 1916. Yet Wanger managed it, Porter later recalled, "with professional éclat."

Then came another about-face. In the fall of 1916, after a year in Marbury's employ, Wanger joined the celebrated thirty-eight-year-old Russian actress Alla Nazimova and her second husband, actor-manager Charles Bryant, to mount the "Nazimova Season." A former violinist and a Stanislavsky student, Nazimova learned English in an astounding six months and proceeded in 1906 to premiere several plays by Ibsen in America, offering, among other triumphs, the first portrayal of the title role of *Hedda Gabler.* A bisexual who subscribed to mysticism, Nazimova capitalized on her enormous dark eyes and an emotional depth that welled up from her small frame, to become one of America's finest actresses. She was also the aunt of the future RKO producer Val Lewton and godmother to Nancy Davis Reagan. In fact, Wanger and Nazimova hired Davis's mother, Edie Luckett, to play a small role in their first production.

The Nazimova Season marked her return to New York after a two-year absence. Wanger first met her at a tea party in New York, which the actress left in a huff after an argument with manager Charles Frohman. She turned to Wanger: "I have a play and I'll do it with you," she told him. It was an extraordinary coup for a first-time producer, but Nazimova was impressed with Wanger's apprenticeship to Barker and taken with his enthusiasm and charm. Their plan was yet another stab at repertory of "international scope," including Russian plays and works by Schnitzler and by Molière, as well as revivals of the actress's past Ibsen successes. The trio told the *New York Dramatic Mirror* in October 1916 that "there is in New York and throughout the country a vast audience ready to accept classic as well as modern drama and that a professional merging of these tastes towards a season of plays of unusual merit will win success."

Yet producing the Nazimova Season proved a difficult chore. After working with both the Shuberts (who had built a theater expressly for her in 1910) and the Syndicate, Nazimova was aware neither one would back her choice of play. Wanger was game to produce it independently, but as he later recalled, "In those days there were no independent theatrical producers." This meant that Wanger had to play the two monopolies off each other to obtain a theater and to obtain funds from "angels" outside the business. The latter gave him no difficulty, as he had "unlimited" backing from a group led by the Guggenheims, who were friends of the Seligmans and the Stettheimers. But securing a theater was a different matter, and Nazimova had begun rehearsing another play before Wanger finally leased the Shubert's Princess Theater in mid-December. Nazimova told the *New York Times* that "had she been willing to appear under other management than her own, and had she not held out for the repertoire [*sic*] idea, she might have obtained a larger theatre and one better suited to her needs."

Nazimova's needs concerned an original new play, *'Ception Shoals,* the second by H. Austin Adams, an Episcopalian preacher turned playwright. *'Ception Shoals* concerned the sexual awakening of Eve (Nazimova), the sheltered, sensitive niece of a lighthouse keeper. Raised in ignorance of such matters, Eve witnesses the birth of a child and falls in love with a ship captain (Bryant). After waiting for his return in anticipation of her future family, Eve learns that her uncle has sent him away. Eve commits suicide "by walking into the sea, clinging to a bit of rag which she fancies to be her child."

This gloomy thesis play, proposing that "it is dangerous to stifle the sex impulse in a normal woman," was a far cry from *See America First*. In fact, the play was of a piece with Dreiser's *Sister Carrie* and resembled Ibsen's dramas, as Nazimova spelled it out for *Theater* magazine:

> There is just as much symbolism of its kind in "'Ception Shoals" as in—say "The Wild Duck" or "Little Eyolf." The little Eve foredoomed at birth to perish for want of light in a lighthouse . . .

Apparently the symbolism was heavy-handed, for after its January 10, 1917, premiere, critics derogated the play's "preachy" passages (particularly its second act) and noted the familiarity of its argument. Yet they were equally unanimous about the quality of the production, what the *New York Dramatic Mirror* called the show's "sincerity, its impressive force, its suggestive atmosphere," and about Nazimova's performance. It didn't hurt the box office to offer a scene in which the stunning actress appeared in a bathing suit. Theatergoers packed the 299-seat Princess for every show (including additional matinee performances Wanger squeezed in) during its four-week run.

The Nazimova Season was cut short, however, first because the lease on the Princess Theater expired and the company had to tour the Midwest while awaiting another New York theater. Also, and more decisively, there was America's entry into the Great War in April 1917. Wanger had planned to produce *Once Upon a Time,* a new play based on the Greek myth of the Golden Fleece, and a musical version of *Snow White* to be written by Frank Oz and designed by poster and book illustrator Maxfield Parrish. Instead, the war ignited Wanger's interest in propaganda. Meanwhile, Nazimova continued with her stage career, appearing in the propaganda film *War Brides.* She eventually adapted *'Ception Shoals* at Metro Pictures as *Out of the Fog* and appeared in several films she produced independently, including *Camille* (1921) and *Salome* (1923), the latter directed by Bryant, the former featuring her good friend, Rudolph Valentino.

Wanger's fascination with the arts of persuasion, evident in his choice of thesis plays such as *The Test* and *'Ception Shoals,* had grown during the summer of 1914, as he prepared to attend Balliol College in Oxford. There he observed the government's mobilization for the Great War. His German heritage meant little in the face of Kaiser Wilhelm II's arrant militarism, and the Wangers' continuing visits to Europe gave him a very immediate sense of the stakes in the conflict. In the fall of 1914, he donated proceeds from a college play to Belgian relief.

Propaganda had monetary rewards too. While working for Marbury in 1916, Wanger negotiated a contract for her client, dancer Irene Castle, to appear in a serial entitled *Patria* for William Randolph Hearst's Cosmopolitan Pictures. For this work, Wanger, whom Marbury paid fifty dollars a week, earned a $1,000 commission, a scale of pay that turned his head. He was also impressed with the film's vivid, melodramatic depiction of anti-Japanese sentiments: Castle portrayed Patria Channing, a hardy American woman who uses her inheritance to lead the American army against invading Japanese (led by the future Charlie Chan, Warner Oland). Released in January 1917, the serial anticipated the disclosure in late February of a proposed alliance between Germany, Mexico, and Japan. *Patria*'s episodes concluded fifteen weeks later just before America's entry into World War I. President Wilson found its jingoistic politics "disturbing": "It is extremely unfair to the Japanese, and I fear it is calculated to stir up a great deal of hostility," he wrote the Hearst company. The film was recut to address Wilson's objections.

After America declared war on April 5, Wanger was appointed Secretary of the Recruiting Committee of New York mayor John Mitchel's Committee on National Defense, which, according to the *New York Times,* oversaw all propaganda in the city "on a scientific basis under a system similar to that evolved in England." Wanger's group gained the cooperation of restaurants, stores, theaters, and the New York Suffragette party to design, print, distribute, and place recruitment posters, including James Montgomery Flagg's "Uncle Sam Wants You." Their efforts climaxed on April 17 with "Wake Up America" day, which commemorated the ride of Paul Revere and the Battle of Lexington in an effort to raise recruitment to fever pitch.

More personally, Wanger exploited family connections in Washington, particularly the Stettheimers' cousin George Beer, an adviser to Colonel House, and obtained letters of recommendation, from Lee Shubert among others, to secure a commission as a second lieutenant in the United States Army's Signal Corps. After sitting in late June for a portrait by his aunt Florine, who was distraught over his enthuasism for getting into battle, Wanger reported to the Massachusetts Institute of Technology for training as a pilot. His Aunt Ettie, seeing him in uniform in August, noted that Walter was "full of excitement and anticipation; doesn't take his job lightly."

The Signal Corps used aviation to collect vital intelligence with photographs of enemy positions, arsenals, and battlefield topography. Wanger, like other Signal Corps trainees, learned piloting without planes at MIT. After several months of on-the-ground preparation, he was shipped with the American Expeditionary Force to France in October 1917. Eventually Wanger was stationed in the Italian equivalent of the Lafayette Escadrille under Fiorello LaGuardia, the future mayor of New York, at Foggia, a city in southeast Italy near the Adriatic Sea. There Wanger quickly gained the ironic title of "the Austrian Ace": "He always told me he was a terrible pilot," Shelley remembered, "and he used to describe how he inevitably crashed his biplane into a ditch that immediately preceded the edge of the runway." Yet Wanger was always unscathed and able to walk away from the wreckage, and there seemed to be an unlimited supply of planes for him to test his skill on. Screenwriter Frances Marion, who met Wanger in Paris at this time, recalled, "Never once was he reprimanded by his superiors, who seemed to admire recklessness and bravado, no matter what the cost."

In April 1918, Wanger's bravado was channeled into intelligence and propaganda work for the Rome office of the Committee on Public Information (CPI). Wanger resisted the move because he was anxious to remain close to combat. Nevertheless, the new assignment, which occasioned a promotion to first lieutenant, involved the movies.

President Wilson had created the CPI on April 13, 1917, just one week after America's entry into the war, at the suggestions of the secretaries of war and the navy. The CPI publicized the country's war aims and methods and drowned out pacifist, pro-German, or anticapitalist sentiments. To head the agency, Wilson selected George Creel, a staunch supporter and a prominent journalist associated most recently with the *Denver Post*. Rapidly, Creel erected a worldwide organization for publicizing America's war efforts and hired a number of brilliant young Americans of the era, including political columnist and adviser Walter Lippmann and Wanger's Ithaca friend, the public relations expert Bernays.

The CPI office in Rome had been created in response to a severe crisis. After the disastrous Battle of Caporetto in October 1917—in which the Italians suffered 40,000 casualties and wounded and 250,000 men were taken prisoner by Austro-Hungarian and German troops—civilian morale plummeted. With Socialists dominating the Parliament, the American government feared that Italy would fall prey to another Bolshevik revolution. Charles E. Russell, the director of CPI operations in England wrote Creel in October 1917: "The consequences [in Italy] that open before us are enough to sober us all with a good, full view of the abyss."

In March 1918, the CPI sent Captain Charles E. Merriam to direct a new Rome office. Author of *A History of American Political Theories* and a student of America's party system, Merriam had been active in recruitment at the University of Chicago. In Italy, he sought to counter what he later called "a tremendous economic pressure upon Italy to end the war," and he aimed "to tell as quickly to as many people as possible, in as vivid a way as possible, the story of America's war preparations and war purposes." Later, in October 1918, the office redirected its efforts toward countering Socialist-inspired unrest.

Taking cabled news items, radio news, and feature articles written under novelist Ernest Poole's direction in London, the Rome office publicized America's efforts in conservation, shipbuilding, industrial work, and recruitment. The office also presented profiles of American farm life which provincial newspapers published, and it deployed 4.5 million postcards, posters, American flags, and speech excerpts to build on President Wilson's extraordinary popularity with the Italians (one author later reported seeing a picture of Wilson in "every shop-window" in Rome). In addition, the Rome office organized a series of special events. Key among these were traveling speakers, such as LaGuardia, who toured the country in a plane, and Samuel Gompers, head of the American Federation of Labor, who spoke to Italians of American labor's support of the war (and whom Wanger escorted to several Roman bordellos).

There is no question that this was the most exciting and fulfilling project in Wanger's already rich life. Merriam was a source of inspiration: he struck Wanger as "marvelous, a Lincolnesque fellow, very honest and forthright." The two men met daily with John Hearley, a burly United Press reporter of Irish descent, in the lobby of Rome's Grand Hotel, which was open only to "ambassadors and royalty and members of the very most exclusive society." There they would plan their strategies and gather information, while "suffering from the best chefs and wine obtainable." Merriam assigned Wanger, who knew French, German, and Italian, to meet with Italian journalists, officials, and aristocrats such as King Victor Emmanuel II, Prince Piero Colonna (a future mayor of Rome), Premier Vittorio Orlando, General Diaz, and General Badoglio. He also escorted American congressmen on tour, one of whom, Wanger liked to recount, thought upon first seeing Venice that "those Huns" had flooded the city.

By no means deskbound, Wanger escorted author Ray Stannard Baker around the front. Baker clandestinely reported on Italy's war efforts to Colonel House in preparation for the peace talks. With Merriam's and the Italian Army's complicity, Wanger at one point obtained and personally copied for Baker a lengthy secret report comparing French and Italian military achievements, a coup that earned Baker's high praise.

Wanger found this invigorating in part because the CPI offices improvised heavily. As one historian described it:

> Main objectives were fixed, but two hours never passed without a new idea for achieving them. Bureaus were thrown together in an evening on the flash of someone's four o'clock inspiration, and on some other day might be as speedily closed down, merged with another office, or directed to assume entirely new duties.

Wanger later characterized the Italian office's work as a kind of "*opera bouffe,*" noting that "we were just blindly in our folly trying to get things accomplished and paying no attention to protocol." This approach had serious consequences, for the American ambassador in Rome, Thomas Nelson Page, resented the CPI office's intelligence gathering and its direct cabling capacity to Washington. At one point Page even threatened to have Wanger reassigned to the front and court-martialed, if Wanger didn't reveal the substance of his intelligence work. He staunchly refused.

Aside from Page's harassment, Wanger thrived in the working conditions of the Rome office. Although he "knew nothing about diplomacy" he earned the loyalty and affection of most of the staff, who wrote him enthusiastic letters when he was reassigned to Paris toward the end of the war and defended him to Creel and President Wilson against Ambassador Page's accusations. Thanks to Hearley, Wanger was "especially commended for efficient and loyal service" in Creel's report on the CPI.

In July 1918, Lieutenant Wanger inaugurated the use of newsreels produced by the Signal Corps for the CPI in New York and Paris (such as the *Inter-Allied Weekly*). He oversaw their retitling in Italian "for popular consumption" at a makeshift lab in Rome, a task that gave him firsthand experience with the art of film editing. The films were distributed to movie theaters, military bases, and schools. Given the urgent situation in Italy and the flexibility of the CPI, Wanger took the initiative of suggesting that the CPI produce a twenty-minute film, likely extracted from newsreel footage. Wanger's film showed

men marching down Fifth Avenue in civilian clothes on their way to our training camps and coming out a few months later in uniform and getting on enormous transports. . . . We gave it to all the theaters in Italy and we enlisted a lot
of the film stars to be at the premiere, which was the 4th of July.

The image of troop recruits before and after training was generic in World
War I newsreels, and Wanger later conceded that some of the newsreels were
"poorly produced and not too effective." Yet,

the feelings of the Italian people were tremendously influenced by those movies
and I am convinced that the ultimate decision of Italy to fight on the side of the
Allies was due, at least to some extent, to the effect of the movies.

The footage for Wanger's film might have been duplicated from an early
Signal Corps film, *The 1917 Recruit*. In any case, Wanger's idea worked and
his office subsequently arranged for films to be distributed on other topics.

In fact, everything the Rome office did during the second half of 1918
seemed to work. When an office employee by chance queried a street speaker
in Florence about United States involvement in the war, the speaker replied
with the most recent statistics circulated by the CPI. The cheering crowds
who greeted Wilson at train stations throughout Italy at the end of the war
were eloquent proof of the effectiveness of Merriam's office.

The CPI experience in Italy at once confirmed Wanger's sense of social responsibility and his optimistic and idealistic attitude toward his work. Most
Americans shared this feeling during the war, for the CPI took much of its
zeal and elevated tone from the Progressive Movement's values of duty and
sacrifice. Such altruism arose from the same moral outlook that had generated
the emphasis on "uplift" in the arts. World War I was an occasion to affirm
the unity of the United States by creating a national identity of selfless sacrifice. Nearly half a century after the fact, Wanger recalled that Armistice Day
was "the most exciting day of my life."

The benefits of Wanger's experience of World War I and the CPI were
many. It provided him, and many government and business leaders, with a
crash course in shaping public opinion and the value of publicity for his films.
There are definite parallels between Wanger's prolific articles, interviews, and
speeches in the late 1930s and Creel's conscious strategy of "expression not
repression," which suppressed negative opinions by flooding the information
services with positive news. From CPI work Wanger also learned the international scope of the movies' potential influence. When America faced World
War II, Wanger was confident that Hollywood could help the cause.

One negative result of the CPI experience is that it exaggerated for Wanger the effectiveness of movies as a means of influencing mass opinion. The
Merriam Office work was undoubtedly successful in the context of the war,

but this did not mean film propaganda would be equally effective in peace-time; in fact, war was the only time most audiences (with their governments' encouragement) tolerated it. In addition, Wanger's war work confirmed his aesthetic preference for direct expression over verisimilitude and subtlety, which often meant that the tone of his films ran contrary to critical and popular standards for entertainment (and entertainment was what brought Italian audiences into the theaters to see Wanger's newsreel in the first place). Subscribing to behaviorist assumptions that were prevalent after the war, Wanger came to believe that the critical reception of movies depended as much on "conditioning" the press and the public's reception of them as on their innate qualities, a conviction that often blinded him to the flaws of his films.

After the war, Wanger worked at the Paris Peace Conference as an aide to Columbia University historian and Wilson adviser James T. Shotwell, who advised the American delegation on international labor problems, standards, and agreements. Wanger again used his multilingual talents to secure from diverse governments the documents Shotwell used in his study. He was once again thrust into the heady atmosphere of international diplomacy: in Shotwell's company alone, Wanger had dinner with Colonel T. E. Lawrence and royalty from the Middle East and attended countless official functions where leaders of twenty-seven nations met. In his book about the conference, Shotwell later described Wanger as "a very jolly boy," who was excited that "we were going to have 'major-generals do our laundering, and all things on a similar scale!'"

Wanger later claimed that he decided to become a film producer after seeing the short film's decisive effects on public opinion in Italy during the war: "That's when I decided that this was going to be my niche." Yet devoted to innovation as he was, Wanger must have considered the movies as a potential career long before he served in the Great War. Unprecedented acclaim and controversy greeted D. W. Griffith's *The Birth of a Nation* when Wanger left Dartmouth in early 1915, and many prominent theatrical managers were involved in film production and distribution (even as films reduced attendance at their theaters).

Moreover, the CPI work, Wilson's high-minded negotiations, and Wanger's enthusiasm and contacts made him consider a career in the Foreign Service. But he found it "too costly. I had to go back and earn some money." When he returned to the United States in the spring of 1919, Wanger resumed his producing career and the struggle to mediate between elite and popular stage productions. First, he extended the run of the Theater Guild's production of St. John Ervine's *John Ferguson,* moving the production uptown to Broadway. A prewar Irish drama that focused on a poor farming family involved in the murder of a landowner, the play became under Wanger's management the greatest success of the Little Theater movement, collecting

$6,000 in weekly ticket sales (well over Wanger's $2,500 expenses). It proved, in Wanger's words, that "a commercial success may have artistic attributes—another triumph for ideals properly business managed."

But Wanger then experienced a run of disappointments. He joined forces with the Syndicate to produce a new comedy, *Five O'Clock,* cowritten by Frank Bacon, a fifty-five-year-old veteran of the San Francisco theater whom Wanger had seen performing when a young man (and the father of film director Lloyd Bacon). In 1918, Bacon had become a star with his own populist comedy, *Lightnin',* about a sharp, cracker-barrel country man, which earned $1,176,000 in three years. His *Five O'Clock* anticipated the plot of Frank Capra's *Mr. Deeds Goes to Town:* it shows the triumphant revenge of an orphan against his greedy relatives, who have placed him in a repressive mental institution for juveniles. Like *Lightnin',* it featured the "exaggerated rural folk of farce," but according to *Variety,* it "would have been better off for another week or two on the road. One author stated that the producer had just muffed a half million by not having the piece doctored." In the competitive 1919 season, *Five O'Clock* ran for only forty-one shows.

Wanger tried producing plays outside of New York with equally disappointing results. *The Purple Slipper,* a mediocre comedy, fizzled in out-of-town tryouts in Scranton and Trenton in October. In November, he leased a shuttered, 350-seat house in Philadelphia to book touring plays, and Wanger quickly changed its name from "The Little Theater" to "The Philadelphian." This move, he told the press, was designed to "rid the theatre of all traces of its previous taint of superiority over all other mere theaters at which art was not capitalized . . . this theater will not be 'high-brow' in any sense of the word." Wanger booked a series of comedies: May Irwin in *On the Hiring Line* and Rupert Hughes's *The Cat Bird* (which featured Janet Beecher, a character actress Wanger would employ in his first independent film *The President Vanishes*), both of which played some variation on reconciling the polarization between rural and urban culture. Wanger found theater management, with its myriad headaches of heating bills, maintenance and cleaning, and paying off licensing fees and taxes, unrewarding. "The theatre of today needs young men like you," Belasco wrote Wanger in 1919, yet his efforts in the theater to negotiate between audience appeal and innovation, between comfortable formulas and elevation, were simply too discouraging for Wanger to continue.

The one bright spot of Wanger's first year after World War I was his marriage on September 13, 1919, to Justine Johnston. Burke recalled Wanger years later as "the boy I knew once whose whole heart and soul was wrapped up in the theatre, even to waiting at the stage door for little red-headed starlets to come out." Johnston was one of those whom he awaited. A twenty-four-year-old lithe, blue-eyed, Swedish blonde, she was dubbed the most beautiful woman in the world after dancing and singing (with her friend

Marion Davies) in the Ziegfeld Follies. The 1916 Version ended in a tableau with Johnston draped in a flag as Columbia. Revues and songs were written for her. Lee Shubert and gambler Diamond Jim Brady were smitten with her. Vaudeville producer Jesse Lasky found her "as Luscious as Marilyn Monroe."

While living with her mother on Central Park West, Johnston starred in several shows, including Lasky's Folies Bergere, in which she led a troupe of topless dancers. Her stardom peaked when she appeared with comedian Ed Wynn and Fred and Adele Astaire in Lee Shubert's wartime revue *Over the Top*. Witty and intelligent, she was like Wanger a progressive idealist, and she was an ardent suffragette and active in the Actor's Fidelity League during the 1919 actors' strike. By the time she married, she was "heart and soul sick of all that 'brainless' beauty category." She shocked Broadway by joining a stock company in Connecticut for acting experience. Wanger promised to help her reach her goal.

And Johnston supported Wanger's decision at the age of twenty-five to join an industry about which he knew little except that it paid exceedingly well and that it could change public opinion overnight. Filmmaking spoke to both Wanger's notions of artistry *and* to the value of topicality as another strategy for producing innovative entertainments. In this sense, the film medium offered the potential for reconciling the irreconcilable terms of the highbrow-lowbrow debate in the theater. "At college we used to dream of a National Theatre for the spoken drama," Wanger told *Moving Picture World* in 1921,

> where playwrights, their incomes assured, might write out their best thoughts and see them produced by the leading actors of the country. And all the time there was an International Theatre, growing in strength every day, that offers big rewards for just this class of work.

At the same time, the constructive engagement of an audience's mind became the key aim of Wanger's efforts at filmmaking, on the liberal assumption he shared with Creel that the American citizen was "rational and capable of wise decisions if properly informed." Wanger articulated these views on December 10, 1921, in an essay published in London's *Daily Mail*. Entitled "films as Foreign Offices," the article is worth quoting at length:

> While the representatives of the nations of the earth sit in conference at Washington searching for formulas which (written on a scrap of paper perhaps) will guarantee to the world everlasting peace, the great masses of those nations are meeting daily or nightly, not in conference to seek formulae, but in kinema [*sic*] houses to see films that will eventually render Washington Conferences unnecessary.
>
> There is at present, at any rate, universal recognition of the futility of wars; there is a very old saying to the effect that the masses never have any quarrel with each other.

Yet . . . [u]niversal peace will come only when there is between all nations and all peoples universal acquaintanceship. And by means of the moving picture we are gaining a knowledge of what the rest of the world knows, what it eats, and, what is more important, *how* it eats; what it wears and, what is of greater importance *how* it wears it.

. . . The written word, the spoken word, have failed to accomplish in a big way what the kine is now accomplishing for the very good and simple and true reason that, after all is said and written, *seeing is believing*. And the moving picture of the real thing is practically as convincing as a view of the thing itself.

It may be argued that nations well acquainted with each other have been known to go to war; also that mere knowledge (which grows so rapidly with the growth of the kinema) is not only no guarantee against international armed conflict but is, on the contrary, the devil's chief lieutenant in devising weapons of torture, mutilation, and death.

The answer to the first part of that argument is that nations *have never known each other as thoroughly as they are now coming to know each other by means of the moving picture.*

The answer to the second part of that argument is that heretofore knowledge has been the possession of the few and the Foreign Office; but henceforth the Foreign Offices of the world will be the picture houses of the world.

For they offer the best means of producing greater world knowledge, world acquaintanceship, and hence, world peace.

All the major concerns of Wanger's future career are alluded to in this short piece: the behaviorist notion that movies could shape attitudes and behavior, the insistence on film's utilitarian purpose in modern society, the vague analogy between diplomacy and international film exhibition, the empirical assumption that to see is to understand, and the assertion that the defining characteristic of the movies is their overwhelming realism. The very object of address—to opinion makers high above the mass of humanity—also demonstrates Wanger's elitist orientation.

These five principles would inform the substance of all Wanger's public pronouncements and guide the majority of his outstanding production choices. To the end of his life, he devoted his efforts to demonstrating their truth. But he did so in ways that often sabotaged his argument.

Part Two

The Executive Apprentice

4

Giving the Movies "Class" (1920–1924)

Sometime during the infamous Actors Equity strike of August–September 1919, Belasco's star actor Holbrook Blinn gave a dinner party at his home in Riverdale. Among his guests were the Wangers and Lasky, then vice-president in charge of production for Famous Players–Lasky (FPL).

Over dinner, Wanger recounted to Blinn and Lasky his triumphs on the Dartmouth campus, his associations with Barker, Marbury, and Nazimova, and the successful propaganda work he had done in Italy. Nearly four decades after that dinner, Lasky recalled how Wanger had impressed him on first meeting as being "bright, suave, and keenly conversant with the legitimate theatre."

Lasky was especially interested in Wanger because he was in a tight spot. FPL financed play production in New York in order to obtain screen rights to the plays. A month earlier, the company had acquired Charles Frohman, Inc., to facilitate this procedure. But with its former manager taken ill, the Frohman company needed someone to oversee operations and select plays. Lasky had neither the time or the desire to do so, and he wanted an executive "of the utmost capability and self-sufficiency." Driving Wanger home in his Stutz-Bearcat, Lasky thought the young impresario would do.

When he proposed this to Wanger the next day at FPL's Manhattan offices, Wanger "was thrilled with the prospect, but even more intrigued with my problems as a studio producer." Lasky elaborated:

> I didn't ask all the questions. With a consuming interest he probed the particulars of my liaison work between the West Coast studio and the Eastern business office. . . .

"Walter," I said after he had repeatedly veered our discussion from the Frohman company to movie-making, "I don't think I'll entrust this post to you after all. Let me think it over."

Lasky instead hired Gilbert Miller, son of the celebrated stage actor Henry Miller and Wanger's lifelong friend. In the interim, Wanger produced *Five O'Clock* and managed the Philadelphian. But Wanger remained intrigued and during the spring of 1920, he advised Lasky on several playscripts being considered for theatrical production. At the end of April, Lasky appointed him "special representative" at FPL, charged with keeping "in close touch with Paramount Artcraft artists and all other phases of production." Artcraft was the brand name under which the studio released its best films with major stars. In this capacity, Wanger watched FPL adapt Barrie's *Sentimental Tommy* and *Dr. Jekyll and Mr. Hyde* with John Barrymore at its several studios in and around Manhattan. In June, Lasky made Wanger temporary head of all production before sailing to England. In November 1920, he named Wanger general manager of FPL production. Wanger was twenty-six years old.

The encounter with Lasky concisely illustrates Wanger's impact on and value to the growing film industry during the 1920s. As this new entertainment form aspired to social acceptance and improved production values, Wanger's personal refinement combined with his experience on the legitimate stage to impress the pioneer studio executives. Immediately, Wanger was set apart from other major studio producers, such as Winifred Sheehan and Samuel Goldwyn, who inspired Bernays to assess the film industry as "a crude, crass, manufacturing business, run by crude, crass men."

Wanger had landed at the top of the top. In 1920 FPL was *the* major company in the field, dominating the business, in the words of film historian Douglas Gomery, "as no company ever had or would." In fact, just a month before Wanger's first meeting with Lasky, the FPL board had approved President Zukor's unprecedented plan to issue $10 million in preferred stock to finance the construction and purchase of fifty first-run movie theaters and for significant investments in hundreds more. Just as Wanger signed on, Zukor was expanding FPL into a vertically integrated firm—one that owned and controlled the production, distribution, and exhibition of films to minimize its investment risks.

The fruits of Zukor's efforts are well known. Within two years (by August 1921), FPL had acquired 303 mostly first-run theaters and could guarantee the showing of all its films on screens around the country. Within another two years, Samuel Goldwyn, Loew's, the Fox Corporation, and the newly formed Warner Bros. all followed Zukor's example.

Even before its domestic theater buying spree, FPL in 1919 collected 30 percent of the movie rentals in the country. This was due in part to a roster of actors that exploited the star system, and in part to its outstanding directors such as Cecil B. deMille. DeMille had left the theater to work with Lasky in films in 1913, when, as Lasky put it, they had seen "some two-reel pictures and decided that if we could not do better than that we ought to be shot." Their first film, *The Squaw Man,* made in Hollywood in 1914, did much better; it initiated a string of successes exceeded only in postwar years when deMille developed a formula for superficially risqué comedies, typically starring Gloria Swanson and Thomas Meighan. In 1919, *Male and Female* netted $1.9 million and *Why Change Your Wife?* nearly $900,000 in profits.

Zukor's empire building and deMille's success was exhilarating, but Lasky required more than deMille specials to fill the theaters twice weekly. Zukor's block-booking policy required unaffiliated (non-FPL) theater managers to book all of FPL's lesser films to get its major star vehicles, and it required Lasky to turn out between seventy and 104 features yearly. The operations were hectic. "This," Lasky later recalled, "was mass production with a vengeance, and need I mention that, if we had been fabricating aircraft, some of them would have been a menace to life and limb."

Lasky and his colleagues met the challenge of high volume production in several ways. They expanded studio facilities in Hollywood. In September 1920, FPL opened a new studio in Long Island City, across the East River from Manhattan, to replace several very cramped spaces in Elmhurst, in Yonkers (the former Triangle studio), in Manhattan proper (at 56th and 125th streets), and in Fort Lee, New Jersey. Larger than Hearst's Cosmopolitan studio in Harlem, Fox's Manhattan studio, or Griffith's Mamaroneck studio, the Astoria, Long Island, facility was capable of shooting up to eight films simultaneously. Studios in Great Britain and India soon followed.

The acquisition of the Frohman company was another way to boost FPL's yearly schedule. In April 1920, Lasky publicly invited playwrights to submit their work: "We want to let every author know that he will have his play produced if it shows any sort of merit. Just so long as a play possesses one good dramatic idea, we are ready to back the writer." Movies had of course long been modeling their production and promotion on the example of the legitimate theater, and the adaptation of literary and theatrical works (such as the *Film d'art*'s *Passion Play* and Laemmle's *Hiawatha*) represented both a reliable source of stories and a shortcut to desirable social prestige.

In turn, the use of literary and stage classics encouraged the innovation of feature-length films of roughly an hour's length in the early to mid-teens. The longer films became standout attractions, and by the late teens, American movies were capable of clearly telling complex stories with multiple plots. They also provided the exhibitor with an excuse to charge higher ticket prices and to increase profit margins.

FPL's New York studio also facilitated the introduction of more sophisticated forms of set design into the movies as directors and studios showed increasing sensitivity to art direction. "A new type of executive," responsible for set construction, the arrangement of furnishings, and costume design, the art director entered the film industry in the mid-teens. In 1914, the Jesse L. Lasky Feature Play Company hired Wilfred Buckland, who had previously designed sets for Belasco, and who used "the most recent theatrical lighting styles," as a studio art designer. While directing *The Blue Bird* and an adaptation of Barker's *Prunella* (both 1918), Maurice Tourneur explicitly invoked as his inspiration the production designs of Craig and Barker. By 1919, Joseph Urban, the Viennese designer who had worked for Florenz Ziegfeld and the Boston Opera Company, worked at Hearst's Cosmopolitan studios, and Robert Haas, a stage designer, worked on the Astoria studio production *Forever*.

Wanger's confident familiarity with the New Stagecraft and the theater generally aided Lasky in every goal for FPL production. He spoke French and Italian and "he knew London like a book," so he could expand the scope of the search for talent and material internationally. A keen and critical judge of new plays, he quickly gained a reputation for his shrewd bargaining tactics for screen rights and was associated with the studio's acquisition of "highbrow" material. Within months of being hired, he made two striking contributions to FPL's operations.

First, Wanger sponsored a fledgling film genre, the orientalist romance, which was derived from the example of the Ballets Russes and their imitators. Wanger's enthusiasm was clearly a product of his exposure to European culture, yet the Middle East had been a staple travelogue subject in the cinema's earliest years. It was a genre inspired by recent archaeological discoveries that reiterated centuries-old imperialist ideologies and that readily translated into short narrative films such as Georges Melies's 1899 *Cleopatre.* During the teens, novels and plays such as Edgar Selwyn's *The Arab* and Edith Hull's *The Sheik* had developed stories set in the Middle Eastern desert—"the locus of irrational primitivism and uncontrollable instincts," in Ella Shohat's phrase—that sustained western nations' visions of empire, foreign conquest, and patriarchal dominance.

FPL, and deMille in particular, were well aware of the box office appeal of exotic spectacle, but they had confined it in past productions to single characters (the Japanese businessman in deMille's *The Cheat,* 1916), biblical interludes in the risqué comedies such as *Male and Female,* or isolated adaptations such as deMille's version of Selwyn's *The Arab* (1914) or Louis Gasnier's *Kismet* (1920). Inspired by the artistry and considerable box office performance of several German costume films such as Ernst Lubitsch's adaptation of Reinhardt's pantomime *Sumurun* (1920), Wanger and enthusiastic story department readers at FPL persuaded Lasky to purchase Hull's *The Sheik.*

The success and notoriety that greeted Valentino's performance in this

FPL film needs no recounting here, but *The Sheik* (1921) is equally notable for the ingenious ways it projects Western narrative formulas into an orientalist setting and for its formulation of a distinctive visual style. Sheik Ahmed Ben Hassan's revealed identity as an orphaned European aristocrat was consistent with the character revelations that informed nineteenth-century melodramas of separated families which Wilde spoofed in *The Importance of Being Earnest*. Similarly, as Gaylyn Studlar has noted, the affair of Lady Diana Mayo (Agnes Ayres) with the sheik conforms to Janice Radway's description of the woman's gradual discovery of her lover's sensitive, affectionate side in the less exotic "women's romance" genre.

Indeed, *The Sheik* was notable for its use of themes and motifs that women's fiction commonly explored during the era and for what Miriam Hansen has called its "ambivalent fantasies of independence and rape." Immediately after a brief prologue, *The Sheik* compares the Arabian women sold on the marriage market "like chattel slaves" to the Lady Diana, who claims that all "marriage is slavery" and who insists on touring the desert alone. As the film progresses, the distinction between the two types of women become blurred, as Lady Diana dresses as an Arabian dancer and is captured and gradually enthralled by the sheik, with whom she is constantly compared through crosscutting. The box office success of this heady mix of the exotic, the dangerous and the sensual inspired Wanger's constant attention to what *Variety* would call "the femme angle," especially since *The Sheik*'s popularity seemed to confirm 1920s estimates that placed women at up to 80 percent of the total film audience.

The Sheik also provided commercial justification for the orientalist genre, within which Wanger worked throughout his career. He was not alone in mining this vein. Hollywood has produced orientalist genre films to the present day, most recently with Disney's *Aladdin* (1992). In the 1920s, all-American Douglas Fairbanks exploited comparable values in the fantasy narrative and William Cameron Menzies's stunning set designs for *The Thief of Baghdad* (United Artists, 1924). That same year Rex Ingram directed *The Arab* on location in Algiers for Metro Pictures. In 1926 Wanger purchased *Beau Geste,* the quintessential tale of the French Foreign Legion. Moreover, the character of the sheik established a durable romantic archetype—the European man trapped, lost, or in flight from his past in Arabia—which peaked with Rick Blaine in *Casablanca* (1943). Be they contemporary adventure films, historical epics and biopics of the Near East, biblical films, Arabian Nights tales, or horror films, these orientalist sub-genre films, like the most shocking performances of the Ballets Russes, transposed uncontrollable desires and risqué stories to exotic locales for the vicarious pleasure of the film audience.

The orientalist films also seduced audiences with their visual splendor, inherited again from visual traditions such as orientalist painting and the set designs of Baskt and Poiret. *The Sheik*'s erotic sensuality derives as much from its labyrinthine voyeurism—a tendency manifest in its penchant for shooting scenes through portals and down passageways—as its suggestion of miscegenation and its sadomasochistic overtones. The mise-en-scène is filled with lush textures: as Valentino and Ayres played their scenes in the sheik's tent, director George Melford constantly composed medium-long shots, inviting the viewer's eye to roam over their costumes and the densely patterned wall hangings, bed covers, pillows, and curtains.

Such images, like the lavish settings of deMille's comedies and melodramas, spoke eloquently to the prevalent materialism of the 1920s. America's moral complacency about Progressive Era achievements and the disillusionment that followed the peace conferences encouraged a self-indulgent ethos that marked a definite shift from Wilsonian idealism and the altruism of the previous two decades, which Wanger, FPL, and other filmmakers eagerly exploited. But Wanger especially recognized how Bakst's work for the Ballets Russes fit well into the adornment of the self and the sexual liberation that marked the decade: his color schemes inspired Cartier to set sapphires and emeralds together in "delirious" combinations, and Poiret's draped dresses, baggy pants with high waistlines and banded ankles became a sensation in European high fashion. No wonder the vertically integrated Hollywood companies built movie palaces with orientalist decor: it cemented the association of movies with *Arabian Nights* fantasies, as evidenced in the title of Terry Ramsaye's 1926 film history, *A Million and One Nights*.

For comparable reasons, Wanger found even greater pleasure in his second contribution to FPL: his ability to upgrade the mise-en-scène of the studio's films. He hired Paul Chalfin, a French expert in architecture, interior decorating, and landscaping best known for designing decorations for the parades that greeted returning American soldiers. Wanger later described this with relish:

> De Mille used to have terrible taste in clothes, in sets, and in representing the ways parties were given. So I signed Paul Chalfin [who] . . . was a man of superb taste, and he had an excellent staff. I sent him out to the Coast to show De Mille how to lay a table, how a butler should behave. De Mille bridled at all this, but I insisted on it. I was young and brash.

The first film to benefit from Chalfin's expertise was probably deMille's *Forbidden Fruit,* released in January 1921. More generally, Wanger's contributions highlighted FPL's claim to "realism": one year later, a studio ad in *Photoplay* boasted, "You know that when the plot calls for a Fifth Avenue mansion, or a Scottish castle, or the interior of a sumptuous yacht, that Paramount gives you the real thing."

The month of *Forbidden Fruit*'s premiere, the studio hired Howard Greer, a former manager at Gordon's studio in Paris and a specialist in Edwardian-era clothing. With Greer and other designers, the studio could give stars trend-setting costume designs instead of speculating on what the fashions would be by the time a film was released. Wanger, having commissioned work from Gordon for his Dartmouth shows, was the only production executive at FPL conversant with the world of Parisian designers. Near the end of his life, he boasted:

> How we changed taste, how we improved sets and clothes, how we finally got great designers interested, that's quite a story! I brought top people from Paris to be interior decorators and now we influence the whole bloody world!

In 1929, he secured dress designs by Poiret for Jeanne Eagels in *Jealousy;* in 1930 he sent French illustrator and interior decorator Paul Iribe to Paramount's Hollywood studio. Iribe was, like Chalfin, a "great arbiter of fashion and style and interior decoration"; he added, in Selznick's words, "general smartness" to the West Coast productions.

Lasky, fully appreciative of the significance of Wanger's contributions, announced his appointment as general manager of production in November of 1920 and noted that Wanger "has shown a grasp of production affairs and a vision for the future that stamp him as one of the really big producing executives of the industry." Indeed, Lasky was Wanger's chief sponsor and cheerleader through 1931, when both men were forced out of the company. In Wanger, Lasky saw a classier image of himself.

Lasky was one of the most congenial production men ever to grace a Hollywood studio. An enterprising cornetist from San Francisco, he and his sister Blanche (the future, first Mrs. Samuel Goldwyn) achieved tremendous popularity on the vaudeville circuit for their duets in military costumes that exploited jingoistic sentiment after the Spanish-American War.

But at the very pinnacle of success, Lasky discovered the appealing pleasures of managing money and productions. Financed by a wealthy theater owner, Lasky became a tireless vaudeville impresario, booking acts, scouting for performing talents in Europe as well as America, and devising and staging as quickly as possible roughly forty musical acts between 1906 and 1910. His later descriptions of himself resemble Chester Kent, the prologue manager depicted by James Cagney in Warner Bros.' *Footlight Parade* (1932), for Lasky took inspiration for his acts from casual conversations. Once, on a bet with his sister that he could elaborate an act from any object she pointed to, Lasky developed a Robinson Crusoe skit from a copy of the book. From his wife's exclamations over dining at the Waldorf Astoria, Lasky conceived a musical skit "At the Waldorf," "the biggest hit we ever had."

It was only in 1913, after his costly failure in the European-styled cabaret Folies Bergere on 46th Street, that Lasky listened to brother-in-law Samuel Goldwyn's (then Goldfish) advice to get into the movies. While deMille supervised production, and Goldwyn handled company finances, distribution, sales, and promotion, Lasky used his vaudeville background to acquire plays and stars—for thirty-six films in their second year of operations. In 1916, they merged with Zukor's Famous Players in Famous Plays.

Up to 1920, Lasky's contact with the legitimate stage had been limited to seeking play scenes and performers to wrench out of context and place on a vaudeville bill. His account of being shut out of play production by legitimate producer Alf Hayman (who subsequently became Lasky's underling with the Frohman company sale) indicates Lasky's painful awareness that his vaudeville background simply was not "high class." In Lasky's eyes, Wanger had all the sophistication that he and the movies lacked.

But for all their differences of class and specialty, Lasky found that he and Wanger were temperamentally similar. Lasky, as his vaudeville work attests, was at heart an idea man; he described his duties for the Jesse L. Lasky Feature Company as acquiring stories and talents, that is, identifying potential script possibilities without necessarily elaborating them into a finished product. Such ideas were the lifeblood of Hollywood film production; writers were signed and stories optioned on the slightest information. Hungarian playwrights could inadvertently sell their work while describing it over lunch in studio commissaries, and movies such as Metro-Goldwyn-Mayer's *San Francisco* (1936) could be conceived on the spur of someone's idea ("Earthquake—San Francisco—Gable and MacDonald—can't you see it . . .").

Idea man Lasky undertook his executive chores with an infectious enthusiasm reminiscent of Barker, though without the latter's high-minded idealism. Rouben Mamoulian, who directed *Applause* at Astoria in 1929, described Lasky as the best kind of audience, the appreciative manager who cannot create:

> Lasky was a showman primarily, rather than a person of premeditated, conscious artistry. He was a showman, but he had a great capacity for appreciating artistry and encouraging and supporting it. This is quite a virtue, you know. He had this more than some of the other pioneers, because he was an idealist, and when he saw something beautiful, he gave you a tremendous reaction to it. . . . He was always burning about something, always excited about something.

Wanger, as his years at Dartmouth and on Broadway amply attested, also could locate and enthusiastically articulate an intriguing idea for production without creative skills. As he bragged in 1950, "I have had no little success working without a story at first but with an idea only." Lasky's example reinforced Wanger's natural predilections in film production.

Another similarity between the two showmen was their experimental approach to new stories and talents. Lasky took chances on directors he did not personally know. He chose James Cruze, instead of any of eleven veteran directors on the lot, to direct the big-budget *The Covered Wagon* because Lasky had heard that Cruze "was supposed to have Indian blood" and was therefore "closer by inheritance to the pioneer days" than the other directors. Likewise, newcomer William Wellman was handed the roadshow film of 1927, *Wings,* because he had flown for the Lafayette Escadrille. The Lasky would even contract the Bolshevik director Sergei Eisenstein to work on an adaptation of Theodore Dreiser's *An American Tragedy,* a property Wanger purchased for the studio (and which his associates regarded, as he later put it, "as though I'd bought something on venereal disease for Shirley Temple"). The scramble for talent was enormous given the pressures of mass production, and Lasky and other executives pursued it in a scattershot approach that often paid off. In the film industry as at Dartmouth, Wanger noted, novelty—the differentiation of product from standardized norms—was the overriding goal.

The most vivid example of Wanger and Lasky's pursuit of product differentiation throughout the twenties involved technological innovations. Both were men of their age, deriving much of their optimism from their certainty that technology would advance civilization with unlimited progress; it certainly would enhance their movies. Lasky used two-strip Technicolor for an adaptation of Zane Grey's *Wanderer of the Wasteland* in 1924 and for portions of *The American Venus* (1925); there was a "gyroscopically controlled" camera in *The Manicure Girl* in 1926, and Lasky directed the studio to experiment with MagnaScope, an intermittent large-screen process for the "roadshow" production of *Old Ironsides* in 1926, as well as for *Chang* and *Wings* (both 1927). From 1926 to 1929, Lasky put MagnaScope designer Lorenzo Del Riccio under contract for technical research on three-dimensional and wide film processes.

Then there was Wanger's idea for "Nocolor," a process, or more precisely a policy, which involved constructing black-and-white sets to facilitate tone control for black-and-white camerawork and to save money on set design and execution. Lasky described it as "a colossal dud" because it negatively affected the performance of the players (the process was tried out for Kay Francis's screen debut in 1929, *Gentlemen of the Press*). Yet Lasky's sympathetic view of Wanger as a "brilliant person who is full of ideas" was based in the security of FPL's vertical integration: "no other company of those times could afford to make such premature and costly experiments. Our position as the foremost motion-picture company was not even remotely threatened." Though Lasky here writes of the early twenties, the Nocolor incident demonstrates that he maintained this ethos even after the rise of MGM and the costly transition to sound production.

Energetic and restless enough to thrive in the hectic pace of volume production at FPL, wide-ranging in his reading and knowledge of production ideas, Wanger was well-suited to work with the man who could conceive a vaudeville sketch on the turn of a phrase. And yet the mutual admiration of Wanger and Lasky was disrupted within three months of Wanger's promotion to general manager of production. In the spring of 1921, *Variety* described FPL officials as "more than pleased with the services Wanger has rendered the organization" and "anxious to retain him." When his promotion came through in November, Wanger began agitating for a raise in pay from $400 to $1,000 weekly. A depressed market for films that fall tied Lasky's hands as the company instituted several economy measures (including closing the Astoria studio). When Lasky proposed a compromise figure, Wanger rejected it.

So in early May 1921, Wanger and Johnston sailed on the Acquitania for England, where they remained for more than three years. Nominally investigating a production of *Richard III* for FPL in England, Wanger hinted to Louella Parsons that he might join the diplomatic corps. Johnston announced plans to make films in England "in defense of her sex" because "she says the women usually shown on the screen are either too noble or else so degraded no one can feel a spark of sympathy. She hopes to strike an average." But nothing came of her plans.

Instead, after briefly visiting FPL studios in Paris and meeting Lubitsch and producer Paul Davidson at Universum-Film Aktiengesellschaft (UFA) in Berlin, Wanger arrived in England to examine FPL's London studio, where Alfred Hitchcock started his film career as title designer and prop maker. Wanger had press releases sent to papers across the country that discussed his Dartmouth education, his work with Nazimova, and his management of *John Ferguson,* a play well-known in England. He shrewdly complimented the British on the country's superior wartime propaganda and constantly asserted the perfect suitability of England for film production. Sewell Collins of the *Daily Express* told her readers:

> I spent an hour with [Wanger] the other day, trying with my best diplomacy to prise out of him something about himself. He seemed such a boy at first that I wanted to call him "Walter" and ask him if his mother knew he was far away in the great city of London alone. When I left him I called him "Mister" and made a curtsy.

With the publicity blizzard, and his pedigree as a former executive at the largest film company in the world, it was easy for Wanger to find work. He took a job with the Stoll Company, a prominent producer-exhibitor. In late fall 1921, he secured a three-month lease on Covent Garden, the three-thousand-seat, dormant opera house and concert hall, and used it as a "super kinema" like the American movie palaces. Wanger was determined to demonstrate in three months' time the appeal of the movies to the city's social elite.

Wanger threw himself into theater management with characteristic vigor. He intrigued and amused the local press—particularly when he tried to obtain insurance against the notorious London fog that was known to invade theaters and block the projector's beam. He shrewdly arranged for his article "Films as Foreign Offices" to appear ten days before the premiere of his first show,

Fairbanks's *The Three Musketeers*. He hired at a weekly cost of £600 conductor Eugene Goossens to arrange and conduct an orchestral film score.

While orchestral accompaniment graced the Drury Lane Theater's showing of Griffith's *Intolerance* and *Way Down East,* Wanger enhanced his presentation with an opening night gala attended by many members of England's nobility who had some personal interest in film: newspaper magnate and movie mogul Lord Beaverbrook, Lord and Lady Birkenhead, the Earl of Pembroke, Lady Cunard, and Lady Diana Duff Cooper. "Will London Society ever patronise the film?" the *Daily Graphic* asked the following day. "Last night may have decided." Wanger's supporter at the *Daily Express* called it a "wholesale miracle of rejuvenation" in which "an audience practically equivalent to that of an operatic first night" came to the theater. Wanger, it was noted, had "no small share of the gallant ideals and temerity of D'Artagnan."

Wanger sought to maintain his momentum with the super kinema by creating a blaze of publicity (through essay writing contests and offering free children's programs on Saturdays). He next booked an epic entitled *The Glorious Adventure,* produced by Vitagraph's J. Stuart Blackton on English soil, photographed in Prizmacolor, and featuring Victor McLaglen and Lady Cooper, an aristocratic amateur. Again, opening night brought "an unbroken procession of crest-bearing motor-cars," and while the film was found to be faulty on many counts, Wanger's showmanship remained unquestioned.

He followed Blackton's film with Jacques Feyder's *L'Atlantide,* an orientalist "romance of the Sahara" that rediscovered the lost city of Atlantis. Thanks to the London subway's banning of a "leggy" advertising poster, and to stunning reviews of the film's atmospheric effects, *L'Atlantide* recovered from a disappointing opening few days. Wanger's last film in March was the Italian *Theodora*. It was the weakest attraction he had yet booked, but he was able to extend the run through April by contracting with Leonid Massine, lately the lead dancer and choreographer of the Ballets Russes, to perform after the film's nightly screenings. To Wanger, Massine and Goossens were "joining hands to help the new industry to higher levels." In May, forced to give up Covent Garden, he took over the recently built 2,500-seat Rivoli in Whitechapel.

Although Wanger was hardly the first exhibitor to use Covent Garden for films, or orchestral accompaniments or prologues, the contemporary press reports—which recalled the tone of his reviews at Dartmouth—indicate that he was the most successful. Some exhibitors questioned the wisdom of his extravagance for provincial houses, but the press could not praise him enough. "The film is the new fashion and Covent Garden is setting the standard," the *Daily Express* exclaimed after the premiere of *The Three Musketeers*. After *L'Atlantide,* the *Times*'s Cinema Supplement of February 21 noted that the Covent Garden theater had "changed from a white elephant to a goldmine."

The *Evening News* hoped Wanger would "teach" theater managers about "the possibilities within their grasp."

The trade press was no less enthusiastic: the *Film Renter and Moving Picture News* "welcomed" Wanger's experiment, noting that "it is attracting an entirely new class of people to the pictures. That it tends to uplift the business is a point everyone connected with it should bear in mind." The *Bioscope* noted his "strength of will and vibrant energy in his piercing, unwavering glance and vice-like handgrip," and called Wanger "a young man of culture and refinement" who "makes a very refreshing contrast from the ordinary Yankee-hustler."

All of this merely confirmed the evidence of Dartmouth campus theatricals, his Broadway partnerships, and his CPI work, that Wanger was his own best promoter. As he put it,

> The successful film publicist so far as the London newspapers are concerned depends very largely upon his personal contact with the critics. Likewise in order to obtain the best possible value of the editorial columns in the provincial press our Managers should be persona grata with local principal editors.

One negative response to Wanger's activities came from F. E. Adams, managing director of the Provincial Cinema Theaters, Limited, at that time the largest vertically integrated film company in England. Wanger, Adams claimed, chastised the British exhibitors out of ignorance of industry conditions and with blithe unconcern for costs. Wanger before the end of 1922 was given a chance to prove Adams wrong, for PCT hired him in July to manage its Regent Theatre in Brighton, advise its board on advertising policies, and use his influence with American distributors to attract a better quality of film. But Wanger got into a nasty dispute with PCT's centralized booker. Naively, he told the company's board he realized that those members who were also prominent in film distribution might unduly influence PCT's booking policies to favor their distribution companies. Looking for some excuse to dismiss Wanger, the directors seized upon this "insult"; but when Wanger sued for breach of contract and recovery of salary, the dispute was settled out of court. PCT paid him an £8,000 settlement.

The stigma of his firing at PCT canceled all the goodwill Wanger had accumulated while managing theaters in London. And after leaving two leading positions with the largest American and British companies, he was tired of the film business. He returned to legitimate stage management, producing in April 1924 Guy Boulting's *Polly Preferred* at the Royalty Theatre in London, starring none other than Johnston (the play was the basis for King Vidor's 1928 *Show People*).

Yet, Wanger found theater management more difficult in London than in New York. There was a theater shortage in London and no "road" to compensate. What was worse to a CPI veteran, the British maintained higher standards of truth in publicity. Hence, Wanger late in the spring of 1924 came to America with a tour of Andre Charlot's revue "Spring Cleaning," starring Gertrude Lawrence, Jack Buchanan, and Beatrice Lillie (and which FPL produced later in the year as *The Fast Set*). In June, Lasky, then visiting London to talk with James Barrie about plans for a film version of *Peter Pan,* invited Wanger to return to FPL and Wanger accepted. On Monday, July 28, 1924, he resumed his post as "general manager of production" with authority over both the Astoria and Hollywood studios. But the company he returned to had changed dramatically.

5

Organizational Demands
(1924–1931)

Personally, Wanger was glad to be back at FPL, for he enjoyed the power and the contacts that his position afforded. Aside from the other studios' most precious performers, such as MGM's Greta Garbo, there was no major talent in, or attracted to, the film industry, from Griffith to George Gershwin, from Eisenstein to Erich Maria Remarque, whom Wanger did not meet, sign up, or work with during the 1920s.

When FPL completed the construction of its new high-rise headquarters over the Paramount Theater in Times Square, Wanger occupied an imposing office with massive wood doors and walnut paneling on the executives' eleventh floor. His annual salary rose from $150,000 to $250,000 yearly between 1924 and 1931, he traveled cross-country first class (sometimes in multimillionaire Lasky's private rail car), and by 1931 owned a Manhattan apartment as well as a home in Great Neck, Long Island, where literary and stage luminaries such as Fitzgerald and Groucho Marx resided or vacationed. As actress Louise Brooks later described him, Wanger in the 1920s was "a brilliant, laughing young man of the world whose heart remained tender."

One of Wanger's many lovers during this period, Brooks understood that Wanger was not the monogamous type. It was another facet of his restless insecurity, but it had become virtually part of a studio head's job. "Since Walter was the head of a studio for so long," agent Robert Lantz notes, "it's not the worst thing to know about an ingredient that is in every movie, the relationship of the sexes." The perennial search for talent justified late nights in Manhattan without Johnston in the company of writers Michael Arlen and Herman Mankiewicz as well as financiers such as Kahn, all of whom favored

Ziegfeld Follies showgirls. Wanger was "a nice enough man under ordinary circumstances," Ginger Rogers—who started her film career in the late 1920s at Astoria—recently recalled. But

> when he arrived on the set for a conference with the director, he always found time to check out the new females. He'd spot a starlet and look her up and down like a horse trader. Most of the crew snickered when they saw him on the prowl.

Tallulah Bankhead later declared, with characteristic directness, that Wanger "had a good cock, but he didn't know how to use it." This would have been news to his countless conquests. With clear gray eyes and dark hair that he combed back off his forehead, Wanger was strikingly handsome, and he enjoyed his share of the fun. Harris described him as a "Persian prince" in the "oriental splendor" of his office. Selznick found him to be a "smiling Casanova."

"He understood women better than anyone I knew," Mehle recalls. "He knew how women thought, how to handle women. He knew women's sensitivities, that they always want to look beautiful and have their best foot forward. I think it was innate although I'm sure dealing with movie divas all those years was excellent schooling." Indeed, young professionals brought out his paternal instincts. He offered encouragement and expert tips on selling manuscripts to Sonya Lubitsch when she began her career as a literary agent. He reassured Leonora Hornblow of her talents as a fledgling novelist in the early 1940s. Charming and generous in his praise, Wanger also flirted outrageously at Hollywood gatherings and easily won over scores of women. At Mack Sennett's parties in the 1920s, Wanger later declared, "if you didn't take the young lady on your right upstairs between the soup and the entree, you were considered a homosexual." There was little doubt about Wanger's preferences. When Marlene Dietrich arrived in New York on her way to Hollywood, Wanger invited her out to dinner and dancing with himself and his wife; showing up without Justine, he wooed Dietrich ardently. She was one of the few who resisted him.

Wanger's blithe spirits derived in part from his easy professional accomplishments. In a matter of months in 1920, he had enormously enhanced the look and feel of FPL films. But in 1924 at the age of thirty, he was still something of a neophyte executive and he struggled arduously to retain his power at the vertically integrated studios. His experiences at FPL guided his conduct as a producer for the rest of his career.

Since the formation of the Jesse L. Lasky Feature Play Company, Lasky had made films under what historian Janet Staiger has called the central producer system. Lasky's role was to single-handedly coordinate and supervise the entire studio output. The system depended on the continuity script written in advance of production for both business and aesthetic reasons. The central producer and his subordinates used the script to map out the needs of the production scene by scene, to facilitate efficient planning, and to keep tabs on the progress and budget of each film. Simultaneously, the continuity script enabled the director and other creative personnel to ensure that set details and spatial relations were consistent from shot to shot and that the film conformed to industrywide standards of verisimilitude and story clarity.

By the late teens, Lasky needed help. The growth in both the number of films produced and in the details of making those films required an increasingly complex managerial hierarchy within the production arm of a studio. Lasky hired Wanger in 1920 not only to improve the studio's production values, but to assume the newly created position of general manager of production, to coordinate the work of FPL's Hollywood, New York, London, and Indian studios. Announcing Wanger's new job, Lasky told the trade press,

> The motion picture has reached a state that demands organization—the big, intricate, highly specialized organization, which alone is capable of producing the type of photoplays that please the public and are successful at the box office.

Under Wanger were the heads of the different studios. Studio heads monitored "supervisors" who oversaw the production of specific films; the supervisors were eventually renamed producers.

Thus when Wanger resumed work in 1924, the division of labor within studio management kept him and Lasky remote from the problems and details of making specific films. Their concerns—like those of Mayer at MGM, Jack Warner at Warner Bros., and Harry Cohn at Columbia—became long-term or "strategic" planning, such as the purchase of story materials, the contracting of talents and the setting of their studio's overall budget. Overseeing the studio's filmmaking fell to studio heads—Irving Thalberg at MGM, Darryl F. Zanuck and Hal Wallis at Warner Bros., and for FPL, Ben P. Schulberg in Hollywood and Hector Turnbull or William Le Baron at Astoria. In 1929, for example, Lasky told an FPL convention that even though he could run the Hollywood studio, "he no longer felt as well qualified [as Ben Schulberg] by any means to do so."

After his frustrating years working in and around the Theatrical Syndicate and the Shuberts, Wanger in 1919 had queried Lasky immediately about FPL's executive hierarchy, specifically, Lasky's "liaison" work between West Coast talents and East Coast management. By the time of Wanger's return to FPL in 1924, that hierarchy had changed thanks to Zukor's theater expansion. Now theater holdings at FPL (as at Loew's and Fox)—especially after the 1925 acquisition of the Balaban and Katz theater chain centered in Chicago—was rising to 90 percent of the company's invested capital and 66 percent of its total assets. The function of filmmaking was only to keep the theaters busy with something to show. This naturally gave distribution and exhibition executives the rationale for dictating terms to the production end. With the encouragement of Lasky's amiable approach to business, President Zukor (and after 1925, Sam Katz) and distribution chief Sidney Kent held what *Variety* called "a whip hand over the production end."

The whip cracked most forcefully at home office meetings in New York in the first quarter of each year. During these sessions, the skeleton of a production schedule was laid out, based not on the properties or talents in FPL's possession, but on purely financial calculations. Kent estimated the number of films his people could sell to exhibitors in the coming season, and they quickly devised a budget for the year's films. The calculations were purely mathematical. For 1927–1928, they had determined to spend $20 million on seventy movies.

The executives then divided their season into three categories of films. There were big-budget, roadshow films (costing anywhere from $500,000 to $2 million, such as *The Covered Wagon, Old Ironsides, Beau Geste,* and *The Rough Riders*), which were sold with advanced seats in specially rented theaters before general distribution. This category evolved in Wanger's absence after the astonishing success of 1923's *The Covered Wagon,* an epic western that surpassed the year-long run of *The Birth of a Nation* at the Criterion Theater in New York. Encouraged by the showing of MGM's *Ben-Hur* in 1925, FPL continued to make the most roadshows of any studio.

Second in prestige, and more numerous, were the "specials," films with major stars costing between $350,000 and $500,000, whose run would be determined only by their popularity. These films (of which FPL proposed to make seventeen for the 1927–1928 season) were the least predictable of the three categories in their profit potential. Finally, there were the $200,000 or less "programmers," films made primarily to lower production and distribution overheads and to fill up the "blocks" of films rented to theaters. There was no magic about the process. As Selznick put it, the pictures' "cost was predetermined, their gross was predetermined. You knew that you could make *x* dollars of profit on each picture you made for *x* dollars."

While helping Lasky provide both studios with a wealth of production possibilities, Wanger assisted studio managers Schulberg, Turnbull, or Le Baron in selecting properties for realization each year, matched stories to specific stars, and made isolated suggestions for their productions. The studio managers followed through, scheduling the films and estimating budgets.

In late spring, Wanger "laid out the schedule" with Lasky for the crucial sales conventions, an annual ritual first suggested by Kent which all the studios soon copied. Here they told distribution people what the next season's films would be, and they sought to create excitement among the men selling the films to the theater managers. As Wanger recalled:

> Lasky would make an address and I'd sit next to him. All the representatives would have beautifully produced books of sales brochures, and Lasky, who was a great showman, would say: "Now boys, before you turn the next page, I just want to say something to you. This is so great I can't believe it myself. What would you think of a picture with Gloria Swanson (and they'd all applaud) . . . Wallace Reid . . ." (and they'd all applaud), and then he'd name about six other stars. He wouldn't know what the hell he was talking about. And then he'd pick a title, or he might make it up, and he'd say "and directed by . . ." and there'd be a big shriek. . . . Sometimes we'd actually make the picture but many of these projects just went on like this from year to year.

In 1925, Lasky and Wanger came up absolutely empty-handed in naming a roadshow special, and Lasky pretended that the title was a trade secret (the studio eventually produced *Pony Express* that year). Their improvisations demonstrated Wanger and Lasky's keen appreciation of production publicity within the company.

Studying Lasky's management style, Wanger found an approach that accorded with his own experiences in the theater: to let the talent create without interference. Lasky personally supervised only roadshow productions such as *Pony Express* or *The Covered Wagon*. Although the executive hierarchy featured the same division of labor that characterized the technicians and creative talents on the studio floor, production heads enjoyed considerable flexibility in their range of responsibilities.

Lasky preferred to "use a director as supervising architect of every phase of production, from writing to cutting, rather than have him serve merely as foreman on the rough construction job." For *The Squaw Man* in 1914, Lasky had remained in New York with his fingers crossed while deMille worked in Hollywood. The policy continued into the mid-twenties, particularly for the studio's most prestigious films and directors. Brooks later recalled that at the Astoria studio, "the writers, directors, and cast were free from all supervision. Jesse Lasky, Adolph Zukor, and Walter Wanger never left the Paramount office on Fifth Avenue, and the head of production never came on the set." When Merian Cooper and Ernest Schoedsack shot *Chang* in Africa they found, as Schoedsack put it, that "we had in Lasky a man who not only let us alone but backed us up to the last degree." Lasky did not let talent do anything: he ordered Erich von Stroheim's *The Wedding March* (1928) cut down to two hours. But he was completely different from the likes of Thalberg, whose complete control over production alienated many talents.

Firmly believing in the romantic conception of the artist who requires special understanding and patience, Lasky was an enlightened exception to the general tendency of studio executives to terrorize talents with their demands:

> The producer must be a prophet and a general, a diplomat and a peacemaker, a miser and a spendthrift. He must have vision tempered by hindsight, daring governed by caution, the patience of a saint and the iron of a Cromwell.

In particular Wanger adopted Lasky's code of diplomacy in the name of keeping the artists "happy." After handling the Elizabeth Taylor–Richard Burton affair on the set of *Cleopatra* in the early 1960s, Wanger recalled how while under Lasky at Paramount, "I got impatient and fired a star." Lasky told him, "Walter, under your contract you have a perfect right to get rid of that star, but that is not what we hired you for. We hired you to get the best out of people, not to fire them." Henceforth Wanger negotiated between the talents and Zukor and Kent, on the assumption that smooth relations would result in better product, no matter what the cost. Such a policy led Wanger, for example, to promise editor Dorothy Arzner a directing opportunity when she planned to join Columbia in the mid-1920s.

Although this was a humane approach to talent management, it had a cruel logic of its own, best illustrated by Griffith's fate at Paramount in 1926 when two of his films, *That Royle Girl* (1925) and *Sorrows of Satan* (1926), went over budget. When Griffith told Wanger that he and Le Baron agreed to conclude *That Royle Girl* with a storm scene, Wanger told Griffith, in the latter's words, that "there was nothing to do but to make it and do the best we could and to spend the money needed to make the best possible picture." But Wanger's reassurances only increased Griffith's shock when Zukor subsequently dismissed him from the studio.

Such duplicity could anger talents as much as confrontations and power plays. H. L. Mencken's protégé and future wife, the short story writer Haardt, spent more than a month in 1927 trying to interest FPL in her script *Way Down South*. Wanger took notice only after she told him she sold the story to Cruze. "In a flash," Haardt wrote Mencken, "all his ingratiating and decorative manner fell away from him. He was simply an excited, grasping Jew who had in some way been outwitted. He took down the telephone and yelled into it, and in two minutes Schulberg was there and they were trying to get me to stay on."

Finally, "diplomacy" could become just plain weak management. Costume designer Greer described the "awe" with which FPL's Polish star Pola Negri was regarded in the Hollywood studio: "She chose her stories, her directors, her actors, and decided what time the day's shooting would begin and when it would end." In 1926 Schulberg found that FPL had

> lost control over the producing units of the studio. Every such unit—the Cecil B. DeMille unit, the Raoul Walsh unit, the James Cruze unit, the Allan Dwan

unit—ran itself as though it were a completely independent business. Combinations of stars and directors would dictate to the company what they would or would not do, how a picture would be fashioned, how it would be cut, how much it would cost.

Schulberg understood that part of his responsibilities as head of Hollywood production was to tame the headstrong talents for greater efficiency. In fact, Schulberg's firm managing techniques eventually made Wanger look inferior.

FPL hired Schulberg at Wanger's suggestion in July 1926 to oversee the Hollywood studio as associate manager in charge of production. British writer-director Ivor Montagu described him as "a strong-looking relaxed man, who resembled an amiable efficient crocodile smoking a large cigar." A scenario writer for Edwin S. Porter and a publicist for Zukor in the early teens, Schulberg wrote scripts for his own Preferred Pictures about fallen society women and subsequently signed Clara Bow and Gilbert Roland to exclusive contracts that he brought to FPL.

FPL saw Schulberg as the studio's answer to upstart MGM's Thalberg, who had guided the studio to a first season that included *Ben Hur,* Vidor's *The Big Parade,* von Stroheim's *The Merry Widow,* and Lon Chaney in *The Unholy Three* and which put FPL to shame; as Lasky admitted to *Variety* in early 1927, MGM had been "outdistancing [FPL] on the quality of product during the year past." Schulberg proved equal to the task, overseeing six outstanding productions in 1927 including *Underworld* and *Wings,* the first film to win a best picture award from the newly formed Academy. He did so in part because he was, in assistant Selznick's words, "a remarkable factory foreman . . . a remarkably efficient man." Schulberg's efficiency disturbed many Paramount talents used to Lasky's relaxed approach, such as directors Allan Dwan and Lucien Hubbard, who either moved back east to Astoria or left FPL entirely.

The departure of senior directors fueled a growing competition between Schulberg and Wanger over the superiority of East Coast versus West Coast production. Although he assisted Lasky in coordinating production on the two coasts, Wanger clearly preferred the principle of East Coast production, and not only because of his fondness for the city. The company put story purchases into production more quickly in New York, and it took advantage of stage talents. Best of all, to Wanger's mind, it provided the egotistical West Coast talents a refreshing and sometimes humbling change of pace from parochial Hollywood. Improvements in indoor lighting technology minimized the technical differences between facilities. By the fall of 1926 New York accounted for 40 percent of studio films, and Wanger seemed to be winning the battle for New York production, but this proved temporary, as the company, at Schulberg's urging, reorganized and expanded the Hollywood facility.

The competition had fruitful results. The two coasts complemented each other in terms of atmosphere. According to Jesse Lasky, Jr., the Astoria studio "took a lot of its tone from Walter, who put a very strong personal stamp on it." In the fall of 1924, Wanger, fresh from England, introduced the ritual of serving four o'clock tea on the sets. Brooks boasted of working with "writers and directors from Princeton and Yale" who would have been completely out of place on the West Coast, where "to love books was a big laugh." To Swanson, Astoria was

> full of free spirits, defectors, refugees, who were all trying to get away from Hollywood and its restrictions. There was a wonderful sense of revolution and innovation in the studio in Queens.

Moreover, according to Jesse Lasky, Jr., Wanger's influence extended beyond studio atmosphere to subject matter: even though the Hollywood studio was better suited to outdoor, action production, "anything that related to Europe and Paris (or something like that) they would have considered (at Astoria) because of Walter Wanger, [who] spoke perfect French, Wanger spoke perfect Italian, Wanger was a European-oriented American." Astoria's output was in fact diverse, ranging from stage comedies and performers (such as W. C. Fields) to melodramas that exploited New York locations. Wanger facilitated a studio style—the sophisticated tone and look rooted in continental dramas and fashions as exemplified by the work of directors Lubitsch and Josef von Sternberg—which FPL maintained into the 1930s.

Yet as the Hollywood studio grew, and as Schulberg's talent for controlling costs became apparent, Astoria seemed expendable. In mid-1927, FPL faced a cost crisis that stemmed from the company's "roadshow" films; between *Old Ironsides, Rough Riders,* and *Wings,* it had spent $5 million dollars that might easily have been applied to more than twenty program pictures, and FPL invested one-third more on production than MGM and twice as much as Fox and First National. Executives at the investment firms underwriting stock flotations and production loans gave "instructions" for "drastic cuts in studio overhead and picture costs" and salaries. FPL's board of directors and executives shut down Astoria, against Wanger's wishes and to the total surprise of its employees. It was a vote of confidence for Schulberg who earned double Wanger's salary anyway. As Haardt noted in the fall of 1927, "it is a fact that [Schulberg] is Wanger's rival and knows much more about pictures than Wanger does."

That fall Wanger used his executive prerogative to supervise, atypically, the initial stages of a script written by Haardt. Haardt's account of their meetings provides a vivid, if sour, look at how Wanger worked with writers when he engaged in production supervision. Conscious of Haardt's intimate relationship with Mencken, Wanger had invited her to Hollywood. Initially dismissive of Wanger because he neglected her, Haardt became more positive about him when they set to work: "I do appreciate his intelligence. He is quick and shrewd, and he knows how to use people." She even conceded that Wanger had made some intelligent suggestions for her first story.

But Wanger subsequently alienated Haardt as she worked on a vehicle for Negri. "I started out with a fairly original idea, within the bounds of the requirement," she wrote Mencken,

> but [Wanger] has gradually made it over into an imitation of Negri's first picture, "Passion," the story of DuBarry. I had Negri cast as a French peasant girl, who was kidnapped off the streets of Paris and chained with six other prostitutes and brought to New Orleans by the officers of the king to populate his colony. It was a marvelous role for Negri, because she is a peasant and acts it. But no, Wanger must have her a mistress of Louis XV, with a lot of meretricious, suggestive stuff that actually lessens the dramatic values of the story. I don't care, of course; I would have made her a sunflower or a dandelion if he wanted her so, but it ruins a possible story.

The man who championed innovations in set designs and technology was less inventive when it came to story lines. "That's all the uplift in the movies amounts to," Haardt concluded, alluding to Wanger's idealistic talk about the potential of the movies. She left the studio that December with $2,000 and a bitter taste in her mouth.

Wanger nearly followed her in early 1928. He later recalled that he "was in the doghouse. . . . They were trying to squeeze me out of the company at that time. Nobody had any traffic with me." He had protested the company's 1927 economies vociferously, and he had berated Kent for not using advertising more effectively. He felt that even Lasky, struggling to keep the growing company unified, was leaving him out of high-level meetings and claiming undue credit for production successes. Schulberg's recent promotion to managing director of production made him Wanger's equal. Lasky's golden boy of 1920 now contemplated leaving the film industry for good.

It was the advent of sound which changed his mind. In August 1927, Warner Bros. had premiered *Don Juan* starring John Barrymore, its first feature-length film using synchronized music on the Vitaphone (sound on disc) system. In October, the studio premiered Al Jolson's hit *The Jazz Singer,* which included several musical scenes with direct sound recorded during principal photography. After three months in general release around the country, *The Jazz Singer* had grossed $1.5 million, proving that sound films had a phenomenal appeal beyond the big city markets.

As Wanger recalled, in April 1928, Zukor called together the FPL (now renamed Paramount) executives and berated them for their ignorance of sound technology. Zukor "was a great guy whenever a crisis developed—crying and making emotional speeches," Wanger recalled, and he recreated Zukor's speech on this occasion:

"Warner's is making this picture [probably *The Lights of New York,* its first all-talkie, as opposed to a film with only musical accompaniment]," he said, "and what have we got? You don't know a goddam thing about sound. A lot of dumbheads. We pay you all money," and so on and on.... I got up at the meeting and said.... "Mr. Zukor, if you will give me the Richard Dix picture that came in today, I guarantee that in six weeks you can have a preview." (It was a baseball picture.) They all looked at me as if I had just come in off a plane from Mars and gave it to me.

The Richard Dix–Jean Arthur picture was a baseball comedy directed by Fred Newmeyer entitled *Warming Up.* Wanger, probably with the help of Paramount's studio engineer Roy Pomeroy, took a print of the film up to a sound laboratory in New Jersey and was able to obtain, reportedly within one week, a track of rudimentary, nonsynchronized effects and music. The film previewed six weeks after the meeting in Zukor's apartment.

Judging from the reviews, *Warming Up* was, like many early sound films, a mediocrity. *The Times* review noted,

The synchronizing is such...that the smack of the ball against a bat is heard some time before [the pitcher] has finished winding up. Mr. Dix's synchronization is better because the balls he throws are never hit.

Variety was characteristically more enthusiastic:

Without the sound effects, which projected the yells of the crowd in the stands, remarks of players at the training camp, etc. the picture is one of the worst duds to ever come out of the Hollywood factory. While the sound record doesn't synchronize with lip movement, it lifts the thing unbelievably. The excitement of the crowd is in some measure transferred to the audience.

Most important, the enthusiasm of the crowd in *Warming Up* was transferred to studio executives who, "at first skeptical over the latest Dix film model, have been reported since the preview to be in raves over the improvement." Wanger remembered the response of Zukor and some Loew's executives to the film:

The people came out. They clapped me on the back, "Genius, how did you do it?" They couldn't understand, even after they saw it. So I was reinstated with new decorations and we started building up Long Island for sound.

Wanger's recollection implies that he single-handedly persuaded the company to adopt sound, yet Paramount executives had been well aware of sound processes since 1924 and were determined to use them, if not own them outright. In March 1927 Paramount cosigned an agreement with the other majors to research the different sound systems available (Warner Bros.' Vitaphone,

RKO's Photophone, and Fox's Movietone) and to adopt one system unanimously. By mid-March 1928, Paramount was poised to sign a contract with Electronics Research Products (ERPI), the subsidiary of Western Electric which handled the licensing and manufacture of sound equipment. In fact, Wanger had used an ERPI lab in New Jersey to synchronize *Warming Up.*

Yet the company's executives were still far more bewildered by the new process than Wanger. He had been friends with Courtland Smith, who had cajoled William Fox into using sound (the Movietone sound-on-film system) for Fox newsreels before implementing it for feature production. During the comparatively free period in late 1927 and early 1928, Wanger had observed the technicians at the laboratory where they prepared sound effects and music for the Movietone newsreels.

If Wanger had not provided sound for *Warming Up,* another studio employee would have done so on another film eventually. But his timing was perfect. *Warming Up* dramatically altered the studio's plans for the coming season. Before the preview, Katz, Kent, and Lasky planned to use sound only in the production of short films (including recordings of Paramount Publix Prologues which Paramount, like Warner Bros., sent to neighborhood theaters and smaller markets). Feature films would remain silent, with sound reserved only for roadshows like *Wings.* Recently, Lasky had told the trade press that intertitles were superior to dialogue. Just one week prior to the *Warming Up* preview, he discussed next season's films without any mention of sound.

What Wanger had demonstrated was that sound would enhance Paramount's plentiful program and special films, or as *Variety* put it, that "sound is of utmost importance as a bolsterer for ordinary product," as well as for the shorts. Within the week following the *Warming Up* preview, Paramount signed the ERPI agreements. In mid-May, Lasky announced that the high volume of ordinary Paramount films—not only its major productions such as *The Patriot* and *The Wedding March*—would be made with synchronized effects and sixty-piece orchestral accompaniments.

Hence Paramount reopened Astoria just over a year after closing it down, while its competitors rushed to New York to establish productions that took advantage of proximity to the New York stage (and faster film stocks that facilitated indoor lighting). Sound also changed Wanger's mind about the movies, for now they more closely resembled the stage. Newly enthused, Wanger resumed his duties at Astoria with greater interest than ever in the logistics of filmmaking.

Wanger's key responsibility during this period was still to scout stories and talents for sound production from the theater. As Robert Florey later recalled, he took "screen tests of actors, explorers, politicians, singers, boxers, clowns, dancers and musicians. From eight in the morning until midnight . . . we shot several kilometers of film." In fall 1930, Wanger's assistant James Cowan told Astoria employees to report on "anyone and anything they see elsewhere that might have value for pictures." The policy paid off: thanks in large part to Wanger's efforts, Paramount signed the Marx Brothers, Maurice Chevalier, Colbert, Rogers, Francis, Jeannette MacDonald, Frederic March, Miriam Hopkins, Frank Morgan, Charles Ruggles, Lillian Roth, Norman Foster, Nancy Carroll, Ruth Chatterton, and Tallulah Bankhead—in short, many of Hollywood's major stars and character actors, as well as the stars of Paramount shorts, also produced at Astoria, such as Burns and Allen, Jack Benny, George Jessell, and radio stars such as Rudy Vallee.

Also at Wanger's suggestion, Paramount signed up countless directing talents from the legitimate stage: George Cukor; the Russian Mamoulian, who had impressed the theater world with his staging of *Porgy and Bess*; and the Frenchman Florey, who handled *Coconuts* with Joseph Santley. In June 1928, Wanger brought graduates of Professor George Baker's Yale Drama Workshop for internships at the studio. Wanger also recruited stage writers Noel Coward, Preston Sturges, Donald Ogden Stewart, and Wanger's associate from 1916, Cole Porter.

As film historian Richard Koszarski has noted, the sound film continued Astoria's silent period search for sources: "nearly every Astoria production was either the direct adaptation of a stage play (*Animal Crackers*) or a testing ground for newly acquired Broadway talent (Helen Morgan and director Rouben Mamoulian in *Applause*)." There were the Marx Brothers' *Coconuts,* Ziegfeld's *Glorifying the American Girl,* Rodgers and Hart's *Heads Up* and *Abie's Irish Rose,* the phenomenally popular play that was recalled from silent movie theaters to be synchronized with sound. The industry shared Astoria's theater-bound choices: for 1929, the first full year of sound films, play adaptations accounted for nearly a third of the films from the largest eleven companies.

As the vogue for musicals subsided in late 1929, the studios were "groping for the public pulse," trying to determine what the national audience wanted. "Sophistication" became the keynote of the Astoria productions under Wanger's stewardship, and Wanger's star during his final years at Paramount rose and fell with it. As his sessions with Haardt suggest, Wanger favored witty comedies of manners and heavily ironic melodrama. Pregnant dialogue, elegant upper-crust or dingy workplace settings, and romances complicated by the hypocrisies of the upper class became key conventions in Astoria's films, especially when Lubitsch became "supervising director."

There was *Gentlemen of the Press*—a biting portrait of cynical journalists produced at the same time as Ben Hecht and Charles MacArthur's *The Front Page*. *The Lady Lies,* featuring Colbert, had "a lot of hells and damns . . . surrounded by a complicated tale of free love and sophisticated children." *Variety* hailed it as "the first peach sophisticater," but one made before audiences could accept it. Forgetting their past excesses and buoyed by huge grosses, studio heads in early 1930 raised the company's overall production budget and increased the number of Astoria films to thirty. Sound films revived the East Coast–West Coast rivalry: in 1929, Wanger had Robert Florey shoot a short film with Chevalier in New York, *Hello New York,* to beat out Schulberg's *Innocents of Paris.* Lubitsch told Zukor in April 1930 that Wanger was responsible for production economies and a spirit of teamwork superior to those in the West Coast studio. By September, Paramount intended to secure "plays and as many of the sophisticated and indoor types of story which can be accommodated at Par's Astoria LI [*sic*] plant," under Lubitsch's oversight. From this shift came numerous comedies—including the Sturges-Stewart scripted *Laughter,* Sturges's *Fast and Loose,* Malcolm St. Clair's *Dangerous Nan McGrew, The Royal Family of Broadway* (codirected by Cukor), Chevalier in *The Big Pond,* and Lubitsch's own *The Smiling Lieutenant.*

Wanger soon diversified Astoria's output to produce films that traded on the lurid appeal of fallen women. *Stolen Heaven* concerned a thief and a prostitute who vacation on a desert island with the proceeds of a factory robbery. There was a series of films starring the languorous Bankhead, about heroines of morally questionable stature: a remake of *The Cheat, My Sin* (about a former nightclub singer from the south), and *Tarnished Lady.* And William Powell in *Ladies' Man* played a gigolo finally killed for seducing a man's wife and daughter. Such films contributed heavily to the widespread protest that moved the Motion Picture Producers and Distributors of America under Will Hays to adopt its celebrated Production Code in March 1930. Having been in the business long before the advent of the code, Wanger intended to ignore it as much as possible.

Although it is an unsatisfying film that was poorly received, Cukor's *Tarnished Lady* illustrates how Astoria approached the fallen woman genre in late 1930. Cukor's first directorial assignment, it was also Paramount's first sound film to star Bankhead. The film embodied the values Wanger had championed within the setting of Manhattan's rich set. Stewart's script concerned Nancy Courtney, a high-society girl who marries formal, dull financier Norman Cravath (Clive Brook) to save her family's ailing fortunes. But Nancy loves a Bohemian young painter ("You're the only thing that isn't connected with money; you're the only thing I want," she tells him), and she marches into her bedroom on her wedding night to a funeral dirge. Pining for the painter, she leaves Norman, coincidentally on the day of the Wall Street crash, only to find her lover otherwise attached and taunting as well. After bearing Norman's child, whom she finds "awfully cute but a terrible nuisance," Nancy supports herself. She bumps into her husband in the dress shop where she works, and they reconcile: walking out the door, her rival tells them, "I hope you two will be very, very unhappy."

The film displays the languorous pace and stylized stasis characteristic of early sound films, but lacks those spectacular values that inform von Sternberg–Dietrich collaborations such as *Shanghai Express*. *Variety*'s review, noting in *Tarnished Lady* a similar tone and pace to British films, speculated that "the producer may have tried to impress a British attitude on the picture for consumption abroad." Indeed, Cukor's direction is informed by a patient use of long takes to record the depths of Nancy's despair, and it buries the irony of Stewart's favorite story twist—better known from *The Philadelphia Story*—in which the upper-class hero proves morally superior to his lower-class rival.

What remains lively in *Tarnished Lady* is its anti–Production Code provocations—the sex angle. From its opening credits with a nude woman's figure on the cover of a magazine, to the scene in which Bankhead discovers her lover in a bathrobe with another woman emerging from his bedroom, the film blatantly showed sexual promiscuity. Stewart's dialogue was highly suggestive, as when Norman talks to Nancy about making a "nest" on Long Island:

> *Nancy:*   And who's going to lay the eggs? . . . Perhaps you're going to buy the eggs.
>
> *Norman:*   There are some things money can't buy.
>
> *Nancy:*   I know the answer to that one.

Like *The Lady Lies, Tarnished Lady* was one of several Wanger-sponsored films that inspired the Production Code coauthor Father Daniel J. Lord to nickname Wanger "our bad boy."

While *Tarnished Lady* went before the cameras in November 1930, however, Paramount production heads faced a new policy dilemma. As reported in *The Dartmouth*, Wanger described to undergraduates how he and his colleagues were puzzling over "just how to cater to the public taste." One option was to produce the kinds of films he favored, which he described as "more sophisticated and somewhat philosophical pictures like 'Holiday,'" a 1930 adaptation of Phillip Barry's idealistic comedy opposing personal happiness and material gain. Another choice was "to release a flood of as he called them, 'hokum' pictures" such as Fox's current hit, *Common Clay,* described as an antiquated melodrama about a bad woman who makes good independently of her wealthy lover.

To every other studio the choice was clear, for *Common Clay* was a box office hit in the fall of 1930. West Coast producers believed, with a conviction that Hays applauded, that "they have finally discovered what talker audiences want": clear-cut morality plays, dying children, and unfairly maligned women. It was time to "strengthen the heart interest," which would strengthen ticket sales at subsequent-run theaters and in small town markets. Wanger had always geared his production ideas to more cosmopolitan audiences in the key markets. As he later put it, Astoria's film versions of plays such as the

Royal Family of Broadway were "a sensation in New York, but in Kansas City, they didn't know what it was all about. . . . Mistakes. . . . Mistakes. . . . Mistakes." The regional audience had become too important to ignore.

The mistakes were not fully apparent until late spring 1931 when the Great Depression—which no doubt influenced moviegoers' revived preferences for "hokum"—finally affected ticket sales. Paramount's net income dropped from $25 million in 1930 to $8.7 million in 1931. By May, Wanger was in Paramount's doghouse again. All the studios reduced their talent rosters, cut salaries, and consolidated production facilities to reduce overhead. Paramount, with extensive debts from its acquisition of five hundred additional theaters between the fall of 1929 and May 1930, was no different, and its economizing was led by the company's widely admired, vigorous, and forceful distribution head Kent, who became Paramount's general manager. As Lehman Brothers partner John Hertz arrived to put Paramount's corporate debt in order, Kent stipulated production policy more forcefully than ever before. Taking a cue from a report filed by newsreel director Emmanuel Cohen, Kent directed Paramount to shut down the Astoria studio in late May because negative costs there averaged $50,000 more than in Hollywood (a recent Astoria film, *Scarlet Hours,* cost $800,000, the most expensive Long Island production ever).

There were other grounds for closing Astoria. By early 1931, West Coast films—such as *The Four Feathers, The Mystery of Fu Manchu,* and the von Sternberg–Dietrich sensations, *The Blue Angel, Morroco* and *Dishonored*—had proven profitable and Schulberg had reestablished his preeminence as a production executive. At Astoria, by contrast, in spite of occasional hits, the unconditional reliance on and promotion of stage performers had proved ill-conceived in many instances. *The Battle of Paris* was a complete failure: "Perhaps the poorest picture to come out of a major studio this season and a terrible break for Gertrude Lawrence." The review of early 1931's *Stolen Heaven* was similarly dismal. *Glorifying the American Girl,* three years in production and featuring scenes in color and large-screen, flopped when released after a lengthy run of backstage musicals. Even Astoria's widely critical successes, such as *Laughter* and *The Royal Family,* proved financial failures and were excoriated by Lasky as "so called 'good' pictures."

Moreover, Wanger's penchant for the compromised woman formula was wearing thin. Carroll had risen to star status on the West Coast in 1930 with sweet ingenue roles in *The Devil's Holiday* and *Honey.* When she came East, Wanger first placed her in the charming comedy *Laughter.* He then off-cast Carroll in films such as *Stolen Heaven* as a prostitute, and as a knowing house servant in *Personal Maid.* None of Carroll's Astoria films proved as commercially successful or unobjectionable as the West Coast productions, and Carroll herself complained to the trade press that she was "made to do and say things that just do not have the proper emotional value or appeal for the women visitors." According to Martin Quigley, Wanger was "credited with practically ruining Nancy Carroll on account of the type of stories given to her." Meanwhile, Schulberg had astonishing success with Bow, Powell, Dietrich, George Bancroft (ranked the biggest box office star in 1929), Esther Ralston, and Gary Cooper.

Off-casting a Paramount star did not by itself count against Wanger, although Warner Bros.' raid on several studio talents (Francis, Powell, and Hopkins) magnified the flaws in Wanger's attempt to modify Carroll's image. Wanger's entire predilection for "sophisticated" material was now out of fashion at the studio. Only months after his dismissal in June 1931, Schulberg told *Variety* that Paramount was de-emphasizing "sophisticated" stories, in favor of "good old hoke tales with a broader sales appeal." Wanger was replaced by Cohen, who let distribution, marketing, and exhibitor sentiment guide his production choices. Ironically, Astoria remained open, following the schedule Wanger had mapped out, through December 1931.

Two weeks after Paramount announced the closing of Astoria, studio counsel Elek Ludvigh informed Wanger that the company had no intention of renewing his contract. Wanger's distress was so great that he had attorney Nathan Burkan draft his inquiry into jobs at other studios. When Stella Stettheimer died the following fall, the "laughing young man of the world" reached the lowest ebb in his career thus far.

Though Wanger left Paramount, Paramount never left Wanger, and like his work at the CPI, his sojourn at the studio created an ambiguous legacy. One benefit was that Wanger gained a superb overview of the talents available in the industry. Universal's chief art director Alexander Golitzen observes that Wanger "knew everybody and everything. For instance, in selecting a cameraman, he knew that this man was good for a polished type of picture, and this man is good for a character study, and so he would hire them accordingly. He knew how to pick people." "He was a great catalyst," Shelley Wanger has commented. "He was clever at putting together talented teams to make his films."

An even more crucial legacy of his Paramount days was Wanger's training as a production executive. Unlike Zanuck at Warner Bros., he did not begin writing scripts. Unlike Selznick, his first studio position was not in middle management. Unlike Thalberg at Universal, he did not start as a twenty-five-dollar a week secretary. Such producers, because of their training in the nuts and bolts of film production, worked closely on the writing, shooting, and editing of the films they produced, often shaping them beyond their talents' efforts.

By contrast, because his personal talents did not extend to creative production and because he began his film work as an executive, Wanger's subsequent conduct as a film producer followed an executive model. Like Lasky, he gave talents virtually complete freedom in the search for innovation. To Golitzen, this was one of Wanger's outstanding traits:

> Once he assigned you, he left you completely alone. Sam Goldwyn and Ross Hunter at Universal, for instance, seemed to want to participate more actively in details of most of the scenes. Wanger left it entirely to the art director, the director, the cameraman.

Even after 1934, when he became an independent producer of specific films, Wanger continued to work this way, typically remote and disinterested—by creative standards—from the writing, shooting, and editing of films. Herein lay his strengths *and* limitations as a producer: the confidence to give creative talents their due without the skills of a Selznick, Thalberg, or Zanuck to improve their work.

From a financial standpoint, as well, Paramount was an ambiguous training ground for a future independent producer, for Wanger worked there sheltered from risk. Although he had struggled with studio politics and resented the dominance of the distribution and exhibition executives at Paramount in the late twenties, Wanger recalled his sojourn there as a golden era and not only because of the enormous power he wielded. As he put it more than three decades later, "Famous Players was simply marvelous to me. I was spoiled. I've never gotten over it":

> Both Mr. Zukor and Mr. Lasky, who controlled the production policy for the entire company, loved talent, adored the theatre, had a deep sense of responsibility to the public. They urged me to sign up anything that would increase the potential of the audience, from writer to dancer, to hat designer, interior decorator, stage director, any talent that would be an asset to making a film more attractive to more people. . . . They had an open door policy. . . . Any idea that was interesting had a hearing and a good chance of being made.

For the rest of his career, Wanger sought to recreate the working atmosphere of experimentation in all his producing ventures. But he did so without the luxury of Paramount's financial resources.

1. Walter Wanger in one of his favorite publicity shots from the 1940s appears as an elegant gentleman producer.

2. Wanger's parents, Sigmund Feuchtwanger
and Stella Stettheimer.

3. Coxswain for the Cascadilla
Boy's School rowing team,
circa 1910.

FULTON THEATRE

46th Street, Just West of Broadway
THE HENRY B. HARRIS ESTATE, Sole Lessee and Manager.

FIRE NOTICE

Look around NOW and choose the nearest Exit to
your seat. In case of fire walk (not run) to THAT Exit.
Do not try to beat your neighbor to the street.
ROBERT ADAMSON, Fire Commissioner.

SPECIAL PERFORMANCES { MONDAY AFTERNOON, FEB. 16, and
TUESDAY AFTERNOON, FEB. 17, 1914

MR. WILLIAM HARRIS, JR. Presents

THE DARTMOUTH PLAYERS

IN

THE MISLEADING LADY

A NEW PLAY,

By CHAS. GODDARD and PAUL DICKEY,

Authors of "The Ghost Breaker."

JACK CRAIGEN..........................GEORGE HENRY TILTON, JR.
JOHN W. CANNELL..................CHESTER BRADLEY JORDAN, JR.
HENRY TRACEY..........................WILLIAM PAUL COSTELLO
SIDNEY PARKER...........................CHARLES MALI CLAEYS
STEPHEN WEATHERBEE............JUSTUS CHRISTIAN DOENECKE
KEEN FITZPATRICK.................GEORGE WESTCOTT HUTCHINS
BONEY...................... ....JAMES MITCHEL KILLEEN
TIM McMAHON............... ....RALPH SANBORN
BILL FAGAN.............................EDWARD TAYLOR PAPSON
"BABE MERILL"...........................ROBERT ALFRED BURLEN
"CHESTY" SANBORN...............WILLIAM ARTHUR MACKIE, JR.
HELEN STEELE............... ....DONALD RICHMOND
MRS. JOHN W. CANNELL..........................ALEXANDER DEAN
JANE WENTWORTH....................DONALD SHAPLEIGH PAGE
AMY FOSTER.............................HUGH LIVINGSTON COLE
GRACE BUCHANAN...............ARTHUR HOLMES LEONARD, JR.

ACT I.—Country Home of John Cannell, on the upper Hudson.

ACT II.—Eagle Lodge in the Wilderness of the Adirondacks. Same
evening.

ACT III.—Same as Act II. Early next morning.

Time—Fall of the year.

Scenery painted by H. Robert Law.
Scenery built by Hudson Construction Co.   Gowns by Fox.

Play staged under the direction of Walter F. Wanger.
Stage Manager, Channing Ellis Harwood.

Program printed, published and controlled by Frank V. Strauss & Co.,
108-114 Wooster Street, New York City.

4. Wanger's greatest coup at Dartmouth: New York's Fulton
Theater presents *The Misleading Lady* in 1914.

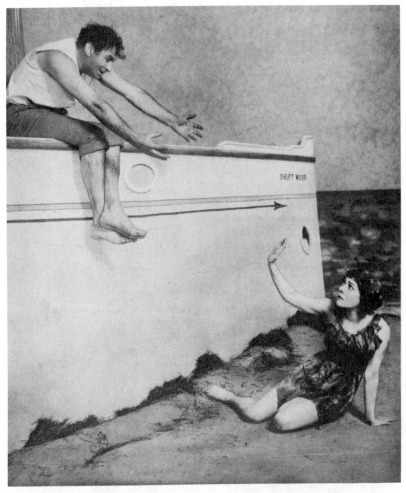

5. Wanger's first professional triumph: *'Ception Shoals*, starring Alla Nazimova, who took to calling Wanger "Bossy."

6. First Lieutenant Wanger, mustachioed like his father for the only time in his life, being reviewed in Italy by the Prince of Wales.

7. Wanger's first wife, Justine Johnston, who was billed as the most beautiful blonde in the world.

8. A fete for Maurice Chevalier in 1931, just before the premiere of Ernst Lubitsch's *The Smiling Lieutenant*. In the front row are Jesse Lasky (holding a cigar), Miriam Hopkins, Tallulah Bankhead, Chevalier, Fredric March, and Wanger.

9. Nancy Courtney (Tallulah Bankhead) discovers her lover (Alexander Kirkland) with another woman in George Cukor's disappointing directorial debut, *Tarnished Lady*.

10. *Washington Merry-Go-Round*, Wanger's first political melodrama, was made at Columbia. Here Button Gwinnett Brown (Lee Tracy in a typical pose) harangues the jaded Alice Wylie (Constance Cummings) about patriotism in front of the Declaration of Independence.

11. Screenwriter Carey Wilson and director Gregory LaCava added this provocative scene to *Gabriel Over the White House*, in which newly elected President Hammond (Walter Huston) plays in the Oval Office with his nephew (Dickie Moore) while the unemployed plead for government help over the radio.

12. A cigarette break with William Randolph Hearst outside the Cosmopolitan building on the MGM lot. Wanger thought Hearst was "a fantastic man."

13. In *Queen Christina*, Greta Garbo as the queen and John Gilbert as Antonio question the maid in the celebrated bedroom sequence at the inn, which Wanger refused to remove from the film's final cut.

14. Publicity still with Jay Paley, the chief backer and financial officer of JayPay Productions, later renamed Walter Wanger Pictures, Inc.

15. Executive assistant Rosemary Foley was intelligent and lively; she kept Wanger's operations in order and charmed everyone who entered his office from 1934 to 1949.

16. President Stanley (Arthur Byron) learns that Congress has declared war at the Annapolis graduation ceremony in *The President Vanishes*, Wanger's debut film as a semi-independent. Cabinet member Osgood Perkins looks on with concern.

17. The logo that preceded virtually every Wanger film in the 1930s and early 1940s was inspired by the National Recovery Administration's eagle.

SCENE 79
EXT. STREET IN POOR SECTION OF WASHINGTON

In a poor section of Washington a small,
shabby automobile stands at the curb.
In the car stands a wild-looking, dark-
haired orator who is talking with many
gestures to the group of unhappy looking
people who have gathered around the car.
In the front seat of the car sits the
driver--apparently unconscious of the
orator's voice.

                              ORATOR (hoarsely)
                                   Fellow-workers, it is your
                                   blood, my blood, the worker's
                                   blood they're after. When war
                                   comes it's you and me that'll
                                   have to bleed! For what? So
                                   that the capitalist blood-
                                   suckers---------

The crowd breaks into a loud
sound of derision.

                              CROWD
                                   Boo!

                              ORATOR
                                   ----yes, so that the Capitalist
                                   blood-suckers can grow richer!
                                   Tomorrow the President goes to
                                   Congress. Maybe he says it is
                                   a shame but we've got to go to
                                   war! Maybe he don't! But I
                                   think he will! But say he don't-
                                   what then? I'll tell you what
                                   then---Congress will say we've
                                   got to fight to protect our
                                   honor!

Again the crowd breaks into a
loud derisive sound.

                              CROWD
                                   Boo!

                    (CONTINUED)

18. Scene 79 from the Final Continuity Script of *The President Vanishes*, in which a
Communist party member urges a mob to resist the war and join the party. Will Hays
insisted that Wanger delete the explicit references to Communism, among other things.

Scene 79 - Continued

                    ORATOR
                         Protect their honor with my
                         blood! Your blood! The workers,
                         you and me! Our blood!

The crowd becomes more tense
and they seem to gather closer
to the car.

                    ORATOR
                         Our blood, I tell you! And for
                         what? For nothing! And there
                         is only one way to stop it!
                         Join the Communist party!

Immediately the crowd breaks out
into cheers and hand-clapping and
whistling.

The orator has a handfull of circulars
and he starts to distribute them among
those nearest the car.

Suddenly from far down the street
we see a large group of Grey Shirts
approaching at a run. We hear their
cry.

                    GREY SHIRTS
                         Union! Union! Union!

At the cry the crowd around the
car jerks into instant action.
They drop their handbills and turn
and run away as fast as possible
yelling as they go.

                    CROWD
                         The Grey Shirts! The Grey Shirts.

They fall over each other in their
mad effort to get away from the
approaching Grey Shirts.

The orator remains standing on his
seat in the car and although the
driver of the car frantically tries
to start the car he is thwarted in
his efforts as the Grey Shirts
descend on both of them.

                    (CONTINUED)

19. A party for the mental hospital staff in *Private Worlds* features Dr. Alec McGregor (Joel McCrea), his wife Sally (Joan Bennett), and vamp Claire Monet (Helen Vinson).

20. Miscegenation in *Shanghai*: Ambassador Lu Sing (Warner Oland) watches as society girl Barbara Howard (Loretta Young) surprises Dimitri Kuslov (Charles Boyer) by wearing his Eurasian mother's favorite dress.

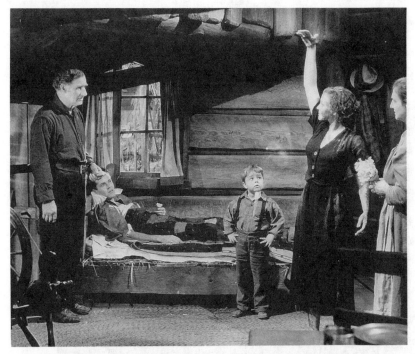

21. *Trail of the Lonesome Pine*: June Tolliver (Sylvia Sidney) describes the tall stranger (played by Fred MacMurray) she has seen in the woods to her father (Fred Stone), her cousin Dave (Henry Fonda), her kid brother (Spanky McFarland), and her mother (Beulah Bondi).

22. Spoiled movie star Cherry Chester (Margaret Sullavan) pretends to be a melancholy reader of long Russian novels to impress a fan magazine writer in *The Moon's Our Home*.

23. Wanger joins the prestigious United Artists team in 1936. From left to right: Douglas Fairbanks, Jr., Charles Chaplin, Samuel Goldwyn, Jock Whitney, David O. Selznick, Mary Pickford, Wanger, Jesse Lasky, Douglas Fairbanks, Sr., and Roy Disney pose for the occasion.

6

Too Much Interference
(1932–1934)

Eight years older than Selznick and Zanuck, five years older than Thalberg, Wanger at thirty-eight was no boy wonder. Some believed that after stepping down from Paramount, Wanger had peaked early in his career. But his reputation as an outstanding scout and his imposing Paramount affiliation made him a valuable asset to any studio. In fact, Wanger spent the next three years bouncing from low-budget Columbia to lavish MGM, searching for an association and a position in the studio hierarchies which could give him the authority to make sophisticated dramas and political melodramas. This quest took him down the ladder of studio management from an executive position at Columbia to a producer's post at MGM, where he gained greater responsibility for individual films. Significantly, he also entered into increasing conflict with studio brass and the industry's Production Code, which in turn pushed him toward independent work.

One would never know it from Paramount's 1920s films, but throughout the decade Wanger retained the idealistic sense of mission that had piqued his interest in the movies. When he arrived in London in 1921, his interviews and publicity hailed him as "a successful businessman with ideals," noting that he read H. G. Wells and "had theories of his own regarding education, sociology and economics." As the British contemplated the meaning of the Fatty Arbuckle and William Desmond Taylor scandals in Hollywood, Wanger published "Films as Foreign Offices." The London *Daily Mail* described him as a "young American who, under a debonair exterior, controls a mind red-hot with ideals and aspirations in regard to the education of the masses by means of the films." And in London Wanger was as good as his word. He sponsored free Saturday performances of Shakespeare for children and screenings of travelogues and nature films. At one of the latter, the *Daily Telegraph* reported, "greatly magnified images of the caterpillar casting its successive skins . . . were greeted with bursts of audible admiration."

Of course Wanger was hardly alone in advocating the educational, social, and diplomatic potential of the film in the 1920s. Art historian John Kouwenhoven argues that American artistic traditions have always displayed a peculiar tendency to approach all forms of cultural expression as inherently useful. Film was no exception. Through the early 1910s, the cinema's champions argued, in Myron Lounsbury's words, that movies overcame "the predicament" of the Protestant work ethic "not by condoning play, but by elevating leisure as a sober preparation for a civilized society." Film's educational function was a logical extension of the notion of "uplift," for it continued the 1910s argument in the theater about how the arts could instill the appropriate virtues in a working class that now had greater leisure time. Since 1915, Griffith had envisioned the use of movies for liberal ends; after 1922, this became the keynote of MPPDA head Hays's public speeches.

From his CPI experience in World War I, Wanger shared the assumption, now considered naive by sociologists and media theorists, that audiences were completely susceptible to mass media "messages" (sometimes known as the "silver bullet" theory). His convictions only intensified when talking pictures arrived, particularly the Fox Movietone newsreels of Shaw and of Charles Lindbergh's takeoff on his transatlantic flight to Paris. In 1929, Wanger discussed making educational films at Paramount with Kahn, Jack Otterson (of Western Electric's sound licensing company), and Dartmouth College president Arthur Hopkins; he claimed the Wall Street crash in October killed the idea. The following year, Wanger told a college newspaper, "The talking motion picture is the greatest step in civilization. . . . It even exceeds the printing press in importance" for it can "bring to the poorest person in the street the greatest academic advantages of the day." He envisioned "classes" with typical catholicity: morning lectures on interior decorating by Elsie de Wolfe, on the theory of relativity by Albert Einstein, and opera concerts the rest of the day. He tried to interest radio's *March of Time* in making films two years before its screen debut.

Then too, Wanger's "Films as Foreign Offices" was an early expression of what became a cliché as the 1920s progressed, that movies could promote world harmony and that trade follows the film. In 1924 the League of Nations established a group to study the impact of movies on intellectual life and in 1930 offered a prize for the film that best promoted "understanding among nations." Benjamin Hampton, hailing Wanger as "one of the keenest minds in American studios," chose to conclude his 1931 industry-financed *History of the American Film Industry* with Wanger's comments on film's potential to achieve this:

Why not put the League of Nations to work? If the League would appoint a committee to encourage, and finally to supervise, the production of text-films, and text-books, to be used all over the world, the problems of mankind could be settled within three generations. Why don't we stop talking about this 'brother-hood of man' idea — why not make it a fact, instead of a dream?

As Paramount's general manager of production, Wanger himself lacked the wherewithal to stop talking and start producing films along these lines. Like the rest of the industry, he viewed educational films as a sideline worth more in prestige than in profits. Yet Wanger's idealistic views set him completely apart from other production executives and impressed many contacts and drinking pals during the 1920s, including the skeptical, acerbic commentator Mencken. When Haardt expressed her greater admiration for playwright-screenwriter Laurence Stallings (a World War I veteran amputee and coauthor of the antiwar *What Price Glory?*), Mencken insisted that "when the time comes to civilize the movies my guess is that Wanger will have more to do with the business than Stallings. He has some schemes, in fact, already." He added:

[Wanger] is highly intelligent, and knows what is wrong with the movies, but his attitude toward them is the usual one: he is getting what he can while the going is good. Discourtesy goes with the business. It was organized by bounders, and is still mainly run by them.

Wanger made a still stronger impression on another visitor to Famous Players' studios: John Grierson, the Scottish philosophy student who subsequently revived the term "documentary" and founded the celebrated British documentary movement of the 1930s. On a Rockefeller fellowship to study the mass media in America, Grierson, at the suggestion of Lippmann, wanted to research the impact of the movies in shaping the immigrant audience's perceptions of current events. Wanger and Grierson discovered two mutual acquaintances: Merriam, Wanger's superior in Rome, was directing Grierson's research at the University of Chicago (and likely sent Grierson to Wanger); and Beardsley Ruml, one of Wanger's best actors at Dartmouth, was administering the Rockefeller grant. Wanger gave Grierson unprecedented access to Paramount's distribution and exhibition reports.

There were more profound instances of mutual interests, for Grierson found Wanger remarkably sympathetic to his views that movies "had the very special public duty to interpret the contemporary scene." They concurred on the necessity for training in film work, as evidenced in FPL's experimental film acting school of the 1920s, Wanger's creation of a script library and film course at Dartmouth in the mid-1930s, and Grierson's training of his protégés at England's Empire Marketing Board. The two men also agreed that movies needed to have popular appeal, and they derogated sentimental "hokum" in favor of uplifting roadshow "epics" such as *The Covered Wagon* and Wanger's special project, *Beau Geste*. They both admired Eisenstein's propagandistic montage editing in *Potemkin* (which Grierson retitled for American viewers).

Moreover, Wanger *had* inaugurated certain enlightened production policies at FPL. As Grierson recalled, "Wanger himself was tied up with Judge Ben Lindsay at Denver [author of the study of contemporary sexual mores, *Revolt of Modern Youth*] about relating the star system to the new youth movement at that time." This led to the scouting of stars who projected positive role models, such as Thelma Todd, Richard Arlen, and Gary Cooper, among others. And Grierson applauded Wanger's sponsorship of exotic documentaries such as Schoedsack and Merian Cooper's *Grass* (1925) and *Chang*, as well as Robert Flaherty's *Moana*. Forty years later, after Wanger's death, Grierson wrote the *London Times* that Wanger "was one of the first important students of the cinema as an active social influence."

Like Grierson, Wanger rejected the political pessimism in Lippmann's argument that the citizens of a modern democracy were incapable of mastering their own political affairs. Like Grierson, Wanger subscribed to the liberal notion that an informed citizenry would make intelligent political choices and that movies were the premiere vehicle of enlightenment. But the two filmmakers subsequently followed different paths. Grierson, with no prior experience in film production, rejected commercial entertainment. He realized that with few exceptions, narrative films trivialized social realities through their ideology of heroic individualism. Part of his achievement as a major figure in the history of documentary was to develop a rhetoric that showed the industrial laborer his or her importance to the national community in the 1930s.

Wanger remained committed to entertainment and narrative formulas that heightened the values of charismatic individualism. Where the films of Grierson's protégés often focused on the working Briton, Wanger centered his message movies on paternalistic political leaders. He aimed to combine enlightenment or sophistication with absurd conventions and happy endings that the industry's recent return to hokum entailed. He sponsored such juxtapositions in the accurate belief that entertainment formulas were essential to attract the mass audience. Yet they tempered the integrity of his message films.

From 1932 to 1934, Wanger tried repeatedly to make precisely the kinds of films that—as Eisenstein's futile sojourn at Paramount had demonstrated—most Hollywood executives did not want. His interest in Haardt's scriptwork testified as much to his interest in supervising individual films as it did to his desire to impress Mencken. To this end, within a week of his dismissal from Paramount, Wanger negotiated to lease the Cosmopolitan studio in Harlem to produce independently. He also considered an offer from Selznick to work as a story and talent scout for a consortium of independents. But after the spring 1931 box office fallout, neither man could find backers for their ventures.

Hence, in late December 1931 Wanger began negotiations with Harry Cohn, who soon became a president also in charge of production at Columbia Pictures. Cohn wanted relief from his scouting duties. Then too, in 1931, Columbia was a low-budget independent studio and former member of "Poverty Row." Cohn believed Wanger would augment his efforts to achieve major studio status. Wanger proved modestly successful, but his efforts were subsequently overshadowed by the phenomenal critical, financial, and Academy Award triumph of Capra's *It Happened One Night* in 1934.

Ex-vaudevillian Cohn had formed Columbia in 1919 with his brother Jack (a newsreel producer for Universal) and attorney Joseph Brandt as CBC Productions. Producing low-budget, $20,000 films (one-eighth of the average Paramount programmer budget), these aggressive men within seven years had established a national distribution network and purchased a studio lot on Gower Street. By 1928 Columbia had joined the MPPDA, and its best films (typically directed by Capra) earned ticket prices in the "$2 top school." The company went public in March 1929, and the stockholders were not disappointed. Even in the early 1930s, Columbia continually earned modest profits ($500,000 to $600,000 through 1934) while Paramount, Fox, Warner Bros., and RKO floundered with million dollar losses.

At Columbia, Wanger faced a low-cost regime that contrasted sharply with the reckless extravagance of his former studio. Cohn kept studio overhead low through special accounting measures, he limited talent contracts to two or three films, and he typically held negative costs to $70,000 to $80,000 per feature, of which no more than $1,000 went to what one executive called "melodramas and unproduced plays or plays that have not clicked." By spring 1931 and the success of Capra's relatively expensive *Dirigible,* the Cohn brothers had a durable policy.

Early in the season, they produced two to four high-quality films (in the 1932–1933 season, these were Irving Cummings's *Night Club Lady* and Capra's *American Madness* and *The Bitter Tea of General Yen*). As one of Wanger's associates explained in August 1932, Jack Cohn and his executives wanted "a real creative production department to turn out a couple of leaders early in the season to enable them to write their usual quota of business, after which they only need a studio to grind out the undelivered pictures at the cheapest possible cost." After the "A" releases in the fall, Jack Cohn sold more than twenty programmers, exploitation films with lots of action, and short comedies for the rest of the year. During the early thirties, they, like most studio heads, reasoned that "a good picture" would return just as much money (if not more) than "the higher cost 'class' production."

In fact, the market conditions in the early thirties proved advantageous to

Columbia. The increased costs of sound filmmaking had forced the major studios to produce fewer films. But decreasing audiences compelled theaters of all grades to change their programs more frequently with more titles. When second- and third-run exhibitors revived double features in 1930, the majors' market dominance, achieved through vertical integration and block-booking, weakened. Low-budget independents such as Mascot and Monogram gained playing time on screens previously denied them. By June 1932, an estimated 40 percent of theaters were using the double feature format, which accounted for up to 75 percent of the independents' bookings.

The major producer-distributor-exhibitors attempted to resist double features, but even Paramount Publix exhibition executives found that in markets such as Toledo, where nothing else seemed to lure people into the theaters, double features worked. The best solution was to distribute more films. With the encouragement of their financiers, the vertically integrated companies began to buy the best low-budget independent films. In 1930, RKO purchased *Today* from Majestic Pictures; in 1931, Paramount distributed F. W. Murnau's *Tabu* and United Artists signed the independent Bela Lugosi vehicle *White Zombie*. Columbia itself had "picked up" two successful outside films, *The Blond Captive* and *Africa Speaks* in the past two years.

The new fluidity between low budget and major studio films enhanced Columbia's standing and its ability to book its movies into the majors' first-run houses, the 16 percent of theaters which collected 70 percent of annual ticket sales. RKO had used Columbia films frequently in its theaters since its overnight formation in 1928. Warner Bros.—First National, the least pretentious of the vertically integrated "Big Five" studios, also used Columbia titles in its theaters. In late 1931, the Cohns saw their chance to break into the extensive, profitable Paramount and Loew's circuits that dominated the New York, New England, southern and upper Midwest markets. They bet that Wanger's sophisticated story taste would help.

Wanger winced at Columbia's salary terms: one thousand dollars weekly over a six-month period, with an option to renew. This was one-third of his Paramount salary, but Cohn wanted Wanger for keeps: he offered him an option to purchase at half price $1 million of Columbia stock (Cohn allegedly bought this stock with mob money). Wanger was well aware of what his status could accomplish for the company: "When I left Paramount for Columbia," he later commented, "everybody thought I was slumming." Morris Safier, brother-in-law to Lewis J. Selznick, noted that Wanger "has too much class for this gang around here and I doubt very much whether they even understand his English." *Variety,* noting the anomaly of Wanger's presence at Columbia alongside the notoriously vulgar Harry Cohn, quipped in mid-February that industry people were "betting that within six months Harry will be carrying the handkerchief in his cuff and Walter will be talking from the side of his mouth." Putting his personality "capital" to use in aiding a parvenu studio, Wanger also expected to have enough freedom to put political melodramas into production.

The hiring of Wanger marked Columbia's plans to spend its biggest budget yet on "fewer and better" films. Cohn reopened the studio's New York story office (closed the preceding May) so that Wanger could scoop talents and stories from the stage. But Wanger also instituted several cost-cutting measures of his own. He urged Cohn to hire young writers on the cheap (like Dore Schary, whom Wanger erroneously assumed from correspondence was a woman, a mistake that Cohn never let him forget). At Wanger's urging, Columbia inaugurated a profit-percentage system for paying directors and stars to reduce negative costs and attract talents freed from the major studios. Within three months, Wanger had signed playwrights Sam Behrman and Sturges and performers Brian Foy, Bert Wheeler, and Robert Woolsey to such contracts.

In April 1932, Cohn asked Wanger to move to Hollywood to assist in overseeing production. There was not much to work with: Capra described the studio as "three cramped stages, a row of shops, an incinerator, a parking place for trucks, and—into a leftover corner—a cubist's nightmare of cutting rooms, film vaults, and projection rooms piled on top of each other." Wanger's move was significant, not simply because he gave up his beloved Manhattan, but because he now assumed a closer relationship to the mechanics of filmmaking.

Wanger supervised several Columbia "specials" through late 1932. He used his pull at Paramount to hire Adolph Menjou and veteran director Cummings for a mystery-thriller "A" production modeled on Paramount's Philo Vance series, *The Night Club Lady*. More notable, because more pretentious, was his purchase of Grace Zaring Stone's best-selling 1930 novel *The Bitter Tea of General Yen*. The studio planned "to throw lots of jack into this filmization . . . stating it will be the most elaborate undertaking in the history of Columbia." It would fit well into a recent cycle of films with Asian settings such as von Sternberg's *Shanghai Express* (1932).

The narrative line of *The Bitter Tea of General Yen* was in many ways a new version of *The Sheik*. It provided the titillating thrill of miscegenation in the relationship between a white woman, American blueblood missionary Megan Davis (Barbara Stanwyck), and a Chinese warlord (Swedish actor Nils Asther), a premise realized in Megan's "dream sequence" in which the general saves her from an Asian bandit and kisses her. The film presented superficially contrasting images of women in the American, independent-minded Davis and the general's slavish concubine whom Davis reluctantly offers to replace at the end of the film. These two aspects of the film, and its portrayal of other myopic missionaries in China, compared the West's hypocritical pieties unfavorably with the mystifying philosophical stoicism of the East. When the Chinese charge d'affaires complained to the MPPDA about dialogue, stating that "human life is the cheapest thing in China," Columbia justifiably replied that "every seemingly derogatory remark about the Chinese is refuted by the story."

Capra inherited this project from Wanger's first-choice director, the silent-era veteran Herbert Brenon (who had directed *Beau Geste* at Paramount). Brenon quit the studio and his profit-sharing contract in early June 1932, and Capra pleaded for the property with Wanger, who in turn demanded the producer's credit. The attraction of *The Bitter Tea of General Yen* for Capra, and for Harry Cohn, lay not just in its message but in its "art appeal," a change of pace from Capra's comedies. As critic Leland Poague has noted, the film has many un-Capra-esque qualities, including its unhappy ending, its sympathetic treatment of the dictator Yen, and its bleak vision of an amoral universe. Completed in November 1932 and opening RKO's new Radio City Music Hall in New York in January 1933—a coup in itself for Jack Cohn—*The Bitter Tea of General Yen* proved one of Capra's few box office failures, due in part to bannings in England and other foreign markets.

Equally significant, Wanger at Columbia pursued "social problem" films, generally associated with the early years of the Great Depression. The genre combined Progressive Era impulses with the entertainment values to which Wanger and Hollywood were unalterably committed. As many critics have observed, they translated impersonal forces (economic trends, governmental policy, the workings of the capitalist system) into melodramatic, interpersonal conflicts (greedy profiteers and corrupt politicians versus morally admirable protagonists and helpless victims). Thus any profound critique of America's social and economic system lay buried under the contingencies of individual personality. As critic Russell Campbell has noted, social problem films were viewed by industry conservatives as "violating the principle of 'pure entertainment' to which the movie capital was held to be dedicated." Liberal industry members such as Wanger, however, felt the genre indicated "that the movie business recognized and was fulfilling its cultural responsibilities."

In the teens such films, according to film historian Kay Sloan, raised "social issues while at the same time containing them in satisfactory bourgeois resolutions." In 1931, Warner Bros., under the guidance of Zanuck and Hal B. Wallis, developed a more sophisticated version of the Progressive Era message movies. Gangster films (*Public Enemy* and *Little Caesar,* both 1931) and the prison film (most notably the 1931 *I am a Fugitive from a Chain Gang*) constructed a kind of realism from their topicality and their low-budget, naturalistic settings that other studios could emulate. The fact that Columbia films played in Warner Bros. first-run houses only encouraged Harry Cohn, Capra, and Wanger to mimic that studio's formula. By spring 1932, Capra had begun a message film, *American Madness,* which dramatized the necessity of "faith" in people and unusual loan policies to stimulate the economy.

The Warner Bros. problem film provided a narrative formula and a visual model: Wanger's innovation was to take new subject matter and plug it in. While Warner Bros. fixed its dramatizations of political corruption at the level of "the mouthpiece" and the city, Wanger focused on national politics. Several comic productions, such as the Marx Brothers' *Duck Soup,* the George M. Cohan vehicle *The Phantom President,* and the stage musical comedy *Of Thee I Sing,* demonstrated a market for such subject matter. In early 1932, MGM shifted the tone to melodrama with *Washington Masquerade,* in which Karen Morley seduces Congressman Lionel Barrymore into betraying his voters.

Wanger's *Washington Merry-Go-Round* (1932) trod similar ground, although its title came from Drew Pearson's muckraking columns and subsequent best-seller that had outlined a series of scandals in the capital. The film unfolds like a crude version of Capra's 1939 *Mr. Smith Goes to Washington,* showing the "education" of an idealistic populist congressman from Georgia, one Burton Gwinnett Brown (played by nasal, early sound star Lee Tracy). Brown's election is sponsored by a bootlegging, murderous ring in Congress, which aims to use him as the perfect facade: to them, he is "all front and no back. He wears star-spangled underwear."

As in *Mr. Smith Goes to Washington,* Brown tours the capital's monuments for inspiration and takes instruction from an attractive but jaded young ingenue named Alice (Constance Cummings), who advises him to attend congressional sessions without reading the bills on which he is to vote. Unlike Mr. Smith, however, Brown comes to Washington with open eyes, and he repeatedly confronts Norton (Alan Dinehart), the leader of the merry-go-round who styles himself an American Mussolini and threatens to marry Alice. Norton has Brown impeached, but in the final moments, Brown persuades a group of Bonus Marchers (homeless, unemployed, World War I veterans) to spy on Norton for eyewitness evidence of his wrongdoing. Norton kills himself rather than be exposed.

To inspire the Marchers to perform the necessary House-cleaning, Brown articulates the need for vigilant citizens:

> This isn't just a Depression. It's a crisis. You've got a Senate and a House of Representatives filled mostly with honest and patriotic men. But they're handicapped, hamstrung by a secret government. An evil marauding crew that has turned the Constitution of the United States into a bill of sale. Your government needs your support, your understanding, your help to throw out the vermin.

To contemporary audiences, the charge of bootlegging alcohol in the Capitol echoed Warren Harding's troubled administration of the early 1920s, particularly the speakeasy activities of Attorney General Harry Daugherty and the Teapot Dome scandal. Released one month before the 1932 presidential election, however, *Washington Merry-Go-Round*'s exhortation to sweep the nation's capital clean had more immediate relevance. *The Nation* described the film as "a significant example of Hollywood's valiant efforts to catch up with the times."

But for all its historical resonance, the film is marred by Brown's bull-headed approach to Washington corruption, which is monotonous and repetitive. As Senator Wylie (Walter Connolly) tells him, "You're a master of attack. Soon you'll learn strategy." But he doesn't learn soon enough. The script by Capra scenarist Jo Swerling lacks plausibility or nuance. It offered an absurd vision of Congress's workings and of members who by dramatic necessity are fatally oblivious to Norton's machinations. Moreover, the film lacks the sympathetic treatment that Capra (and star James Stewart) gave the benighted Mr. Smith and the aesthetic coherence that Capra achieved by paralleling personal betrayal (of Smith by his secretary) and political betrayal of the American people by Congress.

Nonetheless, Wanger rode the political melodrama cycle for all it was worth. Even before *Washington Merry-Go-Round* went into distribution, he secured in July 1932 a Gertrude Purcell screenplay from a Samuel Marx story entitled "Night Mayor." This portrayed a playboy official loosely based on New York mayor Jimmy Walker. Colonel Jason Joy, an administrator of the Production Code, described the character:

> "His Honor" of the story is a wisecracker and something of a Follies-girl chaser, spends little time in his office, and is investigated. Nevertheless he manages to be a good fellow and good mayor in the sense that things get done. The conclusion [in which the mayor avoids scandal by marrying his girlfriend to a muckraking journalist] is very much in the mayor's favor but whether this is good business or bad business I don't know.

Wanger believed it was good business, and he personally assured Joy that Columbia was "willing to assume whatever risks there are as to libel and to criticism by the mayor or his enemies." Starring Tracy and directed by James Flood, the film was completed in mid-August, when the MPPDA deemed it a "well directed, entertaining comedy farce." But three congressmen, the Republican National Committee chairman, and "others of like prominence" complained to Hays about it upon its release.

Whatever its aesthetic or entertainment qualities, *Night Mayor* (1932) was booked to premiere at the Paramount Theater in New York. It seemed that with Wanger's help, Columbia would at last break into a new theater circuit. But between the film's production and its release, Mayor Walker was recalled from office amidst startling revelations about his personal life. Wanger's bravado had backfired. Paramount Publix canceled the booking in fear of reprisals from city and state politicians, and Columbia opened the film in Time Square's Globe Theater, an independent first-run house. None of the circuits would touch the film, sharing *Variety*'s view that it was "a tactless picture to make in the first place" because of its "undiplomatic treatment of a controversial subject."

Meanwhile, *Washington Merry-Go-Round* was hailed by Harry and Jack Cohn as Columbia's "best money getter in gross rentals" during the poor 1932 year, outperforming Capra's more expensive *American Madness*. Even before these accolades, Wanger's contract was renewed in August for another six months, this time at $2,000 a week. Yet he found the second six months less satisfying and productive than the first half year. He later claimed, "I couldn't take [Columbia] because I was used to a much nicer environment [at Paramount]. It was pretty tough there and pretty vulgar." But no matter how crude the Cohn brothers could be, it was company policy, not vulgarity, which made Wanger leave.

Shortly after Wanger's contract renewal, Jack Cohn blocked Harry's nomination of Wanger to Columbia's board of directors. Jack Cohn also persuaded Columbia's board to renege on its big budget plans. Once again, Columbia closed its New York story department and planned a predominantly low-budget season that rebuffed Wanger's policy innovations. Columbia did continue to contract outside talents on a profit-sharing basis for successful films such as Howard Hawks's *Twentieth Century* (1934) and Leo McCarey's *The Awful Truth* (1937). But the quality and type of materials purchased for production in the fall of 1932 became a regular point of contention between the Cohns. In December, Jack complained that Harry was too ambitious and that he had eaten too many lunches with Mayer (although these laid the groundwork for the Clark Gable loan-out for *It Happened One Night*).

Wanger himself had several lunches with Thalberg in early December. Caught between the Cohn brothers, he wanted out. The one unqualified success of his tenure, *Washington Merry-Go-Round,* only confirmed his suspicion that there was a market for political melodrama. Turning down an invitation from Selznick to join RKO, Wanger accepted Thalberg's offer on the twenty-first to work at MGM as an associate producer for $2,000 a week. Wanger left Columbia with few regrets.

MGM was in every way the antithesis of Columbia, taking for granted the lavish filmmaking Harry Cohn struggled to introduce. The company had the highest overhead in the industry (due to such practices as maintaining more than seventy writers on salary), and the biggest per-film negative cost in the industry (estimated at $500,000 per title—$150,000 more than at the other studios). The films, such as the 1932 Academy Award winner *Grand Hotel,* were packed with stars from a stable that ranged from "goddess" Garbo to earthy Wallace Beery. With such policies, the studio successfully turned out more top-quality films in its annual schedule than any of its competitors including Paramount.

Nine years after its formation, MGM had sustained the high caliber of its first season that had so taken Lasky aback. In its 1932 survey of the studio, *Fortune* ascribed its success to high standards of quality (most evident in its performers), executive teamwork, and Thalberg's expert allocation of the studio's generous budgets for production.

Yet Thalberg, like Harry Cohn a year earlier, wanted relief from his duties. The pressure to increase production taxed his abilities and his frail heart. Aside from prestige items and Beery and Marie Dressler movies, Mayer, MGM's vice-president in charge of production, was of little help. In the fall of 1932, Thalberg complained that his associate producers—Harry Rapf, Albert Lewin, and Eddie Mannix, among others—annoyed him with details and that they were not producing films up to his standards. To alleviate Thalberg's problem, MGM hired three producers—Hawks, Sidney Franklin, and Ralph Graves—to produce films with greater autonomy than Thalberg's lieutenants enjoyed. Wanger was a fourth.

Hence, the move to MGM offered Wanger even closer contact with the production of specific films in a studio with resources comparable to those at Paramount. And with his special status, and especially after Thalberg's severe heart problems in early 1933 forced him to take an indefinite vacation, Wanger could do so with a freedom that went beyond any flexibility in a low-budget studio. Both Mayer and Thalberg enshrined the producer—rather than the star, the writer, or the director—as the crucial creative force at the studio. As Mamoulian has said, "MGM was a producer's studio. The director would finish the film, and then the producer and executives would come in and do whatever they felt was necessary." But there were limits to the producer's authority, even at MGM.

Mayer had also welcomed Wanger onto the lot. He asked Wanger, as the latter later recalled, to help him "build up the biggest collection of talent so that this studio can't fail." Wanger regarded Mayer with a mixture of caution and amusement. He was privy to Mayer's futile infatuation with Jean Howard, a Broadway dancer who eventually married agent Charles K. Feldman, for whom Wanger stood as best man at the wedding. The caution came from Mayer's Republican politics and the new political melodrama Wanger planned for his first film. Just days after arriving on the lot in mid-January, he asked MGM's story editor Samuel Marx to purchase *Gabriel Over the White House*.

The novel was written anonymously by Thomas W. Tweed, an aide to former British prime minister David Lloyd George and a liberal champion of governmental activism during the teens. Tweed's book portrayed a prediction often articulated during the early thirties: that American democracy would disappear under the pressure of the Great Depression. Set in the 1980s, it envisioned increased unemployment, crumbling governments around the world which still had not repaid their World War I debts, prohibition and gangsters still fomenting violent crime, and an armed group of army veterans modeled on the Bonus Marchers, who camped in public parks and looted local stores when municipal governments did not meet their demands for food and shelter.

President Hammond is an ordinary, amiable party politician, who after a fatal car accident is revived by God to become a dictator. He dismisses his cabinet and the Congress, repeals Prohibition and punishes gangsters, creates a working corps for the unemployed, enforces disarmament, and creates a new American currency. When felled by a heart attack, Hammond reverts to his former self and tries to rescind his "inspired" actions before he dies. An MGM reader called Tweed's novel "dynamite for picture production," noting that "if we could get Governmental consent, it would be a sensational and world-famous production."

"A sensational picture" was exactly what Wanger hoped to produce. Tweed's novel was an ironic fantasy, but Wanger dropped its future setting and dressed the film up with all the realism that Hollywood could muster, from newsreel footage for Hammond's inauguration to elaborate settings for White House interiors. He directed Carey Wilson, a Thalberg protégé, to streamline Tweed's story flashbacks into a manageable plot and to insert action sequences whenever possible, such as the one in which Hammond crashes his car at ninety miles per hour. In yet another sequence not in the novel, Hammond plays a hide and seek game in the White House with his nephew, completely oblivious to the heartfelt pleas over the radio of unemployed veterans' leader John Bronson for jobs.

Wanger was well aware of Mayer's personal friendship with Herbert Hoover, who had been blamed for the persistence of massive unemployment and Depression. When Wanger, a staunch Roosevelt supporter, approached Thalberg about his differences with Mayer over politics and production ideas, Thalberg had told Wanger, "Don't pay any attention to him." Accordingly, Wanger took several steps to ensure the project's completion. First, he scheduled it for immediate production. With screenwriter Wilson's help, principal photography began in mid-February, just one month after MGM bought the property. The film was shot in under two weeks (from February 16 through the twenty-sixth), and cost roughly $180,000, or the budget for a program picture.

Wanger kept costs low by using, with the exception of Walter Huston and Karen Morley, a cast of faces relatively new to movies, such as Group Theater alumnus Franchot Tone (*Gabriel Over the White House* was his second screen appearance), stage actor Arthur Byron, and David Landau, the brutal warden of *I Am a Fugitive from a Chain Gang,* who played John Bronson, the unemployed veterans' leader. Meanwhile, Huston and Morley, as *New Masses* critic Harry Alan Potamkin noted, reinforced the film's presidential lineage from Huston's appearances in Griffith's *Abraham Lincoln* (1931) and Morley's in *Washington Masquerade.*

Second, Wanger secured the financial backing and endorsement of Hearst after two weeks of script preparation and the assignment of comedy expert Gregory LaCava to direct. Hearst's Cosmopolitan Pictures had operated on the MGM lot with some awkwardness since 1923. His films starring Davies were not always high quality, but they gained valuable distribution and exhibition, while MGM pictures got favorable reviews in the Hearst papers. Wanger had known Hearst socially since the 1910s through Johnston's friendship with Davies and the Wangers' frequent visits to San Simeon. Since Hearst at this point supported Roosevelt, a stance he would later vehemently reverse, he was intrigued by Wanger's project of depicting an activist president. Their friendship now became professional.

Getting Hearst's backing for *Gabriel Over the White House* (1933) also meant allowing Hearst to tamper with the policies enacted by President Hammond. The new phase in script preparation began in early February. It involved downplaying the social ills suggested in Tweed's novel and adding proposed solutions to squatters and war debts, which Hays Office readers immediately recognized as following "very closely the program laid down in the Hearst press." Marx recalls that "Hearst was literally dictating parts of that movie. Writing them out in his own handwriting, in pencil," including Hammond's climactic speech at the international summit conference. This apocalyptic statement, prophesying the destruction of civilization by air bombing, called for men to use "the forces of nature for beneficent purposes." Wanger, committed more to the idea of the production than its specific political implications, was perfectly amenable to Hearst's modifications of the script.

Reading the result, James Wingate, head of the Studio Relations Committee of the MPPDA (the body charged with regulating film content), noted that the Hays Office could not "deny the screen the right to portray a dramatic solution of present-day economic problems." But *Gabriel Over the White House* caused extraordinary concern in the Hays Office largely because of contemporary conditions. In the present "trying times," Wingate noted, the depiction of mobs of men armed and marching on Washington and the talk of revolution "may lead to the radicals and the communists, and others who believe in governmental changes by other than constitutional methods, doing the same thing, thus helping to lessen the confidence of the peons in their form of government." As a New York censor wrote to Hays, "The thing that producers should be careful about in my opinion, is these remarks about revolution. God knows there are enough people who are afraid of something of that sort without stirring it up on the screen." .

The portrayal of venal politicians was even more immediately worrisome, especially the scenes of drinking in the White House during Prohibition and the portrayal of an incompetent and corrupt Congress. Wingate wrote Hays that such a depiction "does not appear to promote a sympathetic attitude of a Congress toward the industry portraying it as inefficient." Several legislators and political leaders had objected vociferously to *Washington Merry-Go-*

Round, and in mid-February 1933, the New York state assembly and senate was considering a bill censoring political films, as a response to movies such as Wanger's *Night Mayor.* Hays felt certain that both state and federal lawmakers would seriously consider taxing or censoring the film industry "if it is felt that a motion picture is offering affront."

Yet another problem concerned international relations. Even during the film's scheduled release, March 1933, Roosevelt's State Department was involved in ongoing conferences in which Germany demanded the right to rearm. Colonel Frederick Herron, in charge of the foreign office of the MPPDA and therefore of securing licenses for exhibiting American films abroad, was outraged by the portrayal of foreign diplomats in *Gabriel Over the White House* as "grovelling and alibiing" and of debtor nations as "bad boys being brought up before the teacher and given a good lecture." A scene in which the cabinet makes an annoying party member the ambassador to England to "get rid of him" was particularly outrageous to another reader:

> We have a hell of a nerve to put anything like this in one of our pictures, and at the same time beg these different Embassies and Legations of ours to help us out and bellyache to the high heavens when we don't get special attention. I just can't understand the type of mind that would put a thing like this into a scenario.

This type of mind enjoyed testing out controversial subject matter, regardless of the consequences. Wanger was counting on the short-term benefits of the film's controversy, and he remained oblivious to complaints about its long-term drawbacks.

What is particularly striking about his determination to see the film through is the fact that Wanger had nothing financially to gain from the production of *Gabriel Over the White House* but the prestige of innovating in political subject matter. (Wanger, following Thalberg's dictum that "credit you give yourself is not worth having," did not receive screen credit for the film.) One week into principal photography on the film, Fred Beetson of the Hays Office visited Wanger and reported that the producer had told him that "the picture, of course, was a strong picture and . . . while he felt the picture might cause criticism, he didn't know what the audience reaction would be, and stated that in the final analysis he felt the great worries we had in mind would not be in the picture." Wanger was perfectly charming to Beetson, who found Wanger "amenable to suggestions, thoroughly aware of our worries," and who felt "he will work harmoniously with us." Never was an MPPDA representative further from the truth about a producer.

Published accounts of the March 1933 Glendale preview of *Gabriel Over the White House* emphasize that Mayer was shocked, finding it to be a slap at the reputation of ex-president Hoover and an endorsement of Roosevelt. If so, Mayer was mistaken, for President Hammond had much more in common with past president Harding as an easygoing, none-too-astute chief of state. "Put that picture in its can," Mayer reportedly told associate producer Mannix, "take it back to the studio, and lock it up!" But the Hays Office had sent red flags to Mayer's office throughout the production, and Mayer had assured them and Loew's New York office that "he would not slow production but he would personally watch the picture carefully" and that neither he nor Hearst would make a film critical of Hoover or Roosevelt.

After the Glendale preview, Hays screened the film repeatedly on March 6 in New York with Loew's executives Nicholas Schenck, J. Robert Rubin, Governor Milliken, and Howard Dietz, coming up with suggestions that he sent to Wingate. Noting that "the whole country is prostrate," Hays wrote:

> The fact is hundreds of thousands of people have one eye on [Roosevelt] and one eye on God and it is a temper and state of mind that in my opinion will resent seriously a reflection on the institution and the factors in government that have to find the solution. The people, in my opinion, will not sense in this picture the fact that it points to the people themselves behind their elected representatives as the source of all government power but will regard it as a direct indictment of the puerility and fallibility of today's government machinery and personnel. . . .
>
> I think it is essential that the picture be so changed in the early footage to indicate that there is some intelligence and some wisdom and some high purpose rather than to avoid even the promises, let alone execution, of proper duty.

Wanger was compelled to concede Hays's point.

Retakes and recutting proceeded to eliminate harsher details about the depiction of Congress, the treatment of foreign leaders, and the references to armed men, anarchists, and revolution. The annoying party member was assigned to Greece instead of England in the first cabinet meeting scene (but the film retained Hammond's incredibly parochial comment about having to wear "short pants" when appearing in the Greek court). The scenes of the unemployed were set in Baltimore rather than Washington, and Hammond's derogatory references to Congress were eliminated.

By March 29, the film had its seal. Wanger, LaCava, and Wilson all expressed their disappointment in the results, but the Studio Relations Committee had done its job: the film received only minor deletions in several states upon its release and earned more than $200,000 in profits. Although national newsweeklies rightly dismissed the film's fairy-tale treatment of serious economic and social problems, *Gabriel Over the White House* got significant attention from political commentators such as Lippmann and *New Republic* editor Bruce Bliven. The *New York Herald Tribune* found it "as frank in its propaganda as any Russian picture," while the *Hollywood Reporter* predicted that it "will probably go down in the history of motion pictures as the most sensational piece of film entertainment the world has ever known." As Wanger later proudly boasted, the film anticipated many of Roosevelt's innovative policies (such as the Works Progress Administration for the unemployed) and his use of radio for fireside chats.

Wanger would have liked nothing better than to produce another propaganda film, but he grew wary of MGM and Hays Office interference. Mayer dismissed out of hand Wanger's recommendation that the studio purchase rights to *Mutiny on the Bounty,* for he didn't want Wanger of all people to develop a story that portrayed mutineers as heroes. Rebuffed, Wanger chose a studio-owned property, *Another Language,* for his second project there. Rose Franken's Broadway hit from spring 1932 concerned the conflict between the artistically inclined, romantic Stella (Helen Hayes) and her small-minded, mediocre in-laws. Wanger secured his former Paramount cronies Mankiewicz and Stewart to adapt the film, which was completed by July.

As directed by Edward H. Griffith, who specialized in Philip Barry adaptations such as the 1930 *Holiday, Another Language* (1933) is an effective if stage-bound comedy-melodrama. Aside from Hayes and Robert Montgomery as her husband Victor, Wanger cast several actors from the Broadway production. John Beal repeated his role as the idealistic nephew who falls in love with Stella. So did Margaret Hamilton (best known as the Wicked Witch of the West in MGM's *The Wizard of Oz,* 1939). Here, she debuted as one of the gossipy sisters-in-law. The film builds to a climactic confrontation between the newlyweds regarding their in-laws and peaks with Stella embracing and kissing, at alarming length, Victor's nephew. In spite of this scene and its $269,000 cost, *Another Language* did not break even.

A more prominent project had begun before Wanger's arrival on the lot. In early October 1932, Thalberg had personally assigned MGM contractee Bess Meredyth to work with Garbo's friend, the Hungarian actress Salka Viertel, on a film concerning Queen Christina, the seventeenth-century Swedish monarch. Hoping to intrigue Garbo, then completing an eight-month vacation, and wary of dull costume pictures, Thalberg encouraged the writers to develop lesbian undertones in the relationship between Christina and Countess Ebba, referring explicitly to the German film *Madchen in Uniform,* as a way of creating "very interesting scenes." Meredyth and Viertel completed their third draft script in early January, three weeks after Thalberg's heart attack.

Wanger took over supervising their script, which was too long and too costly to produce. In true MGM producer fashion, he inaugurated a procession of writers to work on it: Hungarian Ernest Vadja in February to add "Lubitsch touches," British H. M. Harwood in April to give the dialogue "class" and to strengthen the historical backdrop of the story, and finally, in late July 1933, Viertel and playwright Behrman. Mankiewicz supplied rewrites during production from mid-September on.

The historical figure Queen Christina was much more colorful than the Garbo character who emerged from this elaborate process. Raised as a prince rather than a princess, she was bisexual. Her abdication of her throne had nothing to do with a heterosexual romance. Nonetheless, Christina evolved into a quintessential Garbo heroine, a vessel of profound and tragic emotions who pines for love. Mamoulian claims he accepted Mayer's offer to direct the film only after Mayer assigned Wanger to the production. The director of *Applause* knew Wanger would let him work freely.

But Wanger had plenty of other chores negotiating between the demands of talent and Mayer. He, Mamoulian, and especially Mayer wanted Laurence Olivier for the role of the Spanish ambassador. But after just a few weeks of shooting they acceded to Garbo's demands to have her ex-costar and former lover John Gilbert in the part, his second-to-last screen appearance. And as Mamoulian has recounted, during principal photography Mayer objected to the tragic ending for the film, in which Christina abdicates her throne, only to find her lover dead at their rendezvous and sail off anyway. Wanger supported Mamoulian's position; in fact for this affecting scene, Mamoulian may have been inspired by Capra's ending to the Wanger-sponsored *The Bitter Tea of General Yen,* in which Megan Davis, emotionally numb after Yen's suicide, stares offscreen as she sails for New York.

But the greatest test of Wanger's skill at running the obstacle course of studio system production came with the Studio Relations Committee's vehement objections to the depiction of the night shared by the Queen (Garbo) and the ambassador Don Antonio Pimentelli de Parada (Gilbert) at a bawdy country inn. Wingate anticipated that "such scenes of immorality and lack of conventions" would offend both Swedish and American audiences, even if Christina suffers for her transgressions at the end of the film.

New Production Code administrator Joseph Breen agreed. Screening the finished film in late December 1933, he and his associates found "a really fine picture," but one marred by the same scenes and details they had complained of previously. His strongest objections were to the "morning after" scene in which Garbo tactilely "memorizes" her room, from the walls to the pillows, and concludes by comparing her romantic bliss to "how the Lord must have felt when he first beheld the finished world":

> I think Miss Garbo should be kept away from the bed entirely. The scene should be cut from the action at the spinning wheel, at least, and the business of lying across the bed fondling the pillow is, in my considered judgment, very offensive.

Breen complained to Mayer that the scene showed sexual immorality as "attractive and beautiful" and "right and permissible."

Wanger's response to all of these objections—which extended to the scenes in which Garbo kisses Countess Ebba and later vehemently denounces her as a false lover ("Your smiles, your cooing voice and your sympathy—all lies!")—was to nod agreement and then let Mamoulian proceed with the film as scripted. Summarizing the correspondence with MGM, Breen, Wingate's successor, concluded, "It is quite apparent from the examination of the files that Mr. Wanger paid very little attention to our several letters on this, or what was said at the conference." Only when an MPPDA "Hollywood jury" (including Lasky) approved the scene (on the grounds of its period setting, Mamoulian's direction, and historical "accuracy"), did the MPPDA relent. Thus, Wanger had staunchly defended three of the most memorable scenes in all of Garbo's films.

As principal photography on *Queen Christina* (1934) concluded, Wanger supervised his last MGM movie, a charming Davies musical. After Marx and Mayer persuaded Hearst to produce *Going Hollywood* (1933), Wanger asked Stewart to script the film, encouraged Nacio Herb Brown and Arthur Freed to develop the songs and dance numbers, and helped director Raoul Walsh decide on casting. But Wanger displayed a light touch when it came to shooting the film, probably because the more prestigious *Queen Christina* was still in work and Mamoulian "was very extravagant and very meticulous to a degree far beyond what we thought was necessary." Perhaps this was one reason Garbo did not wish to work with Wanger again.

By contrast, Walsh was hardly meticulous. After a week's rehearsals at San Simeon, Bing Crosby later recalled, the film was six months in production. Every day, the orchestra set up at eleven in the morning and accompanied Crosby in songs by Gershwin and Rodgers and Hart for a half-hour:

> Then we'd discuss the first scene with Raoul who, up to that time, might have been leading the orchestra, or practicing driving golf balls into a canvas net on the set, or playing blackjack or rummy with a prop man and an assistant director. By that time it was 12:15 or 12:30. Luncheon was announced for the heads of different departments and the leading players, and we repaired to Marion's bungalow for a midday collation.

After observing Wanger's "supervision" of *Going Hollywood,* Gottfried Reinhardt found him

> a sort of a gentleman producer who, I had the feeling, didn't really care too much about what he was doing. . . . He was very nice, very elegant, more acceptable and more articulate than most of the producers. . . . But there was something of the dilettante about him.

Yet Wanger was attentive enough to get into another scrape with Mayer over a musical sequence (probably the elaborate "We'll Make Hay While the Sun Shines" number) that was photographed, as *Variety* put it, "in defiance of the advice of the technical department heads."

Wanger's relationship with Hearst became equally tense during the production of another Davies vehicle, the Civil War comedy *Operator 13*. Perhaps Hearst was fed up with Wanger and Walsh's dilatory approach to production. In any case, he fired them both ten days into shooting on *Operator 13* in early 1934. After supervising scriptwork on a Myrna Loy spy film *Stamboul Quest* and on an adaptation of Hugh Walpole's gypsy romance *Vanessa* for Hayes, Wanger resigned in mid-May.

"Wanger never really fit in at MGM," Reinhardt recalls. "He didn't get along with Mayer. MGM was sort of a closely knit society, as put together by Thalberg, and Wanger was a bit of an outsider." Mayer never forgave Wanger for his friendship with Feldman and Howard. Wanger and Mayer actually came to blows several years later, when Wanger overcharged Mayer for the loan-out of Charles Boyer. Mayer threw the first punch when Wanger came to his office, and the two men wrestled on the carpet for a minute before they settled down.

Besides his personal struggles with Mayer, Wanger was tired of working for someone else. The previous November, Wanger and Selznick had offered their resignations to Mayer, feeling in *Variety*'s words, that

> the present unit system is not working out as a solo scheme. Claims made [sic] this is due to "too much interference." Inside is that most associate producers on the lot have been seeking full dictatorship and authority over their representative units such as was enjoyed by Irving Thalberg.

Upon resigning from MGM in May 1934, before he had properties to produce, a studio affiliation or even financial backing, Wanger announced his plans to produce independently in the fall—in pursuit of the full dictatorship ideal. Independents were a perennial feature of the American film industry, largely as handicapped competitors of the big studios. But the business environment in 1934 encouraged a new form of independence that promised greater freedom than his previous studio associations had provided. Wanger wasted little time in testing it out.

Part Three

Going "Independent"

7

Semi-Independent Production (1934–1936)

In 1934 as now, Hollywood "independent production" was an umbrella term, something defined negatively. As Staiger has noted, it referred to "a small company with no corporate relationship to a distribution firm" and one that produced only a few films a year. "B" film producers from Poverty Row were one example. "A" film producers whose work was distributed by United Artists—such as Charlie Chaplin and Samuel Goldwyn—were another.

It was the latter brand of independence that Wanger sought upon leaving MGM. But in spite of his brilliant reputation and Wall Street connections, he lacked the multimillion dollar backing of Chaplin, Goldwyn, or even Zanuck. Instead, Wanger embarked on a limited form of independence, which the trade press sometimes called "semi-independence" and which anticipated the form of independence that has flourished in Hollywood from the 1940s through the present day.

Semi-independence is premised on the producer's cooperation with the very studios he or she ostensibly sought to compete with. The industry's belief in the creative power of individual producers or directors was one prerequisite to the system. Disturbing market conditions after 1931—the downturn in weekly audience attendance by 25 percent from 1929 (80 million) to 1932 (60 million), the net losses at all of the major studios except Columbia, and the rise of the double feature—was another. In this context, Wanger ventured into a fragile and risky partnership, whose primary benefit was his own increased visibility with the public and in the trade.

Wanger's "angel" in the summer of 1934 was Jay Paley, the demure, handsome uncle of CBS president William S. Paley. Years earlier, Jay had sold his interests in the family's Congress Cigar Company and CBS, and he had several million dollars at his disposal. He and Wanger were social acquaintances in New York, particularly after the stock swap arranged between CBS and Paramount in the late 1920s. Fond of horse racing, art collecting, and glamorous starlets, Paley was fascinated with the film business. Wanger asked him to manage the "financial and business end" of their new company JayPay Productions, consulting with accountants, attorneys, and distribution executives in New York while Wanger produced films in Hollywood.

They were an engaging team, as one journalist discovered over lunch in December 1934. Wanger compared Paley at the time of his retirement to "one of the lost souls in Dante's *Inferno,* wandering about with nothing to do. We pooled our interests," Wanger continued, "after I had assured Mr. Paley that I could guarantee him more worries than he had ever had in his life." He used what would later become the standard rationale for going independent:

> By the time ideas have passed through 25 or 30 hands, they aren't ideas, they are factory-turned products. I have always felt this, when occupying positions in the major companies as general manager, producer, supervisor, or in whatever capacity they have seen fit to put me. . . . Pictures lose their individuality if too many people are engaged in making them. . . . A small compact unit has a greater chance to discover faults in the story, the scenario, the direction, the acting, the cutting, when just enough people to make the picture are engaged in it. . . . for this reason, Mr. Paley and myself are making one picture at a time. . . . we shall take time to perfect them as much as possible.

Paley replied, "And after they are perfected, as I understand it, it is a tossup whether the public will like them or not." Wanger agreed: "Certainly. That will be another of your worries. If we could hit the bullseye with every picture, we would have so much money we should be tempted to retire again."

The previous summer, the two mapped out their plans in a more sober discussion. They followed the example of former Paramount supervisor and future agent Mike Levee, who formed the Screen Guild company in 1932 with one million dollars in private stock sales to achieve "as much independence as possible." Similarly, Wanger and Paley planned to produce four films for major distribution in one year's time. They financed the films by selling $800,000 of stock to family members (William Paley and Jay's brother Sam Paley; New York banker Paul F. Warburg, who had married one of Wanger's Stettheimer cousins); and to themselves. Paley's total investment, including short-term loans, came to $500,000.

With these funds, JayPay Productions initiated office operations, purchased stories, and contracted with talents for two films. If their films made money, the company would earn 65 percent of the profits, which would be paid in dividends to the stockholders or reinvested in more films. The other 35 percent of JayPay's profits would go to Paramount, through whom Paley and Wanger agreed to distribute their films. They thereby guaranteed their films first-class, nationwide distribution, superior to what United Artists offered its independents. Signing with Paramount also ensured that the studio would pay Wanger $70,000 (from its share of JayPay profits) in back salary stemming from his 1931 breach of contract suit against the company.

Thus, the uncertain business conditions that had prevented Wanger and Selznick from arranging independent production in the fall of 1931 had eased considerably within three years' time. Backers for new film ventures were everywhere. United Artists president Joseph Schenck and other industry insiders financed Zanuck's Twentieth Century Pictures in the spring of 1933. Multimillionaires Jock and Cornelius Vanderbilt Whitney financed Pioneer Pictures, which exploited Technicolor's recently perfected three-strip color process. The following year, Whitney organized a syndicate to finance Selznick International. In 1932, Levee's stock capitalizations and bank loans "radically depart[ed] from orthodox organizational methods in film production"; by 1934 it was a standard mode of operation.

Like Jay Paley, the financiers who contributed to all these stock capitalizations were minimizing their risks by backing former major studio executives such as Wanger. As *Variety* explained, "Producers with former big studio affiliations figure that their reps will command attention from eastern money and first line releases." But the backers also required their independent ventures to receive the superb distribution services of the majors, and the majors were anxious to provide them.

The majors saw in these nominal competitors another solution to the abiding difficulty of meeting the continuing demand for a high volume of feature films. By and large, the demand had remained high because the double-feature phenomenon that had buoyed Columbia's fortunes in the early 1930s persisted in 1934. The majors continued to book the best films from small independents, but since the mid-1920s, they had also sought greater efficiency and higher quality films from their own ranks through the "producer-unit system." And the producer-unit system provided the basic mode of production for the semi-independence that Wanger and others pursued.

Producer-unit production involved organizing all or part of a studio's output into several groups—comprised of a director, writers, and stars who worked under the supervision of one producer—to make several films a year. The unit method was reputed to have several advantages that studio executives in a troubled film market appreciated. It was more efficient than the centralized producer system of the teens and twenties: it facilitated greater cost and quality control by putting a supervisor in charge of fewer films. This is why Columbia and other studios had reinstituted the system in late 1931. It also instilled a sense of teamwork among unit members. In addition, the unit method contributed to product differentiation within a single studio. Each unit organized around a star, a director, or a producer would realize films reflecting his or her distinctive personality. The result would diversify a studio's yearly slate better than the central producer system, where one individual oversaw all of a studio's output. Most prominently at Paramount, Herman Mankiewicz was placed in charge of Marx Brothers films such as *Horsefeathers* and *Duck Soup*, while Le Baron oversaw Mae West movies such as *I'm No Angel*. These outrageously comic films confirmed Lasky's pronouncement in fall 1932: "Small unit producers, unhampered by restrictions and quantity output requirements which inevitably affect large-scale organizations, are the main hope of the industry's future."

Shortly after the revival of unit production in late 1931 came the new group of independent companies. Although they were separate corporate entities, the independents used the same sources of financing, the same technologies, and the same talents as the major studios. Most strikingly, the "A" scale independents of the mid-1930s who produced a few films annually employed the majors' producer-unit system. Like studio units, the semi-independent units were supposed to produce unusual films as determined in part by the personal interests of the producers heading them; as Wanger had put it, an independent company had "just enough hands" to aspire to distinctive perfection. Moreover, like studio units, the semi-independents provided the majors with additional product by turning out anywhere from two to eight films a year. Best of all from the majors' point of view, the semi-independent films cost the studios less than the units. The majors invested in only a portion of the semi-independent's negative costs, or not at all. That was the entire point of going independent: to finance one's own films for greater creative autonomy and a larger share of the profits.

Certainly, this was the logic that motivated Wanger to create JayPay Productions in 1934. He wanted most of all to make another political melodrama like *Gabriel Over the White House* without major studio interference. He also intended to produce two Technicolor films (one starring Ann Harding, the other a remake of his *Beau Geste*), which most studios avoided. When he left MGM, Paramount, which already had unit and semi-independent deals with Charles Rogers, Le Baron, and Schulberg, was the most eager of all studios to accommodate him.

While Wanger was vacationing in Europe in mid-August 1934, the National Recovery Act's Code Authority ruled that the major Hollywood distributors could not tell exhibitors not to show their films on double-bills. The "feeling most prevalent in major ranks since the NRA stand," *Variety* reported, "is that producers will have to turn out what the market demands—which from indications right now, means more and cheaper pictures." The ruling caught Paramount by surprise, since the studio had decided the previous April to eliminate thirteen titles on its schedule. The association with JayPay Productions came just in time. Only weeks after the NRA ruling, the company announced that JayPay Productions would supply four films. Reflecting Paramount's desperate need for product, JayPay's contract specified that the first film be completed by mid-November.

Wanger moved quickly. In mid-August, he hired *Gabriel Over the White House* screenwriter Wilson, who completed his script by mid-September. Renting space at General Service Studios, which advanced its facilities on credit, Wanger hired stage actors such as Byron, who was featured in *Gabriel Over the White House,* and Beecher, who dated back to Wanger's days at the Philadelphian in 1919. Wellman, best known for his vigorous direction of Warner Bros.' seminal gangster film *Public Enemy,* quickly completed *The President Vanishes* (1935) for a December release. Described by Wanger as "the third in my trilogy of political productions" (after *Washington Merry-Go-Round* and *Gabriel Over the White House*), it focused again on corruption in the federal government and opportunistically played upon all the fears and resentments of a population cowed by the Great Depression. It was a startling declaration of independence.

In the second scene of the film a group of American industry leaders—a munitions manufacturer, a newspaper tycoon, a banker, an oil executive, a retired judge, and an ex-senator—gather in a smoke-filled room and decide to drag America into a European war. "What did the last war cost us? A few million casualties. But it also brought us the greatest era of prosperity that this nation has ever seen." Given euphonic names that rhymed with well-known magnates (the steel executive is named Edward Cullen—altered at the request of the Hays Office from Andrew Cullen as too redolent of Andrew Mellon), they earn the sarcastic praise of a lobbyist's wife (Rosalind Russell, in her second film appearance) as "splendid birds," "defenders of the constitution and of the people—especially the right people." As they set down their cigars in the circular ashtray, Wellman dissolves to an irised shot of vultures ringed with fire.

This was the scene that so deeply offended Wanger's cousin, Walter Seligman, that he never spoke to Wanger again; it also offended Wanger's former collaborator, Hearst, since the actor portraying the publisher had Hearst's white hair and physical bulk. Regardless of Wanger's family ties, the negative portrait of business in Wanger's first independent production is striking for its barefaced audacity: up until that film no one in Hollywood had dared to depict the highest levels of American government or industry so directly and critically outside the genres of musical comedy or social satire. The montage following the industrialists' scene of conspiracy, courtesy of Slavko Vorkapich—as high-speed presses and broadcasters reiterate the manufactured slogan, "Save Our Country's Honor" to galvanize the public into a hawkish mood—did not help. For this, Wanger's name was temporarily removed from the invitation list at San Simeon. Thanks to rapid-fire pacing and a general tone that mimicked Warner Bros.' gangster films, the press works like a "silver bullet": the magnates succeed in swaying the country. Congress bows to the industrial leaders and the vice-president is of all things, a corruptible fool.

As an earnest demonstration of the possibilities of semi-independent production, the film had its share of stylistically transgressive moments. Aside from comedies and musicals, a character's acknowledgment of the camera was shunned in classical Hollywood films because it disrupted the fourth wall illusionism that otherwise prevailed. But in *The President Vanishes,* as critic Charles Wolfe has pointed out, the looks at the camera by the media magnate and his broadcasters as they proclaim "Save Our Country's Honor" evoke the factual, authoritative, narrated documentary of the era. When the president triumphs over his opponents in the film's final scene, he looks directly at the camera and explains, "I don't ask your answer because I know it. I have faith in the American people." Such a startling confrontation of the audience was fitting in a film with provocative content.

But of course it was the content of *The President Vanishes* which provoked the greatest discussion, for, thanks in part to Wanger's choice of screenwriter Wilson, it was a virtual remake of the outrageous *Gabriel Over the White House.* Like that first film, this one presumed to show how the president and Congress work and live with corrupt politicians whose pro-war votes are bought by industry leaders. The threat of *Gabriel Over the White House*'s Bonus Marchers becomes *The President Vanishes*'s vigilante Brown Shirts who foment violence on city streets.

The most crucial difference between *The President Vanishes* and *Gabriel Over the White House* involved the former's conception of the president. Unlike President Hammond who openly dismisses Congress and becomes a dictator, this president uses subterfuge to distract the country's attention from the European war cry. Unlike the isolated President Hammond who gets his inspiration from unseen forces, President Stanley, portrayed by the paternalistic Byron, adopts his plan during a domestic poker game with his wife (who suggests he play "another hand"). He even forges an artificial family in his White House staff: his secretary is engaged to his Secret Service bodyguard, and Andy Devine provides comic relief as an idiot milk boy in awe of the Oval Office. When Stanley returns, he thanks them: "No one must know how fine you've been, how much I love you."

Despite such sentimentalism, Stanley's actions in the film had the disturbing implication that the president was simply a more shrewd exploiter of mass sensibilities than his opposition. As *The Nation*'s William Troy pointed out, the film upheld a double standard: hawkish mob manipulators are a menace while the pacifist President is a hero, even though he never responds to the problems of unemployment and trade deficits which the warmongers seek to solve. Then too, the faith this president has in "the people" is unjustified, because their susceptibility to slogans show they do not deserve it—a paradox that informed Wanger's own beliefs about the mass media and its audience.

Other implications were less subtle. The second scene implied, more forcefully than any film up to that time, that America's capitalist economy depended on war. Throughout Vorkapich's montage sequence of the "Save Our Country's Honor" slogan, isolated vignettes of resistance are shown: a family in a rustic cabin, gathered around the radio, dismiss what they hear as hooey, and a mother chastises a group of pro-war women by recounting the loss of her two sons in the last war.

Then the film shows a Communist party member who speaks to a group gathered in the street: "Fellow workers, it is your blood, it is my blood, it is the workers' blood they're after. . . . so that the capitalistic bloodsuckers . . . so that the capitalistic bloodsuckers can grow richer—join the Communist party." The progression of scenes in the montage sequence implies that this speaker has the sympathy of those sensible country folk in the log cabin and the distraught mother. The Communist's speech foments absolute chaos as a group of Brown Shirts, sympathetic to the aims of big business, beats him and terrorizes the crowd. By contrast, President Stanley enforces order, first in the pomp of an early scene at the Annapolis Naval Academy and then in his radio address to reassure the nation in the final scene.

Viewed today, the film is full of outrageous implausibilities, which Wellman's top-speed pacing attempts to obscure. Yet in late 1934, when Father Coughlin every week stirred several hundred thousand listeners with his radio broadcasts, no film was more timely. William Dudley Pelley's silver-shirted vigilantes roamed the streets. *The President Vanishes* also exploited isolationist sentiment. In September, as the film began production, Senator Gerald Nye's committee began its investigation of the arms industry to reveal unsavory profiteering by munitions companies during the Great War; meanwhile, Nazi Germany announced its program of rearmament. Though Wanger himself was hardly an isolationist, President Stanley reassures Americans that "not one American boy carrying gun or bomb in the expectation of death will be sent to foreign soil to leave his blood there as security for your loan."

Equally topical was the representation of the Communist organizer, what with the increasing power of organized labor so much on the country's mind. There had been violent uprisings by unemployed workers in Minneapolis and even by those gainfully employed in New York and the Midwest. The film industry itself was panicked by socialist Upton Sinclair's candidacy for governor of California and targeted his End Poverty in California campaign by producing and distributing anti-Sinclair shorts. As historian William E. Leuchtenberg put it, "In America, the radical tempo quickened not at the bottom of the depression in 1932, when many were dispirited, but in 1934, when things had taken a turn for the better."

The President Vanishes followed that tempo. Even for the tumultuous early thirties, the era of chain gang fugitives, gangsters, shysters, and fallen women, it was both unusual Hollywood fare and testimony to Wanger's ability to cue his story material to contemporary concerns. It was also cause for consternation at the Production Code Administration, that division of the MPPDA under Breen which succeeded the Studio Relations Committee officially in the summer of 1934. Once again the subject of politics was a problem for the Breen Office because the code, focusing on issues of morality and criminality, had no explicit guidelines for the depiction of political situations—a point that underlines how innovative Wanger had been in choosing the subject.

After watching *The President Vanishes* at a Glendale preview, Breen remained uncertain of how to handle it. He told Wanger he thought the film could receive a seal, but that he wanted Hays's advice in New York. Then the trouble began. Wanger assumed that Breen had granted the film a seal, while Hays and several Paramount executives became alarmed about its content. Breen had predicted that the villainous characterizations of businessmen would "give the [film] industry no end of trouble because it is certain to be resented quite forcefully." Indeed, one Charles D. Hilles, a Paramount board member and a "forceful leader" in the Republican Party, demanded cuts in the film.

Hilles had plenty of company. In a letter to Zukor, Hays formulated the problems with *The President Vanishes:*

> The screen as an entertainment medium has a right to deal with the realities of the subject—that is, to show that there are elements in this country as in any other nation who would profit from a European war, whose interest would cause them to espouse our entrance into such a conflict, and whose greed, selfishness or power would lead them to plot for such a consummation.
>
> The industry *has no right,* as a vast popular entertainment medium which must not only reflect correctly our own institutions to our own people but American institutions to the peoples of the world, to present a distorted picture which condemns the banking industry, the oil industry, the steel industry and the newspaper industry per se as war-mongers; which presents the Communist Party as the leading protagonist against these forces, and which indicates such banality and corruption in our governmental and political machinery, that even the Secret Service of the nation cannot be trusted to protect the President of the United States.

Hays also warned Zukor that the film's portrayal of an imbecilic vice-president might incite charges of treason and libel against the film industry. It "would furnish ammunition to the insidious and untrue propaganda now existing in this country that un-American elements influence the motion picture screen."

The President Vanishes surpassed any problem film made up through that time by daring to suggest that American capitalism was at odds with American democracy. The changes needed were clear. *The President Vanishes* should suggest that "only certain elements, not certain industries, nor certain individuals, are under attack in this fictional expose." The Communist's speech had to eliminate the phrases "capitalist bloodsuckers" and "Join the Communist Party." Paramount president Otterson instructed the studio's lab to make a prefatory title indicating that the film was entirely fictional and expressing the hope that the "social forces borne of greed and anarchy" it depicted "will never descend upon us. If they should, the force that is America will rise up to defeat their ends."

Wanger resisted these compromises at every step, but even as a semi-independent, he was contractually bound to let Paramount make changes necessary for censorship purposes. Paramount and the PCA's interference in *The President Vanishes* was precisely the kind of meddling he had chosen semi-independence to avoid. He took revenge by meeting the minimum demands for changes; for example, while the phrase "Join the Communist Party" was eliminated from the film, the phrase "the party" remains, and remains clear enough in its allusions. As Breen noted in late January, the phrase "capitalist bloodsuckers" had also escaped deletion. Warner Bros. had eliminated entirely a comparable scene from *I Am a Fugitive from a Chain Gang,* in which a soapbox orator had praised the collectivist movement in the Soviet Union; Wanger's scene remained in place. In 1930, Schulberg refused to produce Eisenstein's version of *An American Tragedy* because it would make no money and because he felt, as Eisenstein recalled, that "your script is a monstrous challenge to American society." By contrast, *The President Vanishes,* until order is restored in the film's conclusion, took up that challenge. After the MPPDA's requests were met, the film premiered in January 1935.

Wanger later claimed that the effect of the Hays Office and Paramount's interference was to damage the appeal and the coherence of the film, but in fact it remains quite vivid and unmistakable in its implications. Certainly film critics and political columnists, always eager to see and praise "realistic" filmmaking from Hollywood, understood it. *Newsweek* announced that the "movies reached maturity" with its premiere and publicized Wanger and Paley's censorship troubles; Troy in *The Nation* noted "the astonishing advance it makes in Hollywood's willingness to admit what everyone knows." The *New York Times*'s Andre Sennwald hailed *The President Vanishes* as "an exciting example of topical cinema" and "admirably outspoken on topics which Hollywood normally leaves severely alone." Sennwald specifically admired how

> it exposes the ugly truth of Fascism by showing that, on the surface, the Gray Shirts are dedicated to the highest ideals of public service and that, beneath the

surface, their misguided leader is the tool of selfish industrialists. If the photo-play says these things loudly, it is because they are high and important affirmations and because they are worth getting angry about.

Like the newsweeklies, *Motion Picture Herald* praised its timeliness. Discounting the romantic elements as "sustained and necessary contrasting qualities," its reviewer commented:

> While there have been other current history political pictures, none seems to have captured the psychological popular spirit as completely as this. . . . As a matter of fact, during the past year and a half the question "What would happen if something happened to the President?" has been mouthed times without number.

Among the major trades, only weekly *Variety* felt dissatisfied with the result, which it characterized as "sensational in the tabloid sense, without achieving anything vivid or vital, besides visibly and audibly re-creating an already cognizant and exciting state of world affairs." It predicted accurately that it would have "spotty" returns. Though it was not banned in the United States, *The President Vanishes* failed to recover its negative costs. Hollywood would not produce another vision of a domestic fascist conspiracy on a national scale until Capra's *Meet John Doe* and George Stevens's *Keeper of the Flame* in the early 1940s.

But there were other compensations. His independent status and *The President Vanishes* immediately brought Wanger great personal publicity. Just prior to the film's release, he and Paley changed their company name to Walter Wanger Productions, Inc. They took inspiration from Roosevelt and from the National Recovery Administration's insignia—for their corporate trademark, they chose an eagle mounted on a stone pedestal, basking in a diagonal ray of light. It was a dignified, resonant image that contrasted with the greedy vultures portrayed in *The President Vanishes*.

Just before the premiere of *The President Vanishes, New York Times* critic Frank Nugent described Wanger as a maverick who "still burns with the crusader's zeal to go out and break up this entire censorship business." Interviewed under the headline, "Mr. Wanger Hurls a Political Bombshell," Wanger stunned Nugent (as the journalist himself described it) by saying, "I would rather film a new idea fairly well than film an old idea perfectly well." He told another journalist, "It is my humble opinion that we must do something revolutionary if we are to hold a moving picture audience."

Wanger's second film, *Private Worlds* (1935), was almost as startling. He claimed to have been inspired to option the rights to former nurse Phyllis Bottome's novel during his return from Europe in the summer in 1934, when he saw a considerable number of women on the ship reading it. Bottome's conventional melodrama about the love lives of a trio of doctors had an unusual setting—a mental institution. "Such a background can hardly be anything but unpleasant," a PCA reader noted, and the Breen Office warned Wanger that the protagonists' adultery and miscarriages made it totally unacceptable. But Wanger hired Lynn Starling to soften the novel's starker scenes, and the Breen Office accepted the script in early December.

Of course, the German Expressionist *Cabinet of Dr. Caligari* (1919) had made a splash on American screens in the early twenties. But Wanger was by 1935 unique in producing a film on the subject at all. And unlike *The President Vanishes, Private Worlds* presented its material with what Otis Ferguson described as "dignity and honest intelligence" in a "good and grown up job on a difficult theme." The film strikingly suggests that everyone, doctors as well as patients, are susceptible to mental illness. Dr. Jane Everest (Colbert) tells a friend that the patients in the institution differ from the people outside "in only one respect. They have gone so far into their private worlds that most of them are unable to return to reality." The new hospital head, Dr. Monet (Charles Boyer), has left a small town where his sister (Helen Vinson), a Blanche DuBois type, has been involved in a murder. Jane has postponed her emotional life after losing her lover in World War I. Her colleague Alec McGregor (Joel McCrea) is bitter over losing a promotion to Dr. Monet. And Alec's wife Sally (Joan Bennett) most forcefully embodies this equation, for she is closely identified with a disturbed inmate Carrie Flynt. In one of the film's climactic scenes, alone in a thunderstorm, Sally suffers a nervous breakdown: as Carrie's voice calls to her through an echo chamber, Leon Shamroy rotates the camera gyroscopically and Sally falls down the stairs, causing a near miscarriage (during the scene of a patient's violent attack, Shamroy used a zoom lens). And the thin line between sanity and madness provides a rare instance of humor. Monet's flighty sister asks a doctor if her housekeeper is really a former inmate; he replies, "I don't know; I was formerly a patient myself." The sister quickly leaves him.

The similarities between inmates and staff is one way *Private Worlds* construes mental illness not as an involuntary disease but as something patients can fight through sheer willpower. A motif of the dialogue links the patients' difficulties and the staff's romantic problems with "running away from the world." "When life hits you, you hit back," Alec tells one patient. Another patient, leaving after a year's treatment, tells Jane: "Only a year ago I came through that door, depressed in spirit, running away from life like a little child trying to avoid responsibility—I can hardly believe it." In 1935, the analogy had great force: one "problem" that all audiences faced was coping with the Depression.

Given this conception of mental illness as voluntary, the general tenor of both Starling's script and LaCava's direction was to demonstrate the superiority of progressive treatments of the mentally ill. These are endorsed by Jane and Alec, who advocate occupational therapy and group activities, whereas

Dr. Monet and the hospital matron (head nurse) favor corporal punishment and the isolation ward. When the *American Medical Association* reviewed the film in May, it pronounced *Private Worlds* "a real advance in the portrayal of medicine" in films, and praised its refusal to use mental patients with Napoleon complexes for "cheap comedy." One psychologist noted that the patients "calmed down a little too quickly" under Jane's influence, but that "I would give her a job on the staff any time, and that's a standing offer."

In fact, the depiction of Jane is one of the film's most progressive aspects, contrasting with the portrayal of Monet's sister as a classic vamp. The script and mise-en-scène toy with the idea that Jane and Alec are lovers (placing Jane between Alec and Sally in their first scenes), only to confirm that they are just good colleagues. Meanwhile, Monet initially is highly sexist and demotes Jane to outpatient work, but he grows more enlightened as the film progresses. By eliminating a scripted scene of Jane and Monet at the beach, LaCava delineates Monet's growing respect for Jane on a professional rather than romantic basis. After a violent inmate breaks Monet's arm, Jane calms him into submission. Frequently dressed in a hospital coat and tie, Jane casually tells Sally, "Even though a woman is deeply absorbed in her profession, she hates to cease being a woman." Although Jane is paired with (but not married to) Monet at the film's conclusion, she will be able to work *and* be in love without guilt or punishment.

Whereas *The President Vanishes* lacked a name cast, Wanger loaded *Private Worlds* with stars. He secured Colbert from Paramount for $100,000, nearly a quarter of the film's final negative cost. Colbert, hailed by *Variety* in early 1931 as the kind of intelligent actress that sound movies required, had only risen in industry estimates since Wanger had hired her at Astoria. She excelled at portraying strong single women, as in John Stahl's *Imitation of Life* in 1934. Her Oscar-winning work in *It Happened One Night* appeared just prior to *Private Worlds*.

Colbert boosted Boyer, her costar. Boyer at this time was a barely known French stage actor who had tried to work in Hollywood unsuccessfully for several years. He had dubbed the French versions of MGM films and had acted in several of them (he won Jean Harlow in *Red-Headed Woman* where he appeared briefly), but other studios rejected him because of his thick accent. Yet Wanger had seen his roguish carnival barker in Fritz Lang's French version of Frederick Molnar's *Lilliom*. He felt that Boyer's angular features and almond-shaped eyes would make women filmgoers swoon.

Boyer and Colbert had previously appeared together in Berthold Viertel's *The Man From Yesterday,* and they would team up again for the Warner Bros. comedy *Tovarich* in 1937. But the script of *Private Worlds* was tailored to introduce the French actor in the most favorable light possible. Monet is multilingual and speaks Arabic with a dying patient, while Alec complains about Monet's "thick as mud" French accent, an attempt to prepare the audience for

Boyer's diction. In Starling's script, Monet upbraids Sally for wanting to be useful at the hospital; in the film, he encourages her.

The secondary romantic couple was portrayed by equally capable performers. Director LaCava insisted on casting McCrea as Alec over Wanger's preference for Montgomery, who had appeared in *Another Language* at MGM. "I'm rewriting the thing and you're going to do it," LaCava told a concerned McCrea in late 1934. "Just don't worry about it. [Wanger] can stay up there to justify his shiny-top desk, but we'll make the film." With LaCava's help, McCrea admirably portrayed the ambitious young doctor who goes to seed and commits adultery over his denied promotion. His is a resonant depiction of professional disappointment and fears of mediocrity.

Opposite McCrea, Wanger cast his future wife Joan Bennett as Sally. By her own account, Bennett was a reluctant actress, the daughter of the legendary actor Richard Bennett and actress Adrienne Morison. She took her first stage role in *Jarnegan* in 1928 to support her daughter Diana by John Fox, whom she married at the age of sixteen. Sound films proved a great boon for her career. In 1929 alone she appeared in First National's prestigious *Disraeli* with George Arliss and in Goldwyn's enormously popular *Bulldog Drummond* with Ronald Colman, and she played opposite Barrymore in *Moby Dick*. Sally in *Private Worlds* was another ingenue role, but one more demanding than her typical parts in the early 1930s. Bennett rose to the occasion, delineating a character of fragile innocence that became her trademark until the late 1930s.

With *Private Worlds,* Wanger confirmed his reputation as a bold and distinctive producer. Virtually every trade review praised Wanger for his "daring" choice of material, praised Alexander Toluboff's detailed sets and Shamroy's textured use of light and shadow in the hospital scenes. Calling it "one of the finest films of the year," *Motion Picture Daily* opened its review by noting that "with guts and courage" Wanger had dramatized "in celluloid that heretofore untouchable area of the mentally deranged." *The Hollywood Reporter* agreed:

> Viewed from any angle, it's a superb production that will stand a long time as a tribute to the production wisdom and daring of Walter Wanger. . . . It took courage to make and it has emerged a picture with something for everyone.

But New York reviewers, less attentive to Wanger, were evenly and harshly divided on the film's aesthetic merits.

Unfortunately, as *Private Worlds* went into release, Paley decided their semi-independent venture had too many problems for a retired millionaire. *The President Vanishes* recouped a quarter of its costs within weeks of its release, and Paley demanded that Paramount adjust its distribution terms and reduce its share of the profits from 35 to 25 per cent. The studio refused, and

Paley wanted out. Even two years after their release, *The President Vanishes* was still in the red by $147,807, and *Private Worlds,* in spite of Wanger's successful efforts to rescind a ban in Great Britain, made only $10,000 in profits. Loaning Wanger another $110,000, Paley left in March 1935.

Fortunately for Wanger, the demand for feature films remained strong (*Private Worlds* was rushed into distribution in April to fill a gap in Paramount's schedule). Paramount's production arm was now under the direction of Henry Herzbrun and master director Lubitsch. Lubitsch was Wanger's good friend and one of his admirers since the early years of sound at Astoria. He named Wanger godfather to his only daughter Nicole. Lubitsch was keen to keep Wanger, and Wanger was keen to stay on. But there was a significant change in Wanger's operations. He would no longer be functioning as a semi-independent but as a studio employee. Doubling Wanger's salary to $2,000 weekly, Paramount now hired Wanger as a unit producer, funded his films, and took 75 per cent of their profits.

Moreover, with this change in funding, Paramount could dictate stronger operating constraints. As the new contract made clear, Wanger would produce a new film every two months for $300,000, the cost of a low-budget star special. The 1934 agreement granted Paramount no authority over Wanger films beyond recutting the completed film to meet censorship needs. By contrast the 1935 agreement specified that Wanger had to obtain approvals from Lubitsch in Hollywood on virtually all the components of his films: treatments, scripts, composers, lyricists, budgets, directors, and actors. He was also required to make any script, casting, talent, or editing changes demanded by the studio. Although Wanger still shot his films at General Service Studios, Paramount offered

> the services of its artists, directors and technicians, to the same extent as it shall afford and provide such services to its other units at all times consistent with the plans and commitments of the Corporation with respect to its entire production program.

The arrangement benefited both parties: Wanger helped Paramount reduce its overhead while Wanger had a major studio's resources.

The change in Wanger's contractual status from semi-independent to Paramount employee is quite evident in his subsequent films. *The President Vanishes* and *Private Worlds* were based on novels Wanger had read and purchased on his own. By contrast, his subsequent films were either taken from Paramount's story files or quickly scripted for inexpensive production. The studio had abandoned the property "Her Master's Voice" in June 1934; Wanger financed a new script, written by Schary in three weeks, and produced it in 1935 along with another studio property, "Case Against Mrs. Ames."

These films were hardly innovative by any criteria. During the period when Paramount's most notable releases featured the work of Lubitsch, von Sternberg, Dietrich, West, Fields, Cooper, and others, Wanger produced modestly budgeted films ($315,000 on average) with "A" quality production values in standard genre categories: light radio or backstage musicals (*Every Night at Eight, Her Master's Voice, Fatal Lady*), romantic comedies (*The Moon's Our Home, Big Brown Eyes, Spendthrift, Case Against Mrs. Ames,* which was modeled after the Vanderbilt-Whitney custody battle), and melodramas (*Mary Burns, Fugitive, Trail of the Lonesome Pine, Shanghai* and *Smart Girl*).

There were also uneasy generic hybrids. *Fatal Lady* (1936) mixed backstage opera with murder mystery. *Palm Springs* (1936) opens as a college campus musical, but after the heroine (played by radio singer Frances Langford) is expelled for gambling in the locker room, the film quickly shifts to the newly discovered vacation spot. Here it becomes a musical western with Smith Ballew (who dubbed John Wayne's songs in "B" westerns), and the narrative is punctuated six times with the song "Hills of Wyoming." The programmer *Smart Girl* (1935), produced for just $98,000 with newcomer Ida Lupino, abandoned its primary romantic storyline for lengthy, completely irrelevant routines by stage comic Joseph Cawthorn as Lupino's Jewish immigrant boss whose malapropisms ("I've known her since infantry") pepper the film. Cawthorn's coaching of his spineless son to impersonate a Texas oil entrepreneur (where "ticker tape" becomes "tickle you?") postpones resolution of the plot line for twenty minutes.

On the whole, these films were reasonable merchandise that fulfilled their function of lowering Paramount's distribution overhead with more films. They also diminished studio overhead by using contracted talents: actors Edward Everett Horton, Cary Grant (in *Big Brown Eyes,* one of his last Paramount films), Fred MacMurray and directors Walsh, Santley, and Henry Hathaway.

Although Wanger employed a number of different screenwriters, these Wanger-Paramount films frequently employed an oedipal story formula derived from romantic comedy. The stories were typically set in upper-class milieus where "children" (Margaret Sullavan's movie actress in *The Moon's Our Home,* Loretta Young's "most photographed society woman" in *Shanghai,* Peggy Conklin's ex-singer in *Her Master's Voice,* Henry Fonda's naive millionaire in *Spendthrift*) defy the strictures of their wealthier parents, aunts, or grandparents who want to steer them into unwelcomed marriages and restrictive work. In the manner of Capra's *It Happened One Night,* these comedies are resolved happily as class oppositions and familial authorities are reconciled. In *Shanghai* (1935), the terms of these oppositions shift from class to race, as Young falls in love with the mysterious Eurasian Dimitri Kuslov (Boyer) and sadly agrees to leave him.

The Wanger films of this period, scripted and directed without any particular flair, even with the general oversight of Lubitsch, at their best suggest later screen classics. When arguing for the "joys" of the auteur theory, critic Andrew Sarris singled out from Walsh's *Every Night at Eight* (1935), a "maddeningly routine" film, a scene that anticipates a comparable, more expressive moment in Walsh's *High Sierra* (1941). In Walsh's *Spendthrift,* title character Fonda is infatuated with a golddigger who, along with her father, poses as Southern gentry; the entire scenario is a dry run for Sturges's *The Lady Eve* (1941). Similarly, the pretensions and unmasking of characters in *Palm Springs* provide considerable social comedy, but where Sturges or Billy Wilder would heighten those awkward moments of disguise and exposure, director Aubrey Scotto directs them with casual disinterest.

On the whole, the obscurity of Wanger's unit-produced features is well deserved, with two exceptions. *The Moon's Our Home* (1936) is an amusing screwball comedy, directed by William Seiter, who was a comedy veteran (two of his most prominent films are the Astaire-Rogers *Roberta,* 1935, and Laurel and Hardy's *Sons of the Desert,* 1933). The recently divorced Fonda and Sullavan, who according to Fonda nearly remarried during the production, sparred through their physical and verbal fights armed with dialogue by Dorothy Parker and Alan Campbell and a solid dose of physical humor at Sullavan's expense: she spends several minutes stuck head-first in a snowbank, and Fonda wins her back from absentminded Charles Butterworth by enclosing her in a straitjacket.

The Moon's Our Home also offered a witty satire on the whims and publicity efforts of Hollywood stars and the frenzy of fame that was complemented by several striking directorial touches. Unbeknownst to each other, the writer and actress have adjoining rooms on the cross-country train, and Seiter shoots their disparaging remarks about each other and their nightly toilette on a set featuring a cutaway wall. A lengthy, one-take sequence shows them simultaneously before their mirrors, brushing and picking at their teeth and combing their hair. By virtue of the perpendicular camera angle, they appear to be making faces at each other and mirroring the other's gestures in a scene worthy of Jacques Tati's *Play Time* (1968). Subsequently, when a saleswoman tries out a new perfume in a department store where the writer is autographing his books, the camera tracks the mist from the atomizer to Fonda to show his nauseated response (the scent, marketed by Sullavan's character, reminds him of the bubonic plague). Though it opened to lukewarm reviews and failed to recover its costs, the film is slowly being rediscovered.

The one unmitigated triumph of these years for Wanger was *Trail of the Lonesome Pine* (1936) based on a novel by John Fox, Jr., which represented a breakthrough in the technique and conception of how Technicolor could be used. The film's story, first made by FPL in the teens, is a conventional, sentimental melodrama, set in the backwoods of the Kentucky mountains where a multigenerational feud between the Judds and the Tolivers is complicated by the construction of a railroad on their property. Young June Tolliver (Sylvia Sidney) is slated to marry her cousin (Fonda), but she is entranced by the mining engineer (MacMurray) who encourages her to leave the woods for a college education. Their Svengali relationship falters when her younger brother (Spanky McFarland) is killed on the construction site, and June reverts to a passionate rejection of all that contemporary society has to offer.

Even with the leavening presence of a cynical British adviser (Nigel Bruce) to MacMurray's engineer, this is a far cry from the sophisticated settings and tone of Wanger's long-standing production preferences. In fact, it is a classic example of "hokum" and one that Wanger chose by mistake from Paramount's list of available properties. He later told a journalist he had confused it with Fox's Civil War story *The Little Shepherd of Kingdom Come.* Yet with the help of Paramount screenwriting veteran Grover Jones's well-structured script, and the intense performance of Sidney, Wanger produced an affecting drama that the trade press deemed a success aside from the blandishments of Technicolor.

And yet Technicolor was the basis of the film's importance. Associated by the conservative studios primarily with Walt Disney Silly Symphonies, Technicolor's three-strip process was in low demand. Pioneer Pictures's slow and ponderous *Becky Sharp* (1935), the first feature film in color, did not help matters. As *Fortune* noted, "Many companies would prefer to spend the extra $135,000, if necessary, in order to get big names in the cast. For they know that names have a box-office draw and they are not at all sure about color."

But Wanger was. He had admired Pioneer's 1933 live action short *La Cucaracha,* which was designed by Robert Edmond Jones, an important exponent of the New Stagecraft in the teens. Jones told *Fortune* he had "not had so much fun since he did *The Man Who Married a Dumb Wife* eighteen years ago" for Barker. Wanger saw the appeal of Technicolor in the realm of visual design and spectacle, regardless of subject matter, and his convictions carried Wanger through the inevitable arguments with Paramount to shoot the film's exteriors on location.

With color consultant Natalie Kalmus's advice, the color tones of *Trail of the Lonesome Pine* coded the characters' sympathies very subtly, with Sidney's character featured in bright blues and reds against the earth tones of her family and MacMurray's working clothes. Although some critics criticized it in the national newsweeklies, the color scheme and reproduction struck contemporary trade reviewers as perfectly natural and unobtrusive to the story line. The *Hollywood Reporter* noted how "the color is never intrusive" and always accurate. *Variety* wrote that the film explored "the outdoors more extensively for its backgrounds than any previous color picture, it catches with extraordinary fidelity the smokey blues and greys of distance and atmospheric perspective." The film's preview audience "several times rewarded the photography with involuntary gasps of sheer delight, an appreciation more sincere than any applause."

Wanger's accidental choice of subject matter was a lucky break for Technicolor, whose process the studios employed only for sequences in musical comedies, costume films, and fantasies. *Trail of the Lonesome Pine* was a naturalistic outdoor film that expanded Technicolor's applications. As *Fortune* noted in 1936, Wanger's film broke the logjam; as with *Warming Up,* seven years earlier, Wanger had proven the inevitable appeal of a technical innovation. Breaking opening-night records at Paramount's Manhattan theater, *Trail of the Lonesome Pine* inspired "the most active interest producers have shown since the color boom collapsed in 1930." Shortly following its release, Selznick was working on *The Garden of Allah,* and Fox, Paramount, RKO, Warner Bros., Goldwyn, and, in England, Alexander Korda and Herbert Wilcox all reported plans for Technicolor productions. Many of these projects were in preproduction before the release of Wanger's film. Selznick definitively proved the financial benefits of Technicolor production with the consecutive color successes of *A Star Is Born* (1937), *The Adventures of Tom Sawyer* (1938), and *Gone with the Wind* (1939), three films that confirmed the suitability of color in non-musical, non-fantasy genres. Still, as of 1936, *Trail of the Lonesome Pine* was in *Variety*'s words "the best screen color exhibit to date" that "advances the apparently sure coming of the tint era by a great technical stride."

Usually highly critical of Wanger's films, *Variety* gave him his due. Praising performances as well as Hathaway's direction, the trade publication concluded its review:

> And supporting the whole pyramid of outstanding excellence is the courage, the vision, the imagination and showmanly intuition and shrewdness of Walter Wanger paving a further way into the realm of screen color on firm commercial ground.

Ironically, all of the praise and prominence Wanger received for *Trail of the Lonesome Pine* treated him as though he were an independent producer. With his films frequently shot at General Service Studios and his trademarked name and eagle logo appearing before the title credits of his films, Wanger was frequently so misperceived. For publicity purposes, this was the way Wanger preferred it. But like other units, the Wanger operation from 1935 to 1936 was a halfway independent. His experiences at Paramount had demonstrated that from the standpoint of creative autonomy, the difference between working as a semi-independent and as a unit producer was slight indeed.

Wanger himself viewed the unit arrangement with Paramount as strictly temporary. Beginning with *Private Worlds,* he began assembling a staff and a roster of stars under exclusive contract who would remain with him until the late 1930s. Chief among these was scene designer Toluboff, the Russian engineer and architect whom MGM had hired to work on its 1927 film *The Cossack.* For *Rasputin and the Empress* in 1932, Toluboff earned a precedent-shattering screen credit alongside studio department head Cedric Gibbons.

His versatility was apparent in his codesigned glamorous art deco sets for *Grand Hotel,* and his renderings of the castle, the village, and the country inn in Wanger's *Queen Christina.* He specialized in "character design," making newly constructed sets look aged and distressed. Toluboff also excelled at devising highly textured sets despite Wanger's limited budgets and limited facilities at General Service Studios. Wanger recalled how he "always turned over the script to [Toluboff] in its longest and most unwieldy fashion, and received many very constructive ideas on how to cope with and achieve certain values that I had hoped for." Toluboff also integrated his work with Helen Taylor, the costume designer Wanger frequently employed for the rest of the decade.

An equally revealing commitment Wanger made while at Paramount was to put two writers, Gene Towne and Graham Baker, under contract. Although he would not rely on them exclusively for story material, Towne and Baker provided original stories more cheaply than a story or play adaptation and they continually prepared new scripts for shooting. In 1935, a sizable layoff of Paramount writers gave Wanger the chance to sign up the team, and they quickly wrote *Mary Burns, Fugitive, Shanghai,* and *Case Against Mrs. Ames* for Wanger's Paramount productions.

The impulse to resume independence is equally apparent in Wanger's signing of performers such as Alan Baxter, Joan Bennett, Madeleine Carroll, Boyer, Langford, Fonda, and Sidney. Having actors under contract gave Wanger one basis for competing with the majors or for trading loan-outs with them. Wanger signed Boyer after casting him in *Shanghai* and fulfilled his promise to sign Boyer's wife, the British actress Pat Patterson, to her own option contract. The Wanger association marked Fonda and Langford's entrance into the film industry.

Wanger took great pride in securing new (or in the case of Boyer and Bennett, overlooked) talents, selecting them by responding to what he claimed was "simply a matter of supply and demand." Rather than trying to "top" Astaire and Rogers or find "another" Clark Gable, Wanger claimed, his stars offered distinctly different personalities. In spite of Boyer's dismal box office failure in his last American film, Wanger said, "I had seen him in Europe. I knew what he could do and I knew that he had something no one else had on the American screen." About the British-born Madeleine Carroll, Wanger remarked, "The screen needed an actress who looks and acts like a lady. She fills the need." Significantly, Wanger signed both Boyer and Carroll to contracts (and bought the first two properties he produced) while scouting for stories and performers during a visit to Europe in the summer of 1934.

To get Fonda, whom Wanger cast in *Trail of the Lonesome Pine, The Moon's Our Home,* and *Spendthrift,* Wanger relied on his good friend, agent Leland Hayward. Hayward cajoled the New York stage actor into a suite at the

Beverly Hills Hotel in the summer of 1934, just before the actor's break-through success on Broadway in *The Farmer Takes a Wife*. Fonda recalled how he emerged from the shower to a thousand-dollar weekly salary:

> There was a man there with Leland and he introduced me to Walter Wanger. Now the name meant nothing to me, and frankly, Wanger didn't know who the hell *I* was. It made no difference to Leland. . . . Anyway, Wanger and Leland talked, I listened, and all at once I found myself shaking hands with this man on a deal to make two pictures for him next year. He knew I wasn't eager, but he made it clear that I could do theater work *and* movies. He wouldn't stop me. God!

Wanger was signing up Fonda sight unseen in a scouting move worthy of a Lasky protégé.

Similarly, Wanger had to negotiate creatively to attract an established star like Paramount's Sidney in 1935. He offered Sidney $1,500 less than Paramount's $4,000 weekly salary, but as with Fonda, he compensated the actress by permitting Sidney to choose her loan-out assignments (Lang's *Fury* at MGM, *You and Me* at Paramount, and Hitchcock's *Sabotage* in England) and to act on the stage between film assignments. He also demanded fewer performances from her. Sidney had starred in Wanger's *Mary Burns, Fugitive* only to finish her Paramount contract. "I hated the grind," Sidney recently recalled. "Paramount offered me a lot of money to stay on but it was work fifty-two weeks a year. With Wanger, all I would have to do is notify him if I wanted to go off salary. And he would share the overage [the amount above the salary Wanger paid her] with me when I worked for other producers. I loved working for him."

Moreover, the working atmosphere around an independent studio such as General Service was much more intimate than Paramount's "factory." Golitzen recalls how

> in the smaller, independent studios, and at Universal too, you practically had a say in everything. Even Cedric Gibbons didn't dare to approach the wardrobe department at MGM. But at Universal and the smaller studios, the property department was a few feet away from the art department and the wardrobe department was around the corner and we all became very good friends and could coordinate our efforts better.

General Service "was a small studio," Sidney recalls. "They never shot more than two films at a time there, and there weren't a lot of producers or writers around. It was more friendly, it had more of a family feeling among the cast and crew."

Intimate and cordial as his operations were, Wanger was tired of being a unit producer at Paramount. Paramount executives urged him to stay on. His films had greatly augmented the company's volume of production and lowered its distribution and production overheads. In the aggregate they produced gross income of over $5.6 million. This amounted to profits of only $50,000, but losses were Wanger's problem, since Paramount collected distribution fees of more than $1.4 million.

Wanger could not be persuaded. Although *Trail of the Lonesome Pine* had been a sop to his low-budget restrictions, it was not compensation enough. Although his unit films looked superb thanks to Toluboff and Taylor, they were full of narrative flaws and generic formulas and lacked the distinguishing qualities of *The President Vanishes* and *Private Worlds*. Wanger wanted still greater control over his productions, which in his mind meant greater independence. *The President Vanishes* had gone further than *Gabriel Over the White House* in depicting America in disarray, but the objections by Paramount board members and the Breen Office to *The President Vanishes* were identical to what had greeted the studio-produced MGM film. After considering offers from several studios, he chose an affiliation with United Artists which appeared to grant him greater autonomy than ever before to realize his ideals of enlightened moviemaking.

8

A Fine and Daring Producer (1936–1938)

When Wanger moved to United Artists in the summer of 1936, he embarked upon a five-year venture that placed him squarely in the front ranks of progressive and innovative Hollywood filmmaking. He produced an extraordinary run of memorable films, including message movies such as Lang's *You Only Live Once* and William Dieterle's controversial *Blockade;* Ford's stunning *The Long Voyage Home;* box office hits such as Tay Garnett's *Trade Winds,* John Cromwell's *Algiers* and Ford's *Stagecoach;* and his only film to combine entertainment with message making effectively, Hitchcock's *Foreign Correspondent.* Even lesser efforts such as *History Is Made at Night, Stand-In,* and *Eternally Yours* proved superior to his work at Paramount.

Such success did not come immediately or consistently, however. It was rooted in a constellation of factors that ranged from Wanger's new producing arrangement with United Artists to the rumblings of war around the world. In fact there were three distinct phases of Wanger's years at United Artists. From 1936 to 1938, he inaugurated the United Artists affiliation with admirable but profitless work that benefited from his experiment in production financing and from the skills of two screenwriters. There was his peak period from 1938 to 1939, when his public prominence and box office success grew exponentially. Finally, there was the troubled two years through 1941 in which the drawbacks of his independence became evident.

Wanger's value to United Artists in 1936, as with Paramount two years earlier, lay in his ability to supervise a large number of quality films to meet the exhibitors' voracious appetites. Formed purely to distribute films made by stockholders Chaplin, Fairbanks, Mary Pickford, and D. W. Griffith in 1919, United Artists had always required additional producers to fill out its schedule. Goldwyn had joined their ranks in 1926, but by 1935, the product crisis was acute, as the founding generation (except Chaplin) ended their active careers. There were other losses. Walt Disney's company, which had supplied the distributor with popular, Academy Award–winning Silly Symphony cartoons, moved to RKO in 1936 after a contract dispute. Twentieth Century Pictures, which had produced fourteen films over two years, left in 1935 to merge with Fox. To counter these defections, United Artists began distributing the films of Selznick's new company in July 1935 and made the Hungarian émigré Korda a stockholder the following September.

In spite of Korda and Selznick, the company released only fourteen films in the 1935–1936 season (compared with the fifty or more averaged by the producer-distributors). Not owning any theaters, United Artists, like Columbia, made money only if it persuaded the major circuits to premiere and play their films. Between axiomatically unpopular British movies and its few American titles, this was a challenge. Distribution head George J. Schaefer summarized the company's problems in early 1937: "A schedule such as this is not of great importance to the independent theatre or circuit and I am sure you must agree with me it does not help our prestige for the coming season. Neither does it help us meet our distribution cost." To maintain its bargaining position with the independent theaters and to lower its overhead, United Artists required a high volume of product; to maintain its wedge in the affiliated theaters, the company needed quality—major stars and polished productions.

Under these circumstances, Wanger looked very appealing. His first Paramount films in the 1935–1936 season (*Mary Burns, Fugitive*; *Her Master's Voice*; and *Trail of the Lonesome Pine*) showed a total profit of nearly $300,000. From the prestige angle, he had an impressive roster of contracted stars (Bennett, Boyer, Carroll, Fonda, and Sidney among them) who were building their stature with loan-outs to major studios. Art director Toluboff gave each film's sets the appropriate degree of detail and gloss on a limited budget. Best of all, Wanger was prolific: aside from his fourteen films for Paramount in less than two years, he had two scripts—"Three Time Loser" and "History Is Made at Night"—in advanced stages of development that could go into production shortly after his move in August. In 1937, his first five films accounted for 20 percent of the United Artists schedule.

United Artists signed Wanger during a transitional period in its management. President Schenck, who skillfully guided the company through the difficult early years of the Great Depression, had resigned in May 1935 to join Zanuck at Twentieth Century–Fox as chairman of the board. Wanger negotiated with acting head Pickford, and he came aboard when Dr. Attilio H. Giannini, a founder of the Bank of America, assumed the presidency. Industry leaders questioned Giannini's qualifications to run United Artists, but the stockholders were counting on him to facilitate production loans for new producers such as Wanger.

United Artists was so desirous of Wanger's association that it agreed to finance him directly, something the company had never done before. It never had to: Pickford, Chaplin and Fairbanks's phenomenal earnings, and Goldwyn, Korda and Selznick's financial resources had enabled them to fund their films without the distributor's aid. Previously, if United Artists had a strong year, the stockholders collected dividends that they kept or applied to future productions. Moreover, none of the United Artists producers accepted financing from—or shared profits with—the distributor, on the grounds that their financial autonomy prevented United Artists from favoring anyone's films.

Wanger's new company was an experiment for both himself and his distributor. United Artists provided 80 percent of Wanger's capitalization, buying $1.2 million of preferred, nonvoting stock that Wanger applied to his first two productions. Wanger put up $200,500 for the remaining preferred stock. His initial capitalization was thus half the amount of Selznick International. With luck, all these funds would be recouped from profits and the preferred stock retired, leaving just three thousand shares of common stock, which Wanger (and Wanger's old company) and United Artists split equally. In addition, United Artists put up $640,000 in periodic loans for "expenses of running the corporation."

This then appeared to be a corporate and contractual arrangement that gave Wanger more producing freedom than he had ever enjoyed before. The new Wanger corporation, like JayPay Productions, was named and identified as a separate entity from a major distributor. As with JayPay, Wanger had "complete control of all matters involving the production of photoplays"— United Artists did not require consultations on scripts, budgets, or any other preliminaries. Wanger's contract specified that the distributor was restricted to making "only the changes demanded by censors." Wanger was completely in charge as the "executive producer in charge of production" for five years beginning July 6, 1936, at a salary of $2,500 per week ($500 more than his last Paramount contract), plus expenses, making him the twelfth-highest paid producer in the late 1930s. Equally appealing to Wanger, the new arrangement gave him approval over advertising campaigns, whose costs he shared with the distributor. He also had the right to okay the booking contracts negotiated by United Artists with exhibitors. United Artists sold Wanger films singly rather than in blocks. This would make every Wanger film a "special." The distributor even seemed to welcome Wanger's reputation for innovation: publicity boasted that his new contract enabled him, at $750,000 a picture, to "expand all of his theories of the screen unencumbered by restricted negative costs."

But the appearance was deceiving, since the United Artists arrangement in other respects resembled Wanger's unit contract. Where Paramount had financed Wanger's unit films, United Artists guaranteed his bank loans. In both cases, the distributor held significant economic and practical authority over Wanger's work. Most significantly, United Artists had capitalized his company—approximating Wanger's desire to have his old corporation bought up by a distributor. This gave United Artists the right to appoint three of the five members of the Wanger company's board of directors, from whom he would have to seek approvals for large expenditures (more than $750,000 on his films and $150,000 on any single star). By this fact alone, Wanger remained independent in name only.

As at the start of any new venture, United Artists's potential restraints did not worry Wanger, and through the summer of 1938, he worked without interference. He set up shop in the United Artists Studios at 1045 N. Formosa Avenue in Hollywood, with Rosemary Foley, an intelligent, enthusiastic and loyal young woman, as his executive assistant. He hired Harry Kosiner as his New York scout to cover new plays, opening nights, and books as well as to review the booking contracts United Artists negotiated with theaters for the Wanger films. Between them they covered the publishing ground so well that Selznick would complain to his staff by 1941 that "Wanger is beginning to get my goat through seeming to have material [including *Rebecca*] just a little bit earlier than anybody else in the business." Selznick might also have envied Wanger's busy production plans. In the fall of 1936, he had Hecht and MacArthur adapting *Wuthering Heights* for Anatole Litvak to direct; Lewis Milestone was adapting Vincent Sheean's *Personal History,* an account of the correspondent's adventures in the Far East and in Europe during the 1920s; and Ford had agreed to shoot a film about Nazi efforts at mineral hunting in Africa. Ford's project never panned out, Wanger sold the Hecht-MacArthur script to Goldwyn for the classic 1939 version directed by William Wyler, and Wanger had to wait until 1940 for Hitchcock to discard the Sheean book altogether and make *Foreign Correspondent.* But thanks to contracted writers Towne and Baker, and major directors Lang and Frank Borzage, Wanger's first two films made for a striking debut by the new company.

Towne and Baker are obscure names now, but in the 1930s they were two of the most colorful screenwriters in Hollywood. Towne started in the film industry at Vitagraph, and eventually became a title writer and gag man for Sennett; Baker, the more sedate personality, was an ex-reporter and cartoonist for the *Brooklyn Daily Eagle,* the *New York Times,* and the *New York Sun* who joined First National. Shortly after Baker fired Towne from Warner Bros.' story department in the late 1920s they became a team—Towne the wild, cigar-chomping, hyperactive idea man, and Baker, a quiet, more dignified sounding board, who also took dictation. Their ability to crank out scripts provided the backbone of Wanger's program at United Artists, accounting for *You Only Live Once, History Is Made at Night,* two Garnett films *Stand-In*

(1937) and *Eternally Yours* (1939), as well as Wanger's Paramount releases *Mary Burns, Fugitive* (1935), *Shanghai,* and *Case Against Mrs. Ames* (1936).

Devoted to Wanger, for whom they claimed to have turned down more lucrative offers, the team was legendary for their juvenile stunts, which resembled the antics of the Pat O'Brien–James Cagney screenwriting duo in *Boy Meets Girl* (1938). They used toilet paper for note cards as they developed scripts and hung it on the wall to keep track of story progression. Wanger later recalled how, "when they were ready, I'd go up and comment":

> "That seems a little too long. There might be a dead spot there."
> "You're right. You're right."
> They would tear off two pages of toilet paper.

Sometimes, they were hardly this organized. Sidney recalls that they wrote *Mary Burns, Fugitive* daily on the set. According to one anecdote that was also told about Leo McCarey, they once pitched a story to Wanger successfully but then had to rely on the producer to recall it for them after they celebrated their sale with a drunken spree.

As cynical ex-newspapermen, Towne and Baker shared Wanger's healthy irreverence for Hollywood. They were known for working in bathing suits (and sometimes brassieres) during the hot Los Angeles days. Other costumes expressed their loyalty to Wanger:

> They appeared at the studio in smocks such as are worn at gasoline service stations with "Walter Wanger Productions" sewn on the back. During football season they affected white turtleneck sweaters of the collegian manner of 1904 with a crimson block "W" on the front of each.

Towne even helped their Ivy League leader attract actors to their scripts by running around "to every restaurant" telling actors, "Jesus, Wanger's got a great part for you."

Given the perennial problem of finding story material, Towne and Baker were Wanger's saviors, even though he didn't use them for all his films. They gave Wanger strength where he was weakest, his lack of a story sense. Many screenwriters confirm that Wanger had neither the talent for nor the interest in tight or even plausible story construction. Frequently, he was equally disinterested in characterization, to the detriment of *Gabriel Over the White House* and *The President Vanishes,* for these films offer the audience no opportunities for the emotional pleasure of identifying with the characters. For Wanger, the energetic provocateur, such matters were of little concern, and he never evinced any awareness that they might have contributed to his films' poor box office performance.

"He didn't have the instinct of a real moviemaker," Rosten recalls. "I don't think that he read a script with the same sense of story that Ben Hecht, John

Ford, Irving Thalberg—who were movie people to their marrow—did." Philip Yordan, who wrote the screenplay for *Reign of Terror* claimed that Wanger told him, "Scripts are shit. They're nothing. It's the subject matter, the story, the title, the cast, the costumes and the set. That's the picture." Hecht, who admired Wanger immensely and dedicated one of his novels (*A Jew in Love*) to him, was even more emphatic on this point. Wanger and Arthur Hornblow, Jr., were "almost completely devoid of story sense."

> They cannot tell a story. They are like children when it comes to making up a story. They're much inferior to people who are not mortally as smart and cultured as they are. When they make up stories, you think you're listening to a ten year old boy.

Unlike Thalberg, Selznick, or Zanuck, Wanger never rewrote a talent's work or held detailed story conferences about character motivation. He wanted a script he could respond to, and he wanted the job done. In contemporary Hollywood, where films frequently rely on special effects to smooth over story problems, Wanger would thrive. In the classical Hollywood era, he needed help.

Though superior to Wanger's Paramount films, many of his United Artists movies such as the pseudo-musical *52nd Street, Vogues of 1938,* the melodramatic comedy *I Met My Love Again,* and the romantic comedies such as *Winter Carnival, Eternally Yours,* and *Slightly Honorable* are flawed entertainments. This presented something of a problem for Wanger—a drawback that had never been so obvious before. Whereas Paramount specials were guaranteed to pass quickly through the subsequent-run theaters, the United Artists films, because of their budgets and their single bookings, had to be of superior appeal to make profits. At United Artists, as at Paramount, the appeal of Wanger's productions varied, depending on who wrote the script and how well they responded to time constraints. Towne and Baker worked quickly and prolifically (*New York Times* reporter Douglas Churchill quipped that they made the rapid Hecht and MacArthur "look like snails"). They also produced scripts with clear story logic and interesting, ironic situations, which they shamelessly and frequently recycled from film to film (a technique that was part of every screenwriter's arsenal, but which also accounts for Towne and Baker's speed). Their skills were evident in their first realized script at United Artists, "Three Time Loser," released as *You Only Live Once* (1937).

"Three Time Loser" focuses on ex-convict Eddie Taylor (Fonda) and his difficulty in finding acceptance and regular employment in American society. The film underlines at every turn Eddie's predicament as a victim of prejudice and circumstance. After the humorous eviction of Eddie and Joan (Sidney) from their honeymoon hotel, the film takes a more serious turn as Eddie is fired from his truck-driving job for being late while looking over their new house. Eddie is then framed for a bank robbery and the murder of a guard. He is making an escape from death row when he is pardoned, but Eddie cannot believe the truth of what the warden calls out to him in the fogbound prison yard. Shooting the priest who attempts to stop him, Eddie and Joan are forced to live on the run, until they are shot down at the Canadian border.

As directed by Lang, *You Only Live Once* presents a biting vision of American society, whose worst tendencies combine with fate to overwhelm Eddie and Joan. It seems an appropriate film from the master German director of *Dr. Mabuse* (1922), *Metropolis* (1927), and *M* (1931). It was also very similar to his first American film at MGM, *Fury* (1936), which had also starred Sidney. Yet Wanger later claimed that "the entire film was my idea." The story's inspiration was the real Bonnie and Clyde, and at Wanger's suggestion, Towne and Baker reworked their notorious lives into a narrative formula they had previously used for Wanger in a Sidney vehicle at Paramount, *Mary Burns, Fugitive.* The difference between this film and Lang's provides a classic instance of how an auteur could transform generic material into a more personal statement.

In the earlier film, Mary Burns (Sidney), is a countryside coffee shop owner in love with Don "Babe" Wilson (Baxter), who, unbeknownst to her, is a gangster. She is imprisoned as an accomplice to his crimes, but permitted to escape as "bait" so that the police can track Wilson down. The film features violent shootouts between Wilson and the police as well as a sensationalized view of women's prisons in a genre that Sidney came to personify during the early thirties. Scripted and shot in the fall of 1935, the film demonstrates how Hollywood "tamed" the gangster type after the rise of the Breen Office. Mary recoils from Wilson when she learns his true identity, and Wilson compares unfavorably with the gruff, "snowblinded" explorer Alec MacDonald (Melvyn Douglas) whom Mary meets in a Chicago hospital. MacDonald kills Wilson in a shootout at his mountain retreat, mediating between Mary's pastoral purity and Wilson's urban strength and energy.

The similarity in the plight of the victims of circumstance—Mary Burns and Eddie Taylor—is obvious. The differences are quite striking. In *Mary Burns, Fugitive,* the faith of one character, the explorer, is enough to save the heroine; in Lang's film, Joan's faith in Eddie, and even that of the district attorney (Barton MacLaine) and Father Dolan (William Gargan), is powerless to halt Eddie's prosecution and death. More significantly, there is hardly any sense of social injustice in *Mary Burns, Fugitive.* Mary's fate is generically dictated by the fast-paced action of the film and its other gangster accoutrements. *You Only Live Once* dwells on the hypocrisies of secondary characters, such as the cowardly husband who reads true crime magazines for thrills but will not tolerate an ex-con in his hotel, or the gas station attendants who steal money from their boss and blame it on Eddie and Joan.

The greater profundity of the Lang film arose in part from Lang's polishing the script with Towne and Baker in August and September of 1936. Wanger had approached the burly director with sharp brown eyes that summer, having admired Lang's German films, his work with Boyer in *Lilliom* (1934), and his direction of *Fury*. Depicting mob rule in a small midwestern town, *Fury* was probably the most savage, non-comic portrayal of ordinary Americans yet produced in a Hollywood studio. Lang made sure the critics understood—through his rapid direction of it and through interviews—that *Fury*'s incongruously happy ending had been dictated by the studio. But *Fury* earned a respectable box office gross and critical raves for the unconventional director and Sidney's bravura performance as the fiancée of Joe Wilson (Spencer Tracy).

An unconventional director—as well as one who could exploit Sidney's waiflike qualities—was exactly what Wanger sought for his debut at United Artists. He encouraged Lang to surpass *Fury*, distinguishing himself from the MGM executives by agreeing with Lang that a film of "social implications" could mean solid box office receipts. Aware of Lang's distress over the cutting of *Fury*, Wanger told him that he could "do just as he pleases" and assured him "that no other hand will touch it through the editing."

Lang took Wanger's carte blanche as a license to revise Towne and Baker's early drafts into an intriguing social problem film. District Attorney Stephen McCormick became less spitefully jealous of Joan's love for Eddie and Joan's sister Bonnie changed from a social climbing, opera singer manque, whose snobbism rejects Eddie out of hand, to a more pragmatic but compassionate sibling. Revisions also produced some of the most powerful moments in the finished film such as the scene in which Eddie's boss talks complacently about card games to his wife on the phone while Eddie is pleading for another chance on the job.

In principal photography, Lang continued to elaborate on Towne and Baker's script. Where their version of the final scene finished with Eddie and Joan lying together in a "kiss of death," Lang reconceived it to echo the couple's earlier honeymoon scene. There in a hotel garden, Eddie told Joan of how frogs in love always die together, before he picked her up, kissed her in his arms, and carried her up the stairs. In the film's final moments, Fonda again carries Sidney in his arms and stands holding her after kissing her and being shot. Overwhelming backlighting evokes "heavenly gates," and the dead Father Dolan's voice tells Eddie that the "gates are open." They are better off leaving a world that refuses to recognize their essential purity.

Lang's visual style also set *You Only Live Once* apart from *Mary Burns, Fugitive*. The most interesting element of *Mary Burns, Fugitive* is William K. Howard's deployment of the iconography of justice. Under the film's titles is etched the familiar woman blindfolded and holding up scales. Midway through the film, we meet MacDonald, who is blindfolded to protect his eyes. Unlike every other character in the film, he judges Mary by her voice, her personality, (and her coffee)—and not by her associations or circumstances.

Where Howard used a clever visual motif, Lang devised a complex visual strategy for conveying the relativity of perception. As critic George Wilson has shown, Taylor's innocence, Father Dolan's faith, and Joan's affection for Eddie are all ambiguous. Was Eddie Taylor guilty of the bank robbery? Because the scene is shot with fragmenting close-ups and oblique angles, we cannot tell. But Eddie mentions in a previous scene that other ex-cons have invited him to do a robbery, and Lang's narration has shown us Eddie's whereabouts in every previous scene. From the limited camera angles on the bank robbery, in which the robber is identified only by Eddie's hat, through Eddie's desperate behavior after the armored truck crashes—in which he climbs into the window of his new house carrying a pistol—the film implies that Eddie did the job. Lang's play with audience assumptions and the norms of Hollywood narration make *You Only Live Once* one of the most distinctive films that Hollywood ever produced.

These effects are enhanced by Lang's direction of Fonda as a tabula rasa, a skeptical but also lyrical and violently moody unfortunate whose actual innocence is never quite clear—to the audience or to the characters—until it is too late. Here, as in the celebrated point-of-view shot in a police officer's rifle sights before he shoots Eddie in the final scene, Lang implicates the audience in the social prejudices he denounces. Then too, Joan's belief in Eddie seems slightly irrational and Father Dolan's is the product of unthinking faith. Where *Mary Burns, Fugitive* posited a faith in the eventual triumph of justice, Lang realized a film in which such comforting absolutes were impossible. As Nugent put it in the *New York Times*, "in less gifted hands, [*You Only Live Once*] might have been the merest melodrama"—like *Mary Burns, Fugitive*.

Such achievements came at a price. As with *Fury,* the actual production of *You Only Live Once*—which began in September 1936—was arduous for actors and crew. Lang was still adjusting his German working methods to Hollywood. As Lotte Eisner has described, in Berlin Lang got used to working on his own scripts, shooting for long hours with technicians replacing each other in shifts, cutting his own films, and maintaining a unit of performers and crew members. In Hollywood, Lang admitted, "In the early days I was not realizing how it was here. . . . I am working on a scene—I do not want to stop until I am finished. But actors in America are very regular about eating at regular hours." As Sidney recalls, Lang "was a hard taskmaster. He knew exactly what he wanted. He was too bright a man to let discomfort bother him. He got involved in the work."

With *You Only Live Once,* there was only a slight letup. Shamroy, whose camera Lang kept on a crane during shooting, described Lang as "fantastically meticulous" and made an analogy between Lang and "one of those artists who would paint over and over again on the same canvas, covering one painting with another." Fonda couldn't stand him. But even with fifteen days of retakes after a lengthy forty-six days of shooting, Lang completed a film well within Wanger's contracted budget limit at $589,403.

Before the film's premiere, Lang claimed that Wanger prohibited him from shooting a prologue of "social implications," showing how Eddie Taylor came to a life of crime through "bad influences" and an "unfortunate environment." In fact, no such scene appeared in the script drafts, and Lang never mentioned it in interviews during production. On the other hand, five days after completing the shooting script, Towne and Baker expanded Eddie and Joan's dialogue on their honeymoon night to explain Eddie's background as a reform school graduate, first punished for punching a kid who tore a frog's legs off. This dialogue sustains our uncertainty about Eddie better than a sociological prologue would have.

The national newsweekly critics, noting that Lang was finally given the unhappy ending denied him at MGM, were generally admiring: *Newsweek* and *Time* compared it favorably with the seminal gangster film *Public Enemy,* and Nugent commented that the film "within the somewhat theatrical limits of its script" was "an intense, absorbing and relentlessly pursued tragedy which owes most of its dignity to the eloquence of its direction." Wanger, screening the final cut, had been less satisfied, feeling it dragged with "German direction." Between this and Lang's meticulous working methods, Wanger held the director responsible for the film's failure to break even. Whereas Lang told *Variety* that Wanger was "a fine and daring producer," Wanger found Lang an "impossible, dishonest guy." The two did not work together again for nine years.

Just as the melodrama *Private Worlds* followed the message movie *The President Vanishes,* Wanger's second film for United Artists was a romantic comedy designed to diversify his schedule and minimize the risk that his ideals and Lang's film would fail to turn a profit. *History Is Made at Night* was directed by Borzage, the winner of the first director's Academy Award for *Seventh Heaven* in 1927, who had a lyrical touch that was totally different from Lang's paranoid sensibility.

The film opened within a month of *You Only Live Once* and was scripted by Towne and Baker in typical form. When they had worked under Lubitsch at Paramount, their particular forte had become "sophisticated" romantic comedy, in which perfectly decorous visual interactions were informed by sexual connotations that were as outrageous as their working "uniforms." Their first draft for *Case Against Mrs. Ames* was rejected in toto by the Breen Office for depicting pimps, heavy drinking, and a courtroom scene that used prostitutes as character witnesses: as a weary reader put it, "there should be a complete rewrite after someone from this office consults with the writers and explains to them that there is a code which they have violated throughout."

Ordinarily, their skill in skirting the code was superlative: in the comedy of remarriage *Eternally Yours,* which they wrote for Wanger in 1939, a spurned fiancé (Broderick Crawford) tells his wife (Young) on their wedding night, "It's a darn shame I had to trip on that rug and spoil your honeymoon." Enhanced with Irene and Travis Banton's costumes and supporting performances by Billie Burke and comedian Hugh Herbert, Towne and Baker's script was considered a quintessential example of "their sophisticated and accomplished manner."

Wanger especially appreciated Towne and Baker's ability to tailor their work to his contracted stars, writing a role for Carroll as an icy, blonde "rich bitch" in *Case Against Mrs. Ames* after Hitchcock established her persona in *The 39 Steps* and *Secret Agent.* They created sympathetic roles for Sidney in *Mary Burns, Fugitive* and *You Only Live Once.* They conceived a ruthless entrepreneur who was also the victimized progeny of miscegenation for Boyer in *Shanghai.* For *History Is Made at Night,* they built up Boyer's image as a romantic lover by setting him and their story in the upper-class milieu associated with screwball comedy.

Insanely jealous millionaire Steven Vail (Colin Clive) tries to prevent his wife Irene (Jean Arthur) from getting a divorce by compromising her with his chauffeur. Boyer plays Paul, a handsome stranger who rescues Irene by subduing the chauffeur and posing as a jewel thief when Vail breaks in. The connection between thievery and adultery, well established in Lubitsch's *Trouble in Paradise,* constitutes Paul's appeal to Irene and to the audience. According to Joshua Logan's account of the scripting of Borzage's film, Towne, Baker, and Wanger consciously strove for such risqué thrills.

Logan, then hired by Wanger as Boyer's dialogue director on *History Is Made at Night,* was astounded by a story conference he attended between the screenwriters and Wanger. Towne and Baker began with infectious laughter and proceeded to outline the scene they were working on in the crudest terms:

> Here's the great scene, boss. This big, handsome prick charges into this beautiful cunt's bedroom, grabs her by the tit, then throws a fuck into her. Ha, ha, ha. When she grabs him by the balls, the door opens and Mr. Soft Cock husband enters, yelling, 'Shit, shit, shit!' Some scene, eh boss?

Wanger only admired their audacity which he characterized as "genius!"

In subsequent scenes, Towne and Baker had Paul take Irene to the place that has "the best champagne in Paris." Upon arriving at the closed restaurant, Paul persuades the orchestra and the chef to reopen, so they can dine and dance until dawn. Through these expository scenes, Boyer excelled as a romantic sophisticate who charms the girl from Kansas and, presumably, the women in the theaters. His appeals were heightened by the contrasting ethnic comic relief provided by Leo Carrillo (better known as Pancho in television's *The Cisco Kid*) as Paul's sidekick chef. Meanwhile, the chauffeur dies accidentally, and Paul flees to America when accused.

The toilet paper geniuses found writing *History is Made at Night* difficult. It kept veering between comedy and melodrama. During production, the team could not figure out how to resolve the story so that the couple wound up together, a frequent problem in their work. They went so far as to concoct an ocean liner sinking, aping recent films that ended in catastrophe such as MGM's *The Good Earth* and *San Francisco* (both 1936). After an unsuccessful preview and at the suggestion of veteran comedy director Arthur Ripley, they added a scene in which Vail kills his chauffeur and frames Paul. Vail was no longer a jeweler but a steamship line millionaire who commands the captain of the ship bringing his wife and Paul back to Paris to hurry. When the ship speeds into an iceberg, the news makes Vail confess his guilt and commit suicide.

Irene's befuddled responses to the comic and melodramatic plot developments seem like Jean Arthur's reactions to the constructed, synthetic quality of the script. Yet Borzage, unaccustomed to directing murder stories or even the upper-class milieu, kept his focus on Boyer and Arthur, enabling their portrayal of a grand passion to outweigh all other considerations. Their interplay amidst the chaos of the shipwreck and the empty restaurant where they first dance together are quintessential examples of Hollywood romance.

Following *History Is Made at Night,* Towne and Baker drafted one other notable romantic comedy, *Stand-In* (1937). This satire of Hollywood, concerning a Wall Street banker's efforts to save a failing studio, deflates all the pieties of Selznick's *A Star is Born,* released earlier the same year. In the tradition of Hollywood comedies, the secondary characters Towne and Baker created are hilarious caricatures. There's the Russian director, modeled after von Stroheim and von Sternberg (he lies on the floor framing shots with his hands, insists on real edelweiss for a snow blizzard scene, and punches the hero, an investment firm adviser, during a dinner). Nassau (C. Henry Gordon), the financier threatening to buy out Colossal Pictures, interrupts every meeting to hear race results on the radio. Not surprisingly the most dignified member of the Hollywood colony is the alcoholic producer Quintain (Humphrey Bogart), who saves the studio's big jungle film *Sex and Satan* at the editing table by cutting out the star Cherie (Maria Shelton) and inserting more shots of the studio's gorilla. But even Quintain is something of a flake; he carries around his terrier while making impassioned speeches, and on first meeting the studio's Wall Street representative, examines his tennis racket for warping.

Into this vision of decadent, idiotic Hollywood, the script projects a total recluse and ascetic investments adviser, Atterbury Dodd (Leslie Howard), who is immune to the gracefully revealed figure of Miss Plum (Joan Blondell), the stand-in he meets in the studio car. Although it dramatized for the first time Wall Street control over Hollywood, the film's premise closely follows author Clarence Budington Kelland's story, which is in turn very similar to Kelland's "Mr. Deeds Goes to Town," the basis for Capra's 1936 success. Miss Plum capably guides the totally unfamiliar Dodd around Hollywood without demystifying the process of making movies. Dodd in turn is unmercifully subjected to ambitious stage mothers with Shirley Temple clones who insist on demonstrating their talents for him. "Who is Shirley Temple?" he asks Miss Plum. "Skip it," she says hopelessly. As in Sullavan's early scenes in *The Moon's Our Home,* the pretensions of the powerful stars, director, and publicist are all material for fabulous satire: Cherie compliments Dodd that he tangos "divinely" while he puffingly counts out the beat.

But when the Wall Street firm decides to sell out the studio to the corrupt Nassau and put everyone out of a job, Dodd becomes more humane. Taking just a hint from 1935 films about striking workers, such as Warner Bros.' *Black Fury* and MGM's *Riffraff,* the script plants brief references to strike unrest in radio news reports. Meanwhile, Dodd becomes a beneficent capitalist. He stops calling studio employees "units" and he overcomes the technicians and extras' resentment of his "white collar" status with an impassioned speech, begging them to work together without salary to complete a single picture that will save the studio. Having won labor over to capital's side with enlightened management, Dodd seals class harmony with his improbable marriage proposal to Miss Plum.

Stand-In benefits enormously from the trio of Warner Bros.'s stars Wanger obtained in exchange for his loan-out of Boyer for *Tovarich* and of Fonda for *Jezebel.* Blondell conveyed her characteristic, energetic freshness as Dodd's shrewd and unpretentious guide to Hollywood's eccentricities. Bogart is here cast against his predominant gangster type as the alcoholic yet sympathetic Quintain who is hopelessly in love with his leading lady. And Garnett directed Howard with numerous prudish characteristics, ranging from his constant dumping of dirty ashtrays to extensive double takes in close up, raising his glasses in exaggerated shock at the industry's morals and values. *Time's* reviewer hailed the film as "the most human as well as the most biting comedy yet written about Hollywood."

Yet for all their speed, wit, and strong sense of structure, the Towne and Baker scripts earned only meager profits. As his first season at United Artists came to a close, Wanger had in production his most costly film yet, the Technicolor *Vogues of 1938,* and he realized that his films were not selling enough tickets by themselves. As his indebtedness to the Bank of America, United Artists, and two processing labs deepened, he needed further support for his forthcoming $1 million musical. Recalling his personal effect on journalists in London in the early 1920s and the burst of attention he received with the premiere of *The President Vanishes,* Wanger hit upon the solution to his problems—personal publicity.

Actually, Wanger's move to United Artists was preceded by a widely covered press conference in New York, on his return from a visit to Italy, and a forty-five-minute talk with Benito Mussolini. Il Duce encouraged Wanger to establish a production unit in Rome, where the vast Cinecitta was under construction; Wanger offered advice and encouragement to members of the native industry, inviting them to visit Hollywood and study the big studios. The point of this liaison was to pry loose distribution income that was currently blocked by the Italian government—producers could use their funds for English-language films shot in Italy, while American stars could collect their salaries tax-free. To prove his good faith to the Italians, Wanger told a surprised press corps in New York that Mussolini was a "marvelous man," that Italy was completely revitalized under his leadership, and that the Ethiopians had welcomed the Fascists' invasion of their country.

Blinded by his fondness for the country, his admiration for Mussolini, and his economic interests, Wanger made a completely erroneous distinction between Fascism and Nazism and hoped that Mussolini and the Vatican would persuade Hitler to stop persecuting Jews and Catholics. Meanwhile, he urged Sidney, then in England completing Hitchcock's *Sabotage,* to visit with his Italian associates and have her picture taken with Mussolini. The Jewish actress refused. Although Wanger pursued the idea well into 1938, it never got off the ground.

The press charitably forgot this incident when Wanger next came forward in the summer of 1937 to promote *Vogues of 1938.* He gave interviews touting its pastel colors (as opposed to the primary colors that had dominated *Becky Sharp* and *Trail of the Lonesome Pine*). More important, he hired publicist Russell Phelps to circulate a biographical profile that editors ran intact in papers around the country. This was probably inspired by Alva Johnston's four-part profile of Goldwyn and "the Goldwyn touch" in that spring's *Saturday Evening Post.* (The United Artists producers were always learning from each other.) Journalists delighted in covering Wanger. They were entranced by his "New Englandish" accent, his hyperactive intelligence, and his candor. A Boston reporter described what Rosten called his lack of focus:

> He talks rather rapidly, and as he talks wanders about. If you happen to be in a room with him, he rambles to far-off corners. . . . On the street, he talks as he walks and also finds time to peer closely into shop windows and to walk into all interesting store doorways en route.

A reporter for the *Washington Star* noted,

> His associates make Mr. Wanger sound like a sort of Jupiter. Hereafter, that will be quite all right with us. Mr. Wanger is a kind of Jupiter. . . . His vocabulary is

clever and he uses it vigorously in praise of his competitors' pictures when they deserve it and just as vigorously to condemn when he feels that way about them.

When *Time* reviewed his *Stand-In,* its critic noted that Wanger was "always a daring experimenter."

One of two distinguishing features of Wanger's United Artists association was that it gave him a platform, as a semi-independent, for his increased self-promotion. The other was not so much that his new company gave him unprecedented freedom from a distributor's power but that the budgets Wanger could spend on his films enabled him to hire the best talent available to realize his films. Within one year's time, Wanger exploited this setup to arrive at Hollywood's forefront.

9

An Independent in Every Sense of the Word (1938–1939)

In February 1939, *Time*'s critic devoted the bulk of his review of Ford's *Stagecoach* to introducing "a presentable young Dartmouth man," Wanger, who belonged "in the forefront of Hollywood's crusade for social consciousness." After surveying his career, and noting that Wanger was "a prime exception to the rule that a college education is an insuperable handicap in Hollywood," the critic got around to discussing the film. Its sympathetic portrayal of the prostitute Dallas (Claire Trevor), the outlaw Ringo Kid (Wayne), and the inebriated Dr. Josiah Boone (Thomas Mitchell) was evidence not of Ford and Dudley Nichols's inspired dramaturgy, but of Wanger's "contempt for the Production Code." Yet Wanger admitted that he financed the film "without having a hell of a lot to do with it."

Time's review of *Stagecoach* provides the most dramatic evidence of how well Wanger succeeded in projecting the image of an innovative, front-rank producer in the popular press. Beginning with the boycott that had greeted his mediocre message film *Blockade* the year before, Wanger grew into a prominent and omnipresent critic of Hollywood escapism. As fascism spread worldwide, Wanger became Hollywood's man of the moment.

Blockade began as a project for Milestone, who had failed to adapt a shootable script of journalist Sheean's *Personal History* in the fall of 1936. Intent on getting *something* for Milestone's salary, Wanger encouraged him in February 1937 to coauthor with playwright Clifford Odets a script on the Spanish Civil War. They were a formidable creative team: Odets's Group Theater plays *Awake and Sing* and *Waiting for Lefty* were impassioned dramatizations of the necessity for political activism to effect social change, and Milestone was the Oscar-winning director of *All Quiet on the Western Front* (1930, Universal) and *The Front Page* (1931, United Artists). Their most recent production was *The General Died at Dawn* for Le Baron at Paramount, depicting a Chinese warlord who is outwitted by a desperate adventuress and an American; it had proven an effective vehicle for Carroll opposite Cooper.

A Madeleine Carrol–Charles Boyer film was the framework within which Milestone and Odets worked for Wanger. But the very idea of a film on the Spanish Civil War had its roots in liberal Hollywood's concern about the conflict. The war had been raging since the summer of 1936. Although Congressional Neutrality Acts prevented the sale of American arms to either combatant, American Catholics tended to back Franco's brutal Falangist forces while liberals and Communists supported the Loyalists. Hollywood was equally partisan. Industry liberals and radicals—such as Milestone, Nichols, Stewart, March, and Douglas—began fundraising for the Loyalists.

Although they made occasional contributions, Hollywood producers were conspicuously absent from the cause. They respected the federal government's policy stance shaped by influential isolationist congressmen. They were aware of Catholic sympathy with Franco's Rebels—the Legion of Decency boycott that ensured the formation of the Breen Office was only four years past. Documentaries on the subject such as Ernest Hemingway and John Dos Passos's *Spain in Flames* were banned in Pennsylvania and elsewhere. And distribution heads did not want to offend Catholic nations and lose valuable markets. Paramount, MGM, Universal, and Twentieth Century–Fox all had plans to film stories set in the Spanish Civil War by the beginning of 1937, but Paramount's *The Last Train to Madrid* was the only one realized, and its sequence of aerial bombardment by the Rebels remained tangential to the main narrative line.

Wanger's plans were very different: his film would deal directly with the conflict. He had not made a "topical" film since *You Only Live Once* and had the backstage entertainments *Vogues of 1938* and *52nd Street* in production. For all the isolationist sentiment expressed in *The President Vanishes* and the jingoism of *Gabriel Over the White House,* he was an unabashed liberal internationalist with a strong commitment to the fate of Europe. Though he was fooled by Mussolini, he recognized Germany's rearmament as a reprise of events leading to the outbreak of World War I. His elitism and the political fervor in Hollywood encouraged him to challenge isolationist sentiment. In writer John Howard Lawson's words, "Wanger understood the significance of the people's struggle in Spain and believed it was a public service to tell the truth about it."

Wanger's independence made him contractually free to prepare "The River is Blue," the Odets-Milestone script that reworked Ilya Ehrenberg's *The Loves of Jeanne Ney* (filmed by G. W. Pabst in 1927) and transformed Russian expatriates to Spaniards in Paris trying to decide whether to return home. In early 1937, Wanger hired a troupe from the insolvent Group Theater

(Elia Kazan, Phoebe Brand, Luther Adler, and others) under leader Harold Clurman to work as "standbys" reading lines in screen tests (such as those devised for "The River is Blue"). But then the Breen Office instructed Odets and Milestone to ensure that their film's mise-en-scène and dialogue fail "to definitely identify any of the combatants with either faction of the Spanish Civil War." Odets lost interest, and Wanger and Milestone disagreed about the film's casting. Clurman, Wanger's general assistant, was in Kazan's words just "an intellectual ornament" who soon left in frustration. The actors followed him back to New York to produce Odets's *Golden Boy*.

Wanger revived the project the following summer. Perhaps he was inspired by the July screenings of Joris Ivens's *The Spanish Earth* at the homes of March and Viertel. Screenwriter Lawson thought Wanger accepted it out of business necessities created by his independence:

> He was at a disadvantage in competing with the giant corporations, which could invest large sums in stories, stars and advertising campaigns. Wanger's success depended on offering exceptional or controversial films. Therefore, both his social conscience and his economic aims led him to feel that the subject of *Blockade* was sensational enough to bring box office results.

Wanger approached Lawson with the project on Clurman's advice. Lawson's *Success Story*, an ironic Horatio Alger tale of commercial achievement and alienation, had been a triumph for the Group Theater several years earlier, and the Theater Union in early 1937 produced his *Marching Song*, about a sit-down strike in a car factory. Lawson had previously worked for MGM in the late 1920s, but he left Hollywood after organizing the Screen Writers Guild. He was an active supporter of the Spanish Republicans and was the American Communist party's most loyal screenwriter. But this made no difference to Wanger. Lawson dismissed Odets and Milestone's work and proposed the story, inspired by an actual incident, of a town starving because of a blockade by Franco's forces, and whose last hopes die when a supply ship is torpedoed. Wanger accepted the idea "enthusiastically."

In Hollywood lore, Lawson and Wanger made much of the censorship forced upon them, and the common understanding of the film was that, as Fonda put it years later, "It was not the picture that Walter Wanger had thought of making. It was taken away from him." Yet, while an independent at Paramount and at MGM, Wanger ignored Breen Office warnings. By 1937, the Breen Office had more authority than when it was newly formed, but Wanger never had respected the Production Code.

What was different about *Blockade* was that the independence that encouraged him to tackle the subject matter also made him timid about his approach. The fragile United Artists did not appreciate Wanger's decision to halt distribution of his films in Germany in March 1937. Prolific or not, Wanger did the distributor little good if he reduced the market for his films.

As *Blockade* began production, distribution executive Arthur Kelly expressed concern over Wanger's participation in events sponsored by the Hollywood Anti-Nazi League; writing Dr. Giannini, Kelly noted,

> If the people in Hollywood will insist on mixing in international politics then the companies employing such people will have to suffer. This sort of thing has been going on for some time and our companies' pictures have suffered accordingly.

With *Blockade,* Wanger elected to respect both United Artist's needs and his own financial difficulties. "There was no lack of candor in my talks with Walter Wanger concerning the content of the picture and the limitations that were imposed upon it," Lawson later recalled. The screenwriter accepted them "because it was the only way in which the picture could be undertaken." The film's shortcomings stem from Wanger's lack of confidence in a straightforward presentation of issues in the Civil War.

Lawson's *Blockade* script eliminated, with the exception of an opening title specifying Spain in 1936, all references to locations, any precise naming of combatants, or any discussion of causes and politics. This was hardly a problem; in fact this facilitated the film's distortions of the Loyalist forces. The hero Marco is a landowning farmer played by Fonda. His constant declarations of his love of the land motivate his leadership in the Loyalist forces and may have been inspired by Ivens's presentation of a young farmer among the Republicans in *The Spanish Earth.* In the Odets script, written before the release of Ivens's film, Marco was a college-trained chemist.

But as Marjorie Valleau points out, the character Marco's sympathies are misleading since large Spanish landowners almost all sided with Franco. In addition, the scenes showing women sympathetic to the Loyalist cause praying for relief from the blockade were highly inaccurate: the Loyalists ordered all religious shrines closed in the areas they controlled, and they punished pious behavior, sometimes with death. The *Blockade* scenes, by contrast, imply that the women of the port are rewarded for their prayers when the blockade is broken. This proved to be for many Catholics the most infuriating element of *Blockade.* Combined with the film Loyalists' stronger sense of humanity—their constant crowding around war-abandoned babies—this made the Loyalists a much more sympathetic group to the vaguely informed American viewer.

Although Lawson condemned Odets's script as "an inept melodrama" that was totally irrelevant to the realities of the war, his own first script in several years was not much better for it failed, by his own admission, to integrate documentary realism and entertainment formulas. The insistence on a romantic relationship between Marco and Norma was one major concession. Having told his friend Luis how wonderful the land is in the film's opening scene, Marco within a minute of screen time falls in love with Norma after she crashes into a nearby oxcart, and he forgets farming completely. Meanwhile the threat of villain Andre Gallinet (John Halliday, better known as Tracy Lord's father in *The Philadelphia Story*) as a potential lover to Norma is completely unconvincing.

In fact, Norma is virtually identical to the Carroll character in Odets and Milestone's *The General Died at Dawn:* a globe-trotting, world-weary woman without a home, whose aging father spies for Fascist forces in order to finance his dream of retirement, and who waves off all sentiments of fighting for one's country as mere sloganeering. In each film, her character is compelled to emerge from her solipsism into political consciousness in two stages. First, her lover murders her father in self-defense. Later she witnesses the damage her espionage has done to the hero's cause—the torture of Cooper in the Milestone film and the starvation of a port city in *Blockade.*

Lawson had taken his portrayal of Norma as far as he could when his third draft script received Breen Office approval in February (with the deletion of lines such as "They're working with foreigners," which Breen's associates felt were uncomfortably specific references to the Italian- and German-backed Francoists). At that point, Wanger hired Dieterle. The distinguished German actor and protégé of Reinhardt had directed several prestige Warner Bros.'s biopics such as *The Life of Emile Zola* (1937), the recipient of that year's best picture award not least because of its antifascist subtext. Under Dieterle's direction, the core of *Blockade*'s polemical impact resides in its final half hour, which simply shows the effects of the blockade Norma has facilitated on the port town inhabitants: women praying in church, a mother rocking an imaginary baby in her arms, another crying in front of the school where her children were bombed.

The way Dieterle's camera lavishly cranes, dollies, and cuts among the suffering extras in the port indicates his effort—a "conscious" one according to Lawson—to emulate the realism of the great Soviet directors Eisenstein and Pudovkin. The climactic moments in which the villagers gleefully get in their boats and row out to meet the incoming ship resemble the greeting of Odessa residents to the mutinous Battleship Potemkin. After the blockade is broken, Marco protests that "the front is everywhere," and delivers an impassioned speech to the camera: "It's not war. War is between soldiers. This is murder. We've got to stop it. Stop the murder of innocent people! The world can stop it! Where's the conscience of the world?" Sensing the impact of this final half hour, Wanger changed the film's title from "The Rising Tide" to "Blockade" in early May.

Although Wanger's motives for making the film were mixed and its execution was hopelessly compromised, *Blockade* was by 1930s standards a courageous venture. It was the first to attempt a serious statement on the Spanish Civil War, and the major studios viewed it as a litmus test on the subject. MGM's *Idiot's Delight,* from Robert Sherwood's anti-Fascist play, was poised for production, but after seeing *Blockade*'s reception, the studio changed the locale from Switzerland to a fictional country. As Valleau has argued, *Blockade* is the only Hollywood film to question the purposes of the war at all.

As it turned out, *Blockade*'s mediocrity threatened to sink it into oblivion. Breen judged it "an ordinary spy story of a kind which has been done many times before." Virtually every review of the film agreed. *Variety*'s comments were typical: the film was "distinctive, different and provocative. But it misses any claims to greatness because it pulls its punches." Or as one of Wanger's old friends at the London *Daily Mail* put it, "I am very sorry to say that this film bored me. I cannot believe in any of the more successful film stars of Hollywood talking to me about the goodness of working in a field."

Wanger clearly saw *Blockade*'s shortcomings, though he could classify it as an instance of filming "a new idea fairly well." Years later, he recalled telling his publicity director Johnny Johnston in May, one month before the film's scheduled release, "All the way down the line it just misses, although the idea is good." Something had to be done. Johnston started the ball rolling. Shortly before the film's premiere, Johnston, with a daring that would have impressed Creel, created a false telegram to Wanger from friends in England, alleging that spies for Franco had infiltrated the Goldwyn studios to view and destroy *Blockade*. Wanger then sent a copy of the faked cable to Secretary of State Cordell Hull with a telegram full of outrage. Johnston then claimed that Franco had banned the film. "He was a marvel!" Wanger later said of Johnston. "Poor Franco had never seen the picture or heard of it."

Wanger took the ball from Johnston and ran with it. Shortly after the press reported the non-event, Wanger told journalists,

> This is simply another incident in a series, which proves that either Hollywood must assert itself or disappear as a producing center. . . . Not only do we meekly take intimidation from abroad, but we jump obediently when almost anybody in this country says "Frog." . . . It's ridiculous and I for one don't intend to continue. I'm going to release this Spanish picture, as is, and if it's banned in Europe I'll have to take my loss.

As Breen commented in midsummer, much of the controversy about *Blockade* was stirred up by "those exploiting the film."

The Catholic Church did the rest. The New York State Council of the Knights of Columbus, representing five hundred thousand members, called the film "a red trial balloon." They composed a public letter to Hays, citing his own statements that propaganda had "no place" in the movies and demanding that he impose a preface on the film which identified it clearly as "an incursion into the field of Leftist propaganda." The *Catholic News* depicted the film's pacifist sentiments as a "Trojan horse." Protest pamphlets in Flatbush, Brooklyn, claimed the lifting of embargoes implicitly proposed by the film would drag America into war, cited Communist party enthusiasm over the film, and called it "a typical Communist deceit." Wanger was delighted. Rosten recalls that he was "cynical about the true worth of *Blockade,* and laughingly told me the Catholic Church was picketing and organizing protest committees 'all for a mediocre picture.'" The protests spread nationwide.

Publicly, Wanger speciously replied to the Knights of Columbus protest that he was "shocked" that they had "read into" the film "a meaning never a part of its conception." He went on:

> I will admit there is a message in my picture. It is this American message, a message that has been verified by our Congress and by our President and every man and woman: that ruthless bombing of noncombatants, no matter which government does it, is something that is horrible and should not be tolerated. If that thought will "stir up prejudice, bad feeling and contention among many groups of people," then I am guilty.

Meanwhile, the New York Board of Education, the National Educational Association, the Greater New York Federation of Churches, the American Legion Auxiliary, and several other groups of goodwill supported the film and praised the pacifist sentiments of its final half hour.

The controversy neutralized local censors and exhibitors' squeamishness. *Blockade* was banned only in Somerville, Massachusetts. When the Knights of Columbus organized protests in Boston, Wanger, through Roger Baldwin of the American Civil Liberties Union, threatened a lawsuit and persuaded the mayor to allow the film to be shown. (In this effort Wanger also had the aid of celebrated Wall Street attorney Abraham Bienstock, who was counsel to William Paley and the Rothschilds and who became a lifelong friend of Wanger.) The protests tripled ticket sales at Loew's State and the Orpheum. On the other hand, the Fox–West Coast Theater chain refused to book it in first-run houses, and it was widely banned abroad. Wanger took a loss of $130,000.

In fact, the release and controversy over *Blockade* coincided with a crisis in Wanger's company, only two of whose seven films through early summer 1938 had shown a combined profit of $19,000. Although his high output lowered United Artists's distribution overhead and generated healthy fees, the Wanger company itself remained in considerable debt, owing $640,000 to United Artists, several hundred thousand dollars to Consolidated Laboratories for *Vogues of 1938* and *Stand-In* and to the Bank of America for his other films. Much of this debt came from his company's own enormous overhead, including salaries to stars Bennett ($30,000 a film), Boyer ($50,000), Carroll ($75,000), Fonda ($100,000), and Sidney ($240,000). Facing the 1938–1939 season, Wanger needed additional loans and was "very much discouraged."

United Artists, keen to keep Wanger afloat, offered in June to guarantee a $2 million revolving loan from the Bank of America to repay Wanger's debts to Consolidated Film Industries and to finance his upcoming season. Under this financing arrangement, Wanger was forced to concede ultimate control to the distributor. His class A common stock was placed in a voting trust as collateral for the new loans. He hired a new, highly efficient business manager, Clarence Erickson. His activities were now "subject at all times to the approval, control and direction of the board of directors of the Wanger Corporation." He had no choice.

Poor financial earnings were the main reason for the shift in control. Yet the controversy surrounding *Blockade* undoubtedly plays a large role. Giannini and other Bank of America executives were Catholic and almost certainly let their personal beliefs influence their dealings, even over the objections of a progressive United Artists founder such as Chaplin. Asked in 1939, after he left United Artists, about the need for PCA censorship and noncontroversial subject matter, Giannini told *Motion Picture Herald,* "The waters in which the ship of state is now sailing are too disturbed to take any chances." *Blockade*'s controversy only confirmed such wisdom; Wanger had abused his autonomy in undertaking an "offensive" project while still in debt.

United Artists flexed its new muscles immediately. In the spring of 1938, Wanger had assigned Lawson the perennial challenge of adapting Sheean's *Personal History,* and Lawson developed another conversion narrative, in which a callow, rebellious college student (like Wanger himself) is thrown out of school but manages to land a job covering the European conflicts. After reporting on the Spanish Civil War, he moves to Berlin with a new lover, only to find that her Jewish father, a Nobel Prize–winning scientist, is ostracized from the medical community (in a plot development similar to one Goldwyn contemplated for "Exiles"). Resistance work proves futile, and the hero returns home appreciative of democratic freedom.

Many years later, Lawson recalled that Wanger hired Dieterle to direct the film, which would begin production in late June, immediately after the release of *Blockade:*

> The cast was engaged and the sets were built, but two days before the start of production, Wanger called us into his office and announced that the whole thing must be abandoned. The bank had informed him that he would never receive another loan if he proceeded.

Wanger waited a year before commissioning Hitchcock to revive the project. Yet, for all his troubles, Wanger publicly emerged as Hollywood's most independent-minded producer.

As Wanger renegotiated his United Artists contract, the censorship issue quickly transcended *Blockade.* The trigger reaction of the Catholic organizations demonstrated that a reactionary segment of the audience wanted to influence film content. The furor made *Blockade*'s aesthetic flaws irrelevant, as angry film critics within and outside the trade rallied to Wanger's defense. *Time* noted that Wanger's film fell far short of his promised "polemic sensation that would jolt other producers' self-imposed silence on controversial subjects." But while noting *Blockade*'s poor quality, *Time*'s reviewer, like every other critic, excused it, noting that the producer "at least had the nerve to approach an explosive theme." Nugent told *New York Times* filmgoers that *Blockade* "is doing the most we can expect an American picture to do." In a Sunday think piece, he noted that perhaps audiences—and not the industry or the Hays Office—were responsible for Hollywood's neglect of "contemporary problems":

> Most of us have been urging Hollywood to descend occasionally from its cloud-tipped mountain peak, look at the world beneath and make some comment upon the contemporary scene. If every bold producer who does so is to be repaid by misinterpretation, threats and abuse, it is obvious that the road from the mountain will be closed for good.

Many Hollywood above-the-line talents (mostly actors, directors, and screenwriters) were equally vehement. In late July 1938, as the film faced protests around the country, Wanger chaired a meeting of more than 350 people at the Roosevelt Hotel to form the Conference on Freedom of the Screen, conceived to fight censorship action against films in general. Supported by members of the various guilds, the meeting had among its more prominent participants *Blockade*'s director, Dieterle, Herbert Biberman (a future Hollywood Ten blacklistee), Cromwell, and Hollywood's leading director, John Ford. Ford—himself a member of the Knights of Columbus who had just signed to direct *Stagecoach* for Wanger—spoke in protest of "any Nazi or fascistic movement designed to tell Americans what they may or may not see on the screen." Wanger echoed Ford's sentiments:

> Let me advise you with complete honesty that the issue is far greater than the success or failure of the film *Blockade*. . . . It is not *Blockade* they are fighting against but against the fact that if *Blockade* is a success, a flood of stronger films will appear and the films will not only talk but say something.

Such films, he argued, help "the distributor and exhibitor who is falling behind his public and thereby suffering financial loss . . . the time has come for Hollywood to strike back."

In leading Hollywood's anticensorship movement, Wanger became a national celebrity from the summer of 1938 onward. A Los Angeles theater scheduled a "revival cycle of Wanger hits" in July. Nearly a year later, Paramount rereleased *The President Vanishes* on a double-bill, and several reviewers noted how prophetic its vision of mass hysteria and conflicting ideologies was. In November 1938, the *Los Angeles Times* carried his article, "The Wherefore of Movie Ills," in which Wanger played upon growing anti-Fascist sentiment in the country, claiming that giving in to foreign censors was "like having Hitler in the White House." His comments were reprinted in major New York dailies, and he was introduced in the *New York Morning Telegram* as a filmmaker who wished "to make films with a definite point of view on vital social issues, to risk investments in such ventures," and who claimed that the free circulation of ideas was the lifeblood of a democratic nation. He personally made the case for message movies, arguing that Hollywood films promoted democratic and capitalist ideology better than any other mass medium:

> What is entertaining? Any expression of an idea is propaganda for one view point or another. I have never heard any outraged cries over our romantic films glorifying West Point and Annapolis, yet they are just as surely propaganda as films which might attack those institutions for being—which I do not believe they are—incubators for Fascism.

Wanger's rhetorical association of censorship with fascism allied him with progressive and radical activists in the film community who sought his allegiance. "I was very apprehensive about groups from the left," Rosten recalls. "They would try to corral people like Walter for money and support. *Blockade* became the center of their support for him. They tried to lionize him." Apotheosized in the Communist press and labeled as a Communist, Wanger reassured the readers of *Liberty* magazine in September 1938 that he was not a Communist nor a Syndicalist: "I believe in bigger, wetter swimming pools and more polo ponies." Although he allowed the text of his speech to the Committee on Freedom of the Screen to be published in the West Coast *Daily People's World,* Wanger declined to accept in person a "Movie Man of the Year" award from the New York Theater Arts Committee, a group his staff determined was "pink."

Wanger was less suspicious of Films for Democracy, an outgrowth of independent filmmaker and photographer Paul Strand's Frontier Films, which had since 1936 sought to make and distribute independent leftist documentaries. Films for Democracy's sponsors read like a who's who of New Deal internationalism: chaired by New York University dean Ned H. Dearborn, it included Rex Tugwell, Thurman Arnold and Harold Ickes, authors Thomas Mann, Theodore Dreiser, Sherwood Anderson, and Dashiell Hammett; Wanger joined because he was impressed with the list of "scholars and public figures whose judgment is universally respected."

The group's aim reflected a shift in leftist documentary thinking toward commercialization: its specific aim was to produce films for $100,000 or less, using Hollywood techniques to appeal to the broadest possible audience, and to persuade the studios to distribute them, or use local civic groups or trade unions to sponsor screenings. Hollywood members such as Lang and Nichols could in writer Ralph Pearson's words "compensate for their commercial shackles by doing something honest and constructive with their potentially great medium." By March of 1939, the group had raised money for two projected films by Strand on civil liberties (which would become 1942's *Native Land*).

But through the spring of 1939, Films for Democracy came under attack as a Communist front, and Hollywood liberals abandoned it. Wanger held out, taunting Quigley—who was an ardent supporter of the Production Code and whose publication, unlike *Variety* and the *Hollywood Reporter,* was addressed to exhibitors—about "reactionary" tactics. But in early April Wanger withdrew from the group and wrote a letter denouncing its "intellectual straddling" and its refusal to "make a public disavowal of possible Communist sympathies or compromise." Quigley, in a smug editorial in *Motion Picture Herald* entitled "Comes a Dim Dawn," saluted the renunciation of one who "did not know his art from his elbow in the beginning."

But as with his endorsement of Mussolini, Wanger continued his public career undaunted, pursuing the issue of anticensorship. He appeared in a *March of Time* segment presenting his case for free expression in movies. In a June 1939 speech to the American Library Association in San Francisco, Wanger claimed the movies were entitled to the same freedom of speech as the press and reiterated that movies were needed in the antitotalitarian fight. "Democracies, unwisely fearing the power of this medium, have not allowed it to speak for democratic principles," he noted. His "120,000 Ambassadors" (ghostwritten by screenwriter Grover Jones), an essay published in the December 1939 *Foreign Affairs* and widely syndicated, hissed with contempt for the industry's self-regulation and fears of special interest groups:

> So it is that the screen has become obsequious, full of inhibitions, afraid of offending anyone and everyone. It has catered to individuals, to groups, to associations, to politicians, to nations. "Be our friend," it has pleaded on every hand. "Help us keep destruction off our necks."

From January 1939, Wanger's often ghostwritten lectures transcended Hollywood issues as he became a prolific speaker amongst America's intelligentsia. On NBC's highbrow Blue network program "Town Hall of the Air" in February 1939, he could be found sitting beside theologian Reinhold Neibuhr and other Ivy League professors, holding forth on the benefits of radio and the movies for a program entitled, "Has 20th Century Civilization Improved Mankind?" In April he joined forces with Shotwell, his former superior in Paris, to participate in the American Union for Concerted Peace Efforts. In July, he joined in a "study of propaganda" at the Institute of Human Relations in Williamstown, Massachusetts, alongside sociologist Harold Lasswell. He wrote guest columns for syndicated writers Ed Sullivan and Walter Winchell. Everywhere you turned, you could see his byline. Directors and screenwriters were equally active, but no producer in the industry, with the possible exception of Goldwyn, was as visible. None were as openly concerned with using movies as a social force.

In February 1939, Wanger turned his anticensorship efforts on the Breen Office. Fresh from his visit to Dartmouth's Winter Carnival and aiming to publicize the forthcoming release of Ford's *Stagecoach,* Wanger held a small press conference at New York's Ritz Hotel. There he proclaimed that Hollywood should begin a "new era" that did not exclusively produce films that showed "success, money, the girl, happiness without end." Such films, Wanger argued, produced endless profits by catering to an outdated sense of security. Instead, Hollywood should make films that specifically dramatized democratic ideals to counter the propaganda machines of Europe's totalitarian governments. "I do not call this propaganda. I call this a necessary patriotic service."

But the Production Code was an obstacle to Wanger's new era:

> The Production Code functions very well in the case of escapist pictures, for which it was designed. But when it comes to the occasional picture which attempts to deal with actuality—with the problems that afflict our modern world—all is confusion. . . . Democracy depends upon the easy and prompt dissemination of ideas and opinions. The motion picture is potentially one of the greatest weapons for the safeguarding of democracy. But if it is hobbled and haltered—if it cannot speak truthfully and freely where great issues are involved—then it can be a weapon turned against democracy.

Since this was ostensibly a press conference to promote *Stagecoach,* it is hardly surprising that *Time* saw that film as an expression of Wanger's ideas. The circumstantial evidence was overwhelming: the town of Tonto's ugly, self-righteous Temperance League was Wanger's transposition of the Breen Office. But reporters and observers overlooked Wanger's own tepid qualifications to his views, for Wanger admitted the necessity of "pure entertainment," the "backbone of the industry." "For heaven's sake, don't think I believe that all Hollywood films should be in this classification," he had told the Committee for Freedom of the Screen, citing his sponsorship of *The Sheik* and *It* at Paramount in the 1920s. "I understand the escapist film pretty well," he continued. But most accounts of his ideas emphasized only his more controversial condemnation of the Production Code. Critics Nugent, Archer Winsten, Howard Barnes, and Virginia Wright applauded his statements, and Winsten noted, "The most encouraging thing that has happened thus far is that there are the beginnings of controversy among the Hollywoodians."

Syndicated and widely reported by journalists entirely sympathetic to his views, Wanger's remarks on this particular occasion initiated a storm of controversy within the industry. RKO president Schaefer, an enlightened former sales executive at United Artists who knew firsthand the consequences of Wanger's message mongering, publicly countered that propaganda had no place in the movie theater and that the code was just fine. If Wanger wanted to make propaganda films, Schaefer commented, he should rent a theater and show his films with his own money, not with his stockholders'.

Schaefer's position was fiercely applauded by *Box Office Digest* and echoed by Quigley's editorial in *Motion Picture Herald*, which denounced Wanger's speech as irresponsible and unrealistic. In March 1939 Quigley informally polled more than thirty industry executives and exhibitors. The results published in the March 4, 1939, issue indicated rather starkly the climate in which Wanger advanced his case; only two out of more than thirty replies agreed with Wanger.

Although the bulk of the respondents worked in the Midwest (Ohio, Indiana, Michigan, Minnesota, and North and South Dakota), the managers of theaters in more cosmopolitan locales such as Rhode Island, Miami, California, and Manhattan's Paramount Theater also spoke for harmless entertainment. Many exhibitors were hostile to big city culture and "the dizzy heights of Rockefeller Center." Others were clearly isolationist and anti–New Deal. Yet others made valid points about the consequences of message movies from Hollywood: that the exhibitor is "on the spot" when he shows the picture because his patrons assume he endorses it. From Atlanta came the warning that Wanger "and the other advocates of motion picture propaganda" would foment antitrust action against the majors. Among such views, the feelings of a Mrs. Ann Stone from Unity, Saskatchewan, that *Blockade* didn't "quite go far enough" in bringing "to the screen the horrors of the Spanish Civil War" sounded highly eccentric.

The few distribution and production executives who commented on the dispute—Herbert J. Yates of Republic and Barney Balaban of Paramount— firmly disagreed with Wanger. Indeed, Joseph Schenck of Twentieth Century– Fox wrote: "I cannot conceive that Walter Wanger is serious in accusing [Quigley] of a suppressive attitude or that he is even serious in raising the entire controversy." In this, Schenck echoed the sentiments of the Hays Office.

Wanger had written *Time* to protest that its favorable review of *Stagecoach* had exaggerated his anti–Breen Office rhetoric. Although *Time* did not publish his letter, Wanger made sure Breen knew about it. When Kenneth Clark, one of Hays's subordinates, checked Wanger's comments in the press during the February conference, he concluded that if Wanger's public commentary "isn't 'contempt' for the Code I don't know what the definition of contempt is." Clark speculated on Wanger's motives, articulating the inconsistencies of his position:

> Wanger may have meant what he said. On the other hand, he may have been talking with his tongue in his cheek to build up himself in the eyes of the reporters. I just don't know. . . .

> Mr. Wanger subscribes to the Production Code. He is a party to it. There-
> fore, when he criticizes the Code, he is really criticizing himself.

Inconsistencies never stopped Wanger from pressing his case. His public statements had the same quality of new ideas that were poorly thought through which informed his message movies. Nor did inconsistencies prevent the press from lauding Wanger. One publicity profile described him as "Hollywood's champion practical idealist, arch-foe of the cliche in screen entertainment, and talent gambler": "It was his rebellion at rote and rule producing that chiefly motivated his ambition to go on his own and let the chips fall where they may."

Independent articles about him were indistinguishable from his own publicity. A writer for the *Washington Post* called Wanger "one of the most intelligent and most courageous of Hollywood's movie producers" in September 1939 and listed several of his films as evidence of Wanger's ability to put his ideas into practice. A columnist for the *Hollywood Citizen News* the previous August wanted Wanger to "do the things for which he is famous, to shake his fists at tradition, to prophecy." He was "a sort of violent auxiliary to United Artists," who "has himself shown great courage in attempting to put adult ideas and current problems on the screen." He had not received such rave reviews since Dartmouth and Covent Garden.

Though rooted in Wanger's personal frustration with the constraints on production in the movies, his publicity campaign had the effect of differentiating his product, distinguishing his films from those of the competition. This was best illustrated in the September 1938 issue of *Liberty* magazine, which offered across a two-page spread a "debate" of articles by Wanger and Jack L. Warner under the title, "Is Hollywood on the Spot?" Warner's view was complacent: "Despite adverse economic conditions, Hollywood is doing nicely and is in no need of a major operation." Wanger took exactly the opposite position: noting that Hollywood was lacking in "courage" and producing "censored pap," he asked his readers rhetorically, "Where are the new distinctive films?" In the public eye, such statements made Wanger seem to buck the studio system, and his status as an independent producer only enhanced his grandeur. He seemed to be like Goldwyn, a man who functioned completely apart from corporate or financial constraint, a "lone wolf." One journalist called him "the most fearless producer working in Hollywood," whose "pugnaciousness" made him "an independent in every sense of the word."

Hence Wanger's triumphant emergence in Hollywood politics was a personal one. As one reporter noted, Wanger's name "has appeared over so many magazine articles on movies lately that one wonders how he finds time to make pictures." The fact was that Wanger wasn't making them. He had delegated an enormous amount of responsibility to associates and contracted talents. In part this was financial necessity. Wanger had cut his overhead continually since the financial difficulties of summer 1938, releasing stars under contract: *Blockade* was Fonda's last film for Wanger, and Boyer, Sidney, and Bennett soon followed. (Sidney's departure was the most dramatic—she refused to play the secondary gamine role of Ines to Hedy Lamarr in *Algiers*. After a "violent screaming match" and after Wanger sold *Wuthering Heights*—in which Sidney had hoped to play Cathy—to Goldwyn, Sidney broke her contract.) To the same end, he had offered Ford, Garnett, and March profit participation in *Stagecoach* and *Trade Winds* to cut his negative costs. Along with the financial interest, Wanger gave Ford and Garnett complete control over their films. With *Algiers,* these two films boosted the stock of several stars, enhanced Wanger's credibility when he spoke against censorship, and made enough money to cancel virtually all his production debts through the summer of 1939.

Algiers, the remake of the French film *Pepe Le Moko* starring Jean Gabin, concerned a Parisian master thief who holes up in the Casbah until the authorities use a gorgeous tourist to lure him out. The French film was being prepared for American release when Wanger saw it while searching for Boyer vehicles. He bought the distribution rights, and by January of 1938 he had a translation of the script for the Breen Office to reject (because of the "kept" women around the title character). Undeterred, Wanger hired James Cain to work on the opening twenty minutes of exposition and Lawson, after finishing work on *Blockade,* to soften the implications of Pepe's diverse relationships. (Contrary to Lawson's recollections, the *Algiers* assignment was not a result of *Blockade*'s censorship difficulties.) In a month's time, Lawson rearranged the order of several sequences to strengthen the causal relationship between Pepe's love for Gaby and his desire to return to Paris. Lawson also enlarged the role of the informer Regis into a humorously chatty but slimy villain whom actor Gene Lockhart portrayed with appropriate relish. Finally, Lawson revised the ending so that Pepe does not commit suicide but is shot by the police.

Because of Lawson's reworking of the script, the film was not exactly the "shot-for-shot" remake often alleged, but Toluboff recreated many of the French film's sets, and cameraman James Wong Howe mimicked its poetic realist style of soft-focus, low-key lighting that haunts Pepe within the Casbah. To direct, Wanger drafted the capable Cromwell, a former stage actor and triple-threat Paramount contractee of the 1920s, who had just guided Selznick's costume entertainment success *Prisoner of Zenda.* Cromwell took intact the "documentary" sequence of the Casbah in the opening scene and used large swatches of the French score. Boyer later recalled that Cromwell "would run a scene from the original and insist we do it exactly that way. . . . Terrible, a perfectly terrible way to work." But the slavish copying of Julien

Duvivier's film represented a savings in planning time and costs; one year later, it inspired Selznick to remake the Swedish version of *Intermezzo* for Ingrid Bergman's premiere in an American film.

Algiers was praised as "a certain hit" by every major trade publication and by many prominent popular press reviewers. *Variety* predicted its wide appeal—men would like its cops-and-robbers action, and women would like the romance. Nugent called it "clearly one of the most interesting and absorbing dramas of the season." What was apparent to reviewers was the fatalistic overtones of Pepe's existence; all-powerful within the Casbah, he was also bored and trapped there. Even Ferguson of *The New Republic,* who dismissed the bulk of Wanger's films as ridiculous tripe, admired it as "one of those naturals in pictures, having action, romance, strange places and predicaments, and the peg of character to hang it on."

Algiers was above all a triumph for the actors portraying these characters: Hedy Lamarr as Gaby and Boyer as Pepe le Moko. As with Lang two years earlier, MGM had contracted a foreign talent whom its executives could not quite place, this time because Lamarr could not speak a word of English. There was also the notoriety surrounding her nude and lovemaking scenes (shot when she was sixteen) in the forty-minute Czech film *Ecstasy,* which American states' rights distributors circulated just prior to her arrival in New York. When Wanger sized her up at a Hollywood party, he decided Lamarr would be suitable for the part of Ines, the gamine lover whom Pepe deserts for the Parisian Gaby, to be portrayed by Sidney. Lamarr's sultry glamour was instantly apparent in her screen test, and while Sidney broke her contract, *Algiers* made Lamarr a star.

Boyer's character Pepe, an extension of his role in *History Is Made at Night,* was a major success for him. Boyer later complained, "An actor never likes to copy another's style, and here I was copying Jean Gabin, one of the best." Yet, dressed all in black, moving with the tense poise of a professional dancer, Boyer seemed perfectly cast as the lithe, almost superhumanly competent Pepe who escapes the police force, commands absolute loyalty from his gang, and wins Gaby over. His banter with Inspector Slimane (Joseph Calleia) within a Casbah home, where the inspector makes no move to capture him (and in fact lights his cigarette), presented his astounding gentility: "Excuse us while we talk shop," Pepe apologizes to Gaby. Wanger and Cromwell's casting of first-rate character actors Calleia, Alan Hale, Leonid Kinsky, and Robert Greig only built up Boyer's glamour appeal.

Pepe was nothing less than Wanger's bid to make Boyer the Valentino of the 1930s, using a studio-fabricated North African setting to highlight his romantic allure. The film's foreword established the locale as the place "where blazing desert meets the blue Mediterranean and modern Europe jostles ancient Africa." In fact, Wanger planned to star Boyer in a later production of *Arabian Nights*. Within the exotic, labyrinthine, and treacherous Casbah,

Boyer embodied all the mystery and romance of Europe, and as Boyer later complained, the role defined the primary emphasis of his star image for the rest of his career. "Come with me to the Casbah," uttered with a French accent, became a commonplace of American popular culture, even though Boyer himself never spoke the line in the film: "I would say that one line, more than anything else has hampered my career." "Lamarr is beautiful," the *Hollywood Reporter* noted, "but it is Boyer who steals the show, and a Boyer who will sell plenty of tickets from this point on." Unfortunately, *Algiers* would be the last time Boyer sold tickets for a Wanger film.

Algiers was so impressive that several years later Warner Bros. executive Jerry Wald envisioned the unproduced play *Everybody Comes to Rick's* "along the lines of *Algiers*." Wallis renamed the property *Casablanca,* and tried to secure Lamarr to play Ilsa Lund. *Algiers* was a triumph of Wanger's showmanship instincts in casting and in the orientalist vein. By contrast, the adventure comedy *Trade Winds* was entirely a Garnett project, for which Wanger contributed only funds and leading actors. During a worldwide yachting trip after *Stand-In,* Garnett had shot extensive 16mm location footage and he was anxious to use it. He had the merest concept for the film when he broached the subject to Wanger, but Wanger jumped at the chance to replace the canceled Lawson-Dieterle "Personal History." Working with Parker and Campbell, Garnett developed a rambling story about another victim of circumstance. This time a beautiful suspected murderess (Bennett) is chased around the world by a detective (March), who in turn is trying to shake his ex-girlfriend (Ann Sheridan) and an incompetent associate (Ralph Bellamy). Garnett later boasted that nearly 80 percent of the film was shot with process work, and although the film was plied with ridiculous running gags (such as Bellamy's constant insistence, even when sitting with Bennett, that the suspect has fled to Australia), it proved a winner.

Like *Algiers* and Lamarr, *Trade Winds* was a watershed film for Wanger's contracted star Bennett. Since playing Sally in *Private Worlds,* Bennett had not fared well under Wanger's aegis; most of her best roles and appearances were on loan-outs. Wanger still cast her as a sweet blonde, and her subdued talents and appeal were obscured by her more aggressive, shrewd, and flamboyant older sister Constance, who married royalty and negotiated enormous salaries for herself. *I Met My Love Again,* a romantic melodrama focusing on the long-standing affection of a small-town girl and her college professor boyfriend, was calculated by Wanger as a "woman's picture" in which "love triumphs over all." Scripted and directed by Logan and Ripley, the film made hip references to Freud and strained efforts to portray mad Parisian bohemia (Bennett runs off with Alan Marshall, a dashing painter, who works with ketchup and meat sauce for his palette). The result was "a hapless and witless yarn . . . slipshod and saccharine." Bennett, as the small-town girl who doesn't know what she wants, is extremely sweet and likable, but the entire production is a waste of time. *Vogues of 1938* was mounted in Technicolor and featured Bennett as a gorgeous fashion plate for stylish gowns, but its translation of the backstage musical into the world of clothing design houses was a bore.

Occasionally, Wanger did experiment with expanding Bennett's range, however. Her performance as Grant's wisecracking, loyal girlfriend in Walsh's *Big Brown Eyes,* like her appearance in Walsh's *For Me and My Gal* (1932), provided strong evidence of her comic talents, and in Wanger's film she struck *Time*'s reviewer as "virtually indistinguishable from Carole Lombard." Her innocent victim role in *Trade Winds* likewise had considerable vitality and the added shock of her complete change of look. Motivated by her need for disguise from the pursuing police, Bennett's character dyed her hair brunette before fleeing the United States. Her consequent resemblance to Lamarr transformed Bennett from an ingenue to a femme fatale: "After *Trade Winds* where I went from blonde to brunette, my roles got much, much better," Bennett later recalled. "I wasn't the simpering blonde anymore."

In late 1938, Bennett was a final-round contestant for the role of Scarlett O'Hara in Selznick's *Gone with the Wind*. In 1940, Wanger consoled her by casting her in *The House Across the Bay* as the enterprising wife of gangster George Raft. Performing songs and wearing an array of costumes in low-key, moody photography by Merritt Gerstad, Bennett's appearance here and as the empathetic, intelligent Coco in Twentieth Century–Fox's Nazi gothic thriller *The Man I Married* anticipated her transition into the leading ranks of film noir actresses in the 1940s. The shift was completed in Lang's *Man Hunt* (1941), which, like *House Across the Bay*, paired Bennett with Walter Pidgeon.

Not all of Wanger's stars fared so well in his 1930s films. In *Case Against Mrs. Ames* and *Blockade,* Carroll simply performed in a mold and with a persona that she had previously offered in Hitchcock's *The 39 Steps;* Lawson recalled that her limited emotional range frustrated both him and Dieterle during the making of *Blockade*. After leaving Wanger in 1938, she gradually withdrew from performing in film, marrying Sterling Hayden in the 1940s and retiring to private life. By contrast, Fonda, Wanger's first contractee, developed into a major star even though Eddie Taylor remained the only quality role Wanger gave him. His breakthrough came with Warner Bros.' *Jezebel,* and after free-lancing at Fox for *Young Mr. Lincoln* and *Drums Along the Mohawk,* Zanuck signed Fonda to a contract with *The Grapes of Wrath*. Indeed, it was Ford who made Fonda a major star in those three films.

Ford also directed and effectively produced Wanger's third success of 1938–1939 and one of the greatest films Wanger was associated with, *Stagecoach*. As is well known, in April 1936, Ford purchased for a mere $7,500 the rights to Ernest Haycox's "Stage to Lordsburg," a sketchy, subtle short story published in *Colliers*. Producer-director Cooper, best known for *King*

Kong (1933) and his 1920s documentaries *Grass* and *Chang,* had signed Ford to a two-picture contract for Pioneer Pictures. He was willing to let Ford cast the film with Trevor and "B" movie western star Wayne, a personal friend of Ford since the mid-twenties when Wayne was pre-law at USC.

Selznick International inherited Pioneer Pictures and its Technicolor contracts, and sometime in late June 1937, Cooper and Ford presented the package to Selznick. When Selznick insisted on Gary Cooper and Dietrich in the leading roles, the two men quit. Selznick, like Zanuck and Joseph Kennedy at RKO, believed that westerns were the exclusive province of the low-budget studios. The last western to win major acclaim was *Cimarron* (1931), not Warner Bros.'s *Wells Fargo* (1937), and even Ford had not directed a western since 1926. Ford proceeded to work on *Hurricane* for Goldwyn and *Four Men and a Prayer* and *Submarine Patrol* for Twentieth Century–Fox.

When Ford approached him with the property in the summer of 1938, Wanger again took on a project none of his counterparts wanted. Like Ford, he had a long memory—back to the enormous success of *The Covered Wagon* and Ford's 1924 *The Iron Horse*—and a firm belief in recurring film cycles. After struggling through the *Blockade* controversies of the summer of 1938, he was ready to leaven his schedule with quality entertainment. Upon the film's release, he told United Artists publicity director Lynn Farnol:

> I read the story—but after Ford had purchased it and brought it to me. Again, it was Ford who worked with Dudley Nichols in creating a fine script; and John Wayne as the Ringo Kid was also Ford's idea. . . . While I am proud to be the producer of *Stagecoach,* will you please do everything in your power to see that the picture is known as John Ford's achievement.

Although Wanger placed its cost at $1 million when his publicity announced the deal in mid-July 1938, Wanger was pleased by Ford's subsequent estimates that the film would cost less than $500,000.

Ford confirmed Wanger's role before his death:

> I shopped around with ["Stage to Lordsburg"] and got no place. I went to Wanger and gave him the story and he didn't even read it, he said "Go ahead and do it." . . . He said "Who have you got for a writer?" And I said "Dudley Nichols." And he said "Knock it out, let's do it."

One of Ford's favorite collaborators, Nichols was an erudite and diligent freelance ex-journalist who had made his reputation covering the Sacco and Vanzetti trial for the *New York World.* Here again, Wanger allowed Ford free reign, even though Ford's films of Nichols's scripts—*Men Without Women* (1930), *The Lost Patrol* (1934), *The Plough and the Stars* (1936), *Mary of Scotland* (1937)—were not strong box office.

In early October, the Breen Office rejected Ford and Nichols's treatment in toto because of its sympathetic portrayal of Dallas, Doc Boone's constant inebriation, the Ringo Kid's climactic revenge on the three Plummer brothers, and the marshall's assistance in helping him kill the Plummers and escape. Nichols's first draft script, completed by the third week of October, followed Geoffrey Shurlock's suggestion that no "specific references" to Dallas's prostitution be uttered; it further justified both Ringo's shootout and the marshall's assistance by establishing the villainous Luke Plummer's murderous past.

The first draft also involved major departures from Haycox's story. This had the major dramatic situation of a cross-section of society traveling through unsettled territory in the Southwest during an Indian uprising in the mid-1880s, a premise critics have compared to von Sternberg's *Shanghai Express* and which Nichols himself compared to *Grand Hotel*. Haycox had sketched out the main romantic couple (a genial outlaw with "wildness" in his eyes and a compassionate prostitute), a woman joining her fiancé in the army, a gambler, and the whiskey salesman. His story briefly noted the unjust social prejudices of the characters and the quietly heroic deeds of the prostitute.

The heart of the script lay with the fallen creatures, who prove morally superior to their social betters. Hatfield (John Carradine), the former Confederate gentleman, was identified as a dissolute murderous gambler whose protection of Lucy Mallory (Louise Platt) provides a moral victory at his death. Dallas and the Ringo Kid were given parallel backgrounds as loners whose families were destroyed by evil Indians and white men. Most crucially of all, they created, inspired perhaps by Nichols's own drinking bouts, the memorable Doc Boone, the erudite alcoholic who, with the prostitute Dallas, is ousted by the Temperance League in Tonto during the expositional scenes Ford and Nichols added.

During principal photography, from October 31 to December 23, Ford—inspired in part by the silent looks Haycox described among the different characters during the journey—deftly whittled Nichols's script down to what he and Nichols proudly told The *New York Times* was an "unusual economy of dialogue." He also added some of the most amusing scenes in the film, such as Boone's classic line after challenging Luke Plummer in the Lordsburg bar, "Don't ever let me do that again," and his final exchange with the marshall about saving Dallas and Ringo from "the blessings of civilization" and having "just one" drink together.

"If there was ever a picture that was the director's picture," Nichols wrote Ford upon the film's release, "it was that one, and I tried to make that clear to everyone who complimented me in New York." Though Nichols's script was full of careful directions, it was Ford's crew that captured them. Bert Glennon's cinematography ranged from the stunning landscapes of Monument Valley in Arizona to the deep-focus compositions that framed characters down long hallways and in multiple planes, as in the celebrated Dry Forks scene where the passengers debate continuing their trip. Combining chiaroscuro lighting with Toluboff's uncomplicated set designs—as when Dallas waits in the gully by the Lordsburg whorehouse after Ringo leaves her to confront the Plummers—Ford created scenes and gestures that sensitively conveyed character psychology through visuals alone.

Ford's casting was impeccable. From Wanger he took only one suggestion. Platt first appeared in Wanger's *I Met My Love Again* as Bennett's rival for Fonda; here, her refined features, not unlike those of Bergman, made her perfectly appropriate for the strong, restrained Lucy. Like Tim Holt, who played the cavalry officer, Platt was briefly a Wanger contractee. For Gatewood, Ford originally considered Hale, who played Grandpere in *Algiers,* but he settled on Berton Churchill, who had appeared in several earlier Ford films and played a similar role in 1934's *Frontier Marshall.* The choice of Wayne was a tremendous risk that paid off. Wayne was then a star at the lowly Republic Studios, although the *New York Times* reported the studio's loan-out "demands" were so exacting that "Wanger swears he was under the impression he was borrowing Garbo." And from Mitchell (repeating a role in Ford's earlier *Hurricane,* 1937) to Ford's older brother Francis (as Boone's friend Billy Pickett), the cast was paid a pittance—at $15,000 Trevor was the highest-earning performer—totaling $80,000. Ford shot the film in just four days more than its thirty-three-day schedule for under $550,000.

Wayne recalled that the largely UCLA student audience attending a February 1939 preview of *Stagecoach* in Westwood "yelled and screamed and stood up and cheered. I never saw anything like it." Once Ford eliminated a musical sequence (of the passengers singing "Ten Thousand Cattle Gone Astray"), the critics agreed with them. *Stagecoach* received the highest and most unanimous praise of any film Wanger had produced thus far. Mitchell and the film's composers won Academy Awards for their work. Although obscured by *Gone with the Wind*'s award sweep, the film itself, Ford's direction, Toluboff's art direction, Glennon's cinematography, and Otho Lovering, Dorothy Spencer, and Walter Reynolds's editing all received nominations, and Ford received the New York Film Critics' best director award.

As Joseph McBride and Michael Wilmington have noted, the film's success was ironic, since "a film which exalts outcasts over the members of 'respectable' society made the Western respectable." Although *Stagecoach* is often credited with reviving the "A"-scale western, the genre was not completely ignored during the thirties, and major studios such as Warner Bros. and Fox already had westerns—*The Oklahoma Kid* with Cagney, *Dodge City* with Errol Flynn, and *Jesse James* with Tyronne Power—in production when *Stagecoach* premiered. But Ford's film proved the most popular and made a major contribution to the longevity of the genre, which continues intermittently through the present day.

Although the plight of the outcasts in *Stagecoach* resembles that of Eddie Taylor in *You Only Live Once* and even though Wanger applauded the satiric depiction of an anti–New Deal banker who grumbles about government regulation, there was virtually nothing of Wanger in this film; "In fact," John Ford later recalled, Wanger "was away most of the time we were doing *Stagecoach*." But he gave Ford the opportunity to make a "pet project."

He was amply rewarded. *Stagecoach* grossed nearly a million dollars by the end of 1939, providing the largest profits of any Wanger production, nearly $300,000. (Ford collected a 20 percent profit interest of nearly $60,000 on top of his $50,000 salary.) Adding this to the profits on *Algiers* and *Trade Winds,* Wanger's general manager reported in July that the net worth of the Wanger company was $1,440,000, boasting "we now have our capital practically intact again" (i.e., the nearly $1,500,000 initial capitalization of the corporation). Wanger summarized the status of his company by noting "if things continue as they are we should be able to clean up our dividends within a year or so." While United Artists retained a three-two majority on his board, his class A stock was taken out of the voting trust that October, and Wanger secured $8 million in loans from the Bank of America for thirteen more films. Wanger's enlightened policy of letting directors control their films had finally paid off.

Wanger's financial recovery paralleled his personal standing in Hollywood, which reached new heights. "More than a year and a half ago, Walter Wanger started talking Americanism for the screen," Hedda Hopper wrote in June 1939. "Some of our biggies thought he'd gone off the deep end. . . . Now you'll notice they've all gone on his bandwagon." Not all the executives agreed with him. But the press response to his statements and his publicity blitz made him Hollywood's most distinguished representative to the nation.

As the crisis in Europe deepened, Wanger was a harbinger of the industry's internationalism, its gradual move from the silent neutrality out of which he produced *Blockade.* In the fall of 1939, he was elected to the post of Academy president. This was largely a figurehead position, but one that had intangible value for the industry's image in the public mind and which allowed Wanger to articulate Hollywood's highest social aspirations. In February of 1940 he spoke of his mandate to encourage topicality: "the screen is the greatest single social influence, expanding as well as interpreting the American way of living for the whole world. . . . The Academy should and will attempt to present to the world their ideas and ideals with frankness and authority."

In the late 1930s, America and Hollywood increasingly approximated Wanger's ideal of a socially and internationally conscious community. Yet the problems attending his efforts to exploit the shift in public mood grew insurmountable in the early 1940s.

10

Having It All (1939–1941)

Wanger's public glory was completely divorced from his troubled private life. After her London triumphs and performance in *Hush Money* on Broadway in 1926, Johnston decided to abandon her show business career. "I could easily have gone on," she told the *Boston Herald* in 1940, "but suddenly, even more than being a Follies girl, I wanted to be a high school graduate. . . . Beauty without brains buys little happiness or material advantage." While in London, she visited several medical clinics. Back in New York, she began working as a laboratory assistant at the College of Physicians and Surgeons. Under doctors Hirshfeld and Hyman, she participated in the five-day cure for syphillis and in the development of "slow drip" intravenous injections to avoid oxygen bubbles in the bloodstream; in the late 1930s, she devoted her energies to cancer research.

After moving to Los Angeles, she and Wanger grew increasingly alienated. She intensely disliked Hollywood's impoverished culture and parochial social circles. Friends found her warm but reserved. Wanger's extramarital affairs did not help. By 1938, their marriage was in name only, and they agreed that Johnston should sue Wanger for divorce on the grounds of "mental cruelty" to ensure the desired outcome. "When he had dinner engagements he would purposely be late and then he would not join us but just come in, stare at us and go away," Johnston told the court, claiming that he traveled so much, she knew of his whereabouts only from reading newspapers. Wanger agreed to pay several thousand dollars in alimony, and they maintained amicable relations for the rest of their lives.

The year Wanger and Johnston split up, Bennett divorced Twentieth Century–Fox producer and writer Gene Markey, her second husband and the father of her second daughter Melinda. In the twenties Wanger had teased Bennett when he gave her a screen test at Astoria, but he began paying special attention to her during the filming of *Private Worlds:* "It was Claudette Colbert who first enlightened me and told me that Walter never came on the set when I wasn't working," she later recalled. For the rest of the decade, Wanger frequently flew across the country to attend her stage performances. Their relationship had been well noted by gossip columnists since the production of *Vogues of 1938,* which was Wanger's attempt both to emulate *The Goldwyn Follies* and to pay tribute to Bennett's beauty. Late in the night of January 11, 1940, the two were talking on the phone when Wanger suddenly proposed. The following day they took a train to Phoenix with Bennett's friend, publicist (and Louella Parsons's cousin) Margaret Ettinger, and were married by a justice of the peace. Bennett later told her eldest daughter Diana that Wanger "was a hard one to land." Wanger announced the marriage to far-flung friends with a military metaphor: "Impossible to withhold any longer, front lines gave way completely." They made headlines around the country.

Wanger enjoyed Bennett's dry, sardonic sense of humor, and her ability to tell stories on herself. Her shortsightedness was one source of humor. Actress Jane Greer recalls that

> Joan had a system with Walter when they were at dinner parties. He would give her a signal across the table if she made a faux pas. One time when they were out, she started to butter a dinner roll on her plate. She picked it up, looked over at Walter, and he gave her this signal. She looked down and thought to herself, "What have I done?" She looked at her plate. She looked at the silverware. She couldn't figure it out. So she picked up the roll again and finished buttering it. She took a bite. It was a little hamburger.

Casual acquaintances considered her cold and unfeeling, but as Greer points out, "She was blind. She couldn't see across the room. She couldn't see halfway across the room. She couldn't even see two feet away. That's why she didn't say hello to people. She didn't know who was there."

But with her glasses on, Bennett knew how to run a household, especially after her struggles in the twenties as a divorced eighteen-year-old mother. Wanger admired the way she quietly managed the fifteen-room French provincial home she commissioned Wallis Neff to design in Holmby Hills in the late 1930s. She firmly and attentively raised all her daughters to be gracious and poised, and Bennett herself was, in Greer's words, "always stunning. Around her you always felt as if you had a hem sticking out or something." There was also a strong physical attraction: as Wanger once put it, "No one had ever appealed to me the way she did."

They were well matched in many other respects. Wanger was the crusader, the outspoken, opinionated industry leader; sixteen years her elder, he in some ways resembled her loquacious father, the celebrated Richard Bennett, who harangued unappreciative audiences from the stage on the art of the theater. Where Wanger bubbled with excitement over projects and people, Joan Bennett was reserved and cool, hard to impress. Stephanie recalls,

> My father adored that about her. My father always said my mother had no pretenses. If she met the King and Queen of England, well, fine, they were the King and Queen of England. Nobody impressed her. He always loved that about her, because he was impressed with people. He'd meet a great writer and say, "Oh, Lawrence Durrell. wow, wow, wow!" But my mother would say, "So what?"

He, being a creature of habit, liked to get up around six in the morning and go to bed around ten after a quiet evening at home. She preferred to go to Hollywood parties, stay up late reading, and sleep late the next morning. Yet they shared a consuming interest in the film business and spent many hours critiquing movies and plays, discussing the new and exciting talents, and making plans together. "When they first married," Guest reflects, "they had it all really. He was President of the Academy, she was beautiful, he was successful, she knew how to throw dinner parties. I think she had a wonderful time." Not taking Hollywood too seriously, they were one of its most glamorous and dignified couples.

Forty-six years old when they married, Wanger grew more calm and sedate. During countless dinner parties, Hornblow found him thoughtful and focused, where most Hollywood party-goers engaged in social chitchat. Together, Wanger and Bennett lived in what Bennett later described as "something of a rarefied air, often among people who were fascinating, accomplished, and vitally involved in the world around them," such as Carl Sandburg, Wendell Willkie, the Roosevelts, and the Trumans. Though Wanger told Bennett he did not want children of his own, he was thrilled when Stephanie was born in September 1943 and Shelley in July 1948.

The Bennett-Wanger marriage came in the midst of another busy year for the producer. United Artists needed films desperately because its other producers had proven dilatory in completing their projects. The majors were slowing down their production schedules in response to government threats of theater divorcement and to the closing of foreign markets as Hitler marched across Europe. But United Artists had no films at all to distribute from May to July. Murray Silverstone, the company's new president, inaugurated a system of reduced distribution fees to reward its independents with high grosses.

Emboldened by his recent successes and public prominence, and no doubt by Selznick's *Gone with the Wind*, Wanger in the fall of 1939 told the United Artists board of directors, in the words of one observer, that "he was being strangled, was being held down in his contracts, expenditures, and so forth, and wanted more freedom." He had a sympathetic listener in Pickford, and Silverstone proposed an informal arrangement for Wanger. If he would produce several "small" films to fill out the company's schedule, the distributor would give him special consideration, and allow him to proceed on a new version of *Personal History* without board interference.

Indifferent films such as *Winter Carnival* (1939) and *Slightly Honorable* (1940) were Wanger's attempts to cooperate, costing just over $400,000 each. *Slightly Honorable,* the last of his Garnett productions, was a buddy film in which O'Brien and Crawford are framed for murder by a corrupt financier who "kept" the murder victim, O'Brien's old flame. The comedy revealed Garnett's predilection for tiresome running gags, as a naive, squeaky-voiced chanteuse constantly undresses in O'Brien's presence.

Winter Carnival was even less distinguished. Campus movies were a staple of major studio schedules (especially Paramount); there were anywhere between six and thirteen of them every year since 1934, including Wanger's *I Met My Love Again.* Wanger's decision to make a new film at Dartmouth was another publicity move, since no reviewer failed to connect the film with the fact of his attendance there. But it was also part of Wanger's campaign to earn an honorary doctorate from his alma mater, which had begun with his frequent visits to the campus in the twenties and continued through his creation of the Irving G. Thalberg script library.

Partly for this reason as well, Wanger hired and exploited Fitzgerald to work on the screenplay in what became, in Malcolm Cowley's words, Fitzgerald's "biggest, saddest, most desperate spree." The subject was hardly appropriate for Fitzgerald's talents. Since 1910, the Winter Carnival had grown from an inter-class ski meet to a sprawling event with dances, theatrical productions, and visits from nearby womens' colleges. Wanger wanted very much to make his film what he called "an innocent and non–Joe College picture." He also wanted it written by someone with an intimate familiarity with the campus. To this end, he hired Budd Schulberg (the son of his former rival Ben Schulberg), who was a twenty-five-year-old Dartmouth alumnus and a sometime Selznick employee. Schulberg began work in the spring of 1938, advised by Wanger in his words "to try to break away from the cycle of college movies which has depicted higher education as nothing but the necessary background for sophomoric horseplay and last-second victories." By the time of the 1938 carnival, Schulberg still didn't have a story with a "mature romance" that Wanger insisted on. That was where Fitzgerald came in.

The legendary forty-year-old author had come to Hollywood in August 1937 on a six-month contract at MGM, where he bounced between assignments: *A Yank at Oxford,* Borzage's *Three Comrades* (produced and rewritten by producer Mankiewicz), as well as *The Women* and *Madame Curie.* Fitzgerald was never very comfortable with the producers' dominance at the studio, and left it to work for several weeks on Selznick's *Gone with the Wind.* When agent H. N. Swanson contacted Wanger with promises that the writer was on the wagon, Wanger offered $1,500, Fitzgerald's highest weekly salary yet.

Wanger dramatically introduced Schulberg to Fitzgerald after querying the young writer about his knowledge of Fitzgerald's work. "My God, I thought Scott Fitzgerald was dead," Schulberg recalls saying to Wanger. "Not unless your script bored him to death," Wanger quipped. "He's in the next room reading it now."

Schulberg fictionalized the doomed saga of the writing of *Winter Carnival* in his 1951 novel *The Disenchanted.* There, as well as in interviews and an essay, he has recounted the pleasure of meeting and knowing Fitzgerald and the terrible experience the project was for them both, due largely to Wanger's deployment of the prestigious writer to impress the Dartmouth faculty and administration. As Schulberg put it, Fitzgerald at this point in his life was "a kind of dilapidated Model-A roadster, once as shiny and jazzy as they came but now neglected and condemned by public apathy to the used-car lots." Wanger by contrast was at the apex of his career; the trip to Dartmouth came in early 1939 as his public reputation was gathering steam and just prior to his attack on the Breen Office.

Against the ailing Fitzgerald's protests of ill health, Wanger insisted that the two men accompany him to Hanover to freshen their memories of campus life and to suggest background footage for a second unit to shoot. As Schulberg put it, for Dartmouth dropout Wanger, "even a déclassé Scott Fitzgerald would be a calling card on Dartmouth College academicians." Wanger paid for a party sponsored by the English department to show off his literary prize. "I went to that party," recalls Maurice Rapf, Schulberg's childhood friend and Dartmouth classmate. "I saw Fitzgerald in that drunken state, and it was pretty sad, although later that evening he seemed better."

From champagne on the flight east to Fitzgerald's flu and days-long binge in Hanover with Schulberg, no actual writing came out of the project: the premise was entirely uninspiring, and the two writers were too busy discussing contemporary literature, politics, Hollywood, and Wanger ("Ivy on one side, California palm on the other," Fitzgerald reportedly called him). After several embarrassing episodes, including Wanger hauling Fitzgerald out to watch a ski-jumping contest, Wanger came across the two writers later on the steps of the Hanover Inn and fired Fitzgerald.

But Wanger needed a script by April 1, when Warner Bros. star Sheridan and Selznick contractee Richard Carlson were to come to him on loan-out. At Wanger's cajoling, Rapf replaced Fitzgerald, cutting short his prospective honeymoon in Europe to complete a first draft on the cross-country train back to Hollywood. The story line he and Schulberg developed concerned a quintessentially glamorous and wealthy romantic comedy heroine like those of *Shanghai* and *The Moon's Our Home,* in flight from her European husband. She is stranded at the college on her way to Canada and competes with her younger sister, who comes to the carnival unescorted from a nearby women's college.

"My experience with Wanger," Rapf comments, "was that he really wasn't much interested in what was on the pages, as long as they came back" completed. But neither he nor his young writers were pleased with the resulting script. By mid-March, Wanger needed an experienced, quick writer "to pull the thing together so they could shoot it. To hell with it. He lost all interest in making it better at that point." Wanger became desperate and even more imperious than he had been with Fitzgerald. He dismissed Rapf, and when Schulberg threatened to quit in protest, Wanger warned him that he'd never work in Hollywood again. Schulberg remained to work with the future Hollywood Ten member Lester Cole. The result, directed by Charles Reisner, was a mix of cynical newspaper characters and a reasonable, if formulaic love story, with extensive footage of ski jump races and ice sculpture contests photographed long before a storyline existed.

The critical reception of the film was unanimous. The film was tedious, "merely something to be forgotten" as the *Hollywood Reporter* titled its review. The trade paper noted that the film "looks as if it was written, directed, acted and produced by the students of that school, because it has about that much intelligence." Rapf recalls that he couldn't find work for four months after its preview because of his story credit. The film also provided Ferguson with an occasion to let loose a stream of invective against the producer:

> It probably would never have seen the darkness of a New York movie [*sic*] at all if it hadn't been made by Walter Wanger, who has promoted an A.B. degree into one of the fanciest shell games even this industry has seen. With the businessman-gambler sense of any producer, he flushes enough money to get a picture ready for distribution; then he calls in a few ex-legmen and says for release, "Boys, I can't help it if I'm a courageous rebel: I went to *college*! Well it may sound funny but it certainly gets him around . . . the rest of us can either stay away or go and snicker at the joke that was played on so many people the day Walter Wanger got off the train at Hanover.

It was the first Wanger film to receive a critical lambasting tinged with *ad hominem* insults. It was hardly the last.

Wanger's faltering productions were accompanied by his realization that United Artists could not deliver its part of the bargain he had struck with Silverstone. In previous years, smarting from the poor showing of *You Only Live Once* and his musicals, Wanger had argued that the industry should rethink its market and aim its productions at specific audience segments. "Production has been revolutionized since nickelodeon days," he told the *New York Times* in mid-1940, "but there has been practically no change in the method of distributing and exploiting pictures. Pictures are often rushed into and out of theatres before the public has a chance to catch up with them." He suggested to a reporter in Wilkes-Barre, Pennsylvania, that Hollywood "should campaign for certain audiences just as the Buick company, the Cadillac company or the Ford company do for certain purchasers." Producers could thereby attract segments of the audience in smaller theaters rather than try to reach the entire nation in first-run houses. In this, he anticipated the studios post–World War II marketing strategies.

Yet, after his successful 1938–1939 season, Wanger discovered that his problem lay closer to home—at United Artists. Like Selznick and Korda, he felt the distributor, while charging him a 30 percent distribution fee, simply lacked the negotiating power to get the best play dates and rental income for his releases, regardless of their quality. Publicity director Farnol rated *Eternally Yours* Wanger's best film yet and the distributor's strongest attraction for the 1939–1940 season, yet the film represented a $200,000 loss. *Slightly Honorable* had cost him $435,000, but it never got a first-run showing in Manhattan and the Fox West Coast chain booked it only as the bottom half of a double feature (it was therefore distributed on a flat rental basis).

United Artists's inability to book his films into first runs meant that none of the circuits and subsequent runs would pay well for them thereafter. "The very fact that they gave [*Slightly Honorable*] a general release without a New York showing gave the picture a black eye with the trade." The film lost $100,000. As Wanger generalized:

> Because of the United Artists sales set-up, and the fact that they have no circuit of theatres, they cannot demand their prices from the exhibitors and not give them leading attractions. Pictures that Metro, Fox and Paramount would be grateful for, because of their many theatres, cannot show a profit with United Artists distribution.

In early September 1940, the distributor admitted that it was having "trouble" obtaining "satisfactory terms, playing time and theaters" for films produced by Wanger, Edward Small, and Hal Roach. While helping United Artists keep down its overhead with over $3.5 million in distribution fees, Wanger was heading deeper into insolvency.

In early 1940, with foreign markets closing off, the solution appeared to be fewer and better films that could earn large revenues from the domestic audience. For Wanger this meant hiring first-rate talents such as Ford, something his budgets at United Artists allowed him to do. He purchased *So Gallantly Gleaming,* a biography of Jesse Fremont (the wife of one of California's first governors), and *Dynasty of Death,* Taylor Caldwell's novel on the munitions industry. Wanger planned to make both films "big, outstanding pictures and with complete scripts they will create the desire of important directors and artists to work on them." In Wanger's mind, this was "our only salvation as an independent producing unit."

Fortunately, Wanger already had a big production in the works, *Personal History.* After the Bank of America had halted its production in the summer of 1938, Wanger had bided his time. Within a year, American sentiment turned increasingly against the Germans and his company was solvent. By the late summer of 1939, Warner Bros. had released its fast-paced, headline-ridden *Confessions of a Nazi Spy,* what Bernard Dick has called the "first overtly anti-Nazi film," and was about to premiere *Espionage Agent,* while Chaplin had begun work on *The Great Dictator* eight months earlier. Now Wanger had in progress a script of "Personal History" by MGM writer John Lee Mahin. After Germany invaded Poland on September 1, Wanger thought of the project in terms of a quickly made exploitation thriller like *The President Vanishes* and announced on September 3, the same day England declared war on Germany, that he would produce an updated version of Sheean's book to star Boyer and Colbert for November release. His script costs since Milestone first tackled the project in August 1936 had reached an astonishing $140,000.

Shortly after the news from Europe, Wanger approached Selznick about loaning out Hitchcock, whom Selznick had brought over from England. Selznick was willing to loan out his prize director, for he sought additional income for his company while *Gone with the Wind* neared its premiere. Selznick told Wanger that if Hitchcock liked Wanger's project, he could have him after the director completed *Rebecca.* Hitchcock and Wanger lunched together on September 21, and found themselves in good company. They enjoyed each other's boisterous sense of humor. Hitchcock, who felt guilty about sitting out England's entry into the war and was hoping for a project that would justify his presence in Hollywood, appreciated Wanger's desire to make a film about the European conflict.

Wanger was equally eager to have Hitchcock on board. He agreed to Selznick's demand for Hitchcock's $60,000 in advance, plus a payment to the producer of 3 percent of Hitchcock's salary. Hitchcock reported to Wanger on November 26. Since Hitchcock found Mahin's script unshootable, by mid-December, the director discarded it. With Wanger's approval, he set to work on a completely new version for which he hired Charles Bennett, his collaborator on *The 39 Steps, Secret Agent, Sabotage,* and *The Man Who Knew Too Much.*

As Bennett later put it, Sheean's book had "nothing to write a story about," and to Wanger's mind, the writers were on their own. "Hitch was a great idea man," Bennett observed,

> but as regards Walter, well, he had nothing to do with it whatever! He just left us alone. He never bothered us one atom. Hitch and I would get together, we'd have lunch together, we'd have cocktails together, we'd have fun together, we'd talk about the story in the evening. Never met Walter!

On their own, Bennett and Hitchcock developed the story of an ignorant but cheerful American reporter Johnny Jones, renamed Huntley Haverstock (McCrea), who uncovers foreign (implicitly German) agents at work in Europe under the camouflage of a peace organization led by collaborator Stephen Fisher (Herbert Marshall). Jones falls in love with Fisher's daughter Carol (Laraine Day), who helps him expose her father's spy ring.

This plot line was nothing less than a reworking of all of their previous collaborations, particularly *The 39 Steps*. Even though its opening scenes pay homage to the fast-paced, wisecracking tone of the newspaper film, Johnny Jones's complacent but independent-minded crime reporter was derived from Richard Hannay (Robert Donat), the innocent man drawn into an underworld of espionage. The story's trajectory, which leads Jones to seek safety and counsel in the home of Stephen Fisher, echoes Hannay's journey to Scotland and the home of spy mastermind Professor Jordan. And the film's MacGuffin that everyone pursues, the paragraph of a Peace Treaty memorized by the Dutch diplomat Van Meer (Albert Basserman), was a patent recycling of Mr. Memory's knowledge of the thirty-nine steps. Even small details, such as Jones's appearance in Carol's hotel bathroom, and their mutual "kidnapping" in a Cambridge hotel, or the sardonic treatment of official lectures and gatherings by Fisher's "crackpot" movement, echo Hannay and Pamela's enforced tryst and Hannay's improvised political speech. No wonder then that *Foreign Correspondent* is full of reflexive dialogue, such as Jones's comment that his and Carol's immediate declaration of love "cuts down our love scene considerably."

But for all its derivative elements, the convoluted plot took considerable reworking. Wanger allowed Hitchcock to hire writer after writer—Richard Maibaum and James Hilton, Hitchcock's assistant Joan Harrison, and finally Robert Benchley, who played Jones's cantankerous, lazy, and promiscuous associate in London—to elaborate on the plot line and add humorous touches. The heroic figure of Jones became split with British reporter ffolliott (George Sanders), whose dry wit lightens dangerous sequences such as the chase after Van Meer's assassins and the excruciating scene of Van Meer's torture.

The dialogue contains constant jokes about national character, such as the uncomprehending Latvian at the conferences; Jones's constant but inappropriately American desire to have a "show-down" with his enemies; his comment about the British's "air of incorruptibility"; the assassin Rowley's (Edmund Gwenn) description of how royalty like to walk with their bodyguards; and the use of American jazz to torture Van Meer. At the same time, the film had to repress the true identity of the espionage agents. Through all of the screenwriting, Bennett recalled:

> The only time I really remember [Wanger] buzzing in on us was to say, "We can't do an anti-German picture! By God, you've made these people Nazis. This is American propaganda against Germany! It can't be done!" So, what we did was, everybody who spoke German spoke it backwards. . . . The actors were speaking a language that didn't exist! And that satisfied Walter.

The finished film is full of Hitchcock set pieces: an assassination in a rainy Amsterdam square, a tense sequence in a windmill, Jones's escape from assassins on the ledge of a hotel, Rowley's attempt to murder Jones in the tower of Winchester cathedral, and a final plane crash in the North Atlantic. *Foreign Correspondent* is equally enlivened by Hitchcock's flamboyant style and visual ideas: the rapid dolly-shot away from Jones when his boss offers to send him to Europe; the *Potemkin*-like shot of Van Meer's bloodstained face; Stebbins's suggestion that his milk was poisoned; and Van Meer's references to birds in city parks. In fact, *Foreign Correspondent* is a virtual palimpsest of the narrative and visual motifs Hitchcock later elaborated in his American career.

In the end, the film was the most lavish production Wanger had yet undertaken, for he did not restrain Hitchcock when principal photography began on March 18. Hitchcock freely cast the film with loan-outs: veteran German stage actor Basserman came from Warner Bros., nineteen-year-old Day was borrowed from MGM, and Sanders came from Fox. As with *Trade Winds* and *Stagecoach,* the producer gave the director carte blanche. The difference now was that Hitchcock was more demanding than Ford and Garnett put together. Scenes called for seventy-eight three-sided sets. Special plumbing and rerouting of the Colorado River was required to provide water for the rainy scene in which the Dutch diplomat Van Meer is assassinated. Wanger approved an outlay of $47,000 for the transatlantic clipper that crashed in the penultimate sequence. Wanger also allowed Hitchcock to hire Menzies, the celebrated production designer for *Gone with the Wind,* in early March 1940 to shoot second unit work and to design, with Toluboff and Golitzen, the famous plane crash scene. To score the opus, Hitchcock selected Alfred Newman from Fox.

Wanger's willingness to invest heavily in production values and his hands-off approach delighted Hitchcock. Selznick had been exactly the opposite during production on *Rebecca,* sending nonstop memos on everything from scripting to the pacing of scenes and the direction of Joan Fontaine. By contrast, according to Ericksen, Wanger couldn't control Hitchcock even when he wanted to:

> But the big increase in the cost was occasioned by Hitchcock through his taking 71 days to shoot the picture instead of 42, as originally scheduled, and shooting over 250,000 feet of film, and retaking scenes many times. He has had Walter, as well as the rest of us, nearly crazy but no matter what method Walter used to try to speed him up, and notwithstanding his promises to do so, he never did it.

Whereas the Technicolor *Vogues* had cost just over $1 million, Hitchcock's film finally cost $1,484,167, more than double Wanger's average negative costs. As Bennett put it, "Walter trusted us, you see?"

Wanger did receive many benefits from Hitchcock for his money, as Daniel O'Shea resentfully informed Selznick: ˙

> Wanger partly due to his own fault has prevented us from having the use of Hitchcock for an aggregate of almost thirty weeks . . . he got an original story out of Hitchcock while Hitch was working for us on Rebecca . . . as a result of improper supervision while at Wanger's Hitch has gotten a reputation for being an exceedingly slow director greatly affecting his marketability.

Hitchcock also agreed to direct a brief, amusing airplane scene between amateur pilot Pidgeon and an airsick Joan Bennett in *House Across the Bay*.

Wanger reciprocated. For the first time, he published an article on a director as *Foreign Correspondent* went into second- and third-run theaters: "He probably puts more of himself into his pictures than any other director I have known in twenty-one years of producing pictures. His talent is unlimited, his energy and his wit inexhaustible." Wanger's gratitude was sincere, although *Foreign Correspondent* is a minor work in the Hitchcock canon. Leonard Leff persuasively suggests the film suffers from Wanger's slack management of Hitchcock in comparison with Selznick's close supervision of *Rebecca,* and that the Wanger film represents a slip "backwards" to the style of Hitchcock's British thrillers. In fact the British spy thrillers have a focus and energy that *Foreign Correspondent*'s sprawling subplots and characters dilute. But Leff's point is well-taken. *Foreign Correspondent* lacks an emotional core: the profundity of Fisher's betrayal of Carol is glossed over since we hardly care what happens to them. Where Selznick browbeat Hitchcock into exploring the depths and nuances of the characters in *Rebecca,* Wanger had, if anything, even less interest in character than Hitchcock did. He was thrilled with Hitchcock's ingenious set pieces and exciting sequences and allowed Hitchcock, in William Rothman's words, to wrestle with "the problem of making a Hitchcock film in America."

Nonetheless, *Foreign Correspondent* was in many ways the high point of Wanger's career. Here at last was a film that, while it did not propagandize in any direct manner, dealt in a compelling way with the European conflict. Van Meer's faith in "the people" who cannot be forced into war was transformed into faith in the American people in the film's final scene. The June 5 shooting script concluded simply with Jones, Carol, and ffolliott rescued from their plane crash. Jones and ffolliott then speculated on the idea that the Germans had disguised their attack ship as a British fishing boat so that the entire incident would appear as though the British were trying to drag America into the war. Neither Hitchcock, Wanger, nor Charles Bennett had been satisfied with it. As Donald Spoto has indicated, Hitchcock's brief visit to England in late June alerted the director to the threat of an imminent blitz. Upon returning to Hollywood, Hitchcock and Wanger asked Hecht to quickly draft an epilogue that would bring the film up to date.

Virtually overnight, McCrea recalls, Hecht came up with a scene of Jones broadcasting to America in a radio station in London during an air attack that anticipated Edward R. Murrow's celebrated reports. Exhorting America to "hang on to your lights! They're the only lights left in the world," Johnston's monologue reminded Americans that "this is a big story and you're a part of it," a comment that echoes ffolliott's rejoinder to Jones's refusal to fight Fisher, "It's your story." Although otherwise unrelated to the rest of the film, the epilogue—like the prologue dedicated to "those forthright ones who early saw the clouds of war while many of us at home were seeing rainbows"— was vehement enough to suggest the necessity of American defense preparations. One year after the film's release, the House Committee on Interstate Commerce regarded *Foreign Correspondent* as calculated to drag America into war.

Upon the film's August premiere in New York, Wanger told Eileen Creelman of the *New York Sun* that he was "completely happy about 'Foreign Correspondent' and it's the first time he has ever felt that way about a picture." While Wanger was also proud of *Gabriel Over the White House* and *Private Worlds,* the Hitchcock film pleased him most.

> The picture is a melodrama and made for entertainment . . . but I think it also has a deep underlying theme that is not apparent at first. People won't notice until later when they begin thinking about the picture. At least I think they won't, and I think it is there.

Given Academy Award nominations for best picture, supporting actor (for Basserman), original screenplay, special effects, cinematography, and black-and-white art direction, *Foreign Correspondent* also received critical praise nearly equal to that of *Stagecoach. Life* ran a four-page photographic spread on the film and the accompanying text stressed Hitchcock's genius. *Time* found it "easily one of the year's finest pictures." Ferguson rhapsodized about Hitchcock's explorations of "the modern story film," noting that "watching that man work is like listening to music." New York critics Bosley Crowther and Winsten were more critical of the film's narrative plausibility, particularly of the epilogue.

Where most reviewers focused on the director, Winsten called attention to Wanger as the crucial factor in the film's awkward intermixing of melodrama and political components. Winsten singled out Johnny Jones's willingness to throw away a great scoop out of love for Carol Fisher and Carol's acceptance of her father's defamation.

> In the last analysis *Foreign Correspondent*, in addition to its surface of Hitchcock quality, represents the dilemma of Producer Walter Wanger. In his best pictures he is intelligent enough to want to say something significant. But at the same time, apparently desiring not to lose money by quixotic gesture, he tries

to introduce a romantic thread which will carry and make popular the burden of a message. This was even more true of *Blockade* than of *Foreign Correspondent,* and in neither case was the device entirely satisfactory.

Such judgments barely mattered to the die-hard propagandist, for in its opening weeks at the refurbished Rivoli on Broadway, the film grossed $50,000; by the end of the year, after only four months, it had earned $1,810,000 in box office grosses. But because of its huge cost and blocked European income, the film was slow to turn a profit.

While the epilogue for *Foreign Correspondent* was being shot, Wanger's other major production of the 1940 season, Ford's *The Long Voyage Home,* was in principal photography. In fact, McCrea, then performing in the coda to Hitchcock's film, recalled that Ford visited the radio station set, and coached the actor in his reading with his characteristic gruff manner: "'How're you gonna do that? . . . What do you think of it? . . . Throw this line away.' . . . He gave me kind of a reading of it."

There was nothing so strident in Ford's own film. In fact, it is hard to imagine a film more different in tone or implication from the Hitchcock spy thriller. Ford's film was moody and defeatist where *Foreign Correspondent* was buoyant and optimistic. Hitchcock had packed his film with brilliant set pieces like the assassination of Van Meer on the Amsterdam square; Ford's film was full of subtle gestures and techniques.

Ford had signed on to make a film with Wanger in early March while Hitchcock was preparing principal photography on *Foreign Correspondent.* Ford and Merian Cooper had formed Argosy Pictures for semi-independent work, but in early 1940, new independent companies found it difficult to obtain distribution agreements because distributors handled increasingly fewer films. Ford knew that Wanger's slack management style approximated the independence he sought and that Wanger was willing to sponsor virtually anything the director of his greatest success suggested, particularly if *Stagecoach* screenwriter Nichols was involved.

Within a week of signing their contract, Wanger had approved Ford's choice to adapt four one-act sea plays by America's premier playwright Eugene O'Neill. The story of the ragtag crew of the Glencairn, Ford told Wanger, would repeat the critical success of his own *The Informer* (1935) and the excitement of his *Hurricane* (1937). Wanger had publicly noted how high costs, the need to attract large audiences, and negative reviews defeated "experimental" films such as Ford's earlier work, Hecht and MacArthur's *The Scoundrel* (1935), and his own *Private Worlds.* But Wanger was ready to give experimental films a try again.

Wanger sponsored *The Long Voyage Home,* in part because of his and the industry's understanding of its domestic audience. An unsystematic survey of one thousand families undertaken by Warner Bros. in late 1939 indicated that people who did not attend the movies were not going because they lacked the cash for leisure activities or because they simply were not interested in Hollywood's product. As *Variety* noted, producers could do nothing about impoverished moviegoers, but they could try to attract the reluctant segment of Americans, identified as belonging to a higher class and better educated portion of the population, with a new type of film. This was one inspiration for the call to "fewer and better" films in early 1940. In May 1940, evidence that domestic box office attendance had dropped between 5 and 15 percent from the previous year only strengthened Wanger's faith in the project.

Wanger rationalized *The Long Voyage Home* as an answer to this difficulty. In an interview he argued that the loss of more than an estimated 30 million moviegoers could be reversed with "different pictures":

> [Wanger] realized [*The Long Voyage Home*] wouldn't carry the same appeal to the basic 50,000,000 moviegoing group as a picture along the "Collegiate Rhythms of 1939" order, replete with crooners and swing bands; but he was aiming at the marginal 30,000,000.

In his mind, it was a matter of producing a Cadillac instead of a Buick and of appealing "to the classes as well as the masses." In the project's favor was its cultural pedigree. O'Neill had received the Nobel Prize for literature in 1936, just four years before production on *The Long Voyage Home* began. The four plays—*The Moon of the Caribbees* (1917), *Bound East for Cardiff* (1914), *In the Zone* (1917), and *The Long Voyage Home* (1917)—were written as self-sufficient one-acts with the same or similar characters, the crew of the cargo ship Glencairn. A production of all four works in New York in 1929 as *The Long Voyage Home* demonstrated that they could be successfully yoked together as a continuous story.

It took Ford and Nichols two months to develop their script. As Ford later described it,

> Dudley wrote the script after we talked together . . . for six weeks, mulling over photos of real wharves, bars and so forth.
> After these conferences, Dudley locked himself up sixteen hours a day for twenty days and turned out the first draft. Then we took a week and knocked it apart, and then another month to put it back together again. The final script was changed very little during shooting.

Their adaptation updated the story to the present and imposed a linear trajectory on the four self-contained plays, so that the action of the film encompassed one journey from South America to England. After an aborted, raucous bacchanal with rum and women, the ship picks up ammunition in New York to carry to England in the present conflict. A storm kills Yank (Ward Bond), and the crew suspects an upper-class seaman (Smitty, played by Ian Hunter) of espionage. Upon their arrival in England, they again get drunk and save the Swede Ole Olson (Wayne) from being shanghaied onto a "slave ship" so that he can return to Sweden. The next day, his friends prepare to ship out again.

Nichols and Ford "softened" O'Neill's fatalism and his conception of the Glencairn crew, giving them heroic gestures in the face of death, as when Smitty is shot down while directing the sailors' response to the air attack, and making them into a more caring group than they are in O'Neill's plays. Such changes illustrate Peter Bogdanovich's claim that Ford's "most frequently re-curring theme" is "the tragedy of [defeat], but also the peculiar glory inherent in it." As with *Stagecoach,* Nichols and Ford created sequences of silent ac-tion, such as the opening of the film (in which the sailors furtively whisper among themselves) and Smitty's suspicious behavior before the crew interro-gates him. In both these scenes, the audience struggles simply to understand what is going on.

The inexplicit, naturalistic script was enhanced by James Basevi's ab-stracted art direction of the constricting and confining Glencairn set, and Gregg Toland's low-key, shadowy, deep-focus cinematography, which he used most notably in his next assignment, Orson Welles's landmark *Citizen Kane.* His and Ford's framing strategies—most notably when the ship is at-tacked by German planes that remain offscreen for the entire sequence—visu-alize the sailors' impotence more forcefully.

Of course, Ford's conception of the film, including these visual strategies, is in part a consequence of what the director later called "a very small bud-get" for *The Long Voyage Home.* The film cost $682,495, only $6,000 over budget, and was completed ahead of schedule in thirty-seven days almost en-tirely at the Samuel Goldwyn studios. But confining the bulk of the film's ac-tion to the ship creates a constant reminder of the film's source in a stage play. The ship's deck and forecastle, combined with the sailors' restricted point of view from the ship, become a proscenium stage. But what was a convention and a restriction in the theater—only being able to show a single, limited space on the stage—becomes an expressive analogue for the crew's general ineffec-tiveness and their irrevocable attachment to the sea.

Setting aside the actors' awkward Swedish accents, the opening sequence, abstract set design, deep-focus cinematography, and rigorous use of framing all made *The Long Voyage Home* one of the most affecting and visually stun-ning films yet produced in Hollywood. It is a work that approximates the achievements of the post–World War II European art cinema. That it was dis-tinctive was clear to Wanger. He felt that the minimal narration of the open-ing scene, the episodic structure and naturalist causality of the action, and the cyclical implications of the film's conclusion called for some modification. During postproduction, he decided to add prefatory and concluding titles. As scripted by Nichols and shot by Ford, *The Long Voyage Home* was to begin with the opening scene in the Caribbean and end with the final shot of the Donkeyman on the Glencairn deck. Although Wanger tried to enlist Ford's participation in this and other postproduction matters, Ford was either unavailable or uninterested. At Wanger's request, and with the approval of Nichols and Ford, Fox screenwriter Gene Fowler (and previous Ford collaborator) drafted the opening and closing titles. These preserve the fatalistic tone of the film's action and establish prior to the opening scene that sailors forge "the lifelines of nations" but "cannot change the sea." They conclude, with the accompaniment of "Harbor Lights," by noting that for the Glencairn crew "the long voyage home never ends."

Wanger's titles were intended to prepare audiences for the film's unusual qualities. But Wanger's executive assistant Foley felt they were only modestly successful:

> The foreword helps a lot in cleaning up the beginning and it does seem much shorter but you'll forgive me I think if I tell you I just can't like it. Perhaps it is too highbrow. I'll die believing that the audiences should know something about what they are looking at.

By contrast, Wanger sought for the first time in his career as a Hollywood producer to sell a film as high art. He undertook an unusual publicity campaign designed to appeal to those 30 million well-educated Americans who refused to attend Hollywood movies: he commissioned ten canvases by contemporary Regionalist painters. Paid $10,000 each, Thomas Hart Benton, Grant Wood, Raphael Soyer, Ernest Fiene, and others depicted scenes and characters from the film, which were exhibited in galleries in thirty-five cities around the country as the film went into distribution.

"Wanger's portfolio" excited considerable attention and comment at the time. Unlike the opening and closing titles, the paintings were commissioned at the start of the film's production, before he knew what the finished film would look like, and testify to his anticipation of the difficulty in selling the film. The painters were given free access to the sets while Ford directed principal photography ("I didn't like the idea at first," Ford later wrote, "but the artists proved to be a grand bunch of guys"). Their work encased the film in the aura of traditional art in order to appeal to a higher class and more cultured segment of America. Hedging his bets, Wanger and United Artists publicity men hoped the portfolio would also make *The Long Voyage Home*, a film about brawling and barely literate sailors, appealing to women.

Wanger encouraged advance word on the film to raise the reviewers' expectations to the highest level. *Time* reported that "enthusiastic rumors" hailed *The Long Voyage Home* as "the best picture since *The Informer*." Because of its similarities to that Ford "masterpiece," the painting portfolio, and the unconventional features of the film itself, Ford and Wanger created a remarkable consensus about *The Long Voyage Home*. A former United Artists publicity executive remarked in April 1941 that Ford's film was "certain to be called arty." He was right. *Commonweal*, for example, called it "a work of art in cinema technique." The *Hollywood Reporter* was even more emphatic on this point: "It is [arty] in every sense of the word and about as high an art of motion picture as one would find in many days of looking at pictures."

High art was of course what Wanger had shunned since his days on Broadway with Barker and Nazimova. As a liberal internationalist who publicly stated countless times that Hollywood needed to educate its audience, Wanger's use of the term "art" could logically imply its irrelevance to current history. But the "arty" angle was not a pure one in Wanger's hands, and many reviewers praised the film for its "realism," referring to the subject matter, setting, and cinematography. Certainly, Ford and Nichols's updating of the O'Neill plays increased the referential force of the drama: in one scene added to the play, for example, the Glencairn crew learns that it will carry ammunition to Great Britain in the war against the Germans. Significantly, Ford chose to shoot a known location (Wilmington Harbor, California) for the very scene in which the Glencairn crew stumbles into contemporary history. In other scenes, we hear a radio broadcast with war news, and Driscoll (Mitchell) comments that "There's a war on" and "I never was a neutral in my life"; there is an air attack on the Glencairn, and in the final segment in London, the Glencairn crew is denied access to a British soldiers' dancehall. The film manifests an excessive desire to be current when we are shown a London newsboy's placard announcing the Nazi's invasion of Norway, which occurred only weeks before Ford completed principal photography. As Ford and Nichols told a *New York Times* reporter in early 1939, "We've been wanting to do [an anti-Fascist picture] for years."

The topical references in *The Long Voyage Home* only magnify the naturalist conception of the Glencairn crew and their impotence in the face of current world events. Driscoll, Yank, Ole, Swanson, and their mates become all the more pathetic for their unwitting role in the European war. In short, Nichols and Ford's updating of *The Long Voyage Home* compounds the ideological determinism of O'Neill's naturalist dramas, providing a stark contrast with *Foreign Correspondent*. Unlike Hitchcock's film, *The Long Voyage Home* offered a bleak vision of human ineffectiveness to its audiences at a time when Fascist forces were overrunning Europe and when national debate increasingly recognized that their challenge to worldwide democracy demanded a more determined response.

United Artists did not see the logic of Wanger's publicity strategy. When Pare Lorentz gave the film a glowing review in *McCall's,* Kosiner urged distribution executive Kelly to sell the film "as a great motion picture" and book as many dates as possible, "instead of approaching the picture with the fear which we all seem to have." Nonetheless, United Artists issued advertising material that misrepresented it as an adventure film ("the love of women in their eyes . . . the salt of the sea in their blood!"), and Wanger refused to accept highly favorable terms that the distributor negotiated on his behalf with exhibitors. Although Eugene and Carlotta O'Neill praised it as "a grand deeply moving and beautiful piece of work," and though it received Academy Award nominations for best picture, screenplay, editing, cinematography, and musical score, the film's box office was dismal, failing to earn back half of its costs. Apparently, neither artiness nor realism appealed to those 30-million-plus Americans.

The disappointment of *The Long Voyage Home* and the dissatisfying play dates for the Ford and Hitchcock films confirmed for Wanger by January 1941 that his arrangement with United Artists had become wholly unsatisfactory. He needed to either sell his company to United Artists or to adjust his contract. He was urged to this view by stockholder Warburg as well as by attorney Bienstock. After United Artists refused to do either, several disputes in 1941 made him leave.

Wanger's board had tolerated a $1.5 million budget (for *Foreign Correspondent*) in the spring of 1940 for the last time. Wanger never developed *So Gallantly Gleaming* into a successful script; instead, he had purchased the rights to a story by Barrie Lyndon from the *Saturday Evening Post* about the Germans' efforts to smuggle arms to North African natives in an uprising against the British colonial administration. *Sundown* (1941) promised a new combination of Wanger's favorite production elements: a North African setting, a heroine, who like the Sheik appears to be Arabian but turns out to be English, and like *Foreign Correspondent,* a pro-British slant. As Thomas Cripps has shown, Wanger ensured that the anti-Fascist African characters (including those portrayed by Woody Strode and Dorothy Dandridge) were given more progressive and rounder characterizations than was common in Hollywood films of the period. But he also insisted that his screenwriters tag on an epilogue in the manner of *Foreign Correspondent*. Here, Sanders, about to die after successfully suppressing a native uprising, speaks about the glories of the English church and the British army, spilling out a stream of consciousness confession that seems totally absurd after his tight-lipped demeanor throughout the film. Like the later and much more successful *Mrs. Miniver* (1942), *Sundown* then closed in an English church, where Sanders's father delivers the eulogy, and the British air force is seen flying off to further combat. Shot on location and costing more than $1.2 million, the entire project was mismanaged. United Artists took control of it in July 1941. Wanger's board refused to approve the million-dollar budget for Lubitsch's *To Be or Not To Be,* which Wanger turned over to Korda.

Wanger's second planned production for 1941 did not fare much better.

Wanger's 1940 contract with Ford and Cooper's Argosy Pictures called for two films. United Artists wanted a star-studded production after the little-known names of *The Long Voyage Home*. Cooper had a proposal that would allow Wanger to spend his income blocked in England. But it hardly fit United Artists' request.

Cooper, like Wanger, was a World War I pilot, and he proposed a film about the Eagle Squadron, the twenty-four American pilots who joined the Royal Air Force in early 1940. The film's dogma would concern the superior force of air power and the necessity of Anglo-American cooperation. The distinction of the project—what Cooper called "the best showmanship idea of the year"—resided in a documentary method of shooting without a script, which Cooper had followed on *Grass* and *Chang*. When the going got tough on "Eagle Squadron," Cooper constantly reminded Wanger of the *Chang* example: "Schoedsack and I started out with only an idea. That idea was rounded out and constructed and created in the field. This is the same type of picture."

But Wanger and Cooper were also mindful of the celebrated British wartime documentaries. As Academy president, Wanger had created a library of British shorts for Hollywood's appreciation and reference, and films such as Humphrey Jennings's *The First Days,* Harry Watt's *Squadron 990,* and others were screened at the Museum of Modern Art. In attempting to secure government cooperation in England, Wanger's London production manager wrote Ministry of Information head Sidney Bernstein that Wanger wanted to use "real characters wherever we can and real incidents as well, wherever they can be found. Our material will likely be handled with a technique very similar to that used in 'Merchant Seamen.'" *Merchant Seamen* chronicled how British sailors of a torpedoed ship return to Britain determined to ship out again.

The documentary precedents of Cooper's work and the British shorts argued for British collaborators. Jean Renoir had independently drafted a treatment of Antoine de Saint Exupéry's *Wind, Sand and Stars,* but instead Wanger directed Cooper to approach Grierson protégé Harry Watt about working on the project. Cooper secured promises of cooperation and clearance to photograph the squadron at its base in Essex. With Watt's help, Wanger and Cooper felt certain they could elaborate accurately on the hardships of British life under the blitz presented in Watt and Jennings's documentary *London Can Take It:* the routine of sleeping in shelters, firefighting the air raid damage, and the work of the civilian defense units.

Schoedsack replaced Cooper when the latter returned to the States in June 1941 to take up duties with the Army Signal Corps, and the project gradually came unraveled due to the kind of Anglo-American differences that the film sought to collapse. The British Ministry of Information insisted on the submission of a script before granting permission to shoot. The production manager in London had purchased cameras that Schoedsack found "junky." The blitz had ended by the summer of 1941, resulting in few opportunities for ac-tuality footage. The squadron members proved hostile to Schoedsack at first, and by the time he had won them over, they were not generally available for studio work. Those who were, were often killed or missing within weeks of being photographed. Cloudy weather and rain precluded shooting.

Schoedsack and Watt did not get along. By the summer of 1941, Watt was widely hailed and feted for his production of *Target for Tonight,* one of the first films to change the rhetoric of British films from "England can take it" to, in Schoedsack's words, "England can give it too." Schoedsack found that Watt "went prima donna" and as Watt later admitted,

> I was suddenly engulfed in the notoriety of TARGET. It was all too much for me and for the first and only time in my life I went on the town. . . . Heady stuff for a youngster with no particularly strong moral fibre, and it nearly finished me.

Schoedsack often found himself working alone on the "Eagle Squadron" proj-ect. By the fall, the production manager reported that the project went well when the codirectors were kept apart.

But the key conflict between Schoedsack and Watt transcended personali-ties: it entailed their differing conceptions of how documentary films for the war effort could be made. Schoedsack's instructions from Cooper were "to work without a script" and he rejected out of hand a treatment Watt had quickly written up in the spring. Watt had trained under Grierson, who be-lieved that the necessity of a clear symbolism outweighed the virtues of spon-taneous naturalism. Although *London Can Take It* consisted of actuality foot-age, many of Watt's greatest successes, including *Night Mail,* relied heavily on staged scenes shot in a studio.

Schoedsack, working in Hollywood for over a decade since *Chang,* had a more pure conception of documentary practice. He was shocked to discover that Watt's *Target for Tonight* "was 90% interior studio work and trick stuff," including a fuselage from the RAF that Watt used at Denham studios for fly-ing scenes. Watt saw no reason to argue with success; besides, he noted, the conditions under which the Eagle Squadron worked—they went off to almost certain death, in what he and Cooper called a realistic *Dawn Patrol*—was too poignant to shoot with actual pilots.

By the fall of 1941, Watt had completed a treatment that would satisfy the British Air Ministry, but at this point, United Artists had enough. In August 1941, Wanger's representative attended a meeting with the distributor's sales staff and exhibition bookers: "The minute the exhibitors heard that the pic-ture was going to be made in England with an English cast," Wanger's asso-ciate reported, "they became sales resistant." British films, even in the months before Pearl Harbor when American sympathy for Britain had peaked, were poor box office.

In an October 1941 meeting, United Artists stockholders decided that "Eagle Squadron," which they estimated would cost between $1 and $2 million, was "too big a proposition for the Wanger company to undertake at the present time." This was the last straw. Wanger decided to leave. He arranged a swap with the studio that gave him several properties, such as "Eagle Squadron," *Dynasty of Death, So Gallantly Gleaming,* and "Arabian Nights." He in turn gave United Artists the rights and income to all his previous films. As Tino Balio indicates, United Artists got the better part of the deal, since the recovery of blocked income in England made the Wanger company solvent and profitable within a year. The distributor changed the company's name to United Artists Productions and used residuals from the Wanger films to finance other semi-independent producers during the war years. Thus ended an ambitious experiment with independent production.

In the end, the benefit of Wanger's association with United Artists was as much a matter of promotion as of production. In 1941, Rosten named *The Long Voyage Home* among Hollywood's outstanding films (including *Citizen Kane, Fantasia, The Grapes of Wrath, Gone with the Wind,* and *Rebecca*). He placed Wanger alongside Selznick and Clifford Work of Universal as a peripheral but prestigious industry figure whom the most powerful men (Goldwyn, Schenck, Zanuck, Y. Frank Freeman, the Warner brothers, and Harry Cohn) occasionally consulted.

In the early 1940s, intellectuals and artists held Wanger in the highest esteem: as Norman Cousins, editor of the *Saturday Review of Literature,* noted in 1942, Wanger was "associated with new, bold and distinctive advances in the film." "After talking with you," Frank Lloyd Wright wrote him in 1940, "I have more faith in the movies than I ever have before." "There are producers with whom I would not work 'for all the oil in Texas'—and they are a majority," Carl Sandburg wrote Wanger in early 1941. "And you are in the meager minority."

Such praise was ironic given Wanger's business struggles. But these derived from his particular predilections as a producer and especially from United Artists' tentative position in the industry. Although United Artists provided Wanger with the funding to hire the best Hollywood talents in more expensive films, Wanger had not been able to capitalize on it fully. For each of his best films during these years, he turned out what he was more accustomed to producing, movies that were comparable to indifferent Paramount specials.

United Artists, for all its prestige, lacked the clout to get Wanger films— be they good, bad, or indifferent—the best possible bookings among the affiliated theaters. Yet to outsiders such as the federal government, the weak United Artists was grouped with the majors as an oppressive, monopolistic studio. In 1940, the Senate Committee on Interstate Commerce met to consider the Neely Bill, which would strike down block booking, and the Department of Justice pursued an antitrust case against the dominant studios. When Wanger protested to United Artists about its poor bookings on *Eternally Yours* and *Slightly Honorable,* counsel Edward Raftery replied that the distributor

> would be foolhardy to come out with any advertising suggesting that it intends to force an exhibitor to single bill and it would be tremendously bad evidence against them. The entire Government complaint presumes that each of the eight major companies force exhibitors to do things the exhibitor does not wish to do.

Indeed, government investigators, talking with Wanger and Ford in March 1940 about an antitrust suit, concluded:

> These so-called independent producers and all persons who are dependent upon them for their livelihood are so much a part of the thing against which we are complaining that it is and will be a complete waste of time to try to develop anything from them which will be helpful to the Government. . . . Each of them is an integral part of the industry as it now operates and each is dependent upon the present structure and operation of the industry for the maintenance of their respective positions.

Wanger at United Artists was caught in an ambivalent position. As he wrote Frank Nugent in 1938, "an independent producer is someone dependent on the banks, the trade press, the daily press, the radio critics, the theatremen, distributors and lastly—upon the public." He thus expressed the substance of some hard-earned lessons: that his United Artists arrangement was in effect identical to his Paramount program; it was another variant of semi-independence insofar as it exposed him to virtually the same limitations and risks.

In early 1941, Warburg suggested diplomatically that Wanger himself was partly responsible for his difficulties. Looking over a company balance sheet, Warburg noted the popularity of *Algiers, Trade Winds,* and *Stagecoach* and commented that an independent company "cannot afford to take chances by using subjects that are controversial or attempting to make artistic experiments" [such as *The Long Voyage Home*]:

> Experience has shown that the minute you get fancy with ideas, you are bound to take a royal trimming. . . . You must make pictures that the general run of the public understand and you must stick to a formula which is tried and true.

This was not completely accurate, however. Selznick International had similarly suffered through high overhead, managerial inefficiency and United Artists's poor sales efforts for four years, piling up aggregate losses of $779,000 on seven films that emulated tried and true studio formulas. No wonder Selznick disbanded his company after the outstanding success of *Gone with the Wind* and *Rebecca*.

In any case, America's entry into World War II several months later made propaganda the preferred Hollywood formula. Hence Wanger in the war years realized many of his long-standing production ideas—without the dubious benefits of semi-independence.

24. Gene Towne and Graham Baker, fully clothed for once, look enthused about reading one of their scripts.

25. Wanger chats with Fritz Lang and shirtless Graham Baker on the set of *You Only Live Once*.

26. Director Fritz Lang and cinematographer Leon Shamroy (leaning on the camera) watch intently as Eddie Taylor (Henry Fonda) and Joan (Sylvia Sidney) talk about Eddie's unhappy reform school years and the love life of frogs in *You Only Live Once*.

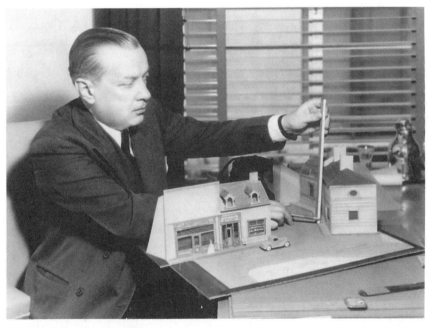

27. Art Director Alexander Toluboff poses with models of the pawnshop–drugstore set and the bank and court building exteriors for *You Only Live Once*.

28. Towne and Baker's romantic triangle in *History Is Made at Night*: Restaurateur Paul Dumond (Charles Boyer) thinks Irene Vail (Jean Arthur) and cruel tycoon husband Bruce Vail (Colin Clive) are laughing at his demeaning work.

29. In his second Technicolor extravaganza, *Walter Wanger's Vogues of 1938*, Wanger again cast Helen Vinson in a rivalry with Joan Bennett, this time for the affections of clothing designer Alan Baxter.

30. *Stand In*: Wall Street whiz Atterbury Dodd (Leslie Howard) is rendered speechless by the histrionics of Colossal Pictures' star director Koslofski (Alan Mowbray), while movie star Cheri (Maria Shelton) and yes-man Potts (Jack Carson) look on.

31. Director William Dieterle coaches Madeleine Carroll and Reginald Denny in a scene from *Blockade*.

32. Shades of *Potemkin*: Residents of the suffering Spanish port town are elated to see a supply ship arriving in *Blockade*.

33. "Excuse us for talking shop." Charles Boyer as Pepe le Moko entrances the Parisian Gaby (Hedy Lamarr) and amuses Inspector Slimane (Joseph Calleia) during a police stakeout of the Casbah in *Algiers*.

34. *Trade Winds*: Bumbling investigator Blodgett (Ralph Bellamy) never suspects that brunette Kay Kerrigan (Joan Bennett) is the blonde murderess he is trying to capture. Sam Wye (Fredric March) does. Bennett dyed her hair permanently after her success in the film.

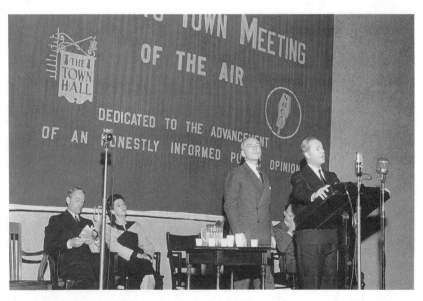

35. In one of his whirlwind public appearances, Wanger speaks on the NBC Blue Network's "Town Meeting of the Air."

36. *Stagecoach*: John Ford and Bert Glennon prepare the famous panning shot from the stagecoach to the group of Apaches preparing to attack in Monument Valley.

37. Wanger confers with director Alfred Hitchcock by the Waterloo Station set for *Foreign Correspondent.*

38. The strident epilogue to *Foreign Correspondent* was quickly drafted by Ben Hecht. Joel McCrea, photographed with costar Laraine Day, took direction from John Ford.

With their hates and desires men are changing the face of the earth — but they cannot change the Sea. Men who live on the Sea never change — for they live in a lonely world apart as

39. Wanger added this prologue, as well as end titles, to Ford's final cut of *The Long Voyage Home* to prepare the audience for its unconventional narrative.

40. *The Long Voyage Home*: Axel (John Qualen), Ole Olson (John Wayne), Davis (Joseph Sawyer), Yank (Ward Bond), and Johnny Bergman (Jack Pennick) comfort Driscoll (Thomas Mitchell), who has hurt his hand in a fistfight.

41. The height of prestige: Wanger officiates at the Academy Awards ceremonies at the Beverly Hills Biltmore Hotel in February 1941 as James Stewart accepts the 1940 Best Actor honor for *The Philadelphia Story*.

42. A 1941 luncheon for Wendell L. Willkie, former presidential candidate (and Twentieth Century–Fox chairman). Darryl F. Zanuck was the host.

43. From the "documentary" prologue of *Eagle Squadron* shot by Ernest Schoedsack: "Phillip Finlow was an oil driller. But he felt that this was his war. He was killed over France."

44. Stanley Cortez's deep-focus cinematography enhanced the studio realism of *Eagle Squadron*, as in this shot of returning flyers at headquarters.

45. Wanger's wartime success, *Arabian Nights*, grossed $3.5 million. Here Ai Ben Ali (Sabu) is teased in the evil Kamar's seraglio.

46. *Ladies Courageous*: Squadron leader Roberta Harper (Loretta Young) gets word that the WAFS will not fly in the air force's "big push" in the Pacific; Gerry (Anne Gwynne), Nadine (Diana Barrymore), and Vinnie (Geraldine Fitzgerald) look on.

47. Princess Delarai (Merle Oberon) reclines in the palace of the porcine King Croesus (Thomas Gomez) in *A Night in Paradise*.

48. A publicity still of Fritz Lang, Joan Bennett, and Wanger to announce the formation of Diana Productions, Inc.

49. A scene Wanger deleted from Fritz Lang's final cut of *Scarlet Street:* Christopher Cross (Edward G. Robinson) is caught by the police while trying to escape from his wife (Rosiland Ivan) and her ex-husband (Charles Kemper).

50. The climactic fire scene from Diana's *Secret Beyond the Door.* Lang refused to use doubles for Michael Redgrave and Joan Bennett.

51. The brutal fistfight between Honey Bragg (Ward Bond) and Logan Stuart (Dana Andrews) in *Canyon Passage*. Young Lloyd Bridges looks on at left.

52. Susan Hayward as alcoholic Angie Evans in *Smash-Up—The Story of A Woman,* the first role to win her an Oscar nomination.

53. Publisher Louis Venable (Robert Cummings) and Father Rinaldo (Eduardo Ciannelli) consider Tina (Susan Hayward) in her austere mode in *Lost Moment*.

54. Susan Hayward as Scarlett O'Hara, or rather Morna Dabney, in *Tap Roots*. Father Hoab Dabney (Ward Bond), suitor Keith Alexander (Van Heflin), and Reverend Kirkland (Arthur Shields) are fiercely proud of her.

11

Wanger at War
(1941–1945)

"I have been struggling with the problem of motion pictures and mass enlightenment ever since the last war," Wanger wrote an official of the Office of War Information seven months after Pearl Harbor. Though all Hollywood producers leaped at the sudden opportunity to prove the value of movies in wartime, Wanger alone acted with the confidence of an alumnus of the Committee on Public Information. Now was the time for Wanger and Hollywood to prove their great potential to elevate, motivate, *and* entertain their audience. As an OWI official wrote Wanger, "It is unfortunate that more of Hollywood's executives do not have the clear picture of their responsibilities and dangers that you do."

Wanger's wartime work was a continuation of his efforts in the late 1930s to produce movies of international scope, yet now Wanger did his part within the framework of studio unit rather than semi-independent production. This was extremely advantageous, for Wanger's association with Universal Pictures from 1941 through 1945 constituted the most stable and unconstrained period of his career since his days at Famous Players–Lasky. An appreciative studio management allowed him to produce a program of heavy-handed combat movies and his beloved orientalist, romantic adventures. In aesthetic terms, these paled next to his best United Artists productions, but Wanger reaped the economic benefits of the industry's wartime boom while remaining in the forefront of Hollywood's leadership.

Although rejected by the army as overage, the forty-seven-year-old Wanger directed his energies into a dazzling array of causes and programs, of which filmmaking was just one. Most striking was his dedication to Jewish concerns. He arranged and financed the escape of numerous Stettheimer and

Feuchtwanger relatives from Nazi Europe. In spite of his assimilated lifestyle and his disdain for the Polish and Russian Jews who led the industry, Wanger matched the contributions of Mayer, Goldwyn, and Selznick to the United Jewish Welfare Fund, whose fundraising campaigns he cochaired with Warner. With Selznick he spearheaded local drives for the United Jewish Appeal for Refugees, by conceiving the idea of soliciting $5,000 donations from top studio executives. In 1945, he raised funds for the establishment of a Jewish state. He also served on advisory panels for several Los Angeles groups, such as B'nai Brith and the Jewish Community Council.

Wanger was equally active in domestic causes. Within the film industry, he served on committees for the Motion Picture Relief Fund (which provided monies for needy ex-industry workers). He served as a consultant to the California State Board of Health. At the request of the surgeon general, he produced a short film featuring newcomer Robert Mitchum on venereal disease, *To the People of the United States* (also known as *The Silent Enemy*). In 1945 alone, Wanger was appointed president of the Dartmouth Alumni Association, served on the United Nations Committee of Southern California, headed a Red Cross drive sponsored by the Academy, and was named a trustee of the Georgia Warm Springs Foundation (an organization sponsored by Roosevelt and dedicated to research on infantile paralysis).

Wanger simultaneously promoted homefront and hemispheric unity. After the release of *Sundown*, he in mid-1942 cosponsored (with Darryl Zanuck and 1940 presidential candidate Wendell L. Willkie) a talk for film producers by his friend Walter White of the NAACP about the industry's humiliating depiction of African Americans. Vice-President Henry A. Wallace praised Wanger for being "very genuine in his ideas about racial tolerance and deeply concerned about the racial friction which exists in many cities." Through mid-1943, Wanger personally served in the Motion Picture Division of the Office of the Coordinator of Inter-American Affairs. This organization, led by Nelson Rockefeller, was formed in the fall of 1940 to counteract Fascist influence in South and Central America. Under Jock Whitney's motion picture division, Wanger reviewed features and short films with South American locales, characters, and concerns to ensure that the films did not offend the nations whose theaters became essential to Hollywood's health when European markets closed off.

To newspaper and magazine editors and radio producers Wanger offered innumerable suggestions on how to bolster homefront morale. In the spirit of the War Advertising Council, he proposed to *Time* editor C. D. Jackson that magazine ads be ribboned with quotations from past American leaders, to offer "an encouragement to all readers that the founders of this country were faced with the same sort of problems that we are faced with and they overcame them by straight thinking, courage and sacrifice." Wanger suggested that the OWI sponsor a July 4, 1943, broadcast to allow soldiers overseas to speak to Americans at home about preparing for the peace and to express their impatience with "flabbiness at home."

As president of the Academy, Wanger was a magnet for government officials seeking industry collaboration, and he had an array of organizational suggestions to offer, including the appointment of Zanuck to oversee Signal Corps film activities for the War Department. Although he voted Republican for Willkie in 1940, Wanger became a vehement Roosevelt supporter after Pearl Harbor, firing off congratulatory telegrams to the president for major policy speeches. In 1943 Dartmouth friend C. F. Palmer, head of the Office for Emergency Management, asked Wanger to film a fireside chat by Thanksgiving for theaters and military bases. This effort "to unite our psychological front" was never realized, but Wanger was honored to be asked.

Indeed, Roosevelt's sensitivity to the importance of the mass media was just one way in which all of Wanger's prewar claims about the role of the movies in American life were vindicated. The entire industry recognized that propaganda served not only the country's war aims but also enhanced the propagandist's stature. In his 1942 annual report, Hays repeated Wanger's 1930s speeches, noting the movies' role in "[t]he dissemination of information about current events and the vicarious experience of war activities." On the September 1942 "Town Hall of the Air," the host described Wanger as

> one of those few people out there on the west coast who had the courage of his convictions to spend an awful lot of money to tell the American people what was the nature of this thing that was about to attack us—and to show us on the screen. He has done it magnificently, and many Americans owe him a great debt of gratitude.

In fact, the film industry was in a sense indebted to the Japanese, for Pearl Harbor rescued Hollywood from an "image problem," derived from 1941 congressional investigations into warmongering among Hollywood liberals and from the trials of labor racketeers William Browne and William Bioff, who collected more than $1 million in bribes from studio executives with threats of theater projectionist strikes. Yet, the unsavory details exposed in the Browne and Bioff case were nothing compared to industry fears about the trust-busting policies of Arnold in the Justice Department. Arnold had forced the majors to sign a 1940 consent decree limiting block-booking to groups of five films. Lowell Mellett, who coordinated Hollywood and Washington's efforts at the OWI, saw Hollywood's eager cooperation as an attempt to delay the progress of the antitrust investigation.

Hence, throughout the war years, Wanger played a prominent role in arguing the industry's case to both the government and the public. He published articles and made speeches denouncing the OWI for rejecting Hollywood's expertise and for appointing leaders who admitted to complete ignorance about film production. In July 1942, Wanger dictated a lengthy letter to OWI Domestic Branch chief Gardner "Mike" Cowles—the publisher of *Look* magazine who helped to persuade the movie companies to distribute Capra's *Why We Fight* in theaters—about how Hollywood could help the administration "sell" the war effort and maintain an acute awareness of wartime needs. In addition to urging the OWI to establish an office in Hollywood (which it did within a month of his letter), Wanger argued that what was being done was good, but not enough:

> We must institute a campaign to make the average American realize how miserably uninformed he is so that it will become unpopular to be an escapist and popular to seek information. "To be a strong nation is to be an *informed* one"— if I may quote from Thomas Jefferson. The trend is going in this direction but it needs more pressure.

He had found support for his ideas in philosopher Mortimer Adler's *Art and Prudence,* published in the mid-thirties, which articulated Wanger's own sentiments that the movies should be appreciated by elites for their inherently democratic values:

> One cannot live in a democracy and despise the popular arts. Here, too, one may wish the impossible and dream of living at a time when the arts were not lowered to the people. But the only genuine practical problem which is raised is one of discovering the undesirable consequences of the popular arts and then seeking if possible, to improve them, not in the spirit of rendering them less evil, but rather hoping to make them greater goods.

That Hollywood's war effort resulted in greater goods became a crucial theme of Wanger's wartime activities. His Academy Award dinners, though still informal by today's standards, became ceremonies to affirm the industry's prestige by association. Dartmouth College President Samuel Adams Hopkins presented the 1939 Irving Thalberg Award to Selznick. Willkie and Chinese Ambassador Hu Shih praised the industry at the 1942 festivities. California governor Earl Warren attended the following year. Most impressively, in early 1941, correspondent Quentin Reynolds presented the screenwriting awards, theater legends Alfred Lunt and Lynn Fontanne announced the acting honors, and Wanger arranged for President Roosevelt to speak by telephone to the gathering. When Roosevelt thanked the industry for its efforts in defense preparations, Academy members in attendance were overwhelmed. Selznick wrote Wanger the next day, "I think you ought to be made president [of the Academy] for life!"

Wanger attempted to boost Hollywood's standing with publicity efforts in other media. He persuaded *Life* magazine to profile the Disney studio's war efforts in mid-1942, and published "Mickey Icarus," an article lauding Disney's filming of Major Alexander de Seversky's *Victory Through Air Power*. On the radio program "Town Hall of the Air" in September 1942, Wanger praised Hollywood stars for their work in Victory Bond drives and characterized them as "willing to do anything to win the war."

That fall, at the invitation of the admiring editor Cousins, Wanger published a series of articles in the *Saturday Review of Literature* on the movies' contribution to the war effort. He took issue with the comments of OWI head Elmer Davis, who had argued that "the easiest way to inject a propaganda idea into most people's minds is to let it go in through the medium of an entertainment picture when they do not realize that they are being propagandized." Davis suggested using elements of mise-en-scène for subtlety: extras could be clothed in military uniforms and store windows could be filled with war-related posters.

By contrast, Wanger argued in "Hollywood and the Intellectuals" that Hollywood's current output was perfectly suitable for the war effort. Reiterating Adler's ideas, Wanger first noted that although at present "not enough liberal philosophy reaches the basic public to produce effect," intellectual leaders should accept the popularity of films as a means to the dissemination of political ideas. As an example of this, Wanger discussed at length MGM's deployment of its stars in *Somewhere I'll Find You,* which shifts abruptly from "a sex-laden comedy" to battle scenes at Bataan:

> Audiences do not find the jump from comedy to drama in [the film] unreal. They sit tense and silent through the "patriotic" scenes; they know life changes like that. . . . The tens of millions who will attend this picture like Gable . . . they like Lana . . . for natural endowments. . . . Too crude an appeal, you say? Yet those audiences, because they saw vividly screen heroism through the eyes of personalities they like, will carry indelibly the impact of what happened on Bataan. Those impressions, filmed on the mind, will prove of great value in that inevitable day when Herr Goebbels launches his carefully prepared propaganda for a patched-up peace.

An associate described Wanger's posture in his essay as "that of the informed liberal who recognizes the good in the medium but can criticize it as well." Actually, Wanger was not criticizing anything, but reiterating his prewar claims that the country was dominated by apathetic, uninformed Americans who enjoyed a vulgar taste level. Then too, the article was a veiled defense of his pet project *Eagle Squadron* and his subsequent war films.

When he left United Artists in November 1941, Wanger claimed that "Eagle Squadron" was "the only thing I am interested in getting set." Yet without stars under contract, Wanger was less appealing to prospective host studios than he had been five years earlier. Moreover, his current project seemed like a bottomless pit. He had spent close to $100,000 on "Eagle Squadron"'s scripting and shooting costs, and he had little to show for it. As it turned out, Universal Pictures was interested in Wanger and was willing to finance "Eagle Squadron," and what began as a single picture deal evolved into a six-year working relationship. Though it was a move comparable to his "slumming it" with Cohn and Columbia Pictures in 1932, Wanger was suitably impressed with Universal to sign on, for like Columbia, Universal sought to upgrade its standing, and it had the financial means to do so.

With the exception of specials such as *All Quiet on the Western Front* and *Showboat* (1936), Universal's production standards throughout the thirties had been comparatively low-budget. Like Columbia and United Artists, it was one of the "little three" majors that owned no theaters. Even though Universal was able to obtain playing time at theaters owned or affiliated with the vertically integrated majors, it relied heavily on contracts with independent circuits and exhibitors for business. Its celebrated horror films starring Lugosi and Boris Karloff accumulated $10 million in domestic profits alone over ten years' time, but the studio showed losses for half of the 1930s.

In 1937, a new executive team led by financier J. Cheever Cowdin and exhibitors Nathan Blumberg and Work began its recovery. Thanks to its upgraded serial films and the fortunate popularity of its first-rank star, the teenage singer Deanna Durbin, the studio in 1940 nearly doubled its pretax profits to roughly $4.4 million. The grosses in 1941 increased yet again by $3 million, buoyed by the box office strength of Durbin, of a one-picture deal with Lubitsch (for *That Uncertain Feeling*), and of their newly contracted comics Abbott and Costello, who were ranked the second highest grossing stars of 1941 (after Gary Cooper). Cowdin and Blumberg applied some of this income to restructuring the company's debt, but they decided in late 1941 when Wanger signed on to use their increased profits to double the number of big-budget films for the coming year. The trend toward larger budgets continued during the war years, fueled by increasing profits and fulfilling the "desires of various interests in U to raise the standards of the company's product."

When the Wanger contract for "Eagle Squadron" was announced in November, Universal had other "outside producers" in tow for upscale productions: Hitchcock was on loan from Selznick to direct *Saboteur,* and LaCava would direct Irene Dunne in *Lady in a Jam.* Universal, like the other majors, had a renewed appreciation for the work of the producer who concentrated on just a few films within the producer-unit system. Claiming that the spring's "important pictures" would come from unit production, *Variety* cited Welles, Lasky, deMille, Disney, Sturges, Korda, Wanger, Howard Benedict, Hunt Stromberg, Jules Levey, Mark Hellinger, and the Cagney brothers as examples of "more or less independent producers." "Fewer pictures mean more personal attention to each," the trade journal noted, "and the best way to achieve that is by the unit system."

The need for fewer pictures derived from one of the industry's chief worries, the November 1940 consent decree that the federal government negotiated with the industry. In forcing distributors to limit their sales blocks to groups of five, Arnold's decree encouraged the major studios to pack films with stars and spend more money on film budgets so that an exhibitor would refuse none of the five films offered in the smaller blocks. Universal benefited from the consent decrees because, like United Artists and Columbia, it was not under their jurisdiction. As the vertically integrated producers lowered their production pace, the "little three" and the "B" studios filled the gaps in the exhibitors' schedules. Universal in particular used the hiring of "outside" producers to finance films that could compete in the more receptive first-run theaters. By October 1942, Universal reported an all-time high in its sales contracts for film exhibition, and all their films enjoyed extended runs.

It was, in short, a fortuitous time for Wanger to join any studio in Hollywood, but the consent decree made a studio of lesser status attractive. Moreover, he benefited from the advantages of studio unit production during the war years. Had he remained at United Artists, Wanger would have had to continue paying interest on production loans from banks, he would have had to vie for technicians in the wake of the draft, and he would have been forced to assert his share of raw stock allocations from the War Production Board and to hold out for his portion of unfrozen foreign revenues. At Universal Wanger faced none of these problems. He produced with Universal City's vast resources and under a contract that rewarded him handsomely.

In Wanger's sweet deal for "Eagle Squadron," Universal assumed all the risks and headaches of financing that Wanger had struggled with at United Artists. The studio recouped from each film's grosses its production, distribution, and advertising costs and fees. Wanger was not liable for budget overruns or for losses. His profit-sharing scheme, on top of his $45,000-per-film salary ($29,000 more than Universal's in-house producers received), was another boon. As an independent at United Artists, Wanger received 75 percent of his profits; at Universal, Wanger received half. Not even the outstanding producer Wallis could equal these terms when he went independent: Paramount provided Wallis with full financing, but cross collateralized his films so that the losses of one film offset the profits of another. Each of Wanger's grosses were computed separately, and Universal alone suffered any losses.

As at Paramount in 1935, Wanger's unit contract entitled Universal to specify contractual and budgetary restrictions on Wanger's work. Producing two films a year, he had to get studio approval at every stage of development; once he obtained that, he was granted "complete supervision and control of the production of the photoplay." In practice, however, all this was irrelevant. Work and his assistant Edward Muhl were exhibitors by training, and they deferred to Wanger's superior wisdom. In fact, they treated him like a king. Unlike Universal's associate producers, who supervised the studio's bread and butter titles, Wanger did not report to executive producers (such as

Joseph Gershenson or Howard Benedict). Like Joe Pasternak, Universal's resident prestige producer, Wanger answered only to Work.

In addition, Wanger used the studio's best personnel or else those he employed were promoted in status. Director Arthur Lubin had been at the company since 1936 and had recently directed the successful Abbott and Costello films. His assignment to *Eagle Squadron* gave him "top director status," leading to his direction of the studio's prestige picture *Phantom of the Opera* (1943). Golitzen followed Wanger to Universal after his work on *Foreign Correspondent* and *Sundown* (and Toluboff's death in 1940). When Universal's art director became ill, Golitzen replaced him. But the best evidence of the royal treatment Wanger received at Universal during the war is the fact that Wanger produced virtually every project he proposed there. United Artists had rejected "Eagle Squadron" and a Technicolor version of *Arabian Nights,* and Wanger had first slated "The Peacock's Feather" for production at Paramount in 1935; he produced all three at Universal.

The one thing Universal could not grant Wanger was big budgets. At a time when Paramount and MGM averaged more than $1 million for their best films, Wanger's Universal productions cost roughly $900,000 ($150,000 more than his contract allowed). While Wanger films cost twice as much as Universal's Abbott and Costello features, Wanger had to work with studio talents. His contracts specified actors of the "Jon Hall and Maria Montez type" and $20,000 directors. Moving his office staff to the Universal lot in November 1941, Wanger knowingly accepted these restrictions. But he also knew that he could accomplish his propaganda aims more easily at Universal than anywhere else.

Universal's indulgence of Wanger was immediately apparent with "Eagle Squadron." Although Universal released its first "yellow peril" film, *Menace of the Rising Sun,* in March 1942, none of the studio executives were convinced of the value of Wanger's project. Nonetheless, they approved Wanger's hiring of Norman Reilly Raine, a Canadian novelist-playwright and former journalist who had written *The Adventures of Robin Hood* and shared an Academy Award for his script of the anti-Fascist *The Life of Emile Zola.* Raine specialized in "conversion narratives" depicting solipsistic characters who suddenly discover a greater purpose in their lives; in his award-winning script, Raine spent nearly half of the film portraying the title character as a complacent, successful writer, stirred from his smug existence by the injustice of the Dreyfus trial. More germane to "Eagle Squadron," Raine, a former pilot, had adopted his formula for the Cagney vehicle *Captains of the Clouds* (1942, Warner Bros.). There, hot dog Canadian bush pilots happen to hear Churchill's "We shall never surrender" speech following the evacuation of Dunkirk and promptly join the RCAF to ferry planes to Britain.

Although he discarded Watt and Schoedsack's previous work, Raine produced a final script for *Eagle Squadron* which realized many of their aims. It follows the fate of a moody young pilot, Chuck Brewer (Robert Stack) who joins the RAF on a lark and sees his best buddy Johnny Coe (Leif Erickson) go down in flames after breaking formation to attack a German munitions depot. Brewer also witnesses the destruction of London under the blitz, and life in war-torn England stirs him out of his pettiness. He falls in love with Ann Partridge, a volunteer communications specialist (played by John Barrymore's daughter Diana, whom Wanger and Universal held to a joint option contract). Ann's mysterious appointments are always revealed to involve war-related work, escorting war orphans on a picnic or searching for her father, an M.P. serving with democratic spirit in the war effort. The self-absorbed American eventually comes to appreciate England's fight and immediately hijacks a deadly new German warplane, the Leopard. Ann is brought to heel as a communications operator who listens in as Brewer flies home. To complete the Anglo-American alliance, Brewer marries Ann.

As the death of Brewer's friend suggests, *Eagle Squadron* was typical of World War II combat films in attempting to negotiate between the competing values of triumphant individualism and cooperative action for effective battle. In the final sequence, Brewer single-handedly completes an aborted commando mission, affirming his unique qualities where it counts. The rest of the film stresses group coordination as a distinctively British value. Arthur Lubin shows the RAF's Battle Command Headquarters in long shots and craning movements that display a beehive of intensive, well-organized activity. During the outing with war orphans, a German attack necessitates unified movements on the part of the children, and Brewer has to rein in an angry child who insists on standing on open ground and hurling stones at the planes. The hospital in which Ann's father resides is attacked during an evening blitz; the blind patients in the hospital are shown with arms on each other's shoulders in single file as a means of getting to safety as quickly as possible.

Yet the formulaic conversion narrative was hardly *Eagle Squadron*'s selling point when it was released in June 1942; fans of aviation films would have seen comparable stories of brash young American protagonists discovering a sense of self-worth and purpose in the British cause in previously released films such as Twentieth Century–Fox's *A Yank in the RAF* and Warner Bros.' *Captains of the Clouds* and *International Squadron*. Moreover, where these films offered the likes of Cagney, Power, and Betty Grable, *Eagle Squadron* had only the young Stack and Barrymore. Wanger hoped to "get away from the traditional air picture and sell (especially to women in the audience) this unknown new force on which the future of the world depends."

But by the time of the film's premiere, the distinctive feature of *Eagle Squadron* highlighted in promotion was "actuality footage" taken from the British documentary *The Pilot Is Safe* and from Schoedsack and Watt's work.

In the film's first lengthy combat sequence of the air raid over German munitions installations, studio close-ups of pilots and their eyelines are edited with distant shots of enemy aircraft, followed awkwardly around the tail of a plane. During the prologue, correspondent Reynolds talks about the Eagle Squadron, first over aerial footage of the British countryside (providing a trace of Wanger's suggestion to Raine that he try to convey the "poetry of flight") and then over a lengthy pan of devastation in London after the blitz. Next Reynolds introduces twelve Eagle Squadron members, who are shown in medium close-ups, shot from low angles against the sky, some looking off camera and some holding letters or pets. As Reynolds introduces them, he indicates their hometowns and gives some detail about them: how many planes they have downed, and most poignantly, whether or not they are still alive.

Reynolds's very presence invariably referred Anglophile audience members to the British wartime documentary. Reynolds had previously narrated *London Can Take It,* which Warner Bros. distributed nationally to widespread critical and Academy acclaim. Following that, he made a lecture tour of the United States and narrated another British documentary, *The Big Blockade,* in early 1941. Wanger also calculated that Reynolds's participation "should help the British market as he is the most popular foreign correspondent there."

The film's narrative furthered this connection by purporting to explain the "stiff upper lip" behind *London Can Take It* and *Listen to Britain* to American audiences. Wanger had greatly admired both these films, and he urged Universal unsuccessfully to distribute the latter film just as *Eagle Squadron* was in postproduction.) But where the work of Watt and particularly Jennings emphasizes the humane and cultured qualities of British citizens who are determined to reaffirm the values they fight for through their daily routines, *Eagle Squadron* melodramatizes the stiff upper lip into an extreme and inhumane pose, a virtual parody of the unemotional professionalism associated with the adventure films of Hawks. When a British flyer tells the squad that his brother has been shot down, the flyer simply pauses in dramatic silence before ordering hot tea. When British flyers joke after Brewer's best friend is shot down, Brewer asks them, "What do you British have for hearts? Carburetors?" As Johnny Coe tries to explain to Brewer, "This island's been taking it for two years." Bosley Crowther commented in his review for the *New York Times,* the filmmakers "had the notion that British resolution was something mystic and hard to explain"; once understood, the hero got "the inspiration for performing a wildly heroic deed."

Hence, given carte blanche to produce what he wanted at Universal, Wanger's first effort was a hodgepodge of documentary footage, formulaic character development, and caricatured national types comparable in its disunities to *Gabriel Over the White House, The President Vanishes,* and *Blockade.* In fact, the most impressive aspect of *Eagle Squadron* remains Stanley Cortez's dazzling work for the studio-shot scenes, of which Wanger was appropriately proud. Fresh from Welles's *The Magnificent Ambersons* (1943), Cortez (who was selected by director Lubin) continued his experiments with deep-focus cinematography, using light-sensitive plus-x film stock, f-stops as small as f/16, and low-key lighting to minimize the artificiality of the studio sets.

Nonetheless, Wanger was outraged by the critical flogging *Eagle Squadron* received. "I wish you would advise your motion picture critic," Wanger wrote his friend Jackson at *Time,*

> that I *was* able to decide whether *Eagle Squadron* should be straight documentary or straight Hollywood. I wanted to make a picture that would have the widest possible circulation in the area where it was needed most, to use as much documentary as possible, but still retain a story that would attract the public.

It was less satisfying aesthetically than *Foreign Correspondent* or than *Mrs. Miniver,* Wyler's Oscar-winning, "womens' picture" paean to "British resolution." This was due in part to the lesser talents (excepting Cortez) at Wanger's disposal. But it was also the result of Wanger's own penchant for message mongering at the expense of verisimilitude. To Cowles, he boasted that the film "is the perfect Hollywood accomplishment—please the masses and serve the country at the same time." Indeed, to his mind, intentions outweighed aesthetic achievement and the critics who panned films like his were practically giving comfort to the isolationists by discouraging exhibitors from booking them. He scolded Jackson that the *Time* critic "should have enough sense to know what the purpose of the picture was," excoriated "the boys who have been sitting in the front row trenches at 21," and preferred to cite the praise of British officials for the film's "realism." In short, the war effort encouraged Wanger to gloss over the whole problem of fully integrating entertainment with propaganda.

In the case of *Eagle Squadron*, Wanger's policy paid off, as the film earned more than $500,000 in profits. The same could not be said of Wanger and Raine's later contributions to the war effort. *We've Never Been Licked* was a portrayal of campus life at Texas A & M University before and during the war. It shifted from the humiliating and ritualistic hazing of freshmen to an espionage plot. A student considered a Japanese collaborator moves to Tokyo and eventually betrays a Japanese air raid on an American carrier by giving his air force college chums the Japanese plans. It drew an analogy between the absurd routines of a highly regimented campus life and the rigors of military training. It implicitly promoted home front vigilance within the espionage plot. But the film's lack of stars and sudden shifts in tone hailed back to the sketchiness of Wanger's least appealing 1930s Paramount films, and its admirers consisted exclusively of A & M alumni.

Ladies Courageous, Wanger's third film depicting the armed forces, is a flawed attempt to glorify women in uniform, a goal many producers embraced after Mellett's call in January 1942 for films that made "the man behind the man behind the gun feel that his work is also exciting and dramatic." MGM produced *Tender Comrade* and *Cry Havoc* (1943), Paramount realized *So Proudly We Hail* (1943) about nurses in the Pacific, and Selznick began work on his first film since *Gone with the Wind, Since You Went Away.*

In early September, Colonel Mason Wright, then head of public relations of the Pictorial Division of the Armed Forces, suggested that Wanger produce a feature on the newly formed Women's Auxiliary Ferrying Squadron (WAFS). This small, experimental group consisted of civilian women pilots who instructed male recruits and flew finished planes from factories to air fields within the United States; the rationale was that in doing so, they freed up male pilots for combat duty. Wanger saw the subject as a "sequel" to *Eagle Squadron*—in fact, a scene in the earlier film featured a British woman pilot flying Chuck Brewer and Johny Coe to headquarters. Wanger agreed to Raine's suggestion that they build their story around a character in journalist Virginia Cowles's book *Looking for Trouble* who was "vain, camera-greedy, press-hungry and publicity-crazy." To collaborate with Raine, Wanger sent short story writer Doris Gilbert to the East to visit the WAFS and talk to officials over several weeks' time.

Gilbert found the WAFS a revelation. Describing the "sorority" spirit of camaraderie among them at one base, she wrote:

> The dialogue is thick and fast and they are definitely devoted to each other. They have to be, because they really feel unwanted at the field. From Mrs. Gillies (a WAFS leader) down, I found the same quiet, proud determination to prove that women in the air deserve the same break as men. "We have to be twice as reserved, twice as business-like, and twice as Army, because we're women."

Gilbert and Wanger discovered that the WAFS was resented by male pilots in training and that its official status was subject to change. Although WAFS leaders such as Nancy Harkness Love awaited official recognition and transatlantic flights, the military brass was slow to respond (their wish was granted just as the film completed postproduction). Wanger's film might enhance the WAFS's chances by presenting it in the best possible light. This is evident in Gilbert's decision to omit any reference to the children left behind while their mothers flew and taught at the air fields.

The "Ladies Courageous" project was as challenging as *Eagle Squadron*. As Wanger put it, the routine duty of the WAFS was not suitable for a narrative film, and "to get any dramatic story at all on which to hang the documentary material was very difficult." Raine responded with two tactics. One was to make a major issue out of the acceptance of women pilots by military officials who wonder how the women will "act in an emergency." Another was what Wanger called "lots of schmaltz"—the melodramatic contortions and distortions set to lush music by Dimitri Tiomkin. Raine's adaptation of Gilbert's treatment exaggerated the pilots' personal problems and sacrifices even beyond their depiction in other wartime films about groups of women. Loaded with flashbacks explaining several fliers' reasons for and fears of their work, it included an ex-actress who crashes a plane during an award ceremony to attract attention to herself and the WAFS's cause, a stunt flier who believes incorrectly her unlucky number is about to come up, and a young flier who, in a situation borrowed from films such as *Cry Havoc,* finds her husband flirting with another woman pilot.

At the film's conclusion, a shortage of men gets the women assigned to a major delivery mission in spite of the squadron's ample problems. But like other homefront films discussed by critic Michael Renov, *Ladies Courageous* suggested the possibility of effective women's action only to deny it emphatically. The air force's Pictorial Division review board eliminated several excessive scenes of the fliers' irresponsibility, yet the script argued implicitly for the dissolution of the WAFS rather than their promotion. As the father of a WAFS pilot wrote Wanger, the women pilots "haven't had any publicity to speak of and what they are getting in your picture they don't deserve." Indeed, the *New York Times* noted that the characters were "a bunch of irresponsible nitwits" whose hysterics, bickering, and "generally unladylike, nay, unpatriotic, conduct" was unprecedented. *Time*'s critic thought the characters were unfit for motherhood: they "cannot be trusted to pilot a perambulator, much less a B-17."

It was something of a paradox, then, that Wanger, the champion of social relevance and propaganda, fared best during the war years when he dispensed with propaganda altogether. Failing to mesh message and entertainment values, Wanger's continued answer was to balance them in alternate productions. In early 1943, he reiterated to a newspaper editor that not all of Hollywood's output should be war related: the "horse operas" and comedies

> have a definite job in an important audience. You can't sell social advances all the time. If you did your theaters would be empty. As a publisher, you know the value of an editorial and how much space should be given the editorial as compared to that given the comic section.

The industry was concerned to maintain its entertainment films anyway, and they acted upon this rationale in different ways; for example, five months after Pearl Harbor, Twentieth Century–Fox announced its plans to increase its number of musicals for the 1942–1943 season. Wanger opted for orientalist fantasies.

Universal's sales staff greeted Wanger's second film, *Arabian Nights* (1942), with relief: as sales head John Joseph told Wanger, "it's more fun to sell dames and horses than Spitfires and heroes." Although United Artists reflected industry wisdom in rejecting the project in 1938, Korda's 1940 *A Thief of Baghdad* grossed $1 million and his *The Jungle Book* in April 1942 had demonstrated a continuing market for orientalist appeals; in fact, Universal approved *Arabian Nights* and Wanger's multifilm contract the very month of *The Jungle Book*'s release. They were also able to hire *Jungle Book*'s John Qualen and, significantly, the handsome, muscular teenage Indian actor Sabu, who had starred in both the Korda films.

Wanger hired Michael Hogan, a British free-lance writer who had worked on adapting *Rebecca,* to script a new version of *Arabian Nights*. Amar Al Amar (Erikson) usurps the position of Chief Caliph of Baghdad from his brother, the noble Haroun Al Rashid (Jon Hall) in order to impress and win the dancer "Sherezade" (*sic,* played by Maria Montez). With the help of acrobat Ali Ben Ali (Sabu), Haroun flees with Sherezade's troupe until he defeats his brother, by which time he has also won Sherezade's love.

Hogan's script owed little beyond character names to the *Arabian Nights*. There, Scheherazade spins the various tales in the framing story of the Arabian Nights to preserve her life, and Haroun Al Rashid is the hero of a cycle of tales, none of which involve conflict with a brother. Hogan's script cut and pasted names from a foreign literature, peppered the dialogue with oaths sworn to Allah and mapped Hollywood genres onto the action. The film's Sherezade's haughty preference for power over love and her gradual recognition of her love for Haroun is in the tradition of Hollywood's 1930s romantic heroines. Sabu's role as cupid repeated his function in *The Thief of Baghdad*. The chase of the performing troupe through deserts and villages by Amar's men, and the character configurations of good and evil brothers closely follow the narrative formula of westerns and of swashbuckling Errol Flynn vehicles. Just prior to production, Wanger hired True Boardman—who had contributed to some Abbott and Costello film scripts and wrote an Arabian Nights radio program for Dietrich—to strengthen character motivation and story structure. Boardman read Hogan's work

> with astonishment and called [Wanger] back saying, "Walter—you can't shoot this script and call it the *Arabian Nights*. It's nothing but a western with camels." To which he replied, "I know that, and it will make a million dollars."

Wanger was right. *Arabian Nights* proved to be the producer's most financially successful film thus far, earning nearly 1.9 million in profits and making Wanger in 1944 the second highest paid Hollywood figure after Mayer. In Cincinnati, one exhibitor wrote Blumberg, in spite of the threats of flooding of the Ohio River, the film broke opening day records; another commented that audiences "just eat it up and I don't know where they all came from." Although *Time* dismissed it as "just another oldtime Sheik picture" and Crowther upbraided the film for its lack of fantasy and fidelity to the literary source (a "gaudy spectacle . . . that seems more inspired by western movies than it does by . . . eastern tales"), *Daily Variety* anticipated its box office success by describing it as "a dazzling prescription for sheer entertainment . . . designed to beguile the mud away from more sober and somber matters."

Clearly the film touched a nerve in the homefront audience, a desire for westerns disguised as exotic fantasy adventures. Haroun Al Rashid's evil brother and the grand vizier Nadam (Edgar Barrier) fulfill a fantastic conception of oriental despotism and break laws in a manner that plays upon the intimate connections between political and erotic power. Where Haroun democratically insists that the acrobat Ali Ben Ali is "not my slave—but my friend," Amar and Nadam ruthlessly exploit and murder their subordinates. In the context of the anti-Fascist struggle, they were a displaced expression of the fear and loathing felt toward the leaders of the Axis powers. As Wanger rationalized while *Arabian Nights* was in postproduction, the film "will make fine propaganda for enlistments in the Middle East." Indeed, the resurgence of the orientalist genre in wartime—embodied in musicals such as MGM's *Cairo* and Warner Bros.'s *Desert Song* and even in the choice of setting for a film such as *Casablanca,* where "life is cheap"—confirmed what the success of *The Sheik* had suggested in 1921; in periods of crisis, it provided a condescending way for America to represent threatening and ancient cultures.

Romanticizing the Near East was only one part of the appeal of *Arabian Nights;* another was its kinship to comedies such as Bob Hope and Crosby's *Road to Morocco* (1942), in effect parodying what Korda's *Thief of Baghdad* had dramatized straightforwardly. Wanger's hiring of Boardman to enhance Hogan's script was significant, for Boardman's forte had been devising sketches for Abbott and Costello. The literary *Arabian Nights* has its share of vulgar, erotic humor, but one can see Boardman's work in the series of comic supporting characters associated with the performing troupe that constantly moans and whines about its deprivations. The troupe's leader Ahmed (Billy Gilbert) is given to bouts of hysteria when Sherezade won't perform. Big and blustery, his contribution to various fights is to pummel Amar's men with his stomach (to the accompaniment of a timpani drum), while he improbably impersonates a blacksmith's daughter ("the Bag of Baghdad") to deceive Amar's guards. The juggler Aladdin (Qualen) drops everything whenever he finds a lamp, in the hope that he will recover his magic genie; no one believes this mousey man's stories. Sinbad, played by future Three Stooges member Shemp Howard, is prone to anachronistic dialogue and to reminisce about his glorious voyages when the troupe is in trouble ("You know, this calls to mind an experience I once had . . ."). They represent what Dana Polan has identified as a hysterical response to the threats of death. Like service comedies such as Abbott and Costello's 1941 hits *In the Navy* and *Buck Privates* or Hope's *Caught in the Draft, Arabian Nights* constructs laughs out of regressive, infantile behavior that refuses to ac-knowledge responsibility and conflict.

Another appeal of *Arabian Nights* lay in the film's lavish production de-sign and erotic mise-en-scène. Universal had not produced color films since the musical sequences in its 1930 *King of Jazz*, and studio executives and technicians were apprehensive about employing three-strip Technicolor. But Wanger had a contractual right to a Technicolor film and argued that Uni-versal's contracted talents would keep the film's negative cost down. With the help of art director Golitzen—who suggested that the final quarter of the film take place in tents rather than in elaborate palace sets—and extensive matte work, the film's sets met wartime restrictions. Wanger awarded Golitzen and Jack Otterson production design credit on *Arabian Nights* and gave Golitzen 5 percent of his own profits.

Hence, Wanger created his first full-blown orientalist fantasy in a campy production that highlighted certain techniques of the Ballets Russes. There was Frank Skinner's score, which, like Miklos Rosza's for *The Thief of Baghdad,* imitated passages and tonal elements of Rimsky-Korsakov's orchestral suite. Golitzen's set designs combined golden-hued carpets with blue pastel in a manner that Bakst would have approved. Black servants and Ali Ben Ali's journey across Amar's seraglio encampment reworked the miscegenational frisson of Nijinsky's golden slave in *Scheherazade.* Sabu's character in this scene is like a kid brother fussed at by harem members, dressed in what Crowther termed "peek-a-boo slacks" for "an obvious come-on."

"You're a lucky stiff, Mr. Smith," distribution head William Scully wrote Wanger after the film's release. "Forget all the sarcastic remarks I made [about the film]." Wanger's share of the profits came to roughly $900,000. Neither he nor Universal took *Arabian Nights* for granted, and executives immediately scheduled Sabu, Hall, and Montez for *White Savage* in July 1942; these films were followed by more profitable, campy orientalist Techni-color fantasies such as *Ali Baba and the 40 Thieves* (1944), *Cobra Woman* (directed by Robert Siodmak, 1944), *Sudan* (1945), and *Tangier* (1946). Uni-versal's mid-decade policy of offering audiences in Chairman Cowdin's words "pictures that provided relaxation from the strains and tension of these troublous times" sustained the cycle, as well as Durbin musicals, produced finally in Technicolor.

Strangely enough, Wanger's subsequent contributions to the trend he had started proved tepid. "The Peacock's Feather" concerned a romance between a haughty Princess Delerai (Merle Oberon, chosen over Wanger's preference for MGM newcomer Ava Gardner) who will marry the porcine, despotic Greek king Croesus (Thomas Gomez). The king's plans are complicated by the lowly shepherd Aesop (Turhan Bey), who appears initially as a wise old man, but is magically transformed into a handsome youth by the princess's love. Retitled *A Night in Paradise* (1946), mounted with heavily matted shots and palatial sets that evoked ancient Greece, as well as the extravagant costumes Wanger commissioned from Travis Banton (who henceforth worked regularly at Universal), the film cost $600,000 more than *Arabian Nights*, due in part to postwar inflation. It lost Universal nearly $800,000.

Similarly, *Salome, Where She Danced* (1945) began as a Merian Cooper–John Ford project in 1941 which Wanger bought. The story focused on an Austrian dancer and spy who is the toast of Europe and catches the eye of Bismarck, but who escapes to the American West for more espionage. Wanger's concept of the film was to reverse the terms of *Arabian Nights*. Veteran screenwriter Stallings submitted a treatment to Wanger noting, "I have faithfully followed the idea of an Arabian nights story in a Western setting." The result was one of Universal's camp classics. Denied the services of Montez, Wanger persuaded Universal's publicity department to mount a much-publicized search for "the most beautiful girl in the world." He eventually chose Yvonne De Carlo, a Paramount contract player, basing his choice, as he had done with Lamarr, solely on her looks (and her resemblance to Bennett): "she was a puppet in our hands." After the film's release, *Variety* ranked De Carlo along with Lizabeth Scott and Lauren Bacall as the "top new stars" of the year.

The critical reception of *Salome, Where She Danced* in the popular press was probably the worst of Wanger's career, bringing to a head the nagging comparisons of Wanger's rhetoric with his films. The *New York Times* review of *We've Never Been Licked* began by noting that Wanger, recently quoted in the paper, "forgets his theories when he makes a film himself." There and in its review of *Ladies Courageous*, its critics noted, "Mr. Wanger should know better." *Script* magazine critic Herb Sterne wondered "how much longer" Wanger could "have the audacity to make public and frequent harangues on what he terms 'the art of the motion picture.'" For *Salome, Where She Danced*, the criticism intensified. John Maynard of the *New York Herald Tribune* wrote "the more I see of Mr. Wanger's latter day output the more I wonder just how much he *really* had to do with 'The Long Voyage Home.'"

David Hanna of the *Los Angeles Daily News* condemned the film, stating that "one's sense of the ridiculous is dulled by the realization that the picture is a creation of Walter Wanger." Hanna continued:

> "Salome, Where She Danced" in a sense, is insulting and certainly a direct contradiction of the theories and ideas allegedly held by producer Wanger. One cannot avoid questioning his integrity or suggesting that he is evading wartime responsibility. . . . "Salome, Where She Danced" is not just a bad picture—it is rank.

Hanna's review arrived on Wanger's desk with an anonymous note that read in part,

This is the way lots of us felt—only David Hanna of the Daily News expressed it better than we could. Those of us who worked on it, and others who didn't work on it but are connected with the industry, sickened at the thought of being connected with it.

Yet after meeting with Wanger, Hanna was moved to publicly retract his criticisms. Wanger shrewdly persuaded Hanna that he made the orientalist films only "to build the value of his trademark," that he was "anything but sympathetic" to that kind of film, and that, somewhat contradictorily, *Salome, Where She Danced* "far from fulfilled his own expectations." Hanna came away "with a better, clearer understanding of the problems of a producer such as Wanger, who has earnestly tried to utilize the resources of the screen for purposes beyond its function as an entertainment medium."

But Wanger could not personally silence all the criticism that appeared about his Technicolor romances: one Washington, D.C., critic noted that Wanger "regularly mentions the need for 'more intelligent films,' and just as regularly turns out Technicolored horrors like 'Night in Paradise.'" When he and Goldwyn told the press in 1946 that American films were losing pace with audience needs, Zanuck snapped back, in a rare derogation of a competitor's product, that Hollywood would thrive if Wanger didn't produce films such as *Salome, Where She Danced*.

The disappointing showings of both *A Night in Paradise* and *Salome, Where She Danced* kept Wanger away from the orientalist genre for several years. But the genre had a life of its own at Universal and Columbia. By the time he pitched *The Adventures of Hajji Baba* to Allied Artists and Twentieth Century–Fox in 1953, a Fox executive noted:

This is a formula story that has been done before and sometimes very successfully. A great deal depends upon who the Princess is and how voluptuous she may look to the morons who like this sort of thing; and, also who the brave Hajji Baba would be. However, for its type I guess it is no worse than its predecessors. This is the kind of picture that is known to the vulgar trade as "t[its] and s[and]."

Wanger's penchant for orientalist romance culminated in *Cleopatra*.

By contrast, Wanger's last financial triumph in wartime for Universal was another combat film, in this case, the 1943 *Gung Ho!* The film was based on the taking of Makin Island from the Japanese by "Carlson's Raiders," 221 Marines under Lieutenant Colonel Evan Carlson in August 1942. Their courageous exploits provided a psychological boost early in the war, and they received additional publicity because James Roosevelt was the second-in-command of the invasion.

When Wanger initially requested the right to film the story, Navy representative Lieutenant Alfred J. Bolton stipulated that the film not single out the characters based on Roosevelt and Carlson. Wanger encouraged veteran producer-director-screenwriter Hubbard to confer with Carlson and closely follow the accounts of the raid. Hubbard and director Ray Enright characterized the Marines selected for the raid as determined killers and sprinkled the film with "yellow peril" jingoism by showing the Japanese as treacherous (pretending to be dead in order to kill Americans at close range) and weak-willed soldiers who fall whenever challenged by Americans. Historians Clayton Koppes and Gregory Black called it "one of the most rabid 'hate the Jap' films made in Hollywood."

With all of its excesses, *Gung Ho!* nonetheless pleased Carlson immensely, particularly for its emphasis on classic Chinese precepts of cooperation which Carlson had emphasized as commander and which the film used to play on the extraordinary sympathy Americans felt toward the Chinese. "From our first meeting," Carlson wrote Wanger,

> I was convinced that you grasped the ideas of cooperation, of tolerance and of self-discipline as a way of life, and that you profoundly believed in their importance as a working basis for an improved social order. Your repeated insistence, in the course of production, that entertainment value be subordinated to authenticity of technique and of fact, and to articulation and illustration of Gung Ho procedure, serve to confirm your sincerity and your courage.

More than *Eagle Squadron, Gung Ho!* balanced the necessity of cooperation with the formulaic demands of individualist heroes.

The Carlson's Raiders story had lost its currency by 1944 but its motif of cooperation could still be utilized as a morale booster. While returning with the men from their mission in the submarine, Colonel Thorwald (Randolph Scott) turns to the camera, in the manner of Wanger's 1930s heroes, and speaks:

> Our course is clear. It is for us at this moment with the memory of the sacrifice of our brothers still fresh, to dedicate again our hearts, our minds and our bodies to the great task that lies ahead. We must go further, and devote ourselves also to the monumental task of insuring that the peace which follows this holocaust will be a just, equitable and conclusive peace.

With this send-off Wanger sought to package *Gung Ho!*, for all its hate-mongering toward the Japanese and its gritty combat sequences, as a plea for postwar unity. Like many industry leaders, Wanger recognized that the enormous value of movies in wartime would "multiply in the *post-war* period when our doctrine will have to be spread rapidly to counteract enemy propaganda."

Louisiana journalist Ulric Bell agreed, and he told Wanger he thought the script for *Gung Ho!* was terrific. His opinion mattered to Wanger not only because Bell had been since 1943 the domestic representative for the OWI in Hollywood but because the two men were active in the Hollywood chapter (founded in 1943) of the liberal internationalist group, the Free World Association. The cooperative message of *Gung Ho!* conformed to the group's call for domestic unity on social and political issues, articulated by members such as Boyer, Cromwell, Hornblow, Jr., Lubitsch, Nichols, Rosten, Schary, Welles, Charles Brackett, William Goetz, John Larkin, Allen Rivkin, and Rosalind Russell (in her liberal days).

Modeled after the international Free World Association organized by French resistance fighter Louis Dolivet, the Hollywood group took as its major theme domestic social and political unity and the creation of a forum like the League of Nations for international cooperation. Claiming itself "a non-partisan, non-political organization," the association included in its policies "an equal and militant fight against Fascism and Communism in the United States of America" and "an end to American isolationism and to that species of false 'nationalism' which history shows has always been used to overthrow democracy." Wanger described the group as "temporary" and "informal," and its activities included dinners, public speakers on international affairs, and roundtable discussions of postwar problems.

But the group's claims of political neutrality were window dressing. Its target was a group of Hollywood conservatives who had been brooding about industry liberalism since the fall 1943 complaints by Republican congressmen that American movies were too supportive of Roosevelt's administration before an election year. Although Free World Association members such as screenwriter Rivkin felt that the association's platform "showed the town we were not a pro-Red outfit, that we aren't concerned with industry level activities," conservatives accused the association of Communist infiltration.

An open clash came in February 1944, one month after *Gung Ho!*'s premiere, when the Hollywood chapter of the association publicly proclaimed its concerns at a dinner held in honor of Vice-President Henry Wallace. The Motion Picture Alliance for the Preservation of American Ideals, led by director Sam Wood and Wanger's Hollywood hero, Disney, held a counter-dinner on the same evening three miles away. At the association's Wallace dinner, Wanger got the biggest applause for putting aside his prepared speech and "attacking" the Motion Picture Alliance for its allegations of Communist influence in the group:

> Let's keep the record straight. We, too, find home-grown communism as odious as home-grown fascism. . . . [But we do not] intend to be misled by the familiar Hitler line by which communism is made the bogey . . . to confuse us.

The Motion Picture Alliance's attack on Hollywood liberals and the Free World Association's counteraccusations became quite heated in the months that followed, and Wanger led the fight. In May, he wrote the alliance that their "unsupported charges of Communism in the motion picture industry" had "linked throughout the nation the words 'Hollywood' and 'Red' and without proof." By the end of the year, he had turned down an offer to work as the head of production at MGM in part because in addition to Mayer and Nicholas Schenck, the studio harbored many Motion Picture Alliance members, such as Wood, Montgomery and James K. McGuinness, who "represent a distinct contradiction to everything I have been fighting for." Wanger campaigned for Congresswoman Helen Gahagan Douglas, for California governor Warren, and heartily for FDR in the 1944 Presidential race. In November, Wanger addressed the Hollywood Democratic Committee, noting that at its core the Republican party stood for prewar isolationism and that it was "hopelessly incapable of dealing with any single phase of the postwar world." His remarks were met yet again with rousing applause.

The Free World Association disbanded when the United Nations was formed, but the Motion Picture Alliance thrived well into the 1950s, and its members had a long memory. The heated political debates were a harbinger of the postwar fragmentation of American society and of Hollywood itself. Like many industry workers, Wanger found that his zealous work, on-screen and off, in support of the nation and of Hollywood, counted for little once the war ended. He retired from the Academy presidency in 1945. Having been at the center of Hollywood's leadership for the past decade, he slipped almost imperceptibly to its margins. There he suffered frustration, neglect, and irreversible personal and professional decline.

Part Four

Bitter Teas and Reckless Moments, 1945–1952

12

Fritz Lang, Incorporated

Diana Productions, Wanger's first postwar semi-independent company, was formed in early 1945 with the highest expectations. Yet three years later, the venture went down in flames. At that time, Wanger sent his friend and attorney Bienstock a lengthy description of his difficulties with Lang. Lang was the company's president, producer-director, and majority stockholder. In executive vice-president Wanger's view, he was also the major reason for Diana's downfall:

> The time he took and the problems he made are really fantastic and beyond human belief. The man is a Prussian to the fingertips when it comes to detail, and worries about something that's been said in a column about him. . . . Although he wouldn't even write a letter without my dictating it for him, he wanted all the credit. It's just been a nightmare.

He further summarized his recent association with Lang as "two and a half years of misery."

Joan Bennett—cofounder of Diana, its second largest nominal stockholder, and the star of its two completed films, *Scarlet Street* (1945) and *Secret Beyond the Door* (1948)—concurred with her husband that Lang was tough to work with. But where Wanger described Lang as a sort of Frankenstein monster unleashed by executive power, Bennett found Lang to be a schizophrenic. He was "a real Jekyll and Hyde character," Bennett later recalled, "calm and purposeful one moment, and off on a tirade the next." Predictably, Lang held a different view of the reasons for Diana's troubles. In November and December 1947, he accused Wanger of dereliction in his duties, condemned

Bennett for sabotaging Diana, and generally asserted that Wanger and Bennett had committed treason against him.

In truth the demise of Diana resulted from more than the clash of strong-willed personalities. Contrary to general perceptions, the highly touted semi-independent producers of the 1940s were, like their 1930s predecessors, adjuncts of the majors, and their fates were tied to those of their nominal competitors. Although Diana was formed when Universal and the film industry were in their strongest economic position, it declined along with Hollywood from early 1947 onward. That year, as Lang struggled to produce *Secret Beyond the Door,* he discovered that semi-independent production in the forties did not dramatically change the way films were made, and it certainly did not enhance his power at a major studio.

Bennett, Lang, and Wanger's aims in forming Diana, Diana's contradictory corporate structure, changing industry conditions, and studio policy management all helped to alienate the partners from one another. No doubt, Lang's alternately authoritarian and pathetic postures inspired Diana's inception, its success with *Scarlet Street,* and its deterioration with *Secret Beyond the Door.* But Diana's melodramatic history is comparable to Lang and Wanger's *You Only Live Once:* a tale of protagonists overwhelmed by external obstacles, bad timing, and misunderstandings.

It had been five years since *House Across the Bay,* and it seemed only logical for Wanger and Bennett to team up again. After leaving Wanger's employ, Bennett went to Twentieth Century–Fox and since 1940 had starred in a series of unremarkable films. The two exceptions, *Man Hunt* (1941) and *The Woman in the Window* (RKO, 1944) were directed by Lang. The success of Bennett's second film with Lang held special importance, since she had interrupted her career to have Wanger's first child, Stephanie, in June, 1943.

Bennett was a devoted mother, but she did not intend to give up acting, and *The Woman in the Window* augured well for her future. In her words, she "performed better under [Lang's] direction than at any other time in my career. Almost always I did what I was told, and we developed a great working rapport." The Diana company would give Bennett greater say in her cinematographer, characters' scripting, and costuming, it would showcase her talents, and it would combine the artistic integrity of Lang's work with Wanger's business acumen. After optimistically titling their company New World Pictures, Lang and Wanger let Bennett to rename it "Diana" in honor of her eldest daughter.

In fact it was Bennett who inspired the new company's formation. She was highly sympathetic to Lang; in fact several of their associates believe that the two were lovers sometime during the mid-forties. Whatever their offscreen relations, in the early 1940s Bennett had witnessed Lang's difficulties with

Fox executives Zanuck and Goetz: "They treated him like just anything," she later recalled, "and he was much more than that." According to Wanger, Diana was formed in part to shield Lang from such conflicts and constraints: "Out of all this came the idea that poor Fritz Lang was an abused soul, and if he only had a company of his own where he could get a chance to express himself, it would make a new man of him and remove all his inhibitions."

Sarcasm aside, Wanger's remarks are a factual summary. Since *You Only Live Once,* Lang had experienced enormous frustration working in Hollywood. He complained to Lewis Jacobs in 1940 that Fox handed him the completed script of *The Return of Frank James* only days before he was to begin shooting. Before working under contracts for Paramount (*Ministry of Fear,* 1944) and International Pictures (*The Woman in the Window*), he had worked as the producer-director for semi-independent Arnold Pressberger on *Hangmen Also Die* (1943), about the Heydrich assassinations. But, Lang told a publicist, the film was "the most difficult picture he ever made" because it was "difficult to cast and to get authentic sets representing Prague."

Lang's dilemma in late 1944 was that, as a perfectionist, he needed to work with the resources and quality facilities of a major studio, but also as a perfectionist, he abhorred the production schedules and protocols he found in Hollywood. Refusing to adjust to the studio system, he was still searching for UFA in America, for an organization that would indulge his need for total authority in filmmaking. Diana Productions held the promise of such an operation, particularly when other plans—such as a thriller starring Bergman for Selznick—fell through after Lang had devoted three weeks to the screenplay. It was a failure that hardened Lang's determination to be in control.

Wanger supported any move that helped his wife's career; he had greatly admired *Man Hunt* for conveying the necessity of a steadfast opposition to Fascism within an adventure format, and he agreed that "Joan's pictures with Lang were about the best she had done in recent years." But Wanger had other, expedient reasons for arranging financing and distribution for Diana: he wished to differentiate his product after four years as a unit producer at Universal. He was tired of limited budgets, contract actors, and minor directors and he was nostalgic for the days when he could afford stars such as Bennett and directors such as Ford and Hitchcock, whose films reflected well on Wanger but who in the postwar period were unavailable to him.

Hence, Wanger served as executive vice-president and as executive producer of Diana films. He secured financing for Lang's films and advised him on studio policy and procedures in exchange for 25 percent of Diana's profit share. As one attorney suggested, Wanger's previous Universal films did not have "directors of the calibre of Fritz Lang or stars of the calibre of Mrs. Wanger. 12½% of a Lang picture [a portion of Wanger's earnings for his work for Diana] may well be worth more than 50% of a Joe Doakes picture."

There was more to joining up with Lang, then, than Bennett's genuine pity for a frustrated artist; it was part and parcel of Wanger's general production strategies during the postwar years.

Bennett, Lang, and Wanger received only encouragement from Universal in their new venture. Like all the major studios, Universal rode the boom market of the war years to what *Variety* termed in early 1946 "the strongest financial position in its history." The end of the war was an especially prosperous period for Universal. The rescinding of the wartime excess profit tax in the fall of 1945 and its 60 percent rise in exhibition contracts over the 1930s increased Universal's 1945 profits to a record high of $3,910,928. It issued 60,000 shares of preferred stock to finance production and to expand its distribution abroad. It renewed its distribution agreement with J. Arthur Rank and ensured playing time and income from British theaters.

Prosperity by itself generated an encouraging environment for production at Universal and a boost for studio morale; of greater significance for Wanger, Bennett, and Lang was that, as in 1941, Universal executives elected to invest a considerable percentage of the company's additional income in production, continuing the studio's efforts to upgrade its product and reach for "big five status," partly by contracting for semi-independent productions from Mark Hellinger, Michael Todd, and, in June 1946, with the impressive Enterprise Productions (which eventually produced Bergman's *Arch of Triumph,* among other films). Diana had plenty of company on the lot.

The tolerance of semi-independent production and the need for prestige product facilitated Diana's formation and the company's emphasis on Lang. The studios' prosperity in wartime only reinforced their and their talents' belief that unit and semi-independent production facilitated greater individual artistry and box office performance. "One has all the money one is allowed to keep," wrote screenwriter Nichols to Lang in March 1945 after seeing *Woman in the Window:*

> Like yourself, I daresay, I'm not interested in just "making pictures." . . . the thing that fascinates is the exceptional story: for me, the attraction is the right story and the right director—and it's been too long since *Man Hunt!*

Nichols signed on to write *Scarlet Street* six weeks later.

In this context, Lang benefited from the notion of authorship and from the mystique of European technique. In 1945, European films were finding a solid audience, presumably one that mainstream Hollywood films did not attract. Olivier's *Henry V* (1944) enjoyed a $1 million American gross, a striking success for a British film, and Roberto Rossellini's *Open City* began its multiple-year run at a single theater in New York City. The continental sensibility, defined primarily as "realism," seemed a viable method of differentiating product for the mature audiences that the foreign films had uncovered. This context gave Lang hope that his work and name could become familiar to American audiences through Diana's operations.

Diana and Lang considered different ways to sell the German director and his "realistic" cinema. Wanger's publicity advisers Mervin Houser and Ted Bonnet suggested in February 1946 a publicity piece that followed Lang as he surveys city life:

> Fritz Lang, the Viennese with the monocle, poking into deadfalls on Main Street, second-hand book shops, talking to or perhaps stealing a stray penny from blind beggars, mixing with the street walkers, grifters, bums, etc.—in other words, a real realist, venturing out beyond the confines of this phoney movie town to find out what life really looks like. Perhaps he could take Susan Hayward or someone else with him.

Lang himself opted for a more dignified strategy. In the summer of 1946, he held a conference with publicist Ettinger about selling Diana's trademark by building up his name. Many of the suggestions made at this meeting were influenced by the success and censorship of *Scarlet Street* earlier in the year. Lang was dissatisfied with Universal's ads for *Scarlet Street,* which hailed him as "the master of the unusual," for this moniker only confused him with Hitchcock's "master of suspense." Lang also noted that *master of the unusual* "seems to connote a mastery of film trickery which bears no relation to the realism of my films." Although he had no catchy phrase to substitute, Lang characterized his "realistic" style in terms of *Scarlet Street,* a film he felt was "of the people" and "for the people."

More significantly, Lang thought his films had special appeal to a mature audience. The minutes of the publicity meeting describe his comments this way:

> Mr. Lang, as producer-director of Diana, unites the culture of Europe with the highly specialized technical achievements of Hollywood. . . . Diana officers do not share the contemptuous opinion that American movie audiences are composed of 14-year-old mentalities. Mr. Lang believes his direction reflects this respect for audiences, for he depends on audience collaboration to a very large extent to give full meaning to his work.

Everyone agreed that Diana needed a slogan to indicate that Lang's films would appeal to "the intellectual upper-crust." The basis of their appeal was "audience collaboration." By this Lang presumably meant the judgments film viewers make about characters and about the consistency and reliability of narration in Lang's films. The director believed that this could be a selling point for Diana Productions.

Like Diana, all the semi-independents of the 1940s—be they Enterprise Productions or James Cagney Productions—followed a method of financing their films which was slightly different from Wanger's arrangements at Paramount and United Artists. Following the example set by Levee's Screen Guild in 1932, they raised up to half of their financing from corporate stock sales and salary deferments. Unlike Wanger's Paramount arrangement, the 1940s semi-independents used loans from banks or other financial institutions. After the war years, the banks no longer required completed films as collateral; a major distribution agreement would suffice for production loans. The major studios advanced them the other half of their production financing, facilities (studio space, technicians, labs), and distribution services. As in the 1930s, the association between the closed semi-independent corporations and the major studios was truly symbiotic. The major difference was that in the 1940s the semi-independents were needed to provide not a high number of films but movies of higher quality.

The relationship Wanger negotiated for Diana with Universal in May 1945 was a textbook example of semi-independent production. Several individuals purchased 1,000 shares of stock in Diana (at seventy-five dollars a share); the $75,000 so raised paid for Nichols's *Scarlet Street* script. Diana, through Wanger, also obtained 60 percent of the money needed for the film's production (generally known as "first money") with a loan from the Bank of America, which it applied to the salaries of the film's talents: Lang ($75,000), Edward G. Robinson ($100,000), Bennett ($75,000), Wanger ($45,000), and Nichols ($50,000). The company also used its loan to pay Universal's monthly 20 percent overhead charges. Diana could not write a single check, however, unless a representative of Universal countersigned it.

Universal's collection of 20 percent overhead charges for more than $350,000 in talent salaries that did not involve studio facilities was inequitable. But the studio took on greater risk with production advances that constituted the more risky "second money"—the difference between the bank loan and the film's final cost, repaid from the film's gross earnings "second" after Diana's bank loan. Nor did Universal charge Diana interest payments on its advances. When the film went into distribution, Universal first reimbursed itself for advertising and distribution costs and took a percentage of the gross (25 percent in North America, 30 percent elsewhere) as a distribution fee. The remaining revenues were to be applied to the bank loan and to the negative cost of the film. If *Scarlet Street* earned any more money, this constituted the profits that Universal and Diana shared equally. Diana's half of the profits was further divided to pay Nichols's deferred salary and to give Wanger one-fourth of Diana's profit share for his services.

Financing was established at the bank, and the cogs of semi-independent–studio machinery began to whir. Nichols's script for *Scarlet Street* was approved in late June 1945 at a budget of $1,149,000, and Universal cleared studio space within six weeks of the script's approval (on July 23) to minimize Diana's costs for idle contracted talent. But the most definitive evidence that cooperating independents such as Diana were closely bound to their host studios was in the contract. Here Lang was given sixty days to complete post-production and view his final cut at a first preview. But it further stipulated that

> [Universal] may recut and re-edit said photoplay in such manner as we may deem necessary or desirable to meet legal, "Hays Office" or censorship require-ments or export requirements or for the purpose of avoiding possible litigation or to enhance its commercial value.

The clause regarding the right of final cut supported a nebulous policy with plenty of room for interpreting "censorship requirements" and "enhancement" of commercial value.

Significantly, the phrasing of this clause was standard in all of Universal's contracts, and it was identical to all of Wanger's own agreements with the studio. Unlike Wanger, Diana had the freedom to develop its scripts with-out Universal's approval. But when it came to the right of final cut, Univer-sal maintained the same discretionary powers over the film from a semi-independent company (responsible for up to 60 percent of its film's financing) as it did over the unit producer whom it financed entirely. Wanger assured Lang that this clause specified a rarely invoked remedy of last resort.

With contracts signed, the production of *Scarlet Street* went smoothly through the postproduction stage. Nichols and Lang developed their story of the middle-class bank cashier and amateur painter Christopher Cross (Robin-son) who grows infatuated with a vulgar prostitute Kitty (Bennett) whose pimp Johnny (Dan Duryea) encourages her to milk Cross for money. Kitty accepts his money and sells his paintings under her own name, until Cross dis-covers Kitty's relationship with Johnny and kills her in a sudden rage. Though Johnny is tried and convicted for Kitty's murder, Cross becomes a derelict haunted by his memories.

While Nichols and Lang worked on the script, Lang cast the bulk of the film and selected Milton Krasner, the cinematographer on *Woman in the Window,* to film it. Lang apparently accepted Universal's selection of other technicians and workers on the film, such as art director Golitzen. Wanger sub-mitted Nichols's script to the Breen Office one month before principal pho-tography began. *Scarlet Street* portrays a murderer who goes legally unpun-ished for his crime, but the completed script, dated July 17, excited little controversy at the Production Code Administration. Nichols was advised to minimize the suggestions that Kitty was a prostitute and Johnny her pimp by playing down her masochistic tendencies. The Breen Office requested fewer scenes in Kitty's bedroom and reminded Lang that the paintings by Cross, such as *Eve Under the Elevated* (actually painted by Lang's friend John Decker), should be done in good taste.

During principal photography, although Lang ran five days behind schedule and $200,000 over budget, neither Universal or Wanger tried to restrain him. When Wanger learned of cost overruns and schedule delays, he sent Lang a copy of the studio memorandum with the note, "Here is key [*sic*] as to how to make quarter of a million dollars. Put this under your pillow." A slight difficulty in scheduling different sets for the film was worked out. The only major controversy concerned Universal's decision to charge Diana increased overhead charges because of the studio workers strike in summer 1945.

Diana smoothly integrated its production into Universal's schedule, but acrimony developed within Diana, according to Wanger, over the final cut of *Scarlet Street*. It was he, not Universal, who elected the right of final cut:

> When it came to the completion of the picture, there was a terrific intrigue and fight over the cutting and Lang accused me of stabbing him in the back because I insisted on the picture's being shortened. He said that I had sided with Universal, and it just took up the god-damndest amount of time and became the most annoying thing.

A comparison of the final script with the released film reveals several elisions.

In the script's opening scene, J. J. Hogarth, Cross's boss, makes a lengthy speech about the "joys" of marriage; this is not in the film. After Chris steals one thousand dollars from Hogarth's firm, in the script he brings it directly to Kitty. Chris finds the copy of *Romeo and Juliet* which Johnny has bought her as a prop for her pose as a struggling actress. Chris reads extensively from the balcony scene as Kitty rolls her eyes. The film omits this scene entirely. In the script, when Chris betrays his wife's first husband, there is considerable action as Chris is caught by the police when he tries to sneak away. The police demand an explanation, assume Chris is Adele's lover, and finally let him go while Adele's first husband swears he'll get revenge on Chris. In the film, Chris sneaks off without incident. Another major deletion is the scene in which Chris watches Johnny's execution from atop a telegraph pole. Chris cries out wide-eyed, "Now, now, now!" when his watch from Hogarth indicates eleven o'clock.

These cuts generally eliminate redundancies and character motivation cues from the story. They also diminish the extremity of Chris's idealism, his humiliating infatuation with Kitty, and his degradation at the conclusion of the film. Publicity stills indicate that several of these scenes were shot: trade advertising for the film as late as December includes a still of Chris reading (*Romeo and Juliet*) to Kitty, and Lang admitted years later that he shot and then eliminated the Sing Sing scene.

It seems unlikely that Lang, who worked intensively on his films at all stages, would allow Wanger to make these changes without a fight. As of

November 1945, however, Lang was at work on *Cloak and Dagger* at Warner Bros., and his absence from Universal, as well as his absorption in directing another film, angered Wanger and facilitated tampering with the final cut. In early November, Wanger received a report from his publicity director Houser on the Universal sales staff's response to *Scarlet Street*. Wanger took their suggestions to heart, for virtually every cut made from script to the finished film is suggested in this memo. Houser reported the staff appraised the film to make "buckets of money," but he argued for better pacing and a running time of 105 minutes—a matter Wanger was sensitive to after the slow "Germanic" direction of *You Only Live Once*. The Universal staff also found the Sing Sing scene strangely humorous, felt that Hogarth's speech in the opening scene was too long, and believed the Shakespeare scene should be omitted.

If Lang objected to the recut version of *Scarlet Street*, Universal accepted it with open arms. After a preview screening of the film, Work, Universal's vice-president and general manager, wrote Universal president Blumberg:

> WITHOUT ANY HESITATION OR EQUIVOCATION I AM HAPPY TO STATE THAT IN MY OPINION THIS IS THE BEST PICTURE THAT HAS EVER BEEN MADE AT UNIVERSAL AND WILL MEASURE UP TO THE STANDARD OF ANY PICTURE MADE IN THE INDUSTRY IN PAST YEARS. . . . IT UNQUESTIONABLY WILL OUTGROSS ANY PICTURE THAT WE HAVE RELEASED IN THE PAST TEN YEARS AND IS THE PICTURE WE HAVE BEEN ANXIOUSLY HOPING TO HAVE ON OUR PROGRAM.

Universal had its prestige production, thanks to Diana. The studio further expressed its enthusiasm by cofinancing a lawsuit against the city of Atlanta for banning the film. The support was well justified: *Scarlet Street* earned back its production costs within six months of release. One year after the film's completion, the book value of Diana's stock had doubled.

With the production of *Secret Beyond the Door*, however, internal relationships at Diana worsened. During the year from January 1946 to the beginning of 1947, Lang and Wanger's personality differences were aggravated by disputes over the roles and contracted responsibilities assigned to them within the corporation. The conflict over the final cut of *Scarlet Street* was only the beginning.

Inevitably, Wanger's supervisory status and Lang's position as major stockholder and company president led to arguments. The capitalization of the company gave Lang 503 of the 1,000 stock shares. Wanger rationalized the granting of majority stock to Lang:

> This was the only way to build the man up so that he wouldn't have this inferiority complex and be so difficult. The idea was that if people once showed confidence in him, he would be very easy to handle.

Wanger claimed that Lang and his attorney Martin Gang insisted that Lang hold the majority of Diana stock and that Wanger not be allowed to own any of it (unbeknownst to Lang, it was actually Wanger's money that Bennett invested in the company).

In practice, Lang was required to accept Wanger's judgment on his budgets, his production choices, and his final cut because Wanger was Diana's executive producer. On the other hand, Lang was legally entitled as Diana president to have Wanger removed from the company (even if it cost him a financing and distribution agreement with Universal—which was the primary reason Lang never did fire Wanger). Wanger and Universal regarded Lang's technically dominant position as nominal or at least irrelevant. But Wanger could not "control" Lang if Diana's producer-director elected to assert his authority more forcefully. And after Wanger cut down *Scarlet Street,* this is what Lang elected to do.

The contract language, like Diana's corporate structure, also supported Lang and Wanger's desire to divide the producer's function into distinct financial and artistic realms. Wanger's March 1945 contract with Diana specified his duties as

> the negotiation of contracts . . . with the banks, distribution organizations and personnel to be engaged by the corporation, and advising the corporation with reference to the performance of its obligations under such contracts. You also shall render your services on behalf of the corporation as supervisor of the aforesaid photoplay and you shall be in charge of all financial phases of the production thereof. . . .

> You agree that you will consult with Mr. Fritz Lang, our producer-director, in connection with problems arising in the course of production; but it is agreed that in case of dispute between you, the judgment of Mr. Lang with respect to matters of a purely artistic nature shall control, while your judgment as to all financial aspects of the production, including matters involving any substantial increase in costs shall be controlling.

Lang's contract with Diana had a clause virtually identical to the second paragraph quoted.

Their contracts sounded reasonable enough, but they ignored several issues. The distinction between executive and creative responsibilities overlooked the complex status of such activities as budgets, casting, final cuts, and publicity, which both men could persuasively claim as their own responsibilities. Then too, the role of an executive, supervising producer, which Wanger was supposed to fill at Diana, was not standardized. It presumably referred to Wanger's duties for securing financing and distribution for the Diana films as he had done for the Ford and Hitchcock films at United Artists. But as Wanger's own career demonstrates, there was nothing rigid about this.

Yet, in the case of *Scarlet Street* and *Secret Beyond the Door,* the contracted allocation of tasks did enable Lang and Wanger to pursue their distinct responsibilities until postproduction. From all indications, Lang threw himself totally into production. Weeks after he and Wanger set up their agreement to produce together, Lang began work in Wanger's office. Foley wrote Wanger, "Now if you could just think of some way to get Fritz Lang out of this office for a few minutes so we could at least vacuum before you return. We like him very much but gosh."

Lang worked at a comfortable pace, spending three months with Nichols on the script of *Scarlet Street* and approximately eight months in earnest work on *Secret Beyond the Door* with Silvia Richards. He spent an extra month dubbing *Scarlet Street* and refused to post a closing date on the second film. Moreover, Lang made the bulk of the creative decisions in production: he chose the properties to adapt, made the casting decisions, and, especially for *Secret Beyond the Door,* requested the technicians he desired. For example, he had Diana borrow Krasner from International Pictures to photograph *Scarlet Street* six weeks in advance of shooting. Lang selected personnel on *Secret Beyond the Door* such as sound engineer Andrew Anderson, editor Arthur Hilton, continuity clerk Dorothy Hughes, composer Rosza, and others. Although such requests were answered according to the supply of talent available—and he deferred to Bennett's preference for Cortez on *Secret Beyond the Door*—the chance to make them was a luxury.

In addition, Lang's proposals for the conduct of Diana business were often adopted. At Lang's suggestion, the company put creative personnel—such as Warner Bros. art director Max Parker (with whom Lang had worked on *Cloak and Dagger*) and screenwriters Silvia Richards, Stuart Lake, and Howard Dimsdale and researcher Andreas Denium—under yearly contracts to ensure their availability. Lang developed publicity ideas for Diana and reviewed Universal's advertising strategies and designs. He requested that *Scarlet Street* be released after Christmas, 1945, rather than during the "dead" period after Thanksgiving. Diana Productions may not have been UFA, but it was about as close as an American company in the studio system could come to recreating the encouraging working environment Lang had enjoyed in Europe.

While Lang attended to production matters, Wanger looked after administrative and financial details. Wanger minimized Diana's overhead by assigning Foley, his accountant George R. Mercader, or his attorney Mendel Silberberg to Diana matters without charging Diana for their services. Moreover, he negotiated distribution contracts and bank loans that would have been otherwise unavailable to the temperamental director. Lang's secretary Min Selvin summed up Lang's dependence on Wanger when she indicated, "On all contractual matters, Mr. Lang feels that Mr. Wanger should sign first." Finally, Wanger worked as a negotiator between "the genius," as Lang was known at the studio, and Universal. Universal's contract with Diana indicated that in the case of any disagreement on the budget between Universal and Diana, "the judgment of Walter Wanger shall be controlling." Universal executives counted on Wanger to represent the interests of both parties as fairly as possible and to "control" Fritz Lang.

Clearly, Lang used Wanger as a buffer between himself and the rest of the industry. The infrequent board meetings of Diana entailed the dictation of Lang's shopping lists: for personnel (such as available cameramen at Paramount), for Technicolor in *Winchester .73,* for James Mason and Michael Redgrave in *Secret Beyond the Door,* and for straightening out with Universal any confusion involving production scheduling or promotion. Since Lang tended to worry when matters were left unsettled, he frequently nagged Wanger in memos. The system left Lang "free" to concentrate on his production plans, but it also made Lang resentful of his dependence on Wanger, particularly when Wanger was not as attentive to Diana matters as Lang wanted him to be.

Their relationship deteriorated badly after Wanger tampered with *Scarlet Street* and the film proved an enormous financial success. The latter inflated Lang's ego considerably, and a tone of impatient condescension entered Lang's memos to Wanger beginning in February 1946. Although Wanger had encouraged Lang's suggestions for the conduct of Diana business, he gradually came to perceive Lang's requests about publicity as harassments and as attempts on Lang's part to overstep his role as the artistic producer. For example, Lang made an effort to have the term "supervisor" removed from Wanger's contract. Wanger accurately saw this as an attempt to circumscribe his authority over Lang and restructure their division of labor. Meanwhile, Wanger felt outnumbered by the presence of Lang's attorney Gang and agent Sam Jaffe on Diana's board, and he attempted futilely to alter the board and stop Lang from acquiring more stock.

The tensions between them emerged most clearly over the issue of proper publicity credit for Lang. The advantages of working with Wanger's company — low overhead and experienced administrators — had their disadvantages as well. Lang was miffed when Universal sent visitors on Diana business to Wanger's offices. Indeed, Wanger's established reputation and association with Universal meant that the hosting studio often confused Wanger's operations with Lang's and that publicity and credit often bypassed Lang as producer of the Diana films. When Hopper announced in the *Hollywood Reporter* that Wanger had told her that Joan Bennett would star in the Wanger production of *Winchester .73,* an outraged Lang naturally turned to Wanger to have the matter corrected, but Wanger had never actually talked to Hopper.

The Hopper item infuriated Lang, and he blew subsequent, similar mistakes out of proportion. When the *Los Angeles Times* reported Diana plans without mentioning Lang's position as president or producer, Lang wrote Wanger that the misinformation "does me great personal harm and injures everything I stand for." Lang continued:

Also, dear Walter, I must again ask that no business contracts or other matters pertaining to Diana be handled by people under contract with your own organization unless they are also identified with Diana. Unless this is done, we will not be able to avoid such misleading and incorrect statements as the above-mentioned one.

Lang's mania for correct credit extended to stationery. Wanger on one occasion brought Lang a memo concerning Diana business. When Lang saw the "Walter Wanger" letterhead on which the memo was written, he had a fit. But Wanger wanted to demonstrate that Lang was getting administrative service free of charge.

The publicity problems with proper credit are a perfect example of the nebulous nature of the producer's role. Apparently, not even industry journalists and Universal's publicity staff understood the obscure distinctions between Wanger and Lang's responsibilities as executive producer and producer. Nor did Diana's officers. From Wanger's point of view, at least, Lang's directives about publicity crossed their neatly defined boundaries of judgment: After all," he wrote in a letter never sent to Gang, "is publicity and exploitation an artistic matter or does that come under my jurisdiction?"

In this atmosphere of melodramatic pettiness and alienation, Lang selected and developed two properties for Diana's next productions, *Winchester .73* and *Secret Beyond the Door.* (Although Lang later claimed that the latter property was forced upon him, Wanger had optioned and purchased the *Redbook* story at Lang's request and pressed him to make it because Diana had nothing else in the works.) Lake, the screenwriter of *The Westerner* and author of the popular 1931 biography *Wyatt Earp, Frontier Marshall,* was hired to develop a treatment for *Winchester .73* early in 1946. For *Secret Beyond the Door,* Lang in April 1946 hired his sometime lover, screenwriter Richards, after *Cloak and Dagger*'s Ring Lardner, Jr., proved unavailable. Richards had written for the radio show "Suspense," and she had coauthored the script for *Possessed* (Warner Bros., 1947), which displayed her expertise with Freudian psychology in its portrait of the obsessive Joan Crawford character. Diana was poised for a busy schedule during the next two years.

But there were delays in writing up the next scripts. Lake turned in a two-hundred-page treatment for *Winchester .73* in April 1946, with thirty pages uselessly devoted to the history of the rifle. Wanger and Lang replaced him with Dimsdale, who started from scratch in late October 1946. The story of *Secret Beyond the Door*—concerning a psychotic architect who is compelled to murder his wife in a reproduction of her room—was, not surprisingly, difficult to rework. In September, Lang and Richards had only the first fifty pages ready for Bennett to use in selecting her wardrobe for the film; this same material was sent to Redgrave (after first choice Mason turned it down) to induce him to play Mark Lamphere, Bennett's husband. Those pages concerned the story's extensive prologue, set in Mexico, where the hero and hero-ine meet and get married. Richards and Lang did not complete the script until November.

Both of these delays drove up Diana's overhead and weakened its bargaining position with Universal for contract renewal. This had dragged on since early 1946, due to the August 1946 merger of Universal and International Pictures and the subsequent reorganization of the studio. In June 1946, a New York federal court issued the consent decree prohibiting film distributors again from selling films in blocks. The majors subsequently faced the prospect of persuading exhibitors to book films on a case by case basis. Universal and International had contemplated creating a new company, United World Pictures, to distribute American and British films worldwide, but realized they could never successfully sell the unpopular British films to American exhibitors under such constraints. The two companies therefore agreed in summer 1946 to dissolve UWP but form a new company Universal-International, with International executives Leo Spitz and William Goetz in charge of studio production.

The merger was the most significant event in Universal's history until the 1960s. *Time* hailed the new corporation as "the first major company formed to produce A pictures exclusively," as Goetz and Spitz announced their plans to eliminate all of Universal's westerns, serials, and "B" films and to produce twenty-five "A" films. These, along with five films from Enterprise and twelve from Rank, would comprise Universal-International's distribution slate for 1947. Thus the International production policy conformed with industry-wide opinion that the most expensive films would prove the most profitable to the studio (*Secret Beyond the Door* was accordingly budgeted at $1,463,500). More significantly, Spitz, who handled contracts and all legal matters of production for Universal-International, insisted on renegotiating all existing contracts so that semi-independent and unit films were subject to cross-collateralization. This meant combining the profits and losses of *Secret Beyond the Door* and *Winchester .73*.

From the beginning of principal photography in mid-February 1947 on *Secret Beyond the Door,* everything seemed to go wrong. There were major difficulties with Universal's costume designer Travis Banton, whom Lang had accused of negligence while working on Hitchcock's *The Paradine Case* during the fall of 1946. Universal-International set costs were miscalculated, effects (such as wind machines at the Lavender Falls train station) constantly broke down, pipes burst during Redgrave's bath scene, and sound units and Mitchell cameras broke down on different days. Universal-International made no attempt to adjust its charges to Diana for these delays. The entire shoot sharply contrasted with the untroubled production of *Scarlet Street,* but it was only the beginning.

While supporting Lang's complaints to Universal-International about these uncontrollable developments, Wanger also kept close tabs on Lang. Production comptroller Mo Slater brought back bad news for Wanger within two weeks of the start of photography, in mid-February 1947: in recent days Lang had printed every fourth take out of as many as twenty-seven takes of single shots. On February 19, Lang shot twenty-four takes of Celia (Bennett) and her friend Edith (Natalie Schaefer) at a Mexican café table. By the third week of production, Lang was five days behind schedule and had completed one-third less footage and one-fifth fewer script pages than scheduled. In the spirit of UFA, he kept people on the set from 7 A.M. to 7:30 P.M.

During production of *Scarlet Street*, Wanger jokingly passed along to Lang studio memos about production overruns; now he composed a lengthy formal memo relating Slater's figures and generally suggesting Lang eliminate scenes to speed up the production. He concluded by reminding the director-producer that the production was in Lang's hands. Lang's response three days later was the result of his "considerable distress and upset." The major problem on the set, he claimed, was cinematographer Cortez. The script called for a constantly roving camera, and Cortez found it difficult to please Lang. "I have never had to worry about split focus, out of focus scenes . . . or out of focus backgrounds." Lang's dissatisfaction led Cortez to work crews overtime to rig setups for the following day's work.

But Lang spared no one blame for production delays on the film: Bennett had rejected Krasner, Lang's first-choice cinematographer, and a recent illness prevented her from working later than five o'clock in the afternoon, which slowed Lang down.

Lang's choicest words remained for Wanger. He indicated that he would not eliminate any sequences in the script and reminded Wanger that he himself had thought the script tightly constructed after the prologue scenes in Mexico. Finally, Lang demanded concrete suggestions from Wanger for improving the production situation and ominously linked their current problems with their past difficulties: "I have repeatedly told you, Walter, that you can be of service and help to me. I have called on you for help in numerous instances, and sometimes in vain." When a meeting was called in mid-March to discuss replacing Cortez, everyone agreed the production was too far along to continue without him. True to form, Wanger subsequently did little more than remind Lang of his schedule and his budget.

If Wanger felt impotent during principal photography, Lang himself was powerless after completing his final cut. Unlike his predecessor Work, International's Goetz, trained by mentor Zanuck, took a hands-on approach to unit and semi-independent production. With Spitz, he dramatically reorganized the studio, dismissing more than thirty-five creative talents associated with Universal's "B" productions. The Spitz-Goetz management team also emphasized efficiency within the studio by coordinating different aspects of production design in day-long budget meetings and assigning one production manager, John Hambleton, to coordinate the look of set design, costumes, wardrobes, hairdressing, and makeup. In their eyes, a director or producer's work could frequently be improved on.

Wanger's memos during production were nothing compared to Goetz's actions during postproduction. When shown to what Lang called an immature, "bobbysox" preview audience on September 3 (i.e., not the adult audience Lang had targeted for Diana films), *Secret Beyond the Door* received terrible responses: "poor," "very poor," "how bad can they get," "beyond human endurance," and two responses of "it stinks." Universal-International executives ignored a second, more favorable preview response on September 11, and Goetz simply took Lang's print and began recutting it. He added bits of voice-over narration supplied by a different screenwriter and had Bennett dub the entire voice-over track, originally recorded by another actress. To make matters worse, Goetz requested that Lang await the completion of his cut before viewing the film.

From a studio executive's standpoint, Goetz's actions made perfect sense. The marketplace had drastically changed. As Lang wound up production on *Secret Beyond the Door* in April 1947, the industry felt the long-expected drops in Hollywood box office take ("Film Biz Dips To 'Only Terrific'; From Used-To-Be 'Sensational,'" *Variety*'s headline read). Studio executives, including Universal's chairman Cowdin, did an about-face on budget policy and called for cost-cutting measures.

As Lang concluded his final cut, the situation was aggravated when England announced in early August its 75 percent ad valorem tax on the projected grosses of all American films. This reduced annual foreign income by an estimated $40 million, and the major studios responded with an embargo of films to Great Britain which lasted through March 1948. At the same time there were firm new calls for reduction of negative costs. Lang's overruns on *Scarlet Street* had been comparable, but the market had changed, and it was a bad time for Lang to bring in a film eighteen days behind schedule and nearly $200,000 over budget.

As it happened, Wanger was conspicuously passive when Goetz recut *Secret Beyond the Door* and even seemed to regard Goetz's action as a legitimate attempt to improve the film. An undelivered note to Gang from this period indicates Wanger's frustration with Lang:

> I have tried to tell him my fears but he is always grasping for more and more— I have conceded everything he has asked on billing, payments—to try to help his operation out but he insists on deluding himself with your help. Universal is his partner & Joan & I are his partners . . . his main objective seems to be to try to convince the world that he alone is responsible for his product.

By now, Diana held a tenuous position at Universal. The influx to the studio of additional semi-independents such as Ramparts Productions (Fontaine and William Dozier) and Garson Kanin, as well as of International's producing, acting, and directorial talent, had decisively diminished Diana's importance to the studio. Wanger informed Lang at a Diana board meeting in November 1947 that Universal-International had decided not to hire any more semi-independent producers and that none of the semi-independents operating earlier on the lot, such as Hellinger and Wanger himself, had their contracts renewed in 1947. By fall of that year, Wanger himself had decided to leave Universal-International. Even if he had wished to defend Lang's cut of *Secret Beyond the Door*, his tenuous position at the studio in late 1947 circumscribed his influence with the new executives.

Besides, Lang had alienated his only remaining supporter at the studio. When the production finished photography on May 10, 1947, over schedule and over budget, there still remained the production of an animated shot of a "dream pool" for the film's opening and conclusion, in addition to postproduction. (When tests by Oskar Fischinger in late spring proved unsatisfactory, the Walt Disney studios produced the shot during the summer.) Advice from other talents on the Universal-International lot confirmed Goetz's instincts: producer (and former editor) Ernest Nims felt the film's prologue was too long, and Leonardo Bercovici found "a lot of foolish, semi-Freudian, unrevealing nonsense—as though author and director were trying to make some profound observations when their materials were quite shallow and at best simply melodramatic." Goetz shortened Lang's final cut by seventeen minutes—eliminating much of the film's opening such as the death of Celia's brother and her trip to Mexico and honeymoon with Mark. The audience at a November 4 preview gave the recut film a gratifying response.

For Lang, all this was a return to the frustrating days of his contract work at Fox under Goetz's supervision. In fact, it contradicted Lang's beliefs about independence:

> I understand that Bill may think he can increase the value of the picture by cutting it, but it seems to me that such extensive cutting is damaging the picture. The value of SECRET lies in the things which are new and different; if these are cut out according to Bill's personal taste, the picture will be just another typical UI release, and our aim to avoid making run-of-the-mill product will not only have been completely defeated but the box-office value definitely lessened.
>
> I cannot help thinking this extensive cutting—certainly unforeseen when we signed the contract with Universal—is against the spirit of the contract. If UI has the right to make such tremendous changes in our pictures, based on personal likes and dislikes, even though I think such changes are damaging, then independent status is of no value whatsoever and our investment is greatly endangered.

Lang later restored a compromise cut after threatening to have his name taken off the film, but the ill will between Diana and Universal, and between Lang and Wanger, was now irreparable.

With *Secret Beyond the Door*'s premiere, the house of cards fell. Universal-International coordinated its distribution poorly, and it proved the studio's lowest grossing film in a terrible business year. When Ohio censors demanded that an imaginary trial sequence in the film be cut, Universal-International consented instantly. The contrast with Universal's handling of the banning of *Scarlet Street* could not have been more striking.

When Lang found he could not control the course of his film's postproduction, he shifted his strategy to obtain control of the corporation. He took the high moral ground and accused Bennett of violating "her duties and obligations as a stockholder" in dubbing the new narration for Goetz. His desire to see Wanger resign was by this time open, but Wanger refused to abandon his $23,000 investment. Lang took to writing informal minutes at Diana director meetings and falsely suggested that Wanger had offered to resign and that Wanger and Bennett had *wanted* Goetz to recut *Secret Beyond the Door*.

In early 1948, Lang extended his option on *Winchester .73* until June. When he failed to complete a script by that time, the property reverted to Universal, where it was produced two years later as an enormous success directed by Anthony Mann and starring James Stewart. Meanwhile, by March, neither of the Wangers had anything to do with Diana. Wanger had moved to the fledgling producer-distributor Eagle-Lion and was supervising postproduction of *Joan of Arc,* his biggest prestige film ever. Lang agreed to buy out "Bennett's" stock for $17,000. This represented a $6,000 loss, but Wanger felt certain the company's value would only diminish with time. Lang maintained Diana for several more years, but its productive period was over.

In the case of Diana, the products of all this sound and fury are equivocal. *Scarlet Street,* produced efficiently in the manner of a standard Hollywood production, is a classic film noir, full of disturbing undertones. It consolidated Bennett's new star image as, in critic David Thomson's words, "the kind of amused, insolent dame who would catch the eye and draw the fantasies of self-consciously respectable men." The film's bitterly satiric portrait of American middle-class life and ideals through the character of Chris Cross is less prominent in Nichols's script than in the treatments by humorist-illustrator Ludwig Bemelmans, Lang's first-choice screenwriter. Yet *Scarlet Street* remains a happy instance of Lang's visual style and narrative technique. Although it outraged censors in key cities, it had the approval of a major studio and the Breen Office.

Given the controversy over the film's postproduction, *Secret Beyond the Door* remains a singular work, quirky and, one could argue, formally incoherent. Its story resembles screenwriter Richards's work on *Possessed*. A heroine who is emotionless until a passionate affair awakes her, a protagonist who in psychotic states imagines committing murders, and the overt invocations of psychoanalysis—these plot components suggest that Lang enthusiastically used Richards's work as a starting point for his own prowling visualization. Wanger noted that Lang agreed with most of Richards's ideas, whereas the director argued often with Nichols on *Scarlet Street;* he attributed this to the fact that Lang and Richards were "more than a writing combination."

The complexities of the film's authorship suggests that Lang used semi-independent production not only to recover a less hurried production schedule, but to "experiment" with new formal concerns. Many years later, Lang claimed that with *Secret Beyond the Door* he was interested in the mood of a fictional space, as Hitchcock had explored it in *Rebecca* (which is no doubt why Lang was so sensitive about comparisons with Hitchcock). The film endorses Mark Lamphere's assertion that a room is well suited to the events that take place within them—even if the events are murders. But Lang was also interested in a new method of narration: the heroine's "thought voice" in voice-over, which Lang had intended to be read by another actress (Colleen Collins).

Moreover, Lang here extended his predilection for the misleading narration that had made *You Only Live Once* so disturbing. After Lang fades out on Celia in the forest with a stranger, the film is narrated for the first time by Mark, as he imagines his trial for killing her. The audience confidently assumes Mark has killed Celia but eventually realizes he is fantasizing an event that never occurred. This was one experiment that semi-independence and Wanger's patronage had facilitated—clearly Goetz would never have allowed it. But in general, though defended by some critics as a triumph of mise-en-scène, the film is an excessive instance of Hollywood's fascination with Freudian psychology, a failed women's gothic film (unlike *Rebecca,* and *Suspicion,* 1941) and a minor entry in the Lang oeuvre.

The fate of these two films in postproduction and distribution also suggests that the majors' reception of the semi-independents changed in accordance with industry conditions. Universal formulated entirely different responses in 1945 and 1947 to comparable aspects of the productions of *Scarlet Street* and *Secret Beyond the Door,* such as cost overruns and local censorship. As had been the case with Wanger's *The President Vanishes* twelve years earlier, semi-independence could not guarantee that filmgoers would see the film as a producer shot it.

Lang's neurotic behavior may have seemed inhuman to his partners at Diana, but actually Lang was highly sensitive to the precarious nature of their enterprise and to the caprice of business conditions. Diana's difficulties in a changing market were a challenge for all semi-independent producers, and the conflicts between Wanger and Lang exacerbated them. Although both agreed that semi-independence provided a means to create the significant, thought-provoking kinds of films that Hollywood had barely touched, Lang's obsession with details of production clashed with Wanger's casual confidence in the Hollywood system. They were ill-matched partners.

Meanwhile, there were more fundamental difficulties that all semi-independents faced in the late 1940s, obstacles that were based in their ambivalent relationship to the major producer-distributors. Each of Wanger's subsequent ventures demonstrated a different dynamic of that ambivalence.

13

Susan Hayward, Past and Present

For Wanger, the four-year period from 1945 to 1949 was as restless as his shifts in the early 1930s from Paramount to Columbia to MGM to Paramount again. Now, however, with remarkable energy, he often maintained affiliations with Universal-International, Eagle-Lion, Columbia Pictures, and RKO simultaneously.

Throughout this interval of musical chairs at the different studios, Wanger produced two types of film in alternation. The first group consisted mostly of Technicolor action films: these included *Canyon Passage* (1946) and *Tap Roots* (1948) for Universal-International and *Tulsa* (1949) and the black-and-white *Reign of Terror* (1949) at Eagle-Lion. Like most historical films, these used history to mythologize American character, to suggest analogies between postwar life and the resilience of earlier Americans, and to promote the wonders of capitalist democracy. These were in effect his message films.

The second group of films had a European flavor. These included the films noir directed by Lang for Diana and the intimate melodramas *Smash-Up* (1947) and *The Lost Moment* (1947) for Universal-International. What these films shared in Wanger's mind was their "adult realism," as seen in the Italian neorealists and the British cinema of quality.

The ideologies of these two types of films contradicted each other, particularly in their differing conceptions of the power of individualism. Yet Wanger thought of them both as depictions of postwar womanhood in the screen persona of Susan Hayward. Throughout his career, Wanger had remained fascinated with women who transgress their traditional social roles in Western culture. From Isadora Duncan to Ziegfeld Follies showgirls, from Nazimova to Hollywood stars such as Bennett, Wanger always admired women whose talents and penchant for self-display expressed a personal liberation. This interest derived from witnessing women's growing social equality in the first decades of the twentieth century, as well as from Wanger's narcissistic appreciation for rebellious individuals.

But Wanger's films, like those of other producers, explored this preoccupation in dramas that raised the specter of a defiant, independent woman only to bring her to heel through the discovery of true love: *Tarnished Lady*; *Queen Christina*; *Mary Burns, Fugitive*; *I Met My Love Again*; *Trade Winds*; and *House Across the Bay*. The heroines of Wanger's orientalist fantasies and aviation films again followed this pattern in response to the unrestrained social and employment conditions women enjoyed on the homefront during World War II. Now after the war, Wanger joined other producers in repeatedly dramatizing the fate of transgressive women as a means of sustaining audience appeal by reaffirming patriarchal values. Hayward's star image distinguished most of Wanger's films from films with Joan Crawford and Bette Davis and other major star vehicles at the other studios.

With or without Hayward, Wanger also believed that both the Technicolor historical films and the melodramas would demonstrate Hollywood's ability to contribute to America's need to maintain national unity and vigilance against the Communist threat. His films, however, did not successfully support his argument. Neither did the film business. After the enormous grosses of the unit-produced *Canyon Passage* and Diana's *Scarlet Street,* Wanger reactivated his semi-independent company in late 1946 to participate in greater domestic and foreign profits. As it happened, Wanger's timing was off, for just months later, the postwar market declined, and the very economic system and industry he aimed to apotheosize came undone. His various ventures fared little better than Diana Productions: returning to semi-independence earned Wanger the privilege of a greater share in over $5.5 million losses on his films. Although he was able to build Hayward from a character actress into a major star, his career began its relentless decline.

Not surprisingly, the war experience changed the kinds of message films Wanger wanted to produce. He was not interested in provoking his audience with visions of catastrophic national leadership or the mendacity of big business as *Gabriel Over the White House* and *The President Vanishes* had done. He was not interested in critiquing American foreign policy by addressing taboo subjects as he had with *Blockade*. Nor did he elect to expose social ills such as religious or racial prejudice as Zanuck did when he sponsored *Crossfire* (1947), the Academy Award–winning *Gentleman's Agreement* (1947), and *Pinky* (1949). On the contrary, Wanger's historical films glorified American individualism and business enterprise.

The most eloquent example of the change in Wanger's message movies is his shifting approach to the unproduced property *Dynasty of Death*. Caldwell's book focuses on the ruthless leader of a munitions firm, and, as Caldwell's husband described it in 1939, it took as its larger theme "the implication of the danger which grew out of the policy of capital run rampant" in the late nineteenth century. Its behind-the-scenes conspiracy bore a strong resemblance to *The President Vanishes*.

In early 1943, however, Wanger directed novelist and budding screenwriter Philip Wylie to "freshen it up and make the hero a fast-talking human type like Adolph Menjou who . . . is a realist who is not afraid of being ahead of the public and who doesn't worry about the common people." The difficulties of capitalist democracy during the Depression now became the heroism of industry leaders in the war effort. Such a change was quite common. Vidor, director of *The Crowd* (1926) and *Our Daily Bread* (1934)—a vision of a farm collective which no major studio would finance—undertook in 1942 *An American Romance*, an immigrant success story that was designed by Vidor and censored by the OWI to create "the best impression of American Industry."

Certainly, Wanger's and Universal's prosperity in 1945 and 1946 gave him good reason to celebrate American capitalism. Even as Lang was preparing *Scarlet Street* for production, Wanger was organizing his first film to express these ideas. The $2.3 million Technicolor *Canyon Passage* turned out to be Wanger's most successful postwar film both financially and aesthetically, picking up where *Trail of the Lonesome Pine* left off ten years earlier. Universal financed its most elaborate on-location schedule yet, the entire month of September 1945 in Oregon, to obtain stunning natural scenery. The studio also hired top talents from off the lot. The cast featured Dana Andrews (from Samuel Goldwyn), Brian Donlevy, and the superlative character actors from some of Ford's best films, Ward Bond and Andy Devine. Singer Hoagy Carmichael, who received much popular acclaim after his appearance in Howard Hawks's *To Have and Have Not* (Warner Bros., 1944), and who later appeared with Andrews in Goldwyn's *The Best Years of Our Lives* (1946), provided comic and musical relief. Wanger borrowed the expert low-budget horror film director Jacques Tourneur from RKO.

Canyon Passage also featured free-lancing Hayward, whom Wanger subsequently signed to a seven-year option contract. Born Edyth Marrener, she was in 1945 a shy, twenty-seven-year-old Hollywood veteran. A working-class Brooklynite, she had a large round face, an impish nose, wavy red hair, and a voluptuous figure that enabled her to flourish in New York as a photography model. She came to Hollywood to test for Scarlett O'Hara in 1937 and remained through the war years when Paramount signed her to a long-term contract. Despite her supporting roles in major films such as deMille's *Reap the Wild Wind* (1942) and in Rene Clair's *I Married a Witch* (1942), Hayward spent most of her contract on loan-out to "B" productions at RKO and Republic.

Wanger first learned of Hayward from his stepdaughter Diana, who had admired her performance as a spoiled society girl in the independently produced *The Hairy Ape* (1944). Married with two children by Universal contractee Jess Barker, Hayward was looking for a new association after her Paramount contract lapsed. Like De Carlo, she struck Wanger as a beautiful talent whom Hollywood had foolishly overlooked. No doubt he found her extremely attractive, but whether or not they were lovers is unclear. Coworkers noted that she always addressed him as "Mr. Wanger," a formality intended to keep things professional. In any case, Wanger had considered using Barker as one of the villains in *Canyon Passage;* instead, he decided to cast Hayward as the heroine.

The story was written by Haycox, and even Ernest Pascal's script was as slight in story events as "Stage to Lordsburg." The main character was, like Sigmund Feuchtwanger, an Oregon general goods distributor named Logan Stewart (Andrews). Logan transports cargo by pack horse between the "booming" trade town of Portland and unsettled Jacksonville. He is a quintessential individualist, constantly on the go and minding his own business, but invariably brought into conflict with men of lesser integrity. When layabout Honey Bragg (Bond) provokes an Indian attack, Logan helps the settlers fight back; when his best friend, the Eastern dandy George Camrose (Donlevy), is accused of cheating at cards and of murder, Logan must respect the town's demands for justice. Spouting a higher sense of purpose in his life than commerce ("Gold is only yellow gravel"), Logan finds that his general store has been burned down in the Indian attack, yet he will make the necessary journeys to restock and rebuild.

During a trip from Portland to Jackson, Logan escorts Lucy Overmire (Hayward) to meet her fiancé Camrose. Although the dialogue suggests that Lucy is an encumbrance (her trademark line is "Logan, would you mind having a woman on your hands?"), Lucy builds up Logan's character, constantly questioning him about his active romantic life, his thriving business, and his sense of fairness. The role is slight as scripted and therefore ruled out a star of greater standing. But Hayward made the most of Lucy, appearing to advantage in Technicolor and giving the character a confident but restrained manner that complemented Andrews's performance. With Goldwyn's permission, her name went above the title.

There was a tension, however, between the requirements of a star vehicle and director Tourneur's pictorialism, especially his tendency to shoot medium and long exterior shots. During location shooting on *Canyon Passage,* Hayward aggressively protested to Wanger that Tourneur was not shooting enough close-ups of her:

THOUGHT MOUNTAINS AND CLOUD STUFF BEAUTIFUL. DEEPLY DISAPPOINTED AUDIENCE DID NOT SEE THIS EMPLOYEE'S FACE. . . .

AS LONG AS WE'RE TO BE HERE TEN MORE DAYS WOULD APPRE-
CIATE IF YOU WOULD ORDER RETAKE OR CLOSEUP. WANT TO DO
BEST POSSIBLE JOB BUT WANT IT TO BE SHOT SO AUDIENCE GETS
WHAT YOU PAY ME FOR.

Indeed, the film is nearly half over before Hayward receives a solo close-up, a shot that Tourneur preferred to save for "important story points." Yet his visual style builds epic implications out of Pascal's threadbare narrative and the grandeur of the Oregon scenery.

Like *The Moon's Our Home, Stand In,* and *Riot in Cell Block 11, Canyon Passage* is one of Wanger's most underrated films. Perhaps this is because it defied the conventional categories of westerns. It was neither an "adult western" like *The Ox-Bow Incident* (1943) nor a nostalgic treatment of the old West like Ford's classic *My Darling Clementine* (1946). The references to Logan's growing pack business and the characters were too specifically tied to the growth of commerce in the West to have universalized meaning. In fact, the film seems slightly revisionist: its opening shots focus on several wagons's struggle simply to cross the muddy Portland streets in a rainstorm. It boasted a remarkably enlightened (for 1945) attitude toward the Indians ("Well, it's their land and we're on it and they don't forget it," as one character puts it). And, like *Stagecoach,* the film betrays a certain distrust of civilization, evident in Camrose's belief that the "human race is a horrible mistake," and in Jacksonville's obvious delight in the brutal fistfight between Logan and Honey Bragg.

Wanger disregarded the film's darker implications. He felt that *Canyon Passage* emphasized the virtues of unity and cooperation which both *Gung Ho!* and the Free World Association had championed during the postwar era. He expressed particular pride over a sequence in which the pioneer community builds a house for a newly married couple on the plains. It is edited at a rigorous pace halted only by humorous vignettes such as Devine lazily resisting the work. "You are right, we did not intend the audience to become too analytical about this film," Wanger wrote *Commonweal*'s critic.

> We did want them to sit back and enjoy the Oregon scenery and the beautiful Technicolor. What we hoped for, though, was that the cabin raising sequence might be taken seriously as we feel it demonstrates the wonderful spirit of tolerance and cooperation of the pioneers—a spirit which should prevail today and, unfortunately, does not. Many reviewers had nothing to say about it at all.

Though appreciative of the film in general, the critics proved impervious to the key motif of Universal's advertising and publicity campaigns. These included tie-ups with housing authority assignments in six cities, accompanied by "propaganda that people should not complain about housing shortages in view of the fact of what pioneers went through." A festive premiere weekend and other promotional activities, including a tribute to Wanger's twenty-five years in Hollywood, produced an astounding $4 million gross.

The apotheosis of American democracy was *the* central subtext of Wanger's Technicolor film, but it did remain a subtext. As Wanger learned in *Foreign Correspondent,* ideas and values need not be stated in to-camera speeches. Arguing for a freer government policy on motion picture exports, he told the press in December 1946:

> Pictures like "Grapes of Wrath," that expose the defects of our social system, or "Mr. Smith Goes to Washington," that poke fun at our Congress, will reveal that a strong democracy can afford to make this sort of self-critical product for entertainment under a capitalistic system. At the same time, we must increase our efforts to make pictures which show the desirable and admirable aspects of our democratic system.

It was in part to pursue this production idea, among others, that Wanger resumed semi-independent production shortly after the premiere of *Canyon Passage.* The unit system by early 1946 had proven too limiting: Wanger resented waiting for Universal to purchase his proposed stories, and the studio was growing exasperated with his big-budget extravaganzas. Lubin later recalled, "The studio was very much against making" *A Night in Paradise* in 1945. Lubin continues: "They would come to me and say, 'Can't you talk him out of making it? Do you need these elaborate sets that Mr. Wanger wants?'" As a semi-independent Wanger could partly finance his films and demand higher budgets.

Most of all, though, Wanger was tired of paying punishingly high income tax rates on his salary and profit shares. This had not been a major factor in creating Diana Productions, although that company's initial success encouraged the reactivation of Walter Wanger Pictures. The capital gains laws of 1946 did likewise. As attorney Guy Knupp noted, under his unit agreement with Universal, Wanger could take home after taxes only 13.5 percent of his profit share, which amounted to a mere $67,500 for every $1 million gross. By contrast, if he were a stockholding semi-independent, he could keep between $94,000 and $215,000 on every million, paying only a 20 percent capital gains tax on the proceeds from the sale of his stock. Scrupulous Bienstock had warned Wanger away from such maneuvers during the war. By 1946 they were standard procedure. Producers at United Artists such as James Cagney, Lester Cowan, and Benedict Bogeaus, as well as Gary Cooper, Leo McCarey, William Wyler, George Stevens, Frank Capra, and countless others at the major studios had become stockholding semi-independents.

Universal executives had promised Wanger they would turn his unit arrangement into an independent deal in the fall of 1944, and in the following year, Wanger began signing up contracted talents again. Besides Hayward and other actors who never caught on, there was cinematographer Cortez and writer-director Martin Gabel, an alumnus of Orson Welles's Mercury Theater, the director of the stage hit *Life with Father* and best known for portraying Strutt in Hitchcock's *Marnie* (1964). By the time Wanger's talks began in February 1946, however, Universal's ardor had cooled, due largely to its negotiations with Enterprise and International Pictures. This changed his relations with the studio considerably.

In early 1943, Bienstock repeated to Wanger the sentiments of Universal board member Matty Fox that "Universal and all the executives just keep 'pinching themselves' to make certain that it is not all a dream and that you really are with them and working as cooperatively and profitably as you have." In 1944, Wanger had told Work that "this has been the happiest association I have ever had in the film industry. . . . I have never worked with a more efficient or more sympathetic group of men." Under Work's administration, Wanger enjoyed a "cordial" and "informal" atmosphere, in which "we did not bother to dispute details regarding the budget, cast and director."

But with the arrival of Goetz and Spitz, the studio's "entire attitude toward my contract and my operations changed. . . . Instead of being in on plans and consulted I was eliminated and obstructed." The two executives did "everything" they could "to make me uncomfortable and to deflate my operation." Spitz "never let up at anytime harassing my operation and planning (which had been independent prior to his arrival)." As with *Secret Beyond the Door,* Goetz recut and reshot all of Wanger's films. And Spitz insisted that Wanger's future films be cross-collateralized, so that his chances of earning profits were cut in half.

Yet Wanger's Americana program appealed as much to the active Goetz and Spitz regime as it did to the laissez-faire Work-Muhl administration. Like *Canyon Passage, Tap Roots* was a paean to American history, but unlike Tourneur's film, it was extremely derivative. Wanger told Universal publicity executives that he wanted no comparisons made with *Gone with the Wind* although his film was "of the same scope." Alan LeMay's screenplay from James Street's best-selling novel concerned the actual Dabney family of Mississippi, whose county seceded from the south upon the outbreak of the Civil War. In fact the characters and story of the new film greatly resembled Selznick's, and Hayward, in the role of Morna Dabney, finally got to portray Scarlett O'Hara, so to speak.

Like many Wanger films, *Tap Roots* has a potentially interesting storyline enlivened by spectacular Technicolor scenery (from location shooting in Asheville, North Carolina) and deadened by merely competent direction (this time by Paramount veteran George Marshall). Hayward again looks stunning in Technicolor, and her intensity is well complemented by Van Heflin's cynicism as the newspaper publisher and expert shot Keith Alexander. Wanger told the studio's publicity staff to promote the film as nothing less than "another great outdoor picture in Technicolor along the lines of, but greater than, Wanger's TRAIL OF THE LONESOME PINE and CANYON PASSAGE, the greatest outdoor picture in Technicolor." But aside from its visual splendor, it was critically lambasted. One of Universal's most expensive efforts, it took years to break even.

By the time *Tap Roots* premiered in the summer of 1948, however, Wanger was long gone from Universal-International. In fact, two months after signing his semi-independent contract there, Wanger began negotiations with Arthur Krim and Robert Benjamin, two young lawyers in charge of the fledgling producer-distributor Eagle-Lion, for a new arrangement. Wanger moved his offices to the Eagle-Lion lot in December 1947, and he brought his Americana program with him.

The very rationale for the formation of the company in late 1945 was a mutual distribution agreement between American railroad magnate and financier Robert Young, who owned the low-budget Producer's Releasing Corporation (PRC) studio, and British film entrepreneur Rank. Although Universal had first choice of Rank's most promising efforts, Wanger shared Rank and Young's hopes that Eagle-Lion could, in Balio's words, "become at least another Universal or Columbia."

Wanger was attracted to Eagle-Lion in part because of his personal admiration for the six-foot, Methodist teetotaler Rank, whose General Cinema Finance Corporation constituted a vertically integrated giant comparable to the American majors. The two enjoyed a lively correspondence throughout the late 1940s that began with Wanger's enthusiasm for Laurence Olivier's *Henry V*. In fact, Rank convinced Wanger to take the plunge with Eagle-Lion; he was a persuasive figure in the late spring of 1947, since he had secured promises from the major studios that his films would be played off in American theaters for $2 million in yearly business. Most important to Wanger, Rank would give preferential treatment to Universal-International and Eagle-Lion releases in the lucrative English market. Wanger also appreciated how the Eagle-Lion association might also facilitate the exchange with Rank of British and American stars; at one point Wanger offered to broker a contract for Rank with Bergman. As a goodwill gesture, he and Bennett hosted a welcoming party for Rank's young star Jean Simmons in 1947. Ever the Anglophile since his years in London, Wanger saw Eagle-Lion as an ideal partner for his new projects.

Then too, after his maltreatment at the hands of Goetz and Spitz, Wanger probably felt he could intimidate Eagle-Lion's capable but inexperienced management team. Max Youngstein was in charge of advertising, publicity, and exploitation (promotional stunts). Attorney Krim came to the new company as a former executive of the theatrical trailer company National Screen Service and a partner in Louis Nizer's law firm, which had provided legal counsel to Paramount. His colleague Benjamin, also a partner with Nizer, had been head of Rank's American operations. They welcomed the chance to run the new operation. It was a trial by fire.

Their 1946–1947 system of two-tiered production—$500,000 films for independent and subsequent-run theaters and Rank films and $1 million titles to break into first-run houses in key markets—didn't work. The A films suffered from a lack of salable stories and name casts: shunned by stars, Eagle-Lion's films featured newcomers or ex-stars such as Richard Basehart, June Lockhart, George Brent, and Louis Hayward. The first-run theaters refused to book them. The Rank films were equally unsuccessful, contributing heavily to 1947's $2.2 million loss.

Just one month prior to his talks with Wanger, Benjamin summed up his frustration in May 1947 by noting that Eagle-Lion did not have "as much as one real attraction on our 1946–47 list." It was time for a change in tactics; as Benjamin wrote to Young in August 1947, "We are all agreed that at this stage of the game there is nothing else for us to do but shift the burden of financial responsibility partially, if not entirely, to outside producers." By October, Eagle-Lion announced a schedule of between fifty-five and sixty films. Twenty-five to thirty titles would be in-house $200,000 productions. Seventeen films would be of $1 million "A" quality: eight Rank releases, six Edward Small films, and two to four films from Wanger.

For Eagle-Lion, the Wanger agreement settled in October 1947 was, in Benjamin's words, of "incalculable importance, especially in regard to the intangible but vital factor of studio prestige" since the forthcoming *Joan of Arc* and *Tap Roots* placed Wanger at "the peak of his career." "It has generally been recognized among exhibitors, producers and other creative talent," Benjamin continued, "that the acquisition of Wanger was positive evidence of the goal for which Eagle-Lion was striving." Wanger brought plans for Technicolor production and two major stars, Bennett and Hayward, to Eagle-Lion. He was Eagle-Lion's best hope for producing films the best theaters would book.

In addition to developing his own projects, Wanger took an active interest in the conduct of Eagle-Lion's affairs as a board member. Hopeful and ebullient, he constantly urged Krim and Benjamin to spend more money, contract with the best talents, and carry on with its first-class aspirations. He set up deals for Ford's Argosy Pictures, although Ford remained at RKO. He tried to interest Selznick in joining producing and distributing forces with Eagle-Lion, but Selznick, in spite of his faltering Selznick Releasing Organization, offered only to let Eagle-Lion rerelease his older films.

Indeed, Eagle-Lion lacked the funds to finance its ambitious plans. The company's weekly revenues in 1948 declined by nearly 9 percent from the previous year. The British half of Eagle-Lion's bid for prestige also ran aground. In 1948, Rank's increased production of films meant less attention to the handling of Eagle-Lion's American releases in British theaters. Krim and Benjamin found new foreign distributors in late 1948, but these groups were nowhere near as efficient, effective, or honest. The studio's cash flow difficulty was so severe, however, that they elected not to sue the duplicitous distributors but collect what income they could.

Before these troubles emerged, however, Wanger sought to take advantage of British distribution. Wanger envisioned more films that showcased Hayward as an autonomous yet out of control woman who needed to be brought to heel. There was "Annie, Queen of the Pirates," a swashbuckling adventure film that depicts a woman pirate's encounters with legendary figures such as Blackbeard, and *Tulsa,* another Hayward vehicle, based on an original story about the oil town in the 1920s. To vary his program, Wanger also had another original story entitled "The Bastille," for which Wanger hoped to use "heavily disguised" sets from his *Joan of Arc* film, and for Joan Bennett, a melodramatic *Ladies Home Journal* story "The Blank Wall," which Wanger shelved when Bennett became pregnant early in 1948 with Shelley.

Eagle-Lion agreed to these projects somewhat reluctantly in mid-May, feeling that their bargaining position was weak with so few other producers on the lot. One month later, however, Young cut off his personal financing of the operation to see if it could float on bank loans. Krim and Benjamin were compelled to revert to the low-budget formula of PRC, "to only entertain doing small pictures that have some sort of sensational exploitation background." The Technicolor *Tulsa* hardly fit this mold, and Krim grew anxious about Wanger's preproduction commitments of an unprecedented $250,000.

On June 12, Krim apologized for putting Wanger "in a terrible spot," but demanded contract revisions and a budget reduction for *Tulsa* on the threat of withdrawing Eagle-Lion financing of the film. Wanger could find no other interested studios. "The Blank Wall" was to be shelved indefinitely. "The Bastille," costing $750,000, and *Tulsa,* costing $1.5 million, were to be cross-collateralized. "Annie, Queen of the Pirates" was canceled (eventually to be directed four years later by Tourneur as *Anne of the Indies,* now a cult film among feminist film critics, for Twentieth Century-Fox).

Wanger carried through at Eagle-Lion with considerable bitterness for the rest of 1948. He faced continuing obstacles in producing *Tulsa,* his first semi-independent film for the company. The studio's production manager placed constant pressure on Wanger and director Stuart Heisler to keep the film within budget. Wanger was upbraided for watching rushes of the film in color rather than in black-and-white. Heisler, an experienced hand who had worked several times before with Hayward (including her Oscar-nominated role for *Smash-Up*), was reprimanded for restoring a musical sequence that Eagle-Lion had deleted. Wanger and Krim argued over the spectacular fire sequence (done with miniatures) that, like the shipwreck in *History Is Made at Night,* concluded an inconsistent story with visual overkill.

Yet, while facing budget constraints, major financial risks, and company difficulties, the two projects Wanger successfully pursued were, like *Canyon Passage* and *Tap Roots,* tributes to the virtues of American capitalism and democracy. For Wanger this theme took on new urgency in the political climate that spawned the National Security Act, the Federal Employee Loyalty Program, and the infamous House investigation of Communist infiltration in the film industry. The first hearings took place in October 1947 as Wanger prepared to move to Eagle-Lion, and his own record was disturbing. His association with Films for Democracy back in the 1930s was one troubling item. His hiring of leftist Dorothy Parker for *The Moon's Our Home* and for the story of his more recent Hayward vehicle *Smash-Up* was another. Then there was the ex-Screen Writers Guild president Nichols, who had written *Stagecoach, The Long Voyage Home,* and *Scarlet Street,* as well as Lawson, the leading member of Hollywood's Communist group, who scripted *Blockade, Algiers,* and *Smash-Up* in 1946.

According to Rapf, Wanger had never been "in any way pro-Communist but, unlike many of his colleagues among producers, he didn't seem to care if the people working for him were known to be reds." To conservatives, it seemed clear where he stood. He had been active in the Hollywood Democratic Committee and the Independent Citizens Committee of the Arts, Sciences and Professions. This and his leadership of the Hollywood Free World Association had antagonized the Motion Picture Alliance for the Preservation of American Ideals, whose members in the spring of 1947 provided the House committee with "evidence." On the first day of October hearings, newspaper editor Howard Rushmore mentioned Wanger, *Blockade,* and Films for Democracy. Alliance leader Wood called the committee's attention to the "interesting organization" the Free World Association and explicitly noted Wanger's leadership of the group.

Though he regarded the HUAC hearings as "certainly a sorry mess," Wanger, unlike Goldwyn, made no public response to these citations, and they did not immediately affect his business dealings. He applauded Schary's denial to HUAC that Communist propaganda infiltrated Hollywood films, cabling Schary that "you stood out like a sore thumb amongst your colleagues." At the Waldorf Astoria in November 1947, he, Goldwyn, and Schary alone opposed the Waldorf statement that inaugurated the studios' blacklisting policy. Wanger and Goldwyn agreed with Schary, as Schary later recalled it, "'Let's take our time. This is a very important issue' . . . But there was nothing we could do about it." Wanger surprised Left-wing writers such as *Winter Carnival*'s Lester Cole when he appeared with Mannix to support Schary at an awkward meeting in Hollywood's Roosevelt Hotel with four hundred members of the Screen Writers Guild to apologize for the Waldorf Statement and to enlist their support in a campaign to counter the charges of Communist infiltration.

But Wanger certainly understood the compromising position in which he and the film industry were placed. In response, he conceived and promoted his Eagle-Lion films as tools in the anti-Communist fight. *Tulsa* was the first of a projected series Wanger planned on airlines, the press, and coal mining, to be financed partly by those industries to promote the idea that "American free enterprise . . . is a fancy name for our individualism," and that "capitalism as an economic term isn't money—it is opportunity."

In the fall of 1948, when *Tulsa* completed principal photography, Wanger told the press, "Hollywood has the medium which can do more in a cold war than anything else" because "we don't need message pictures. Just a picture of well-dressed people walking down Fifth Avenue would show what Americanism can do." *Tulsa* was not quite that subtle. Wanger thought up the project in the wake of *Oklahoma!*'s success on Broadway and after hearing an ABC profile of the city on his car radio. He proceeded to hire Nugent, the *New York Times* film critic-turned-screenwriter (who did his best work for Ford on 1952's *The Quiet Man* and 1956's *The Searchers*). Nugent wrote a script using what Foley described as "Tulsa background, lots of action and dialogue about oil, and a beautiful young girl who comes to the town and gets rich." Wanger wanted it to be a more recent version of *Canyon Passage* starring Andrews (or Mitchum) and Carmichael. But Eagle-Lion's budget-cutting placed Robert Preston (originally cast in a secondary role) in the lead and Chill Wills in the singing part.

After a brief prologue, in which Wills outlines the importance of oil to modern society, the film begins as a revenge tale: Cherokee Lansing (Hayward), after witnessing her rancher father's death at the foot of an oil well, determines to get revenge on the magnate responsible. Her vengeance takes the form of quitting ranching, succeeding wildly in the oil business, and becoming the toast of the city. Although her struggles could have made a compelling drama, all of this occupies only the first thirty minutes of the film. Then Nugent's rambling script portrays Cherokee's uneasy romance with a geologist-conservationist (Preston), her friendship with an Indian rancher (another Ford talent, Pedro Amendariz), and her lust for riches. Like the heroines of *Ladies Courageous* and *Tap Roots,* she misdirects her talents into self-destructive actions. By the film's end, her oil fields are in flames.

Certainly *Tulsa,* by showing Cherokee's meteoric rise in the oil industry, confirmed that America was a land of opportunity, as long as one has the determination of this quintessential, individualist Hayward character. (The always shy Hayward was apparently uninterested in its implications. During principal photography, she refused to act when Bank of America executive Mario Giannini visited her on the set; "Do I go down and watch him foreclose his mortgages?" she asked Wanger.) At the same time, it was a remarkably contradictory film, at once attempting to promote the joys of capitalism while showing its excesses, much in the manner that Wanger had ascribed to *Mr. Smith Goes to Washington.* Wanger dwelt on *Tulsa*'s positive aspects, though, and at the film's premiere in Tulsa in April 1949, articulated once again his desire that his Americana films be read as tools in the fight against Communist propaganda. He alluded to the Marshall Plan, arguing that the United States needed "a very aggressive program to spread the good news of what this wonderful country has and what it is willing to do to assist other countries to build up their industries in order to be able to trade with us." *Tulsa,* he told his audience, was not "the finest picture in the world but it is a sincere attempt in the right direction."

A less sincere attempt was "The Bastille," which Wanger gradually downsized in the spring of 1948 from a big-budget spectacular in the tradition of MGM's *A Tale of Two Cities* (1935) or Korda's *The Scarlet Pimpernel* (1934) to an action melodrama. As with *Tulsa,* the contract revisions of mid-June 1948 made casting the likes of Joan Crawford or Selznick contractee Alida Valli out of the question. Wanger chose MGM starlet Arlene Dahl to play the heroine Madelon. He also signed comedy star Robert Cummings (who had appeared in Hitchcock's *Saboteur*) to play the counterrevolutionary Charles D'Aubigny, who is dispatched by Lafayette to undermine Robespierre and his cronies. D'Aubigny succeeds by revealing to the Commune that Robespierre has all their names listed in his black book for future appointments with the guillotine.

For this project Wanger supervised Aeneas MacKenzie and Yordan's script drafts. He encouraged MacKenzie, a veteran of 1930s Warner Bros. historical films, to research the era carefully. MacKenzie actually drew upon historical figures and incidents from the revolution, including the existence of Robespierre's list, and portrayed the protagonists in a manner consistent with Thomas Carlyle and Charles Dickens's accounts. Then too, Wanger instructed the writer to portray the revolution as neither the liberating overthrow of a decadent aristocracy nor the regrettable destruction of Griffith's *Orphans of the Storm.* Instead, he wanted "the spirit of cheating cheaters that pictures of this type have had in the past, with lots of devices and a great deal of suspense—and loaded with gags."

"This type of picture" apparently meant the action exploitation film, not unlike his own orientalist adventures. In terms of spectacle and ideology, Wanger's postwar Technicolor films took up where the orientalist fantasies left off. Looking over McKenzie's script in May 1948, John Balderston (who had adapted *Dracula, Frankenstein,* and *Gaslight*) warned Wanger that the interjection of "Commune-istes" into a "rough-house sex-chase" formula would "backfire." Perhaps a script by Arthur Koestler, who had documented the horrors of life under Stalin, could make credible a parallel between the Jacobins' reign of terror and Stalinist Russia, "showing . . . how this all happened again in Moscow and could happen here."

The second screenwriter, Yordan, agreed with Balderston that a viewer couldn't follow McKenzie's script unless they were, in Yordan's words, "a student of the French revolution." Hence after Mann begged Yordan to work on the script, Wanger encouraged Yordan to omit the speeches and focus on the action surrounding the black book. With Yordan's additions, "The Bastille," rechristened *Reign of Terror,* became, as historian Richard Maltby has observed, a relentless blend of film noir and gangster film conventions that equate the heroes with the villains at every turn.

Like *Arabian Nights, Reign of Terror* complemented its action and dangerous atmosphere with humor. But where *Arabian Nights'* comedy had been infantile slapstick and vaudeville shtick, director Mann emphasized cynical understatement. Some of the more amusing lines, such as Robespierre's objection to being called "Max," were scripted. But the bulk of its humor came chiefly from the unscripted, wry comments of New York stage actor Arnold Moss in the role of notorious Parisian police chief Fouche. These include his observation, after a murderous attack on himself and Charles that "Paris is never dull"; his advice to Charles and Madelon, "don't stay out too late—there's a revolution going on"; and his comment, echoing the ending of *Casablanca,* that he and Charles (whom he believes to be, like himself, an expert at torture) will "have some great times together."

Once the script was satisfactory, Wanger, busy with *Joan of Arc,* handed over *Reign of Terror* to production designer Menzies, who had last worked for Wanger on *Foreign Correspondent.* Now Menzies agreed to produce, design, and supervise sets, scripting, and direction of the film for an art director's salary. Menzies's collaborator was Mann, a Theater Guild director in the 1930s and a Selznick talent scout for *Gone with the Wind.* After his breakthrough *Desperate* (1947) at RKO, Mann directed *T-Men* for Small at Eagle-Lion, a film that earned four times its negative cost and made Mann the studio's most valued director. He worked quickly—he shot *Reign of Terror* in twenty-nine days from August to September 1948. With *T-Men* cinematographer John Alton, Mann developed a distinctive low-cost noir style, using low lighting levels and omnipresent shadows on minimal decor, bizarre angles (such as a view of a public square from the top of a guillotine), and obvious process photography in the Commune scenes.

Between them, Menzies, Mann, and Alton effectively transformed Wanger's costume epic into an action-packed period film noir. Their work heightened the atmosphere of amorality and constant betrayal which Wanger had envisioned for the film. In postproduction, Wanger reminded Mann to preserve

the spirit of the Revolution—where everything gets out of control and where opportunism reigns supreme, where there is treachery, anarchy—where people try to live to the fullest because they don't know whether they are going to be there tomorrow—where there is distrust and chaos and a carnival of lust.

As Phillip Hartung of *Commonweal* noted, "It has so many thrills, chases, horrors, and accumulations of suspense that one can hardly stand the goings on, and the piece loses a sense of reality."

But Wanger had not forgotten the film's political allegory when it neared its premiere. Citing a news item about author Howard Fast calling anti-Communism in America a reign of terror, Wanger wrote Youngstein in April 1949:

> I think the best way to make a lot of dough with this—I don't know whether you agree with me or not—would be to go all out and maybe have some of the ads warn the public that we will be going through a REIGN OF TERROR in this country if we don't watch out and that there is a REIGN OF TERROR all over the world.
>
> Let this be hailed as the Motion Picture Industry's effort to stop all kinds of to-talitarianism. I think it must be done very carefully because it might be a hell of a HITLER'S CHILDREN [a 1942 RKO exploitation film about the horrific life of German youth] all over again in a romantic dressing.

It is tempting to interpret the depiction of the French revolution in *Reign of Terror* as a commentary on the Red Scare of the forties (with Robespierre's black book as the blacklist). Yet, the film's political connotations are as ambivalent as its mixture of dramatic violence and caustic humor. Like *The President Vanishes*, whose Fascist overtones complicated its New Deal suspicions of big business, *Reign of Terror* celebrated what it ostensibly criticized. It also resembled *Invasion of the Body Snatchers*, whose anti-Communist politics are so displaced and abstracted that they appear to oppose anti-Communist sentiments.

Thanks to diverse promotional campaigns—none of which took up Wanger's suggestion to Youngstein—*Reign of Terror* proved the only profitable postwar Wanger film, although it earned a mere $20,000 after several years in release. *Tulsa* should have done better but didn't. The *Hollywood Reporter* called it "a tremendous, eye-filling spectacle" and an "unqualified success." Eagle-Lion distribution head William Heineman wrote Wanger that exhibitors agreed with him "for the first time since I have been with Eagle-Lion that we definitely have a money picture." Yet the film failed to recover nearly half its negative cost.

Hence, by 1948 the Americana program brought Wanger to a paradoxical position. Eagle-Lion's failure to thrive or even survive resulted from many factors, but primary among them were the barriers to entry facing a new producer-distributor in the monopolistic American film industry. Even as Wanger sought to celebrate American capitalism, his own company and his hosting studio were finding it difficult to survive. In fact, among Wanger's semi-independent projects in the postwar era, his only unadulterated success story was the rise of Hayward. This was partly due to loan-outs to major studios for films such as *They Won't Believe Me* (1947) and *The Saxon Charm* (1948). But Wanger skillfully found scripts appropriate to her talents and her star image.

"I don't think I'm awfully good," Hayward told a reporter in 1946. Under Wanger's tutelage, she didn't need to be. Her characters were never called upon to register any ambiguity or nuance. Instead, the Hayward roles involved the broadest gestures of dismay, resignation or, most commonly, defiance. Passionate, sincere, and determined, the Hayward character was rarely capable of duplicity or of successful deception: in *Tap Roots,* it is Morna Dabrey's coquettish sister Aven (Julie London) who woos away fiancé Clay McIvor (Whitfield Connor) when Morna is not looking. Morna's thoughts, like those of Lucy Overmire or Cherokee Lansing, are readily legible.

In fact, Hayward's star image was primarily that of a survivor, closer to the endurance of Crawford than to the defiance of Bette Davis. Even when her sexuality was initially viewed as threatening, as in *Tap Roots,* it was ultimately domesticated by her leading men, bringing out the good-hearted girl beneath her rage, confusion, or self-destructiveness. Thus Wanger's Americana films highlighted her resilience. *Canyon Passage* ended with an Indian attack that demolishes Logan's store, but Logan with Lucy will work to reestablish his business. The battle of the Dabneys against the Confederate army in *Tap Roots* results in the total destruction of their home, but Morna takes inspiration from the oak tree outside their house and becomes determined to stay on the land and rebuild. *Tulsa* concluded with a fire that destroys Cherokee's oil wells, but she will endure. Hayward's heroines' decision to carry on embodied a strength and determination that was part of Wanger's celebration of pioneer spirit. The destruction of property in all the Hayward films was a displaced metaphor for the battle of World War II. This destruction not only provided the films with a spectacular, rousing climax, it was an implicit exhortation to rebuild America and foreign countries in the wake of World War II.

Like the historical films, Wanger's postwar adult melodramas *Smash-Up* and *The Lost Moment* furthered Hayward's bid for stardom by placing her in roles that embodied the ideas of domesticated passion and emotional resilience. Yet unlike Lucy Overmire, Morna Dabney, or Cherokee Lansing, Angie Evans in *Smash-Up* and Tina Borderau in *The Lost Moment* are overwhelmed by internal rather than external constraints in dramas that Wanger touted for their mature realism.

Where the war experience had changed Wanger's conception of message movies, the postwar cinemas of Europe had influenced Wanger's preference for the frank melodramas in which Angie and Tina appeared. The Italian neorealists' stunning portraits of desperate postwar life, and the candid, adult content of British films such as Sidney Gilliat's *The Notorious Gentleman*

(1945) and David Lean's *Brief Encounter* (1946) were widely praised by critics and filmmakers. They became Wanger's models. In early 1946, Wanger told the group responsible for banning *Scarlet Street* in the city of Atlanta that

> Art is the truth, and the truth never should be censored. Its function is to hold the mirror up to life. It never glamorizes; it never glorifies and it never debases. . . . It is a conscientious response to demands that the American motion picture industry meet its artistic and educational responsibilities to the American people and to the world, that it stop playing with doll-puppets and deal with real people, that it come out of the nursery, grow up and face life honestly.

Similarly, after his November 1946 visit to England with Bennett, who participated in a Royal Command Performance for the Queen, Wanger told the trade press, "Tastes of the people in foreign countries are definitely changing because of the hardships the people underwent during the war and they're now developing more adult and more serious pictures." Other executives in Hollywood were aware of the need to make films that in *Variety*'s words "appealed to a world audience"; but Wanger was more dramatic in pronouncing his own epiphany. He was "changing his entire approach to filmmaking immediately to take advantage of the foreign market." His move to Eagle-Lion eight months later was part of this change.

Of course, what was adult and what appealed to a world audience was open to debate. One possible model was *Smash-Up,* the film Wanger was completing at the time of his return from England. Reputed to be based on the life of Dixie Lee Crosby (which Wanger vehemently denied), the film concerned a budding nightclub performer Angie Evans who marries singer Ken Conway (Lee Bowman). Ken's radio success and busy career drive Angie to drink until a fire and the near death of their child reconciles them.

Following the naturalistic rationale Wanger deployed in defense of *Scarlet Street, Smash-Up* took an unblinking look at alcoholism. Wanger disregarded Breen Office warnings about the "distasteful" and "disgusting" offense of showing a woman drunk on-screen, precisely because those moments of frank portrayal made the film unique: there was a voyeuristic thrill in seeing Angie transformed from a poised, beautiful performer to a distraught, disorderly, and neglected neurotic. Its "realism" was visually emphasized through its "semi-documentary" sequences with location shooting in New York, as when Angie awakens to find herself in a New York tenement. More dramatic interior scenes deployed the studio naturalism exemplified by *Scarlet Street* and *The Lost Weekend.* Cortez, whose work on *Eagle Squadron* Wanger had greatly admired, was the cinematographer. Contrary to descriptions of Hayward "wallowing in softly lit, sumptuously designed luxury," Cortez's often stark lighting techniques give the film a sharp, high-contrast look, most striking in the scene when Ken finds Angie drunk in her darkened bedroom.

Of all of Wanger's postwar "European-inspired" films, *Smash-Up* was the most typical Hollywood production: like problem movies of the postwar years, such as Goldwyn's *The Best Years of Our Lives,* Zanuck's *The Snake Pit,* and *The Lost Weekend, Smash-Up* took the frankness of the neorealists and plugged it into the social problem formula. Lawson's screenplay from an original story by Dorothy Parker and Frank Cavett refused to identify a villain, but offered compassion and understanding instead. Not even the self-absorbed and unsympathetic Ken was to blame; Angie's affliction was just one of those unfortunate occurrences. Doctors and the National Committee for Education on Alcoholism heartily endorsed the film for its explanation of the varied causes and cures for alcoholism.

Angie herself is a classic postwar heroine: she reenacts the shepherding of the homefront woman back from the workplace to the home. She begins the film as a budding singer fond of a nip before performing. She becomes an inebriated housewife. In fact, her doctor accuses her husband of aggravating Angie's alcoholism by making her "idle and useless" and giving her everything she wants. As critic Norman Denzin points out, the film thus meekly implies the repressive potential in family life in patriarchal society; but at the film's end, Angie's doctor has gotten through to Ken, who sits at her hospital bedside and resolves to be more supportive. This entire scene, and the film's flashback structure, were postproduction additions to the film, which otherwise would have proven too pessimistic. The flashback—which provides the patient a means of confronting the past—was a convention of both alcoholic melodramas such as *The Lost Weekend* and those portraits of female hysteria and neurosis typified by *Possessed.*

In *Smash-Up,* Hayward's character turned what critic Michael Renov has called the "double-bind" of the woman's place in postwar culture in upon herself. Although Twentieth Century–Fox in the 1950s developed Hayward's sultry side in a series of biblical epics, this masochistic element was the crucial part of Hayward's star image under Wanger's management. Richard Conte has her perfectly typecast when he tells Hayward in Joseph L. Mankiewicz's *House of Strangers* (1949): "I know your story. You're lonesome. You like to get hurt. Always picking the wrong guy." This was also the key to Hayward's most highly regarded, subsequent performances: the woman left behind by Andrews in *My Foolish Heart* (1949); her portrayal of alcoholics Jane Frohman in *With a Song in My Heart* (1952) and Lillian Roth in *I'll Cry Tomorrow* (1955); and her depiction of Barbara Graham in Wanger's own *I Want to Live!* in 1958. Although film critics pummeled *Smash-Up* for being a "female" version of *The Lost Weekend,* it earned Hayward the first of her five Oscar nominations.

Hayward's next performance for Wanger was equally showy in a less fortunate "adult" film. *The Lost Moment* was Wanger's first semi-independent production for Universal-International after completing *Smash-Up* and returning from England. It was the direct result of his reconnaissance of the foreign market in late 1946. Wanger had purchased Bercovici's free-lance script when a Civil War–era property ("Washington Flyer," eventually directed by Mann in 1951 as *The Tall Target*) fell through. Bercovici, who had robustly criticized the script of *Secret Beyond the Door*, and recently coauthored *The Bishop's Wife* for Goldwyn, freely adapted Henry James's novelette *The Aspern Papers*, in which an American publisher tries to obtain the love letters of a famous romantic poet Jeffrey Aspern. They are held by Aspern's lover, now 104 years old and living with her niece in a Venetian palace.

Wanger envisioned a moody, atmospheric film of a delicate romance that would appeal to international highbrow tastes—James was hardly a household name among moviegoers, and Wanger's first choices for the male lead were continental stars Boyer, Rex Harrison, and John Mills, each of whom he calculated would increase the film's box office in England. Wanger finally hedged his bets by casting Robert Cummings against his light-comedy type as Venable. This he vainly hoped would generate "bobby-sox appeal" for a film the teenage audience would otherwise never go near. Rank, who distributed Universal films in England, expressed some polite admiration for the film. But due largely to curtailed imports in England, it was never shown there.

Wanger's enthusiasm for the film may have been rooted in its subtlety and nuance, but Bercovici's script eliminated these elements by transforming James's dissection of repressed characters into a pseudo-fantasy such as was proving popular in the postwar era. In James's book, the niece Tita is a naive, bland, and spineless matron who hopes very discreetly that the publisher might marry her. An actress such as Fontaine could have essayed the role as James conceived it, but Hayward could not. Bercovici's most prominent, and predictable, alteration of the novelette was a radical reworking of Tita into Tina at the expense of all narrative plausibility. Tina in Bercovici's version is a schizophrenic young beauty. Coldly efficient with publisher Louis Venable during the day, she is under the hypnotic effect of the love letters by night, when she assumes the identity of her aunt and her romance with the poet. She mistakes Venable for her lover and passionately embraces him when he wanders into a room where she plays extravagant nocturnes on the grand piano. Tina can recover a normal life only through the healing effects of the diluted "talking cure" she undergoes with Venable and after the palace and the letters are burned.

The Lost Moment has star vehicle written all over it, with second-rank male stars opposite Hayward to highlight her performance and the opportunity for Hayward to display versatility in portraying diametrically opposed temperaments. From every other standpoint, *The Lost Moment* is ridiculous, not romantic. Similar in tone and logic to the gothic elements of Lang's *Secret Beyond the Door*, *The Lost Moment* was handled by first-time director Gabel, who gave it an "arty," *Citizen Kane*–like visual style of low-key lighting on cavernous palace sets, deep-focus cinematography, and a long-take, roving camera. Tina's 104-year-old aunt, portrayed as a monstrous gargoyle by Gabel's Mercury Theater colleague Agnes Moorehead, completed the effects, but here was a script even more pretentious and preposterous than Lang's and a film that rarely achieved a romantic mood. One preview patron, asked his or her age, wrote "104. Ha-ha." Critics also ridiculed the film.

By the spring of 1948, just prior to the release of *Tap Roots,* Selznick noted that "Susan Hayward is growing almost as rapidly as any young player on the screen." Wanger paid her $35,000 to play Lucy Overmire in 1945; by 1948 he was charging Twentieth Century–Fox double that amount on loan-out. Her successful buildup was the only bright spot in Wanger's immediate postwar years. His perception that audiences at home and abroad would appreciate big-budget celebrations of American history found support in the box office success of Selznick's *Duel in the Sun* (1946) and even Hawks's *Red River* (1948). His logical beliefs about European-style realism and adult subject matter were bolstered by the critical and commercial performance of *The Best Years of Our Lives* and the acclaim that greeted *The Lost Weekend* or *Gentleman's Agreement.*

But, as was often the case, the execution of Wanger's projects fell far below their conception and Wanger's efforts to guide their critical and box office reception proved futile. Whether he worked in this period as a unit or semi-independent producer, Wanger could not hire outstanding talents such as Hawks, Wyler, Wilder, Kazan, or even Hitchcock or Ford. Wanger admired Ford's *My Darling Clementine,* but it "made me sick because you didn't make it with me." Wanger had to settle for actors from the Ford "stock company," George Marshall and Stuart Heisler. Indeed, except for Lang, directors such as Ford no longer needed Wanger; they were forming their own semi-independent units and their access to major distribution and financing made him unnecessary.

Thus, all of Wanger's films apart from Diana Productions, *Canyon Passage,* and *Reign of Terror* proved either mildly entertaining or mediocre, and hardly profitable at that. Now in 1947, Wanger pressed on to produce his most ambitious film ever. Though he made it without Hayward, Wanger conceived *Joan of Arc* in the image of Britain's 1940s cinema and as a meditation on the status of women in Western society.

It was the biggest miscalculation of his entire career.

14

The Price of Anglophilia

At age fifty-two, Wanger saw the $4.5 million *Joan of Arc* as his *Gone with the Wind* and his *Best Years of Our Lives,* the crowning glory of his career and the answer to all of Hollywood's postwar problems. From the selection of the film's property through its roadshow presentation in major cities, *Joan of Arc,* starring Bergman and directed by Victor Fleming, was conceived as a spiritual blockbuster. More significantly, *Joan of Arc* was the first fully independent venture Wanger produced. Using the residuals from his distributed films and the accumulated, unproduced story properties his company held, he was betting all his chips—his achievements of the 1940s—on the success of a single film.

It would be an enormously profitable film centering, like the Hayward vehicles, on a female protagonist. *Joan of Arc,* and *The Reckless Moment* after it, would demonstrate, better than any of Wanger's previous films, Hollywood's capacity to produce films "competitive" in domestic *and* international markets with the distinguished British "quality" cinema of the period.

In retrospect, undertaking a $4 million epic in the midst of the industry's postwar business troubles seems foolhardy. Yet in 1947 it seemed that, with Hollywood's most popular actress in a presold property, *Joan of Arc* could not lose. In 1946, Hollywood's highest-grossing year, Bergman had appeared in four films (including Hitchcock's *Notorious* and *Spellbound* and McCarey's *The Bells of St. Mary's*) which earned $21.7 million. Her films thus accounted for more than 10 percent of the earnings of the sixty highest-grossing movies that year. Apparently, any film starring Bergman made money.

Early in 1946 Wanger persuaded the actress, just released from her contract with Selznick and besieged with other offers, to form an independent company entitled Sierra Pictures (its officers included Bergman's then agent Lew Wasserman, David Tannenbaum, Bergman, Wanger, Fleming, and attorney Silberberg). It was a major coup. As Bennett later recalled, Wanger came home the night of the signing proudly flourishing "the pen that closed the deal with Ingrid Bergman."

Moreover, Bergman had been selling out Broadway crowds since the fall of 1946 in Maxwell Anderson's *Joan of Lorraine*. While pursuing the rights to Shaw's *St. Joan* and commissioning Renoir to draft a treatment about the life of Mary Magdalene, Wanger initiated talks with Anderson about a film of his play when it opened in October 1946. By late December, "virtually all the majors" were contemplating a production about Joan of Arc, for which the participation of Bergman was considered "a must." On director and lover Fleming's advice, Bergman agreed in February 1947 to do an adaptation of Anderson's play for Sierra. The only remaining question was which studio would help finance and distribute the film.

Thus Sierra undertook *Joan of Arc* with the consensus of the industry. Joan of Arc's story had special appeal in the postwar era. As several critics have pointed out, Joan's virginal status, visionary abilities, male coiffure and armor, and martial prowess embody an uncompromising and threatening feminine independence. But like countless heroines in Western literature and Wanger's Hayward vehicles, she is ultimately contained and punished. That this allegory of postwar womanhood was historically true and had spiritual significance (whose box office value had been proven with Fox's 1943 *Song of Bernadette*) only enhanced its appeal as an epic film. As *Variety* noted in late 1946, "Hollywood appears once again to have 'gone significant.' . . . after almost a year-and-a-half of producing escapism." This was certainly true of the producer of *Arabian Nights* and *A Night in Paradise:* it was a classic case of what Robert Ray has called Hollywood's postwar trend toward "inflation" of styles, genres, and subjects.

The conception of *Joan of Arc* entailed an enormous negative cost, following postwar monetary inflation and Hollywood's penchant for more expensive films. Even in May of 1947, when the decline in domestic theater attendance was unmistakable, studio production heads reasoned that "increased production of costly pictures" would reduce their losses. Universal-International had followed this logic in agreeing to cofinance *Tap Roots*. MGM executives argued that the most costly films (such as that studio's *The Yearling* and *The Hucksters*) brought in revenues comparable to 1946 successes. It was MGM that agreed to distribute the Sierra film in April 1947.

Where Wanger's thinking differed from Hollywood's was in the specific "look" he had in mind for the production. His deep admiration for the British cinema had first been stirred by Olivier's *Henry V* in 1944. Wanger had cabled producer Rank:

CONSIDER HENRY THE FIFTH MAGNIFICENT CONTRIBUTION TO
INTERNATIONAL CULTURE. STOP. ACTING, DIRECTION, DECOR,
PHOTOGRAPHY AND COSTUMES SUPERB. . . . IT IS MUCH MORE
THAN A MOTION PICTURE AND SHOULD NOT BE EXPOSED TO THE
KIND OF TREATMENT MOTION PICTURES RECEIVE.

That year, due to his influence as president of the Academy, Wanger engi-
neered the film's special 1945 Oscar. With *Joan of Arc,* Wanger set out to im-
itate the Olivier production in every respect. In early April 1946, shortly after
signing contracts with Bergman and Fleming, Wanger cabled the Cineguild
company in London for the names of the set and costume designers of Olivier's
Henry V. In fact, Wanger asked if the stylized costumes (by Roger Furse) and
sets (Paul Sheriff) from the Olivier film were available for rental or purchase!
Since they weren't, Wanger secured Goldwyn's veteran art director Richard
Day. To design the costumes, Wanger eventually signed commercial artist
Dorothy Jeakins, who subsequently worked on the deMille epics *Samson and
Delilah* and *The Greatest Show on Earth.* To execute Jeakins's designs, he
hired Russian costume maker Barbara Karinska, whose penchant for period
authenticity Wanger had admired in Cukor's *Gaslight,* Mitchell Leisen's Tech-
nicolor adventure film *Frenchman's Creek,* and Dieterle's *Kismet* (all 1944).

Wanger's conception of the Sierra film extended beyond production design
to its exhibition format. Here again, *Henry V* set the example. Wanger had
recognized in Olivier's film the kind of high art production combined with
spectacular, popular entertainment that he had championed at Dartmouth and
at Covent Garden. He foresaw and suggested to United Artists executives that
the Olivier film could be promoted to intellectual elites as "more than a motion picture," by exhibiting it on a roadshow basis in major markets with promotional tie-ins to the Theater Guild and by holding special screenings for
schools and religious groups.

The roadshow method, which dates at least as far back as Griffith's *Birth
of a Nation* (1915) and which Paramount exploited heavily in the 1920s, presents a film as if it were a legitimate theater performance. Numerous varia-
tions on the practice existed, but it usually consisted of advanced ticket sales
at inflated prices, on a schedule of only two showings a day in a legitimate
theater taken over expressly for the run. Using this method and then general
distribution, *Henry V* had grossed more than $1 million in the United States.
As early as October 1946—before Bergman, Wanger, and Fleming had even
agreed on a Joan of Arc film—Wanger mentioned his plan to see his film
"handled. . . . on the model of Henry V." As Tannenbaum described it, *Joan
of Arc* would be "presented in city after city, and year after year."

Independent production ensured that Wanger's conception of the film
would be realized by financing the film with minimal assistance from the majors and without using their facilities. A major studio would have insisted that

Sierra use its resources and personnel rather than copy Olivier's production design. Finding a bank to commit to the film was not difficult. In April, Wanger and Tannenbaum orally settled tentative terms with Loew's, the Security First National Bank, and Banker's Trust for financing the film along the standard lines Wanger had used with Diana Productions and Walter Wanger Pictures. The Sierra Corporation would borrow 75 percent of the film's budget or $3.5 million (whichever was larger) from the banks, using the film as collateral. Loew's agreed to loan Sierra the remaining $1 million, with an unlimited completion bond, for distribution rights worldwide. The precise details of the contract were hashed out over the summer.

The bank loans would not become available until the start of principal photography, however, and Wanger got himself into trouble arranging the funds for scriptwriting and to pay the salaries of Bergman, Fleming, and Anderson, among others. Sierra raised $1 million through stock capitalization—100,000 shares at ten dollars each. Wanger was by far the biggest investor. To encourage Bergman's crucial participation, he financed her purchase of 20,000 shares of company stock by borrowing $200,000 from independent producer Joseph Bernhard (a loan secured by Bergman's stock in Sierra and in the Arch of Triumph Company, which produced the film of the same name). Wanger Pictures purchased 40,000 shares with a $400,000 investment, and Wanger personally spent $50,000 for 5,000 shares.

But this was not all. Wanger negotiated another $200,000 loan from a California investment firm (Pacific Finance Corporation). This he secured with his wartime Universal films, his unproduced story properties, and half of his company's proceeds from the most recent Wanger films, *The Lost Moment* and *Tap Roots*. This arrangement brought Wanger's personal and corporate investment in *Joan of Arc* to $850,000, and cut off half of his income. His blithe approach to obtaining such loans incurred the criticism of his board of directors at Walter Wanger Pictures, and they chastised him for making such arrangements without consulting them. But no one felt that Wanger's commitments to the film were unreasonable or that there was any question of the film's eventual success.

There were numerous production delays during the summer of 1947 once financing was arranged; these resulted from Anderson's inexperience in screenwriting (which necessitated the hiring of another writer, Andrew Solt), the inexpensive but limited facilities at the Hal Roach studios, costuming problems that included the fitting of Bergman's armor, and a strike of costume workers and machine operators in August 1947. Within a month of the revised, September 15 start date, Sierra had yet to cast secondary characters, schedule second-unit work, plan the battle and burning scenes, and hire its cinematographer, editor, and makeup and prop people.

Then Wanger and Sierra were standing on shaky ground. After the August

6, 1947, announcement of Great Britain's 75 percent ad valorem tax, Loew's got cold feet. Sierra's production delays appeared irresponsible, and, with revenues from the British market restricted, the very concept of *Joan of Arc*—an expensive film calculated for international appeal—no longer made sense. Two weeks before shooting began, Loew's president Nicholas Schenck demanded that Wanger renegotiate the terms of Loew's guarantees on Sierra's bank loan. Worse, Schenck demanded that Wanger reduce the budget for the film. Strong-headed, and aware of interest on RKO's part, Wanger refused to do so and, in *Variety*'s words, "then delivered an ultimatum for a decision." Since Sierra's film was not using MGM facilities and because Loew's and Sierra were still debating distribution terms and financing arrangements, they had no binding agreement on paper. Of all the majors, MGM was least amenable to independent deals anyway, aside from Capra's *State of the Union* and Enterprise's *Caught* (1948). Schenck's decision was an easy one.

Suddenly, Wanger was without a distributor for his $4.5 million film and up to his neck in preproduction loans and stock purchases. The Loew's withdrawal required that Wanger negotiate quickly, at a difficult time for independents to settle any deals, let alone the completion monies and distribution of a multimillion dollar epic. Fortunately, RKO signed an agreement with Sierra within four days of the Loew's withdrawal from the project. RKO executive Norman Freeman described the hasty negotiations to production head Ned Depinet:

> One Saturday afternoon in September of 1947, just ten days before the scheduled start of principal photography, Sierra held a discussion with us. . . . The basic terms of the deal were agreed upon that same afternoon subject to approval of the RKO Board. [RKO President] Peter Rathvon took a plane to New York Sunday night and Board approval was obtained on Monday. By the following Saturday, the contract was executed. Sierra was extremely appreciative of the speed which I believe set a record for any such deal (one week from start of negotiations to execution of contract).

The distributor was as anxious as Sierra to secure bank loans for the production and to meet payrolls beginning the following week. Freeman added that the studio "did not use any duress to take advantage of Sierra's desperate situation and Sierra was very thankful of RKO's cooperation and attitude."

The basic agreement between Sierra and RKO resembled the Loew's contract, with one crucial exception. Where Loew's would have provided Sierra with an unlimited completion guarantee of around $1 million, RKO declined to provide Sierra with more than $300,000 in second money or completion money. The bank loan accounted for 75 percent of the film's budget estimate in September 1947; the remaining $1.2 million had to come from the preproduction loans Wanger had already arranged, from partial salary deferrals (by

Wanger, Fleming, and Bergman) equaling $250,000, *and* from additional completion monies to be secured by Wanger.

Wanger arranged one last loan in December, this time from the Landau Investment Company, for $300,000 at 5 percent interest for a profit percentage. In addition, he borrowed $150,000 from Eagle-Lion to repay the Pacific Finance Corporation loan, transferring his debts to a friendlier creditor who was willing to wait for *Joan of Arc*'s profits for repayment. Eagle-Lion's loan was secured with the only remaining collateral Wanger had: the other half-profits due him from *The Lost Moment* and *Tap Roots*. He now had *all* of his income sources tied up in the Bergman film. All of the loans Wanger had arranged had to be repaid before he or any other Sierra stockholder would see profits. Between production and stock purchase loans, and informal contributions from Bennett, Wanger arranged roughly 94 percent of the film's enormous negative cost.

RKO refused to invest more than $300,000 in the costs of *Joan of Arc*. Freeman explained that because of the uncertain market and the roadshow plan, the film would have to gross $10 million before RKO saw a profit: "It will be a long time before the picture will be released and we do not know what the conditions will be at that time so I would feel more comfortable if we should not have the secondary money in the picture."

Thus RKO's squeamishness and Wanger's independent arrangements bought him virtually complete control over the film, including the right of final cut. Although RKO was entitled to view daily rushes, approve major departures from the script, and recut the film once it was in distribution, there were no disputes over the film's production, no interfering studio executives as at Universal-International, and no sudden budget cuts as at Eagle-Lion. Shooting began on September 16, 1947, and ended three months later on December 18, at which time Vorkapich cut the battle sequences. In February, Fleming directed nine days of retakes, funded by the Landau Investment loan; he finished dubbing later in the spring.

Wanger pronounced himself thoroughly pleased with the result when he wrote Fleming in April 1948 that the film was "a serious and profound performance, beautifully mounted and done in a noble manner." To banker Alex Ardrey, Wanger wrote, "If the picture can be sold properly to the American public and is a great commercial success, as well as a spiritual success, it will mean that the motion picture has found itself and from here on in its possibilities are limitless."

Joan of Arc called forth the most optimistic sales pitches Wanger had ever made in his career. "If anyone was expecting Mr. Wanger to be modest about 'Joan,' they were in for a jolt," the *Motion Picture Herald* noted with amusement just prior to the premiere. "It's more than a great motion picture," Wanger had told the paper. "It's a great event. It's bound to break records and make the public proud of the industry." The trade journal's editor Red Kann agreed, opening his review by stating that with *Joan of Arc,* "Motion pictures project themselves onto a plane perhaps higher than they heretofore have attained." *Film Daily* and *Variety* agreed. The "bad boy of the movies" had returned to the fold. Breen wrote Wanger that he was "exhilarated and inspired because of your distinguished achievement." Through the film's premiere, everyone connected with *Joan of Arc* felt certain it would prove immensely profitable, in spite of foreign quotas, reduced revenues, and general criticism of the American film industry.

But they were completely wrong, partly because of the film's realization. Although Wanger had cajoled Anderson, against the latter's will, into scripting *Joan of Arc,* the screenplay by Anderson and Solt was a major departure from the hit Broadway play. *Joan of Lorraine* depicts a contemporary actress struggling to portray and believe in Joan's faith as well as the individual's ability to effect social change; its structure alternates between rehearsal scenes and conversations between the actress and the director. *Joan of Arc* eliminated the play's portrayal of modern-day skepticism and its intriguing use of a framing device for the saint's biography. It presented instead a solemn, straightforward portrayal of Joan of Arc's life.

This decision is even more striking given Wanger's model of *Henry V* for *Joan of Arc,* a fact that only Crowther of the *New York Times* noticed and made the central concern of his review. Olivier's film is admirable in large part for its reflexive qualities, full of overtly stylized sets and colors in its progression from the artificiality of the Globe Theater settings to the cinematic "realism" of the battle scene. By contrast, the Sierra film discarded Anderson's framing device and hence the prestige of an adaptation as such (a component of the British cinema of quality in films such as Lean's *Great Expectations*). The film lacked humor or distance, showing Joan as a pathetic creature preserved only by faith.

Then too, *Henry V* was a misleading model for Wanger. Olivier's film had been a success in part because it was wartime propaganda, even earning British government support through production subsidies. In America, where Anglophilia ran at an all-time high, *Henry V*'s marginal appeal could be broadened slightly for a million-dollar gross. But *Joan of Arc* had to appeal to the general audience to recover its costs. No doubt, popular appeal justified the decision to produce a naturalistic account of the saint's life rather than a more reflexive work. But the film depicted the arduous path from Joan's village to her trial with meticulously researched sets and action in plodding detail. Fleming co-directed *The Wizard of Oz* and *Gone with the Wind* to classic status. But Fleming was less comfortable with Joan's spiritual strength than with Dorothy's innocence and Scarlett's stamina. His drawn-out battle scenes could not relieve the general effect of monotony. Although Bergman's performance was moving and credible, her talents could accomplish only so much.

So could her popularity. *Joan of Arc*'s $4.5 million negative cost made it

Hollywood's most expensive film yet (costing $200,000 more than *Gone with the Wind*). Only *Gone with the Wind, The Best Years of Our Lives,* and *Duel in the Sun* had grossed the $9 million (of which at least $6 million had to be earned domestically) that *Joan of Arc* required to break even. Then there were deferred salaries and profit percentages, all of which RKO treasurer William Clark described as "the most involved contractual situation from the standpoint of the division of receipts of the picture that I have ever witnessed."

Moreover, Wanger had been unrealistically optimistic, in his characteristic way, about the impact of a single film. He had seen propaganda films change public opinion in Italy almost overnight, he had witnessed how Hollywood dictated fashions to worldwide audiences, he had battled the whirlwind surrounding his topical message movies, and he had led the Academy during Hollywood's greatest hour. But as the *Scarlet Street* controversy suggested, in the postwar period, the movies were no longer the central mass cultural event in American society; they could more easily be ignored or derided. Young families had more practical problems to attend to than searching out the movie palaces, and television sets went on the national market the very fall in which *Joan of Arc* premiered.

No one film could single-handedly whitewash the tainting of Hollywood's social prestige in the late forties, pull postwar Americans back into the theaters when they had other leisure preoccupations, or persuade foreign governments and the state department to ensure unhampered foreign distribution. When critics noted the pompous qualities of the production, Wanger privately accused them of being "cynical." Intentions had always been a strong selling point when *The President Vanishes* or *Blockade* had proven compromised, and critics had rushed to Wanger's defense. But intentions were no longer enough. Sierra needed hard cash, not goodwill, to succeed.

Having sunk so much energy and equity into *Joan of Arc,* Wanger refused to accept the possibility that the film did not interest audiences. It opened at the Victoria Theatre in New York on November 11, 1948, not in the roadshow format, but on a "grind" basis, in which the film was shown continuously through the day, with the most expensive seats sold in the evenings for $1.80. But by this time even roadshow films such as *The Best Years of Our Lives* and *Duel in the Sun* were earning grosses below expectations; RKO officials told *Variety* that *Joan of Arc* "may have come along too late to get maximum results at upped admissions, such as a bevy of pix did a couple of years ago."

In spite of RKO's advertising, which included a huge billboard of Bergman over the theater, by the sixth week of its run at the Victoria, *Joan of Arc* was earning only $30,000 and was proving less popular in New York than the MGM musical *Words and Music,* the Cummings-Lamarr comedy *Let's Live a Little,* and Bob Hope's parodic *The Paleface.* RKO felt that perhaps the "dead" period between Thanksgiving and Christmas hurt the film badly, but

Wanger insisted that RKO had not promoted the film in imaginative and thorough ways. Drawing on his personal success in promoting his ventures, he complained that the distributor had not assigned anyone to "contact" critics before *Joan of Arc*'s premiere: "As everyone knows, there is quite a great deal to the way you condition and manage people of the press, and the psychological contact."

Wanger tried to find alternate distributors for the film and to hire consultants to boost its performance, but Sierra's contract with RKO made him powerless to enforce any of his ideas. Since the studio had a minimal investment in the film, there was no incentive to promote the film in a singular fashion. Moreover, the studio had undergone a drastic change in ownership during the summer of 1948 as millionaire Howard Hughes bought up a majority interest and began to involve himself in production. The shift in administration was as harmful as the arrival of Goetz and Spitz at Universal. Idiosyncratic and interfering, Hughes drove production executives Schary and Peter Rathvon away from the studio. Though Wanger believed he had a cordial relationship with Hughes, he could not reach RKO's new owner once the dimensions of *Joan of Arc*'s failure was clear.

Undoubtedly, as Wanger claimed to his friends and colleagues, Bergman's highly publicized affair with Rossellini rendered her casting in the film a blasphemy: she had been denounced on the floor of the Senate, and newspapers nationwide had called for boycotts of her films. Wanger did everything in his power to persuade Bergman to return to Hollywood, to no avail. To his astonishment and anguish, Hughes rushed Bergman's first film with Rossellini, *Stromboli*, into distribution to capitalize on the scandal. It premiered before *Joan of Arc*'s general release in the spring of 1949, when its runs in small towns were termed "murderous."

Although French critics naturally resented Hollywood's temerity in producing a life of its cherished saint, *Joan of Arc* made the strongest showing in foreign Catholic nations of any postwar American film (grossing an extraordinary $900,000 in France alone). But even with packed houses and acting awards for Bergman on the continent, RKO estimated in August that *Joan of Arc* would gross only $7,500,000 from its initial worldwide distribution. The bulk of this went to RKO's distributing and advertising costs and fees. After two years, Sierra still owed the Security First National Bank more than half its negative cost. The second money—$1.1 million in guaranteed loans secured by Sierra stock, Wanger film residuals, and Wanger Pictures properties— would be paid back only with reissues, including the Banker's Trust recut version available on video today.

The disappointment of *Joan of Arc* extended beyond Wanger's finances to his prestige in the industry. Trade reviews were enthusiastic, and industry leaders such as Depinet and Mayer cited *Joan of Arc* as exemplary Hollywood product. Joseph Valentine won an Oscar for his cinematography, and Bergman and Jose Ferrer were nominated for acting honors in the 1948 Academy Awards. But unlike Goldwyn's *The Best Years of Our Lives,* the film itself was denied a best picture nomination (another Olivier film, *Hamlet,* got the best picture award), and Wanger had to lobby for a "Special Award" that was eventually given to him, and not to the film, "for distinguished service to the industry by adding to its moral stature in the world community by his production of *Joan of Arc.*" "People cross the street when they see me," Wanger wrote Bienstock in disgust, "because of this terrible film I have produced." When Wanger publicly upbraided Art Buchwald for his pan in the *New York Herald Tribune,* Buchwald mockingly challenged him to a duel. Wanger was not amused.

Shortly after *Joan of Arc*'s disappointing opening and while *Tulsa* and *Reign of Terror* were in postproduction, Wanger tried to jump-start his last Anglophilic project, "The Blank Wall," ultimately released as *The Reckless Moment.* After giving birth to Shelley in July 1948, Bennett was ready to return to work on Wanger's third Eagle-Lion property. But Krim, facing continuing financing problems at the studio, was forced to shut the studio down on December 21, as Eagle-Lion's production efforts effectively came to an end. Wanger had to go elsewhere.

On the bright side, Wanger by mid-December had secured James Mason for the lead opposite Bennett in what he called "one of the most unusual quality pictures of the year." By late 1948, Mason had completed only unreleased films: Max Ophuls's *Caught* and Vincente Minnelli's *Madame Bovary.* But British exhibitors had ranked him a top box office attraction since 1945, and his performances in *The Wicked Lady, The Seventh Veil* (both 1945), and more recently 1947's *Odd Man Out* had consolidated his position. As Wanger crassly put it when pitching the project to Jack Warner, Mason was worth "three hundred thousand to four hundred thousand pounds in England."

Mason found "The Blank Wall" intriguing, and one afternoon in early December, he conferred with Wanger and scriptwriters Robert Soderberg and Henry Garson at Wanger's house in Holmby Hills. Soderberg later recalled that Mason took their two-page story outline home to confer with his wife Pamela while the writers and Wanger had lunch. After a tense three hours, "Walter's relief was enormous when Mason returned friendly and ready to sign," albeit on the condition that he have script approval and that he could portray Donnelly as a true Irishman and hence trade on his sympathetic role in *Odd Man Out.* His asking price was $150,000 plus 25 percent of the film's profits.

Wanger agreed to Mason's contract terms on December 13 and then sought a producer-distributor to cofinance the film and provide facilities. In the wake of *Joan of Arc*'s performance, he was rejected by RKO and Warner

Bros. Relief for Wanger came, from of all places, Columbia Pictures, whose status had only improved since Wanger had left it in 1933. But neither Rita Hayworth's rise to stardom nor the phenomenal success of 1946's *The Jolson Story* had changed its low-budget orientation. As location manager John Blankenhorn later described it, the studio continued its early 1930s policy of relying on a few outstanding films to carry its lesser pictures:

> Columbia had made its money on very expensive beautifully cast comedies and in those days they were still living on this "one picture a year will do, and we will make a whole bunch of little pictures and we will pay the gas bill and the light bill and the overhead and paint the place and do all those good things. And then when we make the big one, the profit is ours, we don't have to spread it out and support the studio with it."

Because the studio decreased its low-budget output in the wake of the *Paramount* decrees, a Bennett-Mason melodrama would nicely enhance its schedule in the coming year.

By the time he had pitched the project to Columbia, Wanger was desperate to produce it on any basis, independent or unit. Cohn and production head B. B. Kahane were aware of Wanger's position and made stringent demands for a semi-independent project. While securing a first money loan, Wanger had to defer his salary and the reimbursement of his story costs until Columbia had recouped all distribution and advertising expenses as well as production advances. The standing commitment to Mason for 25 percent of the profits would have to come from Wanger's 50 percent. On January 17, 1949, he signed the contract.

Columbia's cost consciousness was apparent from the very first as Mason and Wanger sought a director. Wanger, mindful of Bennett's success with Lang and in Renoir's *Woman on the Beach,* had always hoped for a European director to handle the project and had taken up Mason's suggestion of Renoir. But the French director's demand of $50,000 plus a 5 percent profit share exceeded Columbia's stipulation of a $40,000 director. Ophuls, who had recently worked with Mason on *Caught,* signed a contract on January 17 at a salary of $25,000 with a $5,000 bonus promised if the film finished on time.

Ophuls's extensive experience and achievements as a stage and film director on the continent were barely known in Hollywood, even to Wanger. Born in Saarbrucken in 1902, Ophuls had been a wunderkind director since 1925, growing to prominence in Switzerland and the Burg Theater in Vienna, a worker's theater that persisted into the rise of Nazism. During the early 1930s, he had directed four films in Germany, including the much-admired *Liebelei* (1933) and an adaptation of Smetana's *The Bartered Bride* (1932). Fleeing to France in 1933 to escape anti-Semitism, he proceeded to direct six films, including the Swiss *Mayerling to Sarajevo* (1940), the film by which he was best known in Hollywood when he came to the country during World War II. Beginning with Douglas Fairbanks, Jr.'s *The Exile* (1947), shot at Universal-International while Wanger completed *The Lost Moment,* Ophuls had become a favorite of independent producers, handling Ramparts' *Letter From an Unknown Woman* and Enterprise Productions' *Caught.* He garnered a modest reputation as a director of women's pictures that outweighed in Wanger's mind the rumor that he was a "difficult personality." He was certainly well suited to the property at hand.

"The Blank Wall" was an intimate home-front melodrama about a wartime New England mother Lucia Harper whose errant daughter Bea runs into a blackmail scheme involving the accidental death of her boyfriend. The twist here was that Donnelly, the blackmailer negotiating for the underworld, falls in love with the mother, admiring her sacrifices for her family; she in turn pities him but remains loyal to her husband serving abroad. The Elizabeth Sanxay Holding story was published in the *Ladies Home Journal* in October 1947 and was brought to Wanger's attention by Foley, who felt that if its war background was changed and updated, the role "could be done beautifully by Miss B." Wanger concurred on its appropriateness for Bennett, and in fact, negotiated with Krim a quid pro quo arrangement whereby Bennett would appear in Eagle-Lion's *Hollow Triumph* (opposite Paul Heinreid) only if the studio produced "The Blank Wall."

Wanger saw "The Blank Wall" as "a very human story of a woman's sacrifice to protect her home," but, like *Joan of Arc,* Wanger also saw the film as comparable to the postwar British cinema, a view he articulated very clearly to the talents hired for the project. "Walter Wanger was a man who always wanted to be European," Mason later recalled: "He didn't know how to be European but he wanted to be European so this was rather the kind of film—I suppose, like *Brief Encounter*—that he was trying to make, but it wasn't very good."

Indeed, when Wanger read in January 1948 a first draft script by Leopold Atlas—who had coauthored the earlier Eagle-Lion triumph, Mann's *Raw Deal*—Wanger felt

> that this script will have to be worked over and worked over because its success, in my opinion, will depend on how much we are able to retain the human interest and the slight touches in the same way that they were retained in "BRIEF ENCOUNTER."

He intended to echo Lean and Noel Coward's triumph with the bittersweet, guilt-ridden, near-adulterous affair. The casting of a British lead would be helpful, but even before a treatment was completed in early 1948, Wanger had tried to interest Toland in photographing the film noir look of the film.

In January 1948, Wanger hired RKO's Mel Dinelli, whose script for *The*

Spiral Staircase had demonstrated his knack for crafting domestic suspense films from a heroine's point of view. Dinelli eventually concluded that "The Blank Wall"'s generic innovations would lie in its potential as a thriller without police and without courtroom scenes, and the portrayal of "the effect a murder has on a normal household, without showing the usual routine—question and answer scenes associated with pictures of this type." Yet Dinelli nearly quit in early April, claiming he could not create a "believable" relationship between Lucia and Donnelly—"two characters that I find worlds apart."

After Dinelli completed his script in March, Wanger set the project aside temporarily; the Eagle-Lion contract adjustments of June 1948 put it on hold indefinitely. Late the following fall, he showed Dinelli's script to *New Yorker* author Sally Benson, who specialized in domestic melodrama and comedy, as evidenced in her story for Hitchcock's *Shadow of a Doubt* and for Minnelli's *Meet Me in St. Louis* (MGM, 1944) and the short stories that comprised the best-selling *Junior Miss*. Benson urged Wanger to update the story from wartime, shift its locale to California, and depict its family life with more humor.

Declining the project herself, Benson recommended Garson and Soderberg, two young writers who had worked for Hope, Benchley, and Jolson and who were scripting the weekly radio series "Junior Miss." Like Benson, Garson and Soderberg specialized in prototypical family situation comedy. Rather than presenting a sincere, nostalgic portrait of the middle-class American family, they had cultivated a satiric tone toward their subject. Wanger as usual was happy to hire fresh talent; neither man had ever written a film script.

Once Ophuls was hired to direct, the two young writers set to updating Dinelli's work, fulfilling their radio obligations in the mornings and spending the afternoons on the script. They and Wanger found Ophuls to be a high-spirited collaborator: working on Lucia's false "confession" to Donnelly that she killed Darby (Bea's boyfriend), Ophuls told the writers:

> She doesn't explain to him how that accident happened. She no longer makes up a lie. With his questioning, he half leads her to a confession, and she only says that Darby had come out in spite of her having forbidden it and that she killed him and how she disposed of the body, (Note: ask Mr. Wanger to act out that scene for you—he does it very well) but already in the midst of her explanations, Donnelly no longer believes her and says "You couldn't kill anybody," etc.

Every day, around five or six o'clock, Ophuls came by Soderberg's home in Hollywood Hills to discuss the pages given to him the previous day. Having approved the pages, Ophuls would send the new script portions to

Wanger, highlighting changes with great enthusiasm. And as Garson would later recall, Ophuls discussed his shooting style with the writers for each scene as well: "We wrote it the way he wanted to direct it. We'd go to the set and there weren't many changes, because he knew what he was doing before, he didn't have to rearrange everything." Indeed, their first draft, January 25, 1949, script outline specifies various camera movements, such as the tracking shot with Lucia through the hotel lobby where she meets Darby. Wanger reviewed each day's script pages with great interest, making general suggestions (as did Bennett, Mason, and Mason's wife) such as his request for "tougher" dialogue to generate more "excitement" in the argument between Lucia and Bea at the start of the film.

While they updated the setting of the story, Garson and Soderberg found fertile material in Dinelli's script. Even though set during the war, Dinelli's version depicted American family life in the intrusive, oppressive terms that characterized many of the 1950s family melodramas, such as Nicholas Ray's *Bigger Than Life* (1955), which also starred Mason, or Douglas Sirk's *All That Heaven Allows* (1954) and *There's Always Tomorrow* (1956, which also starred Bennett). Garson and Soderberg left virtually intact Dinelli's early scenes between Lucia and Ted Darby and Lucia and Donnelly (including Mr. Harper's friendliness to the latter) to show the family's vulnerability to corrupt forces. Besides the hardships of wartime rationing and shortages, Dinelli noted in early January 1948, "It would be rather ironic and pathetic to show how Lucia has to get about the business of providing for her family in spite of the fact that she is burdened with the thought of the Darby business."

These are precisely the kinds of scenes that pleased Ophuls and the writers most: the parallels between Bea's illicit relationship with Darby and Lucia's with Donnelly; the bus station background detail of a girl complaining to her grandfather "I want ice cream, not Coke"; Lucia Harper's futile visit to a loan office to obtain funds to pay blackmail and the loan officer's supercilious wish for happy holidays; the unpleasant banter ("I want delivery—not philosophy") in the post office; Lucia's turning to Sybil, the only member of her household, herself subordinated, whom she can trust; and Lucia borrowing a quarter from her blackmailer to phone her sister.

Yet Ophuls, Garson, and Soderberg's updating of the story had telling effects on its ideological implications. In effect, the wartime setting of Holding's story emphasized patriotic values that the wife struggles to maintain and for which the husband fights abroad. Indeed, the first treatments for the film had numerous references to "Japs" and to a racist butcher, and on one occasion Wanger had characterized the story as an American *Mrs. Miniver*. Switching the story to a contemporary period transformed wartime hardships into the repressions and restrictions of domestic life. Where Dinelli's script has Bea sent off immediately to summer camp, away from the distress of

Darby's death and the threat of the police investigation, Garson and Soderberg keep Bea around to intensify Lucia's lack of privacy.

Then too, in Garson and Soderberg's hands, Donnelly's helpful gestures become more tentative and ironic. In the Dinelli script, Donnelly helps Lucia overcome wartime inconveniences. Before their first meeting, he makes a boisterous launderer take back a wash job that is three weeks late and poorly done; later in the script, he finds a more efficient launderer for Lucia to use. He brings the family delicacies such as ham, bacon, and brown sugar through his black market connections. He drives Lucia home from a shopping trip because taxis are in such short supply. Without the wartime setting, Donnelly's generous impulses toward the family in Garson and Soderberg's version become more subtle: offering Lucia's father-in-law a racing tip on their first meeting and expressing concern about Lucia's extensive smoking as Lucia grows even more neurotic in Garson and Soderberg's hands.

Hence, Ophuls, a director celebrated for his depiction of illicit relations and the overwhelming desires of his characters, developed with his writers a film about the blackmailer's restrained passion and the mother's willful obliviousness to it. The resulting film is an outstanding example of domestic melodrama which, like *Brief Encounter,* depicts the repressive aspect of traditional family life. In critic Robin Wood's words, Ophuls's film effects a "subtle subversion of the values and structure of American society." Through his use of camera distance, heavy shadows, and constant bars and other motifs of imprisonment (the staircase railings in the home, the overturned chairs in Darby's hotel), Ophuls develops, in Wood's words,

> a marvelously perceptive portrait of a woman trapped in an ideology which she herself (at least until late in the film) unquestioningly accepts, but from which we, through the distancing of Ophuls's style and the emphasis given by his ironic and unillusioned romanticism, remain detached.

The critical distance was also conceived in relation to the casting. Ophuls and the writers knew that Bennett was not a particularly warm screen personality and that she tended to deliver sharp lines in the wisecracking manner she had used in *Big Brown Eyes.* Soderberg later recalled that Ophuls encouraged the writers to work over "every damned line she had in the picture so that her delivery of it wouldn't come out tough." Sixteen-millimeter footage of the film's production shows Ophuls rehearsing Bennett at the bus station where she confesses her guilt to Donnelly; the director gestures emphatically to Bennett to encourage her outburst. Yet behind those omnipresent sunglasses, Bennett's cool performing style made her all the more appropriate in the role of a complacent, faintly superior, and heavily repressed housewife.

Where the conception of Lucia Harper caused difficulties was in the touchy matter of her relationship with Donnelly, the very crux of Wanger's analogy with *Brief Encounter*. Back in the spring of 1948, Wanger himself was "not completely sold yet on the idea of how far Donnelly and Lucia should become involved in one another." He sensed the threatening implications of Lucia Harper's ability to handle the crises she faces in her husband's absence, and in tangled prose tried to articulate the dynamics of the story's delicate, ideological balancing act:

> I want to change the finish, with the mother having accomplished her mission and not give the impression that she is completely dependent on the husband but she is delighted that he is coming back—she has done her job, but doesn't look forward to any more of the same sort, but that she alone has completed that particular job.

By the time Donnelly has killed his ruthless partner Nagle, Lucia, in the words of the *Framework* critics, "attains some degree of self-knowledge and can bring herself to put her family at risk in order to save Donnelly." But Garson and Soderberg made Donnelly fatally masochistic, refusing to let her do so. Like many stories of the era, *The Reckless Moment* asserted both a woman's independence and her dependence; it challenged the patriarchal order and the family only to reaffirm it.

Dinelli's script had specified that Lucia softens in her attitude toward Donnelly out of pity, not passion. Yet Garson and Soderberg played with the possibilities, particularly in their version of the bus station scene in their February 1, first estimating script draft. After Lucia's confession of causing Darby's death, Donnelly tells her he doesn't want his half of the money, and he promises to return Bea's letters *and* Lucia's jewelry. He then asks Lucia to have dinner or lunch with him. Lucia responds, "almost regretfully" that "I couldn't . . . not possibly." In the final scene by Donnelly's turned-over car, Lucia kisses Martin quickly when he is pinned under the car, and Donnelly tells her, "I'm glad you came." As Lucia walks away from him, Martin asks in shot 370, "Just one thing, Lucia—about that lunch. I never heard your answer." Shot 371 was a medium shot of Lucia standing with her housekeeper Sybil, as Lucia says, "I said 'yes,' Martin," and crying, walks to her car.

This, Soderberg would later recall, was "the closest thing to a love scene" in the film, a scene that would clarify the relationship for the audience and show a "little thrilling moment of two people really wanting to touch, not just the perfect mother and this gentleman blackmailer":

> In it we indicated that her character was emotionally stirred by the man himself. We thought it would indicate that her character would always have a tender scar even though her successful marriage went on. We wanted to pose the unasked question—if Mason *had* lived, would she be free of him? We knew that he was stirred by the woman—but we felt the picture never indicated the emotional impact he had on her.

The scene was omitted from the March 11, final revised script draft, after "a bitter, bitter fight" between the writers and Ophuls in Wanger's office. Wanger sided with his director.

Ophuls told the writers "he could handle it with camera," and in the finished film, Ophuls shows Lucia's growing affections in several ways. Lucia holds Donnelly's wounded arm distractedly after Nagle has stabbed Donnelly in the boathouse. In the penultimate scene, she cries in Donnelly's hair while he exhorts Lucia to leave him there for the police to find; after she returns home, she struggles to rouse herself from crying on her bed to speak on the phone to her husband. Yet the writers still felt Ophuls had obscured the illicit undercurrents in Lucia and Donnelly's relationship by omitting their scene.

Certainly, the Columbia executives would have welcomed any scenes of greater passion. Ophuls completed the film in mid-April under its thirty-day schedule and under budget by nearly $42,000. With Cohn and Kahane's encouragement, Wanger commissioned Garson and Soderberg to redraft new scenes. During eleven days in early May, Ophuls shot these, along with retakes, additional process work, wild sound lines, and silent shooting of the climactic car chase. These scenes were intended to enhance the dramatic points of the story and add some excitement. Cohn had told Wanger, upon approving the additional shooting, that the writers and director should develop what he called a "Stanwyck scene," a scene of great emotional impact between Bea and Lucia (Wanger had previously focused on the same scene); in addition Cohn prescribed "a strong scene between Joan and Mason." Presumably, he was restless in his seat during the screening.

The additional shooting involved the epilogue, affirming Lucia's devotion to her husband; an interrogation scene with the local police to add suspense; and an expansion of Lucia's argument with her daughter Bea (Geraldine Brooks) over the no-account Ted Darby, to indicate that Lucia's husband had rightfully disapproved of Bea's attending art school. But the most important rewrite, to which Bennett, Mason, and his wife Pamela contributed suggestions, came with a new scene in which Donnelly and Lucia talk at some length for the first time, on a ferry boat ride. Kahane, Wanger, and Ophuls agreed that the scene would help motivate Donnelly's admiration for Lucia: Donnelly tells Lucia that her daughter is "lucky to have a mother like you," and Lucia replies, "Everyone has a mother like me. Probably even you had one."

The new dialogue also introduced a marvelously expressive exchange between Lucia and Donnelly which highlighted the writers' view of Lucia's existence. When Lucia tells Donnelly her family is getting suspicious, Donnelly comments, "You're quite a prisoner, aren't you?" When Lucia doubts the existence of Donnelly's cruel partner Nagle, Donnelly replies, "We are all involved with each other. You have your family—I have Mr. Nagle." Lucia responds to this with outrage, for it makes explicit some unsettling parallels between the family in capitalist society and the criminal underworld.

Although Wanger felt "satisfied with the new scenes as written," this was hardly what Cohn had in mind. Through Kahane he relayed to Wanger that "you have failed to take advantage of the opportunity to help the picture by adding a few strong scenes between Lucia and Bea or Lucia and Donnelly." But Wanger, Ophuls, Garson, and Soderberg did not think, in Kahane's words, "that a scene of the kind Harry wants properly fits into the framework of the story." Their subdued melodrama could not tolerate the abrupt effect of a dramatic showdown. For the same reasons, Wanger decided against using a hastily scripted voice-over by Donnelly at the beginning of the film, addressed to Lucia's husband, and ominously hinting at his relationship with Lucia.

Indeed, Wanger spent his sojourn at Columbia running interference between Ophuls and the Columbia executives, even though the Wanger company took all the risks. Estimated in mid-March to cost $895,464, the final budget cost of the film was $881,276, of which the loan from the Bank of America accounted for $528,500. When Columbia repaid itself an overhead charge, their investment was reduced from $283,000 to slightly more than $107,000. Yet Columbia and Irving Briskin were relentlessly cost-conscious. Briskin was Columbia's executive in charge of "B" film production (such as the studio's Boston Blackie series), reassigned to supervise medium-cost films such as *The Reckless Moment* after Columbia revised its production policy away from "B" films. When Ophuls suggested that he could save time if Columbia hired his editor on *Caught* (Robert Parrish), Briskin and the studio instead assigned their Gene Havlick. Ophuls and Wanger requested *Reign of Terror* cinematographer Alton; they got studio veteran Burnett Guffey, with whom they screened previous Bennett films such as *Woman on the Beach* to ensure that Bennett would be photographed to advantage in a low-key, atmospheric style. Though first-rate, both technicians were chosen for economy.

During script preparation, Ophuls wanted to shoot hidden camera footage of downtown Los Angeles for a "documentary" feeling in Lucia's visits to the loan office and Darby's bar. Briskin brusquely responded, "Don't think this should even be questioned by Director—why waste this money?" One of Briskin's underlings reported to Kahane that Ophuls's shooting style obscured Bennett in the scene where Bea returns from her fatal meeting with Darby by the boat house:

> If for no other reason, we will need additional angles in order to understand what the hysterical girl is saying, but there are other reasons, too. Miss Bennett is far from the camera and her back is more or less facing us. It is difficult to feel her reaction. Possibly the director is planning additional angles here, although, judging by his style of shooting, we have been given little reason to expect them.

By contrast, Wanger was willing to give Ophuls his due, frequently allowing the director to use moving camera shots without studio interference.

Yet the budget restrictions, Wanger's limited power at the studio, and his aggravated financial position took their toll. Production tangents that he formerly would have waved off or encouraged now made him angry. When location manager Blankenhorn took Ophuls, Garson, and Soderberg to Balboa for a sense of the setting, Wanger upbraided him for wasting their time. Rather than encouraging the potential publicity for his film, he did not allow Mason to appear in a radio show since it might throw the production behind schedule. To Soderberg, Wanger "was running scared. Hank and I found him to be a very uptight man beneath that urbane exterior."

The Columbia administration was part of the reason. They offered Wanger few benefits. Unlike Universal-International and Eagle-Lion, Columbia refused to pay the salaries of Foley, a secretary, Wanger's accountant, *and* his comptroller. The Wanger company had the burden of paying those salaries at $400 weekly. His offices were "rundown," a set of separate rooms rather than the customary suites assigned to on-the-lot producers. It was humiliating. As Soderberg summarized it, "He was not getting the 'A' treatment there at all."

After *Joan of Arc,* Wanger did not get the "A" treatment anywhere in Hollywood for nearly a decade. *The Reckless Moment* is now one of Wanger's most highly regarded films, but upon its release, it was just another of Wanger's failures. Cohn's instincts proved accurate even after Columbia gave the film a dramatic title. The lack of a Stanwyck-style scene, among other things, proved fatal to the film's financial performance. Late in 1949, Columbia's distribution sales organization in New York held a screening "for every possible New York outlet," and the film failed to get a first-run booking anywhere. Its commercial potential was deemed so poor that Columbia, with its minimal investment assured of a return, opted for a flat rental basis for the film exhibitors in Manhattan. Columbia collected roughly one hundred dollars per booking instead of a percentage of its gross. The film earned merely a third of its negative cost, and its foreign income was blocked by currency restrictions. As a result, Mason and Bennett received only half their salaries. Wanger received none.

Whether his films deployed the ironic undercutting of a genre's surface conventions as Ophuls's work did, or whether they attempted a sincere presentation of the life of a saint, Wanger's plan to beat the British cinema at its own game was a complete failure, even where talents of the magnitude of Bergman, Mason, and Ophuls were involved. Wanger's professional decline continued without relief.

During preproduction on *The Reckless Moment,* Wanger proposed to Ophuls, Garson, and Soderberg that they end the film with a fire in Mason's car. As Soderberg recalls, "We'd seen some Wanger pictures, and we finally went to Max and said, 'Max, this is just Wanger's wanting to burn up the whole place. He does it at the end of every movie.'" Indeed, all of the Americana and the European-modeled films, from *Canyon Passage* to *Reign of Terror,* ended in flames. Wanger and Bennett had survived a serious fire at their home in 1943. Yet, Soderberg remembers, "When we hit Walter with these statistics, he looked shocked—as if he had shown a side of himself he wasn't familiar with either. . . . Isn't that strange? It was his violence, underneath."

15

On the Way Down

"Let me tell you about Hollywood," Wanger once instructed Lantz. "Two sets of bad reviews and the cook quits." Wanger had had more than two. From 1949 onward, every project Wanger undertook and every hope he entertained came unraveled. The failure of *Joan of Arc* was catastrophic, for Wanger had tied all his residual income and nearly all his properties to the fate of that one film. He had been overconfident. "It should never have been made by an independent," he told *Box Office* magazine. By the fall of 1949, he was a man treading water in an industry in decline.

His only major income that year came from selling off his most valuable asset, Hayward. Under the terms of her contract, Wanger was obliged to pay her $4,750 weekly beginning in August 1949 for forty weeks, and he simply did not have the cash to maintain the commitment. He sold the remaining two years of her contract to Fox for $110,000 after her appearance in *House of Strangers*. The funds were applied to his monumental debts and new expenses such as the screening room he and Bennett had installed in their home.

Beginning in 1948, his company operated in a crisis atmosphere that loyal employees found debilitating. One associate recalls, "He was so busy making the deal for the next picture that he didn't pay adequate attention to the development and production of the present project." The Internal Revenue Service inaugurated a series of extensive audits and demanded enormous back payments. This further diminished any remaining income he earned. Accountant Ernest Scanlon clamored constantly about the need for more cash to pay monthly overheads, which accumulated in spite of the loans Wanger obtained from his brother Henry, Goldwyn, and from Gilbert Miller. Upon obtaining a writer's waive of rights to the screenplay of *The Reckless Moment*, Foley informed Wanger that she had accomplished this without lawyers or agents. She concluded, "Well I have to pat myself on the back once in awhile—no one else does!" In the spring of 1950, after fourteen years of steadfast and capable assistance, she left Wanger to get married.

Wanger's dire financial straits and hectic desperation to develop a program in 1949 effectively sabotaged his last great hope for success, a project entitled "Friend and Lover," starring Greta Garbo and planned for production abroad during the spring. Since Garbo's retirement in 1941 after the critical and financial disappointment of Cukor's *Two-Faced Woman*, the trade press carried annual announcements of Garbo's imminent return to the screen. In 1944, it was a Swedish Strindberg adaptation; in 1945, she was to be teamed with Crosby; in 1947, she considered prospects at Columbia, with Korda and with Selznick and Cukor. Wanger's turn came in late June and early July 1948, and he got further than anybody else in pursuing the most elusive prize in the film industry.

As *Tulsa* went into production and *Joan of Arc* was readied for its premiere, Cukor had encouraged Garbo's friend Viertel, screenwriter of *Queen Christina* and other Garbo vehicles, to develop an original script about George Sand which improved upon *A Song to Remember* (1945). The nineteenth-century French novelist's socialist sympathies, sexual emancipation, and love affairs with playwright Alfred de Musset, Franz Liszt, and Frederic Chopin suggested an appropriately colorful character.

Bumping into Viertel at Romanoff's and high on the Bergman epic, Wanger told her that he would be eager to produce a film for Garbo. In spite of Garbo's misgivings over *Queen Christina*, she responded, in Viertel's words, "immediately and wholeheartedly to this offer." When they met, Wanger insisted that Garbo make herself available for more than one picture. He subsequently told Viertel "that he thought a costume picture would be too expensive to make and his bankers were opposed to it." But Garbo refused to do *The Ballad and the Source*, British writer Rosamond Lehmann's best-selling novel, which Wanger had purchased, in a fit of Anglophilia, for $250,000.

At this impasse, in late July, Wanger changed tactics. He enlisted the help of Eugene Frenke, the manager of Robert Cummings's independent production company. Frenke, like Wanger a former aviator, was the husband of Anna Sten, a Russian actress whom Goldwyn had imported in the early 1930s as a potential screen goddess. Since then, Frenke had many accomplishments, due in part to his perseverance, which he applied to Viertel for several weeks.

In Cummings's words, Frenke was "very loyal, he worked very hard and he was very capable, but people didn't take to him." Viertel was initially offended: he "looks like a kind eyed faun, talks like [Gregory] Ratoff [i.e., with a thick accent] and is incredibly persistent." But Viertel was won over by

Frenke's intelligent criticisms of her script, and negotiations resumed. "From then on," she recalled,

Everything began to move rapidly. Wanger called again, Frenke called five times a day and I spent hours and hours on the phone. Then we dined in his house, Greta, Wanger and I—and during a most phantastic [sic] dinner everything was set, [Cukor was] signed, the story bought, Greta happy, etc. etc.

Announcements of the George Sand project appeared in the trade press on August 19. Five days later, Wanger formed Walter Wanger International to join the growing ranks of producers engaged in runaway production (such as Selznick's *The Third Man*). The new company would finance the Garbo film and other projects to be shot in Europe, where Wanger would enjoy access to blocked income and lower production costs. On August 26, Garbo signed a contract for a film to be made by mid-May 1949; she was to be paid $175,000 plus 15 percent of the profits and given approvals of story, director, and cinematographer.

The news was reported by virtually every trade paper and newspaper in the country, although as *Time* magazine commented, "In the Garbo tradition, everybody connected with the deal promptly clammed up or looked studiously vague." Wanger told the magazine, "I had a couple of ideas she liked. She is a very loyal person." Garbo had been dissatisfied with Wanger's supervision of *Queen Christina* back in 1933. Now, she was impressed by Wanger's association with Bergman, and his ability to make a major film independent of the studios. But in fact, George Sand was not Wanger's idea, and Garbo's loyalty had its limits.

She was in many ways the most volatile element in the project. Always ambivalent about her performances in film (which she sometimes characterized as "prostitution"), she was anxious to work again, but uncertain of her talent. At Frenke's request, Cummings approached Garbo during a party at the home of Sir Charles Mendl in early July 1948. As Cummings recalled, "She told me 'I don't want to make films anymore. I can't work anymore. I'm not any good.'" Viertel perceived this uneasiness in Garbo as well: "Greta is impatient to work and on the other side she is afraid of it. I understand this very well after all these years of idleness. Work is a habit and she lost it." Garbo was also contemptuous and suspicious of unenlightened studio management and now in her mid-forties, sensitive to the stakes of her comeback. She told Wanger that she had waited eight years to make another film and that she did not want to make a mistake.

Unfortunately, Wanger was not enthusiastic about Viertel's script, which he thought called for histrionics on the order of "a female Paul Muni." But he agreed to the George Sand story to induce Garbo to sign a contract. Besides, Viertel's work provided a fallback if nothing else turned up. Everyone agreed that Garbo required a project that conformed to the fallen woman genre exemplified by Cukor's own *Camille,* but which provided her with a more sophisticated and ambiguous character. The alternatives kicked around were innumerable, ranging from biographical films of Eleanora Duse, Chauteaubriand's lover Madame Recamier, and Mary Magdalene to Henry James's *Princess Casamissima.* But they all would take too long to develop from scratch.

Cukor was very enthusiastic about the possibilities of adapting Alphonse Daudet's 1884 novel *Sappho,* a property registered by MGM which Wanger had suggested. The novel concerns a French prostitute in her mid-thirties who has posed for a statue of the Greek poetess and who lives unhappily with a younger aspirant to the foreign service. The setting was the decadent bohemian ambience of Paris in the mid-1800s. Cukor felt this was the perfect role for Garbo. "Don't you think it would be wise," he wrote Wanger,

> if Garbo did not take up her career at the same point at which she left off—if she struck a new and bold note? . . . She would achieve the desperation, the pathos, through her performance. The part has such great power and humanity. It should be as distinguished a success for her as "Camille."

While on vacation in Cap Ferrat, Cukor discussed the novel with Somerset Maugham, who made "brilliant" and "constructive" suggestions on its adaptation. But when Cukor took on *Adam's Rib* later that fall, *Sappho* lost its strongest champion.

While Wanger remained in Los Angeles in September 1948, Eugene Frenke and George Schlee, the Russian attorney who had become Garbo's lover, went to Europe to scout properties, writers, and investors. They interviewed Coward, Terrence Rattigan, Sacha Guitry, Jean Anouihl, Jean Cocteau, and the "quality" team of Jean Auranche and Pierre Bost (Wanger's first choice as screenwriters, because of their work with Claude Autant-Lara on *Le Diable aux Corps* with its adulterous liaison). No one was interested. Wanger wrote Cukor, "The thing that is driving me absolutely nuts is who is the right person to do the script of GEORGE SAND so it will really have what it takes."

In late September or early October, Wanger saw the French film of Honoré de Balzac's *La Duchesse de Langeais,* based on a screenplay by Jean Giraudoux. Garbo was enthusiastic about the material, as Wanger put it, "having seen the picture and having a good idea of what she could do with the part." A remake of a French film, such as *Algiers,* would be a safer investment, but Viertel saw Wanger's enthusiasm for the project as politically consistent with his Eagle-Lion films and with *Joan of Arc:* "Wanger, for the usual Hollywood reasons, found the Duchess more 'worthy of Garbo' than the less blueblooded and more Red-oriented George Sand." Balzac's story concerned a flirtatious aristocrat who drives a recently returned Napoleonic officer into a passionate frenzy. He abducts her from a gala court affair, and they plan to elope but are frustrated by bad timing; the duchess enters a nunnery, and the general searches the world for her.

By mid-March 1949, everyone agreed to start production on the Balzac story the following September. Wanger asked Soderberg and Garson to write a treatment. "We didn't think there was enough dramatic story material to hold an audience to the climax," Soderberg recalled, "so we resorted to an old trick. . . . we started with the climax [de Montrivaux's confrontation with the Duchesse at the nunnery], and then went back to show how the characters got there." In May, Wanger signed Benson to write the script in ten weeks, and Garbo made screen tests at the United Artists studio.

With retakes done on *The Reckless Moment* and with Benson at work on the script, Wanger left Los Angeles on May 24 for Europe, where he attempted to establish financing and production arrangements. This was easily accomplished with willing investors in France and Italy. The greater challenge for Wanger lay in combining the Garbo film with a series of films abroad to capitalize on lower costs and his prestige in Europe from *Joan of Arc*. His general plan was to offer limited territorial distribution rights to foreign investors in exchange for their loans, a fund-raising technique that is now routine in film and television production. He hoped to follow the Garbo project with "Annie, Queen of the Pirates" and with Bennett in *The Ballad and the Source*. With his own residuals and properties tied up in *Joan of Arc,* he wooed Italian producers extravagantly to assure them of his resources. "Money meant nothing to him," Cummings recalled. "He sent Frenke these incredible bills for entertaining. He leased two Rolls Royces. When Frenke asked him why, he said, 'I want to get in good with them.' Frenke said, 'Get in good with them! Just say Hello!'"

After many discussions and parties, Wanger opted for production in Italy and established a Rome office in July. Having had a hand in the design of Cinecitta, he felt more confident of the facilities there, which had been rebuilt after wartime destruction. Among his Italian partners was Scalera Films, associated with publisher Angelo Rizzoli. Rizzoli had produced Ophuls's *La Signora di Tutti* back in 1934. Scalera had been active for many years, producing Alessandro Blasetti's *We the Living* in 1942, Welles's *Othello* in 1949, and an elaborate, Italian production of *The Charterhouse of Parma*. Rizzoli would go on with Giuseppe Amato to produce Federico Fellini's *Variety Lights* (1950), Joseph L. Mankiewicz's *The Barefoot Contessa* (1954), and Fellini's *La Dolce Vita* (1960).

Wanger had left Los Angeles in May after reading the first thirty pages of Benson's script. When he returned in late June, he had the unpleasant shock of reading her completed first draft, which was barely a script at all. Benson had been neglecting her work and drinking heavily. When Wanger diplomatically encouraged her with praise, she met his requests for revisions with only minor changes. In July, Wanger was advised to hire another writer. This was a major setback to the project only two months before the start of production.

But other developments were more encouraging. With *The Reckless Moment* finished, both Mason and Ophuls were at liberty. Mason signed on to play opposite Garbo at terms identical to those he had demanded for the first film. Ophuls had already agreed to prepare and direct Bennett in *The Ballad and the Source* in the fall. Wanger had considered many directors for Garbo, including Vittorio De Sica, Carol Reed, and Joshua Logan, whom Wanger had intimidated back in 1936 but had recently directed the Broadway hit *South Pacific*. With limited time left, Wanger asked Ophuls to revise Benson's script.

Ophuls ignored the Breen Office's strenuous objections to the script's depiction of adultery as "right and acceptable" and General de Montrivaux's insistence that the duchess leave the nunnery. In the main, Ophuls found Benson's conception of the duchess too harsh and manipulative, and, taking suggestions from Mason, worked on "humanizing" her and giving her "more dignity, human attractiveness and warmth, because how could this woman be so successful if she was nothing but a matinee La Traviata. She should be able to interest and attract with her intelligence and her heart." When the other directors proved unavailable, Ophuls agreed to postpone *The Ballad and the Source* and take on the Garbo film. To Wanger, the director was "a very fast, clever little fellow and if he has the right people, we will get good results."

As Ophuls worked on the script, Wanger spent the month of August 1949 establishing the basis for production financing. Now titled "Friend and Lover," the film was budgeted to cost roughly $1 million, just slightly more than *The Reckless Moment,* with $125,000 in deferred salaries. Scalera Films would cover two-thirds of the financing, to be obtained in frozen Italian lire in exchange for a combination of interest payments on loans and distribution rights. Wanger's job was to find $300,000 to pay for the above-the-line talents, the cinematographer, and other special technicians and equipment (such as the Mitchell camera).

The chief difficulty of course was that after *The Lost Moment, Tap Roots, Joan of Arc, Tulsa, Reign of Terror,* and *The Reckless Moment,* Wanger had no capital and equity, even in blocked currencies, to put forward beyond the necessary payments for the Ophuls, Garbo, and Mason salaries during the first few weeks of production. An American producer-distributor would be of enormous help. By August 30, Howard Hughes at RKO came forward, and for all his misgivings over RKO's handling of *Joan of Arc,* Wanger agreed to do business with him. Banker's Trust, which had cofinanced *Joan of Arc,* was willing to provide $300,000. With everything in readiness except the bank loans, the production moved to Europe. Garbo arrived in Rome on August 26, and Ophuls arrived there on September 6, with a starting date announced of October 10. Cinematographer James Wong Howe, who had shot Lamarr in *Algiers* and test footage of Garbo the previous June, followed them.

Then, as was the case two years earlier with *Joan of Arc,* the Garbo deal fell apart. Contrary to Wanger's expectations, Banker's Trust refused, even for a Greta Garbo film, to waive its requirement that Wanger pledge world-wide rentals as collateral. Mindful of *Joan of Arc*'s strong foreign and weak domestic box office, the bank sought to protect its investment with foreign income if the Garbo film proved a failure in the United States. But Wanger was in no position to pledge worldwide income, since European grosses were his collateral for the Italian loans.

Then there was trouble with Mason, who was poised in New York to sail to Italy. Wanger was to have RKO send him $75,000 for travel expenses and as proof of the company's commitment to the project by September 8. When, in spite of Wanger's efforts from Rome, the funds were not made available, Mason, on his agent's advice, quit "Friend and Lover." Then Garbo, who had reportedly changed hotels three times in Rome to escape the Italian *paparazzi* and "each time ended up in tears," moved with Schlee to Paris. According to several of Rizzoli's associates, she insisted on her entire salary in advance and a seven-week shooting schedule in Italy and France. Moreover, she met, only reluctantly with Rizzoli and company to discuss her terms in person. She apparently objected to the entire idea of Italian cofinanciers. After this un-friendly gathering, the Italians backed off and RKO withdrew its offer to dis-tribute the film. As *Variety* described it, since "the acquiescence" of each partner (RKO, Banker's Trust, Mason, and the Italians) "hinged on the okay of the other, Wanger was in the position of a juggler." He dropped all the balls.

It was hard to pick them up. In mid-September, Wanger communicated to his new Hollywood attorney Greg Bautzer his willingness to shoot the film in Paris and let RKO take it over: "Time too short for making deals here and for keeping elements together. . . . Realize am giving up great deal but want to see picture made because I know what it will mean to whole European plan." The "European plan" meant Wanger's hopes to produce several films abroad. If he produced the Garbo film for his first runaway production, his prestige in Europe would be immense.

For the rest of the year, he would spend so much time lining up his other films (and trying to get *The Lost Moment* distributed in untouched territories) that he would not be able to reignite Garbo's interest. On September 22, she accepted two weeks' salary and a postponement of the film's starting date until March 1950. In exchange, Garbo required Wanger and Frenke to demonstrate to her MCA agents by January 1, 1950, their ability to finance the film. Failing this, the Garbo agreement would be dissolved.

In late July 1949, Garbo's enthusiasm for making "Friend and Lover" had been strong. Logan told Wanger that she "seems to be very much set on continuing with THE DUCHESSE DE LONGEAIS [*sic*], although she was disappointed with the first script. But she thoroughly believes that it can be solved and that it is a good venture." After the project fell apart in September, however, Garbo was embarrassed. On September 23, she insisted (in an amendment to her contract extension) that Wanger and Frenke issue a precisely worded publicity release that specified the production was postponed "until the Spring in order to allow for more adequate preparation." One week earlier, she told her contact at MCA that "she was dissatisfied with the script, with the lack of a leading man, and with the general conduct of the operation." Her attitude was entirely justified.

Garbo retreated from Wanger, living secretly in France, visiting with aristocratic acquaintances, and letting Schlee handle her business affairs. She rejected Wanger's proposed leading men (Errol Flynn and Louis Jourdain) and claimed that she did not feel physically fit to perform. By mid-October, Wanger in Europe and Frenke in Hollywood were working at cross-purposes, and no script was in progress. At the end of November, Wanger released Ophuls to direct a French film, which ultimately became his celebrated *La Ronde* and led to his steady work in France until his death.

In November, however, things picked up. Before letting Ophuls go, Wanger had on Ophuls's advice hired Jean Jacques Gautier, film editor of *Figaro,* a winner of the Prix Goncourt, and an authority on Balzac. And there was financial help. John Woolf, who had worked previously as Rank's distribution director, had formed Romulus Films with his brother James to make twelve films in England and Europe featuring American stars. The films would be financed through a division of markets: the American producers, typically independents, would be responsible for delivering and financing above-the-line costs in exchange for American distribution rights, while Romulus would finance the rest in exchange for worldwide distribution rights. Among their American productions was Albert Lewin's *Pandora and the Flying Dutchman;* in 1951 Romulus financed John Huston's *The African Queen.* This was the basic scheme offered to Wanger in late 1949. Telinvest, a thriving American firm that specialized in brokering feature film libraries to television stations, agreed to finance Wanger's costs and the completion guarantee if Garbo, Wanger, Frenke, and Ophuls would defer $215,000 in salaries.

Returning to Los Angeles for Bennett's production of *Father of the Bride,* Wanger assumed that Garbo would be satisfied with the new arrangements. He presented his proposition on December 31, 1949, in a letter to Jules Stein at MCA without any official supporting documents such as a contract with Romulus or Telinvest. Although all of this could have been confirmed with a few telephone calls, Wanger's lax presentation provided MCA with a loophole. In spite of Wanger's New Year's Eve visits and telephone calls, Stein decided that the producer had failed to show by the deadline "all of the evidence of your ability to finance the picture" and had failed to set a starting date, both of which were cause for dissolving the contract. Recognizing that there was no point in forcing Garbo to make a film, Wanger's attorneys declined to compel her performance.

Wanger angrily wrote MCA:

> When Garbo made the deal with us, she knew very well that neither Frenke nor myself were the heads of major studios and that this was, to a certain extent, an experiment and an adventure because in her contract, it said she would work *anywhere* in Europe. Now they turn around and expect the stability of Metro-Goldwyn-Mayer or Paramount. It seems a little ridiculous.

Garbo had chosen the wrong producer to manage her comeback. The whole experience was disastrous. In Cukor's words, Garbo found the venture "agonizing, and she felt completely humiliated." Viertel summed it up:

> The display of dilettantism, inflated egos, incompetence, and a hypocritical, indecent disregard for the sensibilities of a great actress had been unsurpassed, even in the history of films. It made Garbo once and for all renounce the screen.

It was equally agonizing and humiliating for Wanger, responsible though he was for its outcome. He had moved his children and Bennett to Europe indefinitely, and now he had no prospects. With *Joan of Arc* having fallen flat, the Garbo project promised to be the most significant and successful venture in his career, and it had slipped away from him because of his limited ability to raise financing, his presumption of goodwill on everyone's part, and his insistence on setting up an entire program. Then there were the hard realities. It was a major burden to repay $84,000 in expenses for the Garbo project.

He pushed on, returning to England in late January and setting up a British production company in the hopes of persuading Garbo to return and of seeing *The Ballad and the Source* into production with Bennett. Lehmann's novel related through multiple flashbacks and narrators the saga of Sybil Jardine, whose determination to live with both her lovers and her children engenders passion, madness, and sacrifice through three generations of women in her family.

Wanger admired the characters' "constant search for happiness and truth in a world shackled by the chains of a bigoted culture," and he thought it would be a superb vehicle for Bergman. But the actress disagreed, telling him, as he later recalled, "Walter, I could never play the part of a woman deserting her child and leaving her husband for someone else, because I could never do a thing like that." Menzies had developed a low-budget script from the Lehmann novel in the spring of 1948, and Wanger had pitched it unsuccessfully as "the greatest mother-love story in many years" to Universal-International, Eagle-Lion, Twentieth Century–Fox, Columbia, RKO, Selznick and to Dozier and Fontaine's Rampart Productions.

But the novel's modernist narration by a fourteen-year-old girl and its anguished subject matter militated against American studio production. Dozier warned Wanger that the story was "pretty dull and rather heavy going." Zanuck and Schenck agreed. To Zanuck it was "not the kind of story I would ever personally produce, mainly because it is the kind of story that for *money* I would never go to see," but he attempted in good faith to interest Fox talents in the project and recommended to Schenck that Fox at least distribute the film if Wanger could make it abroad. Schenck was more emphatic, although apologetic, about the project: "in my humble opinion it's insanity to attempt to produce it as per the treatment or in this [embedded flashback] technique." Schary felt "the series of disasters that occur throughout the picture and some of the construction" made *The Ballad and the Source* a "dubious project."

Since May 1949, Wanger had been concerned to either produce the project or recover his $250,000 investment in it. "I am very anxious to clean this up as I want to get going," he noted at one point, characterizing the film as his "salvation." He circulated a new script by Ophuls in the fall of 1949 after the Garbo project fell apart.

Woolf and Romulus again came through. In the spring of 1950, they were set to finance *The Ballad and the Source* under Ophuls's direction, as the first of four Wanger productions to be made in England in Technicolor. His foreign production program had a starting point now. But the British censors rejected Ophuls's script out of hand for its positive portrayal of adultery. As Woolf put it, "the script must be re-written with basically an entirely different story, following neither the line of the book nor the present screenplay." Though Woolf was eager to work with Wanger, Wanger told him, "all my plans were based on that production," and "I am at present rearranging them."

There was very little left to rearrange, however, in terms of theatrical film production. Naturally enough, Wanger turned to television, the new medium that was stirring interest in the trade even before the widespread marketing of sets in the summer of 1948. Scratching for income to repay his many debts, Wanger had sold his remaining rights to his Universal films to Sol Lesser, who marketed them to television. Now Wanger, like other small producers, explored the prospect of producing a series.

With the guidance of Jennings Lang, Bennett's agent and the head of the Music Corporation of America television division, Wanger proposed an oriental fantasy television series to the American Broadcasting Company. Unlike the live shows broadcast in 1950, Wanger planned to use film. He also wanted to shoot it in Cinecolor, a cheap but effective monopack system that became widely available after Technicolor's monopolistic practices were invalidated by the Department of Justice in February of 1950. ABC provided nearly half the financing for the first half-hour installment, *Aladdin and His Lamp*, which was produced by Wanger's newly formed Citadel Corporation and shot at the Roach studios for $25,000 in the fall of 1950. Although color television sets were still at the development stage, ABC executives were suitably impressed with the production and proceeded to shop the program around to sponsors who might be interested in financing an entire season.

It was on January 9, 1951, during this inconclusive and insecure stage of Wanger's career, that the Bank of America chose to file a petition in United States district court charging Wanger with involuntary bankruptcy. The suit did not involve *Joan of Arc*, as is often alleged; it was due to his failure to repay $178,500 outstanding on *The Reckless Moment*. Wanger later claimed that the bank had mistaken his recovery of a $70,000 trust fund for daughter Shelley as available equity. But bank officials justified the suit as a reaction to Wanger's preferential payments to his *Joan of Arc* creditors. They subsequently attempted to attach Bennett's house in Holmby Hills.

In fact, there was a fairly reasonable, if impersonal logic behind the bank's action. Many banks had pulled tight their loan policies in order to conserve funds to finance industries involved with the Korean War. The Bank of America led the pack. The increasingly stringent demands Wanger had experienced at Universal-International, Eagle-Lion, and Columbia illustrated how inhospitable the business environment had become.

Just one week prior to Wanger's bankruptcy, Ellis Arnall, president of the Society of Independent Motion Picture Producers, noted that independents in Hollywood had little comfort from "the inroads of television, the monopolies in exhibition, the need for strong distributors, the restrictions in foreign markets, increased taxes and cost of production." According to one report, small independent producers had reduced their output by 75 percent since 1946. United Artists, the longstanding host of independent companies, was itself teetering on bankruptcy in 1951. So Wanger was just one more victim of economic hard times. Arthur Mayer, the independent New York exhibitor, sent Wanger a consoling note saying the bank's action was "a terrible commentary on our business, as well as heartbreaking, that the producer of such marvelous pictures as 'The Long Voyage Home' and 'Stagecoach' should be involved in such difficulties."

Then again, the amount for which the Bank of America was suing Wanger was comparatively trivial: $178,500, or less than 20 percent of the budget of *The Reckless Moment* and roughly one-third of the bank loan for the film. This was a paltry sum, especially considering Wanger's credit record of repaying more than $16 million in production loans from the bank during the thirties and forties. There was something particular about Wanger's situation which moved the Bank of America to take its action: his reputation as a liberal activist. Despite all his speechmaking and the promotion of his films to the anti-Communist right, Wanger had a dubious past.

In the fall of 1950, four months before the Bank of America suit, Wanger led the Los Angeles branch of a privately funded, vehement anti-Communist group founded in June 1949 called the Crusade for Freedom. Led by General Lucius D. Clay, who had commanded the American occupying forces as military governor of postwar Germany and had overseen the Berlin airlift, the group supported pro-American broadcasts such as Radio Free Europe and publications distributed behind the Iron Curtain. These were intended, in Clay's words, "to counteract the false Communist propaganda that we in the United States are a nation of war mongers bent on world conquest" and to demonstrate "our true aims of freedom and friendship for all peoples."

The group organized a national fundraising campaign in September 1950 to place an eight-foot-high, ten-ton "Freedom Bell" at the Berlin airport on October 24, United Nations Day. The bell would be accompanied by a "spiritual airlift" of scrolls signed by Americans supporting the group. Wanger focused on Los Angeles city and county, which raised $59,000 and more than 380,000 signatures out of the national total of $1.2 million and 15.5 million signatures. The funds were applied to the purchase of additional radio transmitters. Upon accepting the post, Wanger claimed that his six (futile) months spent in Europe in 1950 convinced him that the crusade was a worthy cause. He employed the familiar imagery of the Cold War that would become the centerpiece of *Invasion of the Body Snatchers:*

> Communism is struggling for the minds of men while we have been sleeping. We cannot continue in our apathy, leaving the contest entirely to government. We are hardly worthy of our freedom unless we are willing to fight and work for it ourselves.

The appointment was an honor, but it proved highly controversial. The zealous anti-Communist California state senator Jack Tenney, who had previously led the California legislature's version of the House Committee on Un-American Activities in 1948, resigned from the crusade, protesting that Wanger had been associated with "subversive" groups earlier in the decade. Tenney noted Wanger's wartime participation in the American Committee for Yugoslav Relief, the Committee for the First Amendment, the Hollywood Independent Citizens' Committee of Arts, Sciences, and the Professions, Mobilization for Democracy, and Russian War Relief.

Most of all, Tenney reminded his audience of Wanger's leadership of the Free World Association and his pointed comments against the Motion Picture Alliance. Several (apparently independent) letters arrived at the Crusade for Freedom's West Coast office seconding Tenney's protest, stating that Wanger was hardly "above reproach" and calling him a "notorious Communist appeaser." As a crusade supporter wrote Wanger in mid-September, "Quite a controversy rages around you." Tenney's accusations further inspired the FBI to open a file on the producer. The agency was particularly concerned with Wanger's distant relation to writer Lionel Feuchtwanger, with the fact that he supported Communist "front" organizations and that Wanger had the telephone numbers of several "representatives" of the Soviet government (Andrei Gromyko among them) and Jacob Malik. The FBI's informant suggested that Wanger's telephone be tapped; apparently the agency chose not to follow through.

Wanger and other liberals in Hollywood had dismissed Tenney as a crank in 1948, but the political picture had changed by the end of the decade with the disclosures of various Soviet spy activities, Alger Hiss's perjury trial, the Soviet Union's detonation of an atomic bomb in 1949, and the start of the Korean War. Tenney himself reached the peak of his political career in 1952 when he ran as vice-president in Gerald K. Smith's presidential bid. In August 1949, columnist Ruth Alexander wrote Wanger:

> It is no news to you that somehow you have been linked with the left-wing point of view in Hollywood for years. I have always defended you and felt you were a New Dealer but definitely not a communist or communist sympathizer. But today it is not enough to be a non-communist. One must be militantly anti-communist.

Wanger attempted to meet the latest accusations head-on. "I have always detested the ideas of communism," he told the Greater Los Angeles Press Club. "You cannot accomplish anything worthwhile if you fear character assassination." He continued:

> It is true that for my efforts I have succeeded in being called a Fascist by the People's World and the Daily Worker and a leftist by the Chicago Tribune and others. However, I can assure you there is nothing about totalitarianism that appeals to me now or ever has . . . and whenever any group that I loaned my name to became the tool of either Fascists or Communists, I withdrew.

None of his protestations had any effect on skeptical listeners. Rabid anti-Communists saw Wanger's participation in the Crusade for Freedom as supplying cover for Communists: one pamphlet claimed that "Wanger, of course, knew perfectly well what he was doing," and responded to his assertion that he had withdrawn from questionable groups by writing, "That is what they all say."

In September 1950, the Motion Picture Alliance, taking its cue from Tenney's action, wrote Wanger a letter welcoming him to the anti-Communist cause and demanding that Wanger recant his condemnation of the Motion Picture Alliance back in 1944. The group had devoted a considerable part of one of its meetings to discussing its tactics in publicly responding to Wanger's position with the Crusade for Freedom. They decided that a public denunciation would be bad publicity and instead drafted a retraction for Wanger to sign. Several newspapers carried his own response, a public disavowal of his past associations.

The Crusade for Freedom drive concluded in October 1950; three months later, the Bank of America took action against Wanger. The Pacific Coast Coordinator for the Crusade was Mario Giannini, who had taken over the bank's management from his brother Attilio, the former United Artists president. The letters that had protested Wanger's crusade appointment were sent to Giannini's desk before being forwarded to Wanger, and Giannini was well aware of Tenney's and others' objections to Wanger's participation; it is entirely possible that the FBI was in touch with him as well. In September 1951, one year after his public flap with Tenney, Wanger met Gianinni to discuss his bankruptcy, and Wanger found that Giannini considered him a "bolshevik, Nihilist and anarchist that had just come from Moscow . . . out to commit fraud and mayhem on the Bank of America."

Gianinni's perception of Wanger as a Communist sympathizer must have influenced the bank's decision keep him at arm's length and embarrass him. The bankruptcy suit brought Wanger's professional career as a semi-independent crashing to the ground. Wanger's personal prestige had always outshone his material assets. By January 1951, Wanger had neither.

His attorneys, accountants, and financial managers advised Wanger to capitulate to the bank's suit, declare himself bankrupt, keep his remaining films and residuals, and start anew. Wanger staunchly refused: "I didn't want to have the stigma of bankruptcy, if I could avoid it." Hence Wanger would not satisfy the bank's claim for another three years.

Now work of any kind was a major priority. The outcome of the *Aladdin* project was crucial and, had ABC found a sponsor for the project, Wanger might well have spent the rest of his career in television production. Here was the market in which Wanger operated best: high volume, low budget, weekly filming, in a series format with guaranteed income, all of which closely resembled the conditions under which he thrived at Paramount in the twenties and thirties. But in May 1951, ABC informed Wanger that no sponsor was interested in a color filmed series when live black-and-white television was the standard.

Shortly after the bankruptcy suit, Wanger had initiated discussions with Steve Broidy, president of the "B" studio, Monogram, about expanding the television pilot into a feature-length film. These plans went into effect on June 12, when Wanger signed a two-year contract to make three films annually as a studio producer. Wanger's contract specified budgets of $250,000, for which he received $12,500 and 14 percent of the profits. He had hit the bottom of the industry.

The studio immortalized by Jean-Luc Godard's homage in *Breathless*

(1959), Monogram had produced "B" films targeted at independent exhibitors and regional markets (largely in the South and the West) since its founding in 1924. After several reorganizations in the 1930s, it flourished with $20,000 films until the mid-forties, when sales chief Broidy stepped up to the presidency. To exhibitors, Broidy pitched his company's films, which he once characterized as "stale bread," for their steady availability. This was not a trivial point after the 1948 *Paramount* case and the majors' production slowdown in response to theater divorcement, for these developments often left theaters with nothing to show their customers. Monogram films could fill the gap.

Exploiting this period of transition, Broidy pressed to change Monogram bookings from flat rental rates to the more lucrative percentage basis. After the success and controversy surrounding the $190,000 *Dillinger,* Broidy also advocated an increase in production budgets for its top films, released under the Allied Artists banner. His policies paid off handsomely in the early 1950s, as Monogram's annual gross rentals hovered at $9 million. In 1951, the company reported an unprecedented net income of more than $1 million, due in part to its sale of its film library (too negligible in quality to reissue theatrically) to television for syndication. Syndication specialist Elliott Hyman of Telinvest put Wanger in touch with Monogram after selling Wanger's two JayPay titles to television.

For Broidy in April 1951, the Wanger association was "the biggest stride forward by the company" in five years. Wanger told one Monogram executive he felt he could upgrade the studio's status as he had previously done at Eagle-Lion, Universal, and Columbia. By the time he came to the studio, the company had a comfortable pattern of production, pitching its films to the family and "juvenile" trade in small towns, to second- and third-run theaters including the new drive-ins, and to "action houses," second-class first-run theaters in the major cities. The staple of its schedule was the low-budget film series: "Bomba, the Jungle Boy" (Bomba was an adolescent version of Tarzan), Bowery Boys comedies, and westerns with Johnny Mack Brown, Whip Wilson, and Wild Bill Elliott.

Complementing the film series were Monogram's more pretentious and costly $250,000 films that Broidy hoped to book in a better class of theater, and this was where Wanger would help out. Under the supervision of Harold Mirisch, a former exhibitor from Wisconsin, and his stepbrother Walter, a graduate of the Harvard Business School, Monogram thrived on exploitation filmmaking, the cost-efficient development of an original idea into a quickly presented narrative, which saved the studio property costs of pre-sold materials.

Wanger was, as always, full of ideas, but he had difficulty realizing several proposals in 1951. "Yellowknife" was one such failure, a romantic Canadian Mountie story that Wanger derived from the "Buccanneer of the Barons" serial in the *Saturday Evening Post.* He had Hecht prepare *Queen of the Uni-*

verse, a story about women who rule the planet Venus and lord it over their male slaves and concubines, but this was not produced until 1958 (as *Queen of Outer Space* with Zsa Zsa Gabor). When the Mirisches turned down Wanger's long-standing properties, such as *Commencement, So Gallantly Gleaming, Dynasty of Death,* and even *The Ballad and the Source,* he changed tactics, proposing several ideas through the fall of 1951 which fit better with Monogram's methods: a production of Cleopatra using footage from Gabriel Pascal's version of the Shaw play, a medieval story exploiting the still standing *Joan of Arc* sets, and a satirical version of *Beauty and the Beast,* like Abbott and Costello's recent *Jack and the Beanstalk.* These projects fell flat as well.

Wanger was eloquent about the advantages of his new affiliation. "With conditions as they are today," he told the press, "there is no better opportunity for an independent . . . because the overhead [estimated at 5 percent] is small and what money is spent on production can be seen on the screen." "I really have analyzed this situation very carefully after our last conversation," he wrote Selznick, "and believe that the setup has really great opportunities. . . . I think, with the market in the condition that it is, I'll be able to make some quick turnovers and keep very active."

Yet for once he could not believe his own rhetoric, and his fall into the arms of Monogram depressed him no end throughout 1951. Bennett recounts, "The damage to his ego and pride was enormous. With the memory of past success, he recoiled violently from present failure." This was not a shrewd move to a smaller studio for greater production control, as had been the case when Wanger came to Columbia, Universal, and Eagle-Lion; this was desperation.

Precipitous falls in the film industry were part of Hollywood's mythic lore. William Fox was on the verge of combining Loew's and his own company into the most powerful presence in Hollywood in 1929, when he was immobilized by a car accident, struggled unsuccessfully through the stock market crash, was halted by an antitrust suit from the Department of Justice, and later indicted for attempting to bribe a judge. B. P. Schulberg, Wanger's erstwhile rival in production at Paramount during the twenties, was unemployed by the forties and had taken out a notorious full-page ad in the trade press begging for work. Lasky's career as an independent was virtually at a standstill and Selznick since 1946's *Duel in the Sun* struggled to produce a few films that turned out unprofitable. Louis B. Mayer retired after a power struggle at MGM in June of 1951. But such comparisons provided little comfort. "It is not easy to be on the way up in Hollywood," Lantz has said. "It is certainly impossible to be on the way down."

In a rare burst of therapeutic writing, Wanger later summarized his situation in 1951:

For two years things had been getting worse and worse. I felt pretty well physically, but ther[e] are just so many disappointments and ordeals, more than one can endure. I was getting weary of cleaning out the Augean Stable. I had had problems before and I always knew something would turn up to straighten them out.

But this time I began to worry . . . maybe my luck was running out. The Bank of America was trying to put me in bankruptcy, involving the house in a mortgage claim that any debt could be put against the house. . . . Senator Tenney trying to make me out a Red sympathizer . . . the fact that I was a Warren supporter is not mentioned on occasions of this sort. . . . My many speeches all over the country were proof enough of my position, but who cared? . . . Hughes taking over RKO out of a clear sky and his putting out "Stromboli" before "Joan of Arc" and ruining its American showing. The coming of television and my not being able to put over my theory regarding films for TV versus live shows. . . . My inability to make any deals that would solve my problems — and on and on they gathered.

I was putting up as brave a front as I could. I went to the new Church — which I loved for its beauty and simplicity, although it was not my church. I prayed and knew there was a solution somewhere — but where? I was getting tired and nervous. I went East. My friends there bored me and I them . . . Long Island . . . New York . . . no solution. My face was twitching and my speech was an effort when tired. I didn't want to drink and didn't.

If I only could get a rest! I hadn't had one in years. New York was strenuous. Europe was a mad rush too. I was never so prolific with good ideas and plans — and much less deserving ones had succeeded in the past — and yet nothing clicked. The Garbo deal even turned against me. I was two years too early with my idea of foreign production to get the finances I needed. If I could only take a trip, but I couldn't afford one with the family — or without. How could I have been so careless to find myself in this dilemma? . . . Where could I go and still be among completely new associations that would revitalize me? . . . Where? . . . When? . . . How?

As Greer observed, "he was besieged by doubt over whether he could do anything again." Unaccustomed to such despair, outraged at the indignities he faced so late in life, feeling helpless among so many developments that were beyond his control, Wanger looked in late 1951 for a situation he could do something about.

According to Bennett, through all his financial difficulties Wanger had resented her steady earnings. Jennings Lang, who had helped Wanger get ABC interested in his *Aladdin* television pilot, arranged frequent television appearances for Bennett. During one of Wanger's trips abroad, Lang had looked after Bennett when she fell ill. By late 1950, Wanger was aware that Bennett's feelings for Lang, in her words, "went beyond our business relationship."

Subscribing to the double standard of the era in which he was raised, Wanger never acknowledged that he in any way contributed to her alienation.

His flirtations and promiscuity while married to Justine Johnston continued unabated during his second marriage. Bennett herself had had her fun before marrying Wanger, but she claimed she was faithful to him. Bennett later recalled that within months of their January 1940 wedding, she had discovered his infidelities but her "deep attachment" to him prevented her from seeking yet another divorce. The birth of their children was another binding tie. Wanger was generous and affectionate with his stepdaughters Diana and Melinda, and he was absolutely devoted to Stephanie and Shelley but Bennett did not consider him a "family man." The fact that virtually every other productive executive was promiscuous was no excuse for his philandering, and she grew tired of his always coming home late from "meetings." She had spent a great deal of time alone at home, loaned him money for *Joan of Arc,* and accompanied him on the abortive trip to Europe in 1949. Although they had never been a physically demonstrative couple, she grew quite cold and formal with him.

Wanger later justified his feelings to his flamboyant and celebrated lawyer Jerry Geisler as the envy of being shut out from her life, not jealousy of Lang:

> I am 57 years old and I loved my wife and family and had no desire for any change—I was not only jealous of Joan I was jealous of our way of life. . . . I was jealous of Joan's forthrightness—I was jealous of her good judgement. . . . I was jealous of the time we had with the family—I was jealous of our liking or disliking a book or play and our reasons—of her interest in my clothes and mine in hers—of her perfume (La Rose) and my cologne (Fraser's)—the way she ran the house, the way she was organized—the efficiency of her means of travel—her interest in my work—my interest in her pictures—the discussion over directors, scripts and all the rest of show business—her desire to entertain well—her love of church and her desire to be with the children—these are all things I was jealous of plus the physical attraction . . . her lack of conceit and willingness to look objectively at her career. . . . I was jealous of all of this which I saw changing from day to day and a hardened new code of behavior and an attitude so foreign and distant and bitter that it was quite obvious to me that our marriage had entered a new phase and a dire one—I did not want to see this change occur and was ready to do all I could to stop it.

He made an absurd distinction between his fleeting affairs and Bennett's one adulterous and loveless liaison and threatened in early 1951 that he would kill anyone who "tried to break up my home." In subsequent months a private detective confirmed that indeed Bennett was having an affair with Lang, meeting him in New Orleans and in the West Indies and during weekday afternoons at a Beverly Hills apartment. This arrangement later inspired Billy Wilder and I. A. L. Diamond to script *The Apartment* (1960). Wanger found it difficult to keep up the proprieties that his wife had maintained for over a decade; he later wrote of his struggle to sit at the dinner table with

Stephanie and Shelley, "knowing where she had been in the afternoon." He told associates that Bennett had threatened to divorce him and take the children with her.

And so Wanger took action, precipitating one of Hollywood's biggest scandals. At 2:30 in the afternoon of Friday, December thirteenth, 1951, he had noticed Bennett's kelly green Cadillac convertible in the MCA parking lot in Beverly Hills. Seeing it there again as he drove by one hour later, Wanger decided to wait for Bennett's return. He was not disappointed. At 5:30, Bennett and Lang pulled up in Lang's car. After Lang helped Bennett into her convertible, he stood talking by her window. Brandishing a .38-caliber pistol issued to him as a civilian deputy of the Los Angeles sheriff's department, Wanger approached the car.

According to a parking lot attendant who witnessed the incident, there was a violent argument between the men, with Bennett yelling, "Get away from here and leave us alone." Bennett later recalled that Lang looked up suddenly from her window and, seeing Wanger raise the gun, said, "Don't be silly, Walter, don't be silly." Wanger, she said, was "standing there like a man hypnotized." Though Lang held up his hands, Wanger was implacable; he fired two shots in Lang's general direction. One went astray against the car; the other struck Lang in the groin, and he collapsed in agony to the ground. The parking lot attendant drove Bennett and Lang to Midway Hospital, where Lang received emergency surgery. Wanger was taken into police custody immediately—the Beverly Hills station was directly across the street. Without remorse, Wanger told the arresting officers, "I've just shot the son-of-a-bitch who tried to break up my home." Friends who called the Wanger home that evening were surrealistically informed, "Yes, the master is in the Lincoln Heights jail." Mike Romanoff tried to ease the hardship by personally serving Wanger dinner in his cell. In the eyes of a *Life* reporter, Wanger's walk that night from his cell to the police desk amidst popping flashbulbs and whirling newsreel cameras resembled Norma Desmond's final descent in Billy Wilder's *Sunset Boulevard*.

Both Lang, who recuperated without major complications, and Bennett anticipated the serious consequences of Wanger's action. On the way to see Lang's doctor they discussed the finer points of what to tell the police and the press and considered the necessity of preserving Wanger's fingerprints on the gun. She consulted with her close friend, publicist Ettinger, who was overheard telling Bennett as they left the jail that first night, "But there is *no way* we can keep it from Louella and Hedda." Bennett graciously tried to downplay the event in a press statement. She hoped that "Walter will not be blamed too much," for he was under great stress after suffering business reversals. She also regretted the negative light the shooting would cast on the Hollywood community, the "vast majority" of which consisted of "good, wholesome and sincere" people. No one fit her description better than Wanger and

Bennett herself. As *Time* put it, this scandal involved "some of Hollywood's shiniest showpieces."

Unaware of Wanger's detective, she and Lang denied the producer's accusations of adultery and declined to press charges against him. The Los Angeles district attorney took up the slack. On the evidence of seven witnesses and after only five minutes of deliberation, a Los Angeles County grand jury on December 18 indicted Wanger for assault with a deadly weapon with intent to commit murder. A conviction would carry up to fourteen years imprisonment. Hollywood's leading studio executives, including several who had turned down many of his projects, quickly gathered around Wanger, generously donating funds to finance his legal costs. Harry and Jack Warner, Goldwyn, Zanuck, Schenck, and agent Feldman each contributed $1,000. Wallis, Lesser, Disney, Work, and Spyros and Charles Skouras, among others, each contributed $500.

On the advice of attorney Geisler, Wanger entered a plea of not guilty by reason of temporary insanity, saying that he fired the gun "in a bluish flash through a violent haze." In mid-April 1952, Wanger agreed to waive trial and threw himself "on the mercy of the court." At his hearing, Geisler read a letter from Zanuck calling him "a man of culture and responsibility" and one from Goldwyn explaining that Wanger has "never chosen the easy way." As Wanger sat "grim and unsmiling," Superior Court judge Harry J. Borde granted Wanger a reduced charge of assault with a deadly weapon; he sentenced him to a four-month sentence to begin the following June at the Castaic Honor Farm two hours' drive north of Los Angeles.

Wanger might have viewed his actions as another type of risk-taking, another fantasy of personal bravado. But acquaintances and friends were bewildered. He was a notorious womanizer, and as Reinhardt observed, "we were all totally baffled by this. It was so inconsistent with everything else we knew about him." It was also inconsistent with the way Hollywood handled adultery. Someone told Greer, "I figure that Walter wanted to read his obituary. He wanted to read what people would say about him. It was his form of suicide. He figured that someone else would take care of him." In their own way, his colleagues in Hollywood had done so. The problem was that he had taken Bennett down with him, and there was no one who could take care of her.

She had a difficult time resuming anything like an ordinary career. Although one could argue that her days of movie stardom had already come to an end, Bennett felt differently. "Without question, the shooting scandal and resulting publicity destroyed my career in the motion picture industry," Bennett wrote. "Suddenly I was the villain of the piece, the apex of a triangle that had driven my husband to a shocking act of violence. I might just as well have pulled the trigger myself."

She had starred to great advantage in Minnelli's *Father of the Bride* (1950) and *Father's Little Dividend* (1951), playing the subdued maternal role in comic situations that *The Reckless Moment* had presented more ironically. The series very probably would have continued had the Lang incident not occurred. Bennett appeared in only five more Hollywood films for the rest of her career. She again played a quiet, competent mother in Sirk's *There's Always Tomorrow*. Two more films were due to the personal insistence of people close to her: Bogart in the case of *We're No Angels* and Wanger himself, who cast her as an officer's spouse who wreaks havoc on a Japanese village in *Navy Wife* (1956). More ominously, she played a murderess in Allied Artists' *Highway Dragnet* (1954). The shooting also ended her television career until the late 1960s.

"To have been publicly, publicly disgraced, for her was just devastating," Guest recalls.

> But again she just pulled herself together and said, "Well, someone's got to work, I've got these kids," and off she went. And she went on these horrid tours, one-night stands, but she did what she had to do. . . . She always wanted us to understand that my father had been the great love of her life and that he had brought this on himself through his philandering.

"Joan and I had often agreed that we could never do anything live," Greer recalls. "I couldn't believe it when she went out on stage, because I knew how nervous it made her."

In April 1952, Bennett replaced Rosalind Russell on the road in *Bell, Book and Candle,* beginning a decade of stage tours. Early on, she was booed on the stage. In Texas, the audience threw tomatoes. Bennett was also taunted in the press, as when the *Los Angeles Herald Express* captioned a photo on Wanger's trial, "Joan Bennett holds press confab in familiar surroundings— parking lot." As Guest summarized it, the Lang shooting "destroyed the life she had so carefully built up."

By contrast, after Harold Mirisch posted the $5,000 bail, Wanger continued his life as before, attending trade screenings, and going to the Bogarts' house for dinner. The day after his release on bail, he visited Edward Lasker and Greer. "Listen, tell me the truth," Wanger asked them. "Where did I hit him? No one will tell me. Did I hit what I was aiming at?" Someone had sent him a sharpshooter's medal. Much to the delight of the local press, Wanger celebrated Christmas 1951 with his daughters in Bennett's house. Having no place to live and no sizable source of income, Wanger found Bennett generous. Although "our lives were separate and we preserved the amenities only for the sake of the girls," Wanger lived with them for several years.

The very day Wanger's indictment was announced in December 1951, Wanger returned to Monogram to resume work. An astonished Walter Mirisch asked him why he was there. "What else can I do?" he asked Mirisch. Mirisch invited him for dinner that night, thinking Wanger should not spend the evening alone. "Walter was a perfect gentleman that evening in my home.

You would never have known what had happened to him that day." All of his friends supported him. Hayward defended him briefly when interviewed by the *New York Times* in the spring of 1952. The Hornblows, Edward Lasker, Mendel Silberberg, and others visited him at the Honor Farm.

The most touching tribute came in June 1952 from Selznick, who himself sensed that his glorious moments in Hollywood were in the past. Selznick had just attended a convention of a new industrywide public relations group. Selznick wrote Wanger that he heard many speakers address the need for "industry ambassadors" to improve Hollywood's image. After making his own speech, Selznick

> then spoke a few minutes on the subject of Walter Wanger. I said that I had heard a great deal at the convention and otherwise about the invaluable services of men like Ronald Reagan and George Murphy; that I agreed that the industry was in the debt of these men; that I also agreed that the industry could use more of them; but that there had been another industry ambassador who had given very greatly and freely of his time and services, named Walter Wanger. I spoke of your long service as the president of the Academy. I then went on to say that you had a picture or two going into release, I believed, although I did not know too much about your recent work or your plans for future production, but that I thought that the industry, including the exhibitors, could well afford to go out of their way to do something for you at this particular time and in the immediate future.

Selznick then reported that he had received an "extraordinarily fine response" to his remarks and that several individuals had agreed to help the Wanger pictures along. He continued:

> I don't have many illusions left as to this business or most of the people in it; but I did think that you ought to know something of the extent of the obvious goodwill toward you, and to have some indication of the many friends that you have.
>
> This summer will be more difficult than either you or I can put into words, I am sure; but in a sense it must be a relief to know that the worst is over, and that instead of having to look forward to the ordeal, it is, day by day, on its way to being finished. And I am sure that when you return to what might laughingly be termed the civilization of Hollywood, you will find everyone rooting that your career reaches unprecedented heights.

What neither Wanger nor Selznick could have anticipated was that Wanger would rebuild his career at low-budget Monogram. But then again, he had nowhere to go but up.

Part Five

Another Comeback:
Three Films

16

Riot in Cell Block 11
(1954)

When the West Coast press corps converged on the Castaic Honor Farm on September 5, 1952, to watch Wanger's release after ninety-eight days of his four-month sentence, the producer offered only one comment for publication: the prison system "is the nation's number one scandal. I want to do a film about it." The harrowing experience of his incarceration, the solitude and inactivity it forced upon him, and the severity of his downfall compelled Wanger to pursue production work on his next major film with more creative interest than ever before. Indomitable, resilient, and impatient to work, he proceeded to make one of the most dramatic comebacks in Hollywood history.

Finally this fortunate, fifty-eight-year-old upper-class gentleman—who had dined with international leaders during the two world wars, debated great minds in print and on radio networks, lived in the most comfortable circumstances, and thrived on the fortunes of the film industry—came to a completely new understanding of the workings of American society. He now became an outsider, humiliated by the circus atmosphere of the press coverage and the trial. Wanger was compelled to acknowledge, if only to himself, his professional and personal collapse.

The shooting solved nothing. At home, though he was alienated from Bennett, he struggled to maintain a loving relationship with his children. "My father was a very reserved man," Shelley Wanger recalls. "He wouldn't fight with my mother in front of us, though she tried to provoke him by constant needling." Screenwriter Richard Collins, invited for dinner shortly after Wanger's release, recalls that Wanger and Bennett communicated by writing notes to each other. "They would sit at dinner and it wasn't too wonderful." Eleven-year-old Stephanie Wanger approached Collins: "I'm so glad that you're friends with daddy," she told him, "because he really needs somebody."

To Wanger's mind the shooting was both accidental and morally justified, because Bennett did have an affair with Lang. By this contradictory logic, Wanger held himself virtually innocent of any wrongdoing: Guest recalls, "My father would say things like, 'If this were France I wouldn't have gone to jail. It was a crime of passion.'" This was one reason that his sentence came as a surprise. The other reason was that he expected Geisler to have him exonerated in a city where influential people quietly escaped punishment. Wanger remained calm for all the trial publicity and his stay in prison. In correspondence and contacts, he joked about his situation, referring to the sentence as "my holiday as a guest of the USA," or signing letters to Harold Mirisch, "Yours on location," noting that the Honor Farm was "like Palm Springs without agents."

But personally, he was deeply troubled. When Wanger visited Stephanie at her Arizona boarding school on weekends,

> He at that point to me seemed a broken man. He was so out of his element in [Castaic], he made the best of it and he didn't complain. But there was a sadness about him. He used to read me *Robinson Crusoe* when he'd come. I thought it was boring but I liked to let him read it because I thought that's the way he felt.

Wanger brooded restlessly at the Castaic Honor Farm, and Silberberg warned him that his "bitterness" might preclude a major studio association upon his release from prison. But Wanger felt that the persistent Los Angeles district attorney had used the trial as an occasion for self-promotion. He noted how accounts of Lang's grave condition at Wanger's hearing affected his sentence, but that "two days after my sentence the press carried stories that Lang was playing tennis and golf at Palm Springs, that he has been frequenting night clubs and parties." He saw the sensationalized press accounts of his trial and sentence (which extended to the national newsweeklies), not as the result of his many years in the public eye, but a humiliating campaign orchestrated by Lang's employer, MCA. After all, MCA's power in the industry seemed to grow exponentially with each year (particularly after the Screen Actors' Guild granted the agency permission to package television shows in a notorious gesture which then-SAG president Ronald Reagan coordinated in 1952).

Wanger had always taken perverse pride in placing himself as the outsider and the loner in Hollywood who was forward thinking while other studio executives were lagging behind him in slothful, ignorant mediocrity. Now, his solitude had negative, destructive consequences. He had a heightened sense of the hypocrisy that punished him but permitted the film industry's most powerful members—in his mind, most prominently, the MCA agents—to act with impunity. From the vantage point of a victim, Wanger felt that many forces and persons were arrayed against him: "It is hard for me to reconcile myself to the acceptance of the theory that might (MCA) makes right," he wrote while serving his sentence. Drawing on the rhetoric of the Cold War, he at one point likened the agency—in its omnipresence and effectiveness—to a Communist conspiracy.

But Wanger was not about to make a melodramatic film about the injustices of Hollywood power plays. He now took the industry too seriously to produce another comedy like *Stand-In*. Instead, as the decade progressed, Wanger gave his most concentrated attention to three projects—*Riot in Cell Block 11, Invasion of the Body Snatchers,* and *I Want to Live!*—whose narrative structure and style expressed a paranoid sensibility, a disillusionment with American society's slack efforts to approximate its social ideals, and a sympathy for those who suffer an arbitrary social ostracism. For the rest of his life, he would refer constantly to the corruption of American society, expanding his elitist contempt for the masses into a comparable disgust with politicians and corporate and intellectual leaders. This was a complete inversion of Wanger's earlier boosterism and pro-American views. The tenor of popular culture and the fortunes of Hollywood in the 1950s were such that Wanger could turn his newfound disillusionment into a professional comeback. First, however, there was the issue of prison reform.

Publicity surrounding *Riot in Cell Block 11* always emphasized that Wanger knew the subject matter of the film from firsthand experience. He willingly exploited his imprisonment, publishing articles in *Pageant* magazine and, most prominently, an article in *Look* magazine that coincided with the release of the film, entitled "West Points of the Underworld." As usual his self-advertisement was an uneasy mix of sincerity and sales pitch. For one thing, there was a striking gap between the conditions he personally experienced in prison and those he would portray in the film. Wanger's greatest hardship came his first night in the Los Angeles County jail, where he found himself harshly handled and sharing a cell with a peeping Tom sniper. Conditions at the Castaic Honor Farm where he spent the summer of 1952 were much more pleasant. Inmates slept in barracks rather than cells and they had considerable freedom of movement. Yet Wanger found the routine intolerable. When they made the two-hour drive to visit Wanger, the Hornblows agreed that the Honor Farm was no picnic. Wanger asked that Leonora wait outside, and they soon understood why. The atmosphere was depressing. Sitting in the parking lot, among the cars of visitors to other inmates, Leonora Hornblow sensed that "the human misery was like a mist that surrounded that place." When her husband came back outside, his face was gray: "He said it was like a Warner Brothers movie." The gifts they had giftwrapped and brought for Wanger—some chocolates, cologne, and a volume of Nadine Gordimer's short stories—were torn open by the guards who demanded, "What have you brought the prisoner?"

Wanger's own complaints about the farm testify as much to his sense of victimization and his privileged lifestyle as it does to penal degradation:

> For nearly 2 months now I have been standing in line 3 times a day to be checked and at night in barracks with 38 other men. Each night a guard walks through and flashes a light in our face to see if we have escaped or not. That we do not sleep between sheets but blankets—that we have no pajamas but sleep in our underwear;—that we line up for chow with a tin plate and cup and have the food doled out to us—we have no knives or milk or sugar to use. I have tasted no red meat since June 4—We can only bathe at certain hours—we are permitted one towel—there is no reading room or recreation hall where one can be by one's self quietly. In the county jail the food is shoveled into the tanks in big metal containers and dished out by a—the best comparison I can give you is to compare it to the way food is served the animals in the zoo. You are not allowed to have books unless they become the property of the county—you cannot subscribe to magazines, mail is censored.

This was hardly the material for a prison melodrama, for which Wanger would have to turn to more depressing penal conditions.

Wanger's minor deprivations at Castaic did reveal certain unenlightened principles of prison management, however, which made the difference between Castaic and San Quentin a matter of degree rather than kind. Primary among these was the dehumanizing treatment of the inmates. This was highlighted by his discovery that prison inmates were mostly free citizens who—like himself—"just happened" to have some "bad luck." As he put it in his notes, the inmates "are not feeble minded or wicked." Having overheard several groups of men talk he noted:

> One group was discussing aviation, another philosophy, another astronomy, another electronics, another motor car construction. These men are . . . engineers, mechanics, plumbers, electricians, blacksmiths, salesmen and they are ambitious.

A "seasoned pickpocket of 30 years experience" gave Wanger several publications on prison conditions and the need for prison reform, such as Harry Elmer Barnes and Negley K. Teetler's 1945 study *New Horizons in Criminology.* Here Wanger read that prison locations, inadequate facilities, and rampant overcrowding were merely the playthings of politicians and the result of public apathy. He learned that no programs existed to give unskilled inmates training or the basic needs of clothing and cash to help the ex-inmate make his or her way on the "outside." He found

> not only the inmates agreeing with me begging for an opportunity not to rot here mentally, but I also talked to the custodians who are so underpaid and [are] prisoners themselves to red-tape . . . that they are stymied by the apathy of the press and public.

If Wanger was impressed with the caliber of his fellow inmates, they were equally taken with him. A model prisoner, he proved diligent in his chores around the yard, in the kitchen, in the latrines, and as the resident librarian. Several inmates gave Wanger cards on his fifty-eighth birthday, and on the occasion of a parole hearing in late July, three wrote letters of support: "His modest behavior—yet his willingness to talk to any one of us at any time, and his genuine interest in our personal problems—has made us respect him as a man." One African-American inmate, Texas editor and journalist Lawrence I. Brockenbury, wrote Wanger upon his departure that he was thrilled to be close to "true greatness":

> I have been inspired by your wisdom, altruism, patience, courage, generosity and humility; and I believe that I am a much better person for having known you. . . . You treated me as a human being, with an equality that members of my racial group have long been striving for.

Shortly after his return to Monogram, Wanger received a letter from a wife of a Castaic Honor Farm inmate:

> It is strange that we (all the mothers and wives) are expecting something from you. You can't be God, but you are a man who can get things done. . . . Maybe you were used as an instrument of mercy in the fact that you had contact with this side of life.

Indeed, having read and experienced the conditions of jails and prisons, Wanger in the fall of 1952 continued work on the Phoenix Project, which he and others designed to help the Castaic Honor Farm prisoners develop technical skills (in electronics and mechanics) and get a job upon their release. Wanger himself hired Brockenbury as a personal assistant when he got reestablished at Monogram. For the rest of the decade, he retained an active interest in the cause of prison reform, at one point participating in the futile movement to obtain a reprieve for death row inmate Caryl Chessman. He was aware that no change would be possible unless the issue of prison reform was publicized, which was the main purpose of the *Pageant* article, published more than a year in advance of *Riot in Cell Block 11*. There he wrote:

> The first thing to be done is for the radio, press, television and motion pictures to throw the searchlight and X-Ray on our Penal System and let the public realize that it is antiquated and under-financed and a dangerous threat to every community, business and family in the United States.

Wanger wanted to change the public's understanding of the inmate first by arguing that "the people who inhabit the jails and prisons of this country are just like yourselves." Second, he wanted to stress that prisons were degrading institutions, keeping convicts idle, mixing first-time offenders comparable to the country's best citizens with pathological cases in overcrowded facilities. Third, Wanger wanted to outline the social forces that resulted in the inadequate prison system—specifically, that prison personnel were underpaid, that the prisons themselves were inadequate and underfinanced facilities, and that all of these problems arose from public neglect.

Though he was bitterly disillusioned with the hypocritical apathy of American society, Wanger retained some measure of his populist idealism about the public. While developing his film, he wrote a state prison commissioner that he felt it

> can be very important and really arouse the public if properly done, without too much propaganda, as the public is pretty smart at realizing what is going on, even though they don't have much chance to express themselves, either through the legislature or through the press, but they still have souls.

Riot in Cell Block 11 was Wanger's appeal to the public, his personal crusade for prison reform, generated at once out of his personal convictions regarding penal conditions, his professional desperation that necessitated an "important" film to restore his reputation, and his disgust with American complacency.

But Wanger also took pains to note that his film should be packaged as an entertainment item to appeal to the audience and to Monogram executives. Wanger's first challenge in the fall of 1952 was to persuade the latter to back a prison film, a genre that had not figured prominently in the studio's output in recent years. Fortunately, his timing was right.

By the fall of 1952, Monogram, like the film industry in general, saw a recovery of fortunes from the low point of 1950. In 1951, a series of blockbusters such as MGM's *Quo Vadis* (shown on the same exhibition basis as *Joan of Arc*), Paramount's *The Greatest Show on Earth,* Warner Bros.'s *A Streetcar Named Desire,* and Twentieth Century-Fox's *David and Bathsheba,* as well as the musicals *Show Boat, An American in Paris,* and *The Great Caruso,* all grossed well over $4 million and combined with increased foreign revenues to make 1951 the first year since 1947 that the industry measured any growth in gross income. The majors had further decreased the volume of films they produced to compensate for waning attendance, declining revenues, and theater divorcement after the *Paramount* case. The films they did produce were either blockbusters or low-budget titles for double-bills that still played in 70 percent of the theaters in the country. As a result, the studios decreased production of moderate "A" films, and a glut of "B" films flooded the market by spring 1952, as Wanger stood trial.

The increased stability of the industry, the decrease in middle-range productions, and the oversupply of "B" films provided encouragement for a low-budget studio such as Monogram to shift to higher budgets for production; Republic Studios did likewise on a larger scale, allocating $15 million in

1952 for Ford's *The Quiet Man* and other films featuring erstwhile major studio stars such as Flynn, Mason, Donlevy, and Trevor. In October 1952, as Wanger was getting reoriented at Monogram, chief executive Broidy jubilantly reported that the company had had the second best year in its history. Profits of more than $589,000 reflected steady domestic and foreign revenues and encouraged Broidy to rename Monogram "Allied Artists" that October, the most decisive change in its image since 1945, in the hopes that it could break into the more profitable urban early-run theaters.

The change in production policy, however, was more gradual than the name change: Allied Artists continued to produce its Bomba, Bowery Boys, and western film series through the mid-1950s. The studio did begin to allocate more funds for $200,000 to $300,000 action films, however, and increased its Cinecolor productions to twelve "Special" films a year, including Walter Mirisch's *Hiawatha; The Rose Bowl Story;* and Mirisch's naval drama *Flat Top,* which *Variety* felt would play well in "key city markets where the company's regular product does not usually play." As Mirisch told the press, the studio was "utilizing more star names, and using more color film in our productions than at any previous period in our history."

Moreover, the policy shift would lead the studio to produce and distribute the kinds of films for which it is best remembered—the violent, low-budget films noir that diversified its audience to include adult viewers. The King Bros.'s *Southside 1–1000* was an isolated instance in 1950. By early 1954 and the premiere of *Riot in Cell Block 11,* Allied Artists also had *Highway Dragnet,* Robert Aldrich's *World for Ransom,* and *Loop Hole.* These were followed by Joseph M. Newman's *Human Jungle* in the fall and *The Big Combo* and *The Phenix City Story* in the first half of 1955. Like *Riot in Cell Block 11,* these films exploited location shooting, newspaper headlines, and an increasing level of violence. This last element also influenced Allied Artists' 1953 westerns. *Son of Belle Star* surprised viewers with an unhappy ending in which the hero was unexpectedly killed. *Variety* described *Jack Slade* as "the violent story of a violent man, too homicidal for the kiddie patrons of the regular western program market and with nothing that can be recommended for general or family audiences."

Hence *Riot in Cell Block 11* was consistent with the Allied Artists production policy in early 1953 when Wanger hired a writer to develop a script. But the studio was serious about closely managing its much-ballyhooed increase in production budgets, which brought the average negative cost up to only $250,000. Since the summer of 1951, Walter Mirisch had overseen the studio's entire output as executive producer, and all company producers from Wanger to the Bowery Boys' Jerry Thomas henceforth were required to obtain his approval at literally every step of production work. Go-aheads and starting dates would be set only if scripts could be made within stipulated budgets.

Wanger wanted more personal authority for his films, more studio support in the form of a full-time production manager and less restrictive budgets. Since *Aladdin and His Lamp,* the studio had established a pattern whereby, in Wanger's words, "I have no authority over any expenditures. They are entirely in the control of [the studio] organization." When approached in the spring of 1953 by NBC radio journalists about collaborating on a prison film, Wanger replied that he was not independent,

> and therefore [I] am subject to quite a few restraints, such as budget and complete operation. . . . I'm sorry to sound so "chintzy" in the whole matter, but this town is in such confusion and I am so limited at the moment, which is a condition I hope to rectify shortly and get back into my own independent operation.

Wanger's desire for greater authority was further complicated by the personal courtesies extended him by Broidy and the Mirisches. Unfazed by the shooting incident and Wanger's sentence, the Monogram executives had assigned him the credit, salary, and profit percentage for three genre films: two westerns (*Fort Vengeance* and *Kansas Pacific*) and a Korean War film (*Battle Zone*). The films were scripted and directed by studio talents, cast with studio perennials such as Sterling Hayden, photographed in two weeks, and edited during the summer and fall of 1952 without Wanger's supervision at a cost of roughly $200,000 each. Wanger's value to the studio had been as much the prestige associated with his name as the quality of his films. The profits and several salary advances gave Wanger nearly $86,000 in badly needed pocket money. As Walter Mirisch later put it, "It was something we did for a friend in trouble."

Still, Wanger was determined to get busy producing as many films as possible, and his key strategy was still to match his interests to the studio's exploitation and serial formulas. He attempted to revive the "Yellowknife" adventure property by approaching Ford, and to activate other comic strip possibilities (such as the action hero Steve Canyon). But the first action film he successfully produced was *The Adventures of Hajji Baba,* based on the popular 1824 novel by British diplomat James Morier that imitated a tale from the *Arabian Nights.* This Wanger hoped would prove as successful as *Arabian Nights* ten years earlier. In mid-January, Wanger hired Collins to write a script for *The Adventures of Hajji Baba* in a "thoroughly ridiculous and tongue and cheek" tone with "a lot of intrigue and Oriental larceny." Cukor praised Collins's work highly; by the time the film went into production in late 1953, Twentieth Century–Fox was so anxious to have more titles in its brand-new widescreen process that it loaned Allied Artists the technology for CinemaScope and Technicolor. Among the cast, Wanger placed his stepdaughter Melinda in a secondary role.

Wanger also took Fox's participation as a rationale for greater expenditures and proceeded to hire two associates of Cukor's from Warner Bros.'s staff of *A Star Is Born* (1954), production designer Gene Allen and color consultant George Hoynigen-Huene. With costume designer Renie, they co-ordinated the set and costume colors on the film. Wanger's presumptuous action triggered several heated arguments with Allied Artists executives. Meanwhile, during January and February, Wanger and Collins discussed a prison film. Keenly interested in the project, Collins turned out to be the most capable writer Wanger had worked with in a long time.

A thirty-nine-year-old former Warner Bros. contractee, Collins had been active in the Communist party through World War II and coauthored the screenplay for MGM's *Song of Russia*. By 1947, he had left the party but was one of the original nineteen Hollywood talents subpoenaed by J. Parnell Thomas's House Committee on Un-American Activities in 1947. By 1951 Collins had become personally convinced of the necessity of anti-Communist vigilance. After consultations with the FBI and HUAC, he was cooperative witness during the hearings in April 1951. This decision he later regretted emphatically as "a mistake," because Collins offered the names of people who had left the party many years earlier, in the belief that they would not suffer any more than the individuals who were dead or already identified.

Testifying did little to alleviate Collins's blacklist status, and he continued to work "under the table" until he coauthored a Don Siegel film, *China Venture*, at Columbia in 1953. As a veteran blacklistee, Collins came cheap ($500 a week under his March contract), which pleased Allied Artists. But he also came with the double ostracism of being blacklisted on the one hand and reviled as an informer on the other. As he would later note, he took to scenes concerning "the burdens and slander of political life . . . like a duck to water." The working relationship between producer and screenwriter was enhanced by their shared sense of alienation.

Wanger cajoled the Mirisches into signing Collins to a contract in March 1953 to develop the prison film script, and he arranged through the offices of Attorney General Edmund "Pat" Brown for Collins to visit several prisons and meet with various authorities on penology "to freshen up on the color and irony of the whole situation." One irony that Wanger saw clearly was that he had previously understood the subject only through the representations of Hollywood's 1930s films, including his own. *House Across the Bay, Mary Burns, Fugitive,* and even *You Only Live Once* had only repeated the generic, melodramatic conception of the hardships of prison life which was divorced entirely from their social and economic causes.

Now Wanger was determined to make a "realistic" film on the subject. "Realism" had always been a primary underpinning to Wanger's enthusiasm for film. But in 1950s Hollywood, the entire industry embraced it as a means of product differentiation as widescreen and color epic and fantasies (such as *The Adventures of Hajji Baba*) became more prevalent. Semi-documentaries and biopics were just two types of films based on "factual yarns" which were prevalent in the early 1950s, and studios continued to save costs with location shooting. *Southside 1–1000,* the King Bros.'s 1950 heist film for Monogram, included scenes shot in San Quentin by cinematographer Russell Harlan, who later worked on *Riot in Cell Block 11.*

Wanger and Collins's most important decision regarding the script of *Riot in Cell Block 11* was to model the film's narrative development closely on the most striking and lengthy of the thirty prison riots that had occurred since mid-1951 in Illinois, Pennsylvania, and Ohio. This was the April 1952 uprising at the prison in Jackson, Michigan, where 2,600 convicts took nine guards hostage, did $2.5 million worth of damage, and demanded that the governor personally guarantee an investigation into their complaints. Interest in the subject was still strong in March 1953 with an NBC radio news series. Wanger and Collins's initial plan was to make a docudrama of events there, but Wanger determined that it would be less costly and litigious simply to leave the prison site unidentified and to capitalize, in true exploitation fashion, on recent headlines.

In fact, the narrative trajectory of Collins's script closely mirrored developments at Jackson. Like Dunn (Neville Brand) and Mike Carney (Leo Gordon) in the film, the leaders of the Michigan action, Earl Ward and his right-hand man "Crazy Jack" Hyatt, were characterized as "psychopaths." Like the film's Warden Reynolds (Emile Meyer), Jackson's Assistant Deputy Warden Vernon Fox was sympathetic to the rioters' demands, and as in the film, the press noted the convergence between the rioters' complaints and Fox's reform agenda. In fact, Fox tried to use the riot to support his own recommendations for constructive changes, but lost his job in the political firestorm that ensued.

Story events in the script also were taken directly from the Jackson uprising. These included the systematic takeover of the prison's isolation unit (in Jackson, called cell block 15), including the actual excuse a prisoner used to get an inexperienced guard to open his cell door to begin the takeover; the inmates' grandstanding for the press; the unproductive discussions with higher-ranking officials (the knife thrown at Commissioner Haskell [Frank Faylen] in the film was at Jackson only threatened); the debate by prison officials on whether or not to march inmates past the rioting cell block in order to feed them; the second riot in the dining hall, sparked by a single shout; the state police's herding the rioters into their cell blocks; the shooting of a single inmate; the riot leader's threat to kill a guard in retaliation and the warden's argument for not doing so; the apparent takeover of the riot by its leader's second in command; the latter's reading of guards' farewell letters over the phone to their hysterical wives; the state officials' plans to dynamite open the cell block; and the governor's signature on the rioters' demands and its subsequent nullification by the state legislature. In the film, the "punk" who is physically restrained from his obvious interest in a younger kid was the barest allusion to the rampant problem of homosexual rapes at Jackson. Among the list of demands read by Dunn to the press, all except the plea for job training, which reflected Wanger's interests in the Phoenix Project, came from the Michigan inmates' list.

Prison riots as early as 1929 had inspired some of the first prison pictures in the sound era such as *The Big House* and *Numbered Men,* but neither of these films had so closely modeled their stories on actual events. One of the intriguing aspects of the message movie and its prison incarnation is how little it changed over two decades' time: the conventions of the romantic interest, of the wrongly accused inmates, and the causal explanation of malevolent characters persisted into the 1950s.

The first prison film convention that Wanger and Collins discarded was the romantic interest. With each rewrite during the spring of 1953, they progressively eliminated all traces of domestic melodrama from their story. The core narrative situation of the completed film—the action of the Michigan uprisings, the inmates' escape, the contrasts between Snyder the psychopath, Dunn, and Mac the intelligent accountant—is present in Collins's first draft. But it is also interlaced with lengthy scenes featuring wives of the warden and the captured guards. The script called for opening with a close-up of a robin in the Warden's wife's garden, only gradually revealing with elaborate camera movement the prison wall that bounds it. It concluded with interrupted dinner scenes and a vehement discussion between the warden and his wife about her desire to leave and the hopeless nature of his work. In the second draft script, Collins replaced the opening scene in the garden with Wanger's suggestion of newsreel footage of prison riots and an interview with California Commissioner of Corrections, Richard A. McGee. Although the scene with the guards' wives remains in the film, it lasts all of thirty seconds as the captured guards are finally released. According to Collins, it was Wanger who insisted that these elements be removed: "I don't want that; I don't want anything *like* that," Collins recalls Wanger telling him, "I want to stay away from the formula as much as I can. Forget the women." For the man who had insisted on romantic subplots in *Gabriel Over the White House* and *Blockade,* this was a major shift.

Similarly, the sympathetic depiction of prison inmates was hardly an innovation of the early 1950s. The Depression-era prison films had always cast the protagonist as a victim of circumstance who "helplessly wallows in frustrating confinement, undergoing harsh punishment for what are only apparent transgressions." The compassionate presentation of James Allen's plight in *I Am a Fugitive from a Chain Gang* (1931) continued in *Brute Force* (Universal, 1947), *Caged* (Columbia, 1950), and the Glenn Ford–Broderick Crawford vehicle *Convicted* (Columbia, 1950), all films that Wanger and Collins screened during the scripting period for *Riot in Cell Block 11.* The tendency to offer sympathetic victims culminated in the whimsical presentation of various nonhomicidal convicts in Stanley Kramer's *My Six Convicts* (an adaptation of a prison psychiatrist's best-seller), which was released in the fall of 1952.

The innocent convict of the prison film is congruent with the message movie's reliance on unfortunate noble victims—the characters who happened to be in the wrong place at the wrong time in a melodramatic coincidence. Angelica in Wanger's own *Smash-Up* is a prime example of this convention. As critic Michael Wood has pointed out, this made it all the easier to condemn the social evil at issue (lynching, prejudice), but implied, conversely, that such actions and attitudes would be fine *if* the scapegoat were in fact guilty. Collins's script for *Riot in Cell Block 11* provides a sympathetic portrayal of the convicts in the riot. With each script draft, Collins's focus shifts from the warden and his domestic problems to the inmates. In fact, journalists and criminologists reading the final revised script complained that the story was "overloaded in favor of the inmates" and that the warden failed to condemn the inmates' violence strongly enough.

But Collins's script also precluded the easy moral and behavioral categorization of types that was so prevalent in the prison film. The inmates are hardly the innocent victims of circumstance seen in other prison films, yet that does not vitiate their right to demand reform. The notion that, in the warden's words, the prison is full of "good and bad—just like the outside," complicates any attempt to generalize about the inmates' status: some of them are psychopaths, and others are perfectly sane. As Richard Combs has perceptively noted, the film offers "a contradiction of viewpoints, of representation." The film's destructive inmates at first resemble the "maddened convicts" described in the newsreel-style prologue, but they gradually prove the inadequacy of that "official" line. As the Colonel (Robert Osterloh) tells Dunn and Carney after their takeover of the cell block is complete, "In the street they think we're wild animals—tonight you proved it." When Carney flings his knife at Haskell, the Colonel yells, "Oh, that's real brilliant Carney—You gave 'em just what they wanted." Similarly, Dunn understands what the newsmen want: "Mad dogs running wild."

If Collins's script questioned generalizations about inmates, it also refused to simplify character motivations. Is the Colonel reluctant to join the riot because he is selfish or because he "used to be brass" in the army and identifies with the guards and warden—two explanations Dunn proposes—or because he truly is repulsed by violence as the Colonel himself suggests? The script does not endorse one explanation over any other.

Yet another instance of complex characterization is Haskell, the closest the film comes to offering a "villain." Haskell wants to impose military discipline and violent repression on the rioters without acknowledging the basis for their complaints (which he calls "without foundation"). The conflict in policy represented by Warden Reynolds and Commissioner Haskell is an updated version of the debate between progressive and reactionary approaches to treating the mentally ill in *Private Worlds* (represented by Alec and Jane and the Matron and Dr. Monet, respectively). In *Riot in Cell Block 11,* however, the debate is much less one-sided. During script preparation, Wanger described Haskell as a composite of reactionary state legislators: one memo noted that he "could be [the right-wing state senator Jack] Tenney in California." But even Haskell's view that negotiating with the convicts will set a bad precedent for other prisons is given its due. Warden Reynolds tells Haskell late in the script, "You'll never stop riots by treating the prisoners worse." Before cutting away to cell block 11, Haskell asks, "Have you stopped them by treating them better?" Like the disagreements among the inmates, the different attitudes of the authorities demonstrate the intricacies of prison reform.

The absence of innocent inmates and clearly evil villains was a major revision of the prison film and the liberal message movie such as *Crossfire, Gentleman's Agreement,* and *Pinky,* or Kramer's *The Defiant Ones* (1958) and *Inherit the Wind* (1960). Such films easily identified a social problem (anti-Semitism, racism, and intolerance) and just as easily found solutions, conforming to Hollywood conventions of the happy ending and the very conception of the social problem as something that individuals can correct. In achieving such happy endings, they deployed what historian Richard Maltby has identified as the validation of "understanding" (of the victims and their malevolent opponents) in place of more rational analysis that would question the workings of the social structures, systems, and processes involved in the problem.

As Peter Roffman and Jim Purdy point out, the prison film differed from other melodramatic genres of the Depression era, such as the gangster and fallen women films, because it took a social institution as its subject. The genre, in principle at least, could offer a nonindividualized critique of the impersonal forces at work in society. But most of Hollywood's prison films—including *Brute Force, Caged,* and other films of more recent vintage—rarely did so and continued to blame regrettable conditions on individual evil officials and guards (*I Am a Fugitive from a Chain Gang* was a modest exception). As late as 1951, Warner Bros.'s program film *Inside the Walls of Folsom Prison* takes the history of the institution as its primary narrative interest and contrasts repressive and progressive administrators in Folsom's history. When the progressive warden is fired, the inmates attempt an escape and all are killed. As *Variety* summarized the film's epilogue, "The resulting hue and cry changes the formula for handling prisoners at Folsom and the institute is now known as a strict, but humane, prison."

For this reason, one of the greatest innovations in *Riot in Cell Block 11* lay in the film's depiction of complex social forces. Unlike previous social problem films, it accomplishes this by denying the audience a single protagonist whose education about an unjust situation provides the audience with a focus for identification. In *Riot in Cell Block 11,* all the main characters know what the problem is, and it is the audience, along with the undifferentiated press corps, who has to learn about the problem and see that no one individual on the screen can rectify it. At the same time, *Riot in Cell Block 11* avoids what critic Alan Lovell has referred to as preachy speechmaking, a feature common to social problem films seeking to dramatize how abstract processes—in this case, public apathy, inadequate funding, hamstrung administrators, and outmoded facilities—contribute to the problem.

Certainly Wanger planned to rely on dialogue to convey many of his points, although he was well aware that "the public" would "shy away from anything they consider propaganda and preachment." He toyed with many prologue speeches and ideas, such as staging a discussion of prison problems by the Folsom Prison Inmates Council at the prison itself. Their talk would challenge, in Wanger's words, "the preconceived notion that anyone in prison is relegated to 'dese' and 'dose' and should remain there forever." The finished film began with newsreels, voice-over narration, and the statement of Corrections Commissioner McGee to establish the film's realistic credentials and put the case for prison reform into words before the story began.

The finished script retained many direct expressions of Wanger's ideas, as in the Warden's recitation of statistics on recidivism (65 percent of released inmates return to jail), or the scene in which the Colonel smacks his fist and says, "If we could just get across that *anyone* could land in prison—just like that!" But in the balance of the script, Collins avoids the speechmaking of the social problem film by packing the didactic component of Wanger's arguments into each scene. Indeed, from the standpoint of Wanger's career, the Collins script continues Wanger's postwar shift into purposeful subtlety and logical, linear narrative development without the to-camera propagandizing and the implausibly formulaic narratives of *The President Vanishes* and *Blockade.*

The exposition of the film is a model for its economical presentation of conditions and causes, which never resorts to talking heads. As at the Jackson riot, Monroe, the first guard overtaken in the cell block, has naively opened the door to deliver a "gift" from an inmate awaiting transfer to another cell. Subsequently, we learn from Warden Reynolds that Monroe is "green" and should not have been posted in block 11. When briefly criticized for making the assignment, an underling replies that even though the block requires six guards, he has trouble finding four. This brief exchange, delivered as Reynolds and his subordinates walk across the yard at night, establishes the desperate lack of staff funding as the weak "link" in the system which the inmates are able to exploit. Similarly, when the riot siren first goes off, a guard loading his gun comments, "Here we go again." His companion replies, "Yeah, and all for fifty bucks a week." Such pithy terseness also contributes to the action orientation of the film.

A final, major innovation in *Riot in Cell Block 11* is its pessimistic resolution. The film's conclusion notes that although public apathy is the primary obstacle to prison reform, public sympathy (as in the liberal message film) is inadequate to solve the problem. Wanger noted that he wished to "shock the people, however, I do not want to make it seem hopeless. I would like the audience to feel that this is their problem and not the problem of the inmates or the custodians." He and Collins worked on the ending continually through the summer of 1953 before arriving at the actual ending—in which Dunn is to stand trial for inciting the riot and no reform is immediately forthcoming, and the warden is hopeful that the publicity of the riot will eventually bring about some good.

Collins's first draft script ended with the Colonel, not Dunn, conferring with the warden, who informs him that the legislature has repudiated the governor and that the warden is being investigated. The Colonel then relays this news to the inmates back in the cell, and someone calls out to ominous general approval, "Next time we'll do it Carney's way." The Breen Office objected to this ending, which they noted, "in effect, thoroughly justifies the evil philosophy dramatized in the character of Carney." In the second draft script, as in the finished film, Dunn will stand trial for his role in inciting the riot, but unlike in the film, he is given a chance to speak on radio before being taken away. As he begins denouncing prison conditions, the radio station cuts him off, moving to an advertisement from Honest Hal, a used-car salesman who boasts that he is "giving these cars away" (a detail that was used early in the finished film). The broadcast then shifts to a society wedding, or in another variant, to the Kentucky Derby.

The radio broadcast scheme, like many of the narrative details of Collins's script, came from Wanger. Never before had he taken such a detailed and definite interest in the course of action in a script. "He was not a writer, but he was an inspirer, in a sense," Collins later recalled. "I mean he really kept you going."

> He would say, "I just feel [the scene is] not right" and he would sort of tell you what he didn't like. He was like many talented men, like Willy Wyler; he couldn't tell you exactly, anymore than Wyler could with an actor. He couldn't tell you exactly what he didn't like, but he had a feeling about it and the big problem was to convey the feeling.

Beyond setting the tone of the film and guiding Collins to its basic narrative, Wanger's contributions to the script were innumerable. He suggested the exchange between inmate Mac and guard Monroe about guards held hostage who want to contact their families and Mac's reply, "Now you know why the

boys fuss over our letters." He suggested using an interview scene between
the Warden and the press—originally conceived just to give background on
the inmates—to voice statistics (the 65 percent recidivism rate is "a number
that proves we haven't been doing the job"). He thought up the inmates' brief
celebration of the governor's capitulation, tossing newspapers around the block
cage in a mild echo of their rampage upon release at the beginning of the
film. To indicate that the prison housed, in Reynolds's words, "good and bad,
just like on the outside," he suggested an inmate reading a psalm and an accountant in prison for forgery who just "reads and reads." In the film, the
accountant's intelligence and altruism are quite striking: "How can you afford
a kid on your salary?" he asks Monroe at one point, with a compassion that
arouses the ire of Carney, who steps on his glasses.

Wanger also wanted to evoke the experience of incarceration through details of mise-en-scène and sound effects. He eliminated details such as sugar
bowls and syrup jars on the prisoners' tables because Wanger did not see
them in "the organization in which I had the pleasure of being entertained."
The Breen Office, as expected, decried the harsh language and violent fights
and persuaded Wanger to eliminate scenes of latrine duty. But Wanger insisted that a toilet bowl be visible in an early shot of the cells on the grounds
that it was "essential and valid in this story" for his message of inmate humiliation; as a concession, all cell scenes after the first were shot facing outward
to exclude toilets from the frame. Wanger told Collins he wanted "to eliminate all trace of Warner Bros. characteristics," those formulaic elements that
didn't ring true, including the depiction of prisons as "big factories only with
inmates instead of workers":

> I never saw anyone nor at any time like a free man—you are watched—
> worried—careful and subservient as well as conscious at all time of your degra-
> dation—you want to get out now. One false move can jeopardize your chances—
> so you take none—unless you blow your top.

He insisted from the outset that the soundtrack feature a steadily growing
symphony of door, cell, and bar clangings, a "mechanical building up of phon-
ing, of loudspeakers, of messengers, of reactions—continuous action to clarify at all times that a battle is in progress and that each camp is trying to
outwit the other." To this end, he urged Collins to script sequences of crosscutting between the scene in which Carney refuses to give the rookie guard
Monroe a cigarette, and the arguments between the warden and Haskell, or
between the governor's assistant's plan to bomb a portion of the cell block
and the inmates tying their hostages to the inside of the wired wall. The
crosscutting adds suspense to the film by creating different levels of knowledge between the audience and the characters. It also gives "equal" time to
inmates and authorities, forestalling audience identification with one side
over the other.

Hence by early July 1953 Collins and Wanger had produced a script that refused or significantly modified many features of the traditional social problem film. In the aggregate, the departures from the prison movie formula outweighed the film's adherence to them. No wonder director Siegel has commented that Wanger

> wanted his contribution to the subject matter to be absolutely honest and uncompromising. No star was allowed to unbalance our casting. . . . We didn't bring any women into the prison. . . . We didn't take sides at all.

Given Wanger's debts to the studio, the influence of Allied Artists on the script was surprisingly slight. Collins recalls that while working on the script, an Allied Artists studio executive sent Wanger a memo with Broidy's endorsement urging Collins to rework the script "to go back to the brutal warden, to the guys trying to get over the wall, all this bullshit we had avoided." Wanger and Collins agreed that following such suggestions would send "everything we were trying to do down the drain" and were allowed to ignore the idea.

The Monogram formula dictated other restrictions, of course. Studio executives wanted a short script of no more than 115 pages, and Wanger noted that they "want mostly action." He intended to oblige by having action right from the film's opening: he wanted "sirens and all of the riot excitement" to be "the very first things we should hear." Budget considerations were another factor. They led to changes in action which were generally immaterial to the film's import. Although Wanger initially hoped to produce the film with Glenn Ford or Van Heflin and to shoot the film in 3-D, this wasn't possible. He eventually endorsed the idea of casting "people that are not too well known, with the exception of perhaps the lead." But the lack of star names only enhanced the film's "realism" and its refusal to posit one central character for audience identification.

Allied Artists' budget limitations coincided with Wanger's efforts to preserve the film's "realism" with location shooting. One of the authorities Wanger contacted, McGee, read the script drafts and agreed to appear in the film's factual prologue. McGee also decided, in mid-June, to allow Wanger's unit to shoot the film at an abandoned cell block in the yard of Folsom Prison. Wanger hired Sam Peckinpah, who came to Wanger with a recommendation letter from Governor Earl Warren, to enhance his cordial relations with state officials. Peckinpah collected extras from gymnasiums in Sacramento for the riot scene. Siegel later recalled, "Wanger said to me, 'Use Sam in any capacity.' . . . The Peckinpah name opened every door."

The door was not held open for long at Folsom Prison: at the request of the California Corrections Office and the command of Allied Artists, location shooting was to occupy no more than two weeks' time at Folsom Prison. Wanger also promised that the company would shoot as little as possible during the night. Finally, Wanger agreed that the script would "minimize all the scenes of the riot, state troopers and yard scenes." These proved difficult to handle, especially when, as Collins recalls, "the prisoners smashed together cans handed them for the scene so they were like little razors that were coming through the air."

While Collins continued polishing the script through early July, Wanger sought a director who could work quickly under such conditions. For all his guardedness about "Warner Bros." characteristics, Wanger on July 22 signed a graduate of that studio, forty-two-year-old Siegel, to direct the film during eight weeks' time for a flat $10,000 fee. A former assistant director, head of montage and second unit director at Warner Bros. (who worked on montage sequences in films such as *The Roaring Twenties* and *Passage to Marseilles*), Siegel had directed low-budget films for that studio, RKO, and Columbia. He had also directed several television pilots and series episodes.

Siegel has been praised and analyzed by countless auteur critics as a director of economical, unpretentious, and stylistically unobtrusive narratives concerning protagonists who are diametrically opposed to society or some social and bureaucratic organization. Yet this and the borderline control that the Siegel protagonist typically struggles to maintain is already present in the early drafts where Dunn is positioned between the forces of instinctual violence represented by Carney and intellectual calm embodied by the Colonel. Like other Siegel trademarks, such as the crosscut sequences of inmates and officials developing their tactics, these were already in the script before Siegel was hired.

This is not to suggest that Siegel made no significant contributions to the film. He and Collins got on well, and Collins welcomed Siegel's suggestions for giving the script a "sense of immediacy," for using inmates' actual vocabulary, and for elaborating Collins's takeover of one guard in cell block 11 into a sequence where several guards are overcome. Siegel also helped nail the troublesome ending into place. In the final shooting script dated August 5, 1953, they had Dunn and the warden talk quietly about Dunn's trial for leading the riot after the state legislature overrides the warden's promises of immunity. Where the warden is quite pessimistic about the future of prison reform, Dunn is hopeful and without bitterness. When the warden reports that the psychopath Carney has been sent to a mental health prison, Dunn says, "You weren't able to do that before the riot."

However, one week later, at Siegel's urging, Collins reversed the dialogue, giving Dunn's cautious optimism to the warden and the bitter lines of resignation to Dunn. Hence, Siegel heightened the irony of what John Belton has called, "defeat in victory," the reverse of John Ford's victory in defeat. The final shot of the film echoes the opening shot under the titles. It thus expresses visually the idea of that defeat, and questions, through its symmetry,

Warden Reynolds's claims that some good has come out of the riot or that anything has changed.

All in all, the qualities most admired and singled out in *Riot in Cell Block 11* are those of its script, and Siegel's unobtrusive style sustained Collins's unsentimental approach to the story. His efficient shooting methods relied heavily on long takes to accommodate the limited budget and the script's "realistic" orientation. Like previous prison-film directors, Siegel exploited the architecture of the abandoned cell block for expressive purposes: numerous medium shots of the metal cell doors among the massive stone walls convey the hardships of prison life. Siegel also integrated the convicts with the building by highlighting the shadows of metal stair meshing on Dunn and Carney as they huddle under a staircase for the opportune moment to overtake another guard and by having Dunn glower through the eye slots in his cell door before he is released. Similarly, Siegel's editing and framing in the opening scenes emphasize the convicts' threat, particularly when the last free guard in cell block 11 comes running down the central corridor in long shot and Carney suddenly drops down from *above* the frame to confront him.

Budgeted to be shot in seventeen days for $289,434, principal photography began August 17, with riot confrontation and mess hall scenes enacted by up to seven hundred prison inmates screened by their leaders (the Inmate Council), the warden, and the captains' guards. The film ran over schedule by only two days and over budget by just $8,805. The additional expense came from dubbing voice-over narration and shooting Dunn and the Colonel's conversation after the inmates' surrender. In postproduction, Wanger noted, "[Siegel] has behaved as if we were paying double salary ever since the picture closed and has been on the job heart and soul."

For all of Allied Artists' low-budget orientation, *Riot in Cell Block 11*'s reception was overwhelmingly favorable in both critical and financial terms. These reviews were the best Wanger had received in years. Critics duly noted the film's departures from the prison genre, and the approval of various academic and governmental officials didn't hurt. For example, *Variety* stated, "It has been some time since the market has had a real good prison melodrama of this voltage," and "the picture doesn't use formula prison plot. There's no inmate reformed by love or fair treatment, nor unbelievable boy-meets-girl gets-same angle. Nor are there any heroes and heavies of standard pattern."

The *New York Times, Time, Newsweek,* and the *New Yorker* all covered the film favorably. To the refined sensibilities of the *New Yorker,* the "unrelenting violence" of the film found justification in the plea for penal reform. *Newsweek* and *Time* praised the film lavishly, making a point of Wanger's personal history. For the former publication, the "message" component of the film was crystal clear, particularly the ending "which emphasizes the incredible slow pace of prison reform in the face of public indifference." The acting by

Brand, Meyer, and Faylen was "continuously fascinating" as were the action sequences. *Time* was no less generous in its praise: "The best prison movie produced in years," it began, highlighting its "semi-documentary" style, its cast, and its factual component. The review was followed by a brief account of Wanger's imprisonment and his hopes for reform.

Allied Artists hired an advertising specialist to coordinate its unprecedentedly high radio and television promotion budget ($350,000). Even so, Wanger exploited connections of his own to promote the film. A few weeks prior to its premiere, *Look* magazine, under Wanger's friend and Henry Luce's protégé Dana Tasker, published "West Points of the Underworld," in which Wanger reiterated the rhetorical points of the film, along with sidebars featuring the comments of McGee and Shaw on the sorry state of Western civilization's penal systems. The article, ostensibly on prisons, mentioned the film in its opening and closing paragraphs and was illustrated heavily with publicity stills of the film's location production. This was unheard-of promotion for a film from a studio that was typically ignored by journals of record and major newsweeklies. Wanger hoped in vain that the film would receive Academy Award nominations for original story, direction, or camerawork.

Wanger also was determined to have "as much as possible of the top brass interested in this picture so that it will really accomplish something." To this end, he kept in constant contact with former California governor and Supreme Court justice Warren, and future governor and attorney general Edmund Brown. Brown wrote Wanger that the film "certainly packs a wallop and will do a great deal to make people understand jails and penal institutions." Murrow was "deeply moved" by the film and called it "a first-rate job." Among the penal authorities, the film was well received. Austin MacCormick, while noting some reservations, wrote Wanger that he "was thrilled by it, and was held spellbound from beginning to end, as everyone in the theater seemed to be."

Wanger also arranged to screen the film at the Edinburgh Film Festival in the summer of 1954, where it was honored with a Diploma of Merit alongside *Salt of the Earth, The Caine Mutiny,* and the Academy Award winner of that year, Kazan's *On the Waterfront.* Due to Wanger's advance work, his personal publicity, and the special radio and television advertising campaign, the film grossed in excess of $1.5 million, producing a profit of nearly $300,000 by the end of its three-year distribution (of which $74,000 accrued to Wanger).

It would be difficult to argue that *Riot in Cell Block 11* had any direct effect on prison reform in California or the nation in the mid-1950s. But the film did enhance the prestige of Allied Artists and the careers of Collins, Siegel, and Wanger. The studio's continuing ambitions to upgrade its status were evident in the fall following *Riot*'s release, as Allied Artists went public with a stock offering. Equally impressive, the studio announced it had agreements with Wilder, Huston, Wyler, and Cooper for independent films. As

Walter Mirisch told the trade press, "Allied Artists now is definitely coming out of its transition, its plans are rapidly materializing and it is scheduling production to release top-caliber pictures one a month." The studio was spending more than $1 million on a single film for the first time in the 1950s, Mirisch's *The Warriors,* starring Flynn and shot in England in CinemaScope. It spent $3 million on Wyler's *Friendly Persuasion,* which, with Wilder's *Love in the Afternoon,* capped the studio's bid for first-run markets.

Meanwhile, Collins and Siegel confirmed with *Riot* their growing reputations, and they continued to work together intermittently during the rest of the decade. After *Riot,* Collins was hired for a Hecht-Hill-Lancaster project, *Until They Sail,* marking his entry into "A"-scale independent production for United Artists. Siegel directed *Annapolis Story,* a Technicolor special for Allied Artists, and *Private Hell 36* for Lupino and Howard Duff. By the end of 1954, he rejoined Wanger to direct *Invasion of the Body Snatchers.*

And Wanger had proven his mettle once again. "I went to lunch with Walter at Romanoff's and the Beverly Hills Hotel," Collins recalls, "and people wouldn't talk to Walter before *Riot in Cell Block 11* was produced. They wouldn't say hello. After *Riot* . . . people began greeting him again."

55. Oil tycoon Bruce Tanner (Lloyd Gough), Indian rancher Jim Redbird (Pedro Armendariz), and engineer Brad Brady (Robert Preston) all love oil entrepreneur Cherokee Lansing (Susan Hayward) in *Tulsa*.

56. *Reign of Terror*: Hero Charles D'Aubigny (Robert Cummings) and the evil Robespierre (Richard Basehart) size each other up in the torture chamber. Police Chief Fouché (Arnold Moss) had the best lines.

57. Ingrid Bergman in the thick of one of Victor Fleming's extensive battle sequences for *Joan of Arc*.

58. Partners in crime: Housewife and mother Lucia Harper (Joan Bennett) comforts her infatuated blackmailer Martin Donnelly (James Mason), seriously wounded after killing his ruthless friend in *The Reckless Moment*.

59. *The Reckless Moment*: Max Ophuls plans a tracking shot of Joan Bennett and James Mason, and then encourages Bennett to make her character's false confession of murder at the bus station.

60. The only footage produced by Walter Wanger International for the "Duchesse of Langeais" project was five minutes of silent test footage of Garbo, shot by James Wong Howe at the Chaplin studios.

61. Joan Bennett with two-year-old Shelley and eight-year-old Stephanie at the side entrance to Bennett's home on Mapleton Drive in Holmby Hills in 1950.

62. Wanger, Joan Bennett, her sister Barbara Randall (previously married to singer Morton Downey), and MCA agent Jennings Lang at El Morroco in mid-1951 in New York. Wanger's forced smile tells the story.

63. Wanger is comforted the night of the shooting by his former partner Eugene Frenke (at left) and attorney Jerry Geisler.

64. Wanger is frisked by
Deputy Sheriff James
Anderson as he checks in
at the Castaic Honor Farm
on June 6, 1952, for his
four-month sentence.

65. Screenwriter Richard Collins
in the 1950s.

66. Wanger and expert location cinematographer Russell Harlan pose for publicity at San Quentin during production on *Riot in Cell Block 11*.

67. Wanger with director Don Siegel on location for the massive confrontation between actual inmates and the national guard in *Riot in Cell Block 11*.

68. *Invasion of the Body Snatchers*: Wanger urged Don Siegel to pick up the pace of the scenes where the townspeople chase Miles (Kevin McCarthy) and Becky (Dana Wynter).

69. "I am not insane!" Miles (Kevin McCarthy) tells a doctor (Whit Bissell) in the prologue scene that Don Siegel deftly directed for *Invasion of the Body Snatchers*. Though Siegel disliked the framing device, Wanger was very much in favor of it.

70. Blindfolded Barbara Graham (Susan Hayward) is guided to the gas chamber by Father Devers (John Marley) in the powerful final minutes of *I Want to Live!*

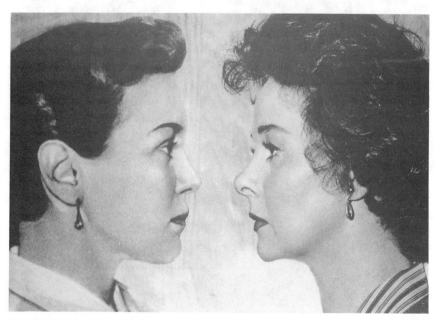

71. A United Artists' publicity collage of Barbara Graham and Susan Hayward for *I Want to Live!* Journalist Ed Montgomery thought their resemblance was striking.

72. "Like a General in the Marines that has to fight his way out of a trap": Wanger addresses the *Cleopatra* crew and some cast members at Cinecittà in the chilly winter months of 1962.

73. The grand procession into Rome, the scene that best exemplified the pageantry that Wanger had envisioned for *Cleopatra*.

74. Wanger and Joseph Mankiewicz remained friends after the production of *Cleopatra*, the film that ended Wanger's career.

75. In May 1966, Wanger received the Commendation of the Order of Merit, Italy's third-highest honor, from Consul General Alvaro V. Bettrani,"for your friendship and cooperation with the Italian government in all phases of the motion picture industry."

17

Invasion of the Body Snatchers (1956)

Wanger was anxious to build on the success of *Riot in Cell Block 11* and 1954 seemed to be the year to do it. The Internal Revenue Service audits finally ended. By mid-1954, distribution expert James Mulvey's Motion Picture Capital Corporation settled Wanger's debts from *Joan of Arc* and *The Reckless Moment*. This was important to Wanger, but something of a Pyrrhic victory:

> I have been able, by breaking my neck, to make a settlement with all of my creditors, so the bankruptcy was never adjudicated and I'm still what is laughingly referred to as a "free man." It's been a tough fight but one worthwhile, because I've always had a horrible feeling about bankruptcy and didn't want to go through it, although it would have been an easy way out and saved about three years of my time.

Indeed the lost time and other debts made Wanger more eager than ever to get to work. The profits from *Riot in Cell Block 11* had only gone to repay Allied Artists for salary advances dating back to his release from prison. He became impatient with the studio's delay in approving his projects:

> I am very grateful for all their past favors and like the association, as well as believing in the future of the company, but they are very smart fellows . . . how do they expect me to live until the pictures pay off and unless I have a program to produce and receive salary?

Just before signing a three-film contract in January 1955, Wanger proposed a unit program centered on Siegel to make several films yearly at a cost of $300,000 each. He felt that due to the fact that so many expensive spectacles are being made—many of them cumbersome and on the dull side—the exhibitors throughout the world are going to be clamoring for this line of goods. I base my calculations simply on the old supply-and-demand business methods.

Wanger outlined six possible projects. These included Adela Rogers St. Johns's 1920s stage hit *Take the Stand, Mrs. Langtry* and Wanger's unproduced script for "Yellowknife."

First and newest among the stories Wanger suggested was one "which everybody seems to like," *The Body Snatchers*. Jack Finney's novel concerned the infiltration of a small town by alien vegetables in the form of giant seed pods that assimilate the bodies of individual residents and absorb their minds while they sleep. Although taking its premise from science fiction, the story's vision of alienation and paranoia was more typical of the romantic strains in detective novels and Hollywood's films noir. In Finney's story, hero Miles Bennell's sense of alienation is the healthiest expression of individualism. His estrangement enables him to resist the pods and persuade them to leave.

Where Hitchcock's *Shadow of a Doubt* focused on one pathological murderer who comes to the small town from outside, *The Body Snatchers* showed an entire community corrupted and conspiring under the veneer of normality. This vision of village life had drawn on classic satires of provincial cruelty and parochialism crystallized by Sinclair Lewis's 1920 *Main Street*. Postwar novels and films continued the pessimistic visions of small town America, in which the opposition of individualism and conformity was increasingly common. From Capra's *It's a Wonderful Life* (1946) to James Jones and Minnelli's *Some Came Running* (1958), main street was a source of hypocritical oppression. Small towns also provided the locus of what critic Stuart Samuels identified as the primary anxieties of the 1950s: the fear of atomic annihilation, the discomfort of "a modern, urban, technologically bureaucratized society," and the fear of the "Red Menace" of Soviet communism. *Invasion of the Body Snatchers* embodied all three concerns.

When Wanger read the installments of Finney's novel from November to December 1954 in *Colliers*, he appreciated their general implications rather than a specific political allegory of a Communist threat. In the 1960s, Siegel admitted that he, screenwriter Daniel Mainwaring, and Wanger were interested in the "general state of mind" depicted in the film. Finney commented that "when people began seeing meanings which aren't really there, I think maybe some of the people concerned with the picture blushed modestly, and didn't deny." Collins, who scripted portions of the film, recalls that *Invasion of the Body Snatchers* was neither anti-Communist nor anti-anti-Communist: "It wasn't either of those things, believe me."

Finney later claimed that he crafted his novel for motion picture production, trying to create a tone and flow that would easily adapt to the screen.

But Wanger was shrewd in seeing its potential, and Allied Artists purchased the screen rights without competing bids from other studios. Yet *Invasion of the Body Snatchers* must have had a very personal appeal to him, for it paralleled Wanger's personal and professional experience of alienation. Moreover, Miles Bennell's stance against capitulation to the alien forces places him as the loner who is rejected by everyone but who is ultimately acting for everyone's benefit. In this regard, Miles resembles Wanger's own professional posture as the lone crusader who thinks only of Hollywood's best interest.

Following his idea of the low-budget unit, Wanger obtained Siegel as director at $21,688—double his salary on *Riot in Cell Block 11*. Siegel readily agreed to work with Wanger again. On the crime melodrama *Private Hell 36*, Siegel was "battling for every decision," whereas with Wanger, Siegel felt, "I had great authority, did whatever I wanted to do." Indeed, Siegel found Wanger to be "by far the most intelligent producer I have worked with in Hollywood." He once elaborated that Wanger "inspired me and he educated one . . . it was a very pleasurable experience working with him. He was always in there thinking, coming up with bright ideas."

When Collins proved unavailable, Siegel and Wanger chose Mainwaring, who had worked previously with Siegel for RKO on the caper-chase film *The Big Steal* (1949) and for Allied Artists on *Annapolis Story* and *The Phenix City Story*. Like Collins, Mainwaring, who sometimes wrote under the pseudonym Geoffrey Holmes, was what Siegel jokingly called a "member (nonpaying) of the older Communist League." For Wanger and Allied Artists, his talent and price were more important.

Director and writer set to work adapting Finney's novel in late December 1954. As Siegel later recalled, he and Mainwaring discussed with Wanger

> our attack on the story, what we wanted to say, the general style, arguing in particular that the pods' infiltration be presented "as normally as possible," with the characters refusing to believe the truth of the invasion until they were actually confronted with physical evidence.

This was a practical consideration of story construction as much as anything else, for as Siegel put it, once the heroes discovered the pods, "it was just an out-and-out chase" well suited to the action emphasis of Allied Artists product. As with Collins's work on *Riot in Cell Block 11*, Mainwaring's writing, in Belton's words, "provides Siegel with a psychological background for his largely physical foreground of chases and action sequences." Wanger was quite content with Finney's narrative and Siegel and Mainwaring's treatment of it; he had few significant suggestions for story events, characters, or details of mise-en-scène.

Siegel and Mainwaring talked at length about each sequence, after which Mainwaring wrote and revised them. Mainwaring was the key link between

Invasion of the Body Snatchers and the rich film noir ethos. With his story and screenplay for *Out of the Past* (RKO, 1947), Mainwaring had formulated a pessimistic scenario of a compromised protagonist struggling futilely against overwhelming odds. This type of story was compatible with what Vivian Sobchack has identified as the predominant logic of low-budget science fiction films such as *It Came from Outer Space* (1953) and *Them* (1954), as opposed to the optimism of big-budget productions like 1950's *Destination Moon*.

In adapting Finney's book, Mainwaring and Siegel not only eliminated the novel's motif of nostalgia for pre–World War II life but made two major alterations in the action. In the novel Becky and Jack and Teddy Belicec help Miles resist the pods until they leave, but Mainwaring and Siegel had all the characters except Miles succumb to the takeover. And where Finney's hero triumphs over the pods, Mainwaring and Siegel's conclusion is more pessimistic as only Bennell is able to escape to a skeptical world.

Yet another significant shift in the process of adaptation concerned its ideological subtext. Finney has maintained that his book was not "a cold war novel, or a metaphor for anything. I wrote it to entertain its readers, nothing more." Yet capitalist values inform the novel: the most generalized symptoms of the invasion are neglect of personal property—front lawns gone to seed, contrary to what Finney naturalizes as "the endless urge to change and improve that marks the human race"—and the slackening of local business activity (the store beneath Miles's office is unrented and poorly maintained). The handout of pods to nearby towns and counties takes place on the town square, a parody of a "bargain jubilee" flea market, where medallions no longer signify boosterism but membership in the pod takeover.

Although Finney's novel suggests that "podism" leads to neglectful entrepreneurship, the film (with the exception of the Grimaldi's run-down vegetable stand) explicitly emphasized its emotional and moral effects. This is crystallized in Miles's evocative statement to Becky: "In my practice I see how people have allowed their humanity to drain away. . . . Only when we have to fight to stay human do we realize how precious it is." And in another speech without precedent in the novel, psychiatrist Danny Kaufman tells Miles and Becky, "Love. Desire. Ambition. Faith. Without them life's so simple, believe me." Actually, these dialogue exchanges were drafted by Collins, who Wanger and Siegel hired in March 1955 during principal photography. *Secret Beyond the Door* screenwriter Richards proposed the equation of the pod takeover and the embrace of conformity to Collins. He recalls that she suggested to him, "Why don't you go at it from the standpoint that these pods are really what's happening to people today?"

But the additional dialogue did not clarify the blurry sense of personal accountability in Finney's book. Critic Glen Johnson has analyzed how the author's "us versus them" scenario "fuzzes the central issue of responsibility for the characters' loss of aspirations and of love" and externalizes the cause for the pods' takeover. In the novel, the voluntary abdication of responsibility takes diverse forms, from using technology for "refining the humanity out of our lives" to the social pressures to get married which Miles struggles against. Although Mainwaring's script retains this conception of external evil, it frequently shows characters yearning for the oblivion of pod-existence, particularly through the comforts of cigarettes and alcohol, from Miles's "very dry" martini at the Skyview Terrace to the constant drinking thereafter.

Siegel and Mainwaring structured the action in effective ways. They eliminated Finney's expressive but unwieldy comparisons between the pods and the town's African-American shoeshine man, and between Santa Mira and the liberated towns of Italy in World War II. The alternation of days and night scenes underline the mystery component of the narrative: Miles, Becky, Jack, and Teddy discover increasing evidence of the pod invasion at night in darkly lit spaces such as Jack's game room, the basement of Becky's house, and Miles's greenhouse. But once the pods have taken over the town, other pods are allocated to nearby towns on a Sunday morning in the town square. The pods chase Becky and Miles into the hills in broad daylight, and the film ends at night, when Becky is taken over and Miles flees to the highway. Similarly, the pursuit of Miles and Becky leads them into progressively smaller hiding spaces, from Miles's office closet to the pit in the ground of the cave.

Mainwaring was able to complete a first draft on February 10, within six weeks of being hired at the studio, and Wanger ignored once more the Production Code Administration warnings about the script. Besides Danny Kaufman's explicit dialogue about how to commit murder with an ice pick, Geoffrey Shurlock found reprehensible the fact that Becky and Miles are both divorced. "There seems to be no particular story point involved," Shurlock wrote Allied Artists on February 21, and on three additional occasions thereafter he urged the studio to change this detail of characterization. Shurlock proved prophetic when the Legion of Decency awarded the completed film a "B" rating, objectionable in part, for its "light treatment of marriage." But as Johnson has pointed out, the divorced status of Miles and Becky in the novel is a moral failure and reflects concern about the decline of the family in the 1950s. In the film, their divorce substantiates Danny Kaufman's claims that love never lasts; but it also becomes a sign of their moral integrity. Miles and Becky are emotionally aware individuals who have the courage to resist the oppressive routine of a failing marriage.

While Mainwaring developed the script, Wanger and Siegel consulted with art director Ted Haworth. Haworth was a fortunate "catch." Although he would later design elaborate sets for Wilder's *Some Like It Hot* (1959) and *The Longest Day* (1962), Richard Brooks's *The Professionals* (1966), several films by Peckinpah, and Siegel's own *The Beguiled* (1970), in 1955 he was an expert in unpretentious realism, designing sets for Hitchcock's *Strangers on a*

Train and *I Confess* and that year's Academy Award–winning *Marty*. Scouting locations for *Invasion of the Body Snatchers* in early January, Haworth and Siegel selected the Los Angeles suburb Sierra Madre after briefly considering Finney's own town, Mill Valley.

Siegel and Wanger also began discussing a cast for the film. Although Wanger had his eye on actors such as Joseph Cotten, Vera Miles, Donna Reed, and Kim Hunter, Allied Artists' budget limit of $382,000 dictated otherwise. Wanger rationalized that new faces would not only be economical for the film, but would enhance its effect: "especially as the kind of names that are available for a moderate price picture [such as Macdonald Carey, Steve Cochran or John Hodiak, all of whom had appeared in studio films] are, in my opinion, simply a Class B identification rather than a box office attraction." When Richard Kiley, who had recently appeared in Allied Artists' *The Phenix City Story,* turned down the role of Miles, Kevin McCarthy accepted a salary of $2,500 a week. The brother of author Mary McCarthy, he achieved notable success at the time, having recently portrayed the adolescent older brother Biff in the British touring company, as well as the film version, of Arthur Miller's *Death of a Salesman;* he had also starred in *Annapolis Story*.

The rest of the cast were Hollywood talents. Carolyn Jones, who played Teddy Belicec, is best known as Morticia on *The Addams Family;* in 1955, she was a Paramount contractee and a television series veteran (most prominently in *Dragnet*). King Donovan, as Teddy Belicec's husband Jack, was an Allied Artists character actor. Opposite McCarthy in the role of Becky was British actress Dana Wynter, whom Twentieth Century–Fox had recently put under contract. Her first major role for Fox, as Richard Egan's high school sweetheart in *The View from Pompey's Head,* resembled that of Becky Driscoll. Wynter subsequently married Wanger's attorney Greg Bautzer.

Though the cast had minimal time to develop characterizations and could not perfect its performances in single takes, the actors portrayed the diverse characters admirably and sometimes under uncomfortable production circumstances. Principal photography on *Invasion of the Body Snatchers* began March 23 with five days of exterior shooting in Sierre Madre. Siegel shot other scenes in and around Los Angeles before returning to the Allied Artists studio. For the lengthy chase sequence near the end of the film, the crew moved on April 7 to Mulholland Drive in the hills northeast of the city (an ordeal the cast and crew called "the battle of Mulholland"). For Miles's climactic scene on the highway, Siegel surrounded McCarthy with expert stunt drivers among whom the actor weaved and bobbed like a deranged man.

The film's low-cost ($3,000) special effects were another hardship for the cast. Ten pods were made of rubber for flexibility during the transformations, including the three for Jack, Miles, and Becky; the remainder were made of plastic. Their manufacture required the actors to lie within a mold, with straws through their nose and mouth to breathe. According to Wynter, the crew set

Jones into her mold and, knowing well her claustrophobia, told her they were breaking for lunch. According to Siegel, Wynter herself was the victim of a practical joke when the crew snuck a pod into the bathroom of her dressing room and watched with amusement when she came running out.

Siegel's shooting and editing strategies worked around the low-budget effects. During the crucial scene of the barbecue at Miles's house when the four main characters confront their pods, Siegel used editing to disguise the improvised special effects. By intercutting reaction shots of Miles, Becky, Jack, and Teddy, the soap bubbles foaming over the pods were not as noticeable. The bursting of the bubbles was shot in slow motion; the bubbles then were processed in reverse to create the effect of forming faces.

Siegel and cinematographer Ellsworth Fredericks used low-key lighting and heavy shadows to visually match Mainwaring's film noir tale. They also chose camera angles and placement for expressive effects. Low-angled shots of Miles in calm authority at the beginning of the film were contrasted with canted angles on his discovery of pods in the greenhouse and on his desperate scene on the highway. Miles and Becky's chatty, blithe descent on the staircase in Miles's office building upon their first reunion is echoed as they later descend the stairs, preparing to act like pods after overcoming Jack and Danny in Miles's office.

Finally, Siegel's camerawork both highlighted the script's oppositions of conformity and individuality and provided greater economy and efficiency in production. Major discoveries, such as the body on Jack's pool table and the pods in Miles's greenhouse, are shot in deep focus. This choice enhances the suspense of seeing characters and their doubles in the same frame, a strategy that is particularly effective when Jack's double awakens on the pool table while Jack sleeps at the bar in the background. Long takes here and in the first scene between Becky and Miles on the sidewalk outside Miles's office visually reinforce their compatibility; by contrast, scenes with pods—such as Jack and Danny in Miles's office, or even Becky herself after she is taken over—are edited in shot-countershot patterns.

Siegel's efficiency was once again evident when principal photography was completed in twenty-three days by April 18. After another month of postproduction work with studio producer Richard Heermance, Siegel told Wanger he felt the film "for what it is and for what has been put in it. . . . is about as good as we could hope it to be." He had a wide range of suggestions for polishing the editing and restoring continuity and rhythm, many of which were followed up on by Heermance. Wanger also made suggestions for fine-tuning. As with *Riot in Cell Block 11,* these concerned a more vivid depiction of the forces conspiring against the individuals—more scenes that could be crosscut into the film showing the pods (Cousin Wilma, the chief of police) conspiring to capture Miles and Becky. He also urged picking up the pace for the climactic chase scenes, which he felt, looked more like a "cross country relay." Such ideas greatly enhanced the film's tension.

The studio immediately recognized the quality of Siegel's work. Viewing a rough cut on June 10, John Flinn, the company's head of publicity, sent a memo to all company distribution exchanges, proclaiming the film a "sure fire box office winner. . . . that should equal or surpass the results of 'Riot.'" Flinn's publicity newsletter for the film in the summer of 1955 had compared the film to the evocative horror films of Val Lewton, Carol Reed's *Dead of Night,* and Carl Dreyer's *Vampyr.* Following its customary desire to get films in distribution as soon as possible, the studio set a release date for September.

It was in perfecting the film's cut that Wanger and Siegel ran into trouble. Siegel has recounted many times that Allied Artists executives imposed a prologue and epilogue on the film. In the prologue, a panicked, sweaty Miles is interviewed in the emergency room of a hospital. In the epilogue, his story is corroborated by a reported accident with a truck carrying pods. The film ends as the doctors contact the FBI. In Siegel's words:

> In addition they forced me, against Mr. Wanger's desire, to shoot a prologue and an epilogue. I resisted shooting this mish-mash as long as I could until they threatened to have one of the janitors shoot it if I refused. In Mr. Wanger's and in my version the last shot of the picture, the very last shot of the picture, was a close shot of Kevin McCarthy pointing his finger directly at the audience, screaming at the top of his lungs, "You're next!" At that moment the picture abruptly and very dramatically ended.

In fact, the attempt to impose a frame story on *Invasion of the Body Snatchers* was not an "us versus them" conflict. In his memos to Wanger, Siegel objected to the framing story but without vehemence. Wanger no doubt assured Siegel that he agreed with him in the name of diplomacy and to ensure that Siegel might work with him again. But, as at Diana Productions ten years earlier, the producer himself took an intermediate stance between the director and the studio hierarchy, and as with Ford's *The Long Voyage Home,* he wanted to temper the film's provocative qualities with forewords and afterwords. The interminable debate over the issue delayed the film's release until early 1956 and added $30,000, nearly 10 percent, to its negative cost.

Allied Artists executives, Wanger, and Siegel all agreed that the film should "prepare and forewarn our audience that something exciting, something impossible, strange and horrible, is going to happen." In their view, the encounter with Jimmy Grimaldi, running away from his mother in front of Miles's car, was not "warning" enough. No doubt, such considerations guided the heavy-handed use of Carmen Dragon's ominous score at various points of major discovery (although Dragon's music also is used to undercut Miles and Becky's pleasant scenes of domesticity). At Wanger's request, in late May

McCarthy dubbed several lines of dialogue in New York, such as Miles's concluding yells on the freeway ("You're next!") and a first-person narration from Finney's book that Miles begins over his arrival at the train station.

With the added introductory and concluding material incorporated into the film, Broidy and the other executives attended a screening. As Wanger described it months later: "When we left the projection room . . . everybody was elated with the picture, and thought it was a great thriller, with the exception of the possibility that the end was too abrupt and not clear and that there should be something done about that."

Several additional previews of the film in late June and early July in Westwood, Encino, and Long Beach proved the remarkable power of the ending in which McCarthy screams for help. As Siegel described the response:

> When the lights came up everyone looked nervously at his immediate neighbor at either side of him and wondered uneasily if he were surrounded by pods. A really sensationally original ending for a film.

Art director Haworth attended the Encino showing on July 1 and wrote Wanger that the film was comparable to *Marty* in its spontaneous effect on the audience; only here the emotions were incredible awe, fright, and tension. "I heard 'Jesus' over and over and over. Also, 'Mother, Mother, I'm scared,' and a hundred other varieties of great reactions." He concluded:

> I have never worked on a suspense film that generated an audience fever like this. They were scared, and they resented it because they were shamed by their own obvious cowardice . . . but would have hated it more if it were an anticipated "all's well that ends well." I could name a thousand reasons for not changing this in any radical way.

Yet, even after the first preview, Wanger remained concerned about orienting the audience for the unusual story. He drafted a hysterical monologue for Miles's secretary Sally and a meandering speech for Danny comparing "our lack of intestinal fortitude" with the fallen Roman empire. Fortunately, neither one was used.

Most significantly, Wanger toyed with the idea of a prologue for the film. After the June 30 preview, he felt that the point of the story was missing. Near the end of Finney's novel, Miles invokes an analogy between his fight against the pods and the anti-Axis struggle of World War II, recalling Churchill's celebrated speech, "We will fight them in the streets, we shall fight them in the hills; we shall never surrender." During the summer of 1955, Wanger planned to use an excerpt from a Churchill speech he had read just before principal photography got underway ("never flinch, never weary, never despair"), but Churchill refused permission.

Wanger considered other possibilities. He became enthused over the idea of a one-minute opening statement of authenticity, such as those in *Eagle Squadron* and *Riot in Cell Block 11*. The idea was to hire a media celebrity associated with either science fiction or broadcast journalism, or preferably both, to deliver a prologue on camera. His first choice was for Welles to link the film to the *War of the Worlds* radio broadcast in a prologue that could also be used in trailers for Wanger's film. Welles could also be used to soften the ending of the film on the highway, easing the audience from the anguish of the film's final scene. In mid-June, Wanger contacted Welles in England, who wanted £10,000 for the chore and then left for the south of France, where he remained incommunicado. Wanger pursued him for three months.

Wanger also considered through September the possibility of other announcers: Murrow, television news host John Cameron Swayze, Lowell Thomas, or Quentin Reynolds. Wanger felt Murrow might be willing to interview Miles using his technique from "Person to Person," Murrow's famous talk show in which celebrities invited CBS cameras into their homes. Wanger felt if the prologue showed Murrow "bringing in his equipment, into a dark room, where Dr. Bennell is recovering from the shock, and commence as if he had been covering the Santa Mira mystery," it would be "a stunning thing to use."

Wanger was equally concerned about the closing. He wanted audiences to understand that Miles is determined to stop the pods because he lost Becky; but he equivocated about how to portray the results of Miles's efforts:

> If the truck [full of pods] is eliminated, and we give the impression that his warning gets over, it'll be much easier for the audience to absorb the idea that he was successful in reaching the outside world before the malignant cancer had spread too far. On the other hand, it must be considered that this [the truck] is quite a shock, and from the horror standpoint makes it a more terrifying picture.

If Murrow participated, he could note at the end of the film that "as long as people believed in faith, decency, and the dignity of man, the world would be safe—or some such thing."

Wanger was unable to secure the participation of any of the prominent journalists he had mentioned. But he established the principle of a need for a prologue and epilogue; in fact, it was a short step from the Murrow "Person to Person" format to the framing scenes in which Miles reports the pods to the authorities in the hospital. The definite decision to use a framing action came after an unhappy preview at the Bay Theater in Encino on August 25. People walked out in groups of four and six. There were unwanted laughs in isolated scenes. Wanger denigrated the film's "sharp, so-called 'B' cutting." He was well aware of the irony of his situation: he alone had doubts about the film's effectiveness when other executives declared themselves satisfied; this latest preview had created what he called a feeling of "panic."

Henceforth, the entire issue of a prologue and epilogue became of primary concern to studio executives. Mainwaring came back to draft the opening and closing scenes and connecting narrating material, and Siegel shot them in September. Although *Invasion of the Body Snatchers* would have been a powerful film without the frame, the opening segment with shots of the police car racing to the hospital and Miles's dramatic scene with the doctors fulfills the low-budget exploitation film's dictum to bombard the audience with action and explain later. As Johnson suggests, the prologue casts doubt on Miles's entire narration by showing his wildly desperate behavior. The epilogue lacked the confrontational shock that Haworth noted was so effective in preview, as it showed the hospital doctors calling the FBI. But Siegel, by portraying Miles anguished and without Becky as he leans back exhausted against a doorway, compromises the reassuring closure. Here again was the "defeat in triumph" that had characterized the ending of *Riot in Cell Block 11*. Siegel himself told Wanger on the twenty-first of September that the frame had "helped" the film. "The rest," he concluded, "is up to you."

Actually, the rest was up to Allied Artists. In late September, Wanger discussed titles with Walter Mirisch, and his proposals lend some insight into his conception of the film. Rejecting Siegel's suggested titles such as "Sleep No More" and "Better Off Dead," Wanger also objected to the studio's proposal, "They Came from Another World." "It puts us in a class with B science fiction pictures." Wanger felt the film's grosses could be enhanced if the film were classified as "something beyond Science Fiction and suspense with a real idea":

> The pod idea and the conformity idea are something that can be exploited and sold. I discussed this with John Flinn and I would be happy to go out on the road and help sell the picture and believe it could become important along these lines, but you cannot sell They Came from Another World.

He proposed a "stunning campaign" with accessories "like buttons saying 'I don't want to be a pod' or 'Are you a pod?'"

But having said his piece for promoting the film as a message movie, Wanger departed for New York to look into other projects and left the decisions entirely in the studio executives' hands. The title "Invasion of the Body Snatchers" was definitely agreed upon by the executives and the sales department on November 23. Wanger's objections to "sharp, so-called B-cutting" went unheeded. In December he protested, "in the interests of commerce and box office returns, not on the basis of an artistic complaint," the studio's decision to release the film in SuperScope. This was an anamorphic process developed by RKO which, unlike CinemaScope, squeezed an ordinary image at the printing stage rather than the shooting stage of production. Predicting that the "dupey" image quality would destroy Wynter's appeal and that a recent series of inferior CinemaScope films would only hurt their ticket sales, Wanger warned that it would be a "costly misadventure." Allied Artists went ahead anyway.

Wanger's decision to withdraw from active engagement with the film is consistent with his trademark casual management style. But given his recognition of its potential status as a "message movie," his behavior is perplexing. Although Allied Artists had financed the production of *Invasion of the Body Snatchers,* Wanger took out a loan for two-thirds of its negative cost in May during postproduction in order to obtain a greater profit share in the new film (the credits accordingly read "Walter Wanger Pictures, Inc. presents"). His financial risk, as well as his desire to move back into the ranks of the majors, makes his passive posture on the film seem puzzling.

But, as always, Wanger was thinking of his future. Various plans to work outside the studio, such as a Tony Curtis–Janet Leigh orientalist film at Columbia, had fallen through. There remained his three-picture deal with Allied Artists, of which *Invasion of the Body Snatchers* was only the first. The more films he could make, the more income he could generate on his $800-a-week salary. In April 1955, he had hired Collins to work on "Adventures in Politics," an optimistic account of an American senator's education in the ways of Congress, based on the career of Oregon's Richard L. Neuberger. As Wanger noted, "The human side of this has rarely been emphasized, particularly as it concerns women and their role in the process." The script was never completed, however.

More promising was "Underworld U.S.A.," a story he felt portrayed "the acceptance of corruption in the United States today, and how it is subverting us beyond all other influences." He persuaded the terminally ill Bogart, a good friend since *Stand-In,* to coproduce it through his independent Santana company for Allied Artists. Wanger got as far as visiting Bogart with Mirisch to discuss the project. Mirisch could see that Bogart was seriously ill with cancer and that the project would never be realized with him. When he told Wanger this, Wanger replied, "But he likes to be involved. He needs to have something to look forward to. And who knows—he may recover." Unfortunately, Bogart did not.

Yet another project was "Mother, Sir!", a mildly humorous account of a navy official's wife who incautiously introduces a Pandora's box of women's freedom to a small Japanese town. Wanger conceived this vehicle for Bennett partly as a penance for her inactivity since the Lang incident. He pushed the project daily, citing the success of Twentieth Century–Fox's 1955 blockbuster *The King and I,* but the sensibly reluctant Allied Artists executives gave him the runaround while *Invasion of the Body Snatchers* was shooting. Wanger hoped to produce the film in Japan and then to follow it with another Garbo film on the last Chinese Empress, Tzu Hsi.

The Garbo idea never got off the ground, and *Navy Wife,* shot at Republic studios, proved entirely mediocre. Cast with Gary Merill and Shirley Yama-guchi, the film was a talky situation comedy that exploited misunderstandings between Americans and Japanese. As several studio employees predicted, it sank into well-deserved oblivion. But as "a chance to get Joan moving again and help the whole situation immeasurably," the film was uppermost on Wanger's mind as he discussed the prologue and epilogue to *Invasion of the Body Snatchers* with the studio.

The limited distribution and press coverage of *Invasion of the Body Snatchers* were an enormous disappointment after the acclaim that greeted *Riot in Cell Block 11*. Not a single Broadway theater would book it for a first run. Those papers that did review the film—the *Los Angeles Examiner* and the trade press—had nothing but praise for its style and its significance. The reviewer for the *Examiner* pointed out the film's suggestion that "maybe, in these hectic times, we have subconsciously been hoping for some . . . escape from worry and fear." Trade press reviewers consistently noted Wanger's touch in the message of the movie. *Variety* credited him for introducing "an element of timely philosophy into this science fiction drama"; *Motion Picture Herald* used the film as an occasion to state that Wanger's career "embraces the production of smash hits in just about every content category." The London popular press was even more enthusiastic. Wanger felt that "the British seem to understand me so much better than the Americans. . . . Why nobody wrote that way over here, I don't know."

Wanger implored the *New York Times* reviewer Crowther to screen the film in May of 1956, after complimenting the critic on a recent think piece on the cycle of monster movies:

> I tried to make it a plea against conformity, and apparently the exhibitor didn't think it was right to have an idea in a picture of this sort, and instead of a Broadway showing, it opened in Brooklyn. . . . No doubt you will see what I'm after in this picture, and apparently the public agrees with us. However, the ever-loving, complaining distributor and exhibitor has missed the chance to really exploit this picture. It's definitely an exploitation picture which they didn't exploit, which is not inconsistent."

Crowther did not gratify Wanger with a review, and the film was slow to recover its costs. Wanger's bank loan was for nought. Yet by 1959, the film was establishing its cult status with television syndication.

With his other film projects stymied, Wanger also made a second concerted effort to work in television. He welcomed the medium and was delighted with the first broadcast of the Academy Awards ceremony in 1958 as "something many of us dreamed of" in the 1940s. He told Crowther that making movies "is more and more comparable to producing plays for Broadway":

Television is killing what amounted to "the road" for movies, just as talking movies killed the road for the legitimate plays. So we are having to produce our pictures for what amount to very selective first runs and hope they will be hits in that area. If they are, we make a lot of money with them. If they aren't we lose darn near the whole investment, just as they do with unfortunate plays.

Wanger had been long enamored with pay-television, which he felt would be "a dream," especially to the independent producer who needed immediate reimbursement for production costs. He became a board director for a closed-circuit, large-screen system called Box Office Television that the Sheraton Hotel chain was developing. But two years after Wanger joined the company, it dissolved, and its technology was acquired by Teleprompter.

Hence by early 1956, Wanger's recovery seemed to reach a plateau. He was on the verge of renewing his contract with Allied Artists, when instead he switched and signed a six-picture, three-year contract with RKO at double his Allied Artists salary with a profit share of 20 percent. Purchased from Hughes by the General Tire and Rubber Company and General Teleradio, the studio was reactivated in September 1955 under producer Dozier. With the $15.2 million proceeds of its historic sale of pre-1948 films for limited television syndication, Dozier in January 1956 began a Ginger Rogers vehicle, *The First Traveling Saleslady,* and planned thirty films (including Fritz Lang's *While the City Sleeps* and *Beyond a Reasonable Doubt*), half of which would be from independents such as Selznick and Wanger.

Wanger pushed several projects. The most poignant one was Lasky's "The Big Brass Band," a story of high school musicians which Lasky himself was powerless to develop because a government lawsuit for back taxes had tied up all his assets. Then coauthoring his autobiography to garner badly needed funds, Lasky wrote Wanger,

I need a last chapter for my book. What a great chapter it would make if the Walter Wanger, who became my assistant in 1918 (I forget the exact year for the moment) could be the means of making it possible for me to put on the screen my last, and it could easily be our most popular picture.

Wanger shopped the project to RKO and NBC, without success. Wanger himself planned to produce "Underworld U.S.A." and "Underdog," a gangster story by W. R. Burnett, concerning an ex-serviceman who falls into illegal activities when he can't readjust to domestic life.

Then something happened that no one could have predicted. Wanger, now sixty-one years old, suffered a heart attack in April. He was incapacitated for several weeks, and Dozier assigned "Underworld U.S.A.," still lacking a shootable script, to another producer, to be directed eventually by Samuel Fuller. By the time Wanger recovered, he had lost his momentum with RKO. This was fortunate, for RKO was gone by 1957. Its production facilities were sold to Lucille Ball and Desi Arnaz to become Desilu Studios.

By August 1956, Wanger had left Allied Artists for good. His timing was fortuitous. The studio's bid for prestige ended with Wyler's *Friendly Persuasion* and Wilder's *Love in the Afternoon*. Wanger had few regrets about ending the association. When Heermance informed Wanger that the studio was reviving his proposal for "Queen of the Universe" that fall, Wanger joked, "I might be able to give you some unusual and expensive ideas which you can reject." Yet, the "B" studio was where Wanger made his recovery. As Walter Mirisch put it, "I always felt that Walter 'got well' while he was with us."

18

I Want to Live! (1958)

Wanger's new partner in September 1956 was one of his oldest acquaintances: Joseph L. Mankiewicz. After a distinguished career at MGM as a writer-producer, supervising many of the studio's most memorable films such as *Fury, Three Comrades* (1938), and *The Philadelphia Story* (1940), Mankiewicz directed his own scripts at Twentieth Century–Fox beginning in 1945. With *A Letter to Three Wives* (1949) and *All About Eve* (1950), he earned writing and directing Academy Awards two years in a row.

In 1951, Mankiewicz moved to New York, shunning Hollywood at the peak of his career. Three years later, he formed an independent company, Figaro, to produce for United Artists release. The NBC television network took a half-ownership in the company, wanting the right of first refusal for any show proposals. Figaro was set up by attorney Bienstock and Mankiewicz's agent Bert Allenberg. The company was managed by Robert Lantz, a German protégé of Allenberg's with whom Mankiewicz became friends in England during World War II.

Mankiewicz planned to produce four films over three years' time, but by mid-1956, he had completed only *The Barefoot Contessa* and had one film in preparation, *The Quiet American*. He asked Wanger that summer to work at Figaro, completely unaware of his success at Allied Artists. Wanger appreciated the invitation:

> Joe is a very sentimental and affectionate man and he's never gotten over the fact that I sent [his brother] Herman out here and protected Herman for many years . . . and he's always felt sort of an obligation to me for some reason or other.

But Mankiewicz also expected Wanger to be a "West Coast Figaro." Wanger later recalled how he, Allenberg, and Lantz "stressed enormously that among the things they wanted me for were ideas, my contacts and my planning." His salary terms at Figaro were only a slight improvement over Allied Artists: $25,000 for each film he produced, but without a profit share.

With characteristic enthusiasm, Wanger was soon overwhelming Figaro with ideas and proposals—to promote *The Quiet American* for snob appeal, like Olivier's *Henry V,* and for film projects such as *West Side Story* and Ian Fleming's *From Russia with Love* (this, five years before the first James Bond film, *Dr. No,* was produced). Within a month of signing on, Wanger had proposed several "spectaculars" for television, such as an all-black musical version of *The Pilgrim's Progress* (starring such performers as Harry Belafonte, Sammy Davis, Jr., Pearl Bailey, and Ella Fitzgerald, and a soundtrack album that NBC could market through RCA records. Figaro turned them down.

Besides offering an entrée into network television, Figaro was promising because it enabled Wanger to participate in the independent production boom on an "A" scale for the first time in nearly a decade. In 1951, Krim, Benjamin, and Youngstein, his former antagonists at Eagle-Lion, took over the failing United Artists. Within four years they converted a $100,000 weekly loss into an industry leader (most dramatically with their $55 million gross in 1955).

One reason United Artists succeeded so dramatically was Krim, Benjamin, and Youngstein's ability to reorganize the company in accordance with a major shift in the studios' mode of production. After World War II, as Hollywood produced increasingly fewer films, major production companies gradually employed the package-unit system, whereby stars, directors, producers, scripts, technicians, and facilities were combined for a single film, usually produced by semi-independents. Selznick had packaged several Hitchcock films in the 1940s. While on long-term contract with Universal, Eagle-Lion, and Allied Artists, Wanger had only dabbled with this system. *The Reckless Moment* was a one-time film package, although Columbia insisted that Wanger employ Columbia's own technicians and facilities. *Joan of Arc* was an exemplary package-unit production, since Wanger assembled the above-the-line talents and technicians not from any one studio but from the talent pool of the entire industry. After 1951 and following the same logic, United Artists, which owned no studios, sponsored package films shot anywhere in Hollywood or around the world.

The United Artists executives succeeded as well because they built on their experiences at Eagle-Lion, particularly their perennial shortage of cash. They decided to take the then unheard-of step of completely financing semi-independent producers under nonexclusive contracts, advancing negative costs, arranging bank loans, and giving producers a considerable profit participation. Krim and company could inaugurate this system in part because of flexible bank loan policies that recognized the film-by-film basis of package-unit production. In short, United Artists eliminated most of the business obstacles, and especially the risks, that Wanger had struggled with as a semi-independent since 1934.

In return for its services, United Artists obtained distribution rights, collected a distribution fee, recovered its outlays from film grosses, and shared profits, if any, with the independent company. With such innovations, United Artists had set an example for all of the major producer-distributors who by 1957, hosted semi-independent units, albeit with differing degrees of autonomy.

United Artists offered their producers the most. As one associate put it, "Once they have agreed to finance you, and the script is okayed, they leave you completely alone until you deliver the negative." Trading on the package-unit system, United Artists policy facilitated many progressive long-term trends in Hollywood of the 1950s—such as a major revision of the Production Code after Otto Preminger's quarrel with the PCA over *The Moon Is Blue* and *The Man with the Golden Arm* as well as the gradual end of blacklisting. Hence the United Artists innovations helped to eliminate many of the institutional constraints on Wanger's past productions.

Wanger's near-bankruptcy, indebtedness, and IRS audits had so incapacitated him that he could not work in the United Artists mold. Yet Wanger remained a champion of independent production, perceiving that the independents produced a cinema of ideas, evident in Sam Spiegel's *Bridge over the River Kwai* (on the futility of war), in Fonda and Reginald Rose's *Twelve Angry Men,* and in Wald's treatment of small-town hypocrisy in *Peyton Place.* To him, the independents were comparable to the Theatre Guild, whose innovative creativity provoked audiences and defied the Shuberts and the Theatrical Syndicate in the teens.

But Wanger returned to "A"-scale independence in the 1950s like Rip Van Winkle, discovering that United Artists' approach to preproduction planning had changed in his absence and that his resources were inadequate. Without his Figaro contract, Wanger would not have been able to work with United Artists, but without his friendship with Susan Hayward, he would never have produced a single film.

Wanger had always been a creature of the vertically integrated studios, and he thrived when a studio plant with enormous overhead and stars under contract encouraged him to put the most nebulous ideas into production so that theaters would have something to show their patrons. With fewer films now in production, ideas were no longer enough, as Wanger discovered in March 1957 when he proposed a Hitchcock-style project entitled "The St. Moritz Affair" for Rita Hayworth and director Charles Vidor. "We have only the idea for [the film] and have so far no story line," Wanger wrote Allenberg. The idea was for "another picture of the type that Rita Hayworth should be in, a la

'Trapeze' or 'Gilda,' with a bit of 'Foreign Correspondent' and 'To Catch a Thief' thrown in." Small details like the story line "could be secured quickly if a deal can be put together. This, of course, like everything else, requires your magic wand." Wanger's choice of language is eloquent: he regarded putting together a package as a kind of sorcery.

Indeed, Wanger wistfully compared current production methods with Paramount's practices in the 1920s. He felt the studio and semi-independent producers should develop "the 'avant-garde' picture and the smaller picture that should be developing new talent and giving opportunities to new writers, new directors, new actors, new producers." The chief barrier to incubating talent and experimentation, in his view, was the prestidigitating agent. For a former studio production head who relied on his personality to cajole talents into work, the agent was a galling go-between who only denied Wanger access to stars, as had happened with Garbo in early 1950. His personal feelings of persecution at MCA's hands only strengthened this conviction. In fact, the Jennings Lang shooting itself was highly symbolic. "You chaps just talk about agents," Wanger once quipped to a group of Twentieth Century–Fox executives. "I'm the only one who ever did anything about them."

But the "problem" of the agent was of course much larger than Lang. The rise of the agent in Hollywood was integral to the package-unit system, which was in turn a consequence of the major's studios' declining power. Packages were put together primarily on the basis of a movie's profit potential. Profit potential was best ensured by securing a major star's participation. And since stars were now free of studio contracts, their agents held enormous brokering power, especially after 1950, when Lew Wasserman secured for James Stewart 50 percent of the profits from *Winchester .73*.

Besides the package-unit system and dealing with agents, the third (and corollary) obstacle to Wanger's successful operations under the United Artists system was the fact that Wanger himself, like the producing studios, was obsolete. The rise of actor-producers, director-producers, screenwriter-producers, and agent-producers provided enormous competition to single-threat producers, even if they were veterans such as Wanger. When Burt Lancaster joined with Harold Hecht, or when Kirk Douglas created Bryna Productions, they obviated the need for the producer as such. Such considerations had helped persuade Zanuck to quit studio work at Fox in 1956. He later complained that "actors have taken over Hollywood completely with their agents. They want approval of everything—script, stars, still pictures. The producer hasn't got a chance to exercise any authority!"

The problem affected independent producers as much as studio executives. As Lantz observed,

> The truth is that any star worth having can get his or her own deal at United
> Artists or any other major studio on terms almost as favorable as those given by

United Artists to Figaro. . . . Figaro, to the Hollywood mind, has nothing to offer that several others couldn't offer, except Joe Mankiewicz.

Krim, Benjamin, and Youngstein were, in Lantz's words, "the nicest men in the business, *haimish,* they were committed." Their grant of autonomy to producers was innovative. But their criteria for financing was, of necessity, conservative. Without a studio plant, United Artists could take or leave any proposed deal, and they favored major star packages and low-budget scripts. By 1955, the company held agreements with the likes of Frank Sinatra, Douglas, Wayne, Lancaster, Mitchum, and Peck. They advanced Douglas $180,000 for *The Vikings* before a script was completed; to Wanger, they advanced nothing. As Mankiewicz recalls, when he told Wanger he would not interfere in any of his projects, Wanger was "delighted. Because he couldn't *demand* power."

Wanger's unsuccessful pitch to United Artists of "Underworld U.S.A." while *Invasion of the Body Snatchers* was in postproduction at Allied Artists in the summer of 1955 starkly demonstrates the distributor's strict financing criteria. Before getting the film on Allied Artists' schedule, Wanger had told Youngstein about it in September 1955, hoping that the distributor would finance a script for $85,000. Youngstein, after looking over the treatment, wrote Wanger that he could not recommend purchasing it "unless I am sure that Bogart, or a star of similar stature, would be willing to commit himself at this stage of the game for the property." Wanger within the week had Bogart on board, but for Allied Artists release. Youngstein was outraged: "I think that United Artists and I, both, have been treated very shabbily." But Wanger read Youngstein's thoughts:

I doubt that you thought I could consummate the deal with Bogart without a script. You know well enough that when you really want something, your letter of September 14th was not the kind of letter you would send. You would certainly have reached me on the phone.

The star made all the difference in United Artists' attitude. In this, the distributor merely reflected industrywide wisdom.

"I'm not saying I am in sympathy with this system of not being able to make pictures without anybody in the world but six stars," Wanger wrote in 1957, "but that seems to be the plan everybody is dedicated to. I am trying to conform." Wanger had to conform, because obtaining financing remained an enormous challenge. Writing a potential investor, Wanger pointed out that it took too long to get back negative costs: "You can get your first money, but getting your second money—your completion—and then waiting so long for your negative recoupment is what dries up nearly every independent production unit." Given the difficulty of obtaining financing and the necessity of national distribution, United Artists remained the dominant partner in its relationships with independent producers, much as it had done with Wanger in the late 1930s. Little had changed. The independents were still semi-independents.

In Wanger's words, Mankiewicz had "complete autonomy with United Artists, a very extraordinary contract . . . that allowed him to make deals without submitting the stories to United Artists." But Mankiewicz's autonomy did not extend to Wanger. Without the interest of a star, Wanger could not obtain United Artists backing to finance script development unless both he and they agreed on the story, the cast, and the director. Then, within Figaro, Wanger could not begin new projects until Lantz obtained the okay of Mankiewicz, Allenberg, and United Artists executives. This Wanger called "United Nations technique," a method of "playing safe and having everybody's approval" which he felt "will not get anybody anything." United Nations technique kept Wanger from developing several projects for Figaro, such as *Border Trumpet,* a Haycox western that Mankiewicz felt held promise to match *Stagecoach* or *High Noon* but which Wanger could not properly script or cast.

After six months with Figaro, in April 1957, Wanger was desperate about his lack of progress on any project:

> I do not like to be told, after coming [to Figaro] . . . that I am too energetic and that I am out of line and that what I am doing means nothing. These things take a great deal of time and effort, and the competition out here for the few stars that the distributors want is tremendous.

But that very month Wanger proceeded with preparations for the one success from his lengthy efforts "to conform" and "package" a film. To accomplish this, he had to act on his own.

The general idea of a Hayward vehicle had always been Wanger's most promising prospect at Figaro. The two had kept in constant contact since Wanger sold Hayward's contract to Twentieth Century–Fox and the studio had built Hayward up. Two years after Wanger sold her contract, Hayward was ranked the biggest grossing female star in Hollywood, with four films (most notably *David and Bathsheba*) together grossing more than $12.5 million. The studio put her into the epic CinemaScope extravaganza *Demetrius and the Gladiators* and the masochistic melodrama *With a Song in My Heart.* After seeing the latter film, Wanger wrote Hayward just one month before entering prison:

> I went to the Beverly Hills theatre, which was packed, and it really made me very happy to hear everyone around me say, "Isn't she divine," "Isn't she just wonderful," "What a magnificent performance," and honestly Susan, it is a wonderful picture and you are just great in it.

After delivering her most widely acclaimed and Oscar-nominated performance in the 1955 Lillian Roth biopic, *I'll Cry Tomorrow,* Hayward worked less frequently as she recuperated from a pill overdose and a lengthy divorce and custody trial against Jess Barker. She signed a non-exclusive contract with Fox for one film a year at $1 million. In February 1957, she inaugurated the happiest marriage of her life to Eaton Chalkey, a wealthy attorney whom she joined in Carollton, Georgia, fifty miles south of Atlanta. She sounded ready to retire when she talked to reporters in early 1958.

Like Mankiewicz, Hayward had a strong sense of loyalty and fondness for Wanger. "I owe everything to Walter," she once observed. "He was the guy who had faith in me." She had told him, "I'll work for you anytime, in anything," and he was taking her at her word. As Wanger wrote Hayward in October 1956, Figaro and United Artists executives were "most excited about the opportunity of eventually working something out with you, and, of course, you know how I feel about that." He kept in constant touch with her about potential projects—*Border Trumpet,* "Underworld U.S.A.," William Gibson's *The Miracle Worker,* and "The Fourth World," a murder mystery set in a backward school for the blind. None of them worked out.

On Thanksgiving in 1956, Wanger joined his daughters in San Francisco visiting Bennett, who was then opening opposite Donald Cook in the stage comedy *Janus.* Wanger there met Edward Montgomery, the *San Francisco Examiner* reporter who had won a Pulitzer Prize for his exposé of tax scandals in Nevada. He was revising a book on the most interesting criminal cases he had covered. After reading it, Wanger thought there was "a very exciting and important picture in the [Barbara] Graham material, although that is passed over rather quickly in the script you gave me."

Graham had grown from a juvenile delinquent and reform school graduate into a party girl who passed bad checks, was addicted to heroin, and led a promiscuous personal life that encompassed three marriages and several children. Vivacious and intelligent, she was comfortable in a demimonde of petty con artists, burglars, and drug dealers, displaying a self-destructive streak and a remarkable loyalty to her acquaintances. After leaving her third, heroin-addicted husband, she lived with "associates," the criminals, and gamblers Emmet Perkins and John Santo. As Mankiewicz wrote Wanger, "*This* is a woman Santo and Perkins could and would frame. A woman whipped, and empty, and unwanted by anybody. . . . Unwanted at birth, suckled by hate, reared by neglect—but somehow moving about on the scummy surface of life."

The trio was arrested for the murder in March 1953 of Mabel Monahan, a sixty-two-year-old widow living in Burbank, who had been bludgeoned to death with a pistol. When captured by the police, Graham refused to give evidence of any kind, in spite of the fact that the men freely admitted their crime and implied that Graham herself had committed the murder. Graham suffered from pre-Miranda circumstances: she was not read her rights by police, she was not supplied an attorney upon her arrest, and the police deceived her into confessing the crime by "entrapment," eliciting a confession from her through an undercover officer who promised to serve as her alibi. The primary witness against Graham in court was John True, a codefendant in the Monahan case who helped the prosecution in exchange for immunity. The local press, including Montgomery, boosted its sales by profiling and closely reporting on the trial and background of "Bloody Babs."

"Barbara Graham was a hard cookie and her playmates were the worst killers this State had had in many years," a deputy police chief told the press in 1958. Yet Montgomery started investigating Graham further after her conviction and found a number of discrepancies with the testimony offered in court, such as the coroner's assertion that the murderer was right-handed, while Graham was left-handed. The reporter also talked with Perkins and Santo, who he came to feel were using Graham as a shield, expecting that the state would never execute a young woman. By the time of Graham's appeal, she had experienced a kind of religious conversion. Her letters to her appeals attorney Al Matthews and to Montgomery beg for an end to the "indignities" of multiple stays of execution. They demonstrate a heightened self-awareness that made her position more poignant: "At times it is still hard to realize that I am the main figure in all this," she wrote Matthews when the Supreme Court refused to hear her case. "Insignificant Barbara Graham. If it wasn't all so serious, it would be funny, but my sense of humor has failed at this point." In another letter, she remarked that she pitied people whose "scope of life is so limited, that they really don't know, what it is to live." The efforts of Matthews and Montgomery proved futile when Los Angeles County refused to reopen the case. Graham was executed at San Quentin on June 3, 1955; Santo and Perkins followed her in the state's first triple execution. Among the witnesses was the officer who had obtained her confession under false pretenses.

If Wanger was intimately involved in the details of scripting *Riot in Cell Block 11,* he now was feverishly prophetic in arguing that Graham's biography could make a compelling film. She struck him as a real-life fallen woman whose transgressions far exceeded those of his Astoria heroines and who received society's ultimate punishment. In director Robert Wise's words, her story "jumped out at him." He immediately envisioned a script from Herman Mankiewicz's son (and Joseph's nephew) Don Mankiewicz, starring Hayward and directed by Daniel Mann, who had guided Hayward's critically acclaimed performance in *I'll Cry Tomorrow.*

Over lunch on January 29, 1957, at Pierre's French Basque, Wanger, Hayward, Matthews (with whom Wanger had corresponded previously on the issue of prison reform), and Graham's physician at San Quentin discussed the project. Wanger reported to Hayward's attorney Gang that the actress "seemed most interested": "I have every reason to believe that this might be the most outstanding picture Susan has done to date, and I think we should get on with it." Montgomery agreed that Hayward "would make an ideal portrayal of Barbara Graham." Impatient after the failure of his other projects, Wanger telephoned Gang daily to proceed.

But Wanger did not wait for the United Nations technique. The standard procedure required Figaro and Hayward to agree on a director before signing any agreements, at which point United Artists would finance script development. Because of the "Border Trumpet" and other failures, Figaro was reluctant to ask United Artists for money until the project was set. If Mankiewicz endorsed the project, United Artists would back it, but Mankiewicz was shooting *The Quiet American* abroad. All Wanger had was his own enthusiasm. Here, Wanger's relationship with Hayward came into play: with Gang's help, Wanger was able to overcome the objections of Hayward's agent Jaffe (who wanted the protection of Mankiewicz's involvement in all scripting and shooting of the film) and persuaded Hayward to commit to the project without a director or a finished script.

Hence, on behalf of Walter Wanger Pictures, Wanger paid $5,000 for Montgomery's story and a new treatment and for Matthews to secure clearances from Graham's friends, family, and acquaintances. Figaro and United Artists' contracts for the project were not signed until July 1957. "If I had listened to Mr. Lantz's instructions, and conformed," Wanger commented in March, "there would not be the deal we now have with Susan Hayward because I acted in the interests of Walter Wanger Pictures when I was not to go forward for Figaro." Lantz agreed that in spite of the risks, "it was helpful that Walter ignored our instructions from New York."

Wanger had contacted screenwriter Don Mankiewicz about revising "Underworld U.S.A." in November 1956; he called him in March about "The Barbara Graham Story." A *New Yorker* writer, Mankiewicz had been a unit publicist on Hitchcock's *Under Capricorn* and the writer of several teleplays Wanger admired, including *The Last Tycoon* for Playhouse 90. Mankiewicz had also written a novel, *Trial,* about a murder case mixed up with Communist infiltration, which he had adapted into a successful film for MGM. Mankiewicz's Columbia University law school training endeared him to Wanger, who told Hayward that Mankiewicz "has a fresh approach, is young, a splendid writer and should do a good, non-Hollywood job on the material." (In later years, Mankiewicz wrote the pilot and many of the shows in Raymond Burr's *Ironside* series; in 1987, he coscripted a television movie version of *I Want to Live!*).

And with no prodding from Wanger, the young writer had his own doubts about the case against Graham:

> Mabel Monahan was killed the same day—or the day before—that my father [Herman Mankiewicz] died. I went out and bought all the papers in which

my father's obituary appeared. I'd brought them home with me from the funeral and I read them. They all had accounts of the death of Mabel Monahan and how the case was developing. And I realized that I knew Mabel Monahan. She was always described as an inoffensive widow lady, and she might have been sweet in other configurations, but I knew her in Gardena and she was a *mean* poker player. And it didn't fit in. As portrayed in the papers, it was just inconceivable that she would have played poker in a commercial casino. I developed a vague feeling that something was wrong with this whole thing.

Armed with his intuitions and Wanger's encouragement, Mankiewicz did thorough research: he read twelve volumes of trial transcripts and interviewed Graham's acquaintances.

Wanger accompanied Mankiewicz on these interviews, and he was tremendously impressed with the many people who came forward to speak about Graham with respect and affection and with the concern that her life be told accurately and sympathetically. Most moving was Graham's best friend from the 1940s, Pat Santa Cruz, who talked with them for two hours over lunch in May,

telling us that "but for the grace of God, there go I," as she shared all the "capers" with Barbara. Never in my life have I listened to a woman so honest and forthright as this friend of Barbara's who came to see us against her priest's advice because she couldn't do otherwise if this would help Barbara who was "all heart" according to Pat and couldn't do a mean thing if she tried. . . . I feel Pat is going to develop into a rich and exciting character in our picture—she will show what, with a little luck, Barbara could also have become.

Santa Cruz's views of Graham were corroborated by other observers whom Montgomery found and who signed releases.

Such testimony only ennobled Graham further in Wanger's mind and gave her the tragic grandeur befitting the unlucky, self-destructive yet resilient mold of Hayward's most memorable performances. "I am really steamed up about this," he wrote Hayward in June, in one of his many letters to keep her interest in the project, "and think it's going to be just right for the greatest actress to make her greatest film yet."

What excited Wanger the most was precisely what had been eliminated from *Riot in Cell Block 11:* in his eyes, Graham was innocent, the victim of circumstance and fate who populated the liberal social problem film. "The material is so fraught with emotion and misunderstanding," Wanger wrote Hayward, "that it is completely enthralling." To Joseph Mankiewicz, he wrote that Graham was "an electronic Becky Sharp. She did what she did because she wanted to but, unfortunately, she couldn't control her inevitable destiny after she got on the toboggan." Graham's trial, incarceration, entrapment, and conviction made her a real life version of Eddie Taylor from *You Only Live Once.* They also paralleled, albeit on a much more devastating plane, Wanger's own run in with the law—in fact, the same deputy district attorneys, Ernest Rolls and Adolph Alexander, had prosecuted Wanger and Graham. As Wanger put it, he felt that Graham "really gets it for not having done anything worse than most of us have done, or would like to do."

"The Barbara Graham Story" offered Wanger the chance to delineate a biopic, star vehicle version of the paranoid and alienated sensibility that had informed *Invasion of the Body Snatchers* as well as *Riot in Cell Block 11*. It was not simply the saga of Graham's life which Wanger wanted to convey, but how a range of forces—the zealousness of the police force, the distortions of the press, and the gullible public—had brought her to the death house. As Don Mankiewicz put it, Wanger "always viewed the Monahan case as a conspiracy":

> If left to his own devices he would have put a disclaimer on that said, from *Dragnet*, "The story you have seen is true. The names have been changed to protect the guilty." . . . He really wanted to portray the cops as anti–Barbara Graham, and they weren't, I don't think. There was a lot of brutality asserted on the part of the police, but I don't think there was any, really, not to speak of.

Yet Wanger saw how the police would fit into the scheme of the film. In early May, he and Mankiewicz listened with dismay to Los Angeles police captains who boasted of the extensive stakeout they used to track down Graham and her associates, Santo and Perkins. Wanger envisioned how the capture of Graham, Santo, and Perkins would open the film,

> letting the audience go along with the feeling that the Police have achieved a great service in catching these three monsters, and how well they have planned and how brilliantly executed the capture (which it was). It was the largest stakeout in the history of California. . . . It will give us an exciting opening and from here we can really twist the audience's arm.

Like the sensationalizing reporters in *Riot in Cell Block 11*, the press was another force against Graham, and for this reason, Wanger wanted to base the script on Montgomery's story even though her case was a matter of public record. Montgomery had become, along with Matthews, Graham's most ardent champion from the time of her appeals and on through her death. As Wanger explained to Hayward, he wanted Montgomery's "story of how he helped condemn the girl and then tried to help her." "A feeling of personal guilt pervaded my mind and a sense of helpless futility swept over me," Montgomery wrote in his treatment. "For the first time in my sixteen years as a crime reporter I felt ashamed. . . . this night [my] reputation [as a Pulitzer Prize winner] seemed a mockery."

Given Wanger's belief in Graham's innocence, he recognized instantly that the project "will be the greatest film ever shot to end capital punishment and the public believing everything it reads about the people apprehended by the law, especially women." In fact, he saw the film as yet another critique of American society, "expressing the hypocrisy and apathy of the American public toward social injustice and at the same time being ultra exciting and suspenseful." He elaborated:

> It is not our idea to make any group but the public the heavies. The police are doing their job of apprehending and investigating; the D.A.'s office their job of getting a conviction; the press their job of selling papers as they see it; the judge makes a decision on the limited information he has. The police resorted to entrapment in the framing of Barbara, which they consider a brilliant piece of police work and they justify it. The D.A.'s office joined the police in convicting. The press, as Montgomery states in his story, poisoned the minds of the public. But, with all this, I don't want to see the picture become hysterical and one-dimensional like "Sweet Smell of Success" or "A Face in the Crowd." Both, in my opinion, missed the boat through sophomoric handling. I hope to see the picture adult and seasoned.

In this sense, "The Barbara Graham Story" would be a top-budget reworking of *Riot in Cell Block 11*. As with the earlier film, Wanger contributed to the mise-en-scène of prison existence, from arranging location shooting at various institutions to describing "the Bolero" of clanging gates and barked orders portraying "that caged-in incarcerated, animal treatment that is supposed to regenerate human beings." But its major star would make "The Barbara Graham Story" a much more conventional film than *Riot in Cell Block 11*. Wanger felt confident that with Hayward's participation, "the saga of a bad girl can be a real 'blockbuster' to use a term beloved of Krim and Youngstein." This time he was right.

Putting this conception into practice was an arduous struggle, however, one that focused on the bane of Wanger's career, the screenplay. Montgomery turned in his treatment on May 13. Mankiewicz completed his first draft script in late August, and it reflected his thorough research, perhaps too comprehensively—it ran 298 pages, beginning with the elaborate stakeout used by the Los Angeles police to track Graham from a laundromat to her hideout with Perkins and Santo. As in Montgomery's treatment, once Graham was in jail, a lengthy noir-esque flashback ensued, covering Graham's life story from her rebellious behavior in reform school as a teenager, to various jobs in which her questionable moral history overwhelmed her efforts to make good, and stay happily married. The flashback ended just before Graham's arrest, and the script concluded after her execution. At one point Wanger suggested that, like the first endings proposed for *Riot in Cell Block 11*, Montgomery cover a society wedding, whose elegant milieu would appear absurdly trivial after Graham's death.

In spite of its lack of focus and excessive length, Wanger was ecstatic with Mankiewicz's first draft. But it was obvious to everyone, including Mankiewicz, that the script lacked "cohesion, structure or dramatic point." With

Hayward's permission, Figaro canceled the November 30 starting date, and Wanger scheduled a script conference with the two Mankiewiczs upon Joseph's return to New York in October.

The elder Mankiewicz made practical suggestions about condensation (of husbands and episodes) and also offered keen insights into Graham's character which the script neglected, such as her hatred for her mother which she transformed into self-destructive tendencies. Such a depiction of Graham would contrast greatly with her partial reformation in prison: "It is then, in the growing awareness of death, that for the first time she becomes aware of life. Of what she could have been—of what she could have done—of what she could have had." Joe Mankiewicz also dismissed Wanger's plans for explicit speech making (prologues, acknowledgments, and so forth) as "the kiss of death." Instead, Mankiewicz suggested, "Both the apathy of the public and the lack of opposition to the savagery of the attacks upon her are strongly motivated if Barbara, at the moment of her incarceration, has no more significance to society than a stray dog thrown into the pound."

As Mankiewicz put it, the Graham story "will be a bastard to get written and prepared in time." Although Don Mankiewicz took many of his uncle's suggestions and whittled the script down to 175 pages by November 1957, he failed to make the story cohere in a satisfactory manner. The delay in completing the script threatened to dissolve the project. What held it all together was Hayward's faith in Wanger. She remained committed to the project without having read a completed script as late as October 1957. United Artists, on the other hand, was not so complacent. The distributor could pull the plug on the project at any time prior to principal photography and charge Figaro with the accumulated costs. The absence of a completed script empowered Krim to specify a budget of $1 million, of which $225,000 (plus 37.5 percent of the profits) were already earmarked for Hayward. Between creative salaries and Figaro's administrative work, "The Barbara Graham Story" faced below-the-line costs of $500,000.

As Figaro fretted over the unfinished script, by December Wanger completed arrangements for Wise to direct the film. Initially he had favored Edward Dmytryk, because that member of the Hollywood Ten "spent a year in the clink in Washington, and I believe that it's very difficult to get the atmosphere that is obligatory for this without the real understanding of what goes on." But he came to agree with Hayward's first choice of Mann. Although other directors—such as Wise, Welles (then completing Universal's *Touch of Evil*), John Sturges, and John Frankenheimer (favored by Krim)—were considered, Mann seemed the most appropriate after Wanger rescreened *I'll Cry Tomorrow*:

I was more impressed even than the first time I saw it . . . it has great bearing on this project. It shows an enormous amount of strength—also is very episodic—

and also shows how ably Susan can portray a woman in her most unattractive moments and how she does it without makeup or any desire to look attractive. . . . "I'll Cry Tomorrow" is our goal to excel.

Although Mann was interested in the project, Krim ruled him out as "too expensive." By contrast, Wise could be hired for $100,000, the fee on his current project, Hecht-Hill-Lancaster's *Run Silent, Run Deep*. Within two days, Wanger set to work on selling Wise on the project that he called "a director's triumph . . . unless both the director and the star get an Academy Award, I'll be very much disappointed." Having admired Wise's Rocky Graziano biopic *Somebody Up There Likes Me* (1956), Wanger initially had contacted the former RKO editor the previous April. For his part, Wise was impressed with Montgomery's four-page synopsis, telling Wanger, "People like a horror story. This is a real life horror story if I ever saw one. Let's go." He agreed, at Wanger's urging, to screen *I'll Cry Tomorrow* and *Riot in Cell Block 11* for ideas on shooting and staging.

Wise also rescued the project from stagnation in the absence of a shootable script. In what he later called "the bleak days of mid-January," Wise recommended Nelson Gidding, who had previously written *The Helen Morgan Story* for Warner Bros. Hayward again approved a delay in production, this time for four weeks. By the start of principal photography on March 27, Gidding had a script of 140 pages.

Gidding used several visual ideas and dialogue lines from Mankiewicz's work, such as using photographs and pennants on Graham's San Francisco apartment wall to evoke her fun times with Santa Cruz. Gidding and Wise also retained from Mankiewicz's version punchy lines of dialogue, such as psychologist Carl Palmberg's conclusions about Graham's amorality ("forgery, perjury, vice—these were her crimes. They are not crimes of violence; they are the crimes of those for whom violence is impossible"), or True's remark to Graham, "I thought there was no such thing as not your type."

At the same time, they dramatically reworked the script's structure, making the film taut, exciting, and dramatic by telescoping episodes prior to her arrest for the Monahan murder and eliminating her first marriage and a trip to Mexico. Gidding created a new scene in which Graham is nearly arrested by an undercover cop for passing bad checks, which simultaneously shows her carelessness, prefigures her entrapment by the false alibi, and inaugurates her relationship with third husband Henry Graham. In another new scene, Barbara learns of the Supreme Court's denial while sitting in a dentist's chair, anticipating her seating in the gas chamber. Drawing on Wise's background as an editor at RKO, the writers condensed Graham's card-shilling days with Perkins into a montage sequence of card games and robberies.

They also found new ways to inflect the paranoia of the film: removing references to Graham's own drug abuse, they built up the scene of her surrender after the police stakeout as a public entertainment in the manner of Wilder's *Ace in the Hole* (1951). As the script directed, "The contrast between this insignificant young woman and the enormous forces arrayed against her are almost comical. It is only her bearing that lends any dignity to the occasion." Both the crowd that greets Graham as she arrives at San Quentin and the spectators surrounding the gas chamber further dramatize how Graham became a spectacle for the viewing pleasure of a perverse American society.

Similarly, Gidding and Wise omitted an early episode in which Barbara eludes Montgomery, who is investigating the activities of her husband, an abortionist. The incident gave Montgomery specific motivation for covering her trial so critically; by omitting it, Gidding and Wise suggest a more general malevolence by the media in sensationalizing her life. Script cutting continued during production. A scene elaborating on Graham's unhappy childhood was cut. On Joseph Mankiewicz's advice, several sequences were eliminated entirely from the film, including a costly dream sequence that Wise transformed into a single, aerial-shot scene of Graham writhing in bed to jarring music.

Most striking, Wise, inspired by a recent visit to a New York nightclub, introduced jazz music as a perennial feature of the film. After interviewing Santa Cruz, Wanger had envisioned showing her "capers" with Graham set to contemporary music. By 1958 jazz was a common element in films with contemporary settings, such as *The Blackboard Jungle, Touch of Evil, The Man with a Golden Arm, I'll Cry Tomorrow, The Glenn Miller Story,* and other jazz biopics. Though motivated by the protagonists' careers, the music had an ominous undertone that, according to critic Jonathan Rosenbaum, was "synonymous with decadence and the forces of darkness."

The importance of the jazz score in *I Want to Live!* is apparent from the opening page of the script. Wise and Gidding disposed of Wanger's scheme to begin with the police stakeout and the flashback sequence. Instead, the film would immediately identify Graham's milieu by opening in a steamy nightclub: "The music is the beat of the beat generation—real cool, cool, jazz, suggesting sex, speed, marijuana, hipsterism and other miscellaneous kicks."

In principal photography Wise elaborated the opening scene into a three-minute sequence of canted angles on the musicians, the patrons, and the marijuana smokers before showing Peg Vincent, Graham's best friend. Serving as a bridge, the music continued under a crane shot from the street to the window of a sleazy hotel room above the club. A reverse angle from inside the room introduces Graham in a dramatic fashion, rising up from below the frame "languidly," and smoking a cigarette in completely backlit silhouette, forging the associations of her vibrant personality with the music coming from outside the window. Such frenetic music was prominent again at a party in Graham's apartment, and a more restrained jazz idiom courtesy of Gerry Mulligan accompanied her stay at Corona prison. Combined with the pulsing rhythm, swish pans, canted angle shots and snappy dialogue, the film's score creates a sense of Graham's life as Wanger's "toboggan" to the death sentence.

One of Wise's proudest boasts about the film was its use of music to forward the narrative. He asked Count Basie alumnus Johnny Mandel to do the score and invited him to script sessions. As Wise later recalled:

> What we wanted to do, what one needs to do in these biographical films so often, is to cut through certain obvious and unnecessary scenes. I hated to have that usual middle scene of a happy marriage and then it goes sour, and then they split up. We had to get on with it; so I got an idea.

Wise asked Mandel: "Can you write me, musically, about the disintegration of a marriage so that in the very next scene I can cut to them breaking up?" Mandel came up with a passage for the scene in which Graham leaves Perkins to get married. The languorous music gets louder as the camera dollies into a house of cards Perkins builds and then destroys. Wise then cuts to Graham's screaming infant and a brutal fight scene between Graham and her husband Henry.

More pointedly, the jazz score became the antithesis of the somber death cell scenes, which were the most significant change Wise and Gidding made in their script. "We knew that somehow the last act had to be her arrival at San Quentin and that last night, the death cell and the next morning," Wise recalls. "But we didn't quite know how to dramatize it." In February, Wise toured San Quentin with art director Haworth and production manager Johnny Johnston in order to prepare a reproduction of the death cell and gas chamber. Wise met with Father McAllister, the priest who attended Graham on her final night.

> So during the conversation I asked, "Father, how did it happen that you left the prison?" He said, "Mr. Wise, I don't suppose you have any idea of the terrible atmosphere, the terrible pall, that descends on the *whole* prison when everybody there knows that preparations are being made to take a life the next day. It was terrible, and I couldn't take it anymore." And that was my clue. I hadn't thought about the preparations to take a life. So I went right back to the prison and I said to the guards, "I want you to take me through every step that you do. Everything. The evening, the very beginning through the next morning." That interview led me to the structure of the last act.

During a later trip, Wise witnessed, with great difficulty, an actual execution, so he could stage Graham's death correctly in the film.

He also was able to interview the nurse who sat with Graham on her final night, who described the ordeal and the impact of preparations and legal maneuvers on Graham. When challenged subsequently by California corrections director McGee on the authenticity of certain events (Graham being allowed to wear her own nightgown, her hostile exchanges with the matron, and whether or not she was served a lavish sundae for her last breakfast), Wise responded point by point, drawing on the testimony of the nurse and others who were with her that last night. Where witnesses differed about the facts, Wise and Gidding freely chose the more dramatic version. In a memo, the director noted he was "taking the time to make these points so that everyone will understand that we did go into this whole matter very thoroughly and make every step of it as authentic as it was dramatically possible for us to do."

The decision to present Graham's last hours was an ethically questionable one, trading as it did on the "pornographic" thrill of filming an execution, something as old as the early Mutoscopes. Yet, placed at the end of the film (with just a brief epilogue outside San Quentin), and shot and edited at a deliberate pace, the sequence gave *I Want to Live!* extraordinary power and gravity. And more than any other change in the script, the decision to spend thirty minutes of screen time in San Quentin clinched the case for implicit rather than explicit moralizing and speech making against capital punishment.

As principal photography proceeded from late March, the problem of how to handle Graham's guilt or innocence in the Monahan case came up yet again. Wanger knew his personal beliefs might impair the film's impact. He had called Graham "an electronic Becky Sharp" and Joseph Mankiewicz reminded him that, like Becky Sharp, Graham "must be guilty as hell—*up to* the end." Lantz was equally emphatic:

> I have always felt that the great dramatic point about this woman's story is that there was doubt, reasonable doubt, increasing doubt, about her guilt—and that as long as such doubt existed, the death penalty must not be imposed. To me, this was the drama and the originality of the story, and never, for one moment, did I think we wanted to establish complete innocence. In any case such complete innocence is highly unconvincing in connection with Barbara.

Yet fashioning a star vehicle for Hayward had its inevitable softening effects. The elimination of crude details, omitting Graham's dirty jokes in her death cell and her sudden need to use the bathroom before walking out to the gas chamber (a detail scripted, but finally not shot on the grounds of bad taste), gave her a more decorous portrait. "We never wanted to say that Barbara was innocent," Wise later recalled, "although the very fact that we got Susan playing the part and she was the lead made it seem that way. That's why we put that line in at the end, where the guard says, 'What was she doing shacked up with those guys in the first place?'"

Indeed, following Lantz's logic, Wise and Gidding decided to suggest superficially that she was innocent by showing the agonizing fight with her husband which Graham later claims took place the night of the murder. The dissolve between scenes of her fight with Henry Graham and her leaving her mother-in-law's house (with headlines in the newspaper by the front door about the Monahan murder) implied her innocence, but only by omission. This ambiguity registered in the film's reviews. For example, Stanley Kauffmann at *The New Republic,* Paul V. Beckley of the *New York Herald Tribune,* and the critic for the *Film Daily* claimed that the film established her innocence unequivocally. But the *Hollywood Reporter* and Arthur Knight of *Saturday Review* felt the film was less definite; the trade paper felt that Barbara's self-delusions about her happy marriage the night before her death "leaves the final question of her guilt or innocence tactfully unsolved."

Similarly, Wanger fretted over the entire issue of police malfeasance. Police reaction was the major concern of the Production Code Administration upon reviewing the script: Wanger and Wise completely disregarded most of its complaints about Graham's opening scene in bed and the violent beating at the hands of Santo. They were urged to downplay suggestions of police brutality (not letting Graham go to the bathroom during her interrogation) and the lesbian demeanor of the inmate involved in her entrapment. Wise and Gidding rescripted and shot these latter scenes accordingly; nonetheless, in spite of Wanger's efforts, both McGee and Brown refused to endorse the film because of its ambiguous portrayal of Graham's innocence.

Thanks to Figaro production manager Johnston, principal photography on *I Want to Live!* went smoothly. Haworth, the art director on *Invasion of the Body Snatchers,* worked with cinematographer Lionel Lindon to use "broadcasts, fancy dissolves, montages, headlines, views of the city, proper views of the prison, our story and magnitude of same," all of which contributed to the pacing of the film. Wise especially appreciated Lindon's ability to capture the textures of many of the film's grim and seedy settings. On the example of *I'll Cry Tomorrow,* Wise cast non-stars from stage and television—Theodore Bikel as psychologist Carl Palmberg, Simon Oakland as Ed Montgomery, and Virginia Vincent as Peg—who fulfilled United Artists' budget strictures and gave "more realism to the picture than a lot of names." Wise concluded the shooting on June 6, just six days behind schedule (due to Hayward's taking ill) and $200,000 over its $1.2 million budget.

Although Wise shot (at Joe Mankiewicz's request) a concluding scene in which Montgomery and Matthews discussed the injustice of the legal system and capital punishment, he and Wanger finally chose the scene he and Gidding had planned. Here, Montgomery receives Graham's letter in the parking lot outside of San Quentin thanking him for his efforts on her behalf. As the journalists rush into their cars and begin honking to get back to their papers, Montgomery pulls out his earplug, creating a dramatic silence in the film, before Mandel's swing score concludes the film. When the two endings were screened, Wise and Wanger chose the less explicit version. As Wanger told Mankiewicz, "If, at this late spot in the film, they don't understand what it's all about, our cause is hopeless and no sermonizing or even the most brilliant dialogue will make the point." They did elect to use Montgomery's assertion, "You are about to see a factual story," at the start and the end of the picture. As Wise observed, "Everybody who has seen the show thinks there is very strong value in the fact that it is a true story. Why not use it?"

Using the Montgomery testimonial only strengthened what everyone at Figaro and United Artists anticipated would be a major success. "I believe we've got something super-colossal," Wanger wrote Figaro's publicity manager Mike Mindlin, Jr. He was fiercely proud of *I Want to Live!* because the film had turned out so well after all of his waiting and cajoling. But his pride was rooted in other reasons as well.

In mid-February, as Gidding and Wise were revising and polishing their script, Wanger had suffered another heart attack. It was hardly as incapacitating as the one he suffered in 1956. In fact, it was mild enough that Wanger could hide it from Figaro and the other talents. He told them that he had simply caught a terrible flu and had to work at home for the entire month, fearful that the insurance company would shut the production down and the film would never get made. Wanger was now sixty-three years old and mindful of his father's premature death. Though as always he put up a brave show, Wanger faced the prospect of his own demise. Were his career to end abruptly, as it easily might, it was desperately important to him to conclude with something besides his relatively obscure Allied Artists films.

In terms of production and final realization, *I Want to Live!* was in many ways the best film—certainly the best combination of message movie and entertainment value—to emerge from Wanger's lifelong working methods as a Hollywood producer. He had found the story, clearly envisioned the interpretation of the material and its implications, pushed incessantly for it, but then let the capable Wise and Gidding shape the film their particular way, which he characterized as "industrious, dedicated and brilliant." Aside from Hayward's star charisma, the film's success lay in its ability, like *The Man with the Golden Arm, The Country Girl,* and Hayward's own vehicles such as *I'll Cry Tomorrow,* to emulate the new standards for naturalism that Hollywood exploited to lure the reluctant audience.

Hence it was hardly surprising that publicity for the film focused on its most provocative elements. (In December 1957, Wanger joked about possible product licensing: "contraceptives, machine guns and all types of firearms, hidden microphones for wiretapping, tear gas bombs, marijuana, opium, heroin and any derivative for chipping, loaded dice.") Figaro's publicity consultant Ted Loeff proposed a two-pronged effort that played upon the ambiguous morality of the decision to show Graham's execution. Loeff noted, "The highlighting of the execution, we feel, will provide the peepshow appeal that will be necessary to entice mass audiences," while the film's careful research and implicit condemnation of capital punishment would preclude censorship and constitute its "long-hair" appeal. United Artists tried to build up ticket sales in New York with a single voyeuristic, "shocking" photo of Hayward, blindfolded and in the gas chamber seat, shot to resemble the *New York Daily News*'s crude picture of Ruth Snyder, who was executed in the 1930s.

The highbrow appeal of the film was more difficult but also more crucial to convey, insofar as it was meant to neutralize charges of vulgar exploitation and factual distortions. Press books stressed the film's authenticity by including court transcript excerpts, a lengthy list of evidence for and against Graham's conviction, and Graham's letter to Matthews stating "I do want to live." Moreover, Wanger successfully lobbied the distributor to postpone the Los Angeles opening at the Fox Beverly Theater until the week of Thanksgiving, so that *I Want to Live!* could garner favorable reviews in the East and Midwest before facing the ire of local police and politicians.

Positive comment on the film began with sneak previews in early September in San Francisco. Marcel Frym, the criminologist whom Wanger had retained as technical adviser on the film, wrote that he'd left the theater speechless. "It is the greatest contribution to our fight against capital punishment," he wrote Wanger, "and unsurpassed in its documentary quality." With Frym's help, Wanger held a special screening of the film at a criminologists' conference; he also arranged a December 1958 screening for several Supreme Court justices, including William O. Douglas—who had granted Graham a stay of execution.

After the film received its October premiere in New York, prominent figures in the world of letters shared Frym's estimate. Playwright Arthur Miller felt the film had "a tremendous presence, an immediacy, a reality which few movies have ever achieved." Screenwriter Paddy Chayefsky and novelist Leon Uris concurred, the latter writing Wanger his "first fan letter," and calling the film "one of the great motion pictures of all time." Nichols "left the theatre stunned." The humane writer of *Scarlet Street* found it "the only real, actual down-to-earth *horror film* I've ever seen" and articulated its implications:

> Your film doesn't say one syllable pro or con, and yet it could be the one thing that would stop capital punishment. The only real propaganda against evil is the truth, just the cold reality, saying "here it is boys, and you're part of it too, sitting out there"—but not uttering one word pro or con.

Most impressively, Albert Camus, who the previous year had coauthored with Arthur Koestler an anti-capital punishment tract in France, praised the film. Camus wrote a grave preface for French distribution, which read in part: "The day will come when such documents will seem to us to refer to prehistorical times, and we shall consider them as unbelievable as we now find it unbelievable that in earlier centuries witches were burned or thieves had their right hands cut off." In Wanger's view, Camus's support gave the film both "the ultimate stamp of quality" and youth appeal, since Camus was a best-selling author and "the darling of the world's youthful intellectuals."

In spite of the film's highbrow appeal, United Artists's $500,000 advertising budget, and Hayward's major American and European city tour, Wanger again felt his distributor had failed to promote the film fully, particularly in England, where censors threatened to delete the final forty minutes. But by the time *I Want to Live!* premiered in New York, Figaro was inactive. Joseph Mankiewicz agreed to direct *Suddenly Last Summer* for Spiegel at Columbia, Lantz resumed his career as an agent, and Wanger was at Twentieth Century–Fox.

I Want to Live! faced minor censorship action: a "C" rating from the Legion of Decency and deletions in Kansas City and Chicago. By far the harshest condemnation came from the Los Angeles Police Department, which especially resented the film's vague treatment of Graham's guilt and the depiction of the press and police as "railroading an innocent woman to her death." Disputing Montgomery's prologue attesting to the film's factuality, the police pilloried certain dramatic sequences such as Barbara's arrest in front of a crowd as "ridiculous" and "100 percent phony": "We trailed Barbara to the hide-out from a meeting she had with a dope peddler. She stopped in a phone booth to take a shot of heroin and then headed for their apartment." *Cavalier* magazine printed an article asserting Graham's guilt, complete with a stomach-turning photo of Mabel Monahan's bludgeoned corpse, and a low-budget company produced "Weep No More for Barbara" with the advice of one of the prosecutors at Graham's trial. Montgomery, who wrote *I Want to Live!*'s paperback tie-in, defended the film publicly, stating that even though the film did not present all of the prosecution's case against Graham, it did not present the defense case in its entirety either. Father McAllister spoke about Graham's religious conversion in prison. Wanger acted detached: "I believe the trial transcript supports our film."

The controversy only helped the film's financial performance. By early August 1959, *I Want to Live!* had a projected gross of $3.1 million. This pleased Wanger particularly because it outperformed the $2.4 million earned thus far by Kramer's *The Defiant Ones,* "which was the choice of U.A. for all honors and boxoffice records." After two and a half years, the film's gross covered losses on Figaro's unproduced scripts and paid Hayward $321,783 in profits.

The trade press gave the film ecstatic reviews. *Motion Picture Daily* remarked that *I Want to Live!* "defied several of the most important conventions of movie-making":

> And, by the very fact that they have utilized as their "innocent" victim of this practice such an amoral and anti-social character as Barbara Graham, they have stripped the issue of all false sentimentality and fuzzy romanticism. They are

saying, in effect, that all God's creatures, including the perjurers and prostitutes, deserve the same compassion.

Variety wrote, "Subtly, inferentially, the creators of the film raise the question
of which is the more degraded, the object of this ordeal or the law that or-
dains it." The *Hollywood Reporter* felt that it went "beyond the question of
innocence to the more haunting and profound one of mercy."

By contrast, Wanger was "furious" with the national newsweekly reviews
and "displeased" with the New York newspaper critics, who denigrated those
melodramatic, liberal aspects of the film that had obscured its general social
criticism. *Time,* pointing out the film's lack of sympathy for Perkins and
Santo, felt the film's social consciousness fatally compromised:

> To judge from the far-out photography, real desperate sound track, and drags-
> ville dialogue that Krylon-spray the whole film with a cheap glaze of don't-
> care-if-I-do-die juvenility, Producer Walter Wanger seems less concerned to
> assist the triumph of justice than to provide the morbid market with a sure-
> enough gasser.

"If the picture came from abroad," Wanger told a publicist, "everyone would
be rubbing Hollywood's nose in it."

Both the trade and general critics agreed that what distinguished the film
from other movies about "mixed-up ladies" was the final forty minutes, the
very portion of the film Wise had added late in preproduction. The film was
"harrowing," "nerve shattering," "grim," "powerful"; *Variety* concurred that
the film was "one of the year's best pictures, and one that sets a milestone for
boldness and realism," and that it was "superb on nearly every count." By
December the film was on several ten-best lists, behind *Anatomy of a Murder,
Some Like It Hot,* and *Some Came Running.*

Much of the acclaim focused on Hayward. In December, she won the Film
Critics Award for best actress of 1958. At the Academy Awards ceremony on
April 6, 1959, at the RKO Pantages Theater in Hollywood, *I Want to Live!*
had many nominees: Bikel, Wise, Gidding and Mankiewicz, Lindon, editor
William Hornbeck and sound engineer Gordon Sawyer. Hayward, nominated
for the fifth time, finally won the best actress award. In her acceptance speech,
she thanked Wanger first.

As an additional token of gratitude, Hayward suggested to Figaro and
United Artists that each party donate 1 percent of their profit share to compensate Wanger for his work in preparing and promoting the film. This added
up to $24,355 and effectively doubled his Figaro salary. After a decade of
neglect from the rest of Hollywood's top stars, Wanger found the gesture
overwhelming, as he wrote Selznick four years later:

> I owe a tremendous loyalty to this girl who has acted just wonderfully toward
> me, as you know. She waited an entire year, against the advice of many of her

advisors, for the script of I WANT TO LIVE and, then after she made it, she was so gracious at the Academy, that I feel very beholden to her. . . . Susan's behavior has been so unusual for a star. . . . I will never do anything but show my gratitude.

He considered the additional income "a God-send."

When the Academy Awards were over, Wise wrote Wanger that his only regret had been that the film had not earned a best picture nomination: The film, "is your baby and wouldn't have existed at all if it had not been for your foresight and perseverance." But Wanger had received a great deal of attention for his work on the film. *Variety* praised his "insight that there was a story in this life of sordid and unappetizing crime." The *Hollywood Reporter* dubbed it Wanger's "resounding comeback." Publicity pieces and interviews focused on his personal views on capital punishment (staying resolutely off the subject of Graham's innocence). He told one reporter that capital punishment was murder and that he considered it "a far more monstrous type in the cold implacable operation of the law than is, say, the unpremeditated crime produced by a momentary, human loss of control." Anyone who recalled the Lang shooting seven years earlier knew exactly what he meant.

I Want to Live! was the culminating instance of Wanger's provocative message movies since *Washington Merry-Go-Round.* As Fonda, star of the botched *Blockade,* observed in 1959, Wanger's *I Want to Live!* "was as good as any [film] he'd made." Wanger told Dorothy Manners he felt the film was "the most exciting picture I have ever had anything to do with, and I'm not forgetting John Ford's great 'Stagecoach' or Charles Boyer and Hedy Lamarr in 'Algiers.'"

"I believe filmmakers must do something revolutionary to hold the audience," Wanger had said in 1934: none of his previous films approached the overwhelming power of the final third of *I Want to Live!* Wanger told Joe Hyams, "I'm one of the old school who believes in the use of propaganda." He continued:

But this isn't a treatise against capital punishment. This is a treatise against the whole social system which we are so apathetic about. There are two things enormously prevalent today in this country—one is the acceptance of corruption and the other is hypocrisy. The sooner we deal with both of those things, the sooner our national and international prestige will improve.

Personal alienation had fueled Wanger's showmanship in the 1950s, and it had served its purposes. "This is my fourteenth career," Wanger told Hyams. "What people here don't realize is that I'm the perennial man-who-came-back." Having made his most successful message movie, he opted, for his next project, to make his biggest entertainment spectacle. In this he succeeded, on-screen and off.

Part Six

Hollywood Merry-Go-Round

19

Arabian Nights
(1958–1961)

The best commentary on *Cleopatra,* the last film Wanger produced, remains writer-director Joseph Mankiewicz's quip: "This picture was conceived in state of emergency, shot in confusion, and wound up in a blind panic." *Cleopatra*'s conception merged Wanger's lifelong infatuation with unruly heroines and sumptuous orientalism, Hollywood's predilection for Technicolor, 70mm Todd-AO spectacle, and Mankiewicz's sense of intimate drama. The emergency and panic was Twentieth Century–Fox's; the resulting confusion was a collaborative effort. The studio set forth the notion, which countless historians and biographers repeat, that *Cleopatra* ruined Fox. But in truth, Fox did itself in, and the film was its most convenient scapegoat.

To contemporary observers, the *Cleopatra* fiasco showed Hollywood in frenzied transition: Vincent Canby wrote that it represented "the end of an era . . . the death rattle of a kind of old-fashioned reckless filmmaking which, in 'Cleopatra,' simply attained a scale never seen before." Different recountings of its troubles allocate the blame to isolated individuals (such as Wanger or Elizabeth Taylor) or particular groups. But *Cleopatra* also demonstrated how essential it was to follow Hollywood's studio system, first consolidated before Wanger joined the film business in 1920. Without its fundamental methods of organization, absolute chaos and overblown expense prevailed.

As Zanuck later put it to Wanger, the making of *Cleopatra* "consistently violated every fundamental or 'kindergarten' production rule." Two violations were outstanding. For nearly three years, the production lacked a shootable script on which to base budgets, operations, and controls. The result was a reported negative cost of over $31 million (more than $90 million in 1994 dollars), the most expensive movie then made in Hollywood and nearly as much as all of Wanger's previous films combined.

Second, *Cleopatra* suffered from the absence of a clear corporate and management hierarchy. This uncertainty was aggravated by Fox's and Wanger's different notions of what a producer does and by Wanger's ambiguous stance between independence and studio affiliation. The turf battles that resulted made the conflicts that had riven Diana Productions look like affectionate teasing. Wanger filed a $2.6 million lawsuit against Fox president and board chairman Spyros Skouras, Zanuck, and the Fox company for breach of contract and libel; Skouras countersued Wanger for libel he found in Wanger's book on the making of the film, *My Life with "Cleopatra."*

In October 1958 when Wanger joined Fox, the studio still operated at nearly full plant capacity. Fox held stars, directors, screenwriters, and producers under non-exclusive contracts, maintained extensive production departments (art direction, costuming, editing), and had a huge backlot, all of which cost several million dollars to maintain annually. The innovations of Krim and Benjamin at United Artists had demonstrated how unnecessary and costly such major studio machinery was in the age of packaging stars, directors, and writers for single films such as *I Want to Live!* But Fox executives had not yet learned this lesson.

What made matters infinitely worse was the fact that Fox in the fall of 1958 lacked a forceful production head to oversee the disbursement of millions of company dollars on worthwhile talents and projects. The brilliant and autocratic Zanuck had been gone for two years, having quit in a fit of exhaustion and depression. Unlike Mayer and Schenck, who in 1933 had ensured that a unit organization at MGM would cover for Thalberg's sudden illness, the Fox studio had no one to take Zanuck's place.

Zanuck's only heir apparent in 1956 was Buddy Adler, the producer of *All the King's Men* (1949) and *From Here to Eternity* (1953) at Columbia, whose forte at Fox had been pre-sold play adaptations and big-budget movies such as 1956's *Bus Stop* and *Anastasia*. Adler was aided by general manager of production Lew Schreiber, story department head David Brown, executive production manager Sid Rogell and the boisterous former exhibition head, Skouras.

In 1951, Fox had led the majors with the most films grossing more than one million dollars, and in 1953, thanks largely to Skouras, it had innovated CinemaScope. In 1958, however, star vehicles such as Huston's *The Barbarian and the Geisha* (starring Wayne), *A Certain Smile* (Fontaine and Rossano Brazzi), and even Zanuck's own *Roots of Heaven* (Flynn and Trevor Howard) were earning pathetic grosses. Zanuck's independent films, starring a series of lover-protégés (Juliette Greco and Irina Demick), generated losses of $7.5 million through 1961. At a studio where executives shunned any discussion of failure, Fox's record of only two to four hits yearly (such as *The King and*

I, 1956, *Three Faces of Eve*, 1957, and *Peyton Place*, 1958) was extremely embarrassing.

Part of the problem was that Adler was not a Zanuck. Screenwriter-producer Nunnally Johnson told an interviewer in July 1959, "I miss Zanuck—I miss him terribly at Fox. No picture-maker, no focal point, no feeling of strength at the top." Screenwriter-director Phillip Dunne noted that Zanuck's "greatest strength was his decisiveness. Right or wrong, he made his decisions quickly and firmly." Adler was quite the opposite: "mistrustful, suspicious, and frightened all the time."

Another part of the problem was that Adler shared his authority in production with Skouras himself. Beyond his preference for family entertainment, Skouras, who was just one year older than Wanger, had little experience with administering an entire studio or realizing an individual film. He had considerable expertise in exhibition and distribution. He had helped to salvage heavily mortgaged Fox and Paramount theaters in the 1930s. His crowning success was to persuade resistant exhibitors to invest in CinemaScope.

On occasion, Dunne recalls, Zanuck locked Skouras out of the projection room. As Zanuck later told a biographer, "about pictures, [Skouras] couldn't tell a good one from a bad one. . . . I've never sent him a script in my life. Never! I showed him pictures, pictures that were edited, scored and finalized." On *Cleopatra*, Skouras constantly commented on the script, urging first director Mamoulian to emphasize "above all action and sex" in the dialogue scenes between the principals.

The hiring of Wanger by Fox was only the first example of the kind of indecisiveness that the Adler-Skouras alliance created. Wanger had been pitching projects to Fox throughout the 1950s, from *The Ballad and the Source* to the low-budget *The Adventures of Hajji Baba*. As Skouras later put it, "This man kept coming; he appealed to me a number of times. He came to my home a number of times. And he was begging me to get him with Twentieth Century–Fox." Before his departure in 1956, Zanuck, according to Skouras, felt Wanger's ideas were "too much of the old school. . . . They didn't believe that he was picking up new subjects." Although Fox executives had been among his firmest supporters after the Lang shooting, they jokingly referred to the well-groomed Wanger as "high button shoes."

Adler agreed at first and declined to sign Wanger when they first met in August 1958. But attorney Greg Bautzer and agent Charles K. Feldman persisted, and Skouras was sympathetic to Wanger because the studio needed as many films as soon as possible to lower its overhead and $100 million operating costs. "We will need one blockbuster a month," Skouras announced at a meeting of Fox production executives in August 1959, as well as "some spectacles with pre-sold names" that "could be made more cheaply than major star vehicles." Adler urged producers to consider remakes.

Wanger was brimming with possibilities, and his contract specified that he use his "best efforts to produce as many photoplays as possible." Since Hayward was committed to Fox for one film each year, Wanger's success with *I Want to Live!* clinched matters. Even Skouras later conceded that Wanger was not hired out of pity. In early October, Adler signed him to his highest weekly salary since World War II—$2,000 with 15 percent of his film's profits.

Contractually, Wanger was on loan-out to Fox from his independent company, sharing the rights to his films with the studio. The arrangement was comparable to those Fox maintained with Wald, Selznick, Zanuck himself, and other "independent producers." But "independent" corporate status meant little beyond profit shares given Fox's contractual and managerial strictures. Skouras and Adler operated in Zanuck's shadow, and in trying to match his record, they copied his style: they rarely delegated authority.

By contract Wanger had to give "due and proper consideration" to Fox's ideas about the script, as well as choices for casts, writers, directors, cinematographers, and composers. Skouras felt that

> producers are responsible to suggest properties . . . to suggest writers, which the studio engages. To suggest directors, cast, and in general, to be fully responsible for the production under the studio management.

The producer's job clearly was the preparation of the film; less clearly, the producer was "responsible" for the film but *under* studio management. This uncertainty regarding where the producer's job left off and studio management's work began informed Wanger's earliest contract discussions: Schreiber told Wanger "that he works strictly under the supervision of the studio." But Wanger clearly recalled Adler's assurances that Fox officials would not be "rigid . . . in controlling me and limiting my production responsibility."

Wanger gradually came to see the obstacle course at Fox as a large-scale version of Figaro's "United Nations" consensus management, in which he could never act freely. The fact that Fox paid him so much money meant that he had to obey Adler and Skouras's restrictions. He had to check with Brown before talking with writers and talk with the casting department before speaking to actors. Above all, he could not communicate with agents. Wanger's hardships at Fox put the Figaro collaboration in a much more positive light; he would exaggerate the contrast between Figaro and Fox in *My Life with "Cleopatra"* when he wrote, "I was soon made painfully aware that even the so-called independent producer at a major studio must be prepared to accept committee rule and interference."

Initially, Wanger acted like the perfect Fox producer. Moving into his offices on October 20, he threw out ideas for the studio to pursue, of which *Cleopatra* was only one (and the first to gain Fox's approval). For Hayward, Wanger proposed "The Fourth World" and a biopic of Eva Peron that delineated "this poor dame who got a hold of mass communications and then developed herself to the most important woman in the world and made her lover

President." He later suggested that Fox distribute Fellini's *La Dolce Vita,* which Wanger felt was "the best sermon that I have heard and seen in many, many years" because it was "a great reflection on the hypocrisy and scandal mongering of our times." Fox rejected both ideas.

Fox did not turn down all of Wanger's proposals. Elaine Dundy's novel *The Dud Avocado* concerned the experiences of a naive but ambitious American young woman (Wanger had Debbie Reynolds in mind) who tries to make her fortune in Paris "and keeps tripping herself up." Wanger envisioned it as "an American *Gigi* in Paris" directed by Blake Edwards in a contemporary setting and as a blockbuster for the teenage audience. With no satisfactory script after a year, Fox shelved the project in December 1959.

But in his waning years and with big studio resources at his disposal, Wanger's keenest ambition was to produce a film in a Middle Eastern setting on the model of the orientalist romance, but one that would overwhelm its audience with spectacular values and profound insights into human nature. (When costume designer Irene Sharaff later suggested that Wanger's *Cleopatra* be done in a campy style (like *Arabian Nights*), Wanger was "not amused.") In September 1958, before coming to Fox, he wanted to take an option on four novels by the poet Lawrence Durrell, who created densely textured prose that was rich in metaphor and mythic reverberations as it described a provocative array of sexual proclivities and degradations. Durrell's *Justine* and *Balthazar* appeared in 1957 and 1958; he completed the quartet with *Mountolive* and *Clea* in early 1959 and 1960.

The Alexandrian quartet concerned the same set of characters, political conspirators in international politics, who met, seduced each other, and variously intersected just prior to and during World War II in Alexandria. Each book was narrated by a different character who revealed personal and political dimensions of the plot's events. The diverse, distinctly written narrators, the disjunctive writing (one volume "reproduced" twenty-nine pages of a character's notebook), and the revelations and recastings of characters' actions and intentions, as well as Durrell's evocative imagery, created a modernist structure that jarred with the prevailing "angry young man" realism of British literature and literature at the end of the fifties. Yet Durrell's achievement was a major literary event of the period; when *Clea* completed the series in April 1960, Gerald Sykes in the *New York Times Book Review* called it "one of the most important works of our time."

To Wanger, the heroines Justine and Clea showed the same amoral behavior and will to survive as Sybil Jardine in *The Ballad and the Source* and Barbara Graham in *I Want to Live!*. After Fox purchased the property, he encouraged writer Ivan Moffat to develop a happy ending:

> To me, Justine is the saga of the resilience of a woman. . . . Justine can do many things that many women do and rise above it—all is maturity. This is what is

going to appeal to the women in my humble opinion. Therefore, [the struggle to create] Palestine is important and a reunion with Nessim [her husband] after all their great trials and excitements is obligatory. Also, the supreme truth that you can overcome anything would be a wonderful inspirational finish. This is an honest story and the author strips the characters nude but then adorns them with humanity, which is his blessing.

At the same time, Wanger was fascinated by Durrell's evocation of a sensuous atmosphere in which the characters pursued their passions and power struggles. The indifferent earnings of *The Adventures of Hajji Baba* had done nothing to diminish his enthusiasm for orientalist romance, and he classified the Durrell quartet, its modernist structure and rich prose aside, in the same category, describing it to Fox's Harry Brandt as "sort of a modern Arabian Nights tale with great suspense and amazing melodramatic situations covered by every sort of passionate adventure."

Selznick agreed, and pleaded Wanger's case with Fox in the hope of landing the role of Justine for his wife Jennifer Jones, writing Fox's Brown that the quartet could become "a kind of adult 'Casablanca,' much deeper in its insight, much richer in its appeal." Wanger did not exactly see Jones in the title role. He did however envision a Technicolor, Todd-AO, four-hour film, "the most beautiful picture ever produced from the standpoint of atmosphere and settings," with one hour for each book of the quartet, a cast of international stars such as Olivier, David Niven, and Grace Kelly, with costumes designed by Oliver Messel or Irene Sharaff, both of whom later worked on *Cleopatra*. He wanted nothing less than the crowning glory of his career.

It says as much about the inroads of European art cinema during the 1950s on Hollywood's consciousness as it does about the difference between Zanuck and Adler that although Zanuck had rejected *The Ballad and the Source* out of hand nearly a decade earlier, the new Fox executives were much more receptive to Wanger's Alexandrian proposal. The studio had frequently produced "arty" films by 1959. That spring, Wald's adaptation of D. H. Lawrence's *Sons and Lovers* was in production in England, and Skouras later approved an adaptation of Jean Paul Sartre's *The Condemned of Altona*. In mid-1962, Wald was preparing a film version of James Joyce's *Ulysses:* "Boy, oh boy," Wald chortled, "how would you like to be in my chair trying to convince everyone that this will be a commercial film?" In the case of the Durrell project, everyone was convinced. Fox persuaded Mankiewicz, who after writing and directing *All About Eve* and *The Barefoot Contessa* was no stranger to multiply narrated stories, to work on the Durrell project beginning in June 1960.

Thus *Cleopatra* was just one of several film ideas Wanger had in the late 1950s at Fox. He had pursued it at Monogram, at RKO, and indeed for any studio executive who would listen. During his Figaro association, he sent a copy of Carlo Franzero's recent *The Life and Times of Cleopatra* to Lantz, noting the entertainment value of Franzero's anachronistic dialogue, Franzero's evocation of Alexandria as the Paris of the ancient world, and arguing for blockbuster casting (Grant as Caesar, Lancaster for Marc Antony, and Sophia Loren or Audrey Hepburn in the title role).

Absurd as the "Cleopatra" project looks in retrospect, in 1958 it had the sanction of other producers, just as all the studios had contemplated a *Joan of Arc* film twelve years earlier. According to Brown, the Fox executives signed Wanger on in part because they had been considering such a film on their own. Unlike "Justine," this film would fit easily into the biblical and ancient epic widescreen spectaculars such as *The Robe* (1953) and *The Ten Commandments* (1956), which were rooted in the Christian epics such as *Joan of Arc* in the postwar era.

With the approval of Adler and Schreiber, Wanger optioned the Franzero book in the fall of 1958. Seeking "the least expensive way to start a project," Brown and Wanger assigned Ludi Claire, a former actress and in Wanger's words "a dedicated eager beaver," to assemble an outline and a first rough draft from the Franzero book. In January 1959, Adler told Wanger that *Cleopatra* "is probably one of our most important projects on the 1959 schedule. . . . what concerns me most is the element of time." They aimed to complete the film by March 1960.

Adler and Skouras's tight schedule presumed that *Cleopatra* would fall well within the $1 million to $3 million range for its "big" films (such as McCarey's *The Devil Never Sleeps* or Mark Robson's *The Inspector*). They wanted an economically made $2 million spectacle with "pre-sold names" such as contractees Joan Collins, Suzy Parker or Joanne Woodward. This clashed with Wanger's big-budget concept and his desire for a voluptuous actress to play the part. As Wanger later explained his "strategy" for getting the film made as he envisioned it, he had "to keep the studio steamed up. . . . [I] had to be selling them all the time."

As Claire worked on the script, Wanger articulated his concept of *Cleopatra*, derived from Franzero's book: neither the "strumpet" of Shakespeare's *Antony and Cleopatra* nor the "silly teenager" in Shaw's *Cesar and Cleopatra,* Wanger saw her as

a fascinating, brilliant, irresistible young woman, admirably reared in rulership. She is a great administrator. She understands military tactics. Her sense of responsibility as a governing chief is enormous. . . . She speaks seven languages and many dialects.

Countless books and plays had been written about her since the 1930s, a phenomenon that cultural critic Mary Hamer argues is "part of an attempt to come to terms with the changing political status of women across the world" (particularly marked by their right to vote). The woman's angle was Wanger's primary justification for tackling a new version: "It can be the last word in opulence, beauty, and art—a picture women will love for its beauty and story."

Like Justine, Peron, and (to some extent) Joan of Arc, Cleopatra's biography provided Wanger with a female star vehicle about a powerful, seductive, destructive heroine in a story full of basic passions and historical reverberations. Cleopatra initiates the film's events as she shrewdly calculates her options for a liaison with Caesar and subsequently with Marc Antony. Contrary to his own claims, Wanger (along with Plutarch, Boccaccio, and Shakespeare) envisioned her as the ultimate femme fatale who, like countless heroines in films noir, leads her lover to self-destruction. "Perhaps this could be a great exploration of the dangers of the American woman who subjugates the American man," Wanger noted at one point, "using Cleopatra as the symbol of fascination, charm and destruction." Her eventual failure was essential to the patriarchal fascination of the "woman ruler." *This* Cleopatra had to be portrayed by a major star.

Wanger also wanted the film to resemble a suspense thriller. Describing Cleopatra's court politics, he evoked the "oily" atmosphere he prescribed for *Reign of Terror* and the *Arabian Nights* films, with "the soothsayers and eunuchs as the lawyers and counsellors [*sic*] of today, maybe the agents":

> The entire picture is one of intrigue, conspiracy, suspense and adventure. It will not be presented—as historical films usually are—in a pompous manner, with endless pageantry, but rather in the speed and tempo and cliff-hanger excitement of an underworld picture. . . . I have never dealt with a piece of material more full of the depths and heights of human emotions.

A big-budget historical film in the thriller vein was certainly a novelty (approximated, perhaps, by the BBC's *I, Claudius* television series). Wanger's first-choice director was Hitchcock, who flatly rejected the project.

To replace the dull pageantry, Wanger suggested the most spectacular values based on his oldest and most powerful production ideals: Diaghilev's Ballets Russes. In the early stages of scripting, he envisioned in the grandest terms the orientalist convention of Cleopatra's triumphant processional into Rome to show off her son Caesarion to Caesar and the city:

> Instead of spending fortunes on parading extras and dull mob scenes, I anticipate introducing the world's most stunning attractions such as great ballets [Les Ballets Africains, the Bolshoi Ballet], great singers, great comedians, great circus acts, as many animal acts as possible, in order to make this the standout visual entertainment for countries where dialogue does not mean so much.

The royal procession of a princess was a staple of the orientalist romance used in Walsh's as well as Korda's respective versions of *The Thief of Baghdad* and in deMille's 1934 *Cleopatra*. And, as with the Ballets Russes in the teens and deMille's film, Wanger recognized that his film's "merchandising potential" was "limitless."

Accordingly, the first phase of Wanger's campaign to produce *his* version of "Cleopatra" was to establish the visual possibilities for a big-budget film. He hired John DeCuir, a former Fox art director whose work on such films as *The King and I* demonstrated a facility with the orientalist aesthetic (by contrast, Wanger felt Fox's head art director was "very theatrical and very cold and not emotional"). DeCuir placed his sketches and set models on display at a small set near the art department, and after lunch one afternoon in mid-February 1959, Wanger "took everybody down [to see them] and they all flipped because it was the God-damnedest thing they had ever seen." As *Newsweek* put it, "By such stratagems, [Wanger] let the company sell itself the idea of a bigger movie." Wanger gloated, "It was my ingenuity against Fox."

Wanger's ingenuity also worked in casting Elizabeth Taylor to portray his reconceived heroine, the second phase of his efforts to sell Fox on his idea. A star since age twelve and her luminous appearance in MGM's *National Velvet* (1945), Taylor in the 1950s began to blossom in sympathetic and often sensuous roles such as Angela Vickers in George Stevens's *A Place in the Sun* (1951) and Leslie Benedict in Stevens's *Giant* (1952). Her portrayal of flustered, manipulative women in *Raintree Country* (1957) and *Cat on a Hot Tin Roof* (1958) marked a new level of acting achievement, for which she received Academy Award nominations. By 1959, her public life was a source of equal fascination. Widowed by Mike Todd's plane crash in 1957, she caused outrage by winning Eddie Fisher away from golden-haired Debbie Reynolds the following year. To Wanger's mind, Taylor's growing acting ability was secondary to her high personal profile; more crucial than either to his conception of Cleopatra was her youthful, beautiful face and full body.

But his casting idea was under siege. In August 1959, at a meeting of Fox executives, Skouras urged Adler to take "a dictatorial attitude" toward the project, undertake a nationwide search for Cleopatra or select his own star, and set a starting date. At the next meeting, Adler suggested that Hayward (or Parker) be cast in the role, that the script pick up Cleopatra's life at the age of thirty-five, and that if Wanger did not like this decision, "he could withdraw from the picture." Skouras replied, in the words of the meeting minutes, "that this was an intelligent decision; that it involved a competent performer, and that the combination would pay off at the box office."

Wanger later claimed that he held out consistently for Taylor in the leading role. But he was in fact far more flexible. After learning of Skouras's stance, Wanger urged Adler to make a big-budget version with Gina Lollabrigida, who had recently starred in United Artists' *Solomon and Sheba*. Still, the Fox executives postponed a final decision. Their hesitation gave Wanger room to maneuver. He called Taylor several times in London, where she was shooting *Suddenly Last Summer* in early September. Taylor asked Wanger for $1 million in salary. She also specified that the film would have to be made abroad for tax benefits. She also had some objections to Cleopatra's characterization in the script.

The Fox executives would not hear of Taylor's demands, but when Wanger again contacted her in Los Angeles in October, she lowered her salary to $750,000 plus a 10 percent interest in the film's gross rentals. "The deal went off the tracks about seven times," Wanger later recounted, "and I had to run around like a messenger boy from [Taylor's agent] Kurt Fringe to Liz to Skouras, to Schreiber." Wanger agreed that if Fox used Taylor, his profit participation would be reduced from 15 percent to 10 percent. Even though Taylor's agent raised her asking price back to $1 million, Fox consented. Taylor would report to Fox next spring after completing her last MGM film, *Butterfield 8*.

Wanger also ensured the look of the film by persuading Fox to let DeCuir follow through with set designs. He scored another coup for Taylor's costumes in persuading the studio to hire Messel, the acclaimed British stage designer who had created costumes for Korda's *The Thief of Baghdad* and worked on Gabriel Pascal's *Cesar and Cleopatra* (1948) and on the sets and Taylor's costumes for *Suddenly Last Summer* (1959). The Fox executives consented to these crucial assignments out of a "tremendous interest" in what Wanger called "getting a great picture as well as an artistic one."

The same consideration led Skouras and Adler to nominate Mamoulian to direct *Cleopatra*. Wanger was hesitant, both because he recalled his past work with Mamoulian on *Applause* and *Queen Christina* and because he was anxious to see "Cleopatra" done as a thriller; yet the only other serious candidate for the job was action director Henry Hathaway. Though Mamoulian had worked intermittently (he directed *Silk Stockings,* MGM's 1957 musical version of *Ninotchka,* but was fired from Goldwyn's *Porgy and Bess*), Wanger knew he was an egotist and willful:

> [Mamoulian] is a great artist but, also, he is a great individualist—and there is no reason for him to be concerned about Company policy as against personal reputation. . . . He is also a very clever man and in a position to take his time about decisions and demands. If this picture is over-shot and slow in terms of technique, I think we will be in a great deal of trouble.

Adler and Skouras secured Mamoulian as director after Taylor signed on in the fall of 1959.

Having persuaded Fox to make a big-budget production focusing on Cleopatra as a brilliant, beautiful, scheming character and having cajoled them into casting Taylor and hiring DeCuir and Messel to design the film, Wanger had made his primary contributions to *Cleopatra*. There were still many decisions to be made for the production. But Fox executives, in the belief that the producer's work consisted only of helpful suggestions, shut Wanger out of their deliberations.

The issue of where to shoot *Cleopatra* was one example. Adler, Schreiber, and Skouras first chose the Fox back lot for the Alexandria set in midsummer 1959, a decision Wanger learned of not by executive memos or talks, but from being alerted by someone on the lot that construction was underway. In late September, studio executives decided they could save $1 million in negative costs and use blocked income if the film was shot in England (a situation that placed the production under the control of Robert Goldstein, Fox's foreign production head).

In early 1960, Adler reversed course once more. He had purchased a completed Italian film, *Cleopatra,* from producer Lionello Santi (whose Galatea films had recently produced Michelangelo Antonioni's *L'Avventura*) to keep it out of the American market. He then decided that Fox's film could be produced cheaply in Italy, especially as a Hollywood actors strike was brewing in February. But the Santi association self-destructed when Fox belatedly realized there were no tax benefits to an Italian production, when Mamoulian discovered insuperable drawbacks to working in Italy, and when Santi took out a full-page ad in *Variety* announcing *his* forthcoming *Cleopatra* production (the one starring Taylor) without mentioning Fox. Adler reassigned the entire production to the Rank Organization's Pinewood studios. The settlement with Santi's company added $275,000 to the film's cost.

While *Cleopatra* was readied for European production, Wanger was to remain in Hollywood preparing his other projects for the studio. Schreiber explained this for the first time to Wanger in November 1959. As a Fox attorney put it later, the company felt that "your services could be used to better advantage if you were tending to your knitting in Hollywood [*The Dud Avocado* and the Durrell quartet] and working on the development of this script." In the fall of 1960, Wanger consulted with Mamoulian on script changes, hired with Mamoulian the British art director John Box and finalized the casting: British actor Peter Finch was to play Caesar, and Stephen Boyd, who had appeared in Zanuck's *The Big Gamble* and as Massala in *Ben-Hur,* would portray Antony.

England proved a disastrous choice. Arriving there at the end of 1959, Mamoulian and Wanger found that Goldstein had greatly exaggerated the size and technical capacity of Rank's Pinewood studios. The ceilings were too low to allow for the massive set design of Cleopatra's palace in Alexandria, there were not enough soundstages for different scenes, the unions were highly restrictive, and the workers expected a break for tea. The larger Denham studio was not available. At Pinewood, none of the technical work would be ready for the August 15 starting date. Skouras, facing a $6 million dollar picture, was unmoved. Mamoulian recalled telling Skouras it was all a mistake:

"but he said, 'Don't you think the president of the company should make that sort of decision?' I said, 'Yes, but you're still wrong.'"

Another producer might have rebelled or quit the project; Wanger, true to form, chose to stay on, quietly absorbing the rebuffs, detaching himself as much as he could from the fray. He had always been a hands-off executive, but his conduct on the Mamoulian *Cleopatra* represented a new extreme in his adherence to this policy. It was partly the mellowing that comes with age. It was also clearly a matter of self-preservation after his second heart attack. Indeed, during principal photography on *I Want to Live!*, Wanger had felt that production personnel were ignoring him "on all matters of budget and production." Yet he never sent his memo of complaint on the subject to Mankiewicz.

Then and now, Wanger knew his position was precarious. He had no other affiliations to fall back on, and he still needed to earn income. "I always had the feeling," Roddy McDowall noted of *Cleopatra,* "that if Walter had had any considerable cash flow, he would have removed himself from the project." Instead, Wanger had to put up with whatever Fox sent his way. And they sent him a producer's nightmare.

When later asked by Fox attorneys why he accepted the major decisions that were made without him (the back-lot construction in the summer of 1959, the hiring of Mamoulian), Wanger replied,

> I was in no position to insist. . . . I wanted to continue as the producer of the picture. . . . I was most anxious to get on with the picture, one way or another. And I was devoted to the subject and this project. . . . and I made allowances all the way down the line and I kept on. . . . I would have liked to have been respected, and I would have liked to have had the control, but if they didn't want that, what could I do about it?

Wanger was hardly unique in feeling the frustration of working at Fox during this time. Actor-producer Mason recalled the hysteria he encountered during the shooting of *Bigger than Life*. Schreiber, Rogell, and Frank McCarthy at one point came shouting at Mason, upset because director Nicholas Ray was shooting scenes that they had not approved. Robson wrote Wanger in December 1960 that "things have been terribly frustrating here in California, too, not only for me, but for most everyone." A joke circulated that producer Andre Hakim had been "given the yellow light to go ahead" with a production. Clearly, Fox executives complicated an already complex undertaking in the production of *Cleopatra*.

A reshuffling of executives in the summer of 1960 did not help. Adler died of cancer in early July. Skouras immediately replaced him with Goldstein, and Skouras asked Wanger to replace Goldstein as head of Fox's European production office. Wanger, smarting from income tax penalties and enjoying his sojourn in England, agreed, but his tenure there was brief. Skouras removed him from the post within weeks of the appointment. Wanger saw this as an act of retaliation. Wanger had given Rogell a copy of Mamoulian's *Cleopatra* script, and Rogell, without Wanger's permission or knowledge, had shown it to a highly critical Zanuck in Paris. Wanger's replacement was Rogell himself.

Fox executives continued to treat Wanger in this arbitrary fashion, most notably with Skouras's refusal to renew officially Wanger's contract with Fox. "Will you clarify this for me or should I go to a Fortune Teller?" Wanger asked his friend Feldman. Feldman found Skouras alternately claiming that Wanger had agreed to no salary raise and then admitting that this was not the truth. Feldman summarized: "It has been this kind of 'talk' which has been going on between Skouras and myself—he at all times telling me, of course, he wants you to stay, etc." to produce *Cleopatra* and "Justine." As Wanger learned, Skouras feared that the $500 increase in Wanger's weekly salary and the 10 percent increase in his profit percentage (to 25 percent) would occasion accusations of extravagance from Fox's disgruntled board of directors.

Wanger later documented such high jinks in *My Life with "Cleopatra"* in detail. He also gave two reasons for the film's incredible costs and confusions: the first was corporate politics that resulted in executive indecisiveness ("conflicting, expensive, on-again, off-again decisions from on-again, off-again groups in power"). The second was that the film went into production "before we had a script or a well-thought-out and practical production plan or organization." Fox's management was clearly responsible for the first difficulty and the lack of organization during the shoot, but the matter of script development was where Wanger contributed to the film's problems.

Like any Hollywood production, *Cleopatra* required a finished script for planning purposes. Yet, as shooting began in the fall of 1960, nearly two years after the project had been approved, there was still no shootable script. Wanger had persuaded Fox to hire British mystery writer Nigel Balchin in the spring of 1959, and he corresponded constantly with Balchin about his work. But ultimately Balchin's work pleased neither Mamoulian or Taylor. Mamoulian, when not seeking locations in Italy (a task that cost a month of script preparations), worked in the spring of 1960 with Durrell, who in Wanger's words had "a better sense of antiquity." But Durrell's work lacked the urgency of the Alexandrian quartet. The scene in Cleopatra's palace when brother Ptolemy's army lays outside the gates had no suspense: Wanger noted, "It seems more like a nice weekend in Surrey where the water is going to be turned off."

Several months' time was lost before Mamoulian signed up Dale Wasserman, who had written a teleplay on Don Quixote (the forerunner of his musical success *Man of La Mancha*). Their revisions continued up until shooting began in the fall of 1960.

"Who had the responsibility for the proper preparation of a script?"

Wanger was asked years later by Fox attorneys. "I had that responsibility," Wanger replied. "Who had the responsibility for a well thought out and practical production plan?" he was then asked. Wanger answered, "I had that, sir, but I didn't have organization." They were interlocking problems. Executive indecision at Fox from 1958 through 1959 about where to shoot the film, whom to cast, and the budget all precluded a confident approach to scripting. Meanwhile, at planning conferences, as Wanger described it, "Mamoulian would go in and give them a lot of double-talk as directors always do and always end up winning, you know."

All of these difficulties resulted in repetitive, interminable preparations for principal photography. "We are just getting ready to start our first set," unit manager Saul Wurtzel reported from England to Rogell on June 17, 1960. "I will close for now, a slightly puzzled man, wondering why we are still arguing points that should have been settled months ago." Two months later, due to script additions ("Cleopatra swimming with crocodiles, the Armenian campaign"), Wurtzel noted, "we may be fairly close now to where we started 8 weeks ago."

Then there was bad luck. When shooting began at Pinewood on September 15, 1960, the company had hopes of completing the film by February 14, 1961. But Taylor immediately contracted a cold from performing in the forty-degree temperatures and high humidity, and her illness cost Fox an additional $2 million. The British hairdressers' union protested the hiring of Taylor's MGM coiffeur Sidney Guilaroff. Messel's costumes for Taylor were still not ready. The crew shot around her, taking matte shots of Egyptian landscapes and shooting dialogue scenes with minor characters.

The results, Mamoulian recalled, were absurdly wrong for a Middle Eastern setting: "The great white columns of that beautiful set were wreathed in light mists; while every time anyone spoke, there were clouds of steam from his mouth. It had a marvelous quality, quite beautiful, but not exactly Alexandria." For the only time in the history of the production, Skouras decided to postpone principal photography. Fox reset the budget at $9 million.

Script problems continued to plague the production. Skouras prevailed upon Nunnally Johnson to work on the script late in 1960 for $140,000, an effort that did not please Mamoulian. At Taylor's suggestion, Wanger sent a copy of the script to Chayefsky, who estimated it would require another six months to improve. They could not afford the delay. As Mamoulian began rehearsing with Taylor in January 1961 before shooting resumed, both she and Finch objected to their scenes, which presented Cleopatra, in Wanger's words, as "a virgin who could only be deflowered by a god." Feldman and Skouras urged Wanger to shoot the script and get retakes later, rather than listening to the complaints of the talents.

By December, Wanger had no love for Mamoulian, however. "In the beginning [those foreign directors] are always sweet—like Fritz Lang," he later commented. Mamoulian, like Lang, had quickly become unmanageable. The director undercut Wanger's authority by calling meetings without him and withholding new script pages. He refused to work overtime or even to discuss the film over a meal, preferring instead to gossip about Fox's politics. Wanger grew tired of what he termed the director's prima donna attitude, his rudeness over unsatisfactory accommodations, and his "quoting the value of Becky Sharp [*sic*] and other pictures of the past." But as with *Applause* and *Queen Christina,* Wanger felt that hiring Mamoulian meant giving the director entire control over the production. Mamoulian felt entitled to ignore Wanger anyway, since Fox, not Wanger, had hired him. Mamoulian was right. Skouras had hired him, and Skouras fired him in mid-January 1961 by unexpectedly accepting Mamoulian's fourth offer of resignation.

At the behest of Fox's management, the lengthy first phase of *Cleopatra*'s production history came to an abrupt end, a victim of bad luck, poor choices, and Wanger's failure to obtain a shootable script. After two years and $7 million—$1.5 million more than the costs of *South Pacific*—Fox had ten minutes of test footage and no script. But the Mamoulian phase was only an exaggerated version of previous confusion and emergencies at Fox in the late fifties. Huston's *The Barbarian and the Geisha* was shot on location without studio supervision—and required extensive reshooting before release. As Johnson put it, if Zanuck had been around, "Huston would never have come up with such rubbish as was brought in." *The Young Lions,* also shot on location, went over budget by $1.3 million due to heavy rains, as did Selznick's *A Farewell to Arms.* Zanuck's own *The Roots of Heaven* exceeded its budget by $1 million.

Nor was such chaos the exclusive domain of the Fox company. The most notable example is *Gone with the Wind,* which drove its talents to acrimony and unnecessary expense, in large part because Selznick could not bring himself to settle on a final version of the script. Perhaps it is not surprising, then, that Fox and Wanger remained determined to complete the picture, and that they would repeat the same mistakes on a much larger scale during the next two years.

20

The Kafka Play
(1961–1962)

The *Cleopatra* that premiered in New York in June 1963 and which critic Judith Crist called "a monumental mouse" was the result not of four year's work and $44 million, but of 222 shooting days in Italy from the fall of 1961 to the summer of 1962 and $24 million in direct costs, exclusive of the Mamoulian phase. The script on which it was based was written in just over a year's time, more than half of it while shooting progressed, and again Fox inaugurated production without the proper preparation. That the film turned out to be as entertaining as it did was nothing short of miraculous. "Naturally," Wanger later commented, "the major credit goes to Joseph Mankiewicz who stubbornly has fought for his beliefs, and who has shown enormous ingenuity, talent, brilliance, humor, integrity and force throughout the two years that he has been working on this picture."

Within six days of accepting Mamoulian's resignation, Skouras had persuaded Mankiewicz to quit his work on "Justine" and take charge of *Cleopatra.* The choice of Mankiewicz was hardly accidental. He had been requested by Taylor; under his direction in *Suddenly Last Summer,* her performance had been nominated for an Academy Award. Based on similar results with Katharine Hepburn, Bette Davis, and the like, Mankiewicz had acquired the status of "immediate acceptability" by the most demanding of the "superstars" in a position to demand.

In December 1960, Mankiewicz read the Mamoulian script and found it "shockingly barren of either scope *or* magnitude—except in the old-fashioned concept of beautiful but dull processional marches to and from thrones, on and off ships . . . an opera without music." He derogated the script's outdated conception of Cleopatra as "a strange, frustrating mixture of an American soap-opera virgin and an hysterical Slavic vamp of the type Nazimova used to play." Intimately familiar with the existing script and having directed *Julius Caesar* for MGM seven years earlier, Mankiewicz agreed to take over the project. The money did not hurt: Skouras paid $3 million to buy out the inactive Figaro company and agreed to give Mankiewicz a profit interest. It was "the typical, killing Hollywood deal," Lantz has noted, "where money is no object. It was an offer he couldn't refuse."

Even before his arrival in London on February 1, Mankiewicz had explained to Wanger, in the latter's words,

> an entirely new, modern, psychiatrically rooted concept of the film. . . . Mark Antony lived always in the shadow of Caesar. . . . JLM sees Antony as a bad replica of Caesar. . . . He sees this inability to match Caesar as the cause of Antony's excessive drinking and eccentric behavior. Antony's conquest of Cleopatra is his only triumph over Caesar. Then he realizes he has not conquered but has been conquered—and this leads to his ultimate self-destruction.

The motif of rivalry, evident in other Mankiewicz films such as *All About Eve,* was the major transformation of the story. Wanger at first resisted the idea of a weak Antony, noting that Caesar's most trusted lieutenant was "a much greater hero . . . as well as the idol of the army." But he was not going to oppose the man who would salvage his most ambitious production, and he persuaded himself that "it can lead to a great picture."

Mankiewicz's new concept meant discarding the Mamoulian script, throwing out the useless ten minutes of footage shot (largely wardrobe tests in 70mm Todd-AO, Technicolor, and sound), dismissing Boyd and Finch, and eventually writing off all of the $7 million in expenditures to that date. Within one month, Mankiewicz outlined a new script, which for the sake of time he then turned over to Durrell (again) and veteran screenwriter Sidney Buchman, a blacklistee who had written *Mr. Smith Goes to Washington* and coauthored *Gone with the Wind.* Each writer separately developed story outlines that closely followed Mankiewicz's work; Mankiewicz in turn developed the detailed screenplay from their outlines. Durrell's work proved useless (again), and Buchman's writing carried the plot to only the first quarter of the finished film, Cleopatra's arrival in Rome. To succeed Buchman, Mankiewicz and Wanger in April hired Ranald MacDougall, who authored the script for *Mildred Pierce* and coauthored with Richards the script for *Possessed.* The hiring of MacDougall confirmed that Mankiewicz shared Wanger's view of Cleopatra as a femme fatale. Moreover, MacDougall had more recently worked as a BBC documentarist. Wanger characterized him as "a hard, fast worker" whom he hoped would provide a sense of immediacy, a "See It Now" flavor, to the film.

For a brief time in the spring of 1961 it seemed as though the writers' efforts were for nought. Taylor suddenly took ill again. First diagnosed with pneumonia of the lungs on the third of March, she was proclaimed fatally ill within days, and doctors performed a tracheotomy to relieve her breathing. Reporters and movie fans mobbed the London Clinic, where Taylor recovered slowly through the month of April. Fox gave up entirely on the idea of a British production and dismantled Box's $600,000 sets at Pinewood. Taylor returned to Hollywood with Fisher, accepted an Academy Award for her performance in *Butterfield 8,* and announced that she was through with shooting abroad. The new sympathy shown Taylor only strengthened Fox's determination to finish *Cleopatra.*

While Taylor recuperated during the summer and underwent plastic surgery on her neck to remove (unsuccessfully) the scar from her tracheotomy, Mankiewicz and Wanger reconstituted a team of above-the-line talents and technicians. Against Fox's wishes, they cast Richard Burton (then appearing in New York in *Camelot*) as Antony (for $300,000, including $50,000 to buy out his year-long contract for *Camelot*), which Mankiewicz called "by far the most demanding and difficult [male role] to play" in the film. For Caesar they secured Rex Harrison (for $200,000), whom Wanger had requested one year earlier because "he can handle costumes and he has strength and sex and, I think, will help Taylor enormously." McDowall, who had played Octavian in a recent stage version of *Julius Caesar,* agreed to play the same role in the new film. An array of sterling British and American actors completed the cast.

While keeping DeCuir, Fox signed veteran cameraman Leon Shamroy (who had shot *You Only Live Once* and *Private Worlds*). To replace Messel, Wanger and Mankiewicz persuaded Fox to sign *Spartacus* designer Vittorio Nino Novarese for the men's costumes and (for Taylor's costumes) Sharaff, who worked on Mankiewicz's *Guys and Dolls* and recently had worked on Broadway and Universal's *Flower Drum Song* (1961); in fact, Shamroy, DeCuir, and Sharaff had all worked on Fox's stunning *The King and I.* To Wanger, Sharaff was

> the most sensitive and most brilliant woman I ever worked with in design. . . .
> She has perfect taste, [is] very sensible, very hard-working and she likes things finished. . . . She is extravagant but it is all in the interest of quality and class.

Sharaff designed sixty costumes, including shoes and jewelry, for Taylor alone, while Renie worked on handmaiden costumes.

With this group assembled, Fox executives decided in late June 1961 to shoot *Cleopatra* entirely in Italy, partly because Fox's back lot was full, partly to take advantage of tax benefits to Taylor and Wanger's production companies, and, as usual, partly because Italy's six-day work week, warm weather, and lower labor costs would save funds. These decisions made, Wanger spent the bulk of the summer months encouraging MacDougall, Sharaff, and DeCuir in their preparations for the Italian shoot and refamiliarizing himself with Fox's studio problems.

Most prominent among these were several Wall Street investment firms whose representatives by the spring of 1961 were dubious about Skouras's management skills. They were also furious about a $15 million loss from 1960's productions plus *Cleopatra*'s $7 million write-off, figures that not even the sale of the bulk of Fox's back lot to real estate developers could obscure. In March, as Mankiewicz and the writers worked on the *Cleopatra* script, hostile board members Robert Lehman (of Lehman Bros.) and Robert L. Clarkson (of American Express) were joined by John Loeb (of Loeb, Rhoades and Co.) and lawyer Milton Gould, representing the investment firm Treves and Co., who with Loeb, Rhoades and Co. held 15 percent of the outstanding studio stock.

The Wall Street board members knew less about moviemaking than Skouras, and their efforts to cut studio overhead and make Fox a more efficient company were at first quixotic. In June 1961, they visited the lot, interviewing "independent producers" such as Selznick, Wald, and Stevens, and surveying the unfamiliar territory with the naïveté of *Stand-In*'s Attebury Dodd. Wanger wrote Mankiewicz during June that the board considered placing Skouras alongside Goldstein in charge of production because "Skouras is so efficient in production." He added dryly, "That's the bankers' latest finding."

The board members quickly wised up. In September, they realized that the studio's high-cost production policy created an annual overhead expense of $9.5 million that was "absorbing all the working cash of the Corporation." They learned that *Cleopatra* and Zanuck's *The Longest Day*—a reenactment of the Allied invasion of Normandy—and several lesser films were also depleting corporate monies. For this, the board blamed Skouras, the only executive continuously overseeing production since Zanuck's departure.

In early May 1961, the board hired the current chief of Fox television (and Skouras's son-in-law), Peter Levathes, to head film production. Levathes had had a string of prime-time successes and he negotiated the landmark 1961 sale of several recent Fox features to NBC. Although Levathes was another neophyte in filmmaking, he assumed his post with the best intentions. "At least Pete is somebody that is human," Wanger wrote Rogell, "a business man who can be talked to and has the backing of the New York office. . . . he seems not to have any desires to interfere in production, but to act as a top administrator. We shall see."

With Levathes learning the ropes, the Fox board took additional action during the summer of 1961 as *Cleopatra* prepared for its September starting date. They canceled dividend payments for the first time in the company's history, threatened to fire Skouras, and began making snap decisions solely on the basis of cost. With *Cleopatra* and *The Longest Day* in preparation and $100 million in Fox's inventories, the Loeb and Treves representatives decided to cancel Stevens's *The Greatest Story Ever Told,* which had accumulated $2.3 million during three years in preproduction. (Stevens produced the project at Paramount in 1965.) As Wanger later observed, "Talking to the people at Fox is like a Kafka play in which you call a number, and no one's at the other end of the phone. . . . You try to reason but discover no one is listening." No one on the board was listening to anything Skouras said, aside from his promises that *Cleopatra* and Zanuck's *The Longest Day* would rectify all of Fox's problems. Under such enormous pressure, he and Levathes insisted that principal photography commence on September 25 and that the film cost only $10 million, not the estimated $14 million required.

Thus most of the major problems that beset the second phase in the production of *Cleopatra* were the consequence of Fox's studio politics. "Skouras had pulled the studio out with CinemaScope," McDowall observes. "That one thing had stemmed the tide of the studio's decline. Now with *Cleopatra,* he was going to do it again. But when you enter into this situation where you depend on 'this one thing,' you are in trouble." Indeed, the demand to begin shooting in September created innumerable problems. The first, and most costly, was that the studio in mid-July sent an inadequate group to prepare for shooting. As Rogell wrote Skouras five months later:

> To attempt to launch Cleopatra with no more than the Director, Unit Manager [Johnny Johnston], Art Director [DeCuir] and [art department] staff without the backing of top-level management, internal controls, legal aides, etc., was nothing less than suicidal. Even the producer was not on the ground until the end of August, with a starting date of Sept 18th.!!

By contrast, MGM spent a year, not two months, in Rome on preproduction for *Ben-Hur.*

Most costly, as Rogell noted, was the fact that Fox sent no administrators ("top level management, internal controls") to the Italian production. As its location staff and salary rolls grew to one hundred people from Fox's lot (*Ben-Hur* had only twenty-six MGM staff members on location), Fox had no one in place to look after the multitude of details to be coordinated. Nor was anyone authorized to oversee expenditures. Comptrollers paid bills from Italian contractors before they could be examined and adjusted. The Italian unit manager overcharged Fox for car, truck, and property rentals and for insurance. As Rogell described it, accountants and production managers were "always three weeks behind [on their estimates], and then they suddenly remember some $300,000 item they forgot to include." The disastrous rainy October weather, which apparently no one anticipated, exacerbated the problem further. Costs rose to more than $135,000 per day.

However, Rogell, in later reports stressed only the most obvious instances of chaotic spending, oversized sets, and rampant expense accounts and featherbedding: "I don't know where the money has gone, but they have thrown away $5,000,000 . . . sets too large and costly, everyone including actors here on salary and living allowances for weeks and months before they were needed." The sets were indeed a problem, but Fox itself had approved costly salaries and expenses for various technicians such as Guilaroff, who received $1,000 a week in salary plus $600 in expenses. But here again, inadequate accounting aggravated the problem, as funds were paid out to personnel even if (like Shamroy's wife) they were no longer on location. McDowall recalls: "We all had our own cars if you could find them, but you could never find your driver. There was a tremendous amount of double-dealing. The important became unimportant, the unimportant became what was really important."

The second major consequence of the September starting date was that shooting was frequently held up because sets, costumes, wigs, or props were not ready on time, a problem that Mankiewicz had warned against in May but which persisted through February 1962. It was, in Wanger's words, "England all over again." The situation was made worse by the fact that production was divided between two locations, the Roman forum set built on twelve acres at Cinecitta and the massive Alexandria set built at Anzio, a hunting estate on the Tyrrhenian Sea owned by Italian prince Borghese (which turned out to be near a NATO practice target). Moreover, DeCuir's massive sets were built as if "intended to remain for all time" on large plankings with innumerable steps that made crowd coordination, lighting, and shooting for proper scale values difficult.

Similarly, costume making was completely disorganized, and Rogell flew over Fox's department head Courtney Haslam to straighten things out. Harrison refused to wear the costumes designed by Novarese. Sharaff, who was hired to design only Taylor's clothes, saved the production considerable delay, in Wanger's words, through "ingenuity and replanning the costumes and doing a very big job . . . even to the extent of building a foundation to build up [Harrison's] slim figure"; she also designed costumes for the dance segment in Tarsus on the barge, upgrading the costumes so that the dancers didn't resemble, too much, "hookers at the Ambassador" hotel.

Finally, and most catastrophically, Skouras and Levathes's rigid adherence to the September starting date meant that production began without a completed script. Mankiewicz claimed it would have cost Fox less, in the long run, if he could have completed the script while the crews finished the sets and costumes. For during the summer's corporate struggles, MacDougall's work on the script had proven entirely unsatisfactory: it veered away from Mankiewicz's story outline (including a segment in which Antony bumps into the Three Magi in the desert). Fox's production department had to prepare its budget estimates from a script outline rather than the script itself. By late September, Mankiewicz had completed 132 pages of script, the equivalent of a one-hundred-minute film and a remarkable accomplishment in six months' time, given his attention to details of production and casting. But another 195 pages remained to be written when shooting began.

As a result, after the September 25 starting date, Mankiewicz shot scenes by day and wrote the script in longhand every night. The strain on the writer-director was considerable, and Mankiewicz resorted to injections and pills for the strength and energy to direct and write. "I spoke to him in Rome," Lantz recalls,

> and I said to him, "Joe, close down the picture for eight days." And he said, "I can't, they won't let me." And I said, "You have to close it down on Friday night, you have to go to bed and sleep Saturday and Sunday, do nothing, and on Monday, untroubled by anything, lock yourself in and rewrite, do what you have to do. You cannot work all night and then shoot the next day with Elizabeth and Rex." And they would not let him do it.

After vehement arguments, Fox allowed him to work five days a week. And in February 1962, burned out from the extraordinary effort he was putting into the film, he rehired MacDougall, who scripted battle scenes (that of Moongate in Alexandria and that of the sea contest at Actium) and the final fifty pages that Mankiewicz lacked the time or energy to compose.

But of equal difficulty to the sheer physical effort was the psychological strain of writing under such circumstances. Mankiewicz was a perfectionist who often rewrote the material scheduled for production. As Wanger recalled it, he

> was being pressed always about his writing—well anybody can write and write and write but are they really going to write something that is going to pay off and working under these circumstances was an enormous agony—agony is the only word I can use—Joseph suffered the agonies of hell because he is conscientious and because he has good taste and he has good judgment and he is very prideful—Also he is very well disciplined and he is very meticulous in what he expects other people to deliver.

Wanger, Rogell, and Skouras were all thrilled with the literate and expressive dialogue and solid structure in the first half of Mankiewicz's script. For the film's second part, however, he had to shoot from a virtual first draft script.

Fox's refusal to wait for a completed script only compounded the film's administrative difficulties (by contrast MGM had a finished script *before* it began its year of preproduction work on *Ben-Hur*). Hence, the filmmakers lacked the control and efficiency of having a continuity script on which to base planning. An estimated additional $7.5 million in costs ensued because Mankiewicz had to shoot in continuity, and as Rogell complained, performers (including Burton and McDowall) found themselves waiting for weeks or months before they were used. Mankiewicz protected himself with scenes and shot angles he thought he might need. Yet he also managed to economize by eliminating or reconceiving various scenes (such as scaling down the desertion of Antony's men to Octavian).

In late October, Rogell's production reports certified that the film would never be finished by March and that it would cost at least $17 million exclusive of studio overhead. This news unfortunately coincided with a spate of minority stockholder suits against Fox. As rain continued to postpone completion of Cleopatra's Rome procession into November, a parade of Fox executives visited the set. They argued heatedly with Wanger during a series of climactic meetings from the sixteenth to the twentieth, exhorting him to take charge with Zanuck-like tyranny.

After this—two months after the start of principal photography, as Mankiewicz began shooting Cleopatra's grand procession into Rome—the weather cleared and European production head Rogell was invested with the studio's authority to control and scrutinize expenditures. Rogell proceeded to cut Fox's location staff by half, institute expenditure accounts and controls in all production departments, and cajole Mankiewicz into finding more cost-efficient ways of shooting his scenes.

To Skouras and Levathes, this was too little too late, especially when a board meeting in late November announced the studio's estimated $22.5 million loss for the year. Again there was talk of Skouras resigning, and Skouras and Levathes needed a scapegoat for their difficulties and for the problems on *Cleopatra.* Mankiewicz, and especially Wanger, were prime candidates. Yet clearly, they had been doing their best to proceed with a chaotic situation that they had not created.

Wanger tried to be the ideal producer, in his words to "be on top of every problem that he can deal with and be active twenty-four hours a day in watching over the picture." But as Wanger later put it, even

> on a much smaller picture than CLEOPATRA the producer is supposed to have a business manager and also a production manager. A producer is not expected to handle every detail of production in person, but is supposed to be properly staffed.

Fox's production staff did not consult Wanger on any of the initial arrangements nor did they equip him for the supervision so desperately needed. For *Cleopatra,* he "used to go around day after day with a long list of items to be checked in connection with the picture, which is really the duty of the production manager and the third or fourth assistants."

DeCuir's set designs were one area where Wanger failed to control the production. To Wanger, DeCuir was (like Sharaff) a perfectionist,

> the kind of man who is never satisfied. He puts up a tower, he wants to put something on top of the tower. He fools around. That's why he is good, but

somebody has to know how to handle him and if he can run between three or four people, he's got you licked.

Wanger conceded that "DeCuir got away from me" and constructed the over-built sets. But Wanger had saved the studio expenses in countless, subtle ways. He prevented the company from renting yet another studio forty-five minutes away from Cinecitta which lacked heat or soundproofing. He rejected the choice of a remote, primitive island to stage the Battle of Actium. He monitored the progress of set constructions and costume making, checked on the scheduling of trips, supervised last minute casting, and made sure that technical problems (humming Todd-AO cameras) were communicated to the studio.

Most of all, and most apparent to the Fox brass, he dealt with above-the-line talents, mediating conflicts such as one he reported between Shamroy's spectacular and Mankiewicz's more intimate aesthetic, or between Mankiewicz and Rogell. He made sure the actors' needs were met, giving them whatever moral support he could. In *My Life with "Cleopatra,"* Wanger, like other directors and producers of epic films, used military metaphors for his work, writing that he sometimes felt "like a chaplain at the front line" during production on the film; privately he felt "like a General in the Marines that has to fight his way out of a trap." Wanger told Levathes in September, "We are really up against a Churchillian task, but everybody's spirits are high and the morale is high." But the toll taken on the group was higher: Johnston took ill in the fall, eventually dying of cancer in Hollywood; in January, Shamroy took a week off from nervous exhaustion while the second unit continued work.

Although Wanger was infinitely more comfortable with Mankiewicz than with Mamoulian, Skouras had personally created an ambiguous hierarchy of command by bypassing Wanger to deal with Mankiewicz. Actually, Skouras had effected this approach with Mamoulian, but that director's personal idiosyncracies had obscured its significance. As in the Mamoulian phase, Fox did not notify Wanger of production meetings on *Cleopatra;* it was Mankiewicz who invited him along. Indeed, executive production manager "Doc" Merman attested that Skouras had told Mankiewicz, "Joe, from you I expect the biggest picture ever made in Hollywood and anything you want you can have and we will all cooperate." Rogell wrote Skouras in December 1962:

> I had no idea that you would turn over to [Mankiewicz] all the business management of the unit, and that's exactly what happened. Joe engaged Johnston, Johnston engaged [Italian production manager] Magli, and they ran it. Joe believed in [them], but they let him down. We, management, are to blame for that, not Mankiewicz!

Skouras denied this until 1963, but Zanuck affirmed it, writing Mankiewicz in 1962:

You were not the official producer, yet in the history of motion pictures no one man has ever been given such authority. The records show that you made every single decision and that your word was law. . . .

I cannot absolve Spyros of his share of the responsibility. He was in a desperate personal situation, but since he was not a picture-maker and since Peter Levathes had no production knowledge, and since both Doc Merman and Sid Rogell were either powerless to act or useless, you were undisputedly in the driver's seat. On this point, I do blame "administration" for giving any one man such unlimited authority.

"Joe has been very considerate and very cooperative with me," Wanger wrote Bautzer in June 1962. "However I have never been in a position where I could make changes other than what I could do through diplomacy and friendship."

Moreover, Wanger had to rely on diplomacy and friendship because Mankiewicz was writing the script as production progressed, a situation Fox's impatience had precipitated. As Wanger noted, he, Rogell, and Merman "couldn't appraise and critique" Mankiewicz's script "intelligently . . . we were not in the position to discipline a director that was writing his script day by day." Levathes and Skouras's visits to Rome were useless in this regard. Rogell wrote Levathes in February 1962 that "the situation is just about the same as it was when you left here. We are completely in the hands of the Director-writer." Merman concurred: "No arguments from me you or President Kennedy is [sic] going to sway Joe from his determination."

Yet even if the script had been completed, and even if Wanger had been given clear authority over Mankiewicz, Wanger was not inclined to pull rank with talent. Rogell complained to Levathes that if he tried to send unnecessary studio personnel back to Hollywood, Mankiewicz "throws a fit" and that "Wanger is no help—goes along with Joe, and begs me to do likewise."

Wanger defended his policy of "going along" with Mankiewicz at several points. During production, he told Fox officials "that the only person who could write the script, and who could direct the picture, was Mankiewicz. Fighting him in the open would get us nothing. The thing is to encourage him, and get on with him." After the film was completed, he told Fox attorneys, "You have to control a director and at the same time you can't beat him down, otherwise you are going to ruin all of this individual imagination. He is supposed to be an artist." A film's producer, he argued,

should be the responsible, militant custodian of the funds and the artistic developments of the film, but, however, of course, if he is a proper producer, he will not belittle or undermine the authority that is due a director and the stars, but will make them do what is required without a crisis . . . so you just don't arbitrarily throw your power around or become a hatchet man. It has to be done with sympathy, understanding, diplomacy and experience."

Even Rogell discovered there was some logic to Wanger's tolerance. When Rogell tried to reduce Harrison's expenses (refusing to pay for his car and his chauffeur, and moving him to a smaller dressing-room trailer), Harrison refused to report on the set and harangued Rogell in front of the entire company. But the adulterous affair between Taylor and Burton tested the limits of Wanger's diplomatic skill and the Fox executives' tolerance of Wanger. "Production I'll straighten out," Merman wrote to Levathes in late February, "but this Taylor thing is dynamite."

The Taylor-Burton romance had started quietly in December 1961, known primarily to Mankiewicz and the actors' most intimate friends. In February it was a general scandal, widely reported in newspapers and magazines around the world; by April, in scenes reminiscent of Fellini's *La Dolce Vita,* the Italian paparazzi fluttered around the lovers as they wandered together on the Via Veneto. Wanger and everyone else assumed it "would be a once over lightly" affair, and Wanger later recalled telling Burton, "I don't care what you do but please don't do it on the front page." But the attraction grew deeper, and Wanger simply could not restrict the lovers' outings, their weekend holidays, or even Taylor's hour-long delays or no-shows on the set. In all, Taylor's illness and indispositions caused thirty-three days of idleness while Fox paid her $50,000 salary plus $3,000 in expenses each week.

Fox had repeatedly used Wanger to cajole Taylor into signing contracts and approving delays and to assure her cooperation in general. But his influence on Taylor in this matter was as limited as Fisher's. When Skouras exhorted Wanger to do something about the situation, Wanger replied that the Screen Actors Guild could discipline Taylor and Burton properly when the film was finished. Skouras didn't want to wait, and he didn't want the additional unfavorable publicity that such action might generate. He wanted Wanger to bring them to heel quietly.

Meanwhile production meetings in Rome between Wanger, Mankiewicz, Rogell, and Merman, as Wanger described them, became costly versions of *Waiting for Godot:* "We would try to find out whether Elizabeth was going to show up the next day—we would all sit around and we would wait to find out and then decide if we could shoot or we couldn't shoot or what the substitution could be." If Taylor or someone else had to cancel a shoot, Mankiewicz spent the day writing additional scenes. Chaplain Wanger meantime consoled Sybil Burton, Eddie Fisher, and Taylor's parents and talked with all the principals about their feelings. "My father was trying to play psychiatrist," recalls Stephanie, who was then attending school in Florence and visiting Wanger on the weekends. "I'd see people camping out in my father's room. There'd be Leon, there'd be Joe and they would all be talking about how they were going to get this thing completed, keep Eddie away and keep Liz happy."

The Fox brass blamed Wanger for the Taylor-Burton affair and the consequent production delays. "The producer on the job, such as you are," Skouras wrote Wanger as negative press on Taylor flooded Fox's New York office, "had the primary responsibility of seeing that this picture proceeded according to schedule." "Walter was treated so miserably," Mankiewicz observed:

> When does a producer get bawled out for things that happen on the set or things that don't happen on the set? . . . Without Walter there would not have been a *Cleopatra*, not conceivably. And I know there must have been times when he took abuse that was meant for me, willingly, without my being there. They weren't doing well and they got pleasure out of a well-bathed, intelligent literate man that they could command at a time when they were not in a position to command anything. They found somebody they could whip with impunity. Walter couldn't hit back. How was he gonna hit back? By quitting? I could hit back. I could hit back by screwing up their entire investment. But he couldn't hit back, and I tried to wrap him up in my skirts.

Wanger perceived the Fox officials' exhortations to discipline the talents as their way of removing him; if he ever alienated Mankiewicz or Taylor, he had no value to Fox. Besides, after the meetings in February 1962, McDowall remembers, "Fox humiliated him into being a maître d' on that film, and it was embarrassing to see someone of that sort of stature being humiliated." Wanger, as if to spite Fox, began spending more time escorting Lady Diana Manners, the Baroness de Rothschild, and the Italian aristocracy onto the Cinecitta sets.

The fretting over Taylor and Burton by Fox executives did have its comical aspects. "[Skouras] worked himself up into a big euphoric state about the fifty million in advance guarantees he was going to get from exhibitors," Selznick wrote Wanger in late February 1962.

> —and then suddenly before my eyes I saw a transition that would make a great scene in a movie: he said, "Of course, if anything happens to that girl . . ." and then he turned white, started to rock from side to side, the tempo of the bead-rolling slowed down as he talked, and then worked up to a fevered pace. I think every time another story comes out of Rome, he gets closer to what with anybody else would be a heart attack—but he really seems to have the strength of ten men, and I am sure will survive everybody else in this business while the activities of Twentieth kill them off in droves.

In the short term, however, Skouras was in deep trouble. He had fended off hostile stockholders in December with twenty minutes of gorgeous rushes from *Cleopatra,* and he had promised the Fox board that the film would shut down in March. This was a promise with no basis in reality. By April 1962, as Taylor and Burton began appearing openly in public, Mankiewicz still had to reshoot Cleopatra's processional into Rome and several battle scenes being scripted by MacDougall. With a half-million-dollar loss posted in 1962's first quarter and the *Cleopatra* budget projected at $27 million, the board's lack of faith in Skouras was absolute.

Various studio releases (*The Innocents, State Fair, Tender Is the Night,* and *Satan Never Sleeps*) had lost money; but *Cleopatra,* Wanger, Mankiewicz, and Taylor were obvious and convenient scapegoats. Rogell's pragmatic and sometimes hysterical communications to Levathes and Skouras undercut Wanger's optimistic letters. Merman's reports faithfully documented disputes with Mankiewicz over where and how to shoot scenes and warned that the film would not close by July if cuts were not made. From Merman's perspective, the director was capricious, insisting on more time to shoot and refusing to cut scenes.

Hence, the executive committee and the board of Fox were determined to pull the plug, just as they had on Stevens's film. With *Cleopatra,* they would simply assemble what had been shot and release the film. Obtaining the approval of Skouras, Fox's executive committee dispatched Levathes and two officials to Rome. Levathes was, in Wanger's words, "hysterical" and insisted on a conference at the Grand Hotel which kept Wanger from spending a weekend with Stephanie in Paris. Wanger recorded in his diary, "For the first time feel really sunk over the whole thing." He told Levathes, "Pete, don't let failure go to your head."

In a heated meeting with Mankiewicz, Rogell, and Wanger, the Fox officials announced three directives from Skouras and the Fox board: first, that Taylor, the most costly talent, had to be closed out of the picture by June 9 regardless of her remaining scenes. On that same date, Fox fired Marilyn Monroe from *Something's Got to Give,* with executives commenting that the studio could ill afford both Monroe *and* Taylor on their payroll; several weeks later Monroe committed suicide.

Second, the studio would cut off all funds for *Cleopatra* on June 30, although the battles of Moongate, Tarsus, and Actium remained to be shot, some of them on location in Egypt. The Battle of Pharsalia, the first scene in Mankiewicz's script, was canceled, even though it was composed "to place the time of the picture and to set up so many interesting speculations in an audience's mind," particularly regarding Caesar's distress at vanquishing his son-in-law Pompey. An ardent telegram from Mankiewicz did not dissuade the Fox board, nor did a generous offer from Harrison to pay the cost of shooting because he resented "very much as an artist the way this man [Mankiewicz] has been treated." These first two directives were written up in a "Memorandum of Understanding" that only Rogell and Wanger signed.

In a third move, the committee informally fired Wanger by discontinuing his salary and expense account, which by this time had amounted to an unprecedented $350,000 for his work on several projects. Although the Fox group in Rome acted sympathetic to Wanger, who was skeptical of the action, a studio executive (Wanger suspected Goldstein) leaked this news to columnist Earl Wilson. But the firing was ambiguous: Fox had never renewed his contract, yet it continued to pay his salary. It was stopping his compensation, but sought his signature on the memorandum of understanding about concluding the film. Fox could legally dismiss Wanger if he refused to abide by their directives, but Wanger remained in Rome and attended and organized meetings to coordinate the remainder of the shooting in Ischia and in Egypt. In fact, up through October 1962, Fox maintained offices for Wanger in a "Cleopatra" bungalow next to Mankiewicz.

Fox's contradictory signals to Wanger may have been rooted in the executives' awareness that they were in a legally tenuous position. And salary aside, they needed Wanger on the job. Mankiewicz read the Wilson column, and he told Merman of his intention to assume the contractually stipulated role of producer and thereby reinstate the photography of several sequences (such as Pharsalia) which Fox had eliminated. Further, the writer-director reported that Taylor and Burton, then en route to Ischia to shoot the Battle of Actium, would coordinate a sit-down strike among talent and crew on the set the next day unless Wanger was reinstated.

Merman, after consulting Levathes in Los Angeles, assured both Mankiewicz and Taylor that "Wanger is the Producer and the salary matter is something of a private nature between Walter and the Studio." With obvious relief, Merman reported that Taylor "sounded very pleased, accepted the situation and promised me she would see me in Ischia today." Wanger, true to his desire to see the film completed, did and said nothing to contradict this. Taylor finished her work on June 23, and the entire production concluded one month later with several battle scenes quickly shot in Egypt.

While the *Cleopatra* group struggled to complete the picture, Skouras lost the battle with his Wall Street critics. Three days after Taylor closed on *Cleopatra*, he resigned from the company. Fortunately for Skouras, Zanuck, who had just completed *The Longest Day*, rescued him. Zanuck's World War II combat drama put the *Cleopatra* operation to shame, for he had completed his epic in ten months with an elaborate, all-star cast for $8 million, and he had it ready for release in the fall of 1962 while Mankiewicz worked on his rough cut.

Buoyed by the experience, Zanuck looked into Fox's corporate affairs in late spring 1962. His family was the largest private stockholder with one hundred thousand shares and had seen the holdings drop from $5 million in the early 1950s to $2 million in the early 1960s. "There is also a little matter called pride," he wrote Wanger in mid-July. "I founded the goddam company with nothing but one secretary and a telephone, and for twenty years it paid dividends and was second to no other company." In June, Zanuck entered the fray as the lone Hollywood insider against the meddling outsiders. "Why does he want a proxy fight?" Gould asked *Newsweek.* "I've been in them before. He hasn't." Zanuck, en route to New York, replied, "I do not believe that stockbrokers or their attorneys are qualified to endorse or pass on annual film proposals." By July, Zanuck had persuaded a board majority to appoint him head of production. "It was a long shot," Joseph Mankiewicz later commented, "a ninety-yard pass from a player thought to be on the sidelines."

To Wanger, Zanuck's return and the dismissal of Fox's troublesome production executives and board members was a much needed, "good, high enema." Zanuck was characteristically vigorous. He replaced Levathes with his son Richard, moved immediately to shut down studio facilities, and reduced payrolls by one-third, with only personnel crucial to television work, *The Woman in July,* and *Cleopatra* remaining. These moves gave him further time to assess Fox's status, review its inventories and plan for the next season's productions.

But Wanger had "no idea as to how [Zanuck] feels about me." In July as he completed postproduction on *The Longest Day* in Paris, Zanuck was very appreciative of Wanger's support:

> I have no illusions about the task that lies ahead. I will need assistance and support from all sides. Knowing that I start with your congratulations and best wishes goes a long way toward me feeling less "lonesome" in the job I have undertaken.

As usual, Wanger began offering suggestions to both Zanucks for projects and publicity, such as a documentary on Monroe and a United Nations endorsement for *The Longest Day.*

Wanger himself was not idle. Through September 1962, he advised Mankiewicz about the five-hour rough cut on *Cleopatra* (from 700,000 feet of rushes to 21,000 feet), supervised dubbing and Alex North's scoring, and composed a lengthy statement in support of a sole screenwriting credit for Mankiewicz. He urged publicity director Charles Einfeld to emulate Todd's promotion of *Around the World in Eighty Days.* Primary among his ideas, which he had first articulated in 1959, involved merchandising, specifically Taylor tie-ins called Cleopatra Enterprises, which would sell "a high quality line of cosmetics and perfumes, plus every type of woman's accessory, jewelry, beauty books, etc., etc." He proposed a lavish souvenir program, book tie-ins, the publication of Mankiewicz's script, and a tour of *Cleopatra*'s costumes, props, wigs, and set designs. Though his contact with Zanuck and Skouras was limited, his relations with them remained cordial. Richard Zanuck seemed to share Wanger's enthusiasm for *Cleopatra.*

Darryl Zanuck did not. When he screened Mankiewicz's four-and-a-half-hour rough cut in September in Paris, he acknowledged the outstanding entertainment values in the bulk of the film, but bluntly expressed "shock" at how much remained to be done. He initially barred Mankiewicz from working on the film. But after he publicized their acrimonious exchanges in the trade press, Zanuck invited Mankiewicz to Paris. Ultimately, Zanuck conceded that many of the sequences Mankiewicz had demanded—connecting material, as well as the battles of Pharsalia and Philippi which would open each half of the film— had to be shot and reshot. In early 1963, the two men went to Spain and England with Burton and Harrison to do so, for an additional $2 million.

From all of this, Wanger was shut out. Completing his study of studio operations, Zanuck had received innumerable reports, particularly from Rogell and Merman, about Wanger's alleged dereliction of duties and his firing. Zanuck agreed wholeheartedly with the perception that Wanger had been negligent and "useless." He wrote Wanger that he could come to Paris, but that Fox would not pay his way.

In reply, Wanger all but groveled to Zanuck:

> I beseech you, Darryl, as the new president of the company not to aggravate this situation and further damage my status as producer of Cleopatra by not bringing me to Paris for the conferences on the cutting and editing of this picture. Not only will this further harm my reputation and status, but I think you, as the new president of Twentieth Century–Fox would not want to further humiliate and degrade me, a fellow producer, in this manner, in the eyes of the entire industry and of the entire world. . . . I appeal to you as a man not to do this to me. I have always been ready, willing and able to perform. This picture has been my life and until it is done, in view of the cost and potential box office, it is impossible for me not to do everything possible to ensure its success, in the same manner as you must have felt toward "The Longest Day."

Zanuck was not moved. In fact, Feldman told Wanger that Zanuck had no intention of doing future films with him, including "Justine." "Walter was wondering what was happening to his film," Mankiewicz later recalled. "Nobody let him know. They treated him contemptuously."

Publicly, it was difficult to tell how isolated Wanger was as Fox prepared *Cleopatra.* He made occasional statements to the press about the film, arguing in February 1963, for example, that Fox could release the film in two two-and-one-half-hour parts (doubling the company's distribution fees for the film and hence offsetting its enormous negative cost) and reasserting that *Cleopatra* would be the first film to gross $100 million. The two-part film idea and his innumerable publicity plans, such as *Cleopatra* cosmetic and coiffure tie-ins, were dismissed in civil but firm replies by Fox (although Fox did promote Taylor's costumes and hairstyles through articles in *Look, Vogue,* and *Life*).

Zanuck not only refused to pay Wanger's way to Paris but infuriated Wanger in several ways. He dismissed Wanger's attorney's inquiries about the cost of the reshooting in Spain: "I am very happy to note that at long last Mr. Wanger is concerned about the production cost of the film CLEOPA-

TRA." Rumors circulated that Wanger had blamed Mankiewicz and Taylor for the film's problems; when Wanger heard that Zanuck believed and repeated them, he wrote Bienstock, "I defended Elizabeth and Joe to such an extent that I got into a terrible battle with the entire New York group. . . . I am so burnt up about it I can't control myself." Meanwhile, he was sickened to see Zanuck and Fox's board "protecting" Fox's new chairman Skouras, a maneuver he found "typical of the hypocrisy of corporate management."

Shut out from postproduction on *Cleopatra* and faced with reports that impugned his ability as a producer, Wanger intended to fight back. "These facts [of Fox's mismanagement] must be brought out one way or another," Wanger wrote Bautzer in July 1962:

> I am not referring to a long lawsuit or anything that is going to hurt Fox as a company, if it is possible to avoid it because it is in my interests and in the interests of the industry to see Fox succeed. I have no personal venom against anybody but I am just revolted by the self-serving carelessness of these negligent and incompetent individuals, except in their own interest.

In September, only Richard Zanuck and publicity head Seymour Poe answered his calls. The editing staff, except for his 1930s employee Dorothy Spencer, avoided him. He had had enough:

> I waited for four months for some sort of recognition and honoring of a contract in connection with a picture which I am entirely responsible for having organized and seen through, notwithstanding the outstanding contributions made by Mankiewicz and the cast, etc. I was the responsible producer from start to finish, although the company did everything that they could to make my work impossible. I have been patient and considerate and now I am ready to move.

The Curse of *Cleopatra*
(1962–1968)

Wanger's "move" in the fall of 1962 was to write a memoir of the *Cleopatra* production and simultaneously to inaugurate a libel and breach of contract lawsuit against Fox. The second gesture was expected, but the first was not. When an excerpt from *My Life with "Cleopatra"* appeared in the *Saturday Evening Post* in April 1963, just two months before the film's premiere, Fox officials were astounded by the candor and embarrassing detail in Wanger's account. But the book was a logical extension of Wanger's courting of the moviegoing public throughout his career.

"Mr. Wanger has a two fold purpose in wanting the book written and published," coauthor Hyams wrote a British publisher: "He hopes to receive a lot of money for it and he is distressed by the studio's attempt to lay the blame for the high cost of 'Cleopatra' at his doorstep." If Darryl Zanuck had allowed Wanger to attend post-production sessions of the film and participate in the publicity campaign, Wanger would never have had time to write the book. Instead, while Zanuck and Mankiewicz fixed up *Cleopatra*, Wanger was restoring his reputation. For the last time in his career, Wanger put to work his most valuable and effective asset—himself, the literate, dignified, worldly producer—and he offered, as he had always done, a disarmingly honest, "outsider" account of what was wrong with Hollywood: studio management.

During production in Italy, several journalists had suggested to Wanger that he write a book that highlighted not only the Taylor-Burton affair but the logistics of location shooting and the corporate politics of the studio. As of fall 1962, only one such exposé, Lillian Ross's *Picture*—about the making of Huston's *The Red Badge of Courage* (1951) for MGM—had been published. It was hard to imagine a Hollywood executive writing anything like it; in many ways, Wanger's book resembles more recent best-sellers such as David McLintick's *Indecent Exposure* (1982) and especially Steven Bach's *Final Cut* (1985).

In October 1962, Wanger contacted Hyams, a reporter for the *New York Herald Tribune* and the Hollywood correspondent for *This Week* magazine. Meeting in New York, they inaugurated a series of lengthy interviews in which Wanger read from his diary entries and discussed the production, the personalities, and the politics behind the film. It was book writing as therapy and revenge, an opportunity to say in print all the things that no one at Fox had been willing to listen to during production meetings. It was as satiric in effect as *Stand-In*: like the 1937 comedy, here was a studio being manipulated by ignorant Wall Street financiers, teetering on bankruptcy and apparently dependent upon the fate of one film and the caprices of its leading actress.

Given Wanger's intentions, the book was misleading in a number of ways both trivial and significant. Although its diary format suggested otherwise, *My Life with "Cleopatra"* was not a carefully reconstructed account of the film's production. Its primary source was not daily production reports but Wanger's diary and correspondence, whose dates and descriptions were condensed for brevity and censored for dignity. Given his strained relations with Fox executives, Wanger had consulted none of them for accurate quotes or permission—nor had he contacted Fisher, Mamoulian, or Taylor to that end. Hyams interviewed Shamroy, Wanger conferred briefly with Mankiewicz, and together they talked with Sharaff.

Many of the book's deceptions related not so much to Wanger's desire to make some money and restore his reputation as to publicize *Cleopatra* and Taylor. As he rationalized it to Fox's attorneys six months after its publication:

> My one purpose in writing this book was to put out a definite piece of material that was pro picture and pro the cast, and especially pro Elizabeth, who was taking a tremendous beating at that time from the press, and nobody had come to glorify her, as I thought should be done for the pivot of a forty-million dollar project.

Taylor and Burton's affair received the most intense, unsolicited publicity in movie history. Wanger recognized that the public was fascinated by their adultery, a phenomenon he compared to the positive effects of Robert Mitchum's 1948 arrest for using marijuana. But Taylor, within two years of earning sympathy for her nearly fatal bout of pneumonia, had reassumed the reputation of Hollywood's most ruthless home wrecker. By the time she closed out on *Cleopatra*, she had been condemned by Vatican City officials, by letters to the print media, and, like Ingrid Bergman in 1948, by American politicians.

Wanger had initially found Taylor and Fisher offensive, describing her as "very vulgar and cheap" and Fisher's friends as "an ugly bunch." He told a friend "we are all on very good terms and I simply do my job, get whatever cooperation I can, and let it go at that." By the time production ended, however, he had nothing but admiration for all of them. He told Hyams that he had "a great deal of respect" for Fisher and that he wanted to give Burton "the same treatment" in the book that he would give Taylor.

Taylor remained the centerpiece of his intentions. "Oh, I'm mad about her," he told Hyams as they began discussing the book:

> I'm crazy about her and I want to get that over, see, and I think that one of the big things that will justify the book is that if she shows that she had so much more guts and much more fortitude and ingenuity than all the people who were talking about her. . . .

Except for his detailed description of a boorish menu at a Fisher gathering, there is no indication in *My Life with "Cleopatra"* that Wanger thought Taylor was crass, unprofessional (and in need of disciplining by the Screen Actors Guild), or anything other than a wrongly pilloried figure. He invoked all the clichés of studio and star publicity, equating Taylor with her screen role and emphasizing her ordinariness as well as her lavish lifestyle (with a bemused account of Taylor sending her Rolls Royce to fetch chicken soup from Wanger's apartment). He stressed her discipline as an actress. He constantly mentioned that she was an avid reader and recounted his trips to English and Italian bookstores on her behalf. He admiringly described her adoption of a handicapped German orphan. "I have lived in several of the great cities of the world during my lifetime," he and Hyams wrote, "and I have known many women considered to be paragons of virtue. I doubt, however, that many of these moral women have strong a code of personal ethics as Elizabeth."

Hyams knew well that the book's mass appeal centered on Taylor and Burton. As Wanger first went over his diary, he discreetly alluded to their relationship by saying only "etc., etc." Hyams pointed out that "etc., etc." was what would sell the book. Wanger admitted in his introduction that he was not a member of Taylor's "inner circle" of friends. But his stance as outsider-looking-in provided a rhetorical illusion of neutrality toward Taylor which obscured his otherwise obvious interest in promoting her as the greatest actress living.

While praising the film and Taylor's personal idiosyncracies to the skies, Wanger calmly savaged the "bungling interference" of "desperate, nervous men" at Fox who preceded Zanuck. (He shrewdly skimmed over the postproduction phase of the film which Zanuck controlled, which was no less strenuous for him than principal photography. After all, he was still hoping to produce "Justine" at Fox.) In adopting this tone, Wanger strove for a model of journalistic immediacy and "neutrality" that appeared to place him above the fray. Early in their talks, Wanger told Hyams:

> This is not a black and white situation. This is a situation full of shades and full of truths—untruths and deviations—and I would like to make all of that clear just as in [*The Making of the President*, 1960] Mr. White made his points very deftly and with great humanity.

Yet Wanger quickly admitted that Skouras was "in many ways . . . the heavy in this whole story, although I do not want to accuse him of that." But Wanger wound up doing so anyway.

Though Wanger warmly praised Skouras's selling ability and described his enormous charm, his deadpan descriptions of Skouras's change of mind on where to shoot the film, his capricious hiring and firing Wanger as head of European production, and his bemoaning Taylor's delays on *Cleopatra* and then urging Wanger to sign her a multi-picture contract were all obviously derogatory. "It's an almost affectionate hatchet job on Skouras," Canby noted in his perceptive review of the book for *Variety*.

Indeed, while talking with Hyams, Wanger was elated to discover in his diary an account of a wasteful expedition Skouras had made to Turkey to scout locations: "This is sensational . . . something that I know everybody has forgotten about. . . . That will really be a shock—I had forgotten all about that myself." His characterizations of Skouras were incredible. He claimed that in their early meetings in the fall of 1958, Skouras brandished an old copy of Fox's script for the 1915 Theda Bara version and told Wanger that it would require "some rewriting" for the new film. The book was loaded with such anecdotes. As a result, Skouras himself had no trouble discerning the book's implication: when examined for the lawsuits, he told Wanger's attorney, "you can pick up anything pertaining to this book and you will find nothing but dishonest statements."

Equally as misleading as the depiction of Taylor as a twentieth-century Sarah Bernhardt was Wanger's evocation of the grace under pressure and team spirit that pervaded cast and crew on the set. From *My Life with "Cleopatra"* there emerges the picture of a few dedicated talents of integrity—Wanger himself, Mankiewicz, Harrison, Taylor, Burton, Shamroy, DeCuir, and Sharaff—who battled it out first with an idiotic administration at the studio and second with the meddling board of directors. Of course, some of this was true, and as Wanger intended, one of the more refreshing things about the book is its attention to the technicians who accomplished so much, far from Fox's back lot. But in fact the pressures of location production and studio in-fighting also fragmented the production team, and each member pursued his or her own advantage. As Wanger described for Hyams his lunches with Sharaff, Merman, Shamroy, and others: "Everybody was very friendly, but they all have their little angles. It was like being with the Borgias. You had to be very careful not to wake up with a knife in your back."

By the time production in Italy had ended, Wanger felt betrayed by everyone, even his long-standing friend and patron, Mankiewicz. His diary entries record feelings of uselessness, exhaustion, and depression. For all his cheerful announcements to the press, he was dubious of the outcome of the film, noting of Mankiewicz's work in late May 1962, "The quality is excellent but much too much of the same thing, and much too much of the same dialogue." The various sessions with Fox officials—particularly the June 1962 meeting of dismissal—were full of "humiliation and treachery" that Wanger found "so bleak in the interests of good business that I have naturally been most upset." Nor was Wanger himself always the soothing father confessor that he appears in the book; Fox art director Jack Martin Smith reported in September that he stopped Wanger in the midst of a harangue against DeCuir for overbuilding the Alexandria sets. In January, Smith himself described Levathes and Wanger as "a team certainly combined to give me hell."

Indeed, Wanger's self-representation was one final crucial area of control in writing *My Life with "Cleopatra."* Hyams on occasion urged him to omit details such as his approval of a gaudy costume because it "clashes with your gentleman image." Reading over the later sections of Hyams's typescript in February 1963, Wanger stated that he wanted "to upgrade the whole attitude and I want to take out some of the indecision as there are too many things that sound as if I didn't know what I was doing, the way it reads to me now."

Wanger was also aware that he had presided over an adulterous liaison with a tolerance he had lacked toward Bennett and Lang. In the book, when he noted that Fisher simply left Italy when the Burton-Taylor affair became more than a fling, he cryptically commented, "I was no expert in solving a similar problem myself." Reading over a draft, he wrote Hyams,

> If I am so compassionate and understanding, somebody with a little brains might say, this is pretty stupid coming from a guy who did what he did [shooting Lang]—why wasn't he so understanding ten years ago? Consequently, I think the preface to my observations must be to the effect that as I reach my more mature years, I realize that there is nothing that can be done to control a man or woman's heart."

He also offered his assessment of the hypocrisy of the American public, in a segment added to the book just before Hyams sent the manuscript to Bantam Books and the *Saturday Evening Post.* This he characterized as "my defense and feelings about Elizabeth and Burton and their morality":

> The American public pretends to be puritanical. But the immense popularity of magazines such as *Confidential,* the peep-hole publications, and fan magazines belies the public puritanism. . . . These are hypocritical times, when men

are permitted to have more than one love at a time and women are castigated for the same kind of behavior. I believe that Elizabeth loves two men. And who is to say that a woman can't love two men at the same time, any more than that a man can't love two women at the same time?

Such ruminations, highly progressive from someone reared at the turn of the century, were Wanger's final expression of his disillusionment with American society since the Lang shooting. Here, they also served to cement the identification of Taylor's affairs with Cleopatra's.

It is impossible to specify the impact of *My Life with "Cleopatra"* on the paying public. The book did quite handsomely, selling more than 136,000 paperback copies in the month before the film opened. Costing the writers roughly $14,000 to prepare, the article excerpt paid $37,500 and the English-language (and Italian) book sales represented more than $42,000. Wanger received proposals to make the book into a film or to adapt it into a musical comedy; German and Dutch translations followed. Fox insiders such as stockholder-distributor Harry Brandt and publicity men Nathan Weiss and Jack Brodsky, who themselves had published a diary of the film, *The "Cleopatra" Papers,* felt certain Wanger's book would add, in Anita Loos's words, "at least ten million dollars to the gross." Edward Bernays wrote of his surprise that nothing had changed "in the motion picture field since I handled Theda Bara in *Cleopatra* in 1916."

By far the most bemused expression of appreciation for Wanger's book by an industry insider came from former Fox director John Ford. Jokingly "forgiving" Wanger for not mentioning *Stagecoach* or *The Long Voyage Home* in the list of past achievements, Ford wrote that *My Life with "Cleopatra"* "for the first time shows the making of a movie, with what you and I, the picture makers and creators, have to contend with." By far the most outraged reader was Skouras, who fumed that "Wanger violated every decent ethics of the amusement world."

The critical reception of the book could not have been better. It was hailed as "probably the best thing of its kind" since Ross's *Picture,* and Wanger's account of the conflicts with Fox "reaches an intensity which most novels about business never approach." Reviewers were equally enamored of Wanger, noting his candor about the Fox follies and how his health did not fail him once during the lengthy production. "He is heroic to say the least," the *Los Angeles Times* reviewer commented. Canby concluded his review by stating,

> Behind it all, of course, is the personality of the author, shrewd, gentlemanly in tone even in times of crude crisis, a much more clever and ruthless fighter than he ever would like to admit. . . . And though he had a heart attack before the film began, [he is] the only person who lived through the film without one sick day. Watch out for him.

After the book's publication, Fox watched Wanger carefully. With his ad-
judged "negligent" performance on *Cleopatra* and especially after all their financial and moral support with the Lang trial, Wanger's public exposure of
the studio's incompetence was stupefying. Accordingly, the Fox executives
did something that upset Wanger as much as their derogation of his talents as
a producer: they ignored him, granting him no more publicity for *Cleopatra*
beyond the minimum required by the Producers Guild and the long-shot photo
and paragraph on him in the souvenir program. The huge billboard ad on
Broadway with the production's signature image—Taylor reclining between
Harrison and Burton—appeared without credits.

Much to Wanger's chagrin, the media followed and magnified Fox's policy. In early May, Wanger read in the *New York Daily News* a series of articles about Zanuck entitled "The Cleopatra Man." An interview on the *Today*
show on June 6, five days before the film's opening, featured behind-the-
scenes footage of the production of *The Longest Day* and the retakes done on
Cleopatra in Spain in February. Zanuck acknowledged that his work on the
film was "very small" but mentioned only Mankiewicz on camera.

Wanger was equally irritated with the acclaim the media accorded Zanuck
for guiding the studio to its successful days. Zanuck *had* imposed order at
Fox where there had only been chaos, but for all of Zanuck's accomplishments, his timing had been impeccable: the studio's fortunes could only rise,
and the media hailed Zanuck as Fox's savior. As Zanuck quipped to Skouras
at a roast held in his honor in February 1964, "Thanks for going out of your
way to look so bad during the last five years so I couldn't help but look good
in this first year." NBC ran "The World of Darryl Zanuck," a special puff
piece that credited Zanuck with Fox's recovery and lauded *The Longest Day*
without reference to his previous failures.

Though he was under doctor's orders to remain calm for his heart condition, Wanger found it hard. "The more I think of it, the more I am irked by
Zanuck's shows," Wanger wrote his attorney, "which to me represent a fla-
grant attempt at stealing credit and hurting my reputation." Small wonder that
in negotiations with his American and British publishers, Wanger insisted
that he be identified as the producer of *Cleopatra* on the book's cover.

Harm to his reputation was one thrust of Wanger's lawsuit against Fox,
which his attorneys at Paul, Weiss, Rifkind, Wharton and Garrison served in
mid-May 1963, with an attempted injunction on the premiere of the film. The
suit grew from very concrete evidence of Wanger's diminished stature in the
industry.

Since Fox had stopped his salary, Wanger was in need of funds, and in
September 1962 he had told Bautzer that he wanted to sell his 10 percent
profit interest in *Cleopatra* for cash. If the film did gross his prophesied $100
million, Wanger's take would be $2,875,000. Bautzer arranged a deal with
Kenneth Hyman, formerly of Telinvest and now head of Seven Arts, which

brokered the sales of post-1948 studio films to television. As Wanger and Hyams discussed their book in December 1962, the sale of Wanger's share in *Cleopatra* to Seven Arts was finalized. Hyman then went on to discuss a multi-film production deal with Wanger.

In early 1963, however, the production talks broke off abruptly: Ray Stark, a Seven Arts representative, "vanished." Bautzer told Wanger that Hyman and his associates had been dissuaded from the deal by Wanger's reputation for extravagance after *Cleopatra*. This confirmed his determination to go forward with the suit, which called for $500,000 for damages to Wanger's reputation, $104,000 in back salary, more than $60,000 in job-hunting expenses, and a multi-million dollar libel judgment against Fox and Earl Wilson for leaking and publishing the news that Wanger had been fired from *Cleopatra*. Even though Wanger's attorneys felt the libel action was weak, they were confident that a jury would be "edified" by "a shocking picture of how Fox management operated," and that Wanger could restore his good name.

The hostilities between Wanger and Fox intensified when the film premiered on June 11, 1963, at the Rivoli Theater in New York. A star-studded group, including Zanuck, Mankiewicz, Harrison, McDowall, Fontaine, Leonard Bernstein, Mary Martin, Tony Randall, Helen Hayes, Red Buttons, Ann Bancroft, Robert Ryan, and Henry Fonda, appeared for an estimated crowd of ten thousand onlookers. Wanger came with daughters Shelley and Stephanie, but was denied the red carpet treatment; instead his group stood on the sidelines with the rest of the moviegoing crowd. The distributor denied the producer his moment of glory and the opportunity to meet with journalists and critics to promote the project that had obsessed him for four years.

The premiere was also Wanger's first glimpse of the film since Mankiewicz had joined Zanuck the previous October in Paris. Wanger was disturbed by rough cutting on the film and felt much of the dialogue was unclear, further evidence in his eyes of Zanuck's casual handling of the film, particularly in comparison with *The Longest Day*. He publicly criticized the length of the film and Zanuck's choppy editing of several scenes, calling it "a preview print." Indeed, Fox did some minor recutting of the film after its opening to clean it up.

There is no question that the release version of *Cleopatra* is a mixed achievement. Although its first half is compelling and exciting, the second half lags in interest. Much of this reflects not only the different conditions under which each was scripted but the different male characters they concern. Caesar, particularly as written by Mankiewicz and portrayed by Harrison, provides the film's greatest emotional strength and intelligence. From the opening Battle of Pharsalia through his death, a poignant sense of loss pervades his scenes, be they his mourning over the death of his son-in-law Pompey or those with Cleopatra. Unlike the frieze images that open each segment, he and Cleopatra, self-proclaimed gods, cannot stop the passage of time, which leads not toward corruption as in a Welles film, but toward the irrevocable acknowledgment of mortality and opportunities lost. Time is the crucial element in Caesar's defense of Alexandria against Ptolemy ("I need this day"), and Cleopatra taunts Caesar for his age and kindles his desire to become emperor. When he leaves Cleopatra and their child Caesarion for Rome, she tells Caesar, "Time is our enemy." "Would you have me conquer time?" Caesar responds. "What plan of battle would you suggest?"

By contrast, although Mankiewicz provided Antony and Cleopatra with intelligent, evocative dialogue, Antony is, as played by Burton, a self-pitying, inebriated adolescent, who compares unfavorably not only with Caesar but with McDowall's inhumanly cool Octavian. Even the spectacles Cleopatra creates in the second half of the film—such as the elaborate Bacchanal with which she greets Antony at Tarsus—barely equal the grandeur of her Rome processional. Unlike the conclusion of *Spartacus*, Cleopatra and Antony's defeat is also anticlimactic: as critic Michael Wood put it, the film "has all the ingredients of a great elegy, a Hollywood swan song, and hardly any of the elements of an epic." In spite of Octavian's reverent command, "The dying of such a man must be shouted, screamed," we can remember little of Antony's conduct that merits such praise. Cleopatra herself is, as Wanger envisioned, more capable and dignified than any of her pervious incarnations, particularly deMille's socialite heroine, but she also remains an orientalist femme fatale.

Aside from its narrative flaws, *Cleopatra* is a sumptuous spectacle, beginning with the grim opening scene at Pharsalia. In Derek Elley's words, "No other historical picture—apart from *The Fall of the Roman Empire*—provides such a feast of costuming, art direction and production design." The first shot of Alexandria pans from Caesar's ship to DeCuir's enormous palace and port with a casual magnificence repeated later in the forum. The cinematography, from the expressionistic lighting during Caesar's epileptic fits to the low-key scene of Cleopatra's secret departure from Rome, is stunning. And Cleopatra's procession into Rome on a sphinx fulfilled Wanger's envisioned series of attractions, with various animals, archers and dancers in golden-plumed bird costumes and an array of talents that show off North African arts to the cheering Romans.

Everybody's hopes were high for the critical reviews of the film, especially after Crowther told Brodsky in June 1962 (in the latter's words) that he expected "to see one of the great films in *Cleopatra*," a movie comparable to *Gone with the Wind*, in large part because "the combination of Mankiewicz and Walter Wanger can't go wrong." None of the critics, especially Crist, were as complimentary as Crowther, who described it as "surpassing entertainment, one of the great epic films of our day." In fact, reviews in all the major national newsweeklies considered *Cleopatra* a middling film. *Time* noted, "As spectacles go, *Cleopatra* goes reasonably well." *Newsweek* called it "neither the greatest film ever created, or the gaudiest, but not the dismal fiasco that was always possible." Hollis Alpert in the *Saturday Review* commented that the film was "not a disaster. Nor is it any kind of triumph."

On the other hand, nearly all the critics had praise for the costumes, set design, and cinematography. In *Time*'s words, "Physically, *Cleopatra* is as magnificent as money and the tremendous Todd-AO screen can make it." Indeed, this was the feature of the film which was most honored at the Academy Awards the following April: DeCuir and Smith's set designs, Sharaff and Novarese's costumes, and Shamroy's cinematography all won awards in the appropriate categories (the film was nominated for best picture, best editing and best sound, as well). Through a mix-up at Fox publicity, none of the many supporting cast members were nominated. Wanger wrote McDowall a conciliatory note, regretting the oversight. McDowall wrote back that the studio had been "merely foolish in relation to me; towards you they were vicious."

Fortunately the critical reviews had little bearing on *Cleopatra*'s box office. As *Newsweek*'s reviewer commented, "One has to see it, as one must climb to the top of Mount Everest, because it is there." Most American moviegoers agreed. Fox spent $22 million distributing the film, but Skouras, in a precedent-shattering move, arranged for $20 million in advance guarantees (more than $1 million of which came from the Rivoli in New York alone) from exhibitors. Skouras also arranged, to Wanger's chagrin, to have the film put into general release immediately after its roadshow premieres so that Fox could quickly recover income from the film.

Skouras's strategy paid off handsomely. By early 1964, *Cleopatra* already ranked ninth in *Variety's* all-time, top-grossing films, earning $500,000 more than *The Longest Day*. After one year in distribution, *Cleopatra* had recovered nearly half its cost. Finally, with its $5 million sale to ABC for two prime-time showings in September 1966, the film broke even. Thanks partially to its theatrical gross, the Fox company was solvent again, reporting a profit in 1963 of $9 million and of $11.5 million in 1964. By 1966, thanks to the nearly $100 million theatrical gross of Robert Wise's *The Sound of Music,* Fox was in healthy condition. In spite of other, later location problems (such as the production of *Dr. Dolittle* in England), Fox never again sunk to the depths of the early 1960s.

The box office performance and the acclaim for *Cleopatra*'s production design only made Wanger more livid with Fox. "The great praise for the 'spectacle' and its lush performance is entirely due to me," he wrote his lawsuit attorney Morris Abrams. "The original sketches and plans before Mamoulian and Mankiewicz prove this." He continued:

> I am really distressed that all of the chances I took and all of my fighting during the film has proven that I was right and instead of acclaiming me for having given them this film they are crucifying me and restricting me from going

ahead in production. I really want to expose them and get what's coming to me
in salaries and damages as well as "Justine."

This, along with his employment difficulties, gave Wanger the momentum
to pursue his suit, and intermittently from late October 1963 through March
1964, he and Skouras gave depositions.

The lawsuits dramatized in a decisive way how elusive a firm definition
of the producer's function in Hollywood was and how elusive Wanger was in
fulfilling it. Fox's attorneys tried to show that Wanger had acted irresponsibly
in supervising the film. In reply, Wanger's attorneys referred to the phrase
"industry custom" in Wanger's contract to describe the standard by which
Wanger's conduct on *Cleopatra* could be judged, aiming to prove that Fox
granted Wanger responsibility without authority because their executives constantly interfered with his work.

What neither side recognized was that there was precious little agreement
on what that "custom" for a producer was beyond developing a script and
finding funds. Wanger had dedicated his book to Stephanie and Shelley, "who
wanted to know what a producer does," but even Wanger had to concede that
Cleopatra did not provide a textbook answer. Skouras and Wanger agreed the
producer was "responsible" for everything in a film's production, but once
the questions became more specific, they had no consensus. Since the 1920s,
there had been a tremendous flexibility in how producers defined their functions in production, and Wanger did not fit the style of a personal producer
enshrined by Fox executives, producers, and writers. To them, Wanger's conduct was incomprehensible, even willfully negligent. "In all sincerity," Skouras
wrote Wanger in May 1962, "I do not believe you have ever felt the responsibility of this venture as I have." "I can never understand Wanger," Fox's
Nunnally Johnson wrote Goldstein in November 1961.

> Whenever I talk to him about *Cleopatra* he talks as if it were somebody else's
> production. Once I said to him: "Is [Taylor] due to work yet?" He replied "I
> hear she's overdue." What the hell does that mean?

But there was nothing inherently wrong with a hands-off producing style.
Given the right circumstances, it could result in superlative films, as Wanger
had demonstrated with *Stagecoach*, Selznick with *The Third Man* and *Notorious*, and Goldwyn with *The Best Years of Our Lives*.

Although the depositions in the suit and countersuit were often heated,
they were also frequently amusing: Skouras revealed that he suspected Wanger of being in a conspiracy with hostile board members and with Brodsky
and Nathan Weiss (of *The "Cleopatra" Papers*) to embarrass him. When
Wanger protested that he felt only pity for the company stockholders, Fox's

counsel replied, "I am sure they will be glad to learn that." Near the end of Wanger's deposition, Fox's attorney noted that "these pleasant meetings we have been having must come to an end. . . . I will miss them." Wanger replied, "So will I. I haven't had a chance to talk about myself so much in years." The lawyers wouldn't miss them at all. Within months of Skouras's deposition, Fox was also handling a lawsuit from Taylor, Burton, and Fisher for improper accountings of their profit shares on the film.

By June of 1965, Wanger felt his attorneys had "no heart" for his lawsuit; in October, he and Fox reached a $100,000 settlement. Wanger issued a generous retraction:

> I want to express my deep regret to Mr. Skouras that anything I have written in my book . . . has done him any injustice and I withdraw any such statement as I hold Mr. Skouras in the highest regard both personally and professionally. I regret that anything I have written has cast a cloud over his outstanding reputation as one of the acknowledged leaders and pioneer executives of the motion picture industry.

The financially more complex suit involving the *Cleopatra* stars was finally settled in late 1967.

The *Cleopatra* curse outlasted the lawsuit. Although he was not, as Fox accused him, primarily responsible for the fiasco of *Cleopatra,* Wanger played his part in exacerbating its problems, and for this he paid an enormous price: he was never able to realize another film. Before *Cleopatra* began, Wanger had several projects to develop. Now, he had to start from scratch. As part of the settlement, he gave up his right to produce the Durrell quartet. Zanuck considered it a "pet project" and assigned it to veteran producer Pandro Berman in the late 1960s. Berman handed it to Cukor, who shot an indifferent version of it in Tunis with costumes by Sharaff and starring Anouk Aimee, Phillip Noiret, and Dirk Bogarde.

In November 1964 before his settlement with Fox, Wanger signed a development deal with Joseph E. Levine's Embassy Pictures, which offered to produce and finance any project it approved. The following month, Wanger signed a contract with MGM to develop several projects under studio supervision, as he had at Fox. Both arrangements undercut his claims of a damaged reputation, but both paid Wanger only when projects were authorized, and, as at United Artists, nothing was approved unless Wanger had a shootable script or a bankable star in hand. Since completing *I Want to Live!* and *Cleopatra,* Wanger had not befriended any new stars or ingratiated himself with the powerful agents. Thus he devoted his efforts to developing appealing scripts.

Although MGM maintained an office for Wanger in Hollywood, Wanger worked out of New York. There he teamed up with an aspiring producer, Gabriel Katzka, to work on several projects: *The Rector of Justin* and *Sylva,* a

Pygmalion story he wanted to do with Jill St. John and which he thought might capitalize on the popularity of *My Fair Lady*. Wanger and Katzka also interested Peck in *The Night of the Short Knives*, a thriller concerning NATO's military preparedness, which Wanger saw as an updated *Foreign Correspondent*. Wanger spent more than $100,000 developing a script by former blacklistees Ring Lardner, Jr., and Ian Hunter. By the end of 1966, MGM had told him to "take it elsewhere," and Wanger failed to sell the project to other, more active producers. He made a third futile attempt to work in television, this time to produce educational programming worldwide before the formation of a national public broadcasting system in the late 1960s.

Though he met and talked several times with younger talents such as Warren Beatty and Peter Bogdanovich, the production trends of the 1960s toward enormously expensive blockbusters passed Wanger by. He was puzzled by the new forms of cultural expression taking shape in the decade. Attending the stage production of *Hair*, he found that he did not care for its lack of propriety, and he was dismayed that for once, a production innovation that spoke to youth had no appeal to him. But he tried to capitalize on the nostalgia craze for earlier films and eras signaled by Wilder's *Some Like It Hot*. He reminisced enthusiastically with historian Kevin Brownlow about the silent era in Hollywood. Up until his death, he and Katzka worked on *Swing Low, Sweet Harriet*, a retelling of the William Desmond Taylor murders for ABC's Palomar Pictures.

The only project they successfully packaged was *Gaily Gaily*, an adaptation of Hecht's ribald autobiography of life in Chicago at the turn of the century, of corrupt politicians who did business in the best whorehouses, and of Hecht's own Candide-like innocence. Wanger optioned this work shortly after Hecht's death. Wanger saw it "directed by Gower Champion, in color, as an American Tom Jones," and newcomer Abram S. Ginnes developed a script. Thinking in terms of a blockbuster like Todd's *Around the World in Eighty Days*, he wanted to cast comics such as Jackie Gleason, Jonathan Winters, Dean Martin, Joe E. Lewis, Martha Raye, and others in secondary roles, and he wanted Robert Morse, who had achieved stardom in *How to Succeed in Business Without Really Trying* on Broadway, to portray Hecht. For Queen Lil, the madame, he approached Carol Channing (then touring on the stage in *Hello, Dolly*) and Lucille Ball, who read Ginnes's script. She turned it down, citing "all these sponsors and networks hanging around my neck." Finally, Wanger and Katzka sold it to producer-director Norman Jewison, who made it in 1969 with Beau Bridges and Melina Mecouri for the Mirisch Corporation. Wanger and Katzka received $125,000 in payments and 10 percent of the profits.

The cash came in handy. Wanger had never stopped living well, and his monthly expenses came to roughly $6,000 a month. Even after the Fox salary and settlement and the sale of his profit share in *Cleopatra*, Wanger found himself cash-poor in the go-go stock market of the 1960s. "I am just flabbergasted when I think of what I have taken in and the way that I have disbursed my monies in the last three years," he wrote his accountant.

> Don't forget that I got $350,000 from Fox, $110,000 from my brother, $100,000 from the Fox settlement; in addition to the book, which, I think, was $50,000 or so. The fact that none of that money has been put to any good use and just disappeared is sort of shocking to me. I know that my expenses are great but on the other hand I don't think that I have used much imagination in manipulating [*sic*]; especially in this market where all of my friends have doubled and tripled their money.

When asked by Haworth, who shared Wanger's clothing size, what he did with his old clothes, Wanger sadly replied, "I wear them." As grandly as he could, Wanger lived off his *Cleopatra* sales income, song royalties from his films, and minor residuals. "I am going through one of my bad periods," he wrote a friend in August 1966. "I am still suffering from the fact that I didn't keep my residuals for t.v. . . . had I hung onto those, I would be on the Riviera, not enjoying ulcers."

There was much to be discouraged about in his final years, such as his diminishing circle of old friends and colleagues. From his Famous Players-Lasky days, Ben Schulberg had died in 1957 and William Le Baron in 1958. His old nemesis Harry Cohn died that year, as did Jesse Lasky, in great debt. Two of his strongest supporters at Fox were also gone. Wald had died in 1962 and Selznick in 1965. The death of Walt Disney in the summer of 1966 made him "very upset." Since his 1958 heart attack, Wanger had had to watch his health closely. During production of *Cleopatra*, he had his blood tested every two weeks, and in his final years he suffered from angina. He had to avoid the cold New York winters. Often while out walking, he had to sit down to rest and take nitroglycerine. Though at times he felt depressed, he never complained about his affliction, nor did he tire his company with accounts of his health.

Like Tennyson's Ulysses, Wanger remained until his death a restless, vibrant, enthusiastic man. He was especially happy to return to the city of his earliest triumphs: "I must say that I get a thrill looking out of my window on Central Park every day," he wrote Stephanie in 1964, before moving to an apartment in the Stanhope Hotel on Fifth Avenue. He enjoyed Manhattan's bookstores, lunches at La Grenouille, dinners at "21," and his haircuts by the Plaza Hotel barber. He was delighted with the opening of Lincoln Center, which to his eyes, repeated affluent New York's patronage of 1908's New Theater. He enjoyed the company of Gilbert Miller, the stage producer who had taken over Famous Players–Lasky's theater operations in 1919.

Living in New York also brought him closer to his children. Bennett had tried to protect Stephanie and Shelley from the unstable life she had had. She was the disciplinarian responsible for manners, schedules, and rules. Wanger was the one who opened up new worlds. When Stephanie was age two, he brought her backstage to bang the piano for Arthur Rubinstein. "He expanded our horizons aesthetically and intellectually," Shelley recalls. "He gave us a love of books, journalism, magazines, art, theater and film. He took me to my first opera, *La Traviata,* when I was 12, and he was always taking me to screenings. He very much included us in his projects and ideas." Partly because he had them so late in life, Wanger doted on his daughters. Wanger was proud of Shelley, who accompanied him to script conference luncheons and whose opinion on new scripts he solicited. He was also pleased to see Stephanie marry the wealthy Frederick E. Guest II, an heir to the Woolworth fortune, in August 1963. Although never one to take a vacation, his family lured him briefly to Jamaica, and he constantly visited London.

Wanger even fell in love again with Aileen Mehle, the beautiful blonde society columnist "Suzy" who then wrote for the *New York Mirror and Journal American.* Married twice before, Mehle hesitated to go out with someone more than thirty years her senior when they first met in 1963. But Wanger pursued her relentlessly, and she quickly forgot about his age. Mehle found him "a wonderful friend. He was an omnivorous reader, he saw every movie and play and was more *au courant* than anyone I knew." He encouraged her with the same enthusiasm he brought to all his projects and loved ones throughout his life. Two years later, after granting Bennett a divorce, Wanger proposed. Though Mehle turned him down, Wanger accompanied her around the city to social gatherings and popular night spots; Wanger was, in *Variety*'s words, "very much the man about town."

Nor did Wanger ever lose his fascination with national and international politics. He liked visiting Washington in his later years. "He had a strong physical feeling for the seat or locus of power," a friend recalled, "and he liked being near it." He applauded Lyndon Johnson's War on Poverty: "Until we clean house domestically, we can never impress the rest of the world with our ability to advise on how they should conduct themselves." In a letter to Sargent Shriver in 1964, he outlined a series of programs to raise the country's standard of living and to engage young people, who are "so advanced and so understanding of what the world problems are, all of this due to television, radio, travel, the motor car, etc." In June 1966, still hoping for the honorary degree that the Lang shooting precluded, Wanger spoke beside General James M. Gavin at Dartmouth in a symposium on world peace and the media.

His lively mind won him countless new friends. Burke Wilkinson, who wrote *The Night of the Short Knives*, was one of them. He saw Wanger in Washington in 1968, when the "Austrian Ace" attended a reunion of World

War I fliers sponsored by the Italian ambassador. Wanger called Wilkinson from his hotel.

> He said the group made him feel old and would I please come and have a drink with him and cheer him up. I dropped everything to go down and there he was in the lobby surrounded by aging fliers (some did look pretty rickety) and their wives. We had a couple of drinks—his favorite Chivas Regal, as usual, and he did cheer up a bit. He had good hopes for *Night of the Short Knives,* and in his indomitable way said, "Burke, we're really going to make this one big."

As late as 1968, Wanger was also trying to make them small. He purchased the screen rights to *The Looters,* John Reese's novel about a group of small-time burglars who rob a bank with Mafia connections. Wanger pitched the material as a low-budget, gritty action film akin to *Riot in Cell Block 11* or "Underworld U.S.A.," and won the backing of Cinema Center, the theatrical film division of the CBS/Broadcast group. Siegel, Wanger's first-choice director, was then busy on *Coogan's Bluff* and recommended Peter Bogdanovich, who had just completed his first feature, *Targets,* for Roger Corman. After screening the film, Wanger was sold and set Bogdanovich to work on the script. To Bogdanovich he remained dignified, "'perfect casting for a wise, elderly professor." And, Bogdanovich noted, "He was a producer in the old tradition. He never quit. He never stopped looking for new things to produce." But Bogdanovich's script went unproduced. (Five years later, Siegel took the project over and directed *Charley Varrick,* with Walter Matthau.)

This was because on Sunday, November 17, 1968, after reading in bed alone, Wanger suffered a heart attack so severe that he could not reach his nitroglycerine. His housekeeper found him the following morning. Services were held four days later at Campbell's in Manhattan. Because Stephanie was then en route by ship to Europe, Shelley Wanger and Frederick Guest made all the arrangements. The service was a small, quiet affair. With Stephanie married, Wanger left his estate of roughly $18,000 to Shelley.

Wanger had asked that at his funeral someone read a monologue from Shaw's *The Doctor's Dilemma,* one of the plays Barker had premiered in America in 1915. Like so many of Wanger's gestures throughout his life, it was an ambiguous choice, the dying speech of the tubercular young painter Louis Dubedat, whom Barker was the first to portray. Modeled after H. G. Wells, D. G. Rossetti, and particularly after Karl Marx's common-law son-in-law Edward Aveling, Dubedat is an amoral scoundrel (Shaw called him a "rascally genius"), who constantly borrows money from the doctors while exposing their hypocritical pieties and who ruthlessly exploits his devoted wife.

To an unsophisticated reader, Dudebat's final speech expresses the credo of an uncompromising artist in the grandest romantic traditions: "I have never done anything wrong, never denied my faith, never been untrue to myself." He affirms his belief "in the might of design, the mystery of color, the redemption of all things made by Beauty everlasting, and the message of Art that has made these hands blessed." At the same time, Dudebat utters several clichéd, self-pitying boasts—"I've been threatened and blackmailed and insulted and starved. But I've played the game. I've fought the good fight,"— and much of his flowery rhetoric seems calculated for its effect on his adoring wife and on a gullible newspaper reporter in the room.

Having worked under Barker in 1915, Wanger was no doubt alert to such ironies in Dudebat's character. But he remained to the end of his life enthralled by the vision of a youthful idealist who believes his devotion to art transcends the petty judgments of society. In any case, Wanger's death was such a shock that his family forgot the request. A few days later, Wanger's body was cremated and placed in a drawer of the Feuchtwanger family plot, the Emanu-El Mausoleum in the Home of Peace Cemetery outside San Francisco.

The vital, tireless man had come to rest.

Conclusion

Like every producer working in a mass medium, Wanger wrestled with the question of what the public wants to see. Selznick, in Schatz's words, favored "lavish production values and cloying sentimentality." Goldwyn usually relied on familiar best-sellers and Broadway successes. Although each of them pursued an ideal of "quality" production, Wanger's answer was novelty.

Upon retiring in 1969, Berman recalled Wanger's admonition forty years earlier that "this year's successes are next year's failures." In the 1920s and 1930s, Schary recalled, Wanger "had a wonderful reputation, even in that era, for trying off-beat subjects." "Don't let anybody interfere with your aggressive thinking," Lasky wrote Wanger on his fifty-fifth birthday, "and someday maybe the industry will catch up with you." Wanger subscribed to dramatic innovation as *the* primary axiom of successful production. In John Ford's words, he was a "sensationalist."

Wanger's brand of sensationalism involved films that highlighted feminine autonomy, spectacular exoticism, and political topicality. He frequently championed the narrative formulas of social liberation articulated by diverse movements of the early twentieth-century theater—the New Stagecraft, the Little Theater, and the Ballets Russes. Personally in revolt against the mores of the late nineteenth century and the conservative strictures of his family, he often chose projects that focused on independent women—the tarnished ladies of Astoria; Mary Burns; Joan Bennett's characters in *Big Brown Eyes* and *Trade Winds*; female, World War II pilots; and Susan Hayward's roles, especially Barbara Graham—who are eventually contained by romance or by some punishment that reestablished their subordinate position within patriarchal society.

392

Most of Hollywood's producers did the same: indeed, the star images of Joan Crawford, Bette Davis, and Katharine Hepburn, among others, were built on such narratives. Aside from Hayward's unique qualities, however, Wanger's approach was further distinguished by his predilection for big-budget films about women who exercised but eventually lost absolute political power—Queen Christina, Joan of Arc, and, of course, Cleopatra.

The linkage of female sexuality and political authority had always held enormous erotic appeal for Wanger since its codification in the progressive thesis plays and stage orientalism that enthralled him in his youth. In this regard, Diaghilev's orientalist aesthetic was an even more distinctive aspect of Wanger's production program. Because it blended modernist expression with shades of prurient vulgarity, the art of the Ballets Russes was already by elitist standards an impure one, especially when compared with Wanger's one-time experiments with adaptations of Henry James and Eugene O'Neill. In Wanger's mind, orientalism was well-suited for reconciling high and mass culture. Encouraged by the phenomenal success of a single film every decade (*The Sheik, Algiers,* and *Arabian Nights*) Wanger crystalized one of Hollywood's most indecorous and campy genres. He preferred those stylish renderings of visual modernism—from Poiret and Chalfin in the 1920s to DeCuir and Sharaff in the 1960s—that could be readily translated into erotic display and consumable goods.

Wanger rationalized the orientalist genre as a means of achieving mass appeal. But "the masses" were often a convenient cover for his own lowbrow predilections. He convinced his colleagues and friends that he needed to compensate for his privileged background and his erudition. Hecht, who dedicated his novel *A Jew in Love* to Wanger, told an interviewer in 1959, "Walter Wanger is one of the most cultured men in the country, one of the most informed human beings we have." But, Hecht continued,

> When he makes a picture, he takes a saw and saws his head off at the neck. He makes pictures so abysmal, so low-grade, that people who can't even understand what he's saying at a dinner table snort with horror at the pictures he makes. . . . I've talked to Walter about that a lot. He made two or three good pictures, because he's been in the business about 40 years. But he says he's a man who's like a convert, he is converted to the idea that there is no chance for intelligent entertainment making any money on a mass scale. He's seen it proved around him a thousand times, so he checks his brains when he makes a picture.

The poor returns on the two films Wanger touted as "off-beat" and "high art" (*Private Worlds* and *The Long Voyage Home,* respectively) or on those modeled on the British example (*The Lost Moment, Joan of Arc,* and *The Reckless Moment*) spoke volumes next to the $3 million gross of *Arabian Nights.*

Zanuck had a similar, well-noted revelation after producing the unpopular *Wilson* in 1943. Henceforth, he claimed, he would produce nothing but Betty Grable musicals.

But after earning his family's disapproval by joining show business, Wanger yearned for the respect of social and cultural elites. During World War I his recognition of the movies' persuasive potential made him conscious of the ideological stakes of filmmaking. "I don't know whether what we do is an art or an industry," Wanger said shortly before he died. "I don't think semantics has a damn thing to do with it. Films are an influence, a tremendous influence." This epiphany, combined with Wanger's personal need for self-justification and his devotion to novelty, persuaded him to undertake the same task that he assigned himself at Dartmouth, on Broadway, and at Covent Garden: to reconcile popular taste with elevated values.

Like Griffith, Zanuck, Schary, and Kramer, Wanger followed through in Hollywood by interspersing his commercial films with one of Hollywood's most pretentious and least profitable genres, the social problem film. This tactic, more than any other, set him apart from other prominent independent producers. "It never has been nor ever should be the function of motion picture producers consciously to educate," Selznick told reporters shortly after forming Selznick International. "Our mission is to discover the nature of the demand and meet it as best we can."

Typically, Hecht once observed, "The producer is sort of a bank guard. He's there to protect the bankroll. His objective is to see that nothing is put on the screen that people are going to dislike. This means practically 99 percent of literature, thinking, probings of all problems." Wanger the sensationalist was neither bank guard nor banker. Selznick and Goldwyn made prestige movies, including Goldwyn's best social problem films such as *Dead End* and the superb *The Best Years of Our Lives,* which major studio executives could be proud to have shown in their theaters. By contrast, the studios and the MPPDA tried to obstruct Wanger offerings, such as *Night Mayor, Gabriel Over the White House, Queen Christina, The President Vanishes, Blockade,* and *Foreign Correspondent.*

Until the early 1950s, however, with the sole exception of *Foreign Correspondent,* Wanger failed to maintain the balance of dramatic interest and instruction which was crucial to aesthetic and box office success. Though Wanger blamed industry institutions such as the Production Code or gun-shy studio executives for his misshapen films full of sketchy politics and hackneyed romances, it was Wanger (particularly his cavalier attitude toward story construction) and the talents he supervised who had missed the mark. Fortunately for Wanger, many influential critics shared his preference for "realism" and his utilitarian views on the potential of the motion picture to enlighten the mass audience. These critics often applauded his efforts, however maladroit, at message movies, a genre reviewers held superior to more apparently superficial genres like musicals and melodramas. Unfortunately, the filmgoers did not agree.

After all, filmgoers flocked to Capra's *Mr. Deeds Goes to Town* and *Mr. Smith Goes to Washington* or Wyler's *The Best Years of Our Lives* or Kazan's *On the Waterfront*. As Kramer once noted, "I found out early in my life really nobody [at the Hollywood studios] objected to messages if you want to call them that. They objected to messages which didn't make money—which makes a big difference." Wanger lacked the skills of a Zanuck, a Schary, or a Kramer to fashion messages that made money. He compensated for this drawback by pairing entertainment films with message movies: *History Is Made at Night* with *You Only Live Once,* or *The Adventures of Hajji Baba* with *Riot in Cell Block 11.*

Wanger also differed from his fellow Hollywood idealists in his assumptions about the challenge he set himself. Given his own affinity for what was often termed lowbrow culture, he wanted influential thinkers and elitists to understand and accept popular taste rather than attempt to raise it. "I really wanted to see our work become a respected calling," he told an interviewer late in life. "I thought it was almost as important as the State Department." Prestige production was rarely one of his policies. Warner Bros. could produce a Reinhardt version of Shakespeare, Selznick might adapt Dickens, and Goldwyn could put violinist Yascha Heifitz in the movies. Wanger would have none of it. "Unless we make films that appeal to the greatest number of people," he stated in a publicity piece in 1961, "we lose the purpose for which production has been designed."

Wanger sought to further distinguish himself from other producers, whether liberal or conservative, by relying to an extraordinary extent on his own self-promotion. Any independent, semi or otherwise, had an inherent advantage in standing apart from other producers. Wanger's efforts make a telling contrast with those of Goldwyn. Goldwyn sought to erase his past by publishing his superficial memoirs in 1923, printing ghostwritten articles on industry matters, and hiring public relations people to "transform him from Mr. Malaprop into an English don." Wanger needed to position himself as Hollywood's most rebellious and erudite producer and to compensate for the failure of his films. "Wanger built his reputation as a movie-maker," Rapf observed, "and then used that reputation to behave like a statesman."

The persona Wanger presented was a variation of his lifelong ambition to be, in the words of *The Dartmouth,* a "practical dreamer." But as Wanger set out to reconcile the high with the low and the innovative with the familiar, he often erred too far on the side of the idealistic and the impractical. His Progressive Era convictions, his comfortable upbringing and exposure to luxury, the incredible resources of the studio system, and Wanger's instant success at Paramount in the twenties gave him an often fatal belief in the power of ideas and his ability to realize and promote them. "Like all first-line salesmen,"

Budd Schulberg wrote of the movie producer modeled partly on Wanger in his *The Disenchanted,* "Milgrim was his own best customer." Wanger's belief that *The Long Voyage Home* would pull in the reluctant audience, especially if he explained his strategy to the press, was just one example. Wanger's faith in *Joan of Arc* nearly destroyed his career.

Hollywood's studio system both empowered and emasculated Wanger's producing program. The studios and his semi-independent company sometimes gave Wanger the authority and the money to prepare films in accordance with his ideals. But frequently, when Wanger had the opportunities, he failed to put his ideas into practice. In this he was not unlike Selznick, who, as David Thomson has pointed out, remained incapable of acting on the perceptive analyses of the industry which he recorded in his memos.

But the two producers had different approaches to their tasks and different limitations. "Selznick's idea of collaboration," Rudy Behlmer has stated, "was to hire first-rate talent, extract certain attributes from that talent, and mold them to suit his vision." Selznick believed in supervising every detail of production, and seemed, in Schatz's words, "to regard filmmaking as a sustained existential dilemma." Wanger was more like Goldwyn, distant and lax in supervising his films. To McDowall, Wanger "was a very competent producer. He had taste, he had charm, he had the ability to pull people together, he was a catalyst, and these were all invaluable skills in that period." But from Selznick's point of view, Wanger was "a man of talent and expert showmanship and ideas and he has been wrongly placed as a personal producer." Wanger was at heart an executive, an idea man, a sponsor.

As a result, as Thomson once put it, "Wanger's record is good, but hit and miss; and the hits coincide with directors of exceptional talent." When lesser or out-of-control talents were involved—Charles Reisner and the screenwriters on *Winter Carnival,* Lang on *Secret Beyond the Door,* Maxwell Anderson on *Joan of Arc,* and Benson on *The Duchesse de Langeais*—Wanger was helpless and the films, if realized, were indifferent. Nunnally Johnson once called Zanuck "the greatest editor of movies, the greatest editor of scripts" in Hollywood, and praised his absolute insistence on getting a script set first. Phillip Dunne praised Zanuck for "his innate ability to handle people. . . . He knew which writer or director best responded to iron discipline, which to sweet persuasion." From Negri to Taylor, Wanger relied almost exclusively on sweet persuasion and diplomacy. The few times when Wanger pulled rank—bulldozing Haardt's writing efforts, yelling at Sidney, and bullying Fitzgerald around Dartmouth—were ugly and unproductive, if not disastrous.

Even when Wanger had disciplined talents working for him and even when he had preconceptions about a project, the tenor of his productions could change dramatically in preparation. (*Riot in Cell Block 11* and *I Want to Live!* were the most significant exceptions to this tendency.) Wanger's hiring and backing of Lang for *You Only Live Once,* Hitchcock for *Personal*

History, and Norman Reilly Raine for *Eagle Squadron* and his endorsement of Mankiewicz's new concept for *Cleopatra* showed how readily Wanger accepted the inflections of his stars, writers, and directors to realize his films. Wanger could rationalize this policy as practical management, but it (along with the various dynamics of the studio system itself) contributed to the contradictory implications of films such as *Gabriel Over the White House, The President Vanishes, Canyon Passage, Tulsa, Reign of Terror,* and *Invasion of the Body Snatchers.*

On the other hand, Wanger's flexibility had its advantages. It enabled him to attract the best talents until the semi-independent boom of the 1940s. "We must select the story and sell it to John Ford," Selznick wrote his associates in the late 1930s when he turned down *Stagecoach,* "instead of having Ford select some uncommercial pet of his that we would be making only because of Ford's enthusiasm. . . . He is an excellent man, but there is no point in treating him as a god." But Wanger revered talent, and although he suffered with *The Long Voyage Home,* he was rewarded with *Stagecoach,* which no one else in Hollywood would produce. To Ford's mind, Wanger "was a nice guy, a great producer to work with" because "he left you alone. . . . He never bothered you." Siegel agreed, calling Wanger "one of the very few producers who, I feel, actively contributes. Not actively contribute in the manner of some idiotic producers. He's never on the set and he would never presume to tell you where to set the camera."

Finally, Wanger's personal idealism precluded the ruthless business sense necessary to thrive in the industry. Where Selznick collected outrageous overages for loan-outs of his talents, Wanger split the difference with his contractees. "Walter was always such a creative man and a wonderful producer," Mehle recalls MCA founder Jules Stein telling her. "He has marvelous ideas, and he's such a man of the world, but he does not have a financial brain. He would be worth a hundred million dollars today if he did, but Walter doesn't think that way." Exclusive of *Cleopatra,* Wanger's films cost approximately $45.5 million (more than *Cleopatra* itself). Once released, they generated $5 million in production losses, but they earned approximately $76 million in gross income (of which roughly $25.3 million represented distribution fees that the major studios collected).

Clearly Wanger's financial performance was mixed, but so was that of most producers. Selznick spent his last few years in mounting debt. (Goldwyn was exceptional. He could net $1 million in a good year from his film activities; Wanger in his best year achieved barely half that amount. At his death, Goldwyn's estate amounted to more than $16 million; Wanger had barely $18,000 and the odd stock to bequeath to Shelley.)

If Wanger had retained his rights to his films, he could have died a multimillionaire, but he pledged the bulk of it away. With the diffusion of television, Selznick repeatedly sold the television rights to his old films (although he had given up his percentage of *Gone with the Wind*). To Wanger, television was a blessing primarily because it could help the producer finance future films. The sensationalist was too busy pursuing his next innovation to guard his past accomplishments. Making money, Wanger told a friend in 1951, "has never been my problem—keeping it has." To Jerry Geisler, Wanger wrote shortly after the Lang shooting, "I often wonder whether I would have been better off if I'd . . . not [been] such a dreamer at times." The consuming intensity of his dreams gave Wanger little time for the details of the business.

Upon Wanger's death, Twentieth Century–Fox won the publicity battle over *Cleopatra,* as obituaries in the national newsweeklies called him "Hollywood's most extravagant producer," as well as the man who shot Jennings Lang. But the truth was more complicated. Many of Hollywood's most successful producers (such as Selznick and Thalberg) were more deserving of that title, and Wanger completed plenty of films at Paramount, United Artists, and Allied Artists on time and within budget.

On the other hand, Wanger's solution to all of Hollywood's woes was more expenditures for promotion and massaging the press. And if a big film was in the making, Wanger—like Selznick, Goldwyn, and Thalberg (who felt an extra $100,000 in production might be worth several million dollars in grosses)—was willing to spend until the film succeeded. When Haworth apologized to Wanger for going over budget on the sets for *I Want to Live!* by $30,000, Wanger told him, "Teddy, if you weren't over budget, I'd be disappointed in you. . . . The more you are over budget the harder you have worked for me and the film." As one director said of Wanger, "Money was not something he liked to think about."

Partly for this reason, Wanger's status as a "semi-independent" had complex and often contradictory ramifications for his production program. Though it made him famous, it certainly did not enrich him as it was alleged to do; he made the most money while a unit producer at Universal during the war years. His exposure to risk as a semi-independent was enormous, especially since he insisted on realizing innovative films that audiences did not want to see. Wanger made *The President Vanishes* and *Private Worlds* without any interference (until after the film was complete), but the failure of either film to make profits rendered his company insolvent. In fact, Wanger's manifold ventures proved that semi-independence, the existence of a corporation separate from the major studios, never guaranteed the producer creative autonomy, since he or she cooperated with the oligopolistic majors.

One of the first producers to arrange a semi-independent deal in the 1930s, Wanger was by temperament and by business conditions an adjunct to the major companies. Selznick went independent in the early 1930s in part because, as Schulberg's assistant at Paramount in the 1920s, he found that the high-volume studio mode of production countered the movies' artistic and commercial potential. Wanger thought the major studio organization and structure was fine; he simply disagreed with the production executives who would not permit him to realize films on the subjects he chose.

Wanger's motivations were closer to the "lone wolf" Goldwyn, who among the most prestigious producers became "the only individual who owns and operates his own studio" so that he could avoid arguing with partners. But Wanger's access to limited financing and semi-independence had many more strings attached than Goldwyn's, and Wanger's semi-independence created only the *potential* for creative autonomy in the preparation of new projects. Therein lay the primary difference (along with guaranteed profit sharing) between semi-independence and unit production under studio control. This difference in potential is what allowed Chaplin to make *Modern Times* and *The Great Dictator,* or Goldwyn to produce films such as *Dead End* and *The Best Years of Our Lives,* or Wanger to prepare and produce *Blockade* when no other studio would touch the subject of the Spanish Civil War.

That potential, however, could be undercut by several contingencies related to the conduct of the corporations involved. The semi-independent's internal management policy was another factor. Goldwyn had no one sitting above him at his company; Selznick did, but his directors were reluctant to challenge him. The United Artists representatives sitting on Wanger's board in the late 1930s allowed him to realize a *You Only Live Once* or a *Blockade.* They also denied him the opportunity to produce a *Personal History* or *Eagle Squadron.* As Wanger put it, at United Artists and Universal "I used to have my own arrangements with the Bank of America and I was free to a degree. But I had to deal with my partners and shareholders just as Skouras does [at Fox]."

The idiosyncracies of the executives at the hosting studio-distributors proved to be another provisional factor in the semi-independent's conduct and autonomy. Wanger thrived in the 1930s largely because his host studios were desperate for films to distribute. Even so, Paramount and United Artists restricted Wanger's budgets, and the successive realization of the unit-produced *Gabriel Over the White House* and *The President Vanishes* showed that semi-independence could at times make little difference to Wanger's ability to put his ideas into production. If the host studio was relaxed, he enjoyed enormous freedom, as in the case of Diana's *Scarlet Street,* but he had comparable autonomy in realizing the unit productions of *Eagle Squadron, Arabian Nights,* and *Canyon Passage.* While a semi-independent he suffered the interference of Universal-International executives, Columbia's low-budget policies for *The Reckless Moment,* and even United Artists' insistence on blockbuster casting in the package for *I Want to Live!* As Skouras put it in his deposition for his lawsuit against Wanger, "when a studio supplies the money, the 'independent producer' is a faulty title."

In short, semi-independence offered different degrees of autonomy which depended on the constellation of social currents (what kinds of production ideas were acceptable to the distributors and the MPPDA), business conditions (the health of the market), and studio conduct (the management structures and policies in effect). Finally, there was the personality of the producer involved. Wanger could capitalize on his semi-independence only rarely, but when he did he managed to make many undeniably daring films. Selznick had far greater freedom than Wanger for most of his career as an independent; in particular he had, in Thomson's words, "stockholders ready to bend over backwards." But Selznick, the neurotic perfectionist who had to control every phase of production by the early 1940s, was insatiable: "Nothing had been enough. He had impeded himself in every way he could find."

It is ironic, given this historical perspective, that more than half of Hollywood's films now are produced under some variant of the package unit system and United Artists' model of semi-independence in the 1950s. Semi-independence today grants producers and directors the kind of autonomy and financing that Wanger and others struggled for so ardently from the thirties onward. Although rampant egos can exploit this system to create unnecessary expense or unsuccessful films (as in the notorious case of Michael Cimino's *Heaven's Gate*), the system remains in place. And semi-independent production still carries the aura of rebellious individuality that Wanger exploited so deftly through the 1950s.

Wanger coped with his personal limitations, the contingencies of the film industry, and the constraints of Hollywood's mode of production in his inimitable fashion, creating a career that was meteoric in its intensity and trajectory. Though he sometimes embodied Hollywood's worst tendencies, though we now take for granted the battles he fought in his time, and though his legacy is a mixed one, Walter Wanger, on- and off-screen, was one of the most humane, significant, and influential producers, studio-employed or semi-independent, in Hollywood history. In their time, Wanger's most notorious films—from *Washington Merry-Go-Round* to *Blockade*—helped to broaden the vocabulary of subjects Hollywood elected to dramatize. His best films—from *Queen Christina* to *I Want to Live!*—remain some of the American cinema's finest achievements. Only a handful of producers from Hollywood's classical era can claim as much.

Bibliographic Notes

A Note on Citations

When I created full and complete citations for the endnotes to this volume, they amounted to a quarter of its length. In the interests of economy, I elected not to use them.

In the comments that follow, I identify the sources of quotations and materials only if they are published in books, major news dailies, and trade publications or are found in selected archival collections.

Any quotations whose source I do not identify are from either interviews or correspondence I conducted with Wanger's associates, friends, and relatives; materials from obscure publications such as *The Dartmouth,* or individual letters from collections where the correspondence I quote is voluminous (specifically the Production Code Administration files, the RKO Archive, or most frequently, the Walter F. Wanger Collection housed at the Wisconsin Center for Film and Theater Research in Madison, Wisconsin).

I will be happy to share specific citations with any interested readers who contact me at the Film Studies Program, Emory University, Atlanta, Georgia 30322.

Abbreviations

AMPAS: Margaret Herrick Library of the Academy of Motion Picture Arts and Sciences, Beverly Hills, Calif.

COHC: The Columbia University Oral History Project, Popular Arts Collection, Butler Library, New York, NY.

DOS: David O. Selznick Collection, Humanities Research Center, University of Texas, Austin, Tex.

Ford:	John Ford Collection, Lilly Library, Indiana University, Bloomington, Ind.
MGM:	MGM Script Collection, Department of Special Collections, Doheny Library, University of Southern California, Los Angeles, Calif.
MLWC:	WFW and Joe Hyams, *My Life with "Cleopatra"* (New York: Bantam Books, 1963).
MPH:	*Motion Picture Herald.*
NYPL:	Billy Rose Theater Collection, Lincoln Center Library for the Performing Arts, New York Public Library.
NYT:	*The New York Times.*
PCA:	Production Code Administration Collection, Margaret Herrick Library, Academy of Motion Picture Arts and Sciences, Beverly Hills, Calif.
RKO:	RKO Archives, UCLA Theater Arts Library, Los Angeles, Calif.
TRT:	Walter Wanger interview in Bernard Rosenberg and Harry Silverstein, *The Real Tinsel* (London: Macmillan, 1970), 80–99.
UA:	United Artists Collection, Wisconsin Center for Film and Theater Research, Madison, Wis.
UA-Addition:	United Artists Collection Addition, 1950–1980, Wisconsin Center for Film and Theater Research, Madison, Wis.
Universal:	Universal Collection, Department of Special Collections, Doheny Library, University of Southern California, Los Angeles, Calif.
V:	*Variety.*
WFW Micro:	Walter Wanger's scrapbook, microfilmed and available at the Wisconsin Center for Film and Theater Research, Madison, Wis.

Epigrams

Louis Dudebat's speech is from George Bernard Shaw's *The Doctor's Dilemma* in *Complete Plays with Prefaces* (N.Y.: Dodd, Mead and Company, 1963), 172–173; Mike Nichols's comment is quoted in John Gregory Dunne, "The Check is in the Mail," *The New York Review of Books,* 17 March 1988: 35.

Preface

The uncharitable observations of Wanger come from Otis Ferguson, "No Visible Means of Support," *The New Republic,* 9 August 1939, in Robert Wilson, ed. *The Film Criticism of Otis Ferguson* (Philadelphia: Temple University Press, 1971), 265; Ezra Goodman's are in *The Fifty Year Decline and Fall of Hollywood* (New York: Simon and Schuster, 1963), 187–188, 243. Ben Hecht's derogatory remarks about producers come from COHC.

The new framework for understanding the work of the Hollywood producer derives from Tino Balio's *United Artists: The Company Built by the Stars* (Madison:

University of Wisconsin Press, 1976; hereafter "Balio I") and *United Artists: The Company that Changed the Film Industry* (Madison: University of Wisconsin Press, 1988; hereafter "Balio II"); Thomas Schatz, *The Genius of the System* (New York: Pantheon Books, 1989) (his comment is on p. 8). An equally profound influence on my work has been David Bordwell, Janet Staiger, and Kristin Thompson, *The Classical Hollywood Cinema: Film Style and Mode of Production, 1917 to 1960* (New York: Columbia University Press, 1986). For an excellent, practical discussion of the contemporary Hollywood producer's functions, see Paul N. Lazarus III, *The Movie Producer* (New York: Barnes & Noble Books, 1985). These same works provide invaluable studies of Hollywood's independent production. The centrality of the tension between individualist and community values in American culture and film receives its fullest treatment in Robert B. Ray, *A Certain Tendency of the Hollywood Cinema, 1930–1980* (Princeton, N.J.: Princeton University Press, 1985). Al La Valley provides a perceptive assessment of Wanger in his *Invasion of the Body Snatchers* (New Brunswick: Rutgers University Press, 1989), 11–14, as does Schatz in *Genius of the System.*

Chapter 1: The Gentleman from the West (1894–1911)

The quote from Jesse Lasky, Jr., comes from his unpublished interview with Richard Koszarski, 17 August 1980, New York, N.Y., Oral History of the New York Motion Picture Industry, Museum of the Moving Image, Astoria, N.Y.

Particularly useful sources for researching Wanger's personality and early life include Russell Phelps, "Uncorking Unknown," 16 January 1938, Sunday Magazine section, *Arkansas Gazette,* "WFW Micro." Published descriptions of Wanger's personality include Henry B. Williams, *Theater at Dartmouth, 1769–1914* (Hanover, N.H.: Friends of the Dartmouth Library, 1987), 165 and Marion Elizabeth Rodgers, ed. *Mencken and Sara: A Life in Letters* (New York: McGraw-Hill Book Company, 1987), 331.

Information on the Feuchtwangers and the Stettheimers derives from Priscilla Fishman, ed. *The Jews of the United States* (Jerusalem: Keter Publishing House, 1974); Robert E. Levinson, *The Jews in the California Gold Rush* (New York: Ktav Publishing House, Inc., 1978); Parker Tyler, *Florine Stettheimer: A Life in Art* (New York: Farrar, Straus and Company, 1963); and Shelley Wanger, "The Stettheimers: A Profile," unpublished essay. Jed Harris's remarks are from his *A Dance on the High Wire* (New York: Crown Publishing, 1979), 8.

The general account of San Francisco stage history is derived from William Issel and Robert W. Cherny, *San Francisco, 1865–1932* (Berkeley: University of California Press, 1986), Edmond M. Gagey, *The San Francisco Stage* (New York: Columbia University Press, 1950) and Dean Goodman, *San Francisco Stages: A Concise History, 1849–1986* (San Francisco: Micro Pro Litera Press, 1986). The *Algiers* dispute is documented in several letters in the *Algiers* File, PCA.

Chapter 2: The Boy Manager (1911–1914)

Background on Dartmouth College derives from Leon Burr Richardson, *History of Dartmouth College,* Vol. 2 (Hanover, N.H.: Dartmouth College Publications, 1932),

756, and John King Lord, *A History of Dartmouth College, 1815–1909* (Concord, N.H.: The Rumsford Press, 1913), 498–505.

Helpful accounts of the work of Edward Gordon Craig, the Ballets Russes, and the Abbey Theater include: Christopher Innes, *Edward Gordon Craig* (Cambridge, Mass.: Cambridge University Press, 1983); Clayton Hamilton, "The New Art of Stage Direction," *Bookman* 35 (July 1912), 485–487 (the description of *The Rising of the Moon* set); "Gordon Craig's New Offensive Against the Modern Theater," *Current Opinion* 65 (September 1918), 163; Lynn Garafola, *Diaghilev's Ballets Russes* (New York: Oxford University Press, 1989); Robert C. Hansen, *Scenic and Costume Design for the Ballets Russes* (Ann Arbor, Mich.: UMI Research Press, 1985), 120; and James Flannery, *W. B. Yeats and the Idea of a Theater* (New Haven, Conn.: Yale University Press, 1976), 239–278.

Wanger's family's encounters with the New Stagecraft are documented in the Florine and Ettie Stettheimer Papers, Beinecke Rare Book and Manuscript Library, Yale University Library, New Haven, Conn., and Danton Walker, "Broadway," *New York Daily News,* 19 February 1939. Henry B. Williams surveys Wanger's work at Dartmouth in his "The Halcyon Years, 1912–1914," in *Theater at Dartmouth, 1769–1914,* 165–181. More immediate descriptions come from Jack Warren, Letter to the Editor, *New Yorker,* 1 April 1954; Henry Tyrrell, "How a New York Freshie at Dartmouth College Succeeded in Putting Hanover, N.H., on the Theatrical Map," *The New York World,* 15 February 1914; and many articles in *The Dartmouth.* The *Eternally Yours* dispute is documented in the *"Eternally Yours"* File of the PCA.

Chapter 3: Finding a Niche (1915–1919)

The discussion of the Little Theater–Theater Monopoly debate derives from "The Greatness of the Little Theater Movement Explained by Its Champions," *Current Opinion* 63 (December 1917), 389–390; Kenneth MacGowan, "America's First Exhibition of the New Stagecraft," *Theatre Magazine* 21, no. 167 (January 1915), 28; Stow Persons, *The Decline of American Gentility* (New York: Columbia University Press, 1973); and Lawrence W. Levine, *Highbrow/Lowbrow* (Cambridge, Mass.: Harvard University Press, 1988), particularly 206–214, 226–231. Michael Budd has explored the currents of social reform in his excellent "The Moments of *Caligari*," in Budd, ed. *The Cabinet of Dr. Caligari: Texts, Contexts, Histories* (New Brunswick: Rutgers University Press, 1990), 84–102.

On Harley Granville-Barker and his American interlude see Eric Salmon, *Granville Barker: A Secret Life* (Teaneck, N.J.: Fairleigh Dickinson University Press, 1983), 114–115; "Granville Barker May Head the New Theatre Here," *Theatre* 21, no. 168 (February 1915), 63; "New York's Excited Impressions of Granville Barker," *Current Opinion* 58 (April 1915): 248–249; Eric Salmon, ed., *Granville Barker and His Correspondents* (Detroit: Wayne State University Press, 1986), 137; "Optimism Feast For Theatre Men," *NYT,* 22 February 1915: 9; and Alexander Woollcott, "The Stage," *New York Morning World,* 23 January 1928.

On Wanger's interlude with Elizabeth Marbury, see her *My Crystal Ball* (New York: Boni and Liveright, 1933); P. G. Wodehouse and Guy Bolton, *Bring on the Girls: The Improbable Story of Our Life in Musical Comedy* (1954; reprint, London: Hutchinson and Co., Ltd., 1980), 12; and Cole Porter, *The Cole Porter Story*

(Cleveland: World Publishing Co., 1965), 13. On *Patria,* see Kevin Brownlow, *The Parade's Gone By* (Berkeley: University of California Press, 1968), 264.

On the Nazimova Season, see "Nazimova in Repertoire," *New York Dramatic Mirror,* 21 October 1916, 1, and "Nazimova Dismisses Company," *New York Dramatic Mirror,* 1 December 1916. On *'Ception Shoals,* see the reviews in *Theatre Magazine,* 25, no. 192 (February 1917); *New York Dramatic Mirror,* 20 January 1917, 7; and *NYT,* 11 January 1917, 13. Nazimova's comments are from "Nazimova—An Apostle of the Drama," *Theatre Magazine* 25, no. 193 (March 1917). For information on Wanger's backers, I relied on several letters: Willard D. Rockefeller to F. K. Reilly, 7 December 1916; F. K. Reilly to Frank Baum, 11 December 1916; and F. K. Reilly to Frank Baum, 26 December 1916, supplied to me by Michael Patrick Hearn.

Wanger's propaganda and war work is documented in "City Leads Nation in Recruiting Work," *NYT,* 9 April 1917: 6; "Women Help Recruiting," *NYT,* 15 April 1917, section 1: 3; and Frances Marion, *Off With Their Heads* (New York: Macmillan, 1972), 60–61. The CPI is discussed in James R. Mock and Cedric Larsen, *Words That Won the War: The Story of the Committee on Public Information* (Princeton, N.J.: Princeton University Press, 1939); the comment on Italy appears on 286. See also Stephen Vaughn, *Holding Fast the Inner Lines: Nationalism, and the Committee on Public Information* (Chapel Hill: University of North Carolina Press, 1980), 18–20.

The Merriam Office is described in Barry D. Karl, *Charles E. Merriam and the Study of Politics* (Chicago: University of Chicago Press, 1974); Merriam's "American Publicity in Italy," *The American Political Science Review* 13, no. 4 (November 1919), 542–544, 549; and various documents in the Charles E. Merriam Papers at the University of Chicago Library. Wanger's work at the Peace Conference is described by James T. Shotwell in his *At the Paris Peace Conference* (New York: MacMillan Company, 1937), 85, 130, 153.

Wanger's descriptions of all these events derive from WFW, Letter to Harold Q. Rugg, 16 January 1915, Walter Wanger Alumnus File Special Collections, Dartmouth College Library, Hanover, New Hampshire; WFW, "Freedom of the Screen," *Dartmouth Alumnus,* October 1947, 13; Kevin Brownlow, unpublished interview with Walter Wanger; Brownlow, "The Early Days of Walter Wanger," *Film* 39 (1964), 10; WFW, Letter to Professor Barry Karl, 28 August 1963; Grover Jones, "Important Fun" (publicity biography); Sewell Collins, "A Wizard of the Films," *Daily Express,* 18 May 1921, WFW Micro; *TRT:* 82, 83; and Edward Weitzel, "Says Walter Wanger, Production Head for Famous Players–Lasky Company," *Moving Picture World,* n.d.

Wanger's postwar career in the theater is documented in *V,* 17 October 1917: 15 and in various clippings in WFW Micro. Information on Justine Johnston comes from Jerry Stagg, *The Brothers Shubert* (New York: Random House, 1968), 150–152; Jesse Lasky with Don Weldon, *I Blow My Own Horn* (Garden City, N.Y.: Doubleday and Co., 1957), 85; "Per Aspera," *The Sun,* 21 June 1919; and "Woman in White," *Harper's Bazaar* (July 1940): 53, 82.

Chapter 4: Giving the Movies "Class" (1920–1924)

The account of Wanger's contact with Jesse Lasky and hiring at Famous Players–Lasky derives from Lasky with Weldon, *I Blow My Own Horn,* 134–135 and *Moving*

Picture World, 1 May 1920: 678, and 12 June 1920: 1448. Bernays's comment comes from his *Biography of an Idea* (New York: Simon and Schuster, 1965), 150. The discussion of Paramount's history and its position in the early 1920s comes from Douglas Gomery, *The Hollywood Studio System* (New York: St. Martin's Press, 1988), 4; Jesse Lasky, "Production Problems," in Joseph P. Kennedy, ed. *The Story of the Films* (Chicago: A. W. Shaw Company, 1927; reprint, New York: Jerome S. Ozer, 1971), 99; *V,* 30 April 1920: 12, *V,* 21 March 1928: 5, and Lasky with Weldon, 126, 129.

The survey of Hollywood's modeling of its feature-length films on the legitimate theater derives from Staiger in Bordwell et al., *Classical Hollywood Cinema,* 129–134, 148 and Austin C. Lescaboura, *Behind the Motion Picture Screen* (New York: Scientific American Publishing Co., 1919), 118. On Maurice Tourneur's admiration for the New Stagecraft, see Richard Koszarski, *An Evening's Entertainment: The Age of the Silent Feature Picture, 1915–1928* (New York: Charles Scribner's Sons, 1990), 120, 225.

Wanger's responsibilities at FPL are described in *V,* 3 June 1921: 47. The discussion of his orientalist efforts is primarily informed by Edward W. Said, *Orientalism* (New York: Pantheon, 1978); Ella Shohat's comprehensive "Gender and Culture of Empire: Toward a Feminist Ethnography of the Cinema," *Quarterly Review of Film and Video* 13, nos. 1–3: 45–84, and Antonia Lant, "The Curse of the Pharoah, or How Cinema Contracted Egyptomania," *October* 59 (Winter 1992): 87–112. See also Gaylyn Studlar, "Discourses of Gender and Ethnicity: The Construction and De(con)struction of Rudolph Valentino as Other," *Film Criticism* 13 (1989): 24–25; Studlar, "The Perils of Pleasure," *Wide Angle* 13, no. 1 (1991): 6–33; Miriam Hansen, *Babel and Babylon* (Cambridge: Harvard University Press, 1991), 256. The film industry's consciousness of consumption and women spectators is discussed in Lary May, *Screening Out the Past* (New York: Oxford University Press, 1980), 200–236; Janet Staiger, "Announcing Wares, Winning Patrons, Voicing Ideals: Thinking about the History and Theory of Advertising," *Cinema Journal* 29, no. 3 (1990): 5; and Diane Waldman, "From Midnight Shows to Marriage Vows," *Wide Angle* 6, no. 2: 40–42.

Wanger's contributions to FPL's art direction are described by Wanger in *TRT:* 83 and evident in *Photoplay* 21, no. 2 (1922): 30; "Fashions Anticipated for Screen Productions," *NYT,* 14 June 1925, section 8: 2; *V,* 28 January 1921: 45; Lasky with Weldon, *I Blow My Own Horn,* 173–174; and David O. Selznick, Memo to M. C. Levee, 4 February 1931, "M. C. Levee" File, DOS.

The description of Wanger's compatibility with Jesse Lasky's approach to production draws on Ivor Montagu, *With Eisenstein in Hollywood* (New York: International Publishers, 1967), 56; Budd Schulberg, *Moving Pictures: Memoirs of a Hollywood Prince* (New York: Stein and Day, 1981), 301; Lasky with Weldon, *I Blow My Own Horn,* 164, 208; *Moving Picture World,* 13 November 1920: 236; Rouben Mamoulian, December 1958, COHC; and Kevin Brownlow, unpublished interview with Walter Wanger.

Wanger's departure from FPL is documented in *V,* 28 January 1921: 47; *V,* 16 February 1921: 46; and Louella Parsons, "Justine Johnstone [*sic*] to Rescue of Her Sex," *New York Morning Telegram,* 3 May 1921: 3. Wanger's sojourn in London is described in "Is This Why?" *Wid's Daily,* 12 December 1921: 1, 2 and several articles in Wanger's microfilmed scrapbooks: Sewell Collins, "A Wizard of the Films,"

London Daily Express, 18 May 1921; "Society and the Film," *Daily Graphic,* 20 December 1921; "Covent Garden Stormed," *Daily Express,* 24 December 1921; "Society's Film First Night," *Evening News,* 17 January 1922; "Picture Theaters," *London Times Cinema Supplement,* 21 February 1922; "Russian Ballet Returns," *London Star,* 22 March 1922; "The Value of West End Exploitation," *Film Renter and Moving Picture News,* 25 February 1922; "From West End to Whitechapel," *Film Renter and Moving Picture News,* 22 April 1922: 10; "Walter F. Wanger To Control the Rivoli," *The Bioscope,* 20 April 1922: 5; "Adams Replies to Weigall," *Kinematograph Weekly,* 12 January 1922; *V,* 23 April 1924: 3; and WFW, "London From the Inside," *NYT,* 20 January 1924, section 7: 2. *V,* 30 July 1924: 21 describes his return to FPL.

Chapter 5: Organizational Demands (1924–1931)

Wanger's personal life is gleaned from Louise Brooks, *Lulu in Hollywood* (New York: Alfred A. Knopf, 1982), 20; Barry Paris, *Louise Brooks* (New York: Alfred A. Knopf, 1989), 71, 87, 89; Julia Pegler, "The Talkies Talk Sense," *College Humor* 74 (February 1930): 49; Ginger Rogers, *My Story* (New York: Harper Collins, 1991), 88–89; Marlene Dietrich, *Marlene,* Salvator Attansio, trans. (New York: Grove Press, 1989), 74; and Irene Mayer Selznick, *A Private View* (New York: Alfred A. Knopf, 1983), 80. Tallulah Bankhead is quoted in Elia Kazan, *A Life* (New York: Alfred A. Knopf, 1989), 158. Selznick's observation is from David Thomson, *Showman: The Life of David O. Selznick* (New York: Alfred A. Knopf, 1992), 102.

The framework for discussing the role of executives at the major studios derives from Bordwell et al., *Classical Hollywood Cinema,* 128–153 and Alfred D. Chandler, Jr., *Strategy and Structure: Chapters in the History of the American Industrial Enterprise* (Cambridge, Mass.: MIT Press, 1962), 8–12; see also Anthony Cutler, Barry Hindess, Paul Hirst, and Athar Hussain, *Marx's "Capital" and Capitalism Today,* Vol. 1 (Boston: Routledge and Kegan Paul, 1977), 308–312.

The division of labor and hierarchies of power among production, distribution, and exhibition arms at FPL are documented in *Moving Picture World,* 12 July 1920: 1469; Erwin Gelsey, Memo to B. P. Schulberg, 25 June 1929, "Erwin Gelsey" File no. 5, RKO-Paramount-MGM Box 2, 1929–1931, DOS; Mae Huettig, "Economic Control of the Motion Picture Industry," in Tino Balio, ed. *The American Film Industry,* 2d ed. (Madison: University of Wisconsin Press, 1985), 292; *V,* 26 March 1924: 22; Lasky in Kennedy, ed., *Story of the Films,* 101; and *V,* 11 August 1926: 3. See also Schatz, *Genius of the System,* 69–81. Selznick's comments are from Kevin Brownlow, *The Parade's Gone By* (Berkeley: University of California Press, 1968), 434; Wanger's description of the sales meetings is from Brownlow, "The Early Days of Walter Wanger": 11. See also Lasky with Weldon, *I Blow My Own Horn,* 198–201.

Wanger and Lasky's laissez-faire approach to production is described by Louise Brooks, who is quoted in Kenneth Tynan, "The Girl in the Black Helmet," *New Yorker,* 11 June 1979: 47; and by Staiger in Bordwell et al., *Classical Hollywood Cinema,* 137. Lasky's prescription for producers is from Leo Rosten, *Hollywood: The Movie Colony* (New York: Harcourt, Brace and Company, 1941), 239. The firing story is from *MLWC:* 167. The Dorothy Arzner incident is recounted in Karyn Kay and Gerald Peary, "Interview with Dorothy Arzner," in Kay and Peary, eds. *Women and the Cinema* (New York: E. P. Dutton, 1977), 157–159. The D. W. Griffith dispute is documented in D. W. Griffith, Letter to Adolph Zukor, 10 November 1926, D. W. Griffith Papers, Reel 14, Microfilm Edition. The lax discipline among FPL talents is discussed in Howard Greer, "My Perils with Pola," *Town and Country,* November 1950: 122; B. P. and Budd Schulberg, *True,* February 1949; clipping in "B. P. Schulberg" File, AMPAS; and Schulberg, *Moving Pictures,* 187–188.

B. P. Schulberg's reign in FPL's Hollywood studio is described in Montagu, *With Eisenstein in Hollywood,* 49; Selznick in Brownlow, *The Parade's Gone By,* 434; Peter Bogdanovich, *Allen Dwan: The Last Pioneer* (New York: Praeger Publishers, 1971), 65–66. The East-West rivalry is discussed in *V,* 1 September 1926: 4; *V,* 25 November 1926: 27; and *V,* 8 December 1926: 4. Wanger's European tone at Astoria is discussed in Koszarski, Interview with Jesse Lasky, Jr.; *V,* 13 November 1924: 26; Tynan, "Girl in the Black Helmet," 47; Brooks, *Lulu in Hollywood,* 21; Gloria Swanson, *Swanson on Swanson* (New York: Random House, 1980), 195–196. For the shutdown of Astoria, see *V,* 9 March 1927: 4. The mid-1927 budget cuts are documented in *V,* 22 June 1927: 8, and *V,* 13 July 1927: 16. Sara Haardt describes her work with Wanger in Marian Elizabeth Rodgers, ed., *Mencken and Sara,* 319, 341–342, 347, 354, 362–363.

Wanger's work during the transition to sound and *Warming Up* are discussed in *TRT:* 94–95, and *NYT,* 26 July 1928: 25; crucial studio announcements were reported in *V,* 2 May 1928: 23; *V,* 16 May 1928: 5; and *V,* 27 June 1928: 14, 31; general background on the major studios' maneuvers during the period comes from Douglas Gomery, "The 'Warner-Vitaphone Peril': The American Film Industry Reacts to Sound," (1976), in Gorham Kindem, ed. *The American Movie Industry* (Carbondale: Southern Illinois University Press, 1982), 119–132. See also Alexander Walker, *The Shattered Silents: How the Talkies Came to Stay* (New York: Morrow, 1978), 40.

The early sound era and Wanger's policies at Astoria are documented in *V,* 23 May 1928: 4; *V,* 6 June 1928: 6; *V,* 25 July 1928: 7; Robert Florey, *Hollywood D'Hier et D'Aujourd'Hui* (Paris: Editions Prisma, 1948, my translation), 147; *V,* 10 September 1930: 3; and *V,* 1 October 1930: 2. For a discussion of Astoria's use of plays, see Richard Koszarski, *The Astoria Studio and Its Fabulous Films* (New York: Dover Books, 1983): 9 and *V,* 30 April 1930: 11.

On Astoria's "Sophisticated" films, see *V,* 11 September 1929: 18; *V,* 4 April 1930: 11; *V,* 13 August 1930: 2; *V,* 20 August 1930: 4; *V,* 25 March 1931: 4; and *V,* 1 April 1931: 7. For a discussion of the fallen woman genre, see Lea Jacobs, *The Wages of Sin: Censorship and the Fallen Woman Film, 1928–1941* (Madison: University of Wisconsin Press, 1991), 3–15. The review of *Tarnished Lady* comes from *V,* 6 May 1931. Father Daniel A. Lord recalls describing Wanger as a "bad boy" in the early 1930s in his Letter to Joseph Breen, 27 September 1938, Father Daniel A. Lord Papers, Jesuit Missouri Province Archives, St. Louis, Mo. The industry's shift to "hokum" is cited in *V,* 3 September 1930: 2 and *V,* 10 September 1930: 4; Schulberg is quoted on the subject in *V,* 17 November 1931: 2. Henry Jenkins III has explored the industry's changing estimate of its market in the early 1930s in 'Shall We Make It for New York, or for Distribution?': Eddie Cantor, *Whoopee,* and Regional Resistance to the Talkies," *Cinema Journal* 29, no. 3 (Spring 1990): 32–48.

Sidney Kent's coup at FPL is documented in *V,* 27 May 1931: 5 and *V,* 23 June 1931: 5. The Astoria films' failures are described in *V,* 1 January 1930: 8; *V,* 12

February 1930: 19; *V,* 28 January 1931: 12; and *V,* 18 February 1931: 14. The Nancy
Carroll issue is discussed in *V,* 8 January 1930: 1; *V,* 9 June 1931: 3; and Martin
Quigley, Letter to Father Daniel A. Lord, 25 June 1931, "Martin Quigley—Movie
Code 1927–1932" File, Father Daniel A. Lord Papers. Wanger's departure from
Paramount is discussed in *V,* 23 June 1931: 4 and *V,* 6 October 1931: 2. His requiem
for the company is in *TRT:* 83.

Chapter 6: Too Much Interference (1932–1934)

Wanger's sustained idealism is documented in Arthur Weigall, "Films: Players
with Ideals," *Daily Mail,* 29 November 1921, and "Films and the Child," *Daily Tele-graph,* 27 February 1922, WFW Micro; Pegler, "Talkies Talk Sense"; and Benjamin
Hampton, *History of the American Film Industry* (New York: Dover Publications,
1931, reprint 1970), 430–431. Its social context is construed from John A. Kouwen-hoven, *The Arts in Modern American Civilization* (New York: Norton, 1948) and
Myron Lounsbury, "Flashes of Lightning: The Moving Picture in the Progressive
Era," *Journal of Popular Culture* 3, no. 4 (Spring 1970): 772; its industry context de-rives from Hampton, *History of the American Film Industry,* 418–425; *V,* 12 Novem-ber 1930: 6; and Earl Hammond, "Short Reels and Educational Subjects" in Kennedy,
ed., *Story of the Films,* 151.

H. L. Mencken's comments on Wanger come from Rodgers, *Mencken and Sara,*
332, 338; John Grierson's views are stated in John Grierson, Letter to the Editor,
London Times, 21 November 1968: 12; Forsyth Hardy, *John Grierson: A Documentary
Biography* (Boston: Faber and Faber, 1979), 36–37; John Grierson, Letter to George
Stevens, Jr., 2 May 1968 (G7: file 33) and *Motion Picture News,* 27 November 1926
(G1A: File 5), both on file at the John Grierson Archive, University of Stirling,
Glasgow, Scotland. Wanger's attempts to go "independent" are documented in *V,* 30
June 1931: 2; *V,* 21 July 1931: 4; and *V,* 28 July 1931: 3.

The general description of Columbia's management and studio is derived from
Gomery, *Hollywood Studio System,* 161–167, and from *V,* 8 January 1930: 81; *V,* 16
February 1932: 64; and *V,* 26 July 1932: 3; and Frank Capra, *The Name Above the
Title* (New York: Macmillan, 1971), 81. On Harry Cohn's mob connections, see David
A. Cook, *A History of Narrative Film,* 2d ed. (New York: Norton, 1990), 293,
footnote.

On the costs of sound filmmaking see *V,* 3 October 1928: 1 and *V,* 13 March 1929:
1. On the return of double-bills, see *V,* 8 October 1930: 4 and *V,* 8 December 1931: 9.
On the increase in low-budget independents, see *V,* 23 May 1928: 5; *V,* 24 October
1933: 2; and *V,* 31 October 1933: 41. For an excellent survey of low-budget indepen-dents during this period, see Paul Seale, "'A Host of Others': Toward a Nonlinear
History of Poverty Row and the Coming of Sound," *Wide Angle* 13, no. 1 (1990):
72–103.

The major studios' booking of outside films and debate on how to handle double-features is documented in *V,* 1 April 1931: 6; *V,* 8 April 1931: 11; *V,* 28 July 1931: 5;
V, 10 November 1931: 5; *V,* 12 January 1932: 5; *V,* 9 February 1932: 4; *V,* 3 May 1932:
21; *V,* 5 July 1932: 5; and *V,* 19 July 1932: 6.

Wanger discusses the anomaly of his presence at Columbia in *TRT:* 93; other observations come from *V,* 2 February 1932: 5 and *V,* 16 February 1932: 5. Morris Safier is quoted in David Thomson, Letter to author, 10 October 1991. Wanger's policy innovations are documented in *V,* 9 February 1932: 3; *V,* 23 February 1932: 5; *V,* 1 March 1932: 50; and *V,* 19 April 1932: 4.

The production history of *The Bitter Tea of General Yen* comes from *V,* 27 May 1931: 5; *V,* 9 February 1932: 4; *V,* 3 May 1932: 21; *V,* 7 June 1932: 7; Joseph McBride, *Frank Capra: The Catastrophe of Success* (New York: Simon and Schuster, 1992), 278–282; "Frank Capra," in Richard Schickel, *The Men Who Made the Movies* (New York: Atheneum, 1975), 70; Capra, *Name Above the Title,* 140; and correspondence in *The Bitter Tea of General Yen* File, PCA. Critical analysis of the film includes Leland Poague, *The Cinema of Frank Capra* (New York: A. S. Barnes, 1975), 138–152, and Ellen Draper, "History, Race and Gender in *The Bitter Tea of General Yen,*" unpublished paper.

The production histories of *Washington Merry-Go-Round* and *Night Mayor* derive from *V,* 22 March 1932: 3; *V,* 13 September 1932: 4; and correspondence in the *"Night Mayor"* and *"Gabriel Over the White House"* Files, PCA. Critical comments come from Alexander Bakshy, "Going into Politics," *The Nation,* 9 November 1932: 466 and *V,* 29 November 1932: 19. Discussion of the social problem film derives from Peter Roffman and Jim Purdy, *The Hollywood Social Problem Film* (Bloomington: University of Indiana Press, 1981), 7; Kay Sloan, *The Loud Silents* (Champaign-Urbana: University of Illinois Press, 1988), 13, 16; and Russell Campbell, "The Ideology of the Social Consciousness Movie: Three Films of Darryl F. Zanuck," *Quarterly Review of Film Studies* 3, no. 1 (Winter 1978): 57. Wanger's departure from Columbia is documented in *V,* 22 November 1932: 4 and *V,* 6 December 1932: 4.

The description of MGM, its producer orientation, and its studio politics in late 1932 and early 1933 comes from "Metro-Goldwyn-Mayer," *Fortune* 6 (December 1932) in Balio, ed. *American Film Industry,* 311–326; Sam Marx, *A Gaudy Spree* (New York: Franklin Watts, 1987), 21; Sam Marx, *Mayer and Thalberg: The Make-Believe Saints* (New York: Random House, 1975), 4, 162; Bosley Crowther, *Hollywood Rajah* (New York: Henry Holt, 1960), 165–166, 193–196; *V,* 27 September 1932: 5; *V,* 1 November 1932: 5; "Dialogue on Film: Rouben Mamoulian," *American Film* (January–February 1983): 67; Schatz, *Genius of the System,* 48–57 and 98–124; and Gomery, *The Hollywood Studio System,* 51–75. Wanger paraphrased Mayer's hopes for Wanger's contribution in Bob Thomas, *Thalberg: Life and Legend* (New York: Bantam, 1967), 255.

The making of *Gabriel Over the White House* is described in "Notes on *Gabriel Over the White House,*" 18 March 1933, *"Gabriel Over the White House"* File 3, MGM; the lengthy correspondence in the *"Gabriel Over the White House"* File, PCA; and "Bills Ask Curb on Political Movies; Sponsors at Albany Say Some Libel Officials," *NYT,* 9 February 1933. See also Robert L. McConnell, "The Genesis and Ideology of *Gabriel Over the White House,*" in Richard Dyer MacCann and Jack Ellis, eds., *Cinema Examined* (New York: E. P. Dutton, 1982), 202–221. For reviews of the film, see Bruce Bliven, *The New Republic,* 19 April 1933: 282; Stark Young, *The New Republic,* 19 April 1933: 280–281; and William Troy, *The Nation,* 26 April 1933: 482–483. Richard Watts, Jr., and Walter Lippmann are quoted at length in "A President After Hollywood's Heart," *Literary Digest,* 22 April 1933: 13. Harry Alan Potamkin's review is reprinted in Potamkin and Lewis Jacobs, *The Compound Cinema*

(New York: Teacher's College Press, 1977), 515–519. Information on *Another Language* comes from *"Another Language"* File 1, MGM, from a statement on production costs and contracts from July 1933 and from a statement of rentals up through August 1, 1935, DOS.

The production history of *Queen Christina* comes from *"Queen Christina"* Files 1 and 4. MGM; Salka Viertel, *The Kindness of Strangers* (New York: Holt, Rinehart and Winston, 1969), 174–175; Leatrice Gilbert Fountain and John R. Maxim, *Dark Star* (New York: St. Martin's Press, 1985), 233–239; John A. Gallagher and Marino A. Amoruco, "An Interview with Rouben Mamoulian," *The Velvet Light Trap* 19 (1981): 20–21; and the voluminous correspondence in the *"Queen Christina"* File, PCA. Jacobs, *Wages of Sin,* provides an excellent account of MPPDA self-censorship policies.

The making of *Going Hollywood* and Wanger's other arguments with Mayer and Hearst and his departure from MGM is documented in Julian Fox, "Going Hollywood," *Films and Filming* 19, no. 9 (June 1973): 34; Raoul Walsh, *Each Man in His Time* (New York: Farrar, Straus and Giroux), 257–258; Gottfried Reinhardt, June 1959, COHC; Marx, *A Gaudy Spree,* 105–106, 111; *V,* 24 October 1933: 5; *V,* 20 February 1934: 3; and *V,* 22 May 1934: 5.

Chapter 7: Semi-Independent Production (1934–1936)

On the formation of JayPay Productions, see Grace Wilcox, "The Bad Boy of the Studios," (unidentified publication), 2 December 1934, WFW Micro and *V,* 6 November 1934: 5, 10. The capitalization of JayPay divided 8,700 shares of preferred stock and 200 shares of common stock between the stockholders.

On the growth of unit production in the early 1930s see Janet Staiger's seminal "The Producer-Unit System: Management by Specialization after 1931," in Bordwell, et al., *Classical Hollywood Cinema,* 320–329. For insightful discussions of independent production in general, see Staiger's analysis in Bordwell et al., *Classical Hollywood Cinema,* 317–319, and Schatz, *Genius of the System,* 176–177. One could argue that internally, semi-independents like Wanger were organized to follow the central producer mode of production. I find the producer-unit more apt given the semi-independent's sparse output and its function in the major's operation. See also *V,* 27 October 1930: 5; *V,* 11 August 1931: 5; *V,* 25 August 1931: 7; *V,* 27 October 1931: 5; *V,* 10 May 1932: 4; *V,* 23 August 1932: 5; *V,* 11 October 1932: 5; and *Film Daily,* 30 September 1932. On the increase of independent deals and Paramount's position in 1934, see *V,* 5 April 1932: 4; *V,* 18 October 1932: 5; *V,* 17 January 1933: 2; *V,* 24 April 1934: 4; *V,* 3 July 1934: 3; and *V,* 21 August 1934: 4.

On the general social context of *The President Vanishes,* see William E. Leuchtenberg, *Franklin D. Roosevelt and the New Deal* (New York: Harper, 1963), 95–97, 111–112 and Robert A. Divine, *The Reluctant Belligerent,* 2d ed. (New York: Wiley, 1975), 9–12. On the PCA controversy see the voluminous correspondence in *"The President Vanishes"* File, PCA, and *V,* 4 December 1934: 4. Eisenstein recalls his talk with Schulberg in "A Course in Treatment" in Sergei Eisenstein, *Film Form,* ed. and trans. Jay Leyda (New York: Harcourt, Brace World, Inc., 1949), 96. For critical assessments of the film, see William Troy, *The Nation,* 26 December 1934: 750; *News-*

week, 15 December 1934: 18–19; NYT, 9 December 1934, section 10: 5; Andre Sennwald, "The Screen Comes to Grips with Life," *NYT,* 16 December 1934, section 11: 5; *MPH,* 24 November 1934; *Hollywood Reporter,* 12 November 1934; and *V,* 11 December 1934. My discussion of the film also drew on Charles Wolfe, "*The President Vanishes* (1934): Direct Address and the Vanishing Point of Narration," unpublished paper.

On *Private Worlds,* see correspondence in the PCA Production File and the Joel McCrea interview in John Kobal, *People Will Talk* (New York: Knopf, 1985), 293–294. For critical reviews, see Otis Ferguson, "Not So Deep As A Well," *The New Republic,* April 1935, in Wilson, ed., *Film Criticism of Otis Ferguson,* 285–286; *Motion Picture Daily,* 6 March 1935; *Hollywood Reporter,* 5 March 1935; *Daily V,* 5 March 1935; *V,* 3 April 1935; and *Film Daily,* 9 March 1935. See also Krin Gabbard and Glen O. Gabbard, *Psychiatry and the Cinema* (Chicago: University of Chicago Press, 1987), 51–52.

Wanger's shift into unit production is documented in *V,* 20 March 1935: 3, 5; *V,* 24 April 1935: 5; *V,* 22 May 1935: 5; *V,* 5 June 1935: 7; *V,* 28 August 1935: 5; *V,* 24 July 1935: 6; and Dore Schary, November 1958, COHC. The Andrew Sarris quote comes from "Notes on the Auteur Theory in 1962," in Gerald Mast and Marshall Cohen, eds. *Film Theory and Criticism,* 3d ed. (New York: Oxford University Press, 1985), 540.

On *The Moon's Our Home,* see Ed Sikov, *Screwball* (New York: Crown, 1990), 48–53 and Henry Fonda with Howard Teichmann, *Fonda: My Life* (New York: New American Library, 1981), 105–106. On *Trail of the Lonesome Pine* and Technicolor, see Gorham Kindem's excellent overview "Hollywood's Conversion to Color: The Technological, Economic and Aesthetic Factors," in Kindem, ed. *American Movie Industry,* 146–158; "What? Color in the Movies Again?" *Fortune* 10 (October 1934): 96; and "Unfinished Business: Technicolor," *Fortune* 13 (June 1936): 40. The critical reception of the film is drawn from *Hollywood Reporter,* 19 February 1936: 3; *Film Daily,* 20 February 1936; *V,* 19 February 1936; and *V,* 26 February 1936.

On Wanger's gradual shift back to semi-independence, see *V,* 6 December 1935: 43; Clarke Wales, "Hollywood's Biggest Gambler," n.d. (circa May 1935), "Walter Wanger Clippings" File, AMPAS; Fonda with Teichmann, *Fonda,* 86; Fonda in Mike Steen, *Hollywood Speaks* (New York: G. P. Putnam's Sons, 1974), 26; and *V,* 7 August 1935: 4.

Chapter 8: A Fine and Daring Producer (1936–1938)

The general history of United Artists comes from Balio I and Balio II: 43. George J. Schaefer's comment on UA's dismal schedule comes in a Memo to Dr. A. H. Giannini, 17 March 1937, Dr. A. H. Giannini Files, Series 5B, Box 4, File 5, UA.

Wanger's negotiating goals are documented in Samuel Briskin, Letter to Leo Spitz, 24 April 1936, "Walter Wanger" File, RKO. Rosten, *Hollywood: The Movie Colony,* 273, provides a listing of producer salaries in 1938. The company Wanger formed for Paramount distribution was called Walter Wanger Productions, Inc.; the company formed with United Artists was called Walter Wanger Productions, Inc. In order to minimize confusion, Wanger changed the name of the first company to Walter Wanger Pictures, Inc., in the fall of 1936. This was the company he reactivated in 1947.

David O. Selznick makes his complaint about Wanger's property scooping in a Memo to Val Lewton and Katherine Brown, 27 January 1941, "Walter Wanger" File, Box 2, DOS. Comments on Wanger's storytelling skills come from Pat McGilligan, "Phillip Yordan: The Chameleon," in McGilligan, ed., *Backstory 2* (Berkeley: University of California Press, 1991), 348 and Ben Hecht, COHC.

On *Fury* and Fritz Lang, see Douglas W. Churchill, "Fritz Lang Bows to Mammon," *NYT,* 14 June 1936; *The New Republic,* 10 June 1936: 130; *Time,* 8 June 1936: 40; and *Newsweek,* 13 June 1936: 40. See Frederick W. Ott, *The Films of Fritz Lang* (Secaucus, N.J.: Citadel Press, 1979), 44–50 and Lotte Eisner, *Fritz Lang,* ed. David Robinson (New York: Oxford University Press, 1977), 162–164, 368, for a description of Lang's working methods.

On *You Only Live Once,* see *TRT:* 85; Paul Jensen, *The Cinema of Fritz Lang* (New York: A. S. Barnes and Co., 1969), 118–124; Cecelia Ager, "Fritz Lang Abhors Propaganda Pix, Favors Originals and Yens for Color," *V,* 17 February 1937: 2; B. R. Crisler, "Film Gossip of the Week," *NYT,* 8 November 1936. Leon Shamroy is interviewed by Charles Higham in Higham's *Hollywood Cameramen: Sources of Light* (Bloomington: Indiana University Press, 1970), 25. Henry Fonda is quoted in Curtis Lee Hanson, "Henry Fonda: Reflections on Forty Years of Make-Believe," *Cinema* (December 1966), cited by Jensen, *Cinema of Fritz Lang,* 120; Fonda also discusses Lang in Steen, *Hollywood Speaks,* 43. Production information comes from "Inside Stuff on Pictures," *V,* 11 May 1927: 22; Lang talks about the deleted sequence in B. R. Crisler, "Film Gossip of the Week," *NYT,* 31 January 1937.

David Bordwell offers a discussion of the film in Bordwell et al., *Classical Hollywood Cinema,* 81–82. The point about Father Dolan and Joan's unbalanced behavior is made in George Wilson's excellent article, *"You Only Live Once:* The Doubled Feature," *Sight and Sound* 46, no. 4 (1977): 221–225. Critical reviews consulted include Frank Nugent, *NYT,* 1 February 1937: 15; *Newsweek,* 30 January 1937: 20; *Time,* 11 January 1937: 56; and *Literary Digest,* 6 February 1937: 123–124.

Information on Towne and Baker comes from the *Film Daily Cavalcade,* 1939, in the "Gene Towne" File at AMPAS; *TRT:* 86; Charles R. Metzger, "Notes," 30 December 1935, *"Case Against Mrs. Ames"* File, PCA; *MPH,* 2 October 1939; and *Film Daily,* 3 October 1939. Joshua Logan describes the making of *History Is Made at Night* in his *Josh* (New York: Delacorte Press, 1976), 104–106. The comment on *Stand-In* comes from *Time,* 8 November 1937: 49.

For Wanger's growing public profile, see Marcia Reed, "Wanger, Love and Mussolini," *New Theater* (August 1936): 23; Regina Crewe, "Zealous About Color, Wanger Feels Story is Vital Film Factor," *Baltimore American,* 22 August 1937; "Mr. Walter Wanger Speaks Up," *Washington Star,* n.d.; and "Calls Each Movie Star a Business," *Boston Post,* n.d., WFW Micro.

Chapter 9: An Independent in Every Sense of the Word (1938–1939)

The *Time* review of *Stagecoach* appears in the 13 March 1939 issue, p. 30; Wanger's comment on the film is from *TRT:* 85.

General background on Hollywood's commitment to the Spanish Civil War (and

Hollywood politics in general) comes from Larry Ceplair and Steven Englund, *Inquisition in Hollywood* (Berkeley: University of California Press, 1986), 70, 108–116. For the production history of *Blockade*, see Larry Ceplair, "The Politics of Compromise in Hollywood: A Case Study," *Cineaste* 7, no. 4 (1978): 4; John Howard Lawson, *Film: The Creative Process* (New York: Hill and Wang, 1967), 125–127 (all of Lawson's comments on the film's production are from p. 125); correspondence in the "*Blockade*" File, PCA; Harold Clurman, *The Fervent Years: The Group Theater and the '30s* (New York: Da Capo Press, 1983), 201; Kazan, *A Life*, 157–158; and Dave Davis and Neal Goldberg, "Organizing the Screen Writers Guild—An Interview with John Howard Lawson," *Cineaste* 13, no. 2 (1977): 4–11. Bernard Dick identifies the actual incident Lawson's story was based on in *Radical Innocence* (Louisville: University of Kentucky Press, 1989), 205 and calls *Blockade*'s opening scene "imitative" of Joris Ivens's *The Spanish Earth*, in Bernard Dick, *The Star-Spangled Screen* (Lexington: University of Kentucky Press, 1985), 18. Henry Fonda is quoted on the film in Colin Shindler, *Hollywood Goes to War* (London: Routledge and Kegan Paul, 1979), 4. United Artists' distress over leftist politics in Hollywood is documented in P. R. Guth, Letter to Arthur Kelly, 26 March 1938, Box 4, File 9 and Arthur Kelly, Letter to A. H. Giannini, Box 2, File 7, Series 5B, A. H. Giannini Files, UA.

The best critical and historical discussions of *Blockade* are Marjorie A. Valleau, *The Spanish Civil War in American and European Films* (Ann Arbor: UMI Research Press, 1982), 154; and Roffman and Purdy, *Hollywood Social Problem Film*, 200–202, 207. Although Valleau argues that Marco represents a positive hero in the socialist realism mode, the similarities of this protagonist to the classical Hollywood hero make it a moot distinction.

Contemporary perspectives on *Blockade* include *V*, 8 June 1938: 17; *V*, 22 June 1938: 1, 55, which notes that the film was a litmus test for Hollywood on the Spanish Civil War; Joseph Breen, Letter to Father Daniel A. Lord, 18 September 1938, "Quigley, Martin—Movie Code 1927–1932" File, Father Daniel A. Lord papers, Jesuit Missouri Province Archives, St. Louis; *London Daily Mail*, 6 June 1938; and Douglas Churchill, "Hollywood's Censor Is All the World," *NYT*, 29 March 1936. Wanger's "'Spies' remarks on "intimidation from abroad" are from "Rush Movie Studio, But It Will Defy Franco's Ire," *New York World Telegraph*, 16 May 1938, clipping in "Walter Wanger" File, AMPAS. The Wanger quote about Johnston's scheme is from *TRT:* 85, but the banning item was also reported in *V*, 10 February 1954: 5.

Domestic censorship of *Blockade* is discussed in Frank Nugent, "Blocking 'Blockade,'" *NYT*, 26 June 1938; "Block 'Blockade'!", Flatbush Anti-Communist League, *Blockade* File, Museum of Modern Art, New York, N.Y..; *Knights of Columbus News*, 4 July 1938: 1, "*Blockade*" File, PCA; "Producer Defends Movie 'Blockade,'" *NYT*, 19 June 1938, which quotes Wanger's speech on *Blockade*'s message; *V*, 20 July 1938: 2; Winchell Taylor, "Hollywood's Secret Censors," *Nation*, 9 July 1938: 38–40; *MPH*, 30 July 1938: 39; *V*, 28 September 1938: 7; *MPH*, 4 March 1939: 17; WFW, "Freedom of the Films," *Daily People's World*, 6 August 1938: 2 (a transcript of Wanger's speech to the Conference on Freedom of the Screen); "Meet for Freedom of the Screen," *Film Survey*, August 1938: 3; "60 Organizations Unite for Freedom of Screen," *Hollywood Now*, 22 July 1938: 1, "*Blockade*" File, PCA. Lawson describes the suppression of *Personal History* in *Film: The Creative Process*, 127. Giannini's comments are from *MPH*, 4 March 1939: 15.

Wanger's newfound celebrity is documented in several articles in WFW Micro: "Revival Cycle of Wanger Hits, *New York Telegraph,* 25 July 1938; "The President Vanishes," *Box Office,* 11 March 1939; WFW, "The Wherefore of Movie Ills," *Los Angeles Times,* 17 November 1938; and William Boehnel, "Hollywood Is Blind to Humanity's Woes," *New York Morning Telegram,* 19 November 1938. Wanger's comments on propaganda are from "Wanger Scores 'Critical Moss Backs' and Urges Pictures for 'Progressive America,'" *Box Office,* 7 January 1938: 10–11. His remarks about "wetter swimming pools" come from WFW and Jack L. Warner, "Is Hollywood on the Spot?," *Liberty,* 10 September 1938: 19–20. On Films for Democracy, see Ralph M. Pearson, "The Artist's Point of View," *Forum* 101, no. 3 (March 1939): 175 and *MPH,* 15 April 1939: 36. Thomas Waugh discusses the shift in the 1930s American documentary movement in his "'Men Cannot Act in Front of the Camera in the Presence of Death': Joris Ivens's *The Spanish Earth,*" *Cineaste* 12, no. 2 (1982): 30–33; and 12, no. 3 (1983): 21–29. Quigley's comments appear in *MPH,* 15 April 1939.

Wanger's American Library Association Speech was published in "Screen Curbs Under Attack," *Los Angeles Times,* 24 June 1939. His omnipresence in the mass media is evident in a number of articles: "120,000 Ambassadors," *Foreign Affairs* (December 1939; the quote is from p. 49); "Wanger Says Films, Radio Have Been Aid to Mankind," *New York Post,* 17 February 1939, WFW Micro; "Wanger to Be Series Lecturer," *Hollywood Citizen News,* 3 April 1939, WFW Micro; WFW, "Hollywood" (Ed Sullivan column), *Washington Times,* 12 March 1939, WFW Micro.

Wanger's anti–Production Code statements were reported in "Wanger Asks New Film Code," *Los Angeles Times,* 24 February 1939; "Wanger Urges Controversial Topics in Films," *The New York Herald Tribune,* 24 February 1939; and Archer Winsten, "To Propagandize or Not to Propagandize," *New York Post,* 22 March 1939, WFW Micro. The Wanger-Schaefer dispute and Quigley's informal poll of industry opinion on the Code were published in *Box Office,* 4 March 1939; *MPH,* 4 March 1939: 12, 14–17; and *MPH,* 1 July 1939. The Hays Office response comes from Kenneth Clark, Memo to Will Hays, 2 May 1939; Joseph I. Breen, Letter to Hon. Will Hays, 22 April 1939, MPPDA Archive on Microfilm.

Published descriptions of Wanger include Alex Gottleib, Publicity Biography, Walter Wanger Productions, Walter Wanger File, AMPAS ("Hollywood's champion practical idealist"); Nelson B. Bell, "The Screen Is Denied Freedom Guaranteed by Constitution," *Washington Post,* 24 September 1939; Morton Thompson, "North By Northwest," *Hollywood Citizen News,* 25 August 1939, WFW Micro; Jay Carmody, "Wanger Adds New Slap at Films," *Washington Star,* 13 January 1939: 1 ("violent auxiliary"); Clara Beranger, "Hollywood's Next Move," *Liberty,* 21 January 1939 ("has himself shown great courage"); and Mary Jane Peak, "Wanger," *Boston Globe,* 17 August 1939, WFW Micro ("an independent in every sense of the word"). The Warner-Wanger debate appears in WFW and Jack L. Warner, "Is Hollywood on the Spot?," *Liberty,* 10 September 1938: 19–20. The remark about Wanger finding time to make movies is from William Boehnel, "Pictures That Say Something," *New York Morning Telegram,* n.d., WFW Micro.

The production history of *Algiers* derives from the Production Code Administration File; the dispute with Sylvia Sidney is reported in A. Scott Berg, *Goldwyn: A Biography* (New York: Ballantine Books, 1989), 320–321. All of the Charles Boyer quotes are from Hollis Alpert, "Movies," *Saturday Review,* April 1960: 15–16. Reviews cited include *Hollywood Reporter,* 24 June 1938; *Motion Picture Daily,* 29 June 1938; *V,* 29 June 1938; *The Film Daily,* 28 June 1938; Frank Nugent, *NYT,* 15 July 1938; and Otis Ferguson, *The New Republic,* 3 August 1938, in Wilson, ed., *The Film Criticism of Otis Ferguson,* 225, 227. *Algiers*'s influence on the conception of *Casablanca* is documented in Aljean Harmetz's *Round Up the Usual Suspects: The Making of "Casablanca"* (New York: Hyperion Books, 1992), 30.

For the reception of *I Met My Love Again,* see *Motion Picture Daily,* 10 January 1938; *MPH,* 15 January 1938; Howard Barnes, *New York Herald Tribune,* 15 January 1938 ("a hapless and witless yarn"); *Hollywood Reporter,* 17 January 1938; and *V,* 13 January 1938. *Time* compared Bennett with Lombard in the issue dated 13 April 1936: 32.

The production history of *Stagecoach* derives from Merian Cooper's account in Ron Haver, *David O. Selznick's Hollywood* (New York: Bonanza Books, 1985), 224. John Ford recalls Wanger, not Selznick, suggesting Cooper and Dietrich in his interview in Bob Thomas, ed. *Directors in Action* (Indianapolis: Bobbs Merrill Company, Inc., 1973), 144; because of its detail, Cooper's account is more persuasive. See also WFW, Letter to Lynn Farnol, 9 February 1939, 1939 Correspondence, Ford (Maurice Zolotow quotes this letter in his *Shooting Star: A Biography of John Wayne* [New York: Simon and Schuster, 1974], 153–154); and *V,* 20 July 1938: 5. John Ford describes his conversation with Wanger in his interview with Dan Ford, Tape 22, Side B; Transcript in Box 11, File 30, Ford; Breen's objections to Nichols's Script are found in Joseph I. Breen, Letters to WFW, 28 October 1938, 9 November 1938, and 14 November 1938, 1938 Correspondence File, Ford; and Dudley Nichols, First Draft Script, 10 October–23 October 1938, Ford. Rudy Behlmer asserts the *Stagecoach* heroes were inspired by characters in Bret Harte's *The Outcasts of Poker Flats.* See his excellent "Bret Harte in Monument Valley: *Stagecoach* (1939)," in *Behind the Scenes* (New York: Samuel French, 1989), 104–118. Other sources include Douglas Churchill, "Home, Home on the Range," *NYT,* 25 December 1938; Bosley Crowther, "John Ford Vs. 'Stagecoach,'" *NYT,* 29 January 1939; Dudley Nichols, Letter to John Ford, 26 March 1939, 1939 Correspondence File, Ford; John Wayne in Bob Thomas, ed. *Directors in Action,* 160; Joseph McBride and Michael Wilmington, *John Ford* (New York: Da Capo Press, 1975), 54; John Ford to Dan Ford, Tape 22, Side B; Transcript in Box 11, File 30, Ford; and Ed Buscombe, *Stagecoach* (London: BFI, 1992).

On Wanger's corporate affairs in 1939, see Clarence Ericksen, Letter to Murray Silverstone, 11 July 1939, Box 37, File 1 and "Resume of Agreement," 8 August 1939, Box 37, File 6, both in Producer's Legal File, UA. On Wanger's emerging industry leadership, see "Hedda Hopper's Hollywood," *Los Angeles Times,* 19 June 1939: 15. Wanger's inaugural address to the Academy is quoted in the *Washington Star,* 1 February 1940, WFW Micro.

Chapter 10: Having It All (1939–1941)

On Justine Johnston and the Wangers' divorce, see Eleanor Early, "Beauties Renounce Stage Glamour for Test Tube," *Boston Herald,* 8 September 1940: 3; "Woman in White" 82; Joan Bennett with Lois Kibbee, *The Bennett Playbill* (New York: Holt, Rinehart and Winston, 1970), 256, 273–274; and "Joan Bennett Weds Film Producer Walter Wanger," *Los Angeles Times,* 13 January 1940.

United Artists' product shortage in early 1939 is documented in *V,* 11 January 1939: 3 and *V,* 29 March 1939: 3. Wanger's complaints to the distributor's board of directors are documented in Louis Calvert, Memo to David O. Selznick and Jock Whitney, 13 September 1939, "Misc. Correspondence 1930s, V-Y," Box 250, DOS. Insights into Tay Garnett's direction in general can be found in Jean-Pierre Courso-don, *American Directors,* Vol. 1 (New York: McGraw-Hill, 1983), 139.

The *Winter Carnival* debacle is described in Budd Schulberg, "Hollywood's Second Generation," *NYT,* 2 July 1939; Schulberg's *Writers in America* (New York: Stein and Day, 1983), 104–140; Matthew J. Bruccoli and Margaret M. Duggan, eds. *Correspondence of F. Scott Fitzgerald* (New York: Random House, 1980), 582; Andrew Turnbull, ed. *The Letters of F. Scott Fitzgerald* (New York: Charles Scribner's and Son, 1963), 579; and Aaron Latham, *Crazy Sundays* (New York: Viking Press, 1971), 219–229. Critical comments on the film are from *Hollywood Reporter,* 20 July 1939; *Motion Picture Daily,* 18 July 1939; *MPH,* 22 July 1939; *NYT,* 28 July 1939; *New York Herald Tribune,* 28 July 1939; and Otis Ferguson's "No Visible Means of Support," in Wilson, ed., *Film Criticism of Otis Ferguson,* 265.

Wanger's thinking on the 1939–1940 season is evident in Thomas Pryor, *NYT,* 11 August 1940; Marguerite Tazelaar, "Wanger Likens Cars to Movie Industry; All in Distribution," *Wilkes-Barre Independent,* 9 January 1938; WFW Micro; Louis Calvert, Memo to David O. Selznick, 10 August 1939, "Misc. Correspondence 1930s, V-Y," Box 250, DOS; and Clarence Erickson, Letter to Murray Silverstone, 28 May 1940, Box 37, File 1, Producer's Legal File, UA. On the changing production trends of 1939–1940, see *V,* 31 January 1940: 1; *V,* 14 February 1940: 3; and *V,* 15 May 1940: 6.

On "Personal History" and the preparation of *Foreign Correspondent,* see Dick, *Star-Spangled Screen,* 59; "News of Screen from Hollywood," *NYT,* 4 September 1939; "Report on Production Costs—'Foreign Correspondent,'" 3 September 1939, Producer's Legal File, UA; Donald Spoto, *The Dark Side of Genius: The Life of Alfred Hitchcock* (New York: Ballantine, 1983), 230 (Spoto's chronology of the writing of the script dates Bennett's script work as beginning one month later than my own research indicates); John Russell Taylor, *Hitch: The Life and Times of Alfred Hitchcock* (New York: Berkeley Books, 1978), 156, 159; and Agreement between Selznick International and Walter Wanger Productions, Inc., 26 September 1939, Producer's Legal File, UA. Donald Spoto, in the most thorough analysis of *Foreign Correspondent,* discusses a number of similarities between this film and Hitchcock's other work in his *The Art of Alfred Hitchcock* (New York: Doubleday, 1979), 97–107.

For information on principal photography of *Foreign Correspondent,* I relied on Spoto, *Dark Side of Genius* and Taylor, *Hitch;* Clarence Ericksen, Letter to Harry Muller, 14 June 1940, Box 38, File 2, Producer's Legal File, UA; Daniel O'Shea, Telegram to David O. Selznick, 7 June 1940, "Walter Wanger" File, Box 1, DOS; and WFW, "Hitchcock, Hollywood Genius," *Current History* 52 (December 1940): 13. On the epilogue, see Spoto, *Dark Side of Genius,* 242–244. For critical assessments of the film, see Leonard Leff, *Selznick and Hitchcock* (New York: Weidenfeld and Nicolson, 1987), 46, 84; William Rothman, *Hitchcock: The Murderous Gaze* (Cambridge,

Mass.: Harvard University Press, 1982), 176–177; Eileen Creelman, "Picture Plays and Players," *New York Sun,* 21 August 1940, "Walter Wanger" File, NYPL; *Life,* 26 August 1940: 42–45; *Time,* 2 September 1940: 31; Otis Ferguson, *The New Republic,* 16 September 1940: 385–386; and *NYT,* 28 August 1940: 15. Archer Winsten's comments come from *New York Post,* n.d., n.p., clipping in "Walter Wanger" File, NYPL.

For documenting the preparation of *The Long Voyage Home* and the downturn in attendance during 1939, I relied on *V,* 10 January 1940: 3; *V,* 17 January 1940: 3; *V,* 19 June 1940: 5; and *V,* 14 August 1940: 5. Wanger's strategy of attracting irregular filmgoers is described in Gladwin Hill, "Revenue 'Non-Profit' Films Sighted," *Hollywood Citizen-News,* 23 August 1940: 8, and Thomas Pryor, "Film News and Comment," *NYT,* 11 August 1940. For a more in-depth analysis of *The Long Voyage Home,* see Matthew Bernstein, "Hollywood's Arty Cinema: John Ford's *The Long Voyage Home* (1940)," *Wide Angle* 10, no. 1 (1988): 30–45. The Ford quote is from John Ford, "How We Made 'The Long Voyage Home,'" *Friday,* 9 August 1940: 21–26. More detailed citations can be found in Bernstein, "Hollywood's Arty Cinema: John Ford's *The Long Voyage Home.*"

Peter Bogdanovich discusses Fordian heroics in *John Ford* (Berkeley: University of California Press, 1968), 23; Robert Carringer discusses Toland's technique in his *The Making of Citizen Kane* (Berkeley: University of California Press, 1986), 78–81. What Carringer calls, on p. 75, the opening shot of the film (which "boldly announces the visual plan of the film") is in fact the second shot of the film; it has been preceded by prefatory titles and a long shot of the Glenncarn at anchor. Peter Lehman focuses on Ford's use of off-screen space in his "An Absence Which Becomes a Legendary Presence," *Wide Angle* 2, no. 4 (1978): 36–42.

Wanger's portfolio of paintings is discussed in Harry R. Salpeter, "Art Comes to Hollywood," *Esquire* 14, no. 3 (1940): 65, 173–174; "Movie of the Week," *Life,* 28 October 1940: 86; Ford, "How We Made," 26; and Lynn Farnol, "Hollywood Build-Up," *Theater Arts Monthly* 25, no. 4 (April 1941): 305. Critical reviews of *The Long Voyage Home* include *Time,* 28 October 1940: 82; *Commonweal,* 25 October 1940: 24; and *The Hollywood Reporter,* 8 October 1940: 3. Eugene O'Neill comments on *The Long Voyage Home* in his Telegram to John Ford, 6 July 1940, "1940 Correspondence" File, Ford. Negative costs came from "Statement," 4 April 1942, Producers Legal File, Box 37, File 2, UA.

For a discussion of *Sundown*'s treatment of African characters, see Thomas Cripps, *Making Movies Black: The Hollywood Message Movie from World War II to the Civil Rights Era* (New York: Oxford University Press, 1993), 35–41. On the preproduction for *Eagle Squadron,* see "British War Documentaries," *NYT,* 11 June 1941; Ian Aitken, *Film and Reform: John Grierson and the Documentary Film Movement* (New York: Routledge, 1990), 108–109; Harry Watt, *Don't Look at the Camera* (London: Paul Elek, 1974), 105; UA Meeting Minutes, 1 October 1941, O'Brien Legal File, Series 2A, Box 6, File 1, UA; and Balio I: 174. Schatz, *Genius of the System,* also discusses this venture, 347–351.

On Wanger's industry standing in 1941, see Rosten, *Hollywood,* 26, 63 and Balio I: 144–146, 179–180. The comments of government officials on Wanger's status vis-à-vis the antitrust action come from Paul Williams, Letter to "Podell," 18 March 1940, cited in Giuliana Muscio, "The Problematic Definition of the Independent Producer," Society for Cinema Studies Conference, Los Angeles, Calif. 1991; Wanger made his

own case for the problems of semi-independence in "Mr. Wanger On the Stand," *NYT,*
15 May 1938.

Chapter 11: Wanger At War (1941–1945)

Valuable background on Hollywood's political status and rhetoric during World
War II includes: Dana Polan, *Power and Paranoia: History, Narrative and American
Cinema* (New York: Columbia University Press, 1986); *V,* 1 April 1942: 6; and Clayton R. Koppes and Gregory D. Black, *Hollywood Goes to War: How Politics, Profits
and Propaganda Shaped World War II Movies* (New York: Macmillan, 1987), which
describes in detail the workings of the OWI; pp. 36–37 features a discussion of the
government's analysis of Hollywood's cooperative attitude. On labor racketeering, see
V, 5 November 1941: 5 and Denise Hartsough, "Crime Pays: The Studios' Labor Deals
in the 1930s," *The Velvet Light Trap* 23 (1989): 49–63, which gives a thorough account of the Browne and Bioff trials within the context of Hollywood labor relations.

On concern about the government's antitrust suit, see *V,* 2 February 1942: 5. Henry
Wallace's comment on Wanger comes from *The Diary of Henry Agard Wallace,* Janu-
ary 18, 1935–September 19, 1946 (Microform, 1946, Butler Library, Columbia Uni-
versity); Elmer Davis's comments on propaganda are quoted in Koppes and Black,
Hollywood Goes To War, 64; Wanger's "Hollywood and the Intellectuals" appeared in
Saturday Review of Literature, 5 December 1942: 11, 40.

For excellent overviews of Universal's history in the 1930s and 1940s, see Gomery, *Hollywood Studio System,* 147–160, and Schatz, *Genius of the System,* 82–97,
228–251, and 340–358. On Universal's financial standing in the early 1940s see *V,*
26 July 1941: 3; *V,* 28 January 1942: 20; and *V,* 28 October 1942: 5. For the studio's
larger production budgets, see *V,* 20 October 1941: 7 and *V,* 8 March 1944: 10. On the
success of Abbott and Costello, see *V,* 31 December 1941: 1, 20 and *V,* 12 July 1944:
21. For Universal's shift to increased unit production and *Variety*'s observations on its
benefits, see *V,* 18 February 1942: 3; on the independents' hardships during the war
see *V,* 24 December 1941: 20 and *V,* 14 July 1943: 5.

Wanger's association with Universal draws on *V,* 22 October 1941: 5; Joseph
Breen, Memo to George J. Schaefer, 21 August 1941, "Walter Wanger" File, RKO; *V,*
3 December 1941: 5; and *V,* 12 November 1941: 6. Hal Wallis's deal is described in *V,*
28 January 1942: 22. Evidence of Universal's generous policy with Wanger is found
in *V,* 7 January 1942: 26 and Martin Murphy, Memo to Edward Muhl, 24 November
1942, Box 256, File 8630, Universal.

If, as Jeanine Basinger claims, *Eagle Squadron* was not a major influence on the
World War II aviation combat film, it is partly because of its focus on British society.
See her *The World War II Combat Film* (New York: Columbia University Press, 1986),
34; Robert Ray postulates *Flying Tigers,* a virtual remake of Howard Hawks's *Only
Angels Have Wings,* as the primary model for World War II combat films. See Ray,
Certain Tendency, 113–125. Professor Brian Winston tells me that the plane models
used in the studio scenes of aerial combat in *Eagle Squadron* are anachronistic and
inaccurate, a fact that further tempers the film's claims to documentary authenticity.
Bosley Crowther's review was published in *NYT,* 2 July 1941: 25.

Ladies Courageous material came from *V,* 14 January 1942: 5 and *V,* 17 June 1942:

16. Reviews include *NYT,* 16 March 1944: 17 and *Time,* 3 April 1944: 92. See also Michael Renov, "From Fetish to Subject: The Containment of Sexual Difference in Hollywood's Wartime Cinema," *Wide Angle* 5, no. 1 (1982): 16–27 for a discussion of the film's position in wartime culture.

On *Arabian Nights* and the escapism context, see *V,* 31 December 1941: 1; *V,* 6 May 1942: 5; Universal Annual Report, 23 October 1944; and Polan, *Power and Paranoia,* 134–135. For reviews, see *Daily V,* 18 December 1942: 3 and *NYT,* 26 December 1942: 15. Peter Wollen has offered a concise, if somewhat cryptic, review of the tradition of oriental despotism in his "Fashion/Orientalism/The Body," *New Formations* 6 (Spring 1987): 15–17. Also see Linda Nochlin, "The Imaginary Orient," *Art in America* (May 1983): 118–132+, for a discussion of the relationship between French academic orientalist painting and French colonialism.

On Wanger's subsequent oriental films, see Yvonne De Carlo with Doug Warren, *Yvonne* (New York: St. Martin's Press, 1987), 85–93; *V,* 9 January 1946: 1; *NYT,* 28 August 1944: 19; *NYT,* 16 March 1944: 17; and *New York Herald Tribune,* 26 May 1945. Herb Sterne is quoted in Goodman, *Fifty-Year Decline and Fall of Hollywood,* 150–151. David Hanna's comments on *Salome, Where She Danced* appeared in *Los Angeles Daily News,* 11 June 1945 and *Los Angeles Daily News,* 25 July 1945, WFW Micro; the Washington, D.C. slap was published in *Washington Daily News,* 21 October 1946, and Darryl Zanuck's insults appeared in *Hollywood Reporter,* 25 November 1946: 1, 4. On *Gung Ho,* see Basinger, *World War II Combat Film,* 202–204, and Koppes and Black, *Hollywood Goes To War,* 264–265.

The background on the Free World Association is from *V,* 13 October 1943: 5 and "The Battle of Hollywood," *Time,* 14 February 1944: 23; see also, "Politics in Hollywood," *The New Republic,* 26 June 1944: 847–848. Wanger's remarks about the Alliance were quoted in a letter draft from Robert Arthur to Wanger, n.d. (circa August 1950), "Walter Wanger" File, Hedda Hopper Collection, AMPAS. His comments on the Republican party appear in "GOP Equals America First, says Wanger, Pal of Willkie," *Los Angeles Daily News,* 6 November 1944, WFW Micro.

Chapter 12: Fritz Lang, Incorporated

Joan Bennett's description of Fritz Lang is in Bennett and Kibbee, *Bennett Playbill,* 283, 286. Lang's problems at Fox are reported in Lewis Jacobs, "Film Directors at Work," *Theatre Arts,* 25, no. 3 (March 1941): 231. Lang's Selznick project is documented in the "Fritz Lang Correspondence, 1945" File of the "General Correspondence: L" Box, DOS.

On Universal's standing, production policies and the Rank deal at mid-decade, see *V,* 30 January 1946: 5; *V,* 17 October 1945: 21; *V,* 31 October 1945: 3; *V,* 5 December 1945: 7; *V,* 16 April 1947: 18; *V,* 12 December 1945: 6; *MPH,* 15 December 1945: 41; and *V,* 5 June 1946: 3.

On the semi-independent phenomenon of the mid-forties, see Janet Staiger's "Individualism versus Collectivism," *Screen* 24, nos. 4–5 (July–October 1983): 69; Ernest Borneman, "Rebellion in Hollywood: A Case Study in Motion Picture Finance," *Harper's* 193 (October 1946): 337–343; George Yousling, "Bank Financing of the Independent Motion Picture Producer," Unpublished MBA Thesis, Graduate

School of Banking, Rutgers University, New Brunswick, N.J., 1948; Terry B. Sanders, "The Financing of Independent Feature Films," *Quarterly of Film, Radio and Television* 9 (1955): 380–389. See also Kevin Hugopian, "Declarations of Independence: A History of Cagney Productions," *The Velvet Light Trap* 22 (1986): 16–32.

Regarding the preproduction of *Scarlet Street:* in his interview with Peter Bogdanovich, Lang claimed that he and Nichols purposely did not choose to screen Jean Renoir's version of *La Chienne* (1931), but this is not the case. Wanger attempted to obtain a print of the film for them through the Museum of Modern Art and the British Film Institute, but no one could locate it. See Peter Bogdanovich, *Fritz Lang in America* (New York: Praeger, 1967), 66. The deletions from Lang's cut are determined from Dudley Nichols, *Scarlet Street,* Final Revised Script, 17 July 1945; Lang in the Peter Bogdanovich interview (p. 69) claims that the telegraph scene was "comic to me" rather than deleted against his will. The *Scarlet Street* ad showing the *Romeo and Juliet* reading can be seen in *MPH,* 15 December 1945.

On the formation of Universal-International, see *V,* 30 January 1946: 5; *V,* 26 June 1946: 6, 28; *V,* 31 July 1946: 3; *V,* 29 January 1947: 4; *V,* 19 March 1947: 12; and "Super, Super," *Time,* 12 August 1946: 88. The production history of *Secret Beyond the Door* is from Daily Production Reports, Box 365, File 3404, Universal; *Hollywood Reporter,* 25 July 1946: 1; *Hollywood Reporter,* 9 September 1946: 1, 17; Lutz Bacher, Interview with James Pratt, 2 September 1978, Sherman Oaks, California; Preview Report, 5 September 1947, Box 659, File 21611, Universal; David Lipton, Letter to Hank Linet, Box 659, File 21611, Universal; *V,* 19 February 1947: 3; and Bogdanovich, *Fritz Lang in America,* 73.

On the 1947 downturn in the film business and Hollywood's response, see *V,* 9 April 1947: 3, 18; *MPH,* 19 July 1947: 13; *V,* 13 August 1947: 1; and *V,* 20 August 1947: 5. On Universal-International's policy toward independents, see *V,* 4 September 1946: 3; *V,* 9 October 1946: 3; and *V,* 19 November 1947: 3.

For an example of the critical standing of Diana's two films, see Michel Mourlet, "Fritz Lang's Trajectory," *Cahiers du cinema* 99 (1959): 19–24; trans. by Tom Milne in Stephen Jenkins, ed. *Fritz Lang: The Image and the Look* (London: BFI, 1981), 12–17. David Thomson's comments on Bennett come from his "Lazy Legs," *Film Comment* 27, 2 (March–April 1991): 55. Foster Hirsch considers *Scarlet Street* a classic *film noir* in his *The Dark Side of the Screen: Film Noir* (New York: DaCapo Press, 1981), 1–8. More detailed citations for this chapter may be found in Matthew Bernstein, "Fritz Lang, Incorporated," *The Velvet Light Trap* 22 (1986): 33–52.

Chapter 13: Susan Hayward, Past and Present

The quotation describing *An American Romance* comes from Koppes and Black, *Hollywood Goes to War,* 143–144. On *Canyon Passage,* one insightful but brief discussion of the film occurs in "The Family in *The Reckless Moment,*" *Framework* 11, no. 4 (Summer 1976): 21; production history comes in part from Maurice Bergman, Letter to David Lipton, 12 June 1946, Box 686, File 23298, Universal and *V,* 4 December 1946: 3. Wanger's statement on exports comes from *Hollywood Reporter,* 4 December 1946: 1, 13 and *Film Daily,* 4 December 1946: 1, 7.

On Wanger's souring relationship with Universal, see Arthur Lubin Interview, TS,

Directors' Guild of America Oral History (interview by James Desmarais), December 1976–January 1977: 29; his new negotiations are reported in *V,* 17 April 1946: 6. Production details for *Tap Roots* come in part from "Summary of Picture Cost," Box 239, File 7874 and Pete Dailey, Memo to Sales Staff, 3 June 1947, Box 544, File 17879, both at Universal.

The discussion of Eagle-Lion derives in part from Balio II, "Prelude at Eagle-Lion," 9–39, specifically 20–21, 37; Robert Murphy, "Rank's Attempt on the American Market, 1944–9," in James Curran and Vincent Porter, eds., *British Cinema History* (Totowa, N.J.: Barnes and Noble Books, 1983), 164–178; *V,* 19 December 1945: 3, 20; *V,* 20 August 1947: 7; *V,* 27 August 1947: 3, 18; *V,* 1 October 1947: 16; and *V,* 8 October 1947: 7. Robert Benjamin's comment on Eagle-Lion's problems is from his Letter to Sam Seidelman, 26 May 1947, UA–Addition; Benjamin's remarks about Wanger are in his Letter to Robert Young, 20 August 1947, "PRC File," UA–Addition. Statements of Eagle-Lion's condition come from "Pathe Industries—1948," UA–Addition; *V,* 8 September 1948: 3; *V,* 3 November 1948: 4; "Weekly Analyses of Comparative Revenue," attached to a memo from William C. MacMillen, Jr. to Robert Benjamin, 12 October 1948; Arthur Krim, Letter to Robert Young, 14 December 1948; Arthur Krim, Letter to Robert Purcell, 18 March 1949, "Gamma Film Deal File," UA–Addition; and Robert Benjamin, Letter to Arthur Krim, 19 April 1948, UA–Addition.

On Wanger's position regarding the infamous 1947 HUAC hearings and the black-list, see Testimony in United States 80th Congress, First Session, October 1947, Committee on Un-American Activities, *Communist Infiltration of the Hollywood Motion Picture Industry,* Vol. 1 (Washington, D.C.: United States Government Printing Office, 1947), 172–173; Dore Schary, COHC; Lester Cole, *Hollywood Red* (Palo Alto: Ramparts Press, 1981), 292; and *MPH,* 11 September 1948: 18.

Leger Grindon, in his "Hollywood History and the French Revolution: from *The Bastille* to *The Black Book,*" *The Velvet Light Trap* 28 (1991): 32–48, discusses Mackenzie and Yordan's historical accuracy and Eagle-Lion's shifting publicity campaigns for the film. Philip Yordan describes how Wanger left town during production, when Yordan informed Eagle-Lion that his script had never been purchased, in McGilligan, ed., *Backstory* 2, 351. Other information on the production of *The Black Book* comes from *V,* 3 November 1948: 3. Critical reviews include Phillip T. Hartung's comments in *Commonweal,* 16 September 1949: 561 and *Hollywood Reporter,* 21 March 1948: 4. In his *Harmless Entertainment* (Metuchen, N.J.: Scarecrow Press, 1983), 140–144, Richard Maltby provides a superb analysis of the film's stylistic, generic, and ideological dimensions.

On Susan Hayward and *Smash-Up,* see John Hobart, "Hollywood Pours Out a Long Drink for Miss Susan Hayward," *San Francisco Chronicle,* 26 January 1947, WFW, Micro; "Daily Progress Reports," Box 220, File 7180, Universal; *V,* 17 September 1947: 23; and *V,* 24 September 1947: 5. Michael Renov articulates the logic of Angie's problem in his essay "*Leave Her to Heaven*: The Double Bind of Post-War Woman," *Journal of Film and Video* 35, no. 1 (1983): 28–36. For an excellent discussion of *Smash-Up* in the context of films about alcoholism, see Norman K. Denzin, *Hollywood Shot by Shot: Alcoholism in American Cinema* (New York: Aldine de Gruyter, 1991), 69–82. For critical comments on *Smash-Up,* see *MPH,* 5 February 1947; Virginia Wright, "Film Review," *Los Angeles Daily News,* 13 March 1947; and

Hollywood Reporter, 14 April 1947: 6. See also Roffman and Purdy, *Hollywood Social Problem Film,* 259, ("wallowing in softly lit . . .").

Wanger's pronouncements on adult films and foreign markets appear in *V,* 6 February 1946: 9; *V,* 13 November 1946: 3, 20; and *Hollywood Reporter,* 19 November 1946. Janet Staiger discusses the critical reception of foreign films in the postwar era in her *Interpreting Movies* (Princeton: Princeton University Press, 1992), 178–195. Some of Wanger's disputes with William Goetz are documented in David Lipton, Letters to Maurice Bergman, 11 July 1947 and 20 September 1947, Box 411, File 12378, Universal. Selznick's comment about Susan Hayward comes from his Letter to Daniel O'Shea, 8 March 1948, "Walter Wanger" File, Box 149, DOS.

Chapter 14: The Price of Anglophilia

The history of *Joan of Arc* is a condensation of Matthew Bernstein, "Hollywood Martyrdoms: *Joan of Arc* and Independent Production in the Late Forties," in Bruce Austin, ed. *Current Research in Film,* Vol. 4 (Norwood, N.J.: Ablex Publishing Co., 1988), 89–113. See Robin Blaetz, "Strategies of Containment: Joan of Arc in Film," (Ph.D. diss., New York University, 1989) for a feminist analysis of the Joan of Arc films. The industry context for the film's inception is documented in *V,* 11 December 1946: 1 ("gone significant"); *V,* 18 December 1946: 3, 29; *V,* 8 January 1947: 1, 8; *V,* 12 February 1947: 1, 4; *V,* 20 March 1947: 4; *V,* 21 May 1947: 3; *V,* 10 September 1947: 3; and Ray, *Certain Tendency,* 129–152.

On Bergman's decision to do a film of Anderson's play see Joseph Steele, *Ingrid Bergman: An Intimate Portrait* (New York: David McKay Company, 1959), 112 and Bennett and Kibbee, *Bennett Playbill,* 295. Roadshown films are discussed in Paul D. O'Brien and Edward Raftery, Memo to Dennis O'Brien, 16 April 1931, O'Brien Legal File, UA; "The Reluctant Audience," *Sight and Sound* 22, no. 4 (April–June 1953): 191–192; Murphy, "Rank's Attempt on the American Market, 1944–9," in Curran and Porter, eds., *British Cinema History,* 168; and WFW, Letter to Maxwell Anderson, 12 October 1946, Maxwell Anderson Collection, Humanities Research Center, Austin, Tex.

Wanger and Tannenbaum's negotiations with the banks, investors, MGM, and RKO are documented in various items in the *"Joan of Arc"* Files 1 and 2, RKO. Production problems on the film are reported in *V,* 23 July 1947: 6; *V,* 30 July 1947: 23; and *V,* 6 August 1947: 16. Red Kann's review appears in *MPH,* 23 October 1948: 14. For a discussion of *Henry V,* see Dudley Andrew, "Realism, Rhetoric and the Painting of History in *Henry V,*" in *Film in the Aura of Art* (Princeton, N.J.: Princeton University Press, 1985): 131–132. See also Bosley Crowther's review, *NYT,* 21 November 1948. Blaetz's "Strategies of Containment," 49–53, 79–86, discusses how Bergman's strength as a performer and Joan of Arc's character are undermined by the film's portrayal of a Joan who "acts in a conventionally feminine way."

For *Joan of Arc*'s distribution problems, see *V,* 13 October 1948: 4; *V,* 8 December 1948: 5; *V,* 22 December 1948: 11; *V,* 12 January 1949: 5; *V,* 11 May 1949: 5; and *V,* 15 June 1949: 5. For evidence of industry praise, see *V,* 9 February 1949: 1 and *V,* 5 January 1949: 9.

On James Mason's popularity, see *MPH,* 6 January 1945: 45; *V,* 11 September

1946: 1; *V,* 16 April 1947: 14; and *V,* 20 August 1947: 3. John Blankenhorn was interviewed by Lutz Bacher, 10 September 1978, Pasadena, Calif.; on the industry's shift away from low-budget films, see *V,* 16 November 1949: 7. James Mason's comments on *The Reckless Moment* come from Rui Nogueria, "James Mason," *Focus on Film* 2 (March–April 1970): 22, 24. Background on Robert Soderberg and Henry Garson comes in part from Lutz Bacher, Interview with Robert Soderberg, 22 July 1979, Santa Barbara, Calif., and Bacher, Interview with Henry Garson, 16 September 1978, Beverly Hills, Calif.

The development of the script for *The Reckless Moment* from wartime to postwar story testifies to the acuity of the analyses in "The Family in *The Reckless Moment,*" *Framework* 11, no. 4 (Summer 1976): 17–24 and in Michael Walker's later comparisons of the film with *Rebecca* and *Since You Went Away* in *Movie* 29, no. 30 (Summer 1982): 54–60; Robin Wood's comments come from his *Personal Views: Explorations in Film* (London: G. Fraser, 1976), 184. I am grateful to Ms. Diana Anderson for allowing me to see footage of the making of *The Reckless Moment.* Lutz Bacher describes the production of *The Reckless Moment* in meticulous detail in his *Travails and Travellings: Max Ophuls in America* (New Brunswick: Rutgers University Press, 1996), 264–320.

Chapter 15: On the Way Down

Wanger's quote on *Joan of Arc* comes from *Box Office,* 9 May 1953: 20. Sources for the Garbo project include: *V,* 1 November 1944: 1; *V,* 24 October 1945: 1; *V,* 8 January 1947: 39; *V,* 5 February 1947: 5; *Time,* 30 August 1948: 72 ("She is a very loyal person"); Salka Viertel, *Kindness of Strangers,* 300; Viertel, Letter to George Cukor, 28 September 1948, George Cukor Collection, AMPAS; *Hollywood Reporter,* 19 August 1948: 13; *Film Daily,* 19 August 1948: 1; *V,* 13 July 1949: 6; *V,* 10 August 1949: 2; *V,* 14 September 1949: 4, 5; *V,* 21 September 1949: 3 ("the acquiescence"); Logan, *Josh,* 251–252; *Los Angeles Times,* 12 September 1949; and Gavin Lambert, *On Cukor* (New York: Capricorn Books, 1973), 158. General details of the Garbo project (Rizzoli's relationship with Ophuls and Garbo) are documented in Bacher, *Max Ophuls in the Hollywood Studios,* 321–327.

On Wanger's bankruptcy and economic conditions in the early 1950s, see *V,* 3 January 1951: 10 (for Arnal's comments); *V,* 10 January 1951; *V,* 17 January 1951: 5; and Thomas F. Brady, "Where the Money Went," *The New Republic,* 31 January 1949: 14. My account of the Crusade for Freedom and Wanger's appointment relies on "Freedom Crusade Will Begin Sept. 4," *NYT,* 28 July 1950; "New Crusade Post Taken by Wanger," *Los Angeles Times,* 21 August 1950: 2; "Summary of Information" regarding Crusade for Freedom, 12 September 1950, FBI Files, Department of the Army Freedom of Information, Privacy Office, Fort Meade, Md.; and Bruce Drake, "Crusade for Freedom...a Front?" WFW Micro. The Motion Picture Alliance's decision to harass Wanger is documented in the "Walter Wanger" file of the Hedda Hopper Collection, AMPAS.

Monogram's studio history is derived from Gomery, *Hollywood Studio System,* 180–182. The Steve Broidy comment about "stale bread" is from his interview in Charles Flynn and Todd McCarthy, eds., *Kings of the Bs* (New York: E. P. Dutton and

Co., 1975), 275. Monogram's position in the early 1950s comes from *V,* 11 April 1951: 4; *V,* 18 April 1951: 5; *V,* 4 June 1952: 7; *V,* 20 June 1951: 3; and *MPH,* 15 September 1951: 26. On Wanger's move to Monogram, see *V,* 13 June 1951: 3; and *MPH,* 4 August 1951: 31.

Joan Bennett's recollections of the Jennings Lang incident and its aftermath appear in Bennett and Kibbee, *Bennett Playbill,* 298–306. It was also reported in "Wanger Gets Off with a Light Term," *Los Angeles Daily News,* 22 April 1952, "Producer at Court's Mercy: No Testimony," *Los Angeles Herald Express,* 15 April 1952: 1, and "Hollywood Cameras Focus on Tragedy," *Life,* 24 December 1951: 17. Susan Hayward's defense of Wanger appeared in Howard Thompson, "Flatbush to Kilimanjaro and Back," *NYT,* 26 April 1952; David O. Selznick reported his remarks in his Letter to WFW, 16 June 1952, "Walter Wanger (and Joan Bennett), Personal or Confidential" File, DOS.

Chapter 16: *Riot in Cell Block 11* (1954)

Bennett and Kibbee in *Bennett Playbill,* 305, quote Wanger's decisive comment on the prison system. For an example of national coverage of his prison sentence, see "Summer Vacation," *Time,* 16 June 1952: 96.

On industry conditions and production policies in the fall of 1952, see *V,* 30 May 1951: 5; *V,* 13 June 1951: 3; *MPH,* 11 August 1951: 13, 21; *MPH,* 22 December 1951: 35; *V,* 16 January 1952: 7; *V,* 12 March 1952: 1; and *V,* 26 March 1952: 3. For discussions of Monogram's condition and the name change to Allied Artists, see *MPH,* 24 November 1951: 24; *V,* 2 April 1952: 71; *V,* 15 October 1952: 5; *V,* 13 November 1952; and Walter Mirisch, "Navy Air Saga Tops New Monogram Policy," *Los Angeles Daily News,* 5 July 1952.

Monogram produced a number of *films noir* during the late 1940s, including *When Strangers Marry* (1944), *Fear* (1946), *Suspense* (1946), *Decoy* (1946), and *I Wouldn't Be in Your Shoes* (1948)—judging from reviews, none of these involved the excessive violence of the 1950s films. These are the films that inspired Jean-Luc Godard's homage in *Breathless* (1959). *V,* 7 December 1955: 3, reports that the Legion of Decency gave "B" ratings to 33.6 percent of all the films reviewed in 1954–1955, up from 22 percent the previous year; *V,* 25 June 1953 and *V,* 15 October 1953.

For Wanger's work at Allied Artists, see Harry Sanford, "Lesley Selander," in Jon Tuska, ed. *Close Up: The Contract Director* (Metuchen, N.J.: Scarecrow Press, 1976), 244 and Thomas Wood, "Battles in 'Hajji Baba' Shot in Different Colors," *New York Herald Tribune,* 23 May 1954.

Richard Collins is quoted on his HUAC testimony in Victor Navasky, *Naming Names* (New York: Penguin Books, 1980), 230; his comment about political life comes from his Letter to Walter Mirisch, 16 June 1955, Richard Collins Papers, Special Collections, Library of the University of Oregon, Portland, Ore. (hereafter "Collins"). On Hollywood's penchant for postwar "'realism," see *V,* 12 March 1952: 7 and William Lafferty, "A Reappraisal of the Semi-Documentary in Hollywood," *The Velvet Light Trap* 20 (1983): 22–26.

Several detailed accounts of the Jackson, Michigan, riot were available during and after Collins's work on the script. Radio journalists Peg and Walter McGraw's three consecutive programs on the riot for NBC's documentary series "Challenge to Our Prisons" were originally broadcast on March 6, 13, and 20, 1953. The McGraws subsequently published their material on Jackson in *Assignment: Prison Riots* (New York: Henry Holt and Co., 1954), 50–135. See also Deputy Warden Vernon Fox's book, *Violence Behind Bars* (New York: Vantage Press, 1956), which expanded his account published in *Colliers*'s July 7, 1952 issue; Bartlow Martin's *Break Down the Walls* (New York: Ballantine, 1954), an expansion of material originally published in the June 1953 *Saturday Evening Post*; and Austin H. MacCormick's *Special Committee to Study the Michigan Department of Corrections—Report* (or "The MacCormick Report"), published on February 12, 1953. Images of the Jackson riot were published in "Convicts Bully A Sovereign State," *Life* 32, 18 (5 May 1952): 27–33. I am grateful to *Velvet Light Trap* editor Dave Pratt for pointing out to me the extent to which Wanger and Collins relied on Jackson events for the script.

While developing *Riot in Cell Block 11*, Wanger was in touch with the McGraws and MacCormick. When the former threatened to sue him for use of material they had assembled for their reports, he wrote a memo, dated 24 July 1953, that categorizes story events in the script according to their source, i.e., from the Michigan uprisings, from Wanger's suggestions, and so forth. At the very least, the McGraws' work indicated that a compelling narrative drama could be derived from the Jackson riots.

The discussion of conventional prison and social problem films draws on: Roffman and Purdy, *Hollywood Social Problem Film*, 25, 29; Michael Wood, *America in the Movies* (New York: Basic Books, 1975), 143–145; Maltby, *Harmless Entertainment*, 239–246; Charles Maland, "The Social Problem Film," in Wes D. Gehring, ed. *A Handbook of Hollywood Film Genres* (New York: Greenwood Press, 1988), 306; John Hill, "The British 'Social Problem' Film—'Violent Playground' and 'Sapphire,'" *Screen* 26, no. 1 (1985): 37; and *V,* 18 May 1951. Russell Campbell in "The Ideology of the Social Consciousness Movie," 61–62, discusses the centrality of ignorant protagonists to the social problem formula. The prison picture actually predates the 1930s Warner Bros. formula, but this was Wanger and Collins's basic framework. See Kevin Brownlow, *Behind the Mask of Innocence* (New York: Alfred A. Knopf, 1990), 239–261, for a description of several such silent films.

Some of Wanger's suggestions to Collins appear in his Memo, 25 May 1953, Collins. Siegel's comment on Sam Peckinpah and the film come from Bernard Drew, "The Man Who Paid His Dues," *American Film* 3, no. 3 (1978): 25; Garner Simmons, *Peckinpah: A Portrait in Montage* (Austin: University of Texas Press, 1982), 25; and Sam Peckinpah, "Don Siegel and Me," in Stuart Kaminsky, *Don Siegel: Director* (New York: Curtis Books, 1974), 299–301. Siegel uses the phrase "sense of immediacy" in his interview with Peter Bogdanovich, *Movie* 15 (1968), quoted in Judith M. Kass, "Don Siegel" in Kass and Stuart Rosenthal, *Tod Browning, Don Siegel,* Vol. 4 of *The Hollywood Professionals* (New York: Tantivity Press, 1975), 96.

Excellent critical discussions of *Riot in Cell Block 11* include Alan Lovell, *Don Siegel: American Cinema* (London: BFI, 1975), 34–35, 53; Richard Combs, "Less Is More: Don Siegel from the Block to the Rock," *Sight and Sound* 49, no. 2 (1980): 117–121; and Andrew Tudor, "Don Siegel," in Christopher Lyon, ed. *International Dictionary of Films and Filmmakers,* Vol. 2 (Chicago: St. James Press, 1987), 500–501. Lovell suggests that Wanger and director Siegel were negotiating between their personal interests and Allied Artists' violent exploitation orientation. Yet violent films were a recent innovation at Allied Artists when *Riot in Cell Block 11* was produced. John Belton's "defeat in victory" phrase comes from his "Don Siegel" in Jean-Pierre Coursodon and Pierre Savage, eds. *American Directors*, Vol. 2 (New York: McGraw Hill Book Co., 1983), 340.

Contemporary reviews of *Riot in Cell Block 11* include: *V,* 8 February 1954; *New Yorker,* 6 March 1954: 62; *Newsweek,* 8 February 1954: 86; *Time,* 15 February 1954: 94. On Allied Artists fortunes in 1954, see *MPH,* 4 September 1954: 17 and *MPH,* 18 September 1954: 20. For more detailed documentation on the film's production history, see Matthew Bernstein, "Individuals and Institutions: *Riot in Cell Block,*" *The Velvet Light Trap* 28 (1991): 3–31.

Chapter 17: *Invasion of the Body Snatchers* (1956)

My production history of *Invasion of the Body Snatchers* is derived in part from two of the best critical discussions of the film: Stuart Samuels, "The Age of Conspiracy and Conformity: *Invasion of the Body Snatchers,*" in *American History/American Film: Interpreting the American Image,* ed. John O'Connor and Martin A. Jackson (New York: Frederick Ungar Publishing Co., 1979), 203–217 and Glen Johnson, "We'd Fight . . . We Had To: *The Body Snatchers* as Novel and Film," *Journal of Popular Culture* 13 (1979): 5–16. Other valuable analyses can be found in Stuart Kaminsky, "Don Siegel on the Pod Society," (1976), in La Valley, ed. *Invasion of the Body Snatchers,* 155. See also Guy Braucourt, "Interview with Don Siegel," in La Valley, ed. *Invasion of the Body Snatchers,* 158–159. La Valley's own production history of the film is excellent. John Belton's comments appear in Coursodon and Savage, eds. *American Directors,* Vol. 2, 336. Vivian Sobchack's remarks on low-budget science fiction films can be found in her essay "Science Fiction" in Gehring, ed. *Handbook of Hollywood Film Genres,* 229–247.

Jack Finney is quoted in Arthur Gacy, "*Invasion of the Body Snatchers:* A Metaphor for the Fifties," *Literature/Film Quarterly* 1 (1978): 69–71. Siegel's comments on Wanger appear in Thomas, ed. *Directors in Action,* 42; his comparison of *Private Hell 36* and *Riot in Cell Block 11* comes from Kaminsky, *Don Siegel,* 96. Contemporary reviews of the film include Sara Hamilton, *Los Angeles Examiner,* 1 March 1956, section 2: 6; *Daily V,* 16 February 1956: 3; *MPH,* 25 February 1956: 794; *Film Daily,* 28 February 1956: 10; and *Showman's Trade Review,* 25 February 1956: 22.

Wanger's comments on television appear in Bosley Crowther, "Hollywood Future," *NYT,* 4 May 1958, section 2 and "Wanger Sees Pay TV as 'A Dream,'" *MPH,* 2 October 1954: 37. On RKO's revival, see *V,* 7 September 1955: 5; *V,* 7 December 1955: 25; *V,* 28 December 1955: 1; *V,* 25 January 1956: 3.

Chapter 18: *I Want to Live!* (1958)

My discussion of United Artists' innovations in the 1950s derives from Balio II, especially pp. 57, 73; Tino Balio, "When Is an Independent Producer Independent?

The Case of United Artists After 1948," *The Velvet Light Trap* 22 (1986): 53–64 and *V,* 26 November 1958: 3. Zanuck's comments on the power of the actors and their agents comes from Rudy Behlmer, *Memo from Darryl F. Zanuck* (New York: Grove Press, 1993), 259; Behlmer's book also provides an excellent overview of Zanuck's career. See also Staiger in Bordwell et al., *Classical Hollywood System,* 330–335, and Schatz, *Genius of the System,* 463–481. On the role of independents in ending the blacklist, see Jeffrey P. Smith, "'A Good Business Proposition': Dalton Trumbo, *Spartacus,* and the End of the Blacklist," *The Velvet Light Trap* 23 (1989): 75–100. Wanger's quip about agents is recorded in David Brown, *Let Me Entertain You* (New York: William Morrow and Co., 1990), 140.

Susan Hayward's comments on and to Wanger come from Beverly Linet, *Susan Hayward: Portrait of a Survivor* (New York: Berkeley Books, 1981), 90, 105; Hayward's box office power in 1951 is reported in *V,* 2 January 1952: 1. The account of her personal life in 1957 derives from Bob Thomas, "Susan Hayward Happy With Life in Georgia's Hills," *Los Angeles Citizen-News,* 7 April 1958.

Wanger's salesmanship to Robert Wise is documented in WFW, Letter to Robert Wise, 13 September 1957, "*I Want to Live!* Correspondence," Robert Wise Collection, USC (hereafter "Wise"). The scriptwriting history of the film is reported in Nelson Gidding, Letter to the Arbitration Committee of the Writers' Guild of America, 10 September 1958, Wise. The discussion of Wise's use of jazz music derives from Jonathan Rosenbaum, "Hollywood's Jazz," *American Film* 3, no. 5 (1978): 69; Wise's comments on Johnny Mandel's contribution comes from Bernard R. Kantor, Irwin R. Blacker, and Anne Kramer, *Directors at Work: Interviews with American Film-Makers* (New York: Funk and Wagnalls, 1970), 397–399.

Contemporary reviews include Stanley Kauffmann, *The New Republic,* 22 December 1958: 21; Archer Winsten, *New York Daily News,* 19 November 1958; Paul V. Beckley, *New York Herald Tribune,* 19 November 1958; *Hollywood Reporter,* 28 October 1958; Arthur Knight, *Saturday Review,* 19 November 1958: 25; Justin Gilbert, *New York Mirror,* 19 November 1958: 36; Bosley Crowther, *NYT,* 19 November 1958: 45; *Time,* 24 November 1958: 94; and John McCarten, *New Yorker,* 29 November 1958: 108–109. For the ten-best lists, see *Film Daily,* 28 March 1960: 1 and Bosley Crowther, "The 'Best' of 1958," *NYT,* 4 January 1959. Trade press reviews include *Motion Picture Daily,* 28 October 1958; *V,* 29 October 1958; and *Hollywood Reporter,* 28 October 1958. Examples of its reception in Los Angeles include Roger Beck, "Police, Prosecutors Blast Film on Barbara Graham," *Los Angeles Mirror News,* 28 November 1958: 1; Gene Blake, "Barbara Graham—Film and Fact," *Los Angeles Times,* 28 November 1958, part 3: 5; Ruth Waterbury, *Los Angeles Examiner,* 27 November 1958, section 2: 8; and Dorothy Manners, "Wanger Betting—on a Murderess," *Los Angeles Examiner,* 10 August 1958: 7, 11. Wanger's comments about Susan Hayward were made in his Letter to David O. Selznick, 29 August 1962, File 59: "Walter Wanger (1953–1963)" DOS. His remarks about how the film would be reviewed if it were a foreign movie come from Joe Hyams, "The Movie They Talk About," *New York Herald Tribune,* 7 November 1958. His comments on capital punishment appear in Dick Williams, "Why Wanger Wars on Death Penalty," *Los Angeles Mirror,* 31 January 1959. Henry Fonda's comment is from COHC.

Chapter 19: Arabian Nights (1958–1961)

Joseph L. Mankiewicz's jibe at *Cleopatra* was reported frequently, but I found it in *Daily V,* 31 October 1962: 18. Vincent Canby's comment comes from his "Hi-Ho, It's the Lone Wanger; His Book Makes Skouras Heavy," *V,* 5 June 1963: 5. Darryl Zanuck's biographers have not delved deeply into *Cleopatra*'s production history. Mel Gussow in *Darryl F. Zanuck: Don't Say Yes Until I Finish Talking* (New York: DaCapo Press, 1980), 239, reasonably notes, "It was certainly cumulative guilt, shared by Skouras, Levathes, producer Walter Wanger, director Joseph Mankiewicz." Leonard Mosley, in *Zanuck: The Rise and Fall of Hollywood's Last Tycoon* (Boston: Little, Brown and Company, 1984), blames various people incorrectly for the film's problems; on p. 325, for example, he credits Wanger with the decision to shoot the Mamoulian version in England. Although Mankiewicz discredited Kenneth L. Geist's *Pictures Will Talk: The Life and Films of Joseph L. Mankiewicz* (New York: Da Capo Press, 1978), it provides the best account of *Cleopatra*. Like all other previous accounts, however, it does not use archival sources.

For background on Buddy Adler, see *V,* 11 January 1956: 4; Zanuck's retirement was reported in *V,* 8 February 1956: 3. James Mason discusses Fox's studio pride in Nogueria, "James Mason," *Focus on Film* (March–April 1970). The Nunnally Johnson remark about Zanuck comes from his July 1959 Oral History, COHC; Phillip Dunne discusses Zanuck in Gussow, *Darryl F. Zanuck,* 142; Dunne describes Adler in Aubrey Solomon, *Twentieth Century–Fox: A Corporate and Financial History* (Metuchen, N.J.: Scarecrow Press, 1988), 124. Dunne reports the projection room incident in Solomon, *Twentieth Century–Fox,* 126; Zanuck is quoted on Skouras in Gussow, *Darryl F. Zanuck,* 140, 178. Fox's operating costs come from Solomon, *Twentieth Century–Fox,* 137.

Wanger's comments on the difficulties of work at Fox come from *MLWC:* 8, 9–10. He describes the Eva Peron project in his letter to David O. Selznick, 29 August 1962, File #59: "Walter Wanger (1953–1963)," DOS. Wanger had even envisioned Luchino Visconti directing it, but anticipated difficulties since the Italian director "is persona non grata with the United States because of his Leftist tendencies and he would make this a very bitter tirade against the way our friends, Mr. Paley and Mr. Luce, use communications."

On the Durrell quartet, see Gerald Sykes, "A Tapestry Woven in Alexandria," *New York Times Book Review,* 3 April 1960: 1; Wanger described some of his plans for it in Murray Schumach, "Hollywood Giant," *NYT,* 10 April 1960: 7. Irene Sharaff discusses *Cleopatra* in her *Broadway and Hollywood* (New York: Van Nostrand, 1976), 105–115.

On *Cleopatra,* see Mary Hamer, *Signs of Cleopatra* (New York: Routledge, 1993) for a concise feminist analysis, particularly of de Mille's films. See also Brown, *Let Me Entertain You,* 74–75. Wanger noted the link in his mind between the Ballets Russes and *Cleopatra* in interviews with Joe Hyams for the draft of *My Life with "Cleopatra."* Wanger's first choice screenwriter for *Cleopatra* was Gore Vidal, who had coauthored the script for MGM's *Ben-Hur* and for *Suddenly Last Summer.* In the spring of 1959, he was scheduled to write a teleplay about Cleopatra's power struggles with Antony to succeed Caesar in Rome. Wanger's comments about "selling" Fox on

Cleopatra come from "The Fortunes of Cleopatra," *Newsweek,* 25 March 1963: 64, probably the best article written on the making of the film. It is also the source for Mamoulian's recounting of his dispute with Skouras over shooting in England.

James Mason recounts the argument over *Bigger than Life* in *Focus on Film* 2 (March–April 1970). Similarly, Richard Zanuck described work on *The Chapman Report* as "green light, then red light" in Gussow, *Darryl F. Zanuck,* 237–238. Wanger's comments on what went wrong with *Cleopatra* come from *MLWC:* 4–5. His remark about Durrell's "better sense of antiquity" is from *MLWC:* 36–37. Mamoulian's description of the British sets for Alexandria comes from "Fortunes of *Cleopatra.*" Nunnally Johnson's remark about *The Barbarian and the Geisha* is quoted in Solomon, *Twentieth Century–Fox,* 123; budget overruns on other Fox films are reported in Solomon, *Twentieth Century–Fox,* 133, 135. It is worth noting that many details in Wanger's account of events on the set and of Fox's administrative and corporate troubles are corroborated by two Fox publicists; see Jack Brodsky and Nathan Weiss, *The Cleopatra Papers: A Private Correspondence* (New York: Simon & Schuster, 1963), which is also sympathetic to Wanger. Some of the quoted material in chapters 19–21 are provided through the courtesy of Twentieth Century–Fox, a division of Twentieth Century–Fox Film Corporation.

Chapter 20: The Kafka Play (1961–1962)

The final tabulation of *Cleopatra*'s costs (including studio overhead) hovered at $31.1 million, of which $7 million were due to the failed Mamoulian version; the remaining $12.9 million represented print and advertising costs. On Fox's hiring of Joseph L. Mankiewicz, see *V,* 22 February 1961: 3. Wanger's description of Mankiewicz's approach to the film comes from *MLWC:* 62–63. His description of Ranald McDougall is from *MLWC:* 73.

On Fox's studio politics in mid-1961, see "Perils of Spyros," *Newsweek,* 21 August 1961: 70; "Skouras Wins Chance to Write New Script," *Business Week,* 4 August 1962: 30–31; "Model City on Old Movie Lots," *Business Week,* 22 April 1961: 123–126; "20th Century City," *Time,* 13 January 1958: 81; *V,* 10 May 1961: 11; *V,* 17 May 1961: 3; "Cut!" *Newsweek,* 18 September 1961: 77. Wanger's description of the Kafka play is from *MLWC:* 88.

Darryl Zanuck's findings of waste in the production of *Cleopatra* were reported in the *Hollywood Reporter,* 29 October 1962: 1 and *Daily V,* 31 October 1962: 1. Wanger's recollections of the November 1961 meetings are from *MLWC:* 101. Wanger described the incident between Rex Harrison and Sid Rogell in *MLWC:* 112–113. Zanuck's letter to Mankiewicz was published in *Film Bulletin,* 29 October 1962, 13, 20. Selznick's description of Skouras comes from his Letter to WFW, 28 February 1962, File 59, "Walter Wanger (1953–1963)," DOS. Fox's 1961 and early 1962 losses are reported in Solomon, *Twentieth Century–Fox,* 143, 144 and "Cut!" 62. Wanger's quip to Levathes is from Brodsky and Weiss, *The Cleopatra Papers,* 116.

Zanuck's exchange with Milton Gould came from "Wrecker or Doctor?" *Newsweek,* 16 July 1962: 64–65. Some of Wanger's public pronouncements on *Cleopatra* are in *V,* 27 December 1961: 5 and *V,* 13 February 1963. Fashion articles about Taylor include "Elizabeth Taylor and the New Cleopatra Look," *Look,* 27 February 1962: 40 and "Elizabeth Taylor as Cleopatra," *Vogue,* 15 January 1962: 93–98.

Chapter 21: The Curse of *Cleopatra* (1962–1968)

Wanger's remarks about Elizabeth Taylor's morality are from *MLWC*: 150; the "desperate nervous men" reference is on *MLWC*: 6. Canby's remarks on *My Life with "Cleopatra"* are from his "Hi-Ho, It's the Lone Wanger." Wanger's comments on Taylor's romantic life are from *MLWC*. Other critical comments are taken from Robert R. Kirsch, "Backstage with 'Cleo's Zany Crew," *Los Angeles Times,* 14 May 1963, part 4: 6.

Zanuck's comment to Skouras on making him look good is quoted in *V,* 19 February 1964: 4; the sale of Wanger's *Cleopatra*'s interest is reported in *V,* 24 April 1963. Wanger's criticisms of the release print of *Cleopatra* appear in *V,* 19 June 1963: 1, 3.

Insightful, critical analyses of *Cleopatra* may be found in Derek Elley, *The Epic Film* (London: Routledge and Kegan Paul, 1984), 93–95; Alexander Walker, *The Celluloid Sacrifice* (New York: Hawthorn Books, 1966), 143 (on Elizabeth Taylor); and Wood, *America in the Movies,* 176–177. The discussion of contemporary reviews of the film draws on: Judith Crist, *New York Herald Tribune,* 13 June 1963; Bosley Crowther, *NYT,* 13 June 1963; *Time,* 21 June 1963: 90; *Newsweek,* 24 June 1963: 25; *Life,* 21 June 1953: 25; Brendan Gill, *The New Yorker,* 22 June 1963: 61–62; Robert Hatch, *The Nation,* 6 July 1963: 197; Francis Russell, *National Review,* 13 August 1963; Stanley Kauffmann, *The New Republic,* 29 June 1963: 27–28; and Hollis Alpert, *Saturday Review,* 29 June 1963: 20.

Cleopatra's grosses are reported in *Hollywood Reporter,* 14 January 1963: 1; "Cleopatra's Lure Helps Fox Film Rise Back into the Black," *Wall Street Journal,* 23 August 1963; *V,* 8 January 1964: 37; and *V,* 31 March 1965: 3. Nunnally Johnson's remark about Wanger comes from Dorris Johnson and Ellen Leventhal, eds. *The Letters of Nunnally Johnson* (New York: Alfred A. Knopf, 1981), 192. On the diversity of approaches to producing films see Richard B. Jewell, "How Howard Hawks Brought *Baby* Up: An *Apologia* for the Studio System," *The Journal of Popular Film and Television* 11, no. 4 (Winter, 1984), 158–165; Schatz, *Genius of the System,* and Staiger in Bordwell et al. *Classical Hollywood Cinema,* 140. The several lawsuits involving Fox are reported in *V,* 1 April 1964: 5; *V,* 29 April 1964; "Liz, Eddie Win Round in Suit on 'Cleopatra,'" *Los Angeles Times,* 11 September 1964: 26; *Hollywood Reporter,* 19 October 1965: 1 (which published Wanger's retraction); and *Daily V,* 20 December 1967: 2. Fox's fortunes and the fate of the Durrell quartet are documented in *V,* 13 February 1963; *V,* 11 November 1964: 4; *V,* 29 June 1966; and *Hollywood Reporter,* 19 January 1967: 1; the "pet project" phrase comes from John Gregory Dunne, *The Studio* (reprint, New York: Limelight Editions, 1981), 98. The "man about town" phrase comes from *V,* 20 November 1968. Discussion of Louis Dudebat derives from Michael Holroyd, *Bernard Shaw Volume II 1898–1918: The Pursuit of Power* (New York: Random House, 1989), 157–172, and Louis Crompton, *Shaw the Dramatist* (Lincoln, University of Nebraska Press, 1969), 130–137.

Conclusion

Pandro Berman is quoted in "Pandro Berman To Retire at 65," *San Diego Union,* 25 November 1969, "Pandro Berman" File, AMPAS; Dore Schary's recollection is from COHC; John Ford called Wanger a "sensationalist" when talking to Dan Ford, Tape 22, Side B; Transcript Box 11, File 30, Ford. Ben Hecht's description of Wanger comes from COHC.

Wanger's comparison of filmmaking to the State Department comes from *TRT*: 92; his discussion of film as an influence are from *TRT*: 86. Selznick's remarks on educating the audience come from Ron Haver, *David O. Selznick's Hollywood* (New York: Bonanza Books, 1980), 174. Stanley Kramer's remarks on message movies come from Stanley Kramer, 14 March 1973, Film History Program, American Film Institute, Microfiche Edition. The description of Milgrim comes from Budd Schulberg, *The Disenchanted* (New York: Random House, 1950), 15.

Selznick's observation about Wanger being "wrongly placed" is in his Telegram to Daniel O'Shea, 2 October 1947, "Walter Wanger" File, Box 149, DOS; David Thomson's comments on Wanger appear in his *A Biographical Dictionary of Film,* 2d ed. (New York: William Morrow, 1981), 644. Nunnally Johnson's remarks about Zanuck the editor are in COHC. Phillip Dunne is quoted on Zanuck's management skills in Gussow, *Darryl F. Zanuck,* 142. Rudy Behlmer's comments about Selznick come from Behlmer, ed. *Memo from David O. Selznick* (1972; reprint, New York: Grove Press, 1981), xv. Selznick's rules on handling John Ford are in Behlmer, ed., *Memo from David O. Selznick,* 116–118; John Ford's remarks about Wanger come from his interview with Dan Ford, Tape 22, Side B, Ford; and Don Siegel is quoted in Paul Mayersberg, *Hollywood: The Haunted House* (New York: Penguin Books, 1969), 61. Ben Hecht's comments on the producer as a bank guard come from COHC. Irving Thalberg is quoted on additional expenditures in *Fortune*'s "MGM" in Balio, 317.

For other examples of specific semi-independent and independent producers, see Schatz's description of Selznick's companies in *Genius of the System,* 176–198, 271–294, 322–339, and 381–407; Thomson, *Showman,* particularly pp. 471–476; Berg, *Goldwyn,* 109, 113, 233, 349, 397; Haver, *David O. Selznick's Hollywood;* and Leff, *Hitchcock and Selznick.* Evidence of independent production's prevalence in contemporary Hollywood comes from *Daily V,* 16 June 1986: 1, 11; and *V,* 27 April 1992: 3, 10. Its perennial status as a source of innovation is apparent in articles such as Vincent Canby, "Rejoice! It's Independence Day," *NYT,* 8 October 1989.

Filmography[1]

At Columbia:

Washington Merry-Go-Round (1932). Director: James Cruze. Screenplay: Joe Swirling from an original story by Maxwell Anderson. Cinematography: Ira Morgan. Editor: Richard Cahoon. Sound: Lodge Cunningham. Technical Adviser: Eugene Thackeray. Release Date: September 29. 75 min.

    Cast: Lee Tracy (Button Gwinett Brown). Constance Cummings (Alice Wylie). Alan Dinehart (Norton). Walter Connolly (Senator Wylie). Clarence Muse (Clarence). Arthur Vinton (Beef Brannigan). Frank Sheridan (Kelleher). Clay Clement (Conti). Sam Godfrey (Martin).

    Cost: NA   Gross: NA   Net: NA

Night Mayor (1932). Director: Ben Stoloff. Screenplay: Gertrude Purcell, from an original story by Sam Marx. Cinematography: Ted Tetzlaff. Release Date: November 26. 65 min.

    Cast: Lee Tracy (The Mayor). Evelyn Knapp (Doree Dawn). Eugene Palette (Hymie Shane). Warren Hymer (Riley). Donald Dillaway (Fred Field). Vince Barnett (Louis Mossbaum). Astrid Allwyn (Patsy). Barbara Weeks (Nutsy). Gloria Shea (Gwen). Emmett Corrigan (Robertson). Tom O'Brien (Delaney). Wade Botejer (Clancy). Harold Minjir (Ashley Sparks).

    Cost: NA   Gross: NA   Net: NA

The Bitter Tea of General Yen (1933).* Director: Frank Capra. Screenplay: Edward Paramore, from the novel by Grace Zaring Stone. Cinematography: Joseph Walker.

---

[1]* indicates the film is available on videotape by a major distributor as of June 1992.

"Cost" refers to the film's negative costs, i.e., the costs required to produce a final cut of the film. "Gross" refers to all rentals paid to Wanger's distributors after theaters subtract their costs and profit share from ticket sales. The "net" refers to any income remaining after distributors subtract their fees, reimburse themselves for print costs, advertising and other charges and after the negative cost of the film is recovered.

Unless otherwise indicated, all figures for film grosses and nets represent worldwide earnings after two to three years in theatrical distribution. They are derived from statements in the Walter F. Wanger papers.

Editor: Edward Curtis. Music: W. Frank Harling. Release Date: January 12. 89 min.
Cast: Barbara Stanwyck (Megan Davis). Nils Asther (General Yen). Gavin Gordon (Dr. Robert Strike). Toshia Mori (Mah-Li). Walter Connolly (Jones). Lucien Littlefield (Mr. Jackson). Richard Loo (Captain Li). Helen Jerome Eddy (Miss Reed). Emmett Corrigan (Bishop Harkness).
Cost: NA   **Gross:** NA   **Net:** NA

At MGM[2]:

Gabriel Over the White House (Cosmopolitan, 1933). Director: Gregory LaCava. Screenplay: Carey Wilson, from the anonymous novel (by Thomas W. Tweed). Additional Dialogue: Bertram Bloch. Cinematography: Bert Glennon. Editor: Basil Wrangell. Art Direction: Cedric Gibbons. Gowns: Adrian. Music: William Axt. Release Date: April 1. 85 min.
Cast: Walter Huston (President Hammond). Karen Morley (Pendola Molloy). Franchot Tone (Hartley Beekman). Arthur Byron (Jasper Brooks). Dickie Moore (Jimmy Vetter). C. Henry Gordon (Nick Diamond). David Landau (John Bronson). Samuel Hinds (Dr. Eastman). William Pawley (Borell).
Cost: $232,400   **Gross:** NA   **Net:** $206,000

Another Language (1933). Director: Edward H. Griffith. Screenplay: Herman J. Mankiewicz and Donald Ogden Stewart, from the play by Rose Franken. Cinematography: Ray June. Editor: Hugh Wynn. Art Direction: Frederic Hope. Gowns: Adrian. Release Date: August 5. 70 min.
Cast: Helen Hayes (Stella). Robert Montgomery (Victor). Louise Closser Hale (Mom). John Beal (Jerry). Henry Travers (Pop). Margaret Hamilton (Helen). Willard Robertson (Harry). Irene Cattell (Grace). Minor K. Watson (Paul). Hal Dawson (Walter). Maidel Turner (Etta).
Cost: $269,600   **Gross:** $467,193   **Net:** NA

Going Hollywood (Cosmopolitan, 1933). Director: Raoul Walsh. Screenplay: Donald Ogden Stewart from an original story by Frances Marion. Cinematography: George Folsey. Editor: Frank Sullivan. Art Direction: Merrill Pye. Gowns: Adrian. Songs: Nacio Herb Brown and Arthur Freed. Musical Direction: Lennie Hayton. Dance Direction: Albertina Rasch. Release Date: December 22. 75 min.
Cast: Marion Davies (Sylvia Bruce). Bing Crosby (Bill Williams). Fifi D'Orsay (Lili Yvonne). Stuart Erwin (Ernest B. Baker). Ned Sparks (Conroy). Patsy Kelly (Jill). Bobby Watson (Thompson). Three Radio Rogues (Themselves).
Cost: NA   **Gross:** $583,232   **Net:** NA

Queen Christina (1933).* Director: Rouben Mamoulian. Screenplay: Salka Viertel and H. M. Harwood, from an original story by Viertel and Margaret P. Levino. Dialogue: S. N. Behrman. Cinematography: William Daniels. Editor: Blanche Sewell. Art Direction: Alexander Toluboff. Gowns: Adrian. Music: Herbert Stothart. Release Date: December 28. 96 min.

---

[2]Figures for Wanger's MGM films are from p. 261 of Samuel Marx's *Mayer and Thalberg: The Make-Believe Saints* and documents in the David O. Selznick collection. Profit and loss figures are based on worldwide earnings after two to five years in distribution.

Cast: Greta Garbo (Queen Christina). John Gilbert (Antonio). Ian Keith (Magnus). Lewis Stone (Oxenstierna). Elizabeth Young (Ebba). C. Aubrey Smith (Aage). Reginald Owen (Charles). George Renevent (French Ambassador). David Torrence (Archbishop). Gustav von Seyffertitz (General). Ferdinand Munier (Innkeeper).
Cost: $1,144,000   Gross: $2,887,285   Net: $632,000

At Paramount:

The President Vanishes (1935). Director: William Wellman. Screenplay: Carey Wilson and Cedric "Worth," from the novel by Rex Stout. Dialogue: Lynn Starling. Cinematography: Barney McGill. Special Effects: Slavko Vorkapich. Editor: Hansen Fritsch. Music: Hugo Reisenfeld. Release Date: January 11. 80 min.
    Cast: Arthur Byron (President Stanley). Janet Beecher (Mrs. Stanley). Paul Kelly (Chick Moffat). Peggy Conklin (Alma Cronin). Rosalind Russell (Sally Voorman). Edward Arnold (Secretary of War Wardell). Osgood Perkins (Harris Brownell). Edward Ellis (Lincoln Lee). Andy Devine (Val Orcott).
    Cost: $290,056   Gross: $391,542   Net: –$145,948
Private Worlds (1935). Director: Gregory LaCava. Screenplay: Lynn Starling and LaCava, from the novel by Phyllis Bottome. Additional Dialogue: Gladys Unger. Cinematography: Leon Shamroy. Editor: Aubrey Scotto. Art Direction: Alexander Toluboff. Technical Adviser: Dr. Samuel Marcus. Release Date: April 19. 84 min.
    Cast: Claudette Colbert (Jane Everest). Charles Boyer (Charles Monet). Joel McCrea (Alex MacGregor). Joan Bennett (Sally MacGregor). Helen Vinson (Claire).
    Cost: $435,032   Gross: $819,118   Net: –$10,458
Shanghai (1935). Director: James Flood. Screenplay: Gene Towne, Graham Baker, and Lynn Starling. Cinematography: James Van Trees. Editor: Otho Lovering. Art Direction: Alexander Toluboff. Music: Frederick Hollander. Musical Direction: S. K. Wineland. Technical Adviser: Joseph Moody. Release Date: July 19. 75 min.
    Cast: Loretta Young (Barbara Howard). Charles Boyer (Dimitri Kuslov). Werner Oland (Ambassador Lun Sing). Fred Keating (Tommy Sherwood).
    Cost: $260,601   Gross: $511,225   Net: $142,246
Smart Girl (1935). Director: Aubrey Scotto. Screenplay: Francis Hyland. Additional Dialogue: Wilson Collison. Cinematography: John Mescall. Editor: Tom Persons. Art Direction: Alexander Toluboff. Release Date: July 26. 74 min.
    Cast: Ida Lupino (Pat Reynolds). Kent Taylor (Nick Graham). Gail Patrick (Kay Reynolds). Joseph Cawthorn (Karl Krausemeyer).
    Cost: $98,823   Gross: $245,153   Net: $88,511
Every Night at Eight (1935). Director: Raoul Walsh. Screenplay: Stanley Carey, Gene Towne, and Graham Baker. Additional Dialogue: Bert Hanlon. From the story "Three on a Mike" by Stanley Garvey. Cinematography: James Van Trees. Editor: W. Donn Hayes. Art Direction: Alexander Toluboff. Costumes: Helen Taylor. Music: James McHugh and Dorothy Field. Release Date: August 8. 81 min.
    Cast: George Raft ("Tops" Cardona). Alice Faye (Dixie Foley). Frances Langford (Susan Moore). Patsy Kelly (Daphne O'Connor). Walter Catlett (MC).
    Cost: $266,956   Gross: $507,117   Net: $148,782
Mary Burns, Fugitive (1935). Director: William K. Howard. Screenplay: Gene Towne and Graham Baker. Continuity: Louis Stevens. Cinematography: Leon Shamroy.

Editor: Hanson Fritsch. Art Direction: Alexander Toluboff. Costumes: Helen Taylor. Musical Direction: Heinz Roemheld. Release Date: November 15. 84 min.

Cast: Sylvia Sidney (Mary Burns). Melvyn Douglas (Alec MacDonald). Alan Baxter (Don "Babe" Wilson). Wallace Ford (Harper). Brian Donlevy ("Spike").

Cost: $337,152   Gross: $513,176   Net: $29,089

Her Master's Voice (1935). Director: Joseph Santley. Screenplay: Dore Schary and Harry Sauber, from the play by Clare Kummer. Cinematography: James Van Trees. Editor: Bob Simpson. Art Direction: Alexander Toluboff. Costumes: Helen Taylor. Music: James McHugh and Gus Kahn. Release Date: January 17. 87 min.

Cast: Edward Everett Horton (Ned Farrar). Peggy Conklin (Queena Farrar). Laura Hope Crews (Aunt Min). Elizabeth Patterson (Mrs. Martin). Grant Mitchell (Twilling). Ruth Warren (Phoebe).

Cost: $161,829   Gross: $214,464   Net: –$2,300

The Trail of the Lonesome Pine (1936). Director: Henry Hathaway. Screenplay: Grover Jones. Adaptation: Horace McCoy and Harvey Thew, from the novel by John Fox, Jr. Cinematography (Technicolor): Howard Green and Robert C. Bruce. Editor: Robert Bischoff. Art Direction: Alexander Toluboff. Costumes: Helen Taylor. Music: Hugo Friedhofer and Gerrard Cabonara. Musical Direction: Boris Morros. Songs: Lou Alter and Sidney D. Mitchell. Release Date: March 13. 102 min.

Cast: Sylvia Sidney (June Tolliver). Henry Fonda (Dave Tolliver). Fred MacMurray (Jack Hale). Fred Stone (Judd Tolliver). Nigel Bruce (Thurber). Beulah Bondi (Melissa Tolliver). Spanky McFarland (Buddie Tolliver). Fuzzy Knight (Tater).

Cost: $621,864   Gross: $1,665,838   Net: $522,620

Big Brown Eyes (1936). Director: Raoul Walsh. Screenplay: Raoul Walsh and Bert Hanlon, from stories by James Edward Grant. Cinematography: George Clemens. Editor: Robert Simpson. Art Direction: Alexander Toluboff. Costumes: Helen Taylor. Musical Direction: Boris Morros. Release Date: April 3. 78 min.

Cast: Joan Bennett (Eve Fallon). Cary Grant (Danny Barr). Walter Pidgeon (Scola). Lloyd Nolan (Corsig). Alan Baxter (Carey Butler).

Cost: $289,696   Gross: $359,009   Net: –$14,645

The Moon's Our Home (1936). Director: William A. Seiter. Screenplay: Isabel Dawn and Boyce DeGaw, from the novel by Faith Baldwin. Additional Dialogue: Dorothy Parker and Alan Campbell. Cinematography: Joseph Valentine. Editor: Dorothy Spencer. Art Direction: Alexander Toluboff. Costumes: Helen Taylor. Musical Direction: Boris Morros. Release Date: April 10. 83 min.

Cast: Margaret Sullavan (Sarah Brown). Henry Fonda (John Smith). Charles Butterworth (Horace van Steedan). Beulah Bondi (Mrs. Boyce Medford). Margaret Hamilton (Mitty Simpson). Walter Brennan (Lem).

Cost: $402,573   Gross: $417,663   Net: –$111,845

Case Against Mrs. Ames (1936). Director: William A. Seiter. Screenplay: Gene Towne and Graham Baker, from the book by Arthur Somers Roche. Cinematography: Lucien Andriot. Editor: Dorothy Spencer. Art Direction: Alexander Toluboff. Costumes: Helen Taylor. Release Date: May 8. 89 min.

Cast: Madeleine Carroll (Hope Ames). George Brent (Matt Logan). Arthur Treacher (Griggsby). Alan Baxter (Lou). Beulah Bondi (Mrs. Livingston Ames). Alan Mowbray (Lawrence Waterston).

Cost: $334,971   Gross: $339,443   Net: –$38,869

Fatal Lady (1936). Director: Edward Ludwig. Screenplay: Samuel Ornitz, from a story by Harry Segall. Adaptation: William R. Lipman. Additional Dialogue: Tiffany Thayer. Cinematography: Leon Shamroy. Editor: Ernest Nims. Art Direction: Alexander Toluboff. Costumes: Helen Taylor. Songs: Sam Coslow and Victor Young. Release Date: May 15. 77 min.

   Cast: Mary Ellis (Marion Stuart, Maria Delasaro, and Malevo). Walter Pidgeon (David Roberts). Ruth Donnelly (Melba York). Alan Mowbray (Uberta Malia). Edgar Kennedy (Rudy).

   Cost: $431,862   **Gross:** $201,707   **Net:** –$296,665

Palm Springs (1936). Director: Aubrey Scotto. Screenplay: Joseph Fields. Adaptation: Humphrey Pearson, from the story "Lady Smith" by Myles Conolly. Cinematography: James Van Trees. Editor: Robert Simpson. Art Direction: Alexander Toluboff. Costumes: Helen Taylor. Songs: Ralph Rainger and Leo Robin, and Mack Gordon and Harry Real. Release Date: June 5. 74 min.

   Cast: Frances Langford (Joan Smyth). Smith Ballew (Slim). Sir Guy Standing (Captain Smyth). Ernest Cossart (Starkey). David Niven (George Britell). Sterling Holloway (Oscar).

   Cost: $328,818   **Gross:** $225,637   **Net:** –$154,089

Spendthrift (1936). Director: Raoul Walsh. Screenplay: Raoul Walsh and Bert Hanlon. Cinematography: Leon Shamroy. Editor: Robert Simpson. Art Direction: Alexander Toluboff. Costumes: Helen Taylor. Music: Boris Morros. Release Date: July 10. 80 min.

   Cast: Henry Fonda (Townsend Middleton). Mary Brian (Sally Barnaby). Pat Paterson (Boots O'Connell). June Brewster (Topsy). J. M. Kerrigan (O'Connell).

   Cost: $344,332   **Gross:** $278,085   **Net:** –$126,925

At United Artists:

You Only Live Once (1937).* Director: Fritz Lang. Screenplay: Gene Towne and Graham Baker. Cinematography: Leon Shamroy. Editor: Daniel Mandell. Art Direction: Alexander Toluboff. Costumes: Helen Taylor. Music: Alfred Newman. Release Date: January 27. 85 min.

   Cast: Henry Fonda (Eddie Taylor). Sylvia Sidney (Joan Graham). Barton MacLaine (Stephen Whitney). Jean Dixon (Bonnie Graham). William Gargan (Father Dolan). Jerome Cowan (Dr. Hill). Chic Sale (Ethan). Margaret Hamilton (Hester). Warren Hymer (Buggsy). Gunn Williams (Roger). John Wray (Warden). Walter De Palma (Monk).

   Cost: $589,503   **Gross:** $628,138   **Net:** –$48,045

History is Made at Night (1937).* Director: Frank Borzage. Screenplay: Gene Towne and Graham Baker. Additional Dialogue: Vincent Lawrence and David Hertz. Cinematography: Gregg Toland. Special Photographic Effects: James Basevi. Editor: Margaret Clancey. Art Direction: Alexander Toluboff. Costumes: Bernard Newman. Music: Alfred Newman. Release Date: March 8. 97 min.

   Cast: Charles Boyer (Paul Dumond). Jean Arthur (Irene Vail). Leo Carrillo (Cesare). Colin Clive (Bruce Vail). Ivan Lebedeff (Michael). George Meeker (Norton).

   Cost: $821,791   **Gross:** $948,500   **Net:** $17,450

Walter Wanger's Vogues of 1938 (1937). Director: Irving Cummings. Screenplay: Samuel and Bella Spewack. Cinematography (Technicolor): Ray Rennahan. Editors: Otho Lovering and Dorothy Spencer. Production Design: Alexander Toluboff. Costumes: Jaeckel, Inc., Irene, Omar Kiam, Sally Victor, John-Frederic Trabert and Hoeffer, and I. Miller and Sons. Makeup: Max Factor. Dance Director: Seymour Felix. Musical Direction: Boris Morros. Music and Lyrics: Lew Brown and Sammy Fain, Frank Loesser and Manning Sherwin, and Louis Alter and Paul F. Webster. Release Date: August 7. 105 min.

Cast: Warner Baxter (George Curson). Joan Bennett (Wendy Van Klettering). Helen Vinson (Mary Curson). Mischa Auer (Prince Muratov). Alan Mowbray (Mr. Morgan). Jerome Cowan (Mr. Brockton).

Cost: $1,048,435   **Gross:** $1,089,956   **Net:** –$256,207

Stand-In (1937).* Director: Tay Garnett. Screenplay: Gene Towne and Graham Baker, from a story by Clarence Budington Kelland. Cinematography: Charles G. Clarke. Editors: Otho Lovering and Dorothy Spencer. Art Direction: Alexander Toluboff. Costumes: Helen Taylor. Musical Direction: Rex Rommell. Release Date: October 5. 90 min.

Cast: Leslie Howard (Atterbury Dodd). Joan Blondell (Lester Plum). Humphrey Bogart (Quintain). Alan Mowbray (Koslofski). Maria Shelton (Cheri). Jack Carson (Potts). C. Henry Gordon (Nassau).

Cost: $523,613   **Gross:** $617,521   **Net:** $9,274

52nd Street (1937). Director: Harold Young. Screenplay: Grover Jones. Additional Dialogue: Sid Silvers. Cinematography: George Schneiderman. Editors: Otho Lovering and William Reynolds. Art Direction: Alexander Toluboff. Costumes: Helen Taylor. Choreography: Danny Dare. Songs: Harold Bullock and Harold Spina. Release Date: November 17. 80 min.

Cast: Ian Hunter (Rufus Rondell). Dorothy Peterson (Adela Rondell). Zasu Pitts (Letitia Rondell). Pat Paterson (Margaret Rondell). Leo Carrillo (Fiorello Zamarelli). Kenny Baker (Benjamin Zamarelli). Marla Shelton (Evelyn Macy). Ella Logan (Betty).

Cost: $523,869   **Gross:** $598,384   **Net:** –$4,392

I Met My Love Again (1938). Directors: Arthur Ripley and Joshua Logan. Screenplay: David Hertz, from the novel *Summer Lightning* by Allene Carliss. Cinematography: Hal Mohr. Editors: Otho Lovering and Edward Mann. Art Direction: Alexander Toluboff. Music: Heinz Roemheld. Release Date: January 8. 79 min.

Cast: Joan Bennett (Julie). Henry Fonda (Ives). Dame May Whitty (Aunt William). Alan Marshall (Michael). Louis Platt (Brenda). Alan Baxter (Tony). Tim Holt (Budge).

Cost: $428,800   **Gross:** $416,687   **Net:** -$64,104

Blockade (1938). Director: William Dieterle. Screenplay: John Howard Lawson. Cinematography: Rudolph Mate. Special Photographic Effects: Russell Lawson and James Basevi. Art Direction: Alexander Toluboff. Costumes: Irene and John Frederics. Editors: Otho Lovering and Dorothy Spencer. Musical Direction: Boris Morros. Music: Werner Jannsen. Release Date: June 9. 73 min.

Cast: Madeleine Carroll (Norma). Henry Fonda (Marco). Leo Carrillo (Luis). John Halliday (Andre Gallinet). Vladimir Sokoloff (Basil). Reginald Denny (Eduard Grant).

Cost: $692,087   **Gross:** $665,523   **Net:** -$135,672

Algiers (1938).* Director: John Cromwell. Screenplay: John Howard Lawson, from the novel by Roger Ashelbe. Additional Dialogue: James M. Cain. Cinematography: James Wong Howe. Editors: Otho Lovering and William Reynolds. Art Direction: Alexander Toluboff. Wardrobe: Omar Kiam and Irene. Music: Vincent Scotto and Mohammed Igorbouchen. Release Date: June 28. 95 min.

Cast: Charles Boyer (Pepe Le Moko). Hedy Lamarr (Gaby). Sigrid Gurie (Inez). Joseph Calleia (Slimane). Alan Hale (Grandpere). Gene Lockhart (Regis).

Cost: $691,833   **Gross:** $951,801   **Net:** $150,466

Trade Winds (1938).* Director: Tay Garnett. Screenplay: Dorothy Parker, Alan Campbell, and Frank R. Adams, from a story by Garnett. Cinematography: Rudolph Maté. Special Photographic Effects: James R. Shackleford. Editors: Otho Lovering and Dorothy Spencer. Art Direction: Alexander Toluboff. Costumes: Irene and Helen Taylor. Musical Director: Alfred Newman. Release Date: December 28. 93 min.

Cast: Frederic March (Sam Wye). Joan Bennett (Kay Kerrigan). Ralph Bellamy (Blodgett). Ann Sothern (Jean). Sidney Blackmer (Thomas Bruhm II). Thomas Mitchell (Police Commissioner). Robert Elliott (Faulkiner). Joyce Compton (Mrs. Johnson).

Cost: $738,733   **Gross:** $964,404   **Net:** $71,129

Stagecoach (1939).* Director and Producer: John Ford. Screenplay: Dudley Nichols, from a story by Ernest Haycox. Cinematography: Bert Glennon. Editors: Otho Lovering, Dorothy Spencer, and Walter Reynolds. Art Direction: Alexander Toluboff. Costumes: Walter Plunkett. Music: Richard Hageman, W. Franke Harling, John Leipold, Leo Shuken, and Luis Gruenberg. Release Date: February 15. 95 min.

Cast: Claire Trevor (Dallas). John Wayne (Ringo Kid). Thomas Mitchell (Dr. Boone). John Carradine (Hatfield). Andy Devine (Buck). Donald Meek (Samuel Peacock). Louise Platt (Lucy Mallory). Tim Holt (Lt. Blanchard). George Bancroft (Sheriff Wilcox).

Cost: $531,374   **Gross:** $1,103,757   **Net:** $297,639

Winter Carnival (1939). Director: Charles Reisner. Screenplay: Lester Cole, Budd Schulberg, and Maurice Rapf, from a story by Schulberg and Rapf, based on "Echoes that Old Refrain" by Corey Ford. Cinematography: Merritt Gerstad. Process Photography: Ray Binger. Editors: Otho Lovering and Dorothy Spencer. Art Direction: Alexander Toluboff. Music: Werner Jansen. Release Date: July 20. 91 min.

Cast: Ann Sheridan (Jill Baker). Richard Carlson (John Weldon). Helen Parrish (Ann Baxter). James Corner (Mickey Allen). Alan Baldwin (Don Reynolds). Robert Armstrong (Tiger Reynolds). Marsha Hunt (Lucy Morgan). James Butler (Larry Gray). Virginia Gilmore (Margie Stafford).

Cost: $412,640   **Gross:** $474,286   **Net:** -$33,696

Eternally Yours (1939).* Director: Tay Garnett. Screenplay: Gene Towne and Graham Baker. Additional Dialogue: John Meehan. Cinematography: Merritt Gerstad. Art Direction: Alexander Toluboff. Music: Werner Janssen. Release Date: October 3. 99 min.

Cast: Loretta Young (Anita). David Niven (Tony). Hugh Herbert (Benton).

Billie Burke (Aunt Abby). C. Aubrey Smith (Bishop Peabody). Broderick Crawford (Don Barnes). Virginia Field (Lola DeVere). Zasu Pitts (Mrs. Bingham). Raymond Walburn (Mr. Bingham).

Cost: $790,878   **Gross:** $683,131   **Net:** –$200,281

Slightly Honorable (1940). Director: Tay Garnett. Screenplay: Ken Englund, from the novel *Send Another Coffin* by F. G. Presnell. Cinematography: Merritt Gerstad. Editors: Otho Lovering and Dorothy Spencer. Art Direction: Alexander Golitzen. Gowns: Travis Banton. Music: Werner Janssen. Release Date: January 9. 83 min.

Cast: Pat O'Brien (John Webb). Edward Arnold (Cushing). Broderick Crawford (Rus Sampson). Ruth Terry (Ann). Alan Dinehart (Commissioner Joyce). Claire Dodd (Alma Brehmer). Douglas Dumbrille (George Taylor). Eve Arden (Miss Ater). Ernest Truex (P. Hemingway Collins). Janet Beecher (Mrs. Cushing).

Cost: $434,874   **Gross:** $386,116   **Net:** –$107,709

House Across the Bay (1940).* Director: Archie Mayo (airplane flight scene directed by Alfred Hitchcock). Screenplay: Katheryn Scola, from a story by Myles Connoly. Cinematography: Merritt Gerstad. Special Photographic Effects: Ray Binger. Editors: Otho Lovering and Dorothy Spencer. Art Direction: Alexander Golitzen. Gowns: Irene. Music: Werner Janssen. Release Date: March 1. 86 min.

Cast: George Raft (Steve Larwitt). Joan Bennett (Brenda Brentley). Lloyd Nolan (Slant Kolma). Gladys George (Mary Bogales). Walter Pidgeon (Tim Nolan).

Cost: $713,965   **Gross:** $684,374   **Net:** –$101,334

Foreign Correspondent (1940).* Director: Alfred Hitchcock. Screenplay: Charles Bennett and Joan Harrison. Dialogue: James Hilton and Robert Benchley. Cinematography: Rudolph Maté. Special Photographic Effects: Paul Eagler. Editors: Otho Lovering and Dorothy Spencer. Art Direction: Alexander Golitzen. Special Production Effects: William Cameron Menzies. Costumes: L. Magnin and Co. Music: Alfred Newman. Release Date: August 29. 119 min.

Cast: Joel McCrea (Johnny Jones/Huntley Haverstock). Laraine Day (Carol Fisher). Herbert Marshall (Stephen Fisher). George Sanders (Herbert ffoliott). Robert Benchley (Stebbins). Albert Basserman (Van Meer). Edmund Gwenn (Rowley). Eduardo Ciannelli (Mr. Krug). Harry Davenport (Mr. Powers).

Cost: $1,484,167   **Gross:** $1,598,435   **Net:** –$369,973

The Long Voyage Home (1940).* Producer: Argosy Corporation. Director: John Ford. Screenplay: Dudley Nichols, from *Four Sea Plays* by Eugene O'Neill. Cinematography: Gregg Toland. Special Effects: R. T. Layton and R. O. Binger. Editor: Sherman Todd. Art Direction: James Basevi. Music: Richard Hageman. Release Date: October 9. 105 min.

Cast: John Wayne (Olsen). Thomas Mitchell (Driscoll). Ian Hunter (Smitty). Barry Fitzgerald (Cody, the Steward). Wilfred Lawson (Captain). John Qualen (Axel). Ward Bond (Yank). Arthur Shields (Donkeyman). Joseph Sawyer (Davis). J. M. Kerrigan (Crimp). Mildred Natwick (Freda). Rafaela Ottiano (Bella). Carmen Morales (Girl).

Cost: $682,495   **Gross:** $580,129   **Net:** –$224,336

Sundown (1941).* Director: Henry Hathaway. Screenplay: Barre Lyndon, from his magazine serial. Adaptation: Charles G. Booth. Cinematography: Charles Lang. Special Photographic Effects: Ray Binger. Editor: Dorothy Spencer. Art Direction:

Alexander Golitzen. Gene Tierney's Costumes: Walter Plunkett. Music: Miklos
Rozsa. Release Date: October 21. 90 min.
   Cast: Gene Tierney (Zia). Bruce Cabot (Crawford). George Sanders (Major
Coombes). Sir Cedric Hardwicke (Bishop). Harry Carey (Dewey). Joseph Calleia
(Pallini). Reginald Gardner (Lt. Turner). Carl Esmond (Kuypens).
   Cost: $1,242,639   **Gross:** $873,808   **Net:** –$658,824

Unit Production at Universal[3]:

Eagle Squadron (1941). Director: Arthur Lubin. Screenplay: Norman Reilly Raine,
from a story by C. S. Forrester. Cinematography: Stanley Cortez. Special Photo-
graphic Effects: John Fulton. Editor: Philip Cahn. Art Direction: Jack Otterson and
Alexander Golitzen. Music: Frank Skinner. Technical Adviser: John M. Hill, RAF.
Release Date: June 16. 108 min.
   Cast: Robert Stack (Chuck Brewer). Diana Barrymore (Ann Partridge). Nigel
Bruce (McKinnon). Leif Erikson (Johnny Coe). Edgar Barrier (Wadislaw Borow-
sky). Jon Hall (Hank Starr).
   Cost: $908,768   **Gross:** $2,607,422   **Net:** $697,607
Arabian Nights (1942).* Director: John Rawlins. Story and Screenplay: Michael Ho-
gan. Additional Dialogue: True Boardman. Cinematography (Technicolor): Milton
Krasner, William B. Skall, and Howard Greene. Editor: Philip Cahn. Art Direc-
tion: Alexander Golitzen. Production Design: Jack Otterson and Alexander Golit-
zen. Set Decorations: Russell A. Gausman. Women's Costumes: Vera West. Music:
Frank Skinner. Release Date: December 23. 86 min.
   Cast: Sabu (Ali Ben Ali). Jon Hall (Haroun-Al-Rashid). Maria Montez
(Sherazade). Leif Erikson (Kamar). Billy Gilbert (Ahmad). Edgar Barrier (Nadan).
Richard Lane (Corporal). Turhan Bey (Captain). John Qualen (Aladdin). Shemp
Howard (Sinbad).
   Cost: $904,765   **Gross:** $3,453,416   **Net:** $1,851,921
We've Never Been Licked (1943). Director: John Rawlins. Screenplay: Norman Reilly
Raine and Nick Grinde, from a story by Raine. Cinematography: Milton Krasner.
Special Photographic Effects: John P. Fulton. Editor: Phillip Cahn. Art Direction:
John Goodman and Alexander Golitzen. Gowns: Vera West. Technical Adviser:
Col. J. K. Boles, U.S. Army. Musical Direction: Charles Previn. Release Date:
August 3. 101 min.
   Cast: Richard Quine (Brad Craig). Noah Beery, Jr. (Cyanide). Anne Gwynne
(Nina). Martha O'Driscoll (Dedee). Edgar Barrier (Nishikawa). William Frawley
(Fat Man). Harry Davenport ("Pop" Lambert).
   Cost: $918,175   **Gross:** $1,109,186   **Net:** –$283,724
Gung Ho! (1943).* Director: Ray Enright. Screenplay: Lucien Hubbard, from a story
by Capt. W. S. LeFrancois, USMC. Additional Dialogue: Joseph Hoffman. Cine-

[3]Income for all of Wanger's Universal productions, unit and independent, is as of 1954 and
represents earnings after from six to twelve years in distribution.

matography: Milton Krasner. Special Photographic Effects: John P. Fulton. Editor: Milton Carruth. Art Direction: John B. Goodman and Alexander Golitzen. Music: Frank Skinner. Technical Advisers: Lt. Col. Evans F. Carlson, USMCR, Lt. W. S. Le Francois, USMC, and Gunnery Sgt. Victor Maghakian, USMC. Release Date: December 20. 88 min.

   Cast: Randolph Scott (Col. Thorwald). Grace McDonald (Kathleen Corrigan). Alan Curtis (John Harbison). J. Carrol Naish (Lt. Cristoforus). David Bruce (Larry O'Ryan). Peter Coe (Kozzarowski). Robert Mitchum (PigIron). Rod Cameron (Rube Tedrow). Sam Levene (Transport).

   Cost: $866,898   **Gross:** $2,176,489   **Net:** $577,460

Ladies Courageous (1944). Director: John Rawlins. Story and Screenplay: Norman Reilly Raine and Doris Gilbert, suggested by the book *Looking for Trouble* by Virginia Cowles. Cinematography: Hal Mohr. Special Photography: John P. Fulton. Editor: Philip Cahn. Art Direction: John B. Goodman and Alexander Golitzen. Gowns: Vera West. Technical Advisers: Marjorie Kumler and Capt. Charlton Fincher. Release Date: March 24. 95 min.

   Cast: Loretta Young (Roberta Harper). Geraldine Fitzgerald (Vinnie Alford). Diana Barrymore (Nadine). Anne Gwynne (Gerry Vail). Evelyn Ahern (Wilhelmina). Phillip Terry (Tommy Harper). David Bruce (Frank Garrison).

   Cost: $834,260   **Gross:** $1,072,763   **Net:** –$186,691

Salome, Where She Danced (1945).* Associate Producer: Alexander Golitzen. Director: Charles Lamont (replaced by Erle Kenton). Screenplay: Laurence Stallings, from a story by Michael J. Phillips. Cinematography (Technicolor): Hal Mohr and Howard Greene. Editor: Russell Schoengarth. Art Direction: John B. Goodman and Alexander Golitzen. Gowns: Vera West. Music: Edward Ward. Release Date: April 17. 90 min.

   Cast: Yvonne De Carlo (Salome). Rod Cameron (Jim). David Bruce (Cleve). Walter Slezak (Dimitrioff). Albert Dekker (Von Bohlen).

   Cost: $1,159,225   **Gross:** $2,598,964   **Net:** $149,387

A Night in Paradise (1946). Associate Producer: Alexander Golitzen. Director: Arthur Lubin. Screenplay: Ernest Pascal. Adaptation: Emmet Lavery, from a novel by George Hellman. Cinematography (Technicolor): Hal Mohr and W. Howard Greene. Special Photographic Effects: John P. Fulton. Editor: Milton Carruth. Art Direction: John B. Goodman and Alexander Golitzen. Set Decorations: Russell A. Gausman and E. R. Robinson. Costumes: Travis Banton. Music: Frank Skinner. Release Date: April 13. 84 min.

   Cast: Merle Oberon (Delarai). Turhan Bey (Aesop). Thomas Gomez (Croesus). Gale Sondergaard (Attossa). Ray Collins (Leonides). George Dolenz (Frigid Ambassador). John Litel (Archon). Ernest Truex (Scribe). Douglass Dumbrille (High Priest).

   Cost: $1,602,641   **Gross:** $2,032,486   **Net:** –$790,711

Canyon Passage (1946). Associate Producer: Alexander Golitzen. Director: Jacques Tourneur. Screenplay: Ernest Pascal, from the story by Ernest Haycox. Cinematography (Technicolor): Edward Cronjager. Special Photography: D. S. Horsley. Editor: Milton Carruth. Art Direction: John B. Goodman and Richard H. Reidel. Costumes: Travis Banton. Musical Direction: Frank Skinner. Songs: Hoagy Carmichael and Jack Brooks. Release Date: July 15. 99 min.

Cast: Dana Andrews (Logan Stuart). Brian Donlevy (Camrose). Susan Hayward (Lucy Overmire). Hoagy Carmichael (Hi Lennet). Andy Devine (Ben Dance). Ward Bond (Honey Bragg). Patricia Roc (Caroline).
Cost: $2,623,925   Gross: $4,263,651   Net: –$63,784

Smash-Up—The Story of a Woman (1947). Director: Stuart Heisler. Screenplay: John Howard Lawson, from a story by Dorothy Parker and Frank Cavett. Additional Dialogue: Lionel Wiggam. Cinematography: Stanley Cortez. Editor: Milton Carruth. Art Direction: Alexander Golitzen. Gowns: Travis Banton. Music: Frank Skinner. Songs: Edgar Fairchild and Jack Brooks, and Jimmy McHugh and Harold Adamson. Release Date: March 1. 103 min.
Cast: Susan Hayward (Angie Evans). Lee Bowman (Ken Conway). Marsha Hunt (Martha Gray). Eddie Albert (Steve). Carl Esmond (Dr. Lorenz). Carleton Young (Mr. Elliot).
Cost: $1,360,286   Gross: 2,301,555   Net: –$111,664

Diana Productions, Inc., at Universal:

Scarlet Street (1945).* Producer and Director: Fritz Lang. Screenplay: Dudley Nichols, from *La Chienne* by Georges de la Fouchardiere. Cinematography: Milton Krasner. Editor: Arthur Hilton. Art Direction: Alexander Golitzen. Costumes: Travis Banton. Music: Hans J. Salter. Release Date: December 28. 102 min.
Cast: Edward G. Robinson (Christopher Cross). Joan Bennett (Kitty). Dan Duryea (Johnny). Margaret Lindsay (Millie). Rosalind Ivan (Adele). Samuel S. Hinds (Charles Pringle). Jess Barker (Janeway). Arthur Loft (Dellarowe). Vladimir Sokoloff (Pop Lejon).
Cost: $1,202,007   Gross: $2,948,386   Net: $540,575

Secret Beyond the Door (1948). Producer and Director: Fritz Lang. Screenplay: Silvia Richards, from the novel *Museum Piece No. 13* by Rufus King. Cinematography: Stanley Cortez. Editor: Arthur Hilton. Production Design: Max Parker. Gowns: Travis Banton. Makeup: Bud Westmore. Music: Miklos Rozsa. Release Date: February 1. 99 min.
Cast: Michael Redgrave (Mark Lamphere). Joan Bennett (Celia). Ann Revere (Caroline). Barbara O'Neil (Miss Robey). Natalie Schaefer (Edith Potter). Paul Cavanaugh (Rick Barrett).
Cost: $1,463,500   Gross: NA   Net: –$1,145,000

Walter Wanger Pictures, Inc., at Universal:

The Lost Moment (1947).* Director: Martin Gabel. Screenplay: Leonardo Bercovici, from "The Aspern Papers" by Henry James. Cinematography: Hal Mohr. Editor: Milton Carruth. Art Direction: Alexander Golitzen. Gowns: Travis Banton. Makeup: Bud Westmore. Music: Daniele Amfitheatrof. Release Date: October 25. 88 min.
Cast: Robert Cummings (Louis Venable). Susan Hayward (Tina Borderau).

Agnes Moorehead (Juliana Borderau). Joan Lorring (Amelia). Eduardo Ciannelli (Father Rinaldo). John Archer (Charles).

Cost: $1,313,775   **Gross:** $734,357   **Net:** –$886,494

Tap Roots (1948). Director: George Marshall. Screenplay: Alan LeMay, from the novel by James Street. Additional Dialogue: Lionel Wiggam. Cinematography (Technicolor): Lionel Lindon and Winton C. Hoch. Editor: Milton Carruth. Production Design: Alexander Golitzen. Art Direction: Frank A. Richards. Costumes: Yvonne Wood. Music: Frank Skinner. Release Date: August 1. 109 min.

Cast: Van Heflin (Keith Alexander). Susan Hayward (Morna Dabney). Boris Karloff (Tishimingo). Julie London (Aven Dabney). Whitfield Connor (Clay MacIvor). Ward Bond (Hoab Dabney). Richard Long (Bruce Dabney). Arthur Shields (Reverend Kirkland). Ruby Dandridge (Dabby). Russell Simpson (Sam Dabney).

Cost: $2,118,688   **Gross:** $3,293,658   **Net:** –$380,385

Sierra Pictures, Inc.:

Joan of Arc (1948).* Director: Victor Fleming. Screenplay: Maxwell Anderson and Andrew Solt, based on the play *Joan of Lorraine* by Anderson. Cinematography (Technicolor): Joseph Valentine, Wm. V. Skall and Winton Hoch. Special Photographic Effects: John Fulton and Jack Cosgrove. Editor: Frank Sullivan. Art Direction: Richard Day. Set Decorations: Edwin Roberts and Joseph Kish. Costume Design: Karinska and Dorothy Jankins. Costume Supervision: Herschel. Music: Hugo Friedhofer. Release Date: October 30. 150 min.

Cast: Ingrid Bergman (Jeanne D'Arc). Jose Ferrer (Dauphin). Francis L. Sullivan (Count-Bishop of Beauvais). J. Carrol Naish (Count of Luxembourg). Ward Bond (La Hire). Shepperd Strudwick (Father Massieu). Hurd Hatfield (Father Pasquerel). Gene Lockhart (Georges de la Tremouille). John Emery (Jean, Duke d'Alencon). George Coulouris (Sir Robert). John Ireland (Captain Jean de la Boussac). Cecil Kelloway (Inquisitor of Rouen).

Cost: $4,650,506   **Gross:** $5,768,142   **Net:** –$2,480,436

Walter Wanger Pictures, Inc., at Eagle-Lion:

Tulsa (1949).* Associate Producer: Edward Lasker. Director: Stuart Heisler. Screenplay: Frank Nugent and Curtis Kenyon, suggested by a story by Richard Wormser. Cinematography (Technicolor): Winton Hoch. Special Photographic Effects: John Fulton. Editor: Terrell Morse. Art Direction: Nathan Juran. Costumes: Herschel. Music: Frank Skinner. Release Date: April 13. 90 min.

Cast: Susan Hayward (Cherokee Lansing). Robert Preston (Brad Brady). Pedro Armendariz (Jim Redbird). Lloyd Gough (Bruce Tanner). Chill Wills (Pinky Jimpson). Ed Begley (Johnny Brady).

Cost: $1,158,035   **Gross:** $2,340,336   **Net:** –$746,099

Reign of Terror / The Black Book (1949).* Producer: William Cameron Menzies.

Associate Producer: Edward Lasker. Director: Anthony Mann. Screenplay: Phillip Yordan and Aeneas McKenzie. Cinematography: John Alton. Special Photographic Effects: Roy W. Seawright. Editor: Fred Allen. Art Direction: Edward Ilou. Music: Sol Kaplan. Release Date: June 10. 89 min.

Cast: Robert Cummings (Charles D'Aubigny). Arlene Dahl (Madelon). Richard Hart (Francois Barras). Arnold Moss (Fouche). Richard Basehart (Robespierre). Jess Barker (Saint Just). Norman Lloyd (Tallien). Wade Crosby (Danton). Beulah Bondi (Grandma).

Cost: $771,623   Gross: $692,621   Net: NA

Walter Wanger Pictures, Inc., at Columbia:

The Reckless Moment (1949). Director: Max Ophuls. Screenplay: Henry Garson and Robert Soderberg. Adaptation: Mel Dinelli and Robert E. Kent, from "The Blank Wall" by Elizabeth Sanxay Holding. Cinematography: Burnett Guffey. Editor: Gene Havlick. Art Direction: Cary Odell. Gowns: Jean Louis. Music: Hans Salter. Musical Director: Morris Stoloff. Release Date: October 30. 81 min.

Cast: James Mason (Martin Donnelly). Joan Bennett (Lucia Harper). Geraldine Brooks (Beatrice Harper). Henry O'Neill (Mr. Harper). Shepperd Strudwick (Ted Darby). Daniel Bar (David Harper). Roy Roberts (Nagle). Frances Williams (Sybil).

Cost: $882,653   Gross: $717,188   Net: -$565,775

At Allied Artists:

Riot in Cell Block 11 (1954).* Director: Don Siegel. Story and Screenplay: Richard Collins. Cinematography: Russell Harlan. Special Effects: Ray Mercer. Editor: Bruce B. Pierce. Art Direction: David Milton. Music: Herschel Burke Gilbert. Release Date: February 10. 90 min.

Cast: Neville Brand (Dunn). Emile Meyer (Warden Reynolds). Frank Faylen (Haskell). Leo Gordon (Carnie). Robert Osterloh (The Colonel). Paul Frees (Monroe). Don Keefer (Reporter). Alvy Moore (Gator). Dabbs Greer (Schuyler). Whit Bissell (Snader). Joel Fluellen (Al). Joe Kerr (Mac).

Cost: $298,780   Gross: $1,531,755   Net: $297,702

The Adventures of Hajji Baba (1954). Director: Don Weis. Screenplay: Richard Collins, "suggested" by the James Morier novel. Cinematography (DeLuxe Color, Cinema-Scope): Harold Lipstein. Editor: William Austin. Production Design: Gene Allen. Special Color Consultant: George Hoyningen-Huene. Costumes: Renie. Music: Dimitri Tiomkin. Song "Hajji Baba" by Tiomkin and Ned Washington, sung by Nat "King" Cole. Release Date: October 30. 92 min.

Cast: John Derek (Hajji Baba). Elaine Stewart (Fawzia). Rosemarie Bowe (Ayesha). Thomas Gomez (Osman Aga). Paul Picerni (Nur-El Din). Donald Randolph (Caliph). Amanda Blake (Banah). Linda Danson (Fabria).

Cost: $816,813   Gross: $2,019,100   Net: $673,593

Invasion of the Body Snatchers (1956).* Director: Don Siegel. Screenplay: Daniel Mainwaring (Richard Collins, uncredited), from "The Body Snatchers," a *Colliers* serial by Jack Finney. Cinematography (SuperScope): Ellsworth Fredericks. Editor: Robert S. Eisen. Art Direction: Ted Haworth. Music: Carmen Dragon. Release Date: February 26. 80 min.

    Cast: Kevin McCarthy (Dr. Miles Bennell). Dana Wynter (Becky Driscoll). Larry Gates (Danny Kaufman). King Donovan (Jack Belicec). Carolyn Jones (Teddy Belicec). Jean Willes (Sally). Ralph Dumke (Nick). Virginia Christine (Wilma). Tom Fadden (Ira). Kenneth Patterson (Mr. Driscoll). Guy Way (Sam). Doctor: Whit Bissell.

    Cost: $416,911   **Gross**: $1,200,000[4]   **Net**: NA

Navy Wife (1956). Director: Edward L. Bernds. Screenplay: Kay Leonard, from the novel *Mother, Sir!* by Tats Blain. Cinematography: Wilfrid Cline. Editor: Richard Cahoon. Art Direction: David Milton. Music: Hans Salter. Song: "Mother, Sir!" by Jack Brooks and Salter. Release Date: June 12. 82 min.

    Cast: Joan Bennett (Peg Blain). Gary Merrill (Jack Blain). Shirley Yamaguchi (Akashi). Maurice Manson (Capt. Arwin). Judy Nugent (Debby Blain). Teru Shimada (Mayor Yoshida). Robert Nichols (Oscar). John Cravern (Dr. Carter).

    Cost: $353,300   **Gross**: NA   **Net**: NA (–)

At Figaro, for United Artists:

I Want to Live! (1958).* Director: Robert Wise. Screenplay: Nelson Gidding and Don Mankiewicz, based on articles by Ed Montgomery and letters of Barbara Graham. Cinematography: Lionel Lindon. Editor: William Hornbeck. Art Direction: Ted Haworth. Costumes: Wesley Jeffries and Angela Alexander. Music: Johnny Mandel. Release Date: October 29. 120 min.

    Cast: Susan Hayward (Barbara Graham). Simon Oakland (Ed Montgomery). Virginia Vincent (Peg). Theodore Bikel (Carl Palmberg). Wesley Lau (Henry Graham). Philip Coolidge (Emmett Perkins). Lou Krugman (John Santo). James Philbrook (Bruce King). Barlett Robinson (District Attorney). Gage Clark (Richard G. Tibrow). Joe De Santis (Al Matthews). John Marley (Father Devers). Gavin McLeod (Lieutenant).

    Cost: $1,383,578   **Gross**: $5,641,711   **Net**: $2,455,570

At Twentieth Century-Fox:

Cleopatra (1963).* Director: Joseph L. Mankiewicz. Screenplay: Joseph L. Mankiewicz, Ranald MacDougall, and Sidney Buchman, based on histories by Plutarch, Suetonius, and Appian and *The Life and Times of Cleopatra* by C. M. Franzero.

---

[4]*Invasion of the Body Snatchers's* gross income listed is domestic only and reported in *V,* 2 January 1957.

Cinematography (Deluxe Color, Todd-AO): Leon Shamroy. Editor: Dorothy Spencer. Production Design: John DeCuir. Art Direction: Jack Martin Smith, Hilyard Brown, Herman Blumenthal, Elver Webb, Maurice Pellig, and Boris Juraga. Costume Design: Vittorio Nino Novarese (for men), Renie (for women), Irene Sharaff (for Elizabeth Taylor). Music: Alex North. Second Unit Directors: Ray Kellogg, Andrew Martin. Release Date: June 11. 243 min.

   Cast: Elizabeth Taylor (Cleopatra). Richard Burton (Marc Antony). Rex Harrison (Caesar). Pamela Brown (High Priestess). George Cole (Flavius). Hume Cronyn (Sosigenes). Cesare Danova (Apollodorus). Kenneth Haigh (Brutus). Andrew Keir (Agrippa). Martin Landau (Rufio). Octavian (Roddy McDowall). Robert Stephens (Germanicus). Francesca Annis (Eiras). Gregoire Aslan (Pothinos). Martin Brenon (Ramos). Herbert Berghof (Theodotus). Jacqui Chan (Lotos). Isabelle Cooley (Charmian). Michael Holdern (Cicero). Carroll O'Connor (Casca). Gwen Watford (Calpurnia). Jean Marsh (Octavia).

   Cost: $31,115,000   Gross: NA   Net: NA

In September 1966, Twentieth Century–Fox announced that the $5 million sale of television rights for *Cleopatra* to ABC enabled the film to break even.

Other Credited Films

The Lady in the Iron Mask (1952) Distribution: Twentieth Century–Fox. Producer: Eugene Frenke. Executive Producer: Wanger. Director: Ralph Murphy. Screenplay: Jack Pollixfen and Aubrey Wisberg. Cinematography: Ernest Laszlo. Editor: Bruce Pierce. Music: Dimitri Tiomkin. Release Date: July 26. 78 min.

   Cast: Louis Hayward (D'Artagnan). Patricia Medina (Princess Ann). Alan Hale, Jr. (Porthos). Steve Brodie (Athos).

   (Note: As a favor to his former associate Eugene Frenke, Wanger secured distribution for this film through Twentieth Century–Fox.)

   At Allied Artists, Wanger received credit for the following films that the associate producers actually produced.

Aladdin and His Lamp (1952). Associate Producer: Ben Schwalb. Director: Lew Landers. Screenplay: Howard Dimsdale and Millard Kauffman. Cinematography (Cinecolor): Gilbert Warrenton. Editor: Jack Ogilvie. Music: Martin Skiles. Release Date: February 7. 67 min.

   Cast: Patricia Medina (Jasmine). John Sands (Aladdin). Richard Erdman (Mizra). John Dehner (Bokra).

Battle Zone (1952). Director: Lesley Selander. Screenplay: Steve Fisher. Cinematography: Ernest Miller. Editor: Jack Ogilvie. Music: Martin Skiles. 81 min.

   Cast: John Hodiak (Danny). Linda Christian (Jeanne). Stephen McNally (Mitch). Martin Milner (Andy).

Kansas Pacific (1953). Associate Producer: Edward Morey, Jr. Director: Ray Nazarro. Screenplay: Dan Ullman. Cinematography (Cinecolor): Harry Neumann. Editors:

William Austin and Walter Hannemann. Music: Albert Sendrey. 73 min.

   Cast: Sterling Hayden (John Nelson). Eve Miller (Barbara Bruce). Barton MacLane (Calvin Bruce).

Fort Vengeance (1953). Director: Lesley Selander. Screenplay: Dan Ullman. Cinematography (Cinecolor): Harry Neumann. Editor: Walter Hannemann. Music: Paul Dunlap. 75 min.

   Cast: James Craig (Dick). Rita Moreno (Bridget). Keith Larsen (Carey). Reginald Denny (Major Trevett).

Illustration Credits

Index

Matthew Bernstein teaches film studies at Emory University. He has edited *Controlling Hollywood: Censorship and Regulation in the Studio Era* and coedited *Visions of the East: Orientalism in Film.* He is associate editor of *Cinema Journal* and has served on the editorial boards of *The Velvet Light Trap* and *The Journal of Film and Video.*

Robert Wise is an award-winning editor and director whose films include *Citizen Kane* (editor), *The Magnificent Ambersons* (editor), *The Sound of Music, West Side Story, The Andromeda Strain,* and *Star Trek: The Motion Picture.*

Designer: U.C. Press Staff
Compositor: Prestige Typography
Text: 10/12 Times Roman
Display: Helvetica
Printer: Edwards Bros.
Binder: Edwards Bros.